TEACHER'S EDITION

D'accord! 1A

LANGUE ET CULTURE DU MONDE FRANCOPHONE

VISTA
HIGHER LEARNING

Boston, Massachusetts

Cover photos: clockwise from top left: characters from the **D'ACCORD!** **Roman-photo** video program in Aix-en-Provence, France; honey shop, Provence, France; artichokes at a local market, Paris, France; Mont Saint Michel, Normandy, France

Publisher: José A. Blanco
Vice President, Editorial Director: Amy Baron
Executive Editor: Sharla Zwirek
Senior National Language Consultant: Norah Lulich Jones
Editorial Development: Diego García
Rights Management: Jorgensen Fernandez, Annie Pickert Fuller, Caitlin O'Brien
Technology Production: Paola Ríos Schaaf, Erica Solari
Design: Mark James, Andrés Vanegas
Production: Manuela Arango, Oscar Díez, Jennifer López

Copyright © 2016 by Vista Higher Learning, Inc.

All rights reserved.

No part of this work may be reproduced or distributed in any form or by any means, electronic or mechanical, including photocopying and recording, or by any information storage or retrieval system without prior written permission from Vista Higher Learning, 500 Boylston Street, Suite 620, Boston, MA 02116-3736.

Student Text ISBN: 978-1-68004-105-7
Teacher's Edition ISBN: 978-1-68004-107-1
Printed in the United States of America.

1 2 3 4 5 6 7 8 9 RW 20 19 18 17 16 15

TEACHER'S EDITION

Table of Contents

D'accord! Program Scope and Sequence	T4
Articulation from French 1 to Advanced	T8
Program Overview	T10
D'accord! At-a-Glance	T13
The VHL Story	T27
How **D'accord!** Works	T28
Differentiation	T28
Best Practices	T29
Assessment	T30
Student Objectives	T31
Integrated Performance Assessment	T32
D'accord! and the *Standards for Foreign Language Learning*	T35
Pacing Guide: Traditional Schedule	T36
Pacing Guide: Block Schedule	T40
Index of Cultural References	T44

Front Matter to the **D'accord!** Student Edition

Table of Contents of the Student Edition	iv
Map of the Francophone World	viii
Map of North and South America	x
Map of France	xi
Map of Europe	xii
Map of Africa	xiii
Using **D'accord!**	xiv
Studying French	xviii
Getting Started	xxv
Acknowledgments	xxviii
The Student Edition with instructional annotations	1

D'accord! 1A & 1B Scope and Sequence

1A

Unit/Lesson	Contextes	Structures	Culture/Panorama
Unité 1 Salut!			
Leçon 1A	Greetings and goodbyes Introductions and expressions of courtesy	Nouns and articles Numbers 0–60	Greetings and manners
Leçon 1B	People and things around a classroom	The verb **être** Adjective agreement	French diversity **Le monde francophone**
Unité 2 Au lycée			
Leçon 2A	Academic life	Present tense of regular –**er** verbs Forming questions and expressing negation	French school life
Leçon 2B	Everyday activities	Present tense of **avoir** Telling time	**Le bac** **La France**
Unité 3 La famille et les copains			
Leçon 3A	Family, friends, and pets	Descriptive adjectives Possessive adjectives	The family in France
Leçon 3B	More descriptive adjectives Professions and occupations	Numbers 61–100 Prepositions of locations and disjunctive pronouns	Relationships **Paris**
Unité 4 Au café			
Leçon 4A	Places and activities around town	The verb **aller** Interrogative words	Popular leisure activities
Leçon 4B	Going to a **café**	The verbs **prendre** and **boire**; Partitives Regular –**ir** verbs	**Café** culture **La Normandie** **La Bretagne**

1B

Unit/Lesson	Contextes	Structures	Culture/Panorama
Reprise			
A brief overview of the contexts and grammar from Level 1A			
Unité 5 Les loisirs			
Leçon 5A	Leisure activities	The verb **faire** Irregular –**ir** verbs	Soccer in France
Leçon 5B	Weather	Numbers 101 and higher Spelling-change –**er** verbs	Public spaces in France **Les Pays de la Loire** **Le Centre**
Unité 6 Les fêtes			
Leçon 6A	Parties and celebrations	Demonstrative adjectives The **passé composé** with **avoir**	**Carnaval**
Leçon 6B	Clothing and colors	Indirect object pronouns Regular and irregular –**re** verbs	Fashion **L'Aquitaine** **Le Midi-Pyrénées** **Le Languedoc-Roussillon**
Unité 7 En vacances			
Leçon 7A	Travel arrangements Transportation	The **passé composé** with **être** Direct object pronouns	Tahiti
Leçon 7B	Hotels and accomodations	Adverbs The formation of the **imparfait**	Vacations **Provence-Alpes-Côte d'Azur** **Rhône-Alpes**
Unité 8 Chez nous			
Leçon 8A	Parts of the house Furniture	The **passé composé** vs. the **imparfait**	Housing in the Francophone world
Leçon 8B	Household chores	The **passé composé** vs. the **imparfait** The verbs **savoir** and **connaître**	Household interiors **L'Alsace** **La Lorraine**

D'accord! 1 Scope and Sequence

Unit/Lesson	Contextes	Structures	Culture/Panorama
Unité 1 Salut!			
Leçon 1A	Greetings and goodbyes Introductions and expressions of courtesy	Nouns and articles Numbers 0–60	Greetings and manners
Leçon 1B	People and things around a classroom	The verb **être** Adjective agreement	French diversity **Le monde francophone**
Unité 2 Au lycée			
Leçon 2A	Academic life	Present tense of regular –**er** verbs Forming questions and expressing negation	French school life
Leçon 2B	Everyday activities	Present tense of **avoir** Telling time	**Le bac** **La France**
Unité 3 La famille et les copains			
Leçon 3A	Family, friends, and pets	Descriptive adjectives Possessive adjectives	The family in France
Leçon 3B	More descriptive adjectives Professions and occupations	Numbers 61–100 Prepositions of locations and disjunctive pronouns	Relationships **Paris**
Unité 4 Au café			
Leçon 4A	Places and activities around town	The verb **aller** Interrogative words	Popular leisure activities
Leçon 4B	Going to a **café**	The verbs **prendre** and **boire**; Partitives Regular –**ir** verbs	**Café** culture **La Normandie** **La Bretagne**
Unité 5 Les loisirs			
Leçon 5A	Leisure activities	The verb **faire** Irregular –**ir** verbs	Soccer in France
Leçon 5B	Weather	Numbers 101 and higher Spelling-change –**er** verbs	Public spaces in France **Les Pays de la Loire** **Le Centre**
Unité 6 Les fêtes			
Leçon 6A	Parties and celebrations	Demonstrative adjectives The **passé composé** with **avoir**	**Carnaval**
Leçon 6B	Clothing and colors	Indirect object pronouns Regular and irregular –**re** verbs	Fashion **L'Aquitaine** **Le Midi-Pyrénées** **Le Languedoc-Roussillon**
Unité 7 En vacances			
Leçon 7A	Travel arrangements Transportation	The **passé composé** with **être** Direct object pronouns	Tahiti
Leçon 7B	Hotels and accomodations	Adverbs The formation of the **imparfait**	Vacations **Provence-Alpes-Côte d'Azur** **Rhône-Alpes**
Unité 8 Chez nous			
Leçon 8A	Parts of the house Furniture	The **passé composé** vs. the **imparfait**	Housing in the Francophone world
Leçon 8B	Household chores	The **passé composé** vs. the **imparfait** The verbs **savoir** and **connaître**	Household interiors **L'Alsace** **La Lorraine**

D'accord! 2 Scope and Sequence

Unit/Lesson	Contextes	Structures	Culture/Panorama
Reprise			
	Review of Level 1 vocabulary	Review of Level 1 grammar	Summer vacation activities
Unité Préliminaire Chez nous			
Leçon PA	Parts of the house Furniture	The **passé composé** vs. **the imparfait**	Housing in the Francophone world
Leçon PB	Household chores	The **passé composé** vs. **the imparfait** The verbs **savoir** and **connaître**	Household interiors **L'Alsace** **La Lorraine**
Unité 1 La nourriture			
Leçon 1A	Food	The verb **venir** and the **passé récent** **Devoir, vouloir, pouvoir**	French gastronomy and the **Guide Michelin**
Leçon 1B	Dining Specialty food shops	Comparatives and superlatives of adjectives and adverbs Double object pronouns	French meals **La Bourgogne** **La Franche-Comté**
Unité 2 La santé			
Leçon 2A	Parts of the body Daily routine	Reflexive verbs Reflexives: **Sens idiomatique**	Healthcare in France
Leçon 2B	Maladies and remedies	The **passé composé** of reflexive verbs The pronouns **y** and **en**	**La sécurité sociale** **La Suisse**
Unité 3 La technologie			
Leçon 3A	Computers and electronics	Prepositions with the infinitive Reciprocal reflexives	Technology
Leçon 3B	Cars and driving	The verbs **ouvrir** and **offrir** The **conditionnel**	Cars **La Belgique**
Unité 4 En ville			
Leçon 4A	Errands	**Voir, croire, recevoir,** and **apercevoir** Negative/Affirmative expressions	Small shops
Leçon 4B	Giving and getting directions	**Le futur simple** Irregular future forms	French cities and towns **Le Québec**
Unité 5 L'avenir et les métiers			
Leçon 5A	At the office Making phone calls	**Le futur simple** with **quand** and **dès que** The interrogative pronoun **lequel**	Telephones in France
Leçon 5B	Professions	**Si** clauses Relative pronouns **qui, que, dont, où**	Unions and strikes **L'Afrique du Nord**
Unité 6 L'espace vert			
Leçon 6A	Environmental concerns	Demonstrative pronouns The subjunctive	The ecological movement in France
Leçon 6B	Nature	The subjunctive Comparatives and superlatives of nouns	National parks **L'Afrique de l'Ouest** **L'Afrique centrale**
Unité 7 Les arts			
Leçon 7A	Performance arts	The subjunctive Possessive pronouns	Theater in France
Leçon 7B	Literary arts TV and movies	The subjunctive	Haitian painting **Les Antilles** **La Polynésie française**

D'accord! 3 Scope and Sequence

Lesson	Contextes	Structures	Imaginez/Culture	Film/Littérature
Reprise	Review of Levels 1 and 2 vocabulary	Review of Levels 1 and 2 grammar		
Leçon 1 Ressentir et vivre	Relationships	Spelling-change verbs The irregular verbs **être**, **avoir**, **faire**, and **aller** Forming questions	Les États-Unis Les francophones d'Amérique	**Court métrage:** *À tes amours* (France) **Littérature:** *Il pleure dans mon cœur* de Paul Verlaine
Leçon 2 Habiter en ville	Towns and cities	Reflexive and reciprocal verbs Descriptive adjectives and adjective agreement Adverbs	La France Rythme dans la rue: La fête de la Musique	**Court métrage:** *J'attendrai le suivant* (France) **Littérature:** *Mai 1968* de Jacques Prévert
Leçon 3 L'influence des medias	News and media	The **passé composé** with **avoir** The **passé composé** with **être** The **passé composé** vs. the **imparfait**	Le Québec Guy Laliberté, un homme hors du commun	**Court métrage:** *Le Technicien* (Canada) **Littérature:** *99 Francs* de Fréderic Beigbeder
Leçon 4 La valeur des idées	Human rights Politics	The **plus-que-parfait** Negation and indefinite adjectives and pronouns Irregular **–ir** verbs	Les Antilles Haïti, soif de liberté	**Court métrage:** *La révolution des crabes* (France) **Littérature:** *Discours sur la misère* de Victor Hugo
Leçon 5 La société en évolution	Contemporary life	Partitives The pronouns **y** and **en** Order of pronouns	L'Afrique de l'Ouest La jeunesse africaine va à l'école sur Internet	**Court métrage:** *Samb et le commissaire* (Suisse) **Littérature:** *Le marché de l'espoir* de Ghislaine Sathoud
Leçon 6 Les générations que bougent	Families Stages of life Food	The subjunctive: impersonal expressions; will, opinion, and emotion Demonstrative pronouns Irregular **–re** verbs	L'Afrique du Nord et le Liban Jour de mariage	**Court métrage:** *De l'autre côté* (Algérie/France) **Littérature:** *La logique des grands* de Olivier Charneux
Leçon 7 À la recherche du progrès	Technology and inventions The sciences	The comparative and superlative of adjectives and adverbs The **futur simple** The subjunctive with expressions of doubt and conjunctions; the past subjunctive	La Belgique, la Suisse, et le Luxembourg CERN: À la découverte d'un univers particulier	**Court métrage:** *Le Manie-Tout* (France) **Littérature:** *Solitude numérique* de Didier Daeninckx
Leçon 8 S'évader et s'amuser	Leisure activities Sports Shopping	Infinitives Prepositions with geographical names The **conditionnel**	L'océan Indien La Réunion, île intense	**Court métrage:** *Le ballon prisonnier* (France) **Littérature:** *Le football* de Sempé-Goscinny
Leçon 9 Perspectives de travail	At the office Banking and finances	Relative pronouns The present participle Irregular **–oir** verbs	L'Afrique Centrale Des Africaines entrepreneuses	**Court métrage:** *Bonne nuit Malik* (France) **Littérature:** *Profession libérale* de Marie Le Drian
Leçon 10 Les richesses naturelles	Nature The environment	The past conditional The future perfect **Si** clauses	La Polynésie française, la Nouvelle-Calédonie, l'Asie Les richesses du Pacifique	**Court métrage:** *L'homme qui plantait des arbres* (Québec, Canada) **Littérature:** *Baobab* de Jean-Baptiste Tati-Loutard

Articulation from French 1 to Advanced

An extended sequence of study **that just makes sense.**

Middle School

Level 1

Level 2

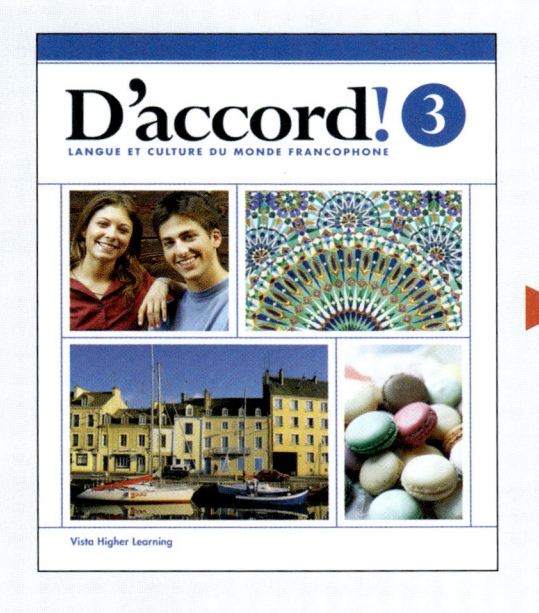

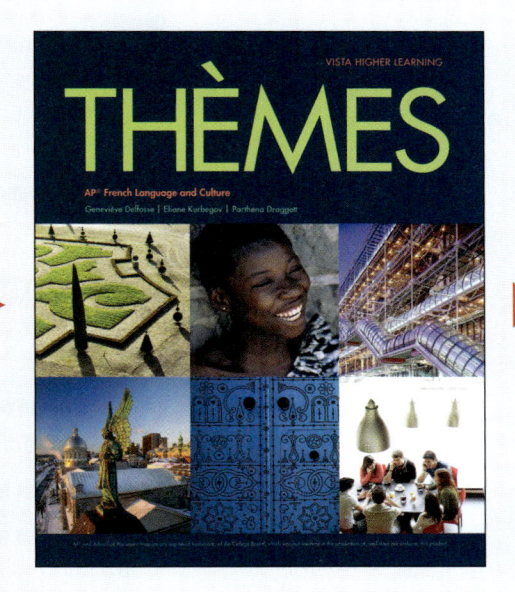

Level 3 → Advanced Placement → Advanced Conversation

- Sequenced instruction builds interpretive, interpersonal, and presentational communication skills
- Consistent pedagogy enables a seamless transition from year to year
- Focus on personalized language learning enhances the student experience
- A single technology platform—the Supersite—built specifically for world language education

D'accord! 1A Program Overview

Program Components

For you
- Teacher's Edition
- Teacher Supersite
- Video Program DVD
  - *Roman-photo*
  - *Flash culture*
- Testing Program
- Answer Key
- Activity Pack
- Middle School Activity Pack

For your students
- Student Edition with Supersite Plus (vText)
- *Cahier de l'élève*
- *eCahier* online workbook
- vText interactive, online textbook

Supersite

Integrated content
means a better student experience

- All textbook "mouse-icon" activities and additional online-only practice activities
- Immediate feedback for most activities via auto-grading
- Interactive French Grammar Tutorials
- Partner Chat tool for recording live student conversations and submitting to the gradebook
- My Vocabulary tool for compiling, saving, and organizing words
- Virtual Chat activities for simulating conversations that build students' confidence
- Streaming video of the *Roman-photo* episodic series, *Le Zapping* authentic TV clips, and *Flash culture*
- Textbook and Audio Program MP3s
- Audio-sync readings for all Lecture selections
- Oral record-submit activities
- Internet search activities
- Reference resources: online dictionary, audio flashcards
- iPad®-friendly for on-the-go access
- **vText**—the online, interactive Student Edition

Visit: **vistahigherlearning.com/demo-request-SE** for trial access.

Supersite

Specialized resources
ensure successful implementation

- Online assessments
- Answer Keys
- MP3 files of the complete Textbook, Audio Program, and Testing Audio Programs
- Audio and video scripts with English translations
- Activity Pack (PDF) with communicative and directed activities for every lesson
- Middle School Activity Pack (PDF)
- Lesson Plans in an editable format
- Grammar Presentation slides
- Digital Image Bank (PDFs)

Online tools
facilitate instruction

- A gradebook to manage classes, view rosters, set assignments, and manage grades
- Online administration of quizzes, tests, and exams
- A communication center for announcements, notifications, and responding to help requests
- Live Chat tool for instant messaging, audio, and video chat with students
- Voiceboards for oral assignments, group discussion, and projects
- Tools to add your own content to the Supersite
    - Create, assign, and grade your own Partner Chats, open-ended activities, and assessments
    - Incorporate your own or external video
    - Add your own notes to existing content
- Single sign on for easy Blackboard integration
- Reporting tools for summarizing student data
- Complete access to the Student Supersite

Also available:

- *eCahier* Interactive, online version of the *Cahier de l'élève* with full integration with the Supersite gradebook

D'accord! 1A Program Overview

Communication beyond the classroom

A major goal of language instruction is to help students express themselves efficiently and appropriately during oral conversation. **Virtual Chat** and video **Partner Chat** features help accomplish that goal in a way that's familiar to students—after all, online chatting is part of their everyday lives!

Supersite chat activities provide:

- A communication tool that today's students prefer to use
- Increased opportunities for spoken production, beyond the face-to-face classroom
- A portal that helps reduce students' affective filter and build confidence
- An easy-to-use grading tool that makes grading a breeze
- Integration with the Supersite, so that chat activities can be assigned, and graded work flows into the gradebook
- A recorded portfolio of students' spoken work

A fresh approach to grammar

Interactive **French Grammar Tutorials** entertain and inform students by pairing grammar rules with fun explanations and examples.

Featuring *le professeur*—an amusing character who grabs students' attention with his humorous gags and lighthearted approach to grammar—, these assignable, interactive presentations are a handy reference tool and support students' independent study. Interactive questions help check understanding, plus end-of-tutorial activities can be submitted for a grade.

Lighten backpacks!
The Supersite and vText are iPad®-friendly.*

* Students must use a computer for audio recording and select presentations and tools that require Flash or Shockwave.

D'accord! 1A At-a-Glance

Beginning with the student in mind

All chapters open with images that provide visual context for the chapter theme.

Au lycée

Unité 2

Leçon 2A

- **CONTEXTES** ..... pages 46–49
  - Academic life
  - Liaisons
- **ROMAN-PHOTO** . pages 50–51
  - Trop de devoirs!
- **CULTURE** .... pages 52–53
  - Au lycée
  - Flash culture
- **STRUCTURES** .... pages 54–61
  - Present tense of regular -er verbs
  - Forming questions and expressing negation
- **SYNTHÈSE** ...... pages 62–63
  - Révision
  - Le Zapping

Leçon 2B

- **CONTEXTES** ..... pages 64–67
  - Everyday activities
  - The letter r
- **ROMAN-PHOTO** . pages 68–69
  - On trouve une solution.
- **CULTURE** .... pages 70–71
  - Le bac
- **STRUCTURES** .... pages 72–79
  - Present tense of avoir
  - Telling time
- **SYNTHÈSE** ...... pages 80–81
  - Révision
  - À l'écoute

Savoir-faire ... pages 82–87
- Panorama: La France
- Lecture: Read an academic brochure.
- Écriture: Write a description of yourself.

Pour commencer
- Which room at school is pictured?
  a. la bibliothèque b. la salle de classe c. le café
- What are the students looking at?
  a. un cahier b. un professeur c. un livre
- How do the students look in this photo?
  a. intelligents b. sociables c. sérieux
- Which item is not visible in the photo?
  a. une table b. une fenêtre c. un ordinateur

Content summaries provide an at-a-glance view of the vocabulary, grammar, and cultural topics covered in the chapter.

Each chapter includes two lessons and an end-of-chapter *Savoir-faire* section.

Pour commencer activities jump-start the chapters, allowing students to use the French they know to talk about the photos.

Look for the **S** located at the beginning of every section to see the corresponding resources available on the Supersite!

D'accord! 1A At-a-Glance

Setting the stage for communication

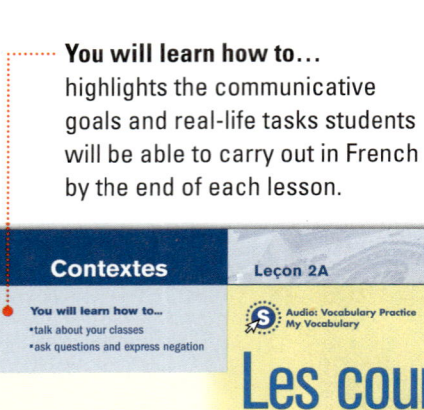

You will learn how to… highlights the communicative goals and real-life tasks students will be able to carry out in French by the end of each lesson.

Theme-related vocabulary is introduced through expansive, full-color illustrations and easy-to-reference lists.

Mise en pratique starts the lesson's activity sequence with controlled practice.

Ressources boxes reference additional print and digital student resources.

Mouse icons indicate activities that teachers can assign on the Supersite. All close-ended practice activities are auto-graded with immediate feedback.

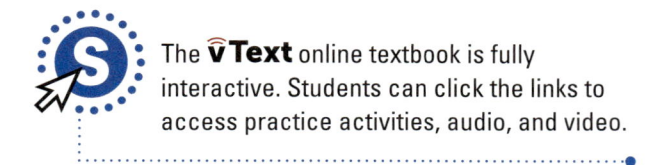

The **vText** online textbook is fully interactive. Students can click the links to access practice activities, audio, and video.

T14 Teacher's Edition • D'accord! At-a-Glance

Visually engaging formats

The **Communication** section includes personalized communicative activities that allow students to use the vocabulary creatively in interactions with a partner, a small group, or the entire class.

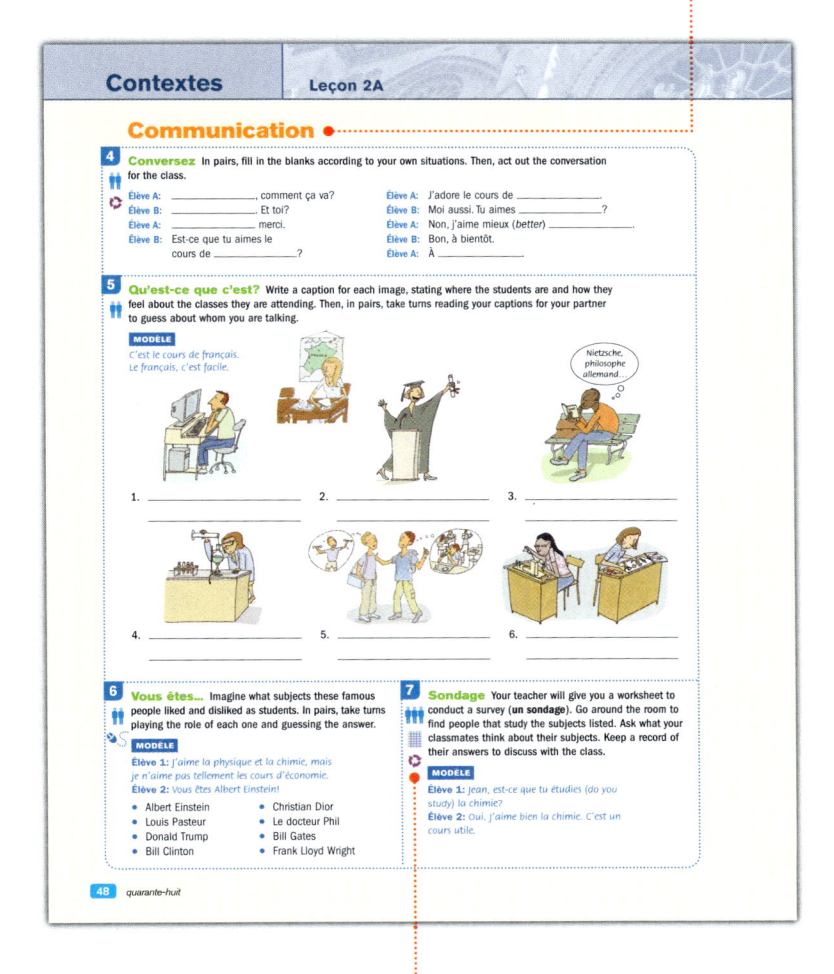

Hands-on activities encourage interaction and communication.

Build students' oral language skills through assignable **Virtual Chat** and **Partner Chat** activities.

D'accord! 1A At-a-Glance

Pronunciation and spelling practice

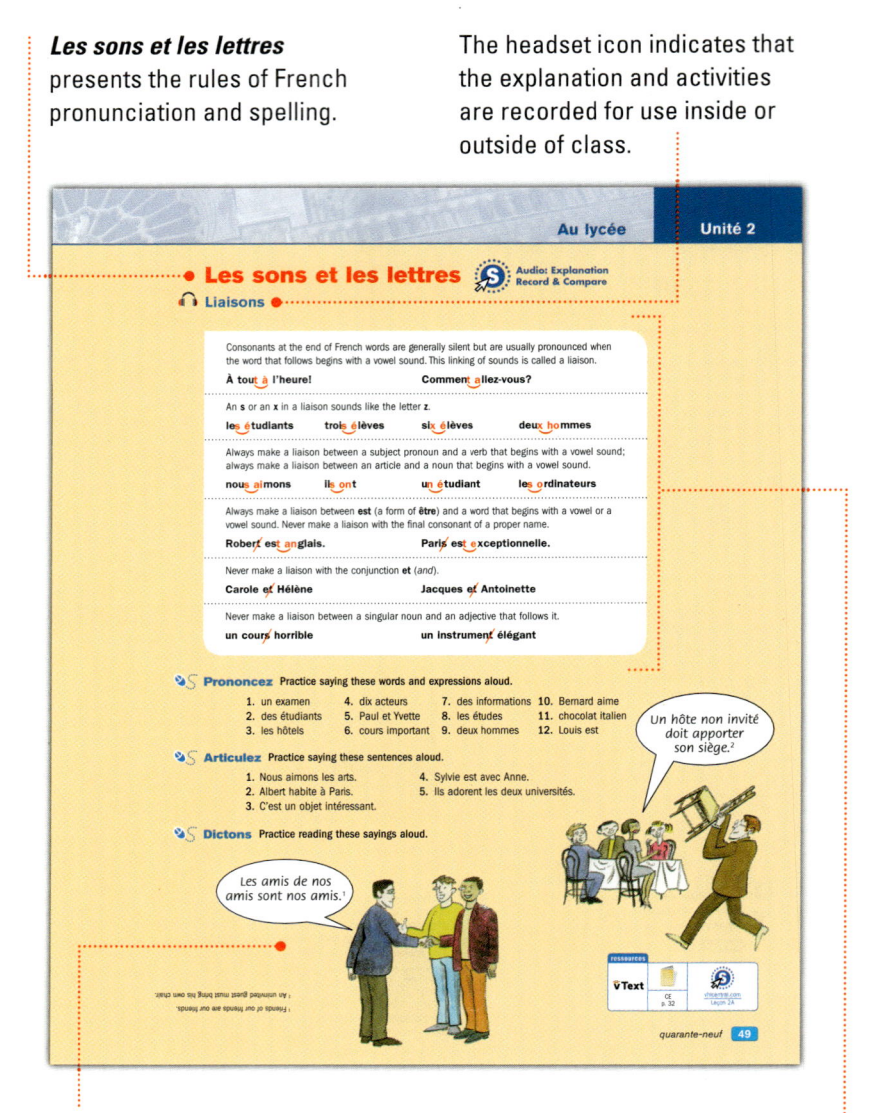

Les sons et les lettres presents the rules of French pronunciation and spelling.

The headset icon indicates that the explanation and activities are recorded for use inside or outside of class.

The last activity features illustrative sayings and proverbs to practice the pronunciation or spelling point in an entertaining cultural context.

An abundance of model words and phrases focus students' attention on the target sounds and letters.

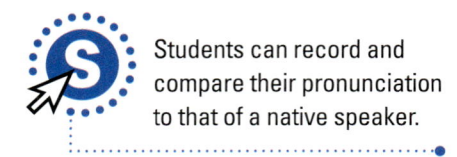

Students can record and compare their pronunciation to that of a native speaker.

Roman-photo bridges language and culture

Follow characters through all the levels of **D'accord!**.

Roman-photo storyline video brings lesson vocabulary and grammar to life. Students experience local life with a group of students living in Aix-en-Provence, France.

Products, practices, and perspectives are featured in every episode.

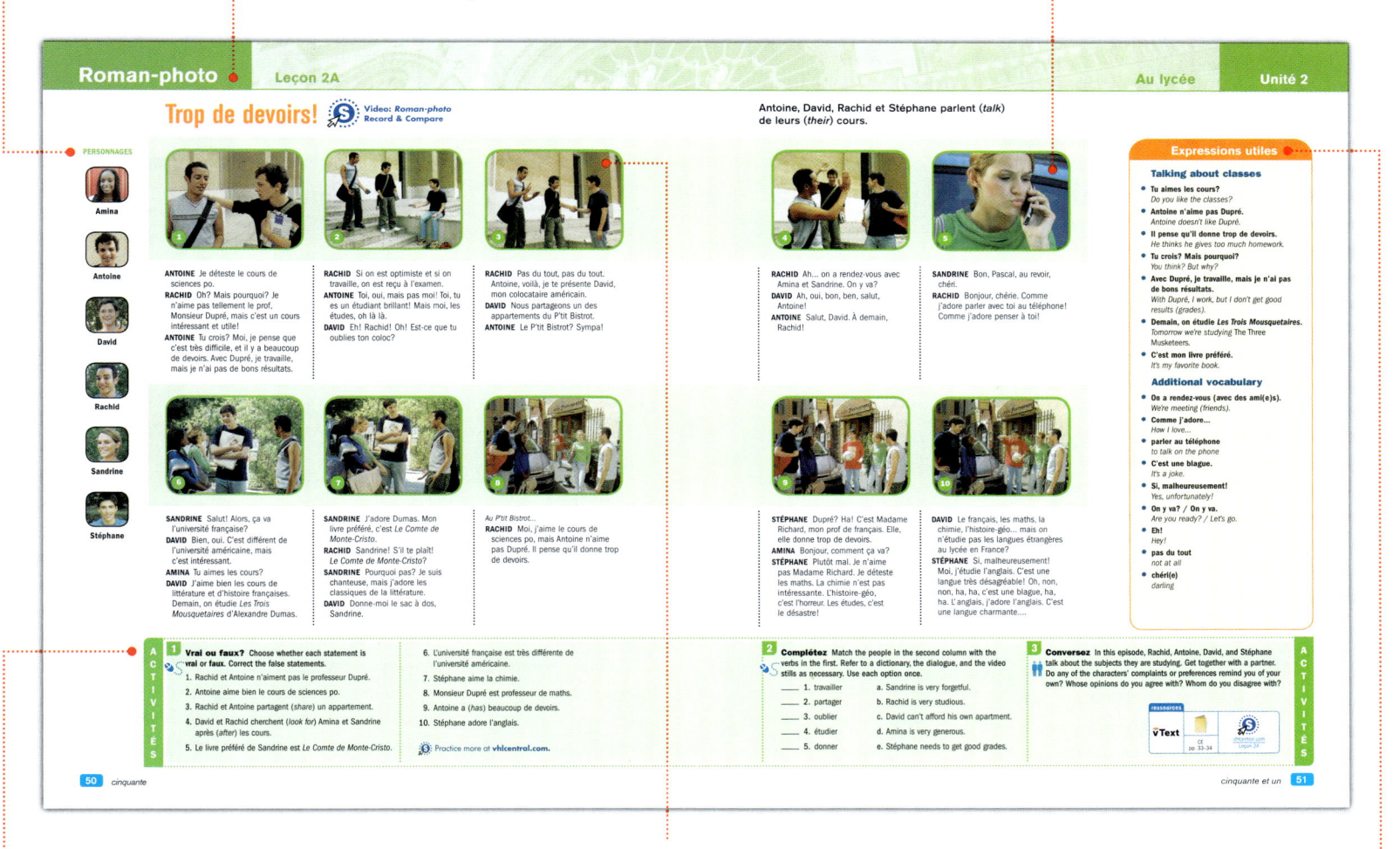

Activities feature comprehension questions, a communicative task, and a research-based task.

The easy-to-follow storyboard sets the context for the video and the dialogue boxes reinforce the lesson's vocabulary and preview the language structures that will be covered later in the lesson.

Expressions utiles organizes the most important words and expressions from the episode by language function, showing how students can apply them in real, practical ways.

Assign pre- and post-viewing activities to test student comprehension of lesson vocabulary and key language functions.

Teacher's Edition • **D'accord!** At-a-Glance   T17

D'accord! 1A At-a-Glance

Culture presented in context

Culture à la loupe explores the chapter's theme in-depth—in English in early chapters of level 1A and in French thereafter for true cultural comprehension.

Le monde francophone continues the exploration of the lesson's cultural theme, but with a regional focus.

Le français quotidien presents familiar words and phrases related to the lesson's theme that are used in everyday spoken French.

Portrait focuses on Francophone personalities and places of high interest to students.

Comprehension activities solidify learning.

Sur Internet features additional cultural explorations online.

Coup de main boxes provide handy, on-the-spot language or grammar information that supports student learning.

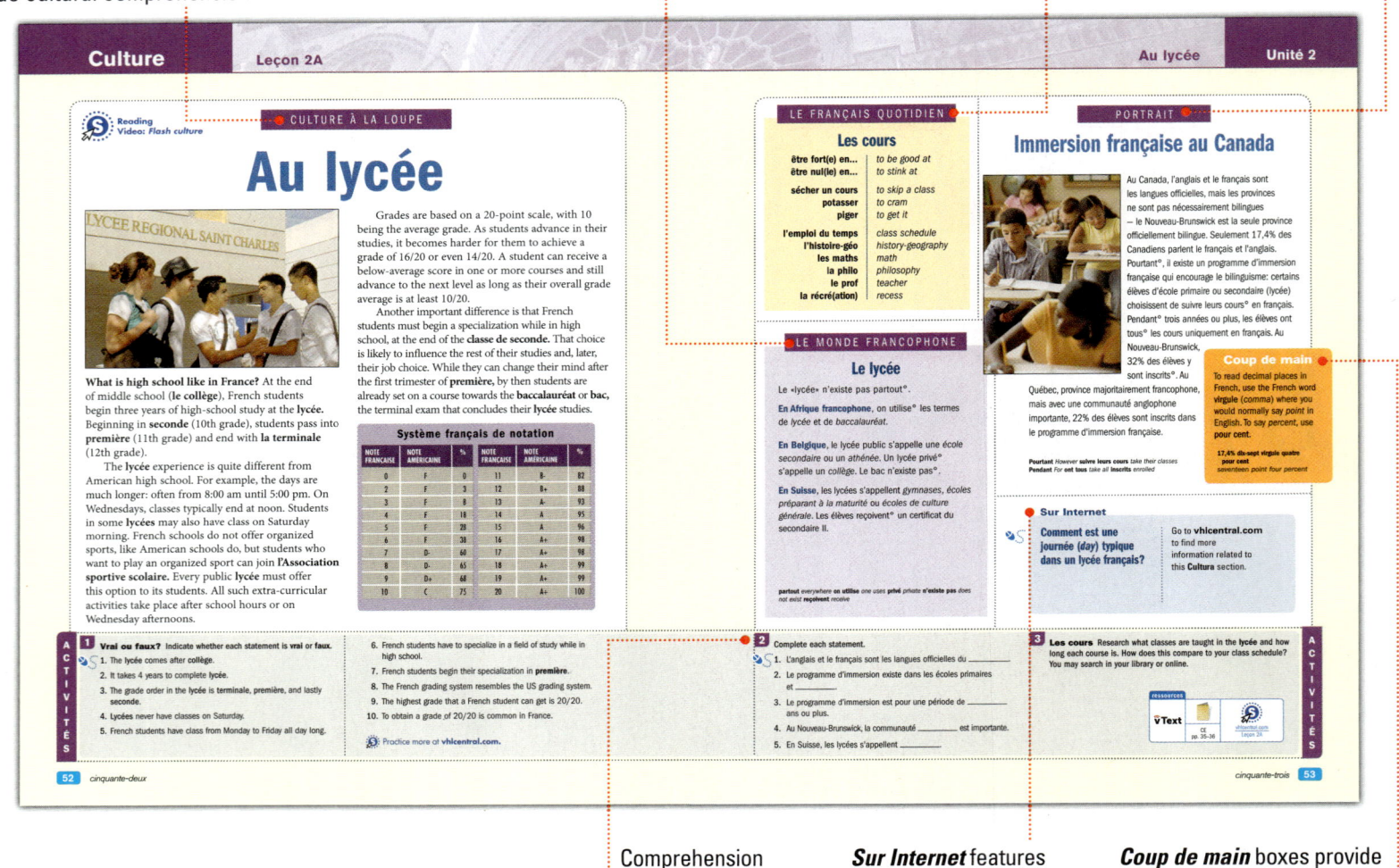

Students don't just read about Francophone culture, they experience it themselves by watching the **Flash culture** video.

Grammar as a tool not a topic

The **Structures** sections include two grammar points, each with an explanation and practice activities.

Boîte à outils boxes provide additional information about the grammar.

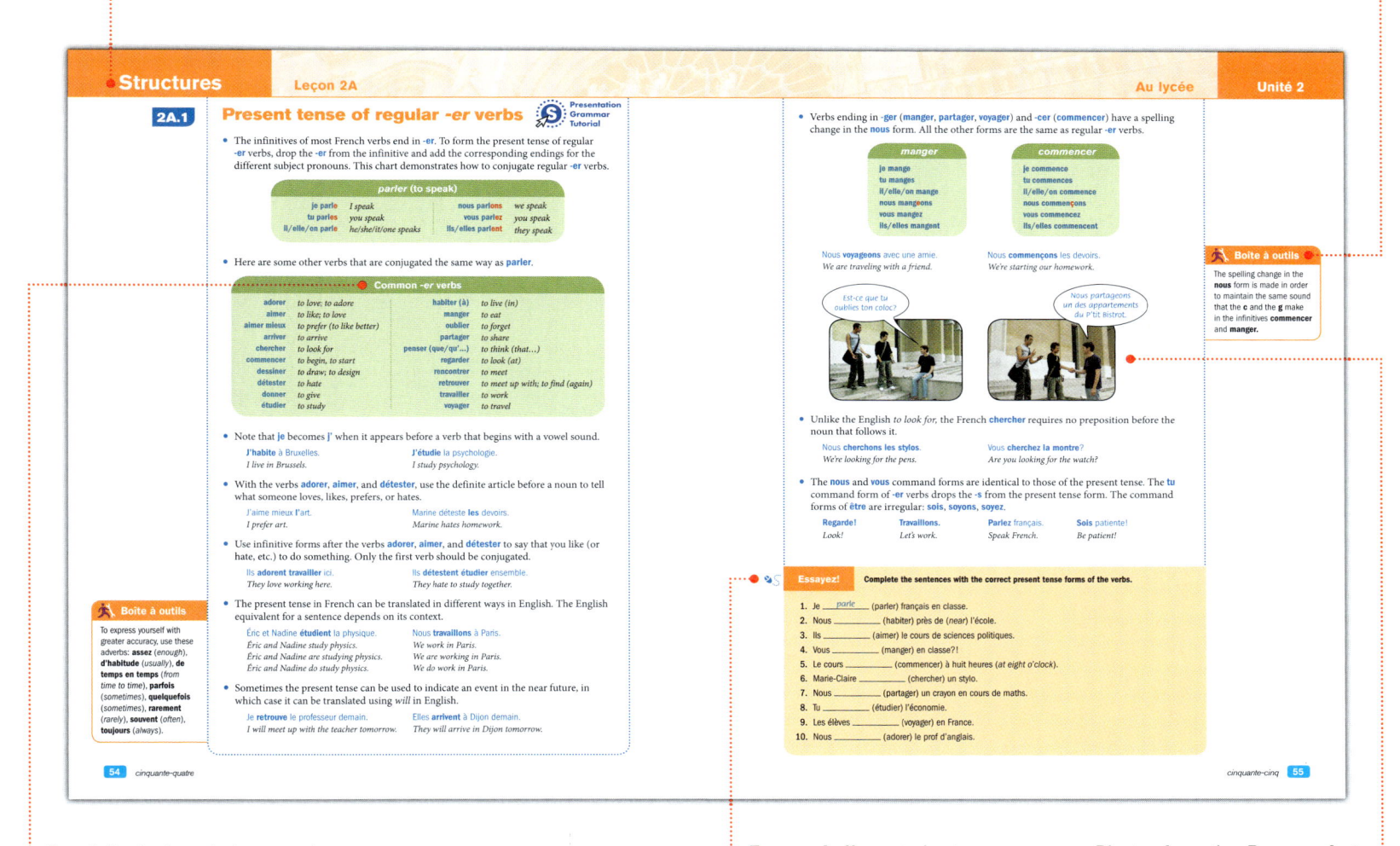

Carefully designed charts and diagrams call out key grammatical structures and forms, as well as important related vocabulary.

Essayez! offers students their first practice of each new grammar point.

Photos from the **Roman-photo** show the grammar in context.

Students can watch the grammar rules come alive with 60 brand-new, animated **French Grammar Tutorials** featuring *le professeur*.

D'accord! 1A At-a-Glance

Carefully scaffolded activities

Mise en pratique sections include contextualized, personalized activities.

Communication sections feature pair and group activities for interpersonal and presentational practice.

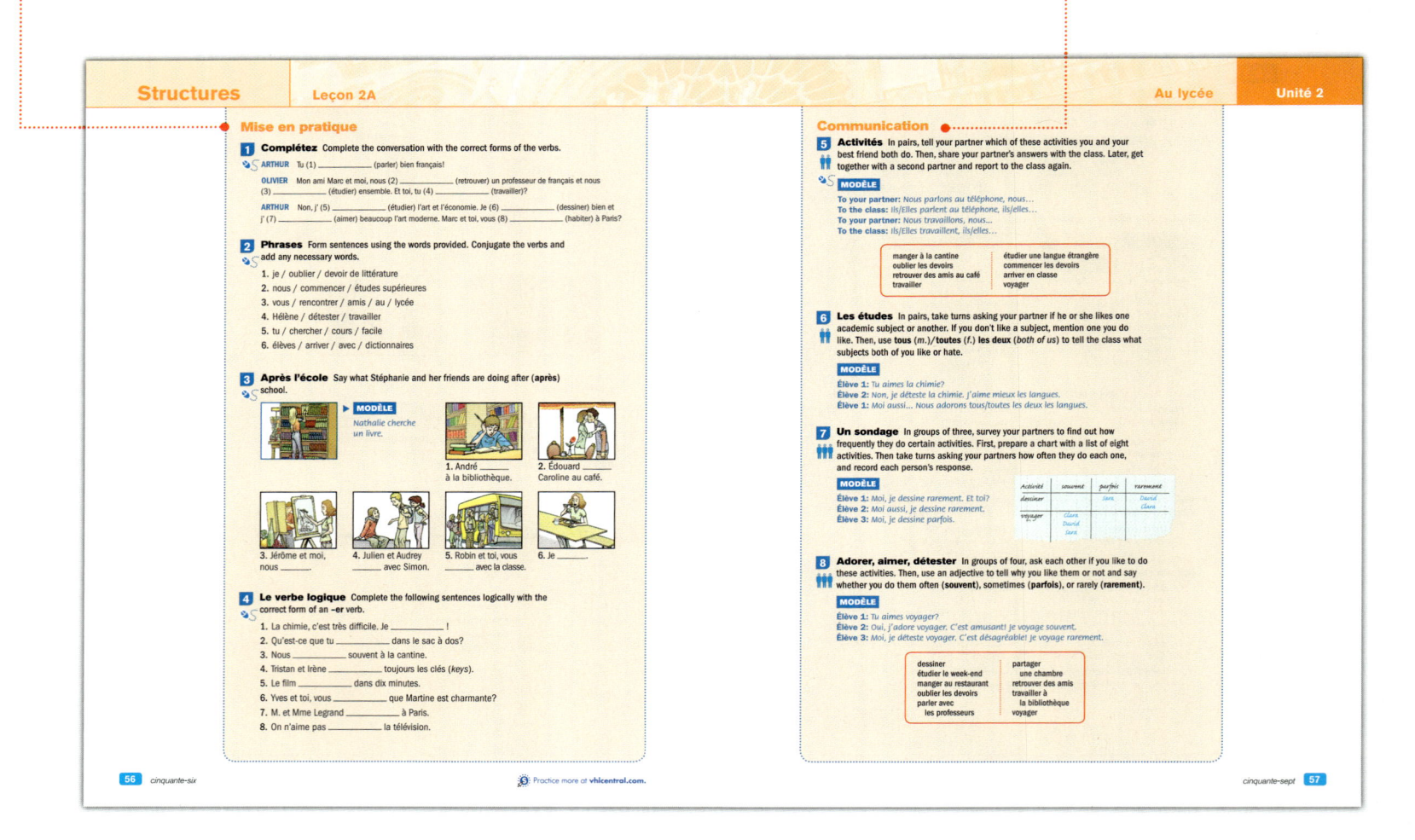

Middle School Activity Package
Additional in-class games and activities for beginning-level students.

Targeted review and recycling

Révision activities integrate the lesson's two grammar points with previously learned vocabulary and structures, providing consistent, built-in review and recycling as students progress through the text.

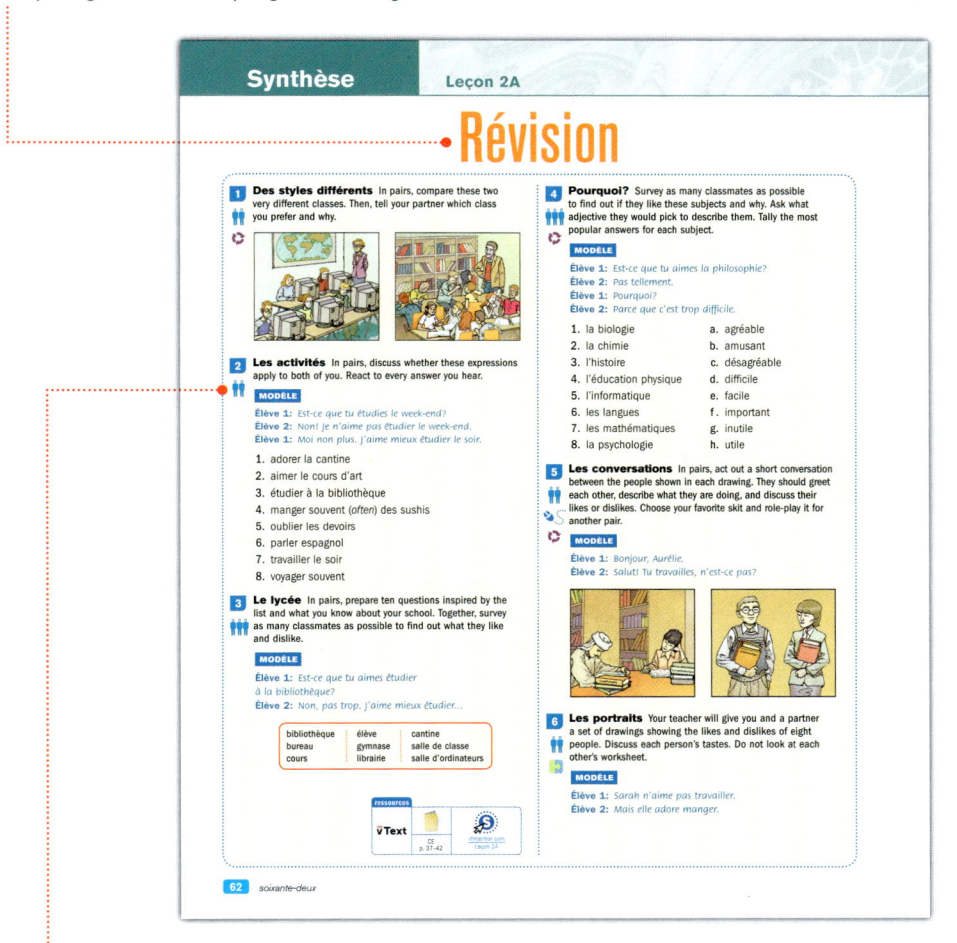

Interpersonal activities encourage students to demonstrate proficiency with the chapter's vocabulary and grammar. Activity types include situations, role-plays, games, personal questions, interviews, and surveys.

The **Activity Pack** in the Teacher Resources section of the Supersite contains the student worksheets for the **Info Gap activities**. In the Student Edition, these are identified by the interlocking puzzle pieces.

D'accord! 1A At-a-Glance

Authentic media and listening for interpretive communication

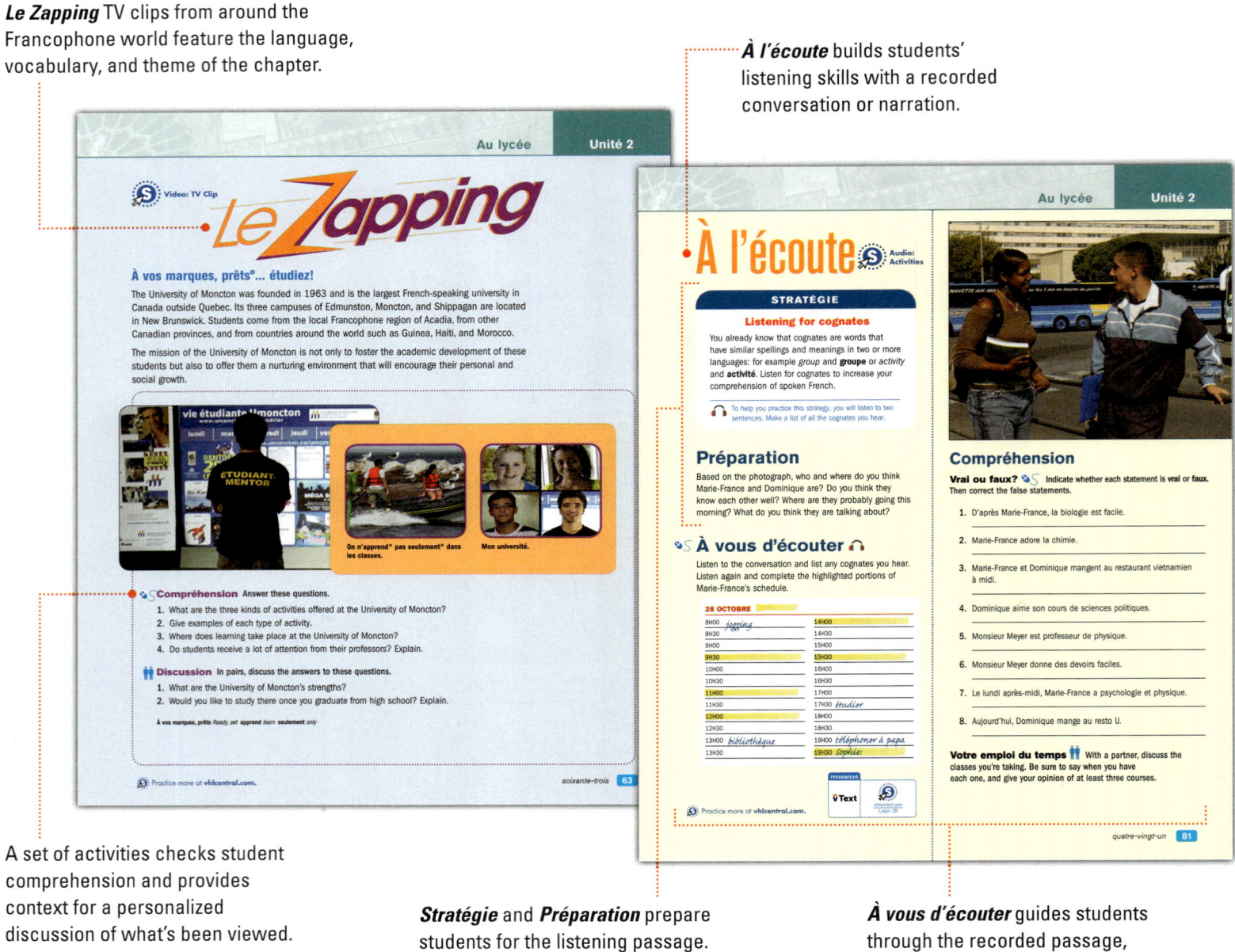

Le Zapping TV clips from around the Francophone world feature the language, vocabulary, and theme of the chapter.

À l'écoute builds students' listening skills with a recorded conversation or narration.

A set of activities checks student comprehension and provides context for a personalized discussion of what's been viewed.

Stratégie and *Préparation* prepare students for the listening passage.

À vous d'écouter guides students through the recorded passage, and *Compréhension* checks their understanding of what they heard.

Generate lively discussions by playing the TV clip in class.

Perspective through geography

Panorama presents interesting details about Francophone countries and regions.

Maps point out major cities, rivers, and other geographical features and situate the featured place in the context of its immediate surroundings and the world.

Art, history, and daily life are vividly described through language-rich text and photos.

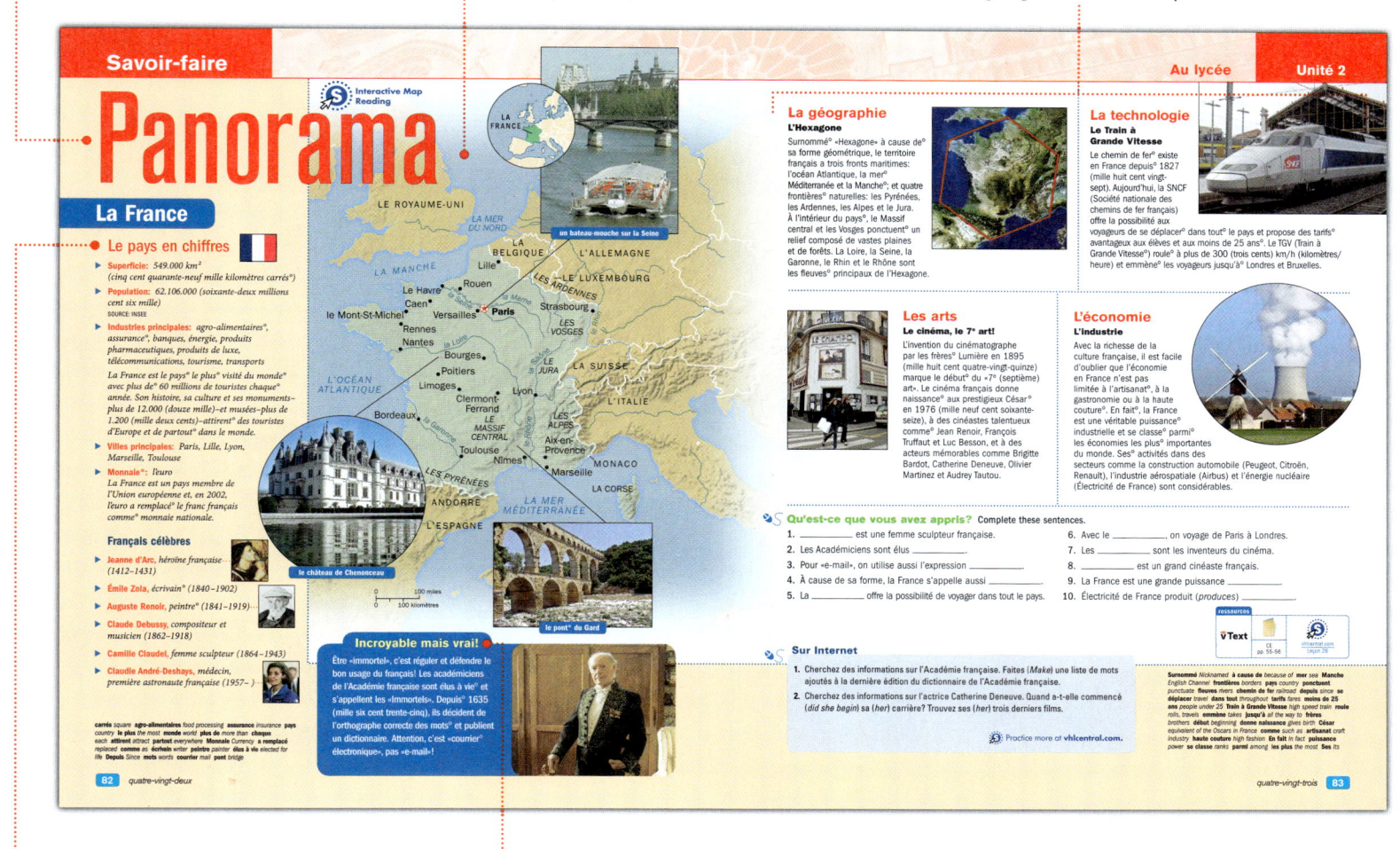

La ville/Le pays/La région en chiffres provides interesting key facts about the featured city, country, or region.

Incroyable mais vrai! highlights an "Isn't that cool?" fact about the featured place or its people.

Assign **Sur Internet** online research activities about a Francophone region of the world.

Teacher's Edition • **D'accord!** At-a-Glance   T23

D'accord! 1A At-a-Glance

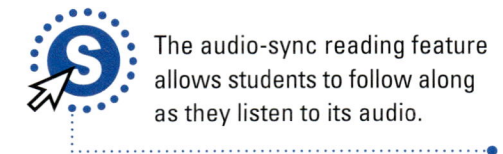

Reading skills developed in context

Avant la lecture presents valuable reading strategies and pre-reading activities.

Context-based readings pull all the chapter elements together.

Après la lecture activities include comprehension checks and post-reading expansion exercises.

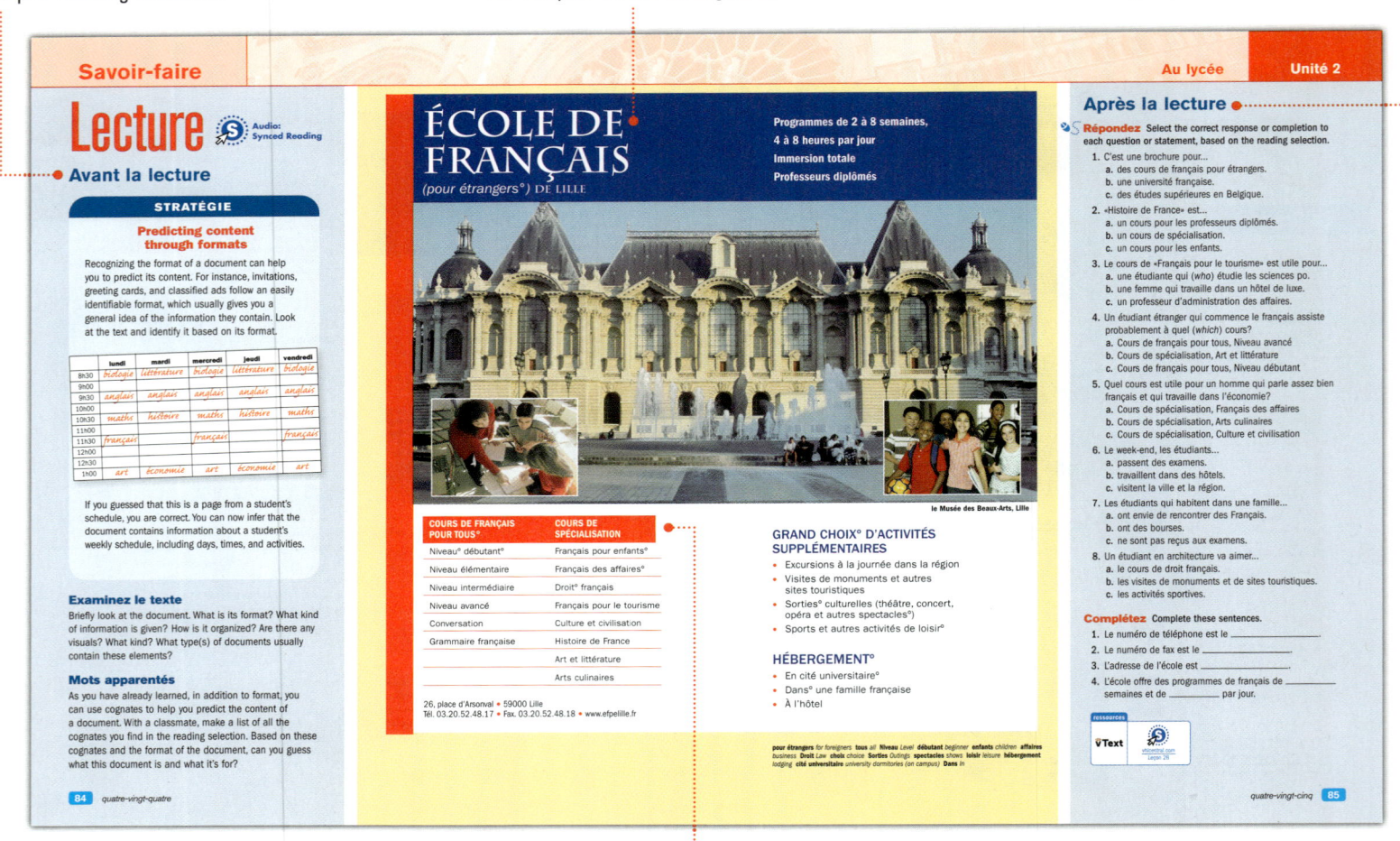

Graphic organizers, photos, and other visual elements support reading comprehension.

The audio-sync reading feature allows students to follow along as they listen to its audio.

Writing skills developed in context

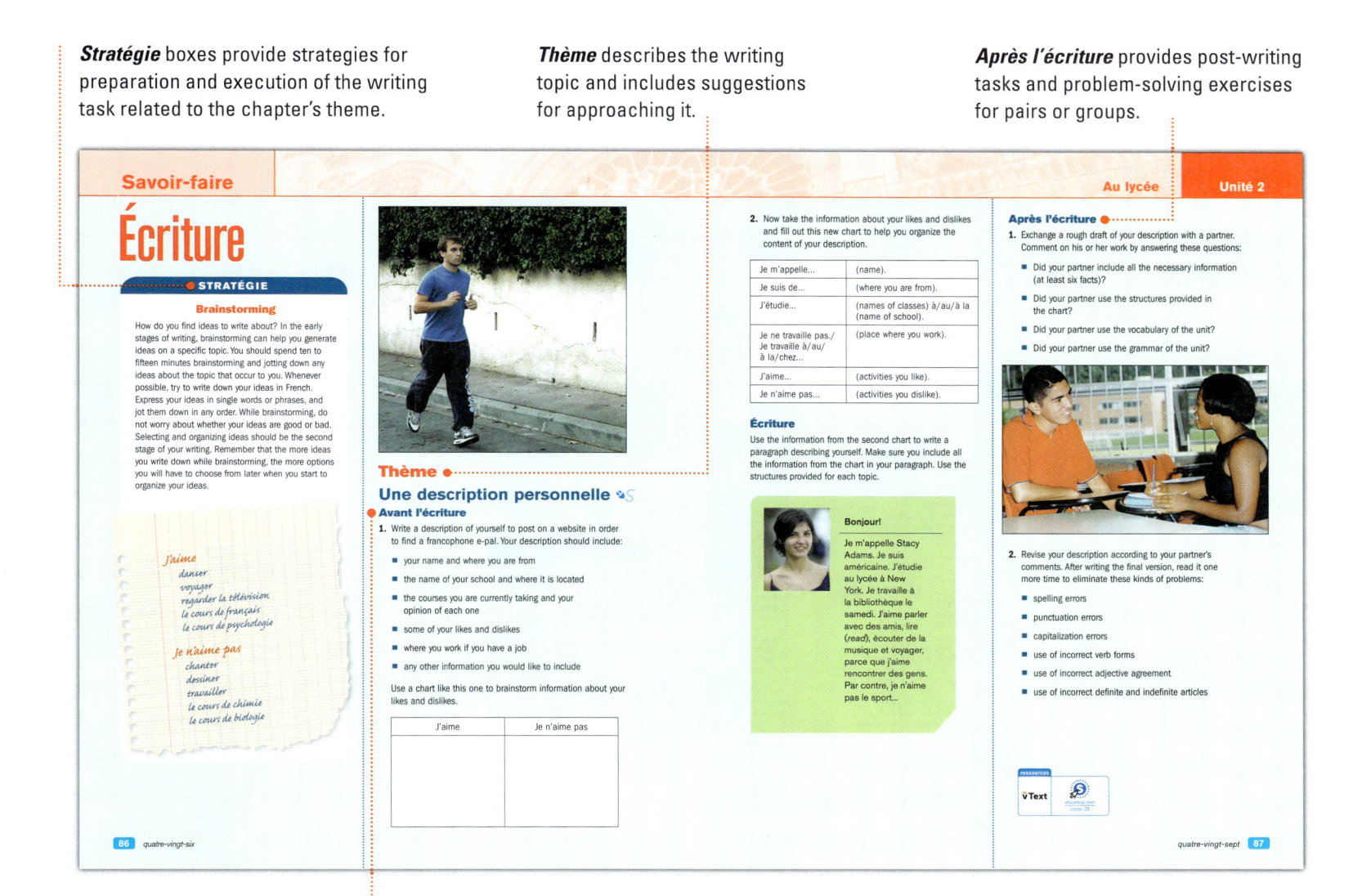

Stratégie boxes provide strategies for preparation and execution of the writing task related to the chapter's theme.

Thème describes the writing topic and includes suggestions for approaching it.

Après l'écriture provides post-writing tasks and problem-solving exercises for pairs or groups.

Avant l'écriture includes step-by-step tasks and problem-solving exercises for pairs or groups.

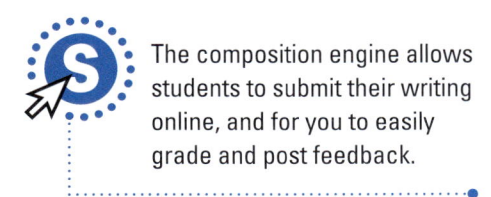

The composition engine allows students to submit their writing online, and for you to easily grade and post feedback.

D'accord! 1A At-a-Glance

Vocabulary as a reference and study tool

Vocabulaire summarizes all the active vocabulary in the chapter.

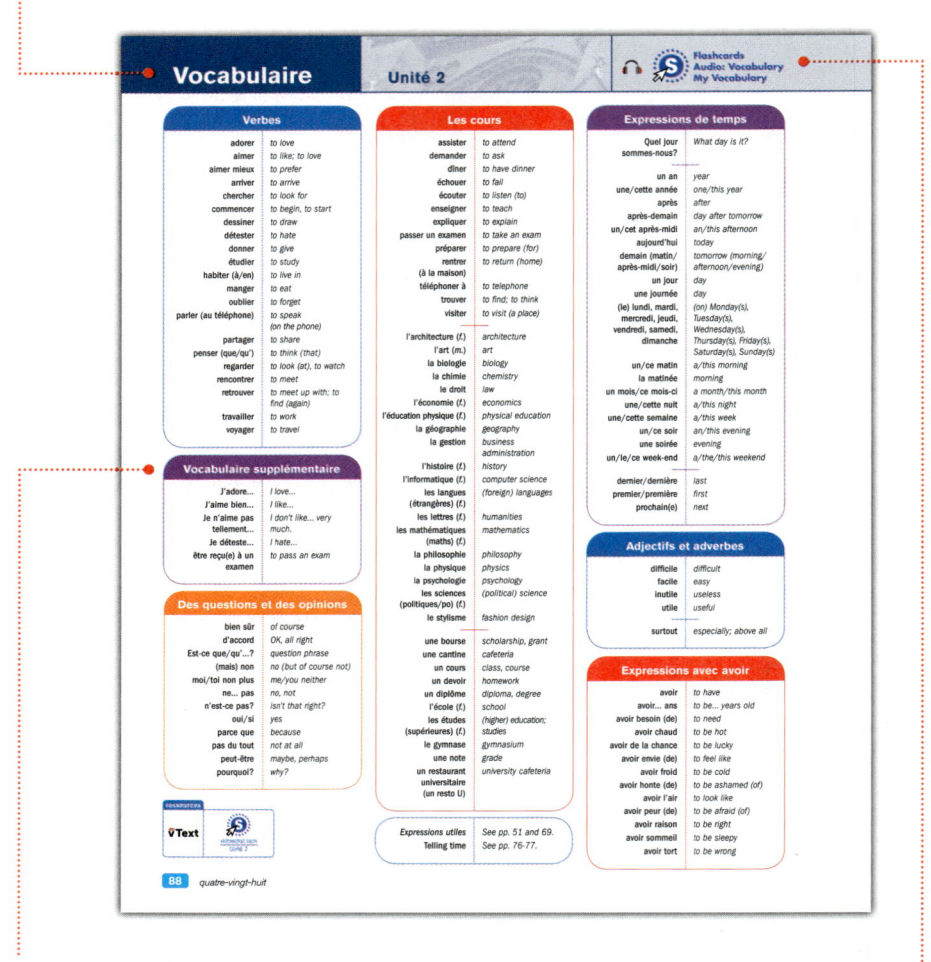

Each grouping includes active vocabulary that ties to the **You will learn how to…** goals presented at the beginning of each lesson.

Active vocabulary is recorded for convenient study and practice.

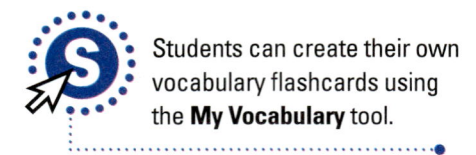

Students can create their own vocabulary flashcards using the **My Vocabulary** tool.

The Vista Higher Learning Story
Your Specialized Foreign Language Publisher

Independent, specialized, and privately owned, Vista Higher Learning was founded in 2000 with one mission: to raise the teaching and learning of world languages to a higher level. This mission is based on the following beliefs:

- It is essential to prepare students for a world in which learning another language is a necessity, not a luxury.
- Language learning should be fun and rewarding, and all students should have the tools they need to achieve success.
- Students who experience success learning a language will be more likely to continue their language studies both inside and outside the classroom.

With this in mind, we decided to take a fresh look at all aspects of language instructional materials. Because we are specialized, we dedicate 100 percent of our resources to this goal and base every decision on how well it supports language learning.

That is where you come in. Since our founding, we have relied on the invaluable feedback of language teachers and students nationwide. This partnership has proved to be the cornerstone of our success, allowing us to constantly improve our programs to meet your instructional needs.

The result? Programs that make language learning exciting, relevant, and effective through:

- unprecedented access to resources
- a wide variety of contemporary, authentic materials
- the integration of text, technology, and media
- a bold and engaging textbook design

By focusing on our singular passion, we let you focus on yours.

The Vista Higher Learning Team

VISTA®
HIGHER LEARNING

500 Boylston Street, Suite 620, Boston, MA 02116-3736 TOLL-FREE: 800-618-7375
TELEPHONE: 617-426-4910 FAX: 617-426-5209 www.vistahigherlearning.com

How D'accord! Works

Differentiation

Knowing how to appeal to learners of different abilities and learning styles will allow you to foster a positive teaching environment and motivate all your students. Here are some strategies for creating inclusive learning environments. Consider also the ideas at the base of the Teacher's Edition (TE) pages. Extension and expansion activities are also suggested.

Learners with Special Needs

Learners with special needs include students with attention priority disorders or learning disabilities, slower-paced learners, at-risk learners, and English-language learners. Some inclusion strategies that work well with such students are:

Clear Structure By teaching concepts in a predictable order, you can help students organize their learning. Encourage students to keep outlines of materials they read, classify words into categories such as colors, or follow prewriting steps.

Frequent Review and Repetition Preview material to be taught and review material covered at the end of each lesson. Pair proficient learners with less proficient ones to practice and reinforce concepts. Help students retain concepts through continuous practice and review.

Multi-sensory Input and Output Use visual, auditory, and kinesthetic tasks to add interest and motivation, and to achieve long-term retention. For example, vary input with the use of audio recordings, video, guided visualization, rhymes, and mnemonics.

Additional Time Consider how physical limitations may affect participation in special projects or daily routines. Provide additional time and recommended accommodations.

Different Learning Styles

Visual Learners learn best by seeing, so engage them in activities and projects that are visually creative. Encourage them to write down information and think in pictures as a long-term retention strategy; reinforce their learning through visual displays such as diagrams, videos, and handouts.

Auditory Learners best retain information by listening. Engage them in discussions, debates, and role-playing. Reinforce their learning by playing audio versions of texts or reading aloud passages and stories. Encourage them to pay attention to voice, tone, and pitch to infer meaning.

Kinesthetic Learners learn best through moving, touching, and doing hands-on activities. Involve such students in skits and dramatizations; to infer or convey meaning, have them observe or model gestures such as those used for greeting someone or getting someone's attention.

Advanced Learners

Advanced learners have the potential to learn language concepts and complete assignments at an accelerated pace. They may benefit from assignments that are more challenging than the ones given to their peers. The key to differentiating for advanced learners is adding a degree of rigor to a given task. Examples include sharing perspectives on texts they have read with the class, retelling detailed stories, preparing analyses of texts, or adding to discussions. Here are some other strategies for engaging advanced learners:

Timed Answers Have students answer questions within a specified time limit.

Persuading Adapt activities so students have to write or present their points of view in order to persuade an audience. Pair or group advanced learners to form debating teams.

Pre-AP®

While Pre-AP® strategies are associated with advanced students, all students can benefit from the activities and strategies that are categorized as Pre-AP® in **D'accord!** Long-term success in language learning starts in the first year of instruction, so these strategies should be incorporated throughout students' language-learning career.

D'accord! is particularly strong in fostering interpretive communication skills. Students are offered a variety of opportunities to read and listen

Pre-AP is a registered trademark of the College Board, which was not involved in the production of, and does not endorse, this product.

to spoken language. The *Lecture* sections provide various types of authentic written texts, and the *Le Zapping* and *Flash culture* videos feature French spoken at a natural pace. Encourage students to interact with as much authentic language as possible, as this will lead to long-term success.

Heritage Language Learners

Heritage language learners are students who come from homes where a language other than English is spoken. French heritage learners are likely to have adequate comprehension and conversation skills, but they could require as much explicit instruction of reading and writing skills as their non-heritage peers. Because of their background, heritage language learners can attain, with instruction adapted to their needs, a high level of proficiency and literacy in French. Use these strategies to support them:

Support and Validate Experiences Acknowledge students' experiences with their heritage culture and encourage them to share what they know.

Develop Literacy and Writing Skills Help students focus on reading as well as grammar, punctuation, and syntax skills, but be careful not to assign a workload significantly greater than what is assigned to non-heritage learners.

Best Practices

The creators of **D'accord!** understand that there are many different approaches to successful language teaching and that no one method works perfectly for all teachers or all learners. These strategies and tips may be applied to any language-teaching method.

Maintain the Target Language

As much as possible, create an immersion environment by using French to *teach* French. Encourage the exclusive use of the target language in your classroom, employing visual aids, mnemonics, circumlocution, or gestures to complement what you say. Encourage students to perceive meaning directly through careful listening and observation, and by using cognates and familiar structures and patterns to deduce meaning.

Cultivate Critical Thinking

Prompt students to reflect, observe, reason, and form judgments in French. Engaging students in activities that require them to compare, contrast, predict, criticize, and estimate will help them to internalize the language structures they have learned.

Encourage Use of Circumlocution

Prompt students to discover various ways of expressing ideas and of overcoming potential blocks to communication through the use of circumlocution and paraphrasing.

How D'accord! Works

Assessment

As you use the **D'accord!** program, you can employ a variety of assessments to evaluate progress. The program provides comprehensive, discrete answer assessments, as well as more communicative assessments that elicit open-ended, personalized responses.

Testing Program

The **D'accord!** Testing Program offers two quizzes for each **Contextes** section and every grammar point in **Structures** in Levels 1 and 2. Each **Quiz I** uses discrete answer formats, such as multiple-choice, fill-in-the-blanks, matching, and completing charts, while **Quiz II** uses more open-ended formats, such as asking students to write sentences using prompts or respond to a topic in paragraph format. There is no listening comprehension section for the **Quizzes**. Level 3 **Quizzes** for the **Pour commencer** and **Structures Quizzes** follow a similar format to those in Levels 1 and 2.

Two **Lesson** and **Unit Tests** are available for Levels 1 and 2. Versions **I** and **II** are interchangeable, for purposes of administering make-up tests. All of the **Tests** contain a listening comprehension section. Level 3 has one **Test** for each lesson. Cumulative **Exams** in all three levels encompass the main vocabulary fields, key grammar points, and the principal language functions covered in corresponding textbook chapters. All levels contain **Optional Test Sections**.

The Testing Program is also available on the Supersite so that you can customize the components by adding, eliminating, or moving items according to your classroom and student needs.

Portfolio Assessment

Portfolios can provide further valuable evidence of your students' learning. They are useful tools for evaluating students' progress in French and also suggest to students how they are likely to be assessed in the real world. Since portfolio activities often comprise classroom tasks that you would assign as part of a lesson or as homework, you should think of the planning, selecting, recording, and interpreting of information about individual performance as a way of blending assessment with instruction.

You may find it helpful to refer to portfolio contents, such as drafts, essays, and samples of presentations when writing student reports and conveying the status of a student's progress to his or her parents.

Ask students regularly to consider which pieces of their own work they would like to share and help them develop criteria for selecting representative samples. Prompt students to choose a variety of media to demonstrate development in all four language skills.

Strategies for Differentiating Assessment

Here are some strategies for modifying tests and other forms of assessment according to your students' needs.

Adjust Questions Direct complex or higher-level questions to students who are equipped to answer them adequately and modify questions for students with greater needs. Always ask questions that elicit thinking, but keep in mind the students' abilities.

Provide Tiered Assignments Assign tasks of varying complexity depending on individual student needs.

Promote Flexible Grouping Encourage movement among groups of students so that all learners are appropriately challenged. Group students according to interest, oral proficiency levels, or learning styles.

Adjust Pacing Pace the sequence and speed of assessments to suit your students' needs. Time advanced learners to challenge them and allow slower-paced learners more time to complete tasks or to answer questions.

Student Objectives

Students can assess their own progress by using "I Can" (or "Can-Do") Statements. The template below may be customized with the Student Objectives found in **D'accord!** to guide student learning within and between chapters, and to train students to assess their progress.

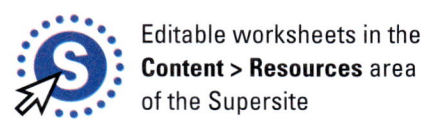

Editable worksheets in the **Content > Resources** area of the Supersite

---

STUDENT OBJECTIVES
Leçon 1A D'accord! 1

Nom _____ Date _____

Objectifs: Contextes	Date	Barème
1. I can use basic greetings and farewells.		
2. I can introduce myself and others.		
3. I can respond appropriately to people.		

Barème:

4 Formidable!: I know this well enough to teach it to someone.
3 Très bien: I can do this with almost no mistakes.
2 Assez bien: I can do much of this but I have questions.
1 C'est dur: I can do this only with help.
0 Au secours!: I do not understand this, even with help.

Commentaire: _____
_____
_____
_____

How D'accord! Works

Integrated Performance Assessment

Integrated performance assessments (IPA) begin with a goal—a real-life task that makes sense to students and engages their interest. To complete the task, students progress through the three modes of communication: they read, view, and listen for information (interpretive mode); they talk and write with classmates and others on what they have experienced (interpersonal mode); and they share formally what they have learned (presentational mode). A critical step in administering the IPA is to define and share rubrics with students before beginning the task. They need to be aware of what successful performance should look like.

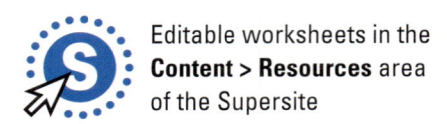

Editable worksheets in the **Content > Resources** area of the Supersite

assessment

Unité 2

Integrated Performance Assessment Rubric

	5 points	3 points	1 point
Interpretive	The student has identified a substantial list of classes and additional activities for the brochure.	The student has identified a short list of classes and additional activities for the brochure.	The student has difficulty identifying classes and additional activities for the brochure.
Interpersonal	Using grammatically-correct French, students compare their lists and agree on the best items to include in the brochure.	Students compare their lists and agree on the best items to include in the brochure, but with some errors in French.	Students have difficulty comparing their lists and agreeing on the best items to include in the brochure.
Presentational	The brochure has an appropriate and substantial list of classes and additional activities. The brochure is attractively laid out, with all relevant information and attractive use of imagery.	The brochure has an adequate list of classes and additional activities. The brochure is attractively laid out, with some relevant information and some imagery.	The conversation does not include an appropriate list of classes and additional activities. The brochure is not attractively laid out, with little relevant information and few images.

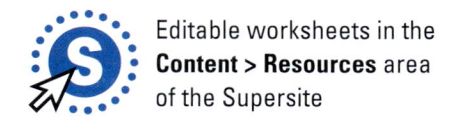

> Editable worksheets in the **Content > Resources** area of the Supersite

performance task — Unité 2

All responses and communication must be in French.

Context
A French student exchange program wants to evaluate the class offerings at your school to see if it would be a good place to send French students. You and your classmates need to create a brochure for your school to attract exchange students.

Interpretive task
Read the **Lecture** section on pages 68–69 of the textbook, paying particular attention to the course listings. Make a list of the classes you would include on the brochure, as well as additional activities you think would be attractive to a French exchange student.

Interpersonal task
Compare your list with a partner, asking each other if each course on the individual lists should go in the brochure. Come to an agreement on the classes you want to include in your brochure, as well as several supplementary activities.

Presentational task
Compile your information into an attractive brochure for your school, including photos, using the model shown on pages 68–69.

Within the **D'accord!** activity sequence, you will find several opportunities for performance assessment. Consider using the Voiceboard tool or Partner Chat activities as the culmination of an oral communication sequence. The *Écriture* assignment in the *Savoir-faire* section has students apply the chapter context to a real-life task.

How D'accord! Works

Six Steps in Using the D'accord! Instructional Design

Step 1: Context

Begin each lesson by asking students to provide *from their own experience* words, concepts, categories, and opinions related to the theme. Spend quality time evoking words, images, ideas, phrases, and sentences; group and classify concepts. You are giving students the "hook" for their learning, focusing them on their most interesting topic—themselves—and encouraging them to invest personally in their learning.

Step 2: Vocabulary

Now turn to the vocabulary section, inviting students to experience it as a new linguistic *code* to express what they *already know and experience* in the context of the lesson theme. Vocabulary concepts are presented in context, carefully organized, and frequently reviewed to reinforce student understanding. Involve students in brainstorming, classifying and grouping words and thoughts, and personalizing phrases and sentences. In this way, you will help students see French as a new tool for self-expression.

Step 3: Media

Once students see that French is a tool for expressing their own ideas, bridge their experiences to those of French speakers through the *Roman-photo* section. The *Roman-photo* Video Program storyline presents and reviews vocabulary and structure in accurate cultural contexts for effective training in both comprehension and personal communication.

Step 4: Culture

Now bring students into the experience of culture as seen *from the perspective* of those living in it. Here we share Francophone cultures' unique geography, history, products, perspectives, and practices. Through *Flash culture* (instructional video) and *Le Zapping* (authentic video) students experience and reflect on cultural experiences beyond their own.

Step 5: Structure

We began with students' experiences, focusing on bridging their lives and language to the target cultures. Through context, media, and culture, students have incorporated both previously-learned and new grammatical structures into their personalized communication. Now a formal presentation of relevant grammar demonstrates that grammar is a tool for clearer and more effective communication. Clear presentations and invitations to compare French to English build confidence, fluency, and accuracy.

Step 6: Skill Synthesis and Communication

Pulling all their learning together, students now integrate context, personal experience, communication tools, and cultural products, perspectives, and practices. Through extended reading, writing, listening, speaking, and cultural exploration in scaffolded progression, students apply all their skills for a rich, personalized experience of French.

D'accord! and the *Standards for Foreign Language Learning*

D'accord! promotes and enhances student learning and motivation through its instructional design, based on and informed by the best practices of the *Standards for Foreign Language Learning in the 21st Century* as presented by the American Council on the Teaching of Foreign Languages (ACTFL).

D'accord! blends the underlying principles of the five Cs (Communication, Cultures, Connections, Comparisons, Communities) with features and strategies tailored specifically to build students' speaking, listening, reading, and writing skills. As a result, right from the start students are given the tools to express themselves articulately, interact meaningfully with others, and become highly competent communicators in French.

Key Standards annotations, at the beginning of each section in the TE, highlight the most important standards met in that section. Below is a complete list of the standards.

The Five Cs of Foreign Language Learning

1. Communication
Students:
1. Engage in conversation, provide and obtain information, express feelings and emotions, and exchange opinions. (Interpersonal mode)
2. Understand and interpret written and spoken language. (Interpretive mode)
3. Present information, concepts, and ideas to an audience of listeners or readers. (Presentational mode)

2. Cultures
Students demonstrate an understanding of the relationship between:
1. The practices and perspectives of the culture studied.
2. The products and perspectives of the culture studied.

3. Connections
Students:
1. Reinforce and further their knowledge of other disciplines through French.
2. Acquire information and recognize distinctive viewpoints only available through French language and cultures.

4. Comparisons
Students demonstrate understanding of:
1. The nature of language through comparisons of the French language and their own.
2. The concept of culture through comparisons of the cultures studied and their own.

5. Communities
Students:
1. Use French both within and beyond the school setting.
2. Show evidence of becoming life-long learners by using French for personal enjoyment and enrichment.

Adapted from ACTFL's *Standards for Foreign Language Learning in the 21st Century*

D'accord! 1A Pacing Guide

DAY	Warm-up / Activate	Present / Practice / Communicate	Reflect / Conclude / Connect
1 Context for Communication	• Evoke student experiences & vocabulary for context; present **Pour commencer** [5] *5 minutes*	• Hand out Student Objectives Worksheet for **Contextes**. Explain how they can track their own progress using the Worksheet [5] • Present vocabulary through illustrations, phrases, categories, association [20] • Student pairs begin **Mise en pratique** [15] *30 minutes*	• Students restate context [5] • Introduce homework: Complete **Mise en pratique** Act. 1 (text/**Supersite**) [5] *10 minutes*
2 Vocabulary as a Tool	• Review vocabulary [5] *5 minutes*	• Do the **Écoutez** activity with the whole class, playing the audio as many times as needed [15] • Have student pairs finish **Mise en pratique** [15] *30 minutes*	• Students review and personalize key vocabulary in context [5] • Introduce homework: **Supersite** flashcards, context illustrations & audio; end-of-chapter list with audio [5] *10 minutes*
3 Vocabulary as a Tool	• Student groups review **Mise en pratique** [5] *5 minutes*	• Students do **Communication** [20] • Choose one activity from the Middle School Activity Pack as a class activity [10] *30 minutes*	• Students review and personalize key vocabulary in context [5] • Introduce homework: **Supersite** flashcards, context illustrations & audio; end-of-chapter list with audio; remaining auto-graded activities (as applicable) [5] *10 minutes*
4 Vocabulary as a Tool	• Student groups review **Communication** [5] *5 minutes*	• Present **Les sons et les lettres** (**Supersite**/CD) [15] • Allow all students to check their pronunciation through classroom practice and repetition [15] *30 minutes*	• Have students check their progress on their Student Objectives Worksheet [5] • Introduce homework: Continue practicing pronunciation on the **Supersite**; My Vocabulary; end-of-chapter list with audio; remaining auto-graded activities (as applicable) [5] *10 minutes*
5 Media as a Bridge	• Assessment: **Contextes** [5] *5 minutes*	• Distribute the **Roman-photo** activities in the **Cahier**. Answer the questions in the **Avant de regarder** [5] • Orient students to **Roman-photo** and **Expressions utiles** through video stills with observation, role-play, and prediction [10] • Read the storyboard in the Student Edition [20] *35 minutes*	• Introduce homework: **Roman-photo** activities (Text/**Supersite**) [5] *5 minutes*
6 Media as a Bridge	• Go over the activities in **En regardant la vidéo** (**Cahier**) [10] *10 minutes*	• View **Roman-photo** while students answer the questions from the **Cahier** [25] • Check comprehension and practice using the activities in the Student Edition [10] *35 minutes*	• Introduce homework: **Roman-photo** activities (**Supersite**) [5] *5 minutes*
7 Media as a Bridge	• Distribute the **Flash culture** activities in the **Cahier**. Answer the questions in the **Avant de regarder** [5] *5 minutes*	• View **Flash culture** while students answer the questions from the **Cahier** [25] • View, discuss, re-view **Flash culture** [10] *35 minutes*	• Introduce homework: Students complete **Flash culture** activities (Text/**Supersite**) [5] *5 minutes*
8 Culture for Communication	• Review **Flash culture** activities [5] *5 minutes*	• Present (select) **Culture** features in whole class or small groups, jigsaw, numbered heads together, etc. [20] • Assign Activity 3 to student pairs, allowing time for students to present their work to the whole class [15] *35 minutes*	• Introduce homework: **Sur Internet** or **Activités** (Text/**Supersite**) [5] *5 minutes*
9 Structure as a Tool	• Student pairs/groups review **Culture** activities [5] • Assessment: **Roman-photo**, **Culture** [5] *10 minutes*	• Present about half of grammatical concept A.1 using text, **Supersite** (slides), and **Roman-photo** segments [10] • Do a whole class quick check to ensure students understand the explanation [5] • Present the balance of grammatical concept A.1 [10] • Do a whole class quick check to ensure students understand the explanation [5] *30 minutes*	• Introduce homework: Students complete **Essayez!** (text/**Supersite**) [5] *5 minutes*

Traditional Schedule

DAY	Warm-up / Activate	Present / Practice / Communicate	Reflect / Conclude
10 **Structure in Context**	• Go over **Essayez!** [5] **5 minutes**	• Hand out Student Objectives Worksheet for **Structures** [5] • Re-present grammar topic using the Grammar Tutorial (**Supersite**) [10] • Students pairs do assigned activities from A.1 **Mise en pratique** and **Communication** [20] **35 minutes**	• Introduce homework: Students complete A.1 **Mise en pratique** and **Communication** (text/**Supersite**); watch tutorials (**Supersite**) [5] **5 minutes**
11 **Structure in Context**	• Review Homework [5] **5 minutes**	• Choose a class game/activity from the Middle School Activity Pack or TE wrap [20] • Students do A.1 **Cahier** written activities [15] **35 minutes**	• Introduce homework: Students complete **Cahier** (written) activities (text/**Supersite**) [5] **5 minutes**
12 **Structure in Context**	• Review Homework [5] **5 minutes**	• Students do A.1 **Communication** [15] • Complete selected **Cahier** audio activities [15] • Start **Révision** activities [5] **35 minutes**	• Introduce homework: Students do selected **Révision** activities (text/**Supersite**) [5] **5 minutes**
13 **Structure as a Tool**	• Review Homework [5] • Assessment: **Structure A.1** [5] **10 minutes**	• Present about half of grammatical concept A.2 using text, **Supersite** (slides), and **Roman-photo** segments [10] • Do a whole class quick check [5] • Present the balance of grammatical concept A.2 [10] • Do a whole class quick check [5] **30 minutes**	• Introduce homework: Students complete **Essayez!** (text/**Supersite**) [5] **5 minutes**
14 **Structure in Context**	• Go over **Essayez!** [5] **5 minutes**	• Hand out Student Objectives Worksheet for **Structures** [5] • Re-present grammar topic using the Grammar Tutorial (**Supersite**) [10] • Students pairs do assigned activities from A.2 **Mise en pratique** and **Communication** [20] **35 minutes**	• Introduce homework: Students complete A.2 **Mise en pratique** and **Communication** (text/**Supersite**); watch tutorials (**Supersite**) [5] **5 minutes**
15 **Structure in Context**	• Review Homework [5] **5 minutes**	• Choose a class game/activity from the Middle School Activity Pack or TE wrap [20] • Students do A.2 **Cahier** written activities [15] **35 minutes**	• Introduce homework: Students complete **Cahier** (written) activities (text/**Supersite**) [5] **5 minutes**
16 **Structure in Context**	• Review Homework [5] **5 minutes**	• Students do A.2 **Communication** [15] • Complete selected **Cahier** audio activities [15] • Start **Révision** activities [5] **35 minutes**	• Introduce homework: Students do selected **Révision** activities (text/**Supersite**) [5] **5 minutes**
17 **Authentic Media**	• Student groups present and complete **Révision** [10] **10 minutes**	• Introduce, guide discussion of **Le Zapping**; show clip via **Supersite** [10] • Student pairs do post-viewing activities; show clip again as necessary [15] **25 minutes**	• Student pairs/groups use unit context to review grammar concepts [5] • Introduce homework: Prepare for **Structures** assessment [5] **10 minutes**
18 **Context for Communication**	• Assessment **Structures** [10] **10 minutes**	• Hand out Student Objectives Worksheet for **Contextes** [5] • Present vocabulary through illustrations, phrases, categories, association [20] • Student pairs begin **Mise en pratique** [5] **30 minutes**	• Introduce homework: Complete **Mise en pratique** Act. 1 (text/**Supersite**) [5] **5 minutes**
19 **Vocabulary as a Tool**	• Review vocabulary [5] **5 minutes**	• Do the **Écoutez** activity with the whole class, playing the audio as many times as needed [15] • Have student pairs finish **Mise en pratique** [15] **30 minutes**	• Students review and personalize key vocabulary in context [5] • Introduce homework: **Supersite** flashcards, context illustrations & audio [5] **10 minutes**
20 **Vocabulary as a Tool**	• Student groups review **Mise en pratique** [5] **5 minutes**	• Students do **Communication** [20] • Choose one activity from the Middle School Activity Pack as a class activity [10] **30 minutes**	• Students review and personalize key vocabulary in context [5] • Introduce homework: context illustrations & audio; remaining auto-graded activities (as applicable) [5] **10 minutes**

D'accord! 1A Pacing Guide

DAY	Warm-up / Activate	Present / Practice / Communicate	Reflect / Conclude / Connect
21 Vocabulary as a Tool	• Student groups review **Communication** [5] 5 minutes	• Present **Les sons et les lettres** (**Supersite**/CD) [15] • Allow all students to check their pronunciation through classroom practice and repetition [15] 30 minutes	• Have students check their progress on their Student Objectives Worksheet [5] • Introduce homework: Continue practicing pronunciation on the **Supersite**; remaining auto-graded activities (as applicable) [5] 10 minutes
22 Media as a Bridge	• Assessment: **Contextes** [5] 5 minutes	• Distribute the **Roman-photo** activities in the **Cahier**. Answer the questions in the **Avant de regarder** [5] • Orient students to **Roman-photo** and **Expressions utiles** through video stills with observation, role-play, and prediction [10] • Read the storyboard in the Student Edition [20] 35 minutes	• Introduce homework: **Roman-photo** activities (Text/**Supersite**) [5] 5 minutes
23 Media as a Bridge	• Go over the activities in **En regardant la vidéo** (**Cahier**) [10] 10 minutes	• View **Roman-photo** while students answer the questions from the **Cahier** [25] • Check comprehension and practice using the activities in the Student Edition [10] 35 minutes	• Introduce homework: **Roman-photo** activities (**Supersite**) [5] 5 minutes
24 Culture for Communication	• Review **Roman-photo** activities [5] 5 minutes	• Present (select) **Culture** features in whole class or small groups, jigsaw, numbered heads together, etc. [20] • Assign Activity 3 to student pairs, allowing time for students to present their work to the whole class [15] 35 minutes	• Introduce homework: **Sur Internet** or **Activités** (Text/**Supersite**) [5] 5 minutes
25 Structure as a Tool	• Student pairs/groups review **Culture** activities [5] • Assessment: **Roman-photo**, **Culture** [5] 10 minutes	• Present about half of grammatical concept B.1 using text, **Supersite** (slides), and **Roman-photo** segments [10] • Do a whole class quick check to ensure students understand the explanation [5] • Present the balance of grammatical concept B.1 [10] • Do a whole class quick check to ensure students understand the explanation [5] 30 minutes	• Introduce homework: Students complete **Essayez!** (text/**Supersite**) [5] 5 minutes
26 Structure in Context	• Go over **Essayez!** [5] 5 minutes	• Hand out Student Objectives Worksheet for **Structures** [5] • Re-present grammar topic using the Grammar Tutorial (**Supersite**) [10] • Students pairs do assigned activities from B.1 **Mise en pratique** and **Communication** [20] 35 minutes	• Introduce homework: Students complete B.1 **Mise en pratique** and **Communication** (text/**Supersite**); watch tutorials (**Supersite**) [5] 5 minutes
27 Structure in Context	• Review Homework [5] 5 minutes	• Choose a class game/activity from the Middle School Activity Pack or TE wrap [20] • Students do B.2 **Cahier** written activities [15] 35 minutes	• Introduce homework: Students complete **Cahier** (written) activities (text/**Supersite**) [5] 5 minutes
28 Structure in Context	• Review Homework [5] 5 minutes	• Students do B.1 **Communication** [15] • Complete selected **Cahier** audio activities [15] • Start **Révision** activities [5] 35 minutes	• Introduce homework: Students do selected **Révision** activities (text/**Supersite**) [5] 5 minutes
29 Structure as a Tool	• Review Homework [5] • Assessment: **Structures B.1** [5] 10 minutes	• Present about half of grammatical concept B.2 using text, **Supersite** (slides), and **Roman-photo** segments [10] • Do a whole class quick check [5] • Present the balance of grammatical concept B.2 [10] • Do a whole class quick check [5] 30 minutes	• Introduce homework: Students complete **Essayez!** (text/**Supersite**) [5] 5 minutes

Traditional Schedule

DAY	Warm-up / Activate	Present / Practice / Communicate	Reflect / Conclude
30 Structure in Context	• Go over **Essayez!** [5] **5 minutes**	• Hand out Student Objectives Worksheet for **Structures** [5] • Re-present grammar topic using the Grammar Tutorial (**Supersite**) [10] • Students pairs do assigned activities from B.2 **Mise en pratique** and **Communication** [20] **35 minutes**	• Introduce homework: Students complete B.2 **Mise en pratique** and **Communication** (text/**Supersite**); watch tutorials (**Supersite**) [5] **5 minutes**
31 Structure in Context	• Review Homework [5] **5 minutes**	• Choose a class game/activity from the Middle School Activity Pack or TE wrap [20] • Students do A.1 **Cahier** written activities [15] **35 minutes**	• Introduce homework: Students complete **Cahier** (written) activities (text/**Supersite**) [5] **5 minutes**
32 Structure in Context	• Review Homework [5] **5 minutes**	• Students do B.2 **Communication** [15] • Complete selected **Cahier** audio activities [15] • Start **Révision** activities [5] **35 minutes**	• Introduce homework: Students do selected **Révision** activities (text/**Supersite**) [5] **5 minutes**
33 Skill Synthesis: Interpretive (Listening)	• Share & discuss **Révision** [5] • Assessment: **Structures** [5] **10 minutes**	• Guide students through **Stratégie** and preparation in **À l'écoute**; present selection [20] • Students (individuals, pairs, or small groups) do **Compréhension** activities [10] **30 minutes**	• Introduce homework: Complete **À l'écoute** (text or **Supersite**) [5] **5 minutes**
34 Geographical Context	• Review content & context of **À l'écoute** [5] **5 minutes**	• Use the Interactive Map on the **Supersite** to situate the featured area geographically [10] • Present **Panorama** through whole class or small groups, jigsaw, numbered heads together, etc. [20] • Student pairs/groups begin activities [5] **35 minutes**	• Introduce homework: **Sur Internet** activity (text/**Supersite**) [5] **5 minutes**
35 Skill Synthesis: Interpretive (Reading)	• Have student report and compare their answers to the **Sur Internet** activity [10] **10 minutes**	• Guide students through **Avant la lecture** [15] • Students read **Lecture** (whole class or small groups) [15] **30 minutes**	• Introduce homework: begin **Après la lecture** activities (text/**Supersite**) [5] **5 minutes**
36 Skill Synthesis: Interpretive (Reading)	• Discussion/assessment: **Panorama** [10] **10 minutes**	• Go over homework and then do the second **Après la lecture** activity [15] • Assign student pairs or groups to the interpersonal activity at the end of the activity sequence [15] **30 minutes**	• Introduce homework: begin **Cahier** activities (**Cahier/Supersite**) [5] **5 minutes**
37 Skill Synthesis: Presentational (Writing)	• Discussion/assessment: **Lecture** [10] **10 minutes**	• Guide students through **Écriture**, including **Stratégie** and **Thème**, connected to unit context [15] • Students prepare writing plan, sharing with partner [15] **30 minutes**	• Introduce homework: First draft of **Thème** of **Écriture** [5] **5 minutes**
38 Skill Synthesis: Presentational (Writing)	• Student groups present drafts of **Thème** of **Écriture** [15] **15 minutes**	• Student pairs exchange papers and work through **Après l'écriture** [15] • Students discuss their partners' comments and corrections [10] **25 minutes**	• Introduce homework: Final draft of **Thème** of **Écriture** [5] **5 minutes**
39 Communication-based Synthesis and Review	• Have students report on how the **Stratégie** helped them on their writing assignment [5] **5 minutes**	• Connect unit context to language structures & communication via a synthesis of grammar, vocabulary, & skills to prepare for the test [30] **30 minutes**	• Confirm understanding of assessment content & grading rubric [5] • Introduce homework: prepare for lesson test using text & **Supersite**; complete **Thème** [5] **10 minutes**
40 Assessment	**Orientation** Students look over lesson content in preparation **5 minutes**	Lesson Test: 40 minutes	

D'accord! 1A Pacing Guide

DAY	Warm-up / Activate	Present / Practice / Communicate
1 — Context for Communication	• Evoke student experiences & vocabulary for context; present **Pour commencer** [10] 10 minutes	• Hand out Student Objectives Worksheet for **Contextes**. Explain how they can track their own progress using the Worksheet [5] • Present vocabulary through illustrations, phrases, categories, association [20] • Student pairs begin **Mise en pratique** [5] 30 minutes
2 — Vocabulary as a Tool	• Student groups review **Mise en pratique** [10] 10 minutes	• Students do **Communication** [20] • Choose one activity from the Middle School Activity Pack as a class activity [10] 30 minutes
3 — Media as a Bridge	• Assessment: **Contextes** [10] 10 minutes	• Distribute the **Roman-photo** activities in the **Cahier**. Answer the questions in the **Avant de regarder** [5] • Orient students to **Roman-photo** and **Expressions utiles** through video stills with observation, role-play, and prediction [10] • Read the storyboard in the Student Edition [15] 30 minutes
4 — Media and Culture	• Distribute the **Flash culture** activities in the **Cahier**. Answer the questions in the **Avant de regarder** [10] 10 minutes	• View **Flash culture** while students answer the questions from the **Cahier** [20] • View, discuss, re-view **Flash culture** [10] 30 minutes
5 — Structure as a Tool	• Assessment: **Roman-photo, Culture, Flash Culture** [10] 10 minutes	• Present about half of grammatical concept A.1 using text, **Supersite** (slides), and **Roman-photo** segments [10] • Do a whole class quick check to ensure students understand the explanation [5] • Present the balance of grammatical concept A.1 [10] • Do **Essayez!** [5] 30 minutes
6 — Structure in Context	• Review Homework [10] 10 minutes	• Choose a class game/activity from the Middle School Activity Pack or TE wrap [15] • Students do A.1 **Cahier** written activities [15] 30 minutes
7 — Structure as a Tool	• Assessment: **Structure A.1** [10] 10 minutes	• Present about half of grammatical concept A.2 using text, **Supersite** (slides), and **Roman-photo** segments [10] • Do a whole class quick check to ensure students understand the explanation [5] • Present the balance of grammatical concept A.2 [10] • Do **Essayez!** [5] 30 minutes
8 — Structure in Context	• Review Homework [10] 10 minutes	• Choose a class game/activity from the Middle School Activity Pack or TE wrap [15] • Students do A.2 **Cahier** written activities [15] 30 minutes
9 — Authentic Media / Context for Communication	• Assessment **Structures** [10] 10 minutes	• Introduce, guide discussion of **Le Zapping**; show clip via **Supersite** [15] • Student pairs do post-viewing activities; show clip again as necessary [15] 30 minutes
10 — Vocabulary as a Tool	• Review vocabulary [10] 10 minutes	• Do the **Écoutez** activity with the whole class, playing the audio as many times as needed [15] • Have student pairs finish **Mise en pratique** [15] 30 minutes

Block Schedule

Reflect	Present / Practice / Communicate	Reflect / Conclude	DAY
• Students pairs restate context of vocabulary [5] **5 minutes**	• Do the **Écoutez** activity with the whole class, playing the audio as many times as needed [15] • Have student pairs finish **Mise en pratique** [15] **30 minutes**	• Students review and personalize key vocabulary in context [5] • Introduce homework: **Supersite** flashcards, context illustrations & audio; end-of-chapter list with audio [5] **10 minutes**	1
• Students review and personalize key vocabulary in context [5] **5 minutes**	• Present **Les sons et les lettres** (**Supersite**/CD) [15] • Allow all students to check their pronunciation through classroom practice and repetition [15] **30 minutes**	• Have students check their progress on their Student Objectives Worksheet [5] • Introduce homework: Continue practicing pronunciation on the **Supersite**; **My Vocabulary**; end-of-chapter list with audio; remaining auto-graded activities (as applicable) [5] **10 minutes**	2
• Student pairs restate media's use of vocabulary in context [5] **5 minutes**	• View **Roman-photo** while students answer the questions from the **Cahier** [20] • Check comprehension and practice using the activities in the Student Edition [10] **30 minutes**	• Introduce homework: **Roman-photo** activities (**Supersite**) [5] **5 minutes**	3
• Student pairs restate media's use of vocabulary in context [5] **5 minutes**	• Present (select) **Culture** features in whole class or small groups, jigsaw, numbered heads together, etc. [20] • Assign Activity 3 to student pairs, allowing time for students to present their work to the whole class [15] **35 minutes**	• Introduce homework: **Sur Internet** or **Activités** (Text/**Supersite**) [5] **5 minutes**	4
• Student pairs restate grammar concept to each other [5] **5 minutes**	• Hand out Student Objectives Worksheet for **Structures**. Explain how they can track their own progress using the Worksheet [5] • Re-present grammar topic using the Grammar Tutorial (**Supersite**) [10] • Students pairs do assigned activities from A.1 **Mise en pratique** and **Communication** [20] **35 minutes**	• Introduce homework: Students complete A.1 **Mise en pratique** and **Communication** (text/**Supersite**); watch tutorials (**Supersite**) [5] **5 minutes**	5
• Student pairs restate grammar concept to each other [5] **5 minutes**	• Students do A.1 **Communication** [15] • Complete selected **Cahier** audio activities [15] • Start **Révision** activities [5] **35 minutes**	• Introduce homework: Students do selected **Révision** activities (text/**Supersite**) [5] **5 minutes**	6
• Student pairs restate grammar concept to each other [5] **5 minutes**	• Hand out Student Objectives Worksheet for **Structures**. Explain how they can track their own progress using the Worksheet [5] • Re-present grammar topic using the Grammar Tutorial (**Supersite**) [10] • Students pairs do assigned activities from A.2 **Mise en pratique** and **Communication** [20] **35 minutes**	• Introduce homework: Students complete A.2 **Mise en pratique** and **Communication** (text/**Supersite**); watch tutorials (**Supersite**) [5] **5 minutes**	7
• Introduce homework: Students complete **Cahier** (written) activities (text/**Supersite**) [5] **5 minutes**	• Students do A.2 **Communication** [15] • Complete selected **Cahier** audio activities [15] • Start **Révision** activities [5] **35 minutes**	• Introduce homework: Students do selected **Révision** activities (text/**Supersite**) [5] **5 minutes**	8
• Student pairs restate media's use of vocabulary in context [5] **5 minutes**	• Hand out Student Objectives Worksheet for **Contextes**. Explain how they can track their own progress using the Worksheet [5] • Present vocabulary through illustrations, phrases, categories, association [20] • Student pairs begin **Mise en pratique** [5] **30 minutes**	• Introduce homework: Complete **Mise en pratique** Act. 1 (text/**Supersite**) [5] **5 minutes**	9
• Students review and personalize key vocabulary in context [5] **5 minutes**	• Students do **Communication** [20] • Choose one activity from the Middle School Activity Pack as a class activity [15] **35 minutes**	• Introduce homework: **Supersite** flashcards, context illustrations & audio; end-of-chapter list with audio; remaining auto-graded activities (as applicable) [5] **5 minutes**	10

D'accord! 1A Pacing Guide

DAY	Warm-up / Activate	Present / Practice / Communicate
11 Vocabulary and Media	• Student groups review **Communication** [10] *10 minutes*	• Present **Les sons et les lettres** (**Supersite**/CD) [15] • Allow all students to check their pronunciation through classroom practice and repetition [15] *30 minutes*
12 Media and Culture	• Assessment: **Contextes** [10] *10 minutes*	• View **Roman-photo** while students answer the questions from the **Cahier** [20] • Check comprehension and practice using the activities in the Student Edition [10] *30 minutes*
13 Structure as a Tool	• Assessment: **Roman-photo, Culture** [10] *10 minutes*	• Present about half of grammatical concept B.1 using text, **Supersite** (slides), and **Roman-photo** segments [10] • Do a whole class quick check to ensure students understand the explanation [5] • Present the balance of grammatical concept B.1 [10] • Do **Essayez!** [5] *30 minutes*
14 Structure in Context	• Review Homework [5] *5 minutes*	• Choose a class game/activity from the Middle School Activity Pack or TE wrap [20] • Students do B.2 **Cahier** written activities [15] *35 minutes*
15 Structure as a Tool	• Assessment: **Structures B.1** [10] *10 minutes*	• Present about half of grammatical concept B.2 using text, **Supersite** (slides), and **Roman-photo** segments [10] • Do a whole class quick check to ensure students understand the explanation [5] • Present the balance of grammatical concept B.2 [10] • Do **Essayez!** [5] *30 minutes*
16 Structure in Context	• Review Homework [5] *5 minutes*	• Choose a class game/activity from the Middle School Activity Pack or TE wrap [20] • Students do A.1 **Cahier** written activities [15] *35 minutes*
17 Skill Synthesis	• Assessment: **Structures** [10] *10 minutes*	• Guide students through **Stratégie** and preparation in **À l'écoute**; present selection [20] • Students (individuals, pairs, or small groups) do **Compréhension** activities [10] *30 minutes*
18 Skill Synthesis: Interpretive (Reading)	• Discussion/assessment: **Panorama** [10] *10 minutes*	• Guide students through **Avant la lecture**, including **Stratégie** [15] • Students read **Lecture** (whole class or small groups) [15] *30 minutes*
19 Skill Synthesis: Presentational (Writing)	• Discussion/assessment: **Lecture** [10] *10 minutes*	• Guide students through **Écriture**, including **Stratégie** and **Thème**, connected to unit context [15] • Students prepare writing plan, sharing with partner [15] *30 minutes*
20 Assessment	• Student groups present **Écriture** [15] *15 minutes*	• Connect unit context to language structures & communication via a synthesis of grammar, vocabulary, & skills to prepare for the test [20] *20 minutes*

Block Schedule

Reflect	Present / Practice / Communicate	Reflect / Conclude	DAY
• Have students check their progress on their Student Objectives Worksheet [5] **5 minutes**	• Distribute the **Roman-photo** activities in the **Cahier**. Answer the questions in the **Avant de regarder** [5] • Orient students to **Roman-photo** and **Expressions utiles** through video stills with observation, role-play, and prediction [10] • Read the storyboard in the Student Edition [20] **35 minutes**	• Introduce homework: **Roman-photo** activities (Text/**Supersite**) [5] **5 minutes**	11
• Student pairs restate media's use of vocabulary in context [5] **5 minutes**	• Present (select) **Culture** features in whole class or small groups, jigsaw, numbered heads together, etc. [20] • Assign Activity 3 to student pairs, allowing time for students to present their work to the whole class [15] **35 minutes**	• Introduce homework: **Sur Internet** or Activités (Text/**Supersite**) [5] **5 minutes**	12
• Student pairs restate grammar concept to each other [5] **5 minutes**	• Hand out Student Objectives Worksheet for **Structures**. Explain how they can track their own progress using the Workshee. [5] • Re-present grammar topic using the Grammar Tutorial (**Supersite**) [10] • Students pairs do assigned activities from B.1 **Mise en pratique** and **Communication** [20] **35 minutes**	• Introduce homework: Students complete B.1 **Mise en pratique** and **Communication** (text/**Supersite**); watch tutorials (**Supersite**) [5] **5 minutes**	13
• Student pairs restate grammar concept to each other [5] **5 minutes**	• Students do B.1 **Communication** [15] • Complete selected **Cahier** audio activities [15] • Start **Révision** activities [5] **35 minutes**	• Introduce homework: Students do selected **Révision** activities (text/**Supersite**) [5] **5 minutes**	14
• Student pairs restate grammar concept to each other [5] **5 minutes**	• Hand out Student Objectives Worksheet for **Structures**. Explain how they can track their own progress using the Worksheet [5] • Re-present grammar topic using the Grammar Tutorial (**Supersite**) [10] • Students pairs do assigned activities from B.2 **Mise en pratique** and **Communication** [20] **35 minutes**	• Introduce homework: Students complete B.2 **Mise en pratique** and **Communication** (text/**Supersite**); watch tutorials (**Supersite**) [5] **5 minutes**	15
• Student pairs restate grammar concept to each other [5] **5 minutes**	• Students do B.2 **Communication** [15] • Complete selected **Cahier** audio activities [15] • Start **Révision** activities [5] **35 minutes**	• Introduce homework: Students do selected **Révision** activities (text/**Supersite**) [5] **5 minutes**	16
• Student pairs connect **Á l'écoute** selection to unit content [5] **5 minutes**	• Use the Interactive Map on the **Supersite** to situate the featured area geographically. Review (or teach) country names, capitals, and bordering nations. [10] • Present **Panorama** through whole class or small groups, jigsaw, numbered heads together, etc. [20] • Student pairs/groups begin activities [5] **35 minutes**	• Introduce homework: **Sur Internet** activity (text/**Supersite**) [5] **5 minutes**	17
• Student pairs begin **Après la lecture** activities [5] **5 minutes**	• Complete the second **Après la lecture** activity [15] • Assign student pairs or groups to the interpersonal activity at the end of the activity sequence, giving students time to prepare and practice [15] **30 minutes**	• Introduce homework: begin **Cahier** activities (**Cahier**/**Supersite**)[5] **5 minutes**	18
• Student pairs confirm understanding of assessment content & grading rubric [5] **5 minutes**	• Student pairs exchange papers and work through **Après l'écriture** [15] • Students discuss their partners' comments and corrections [10] **25 minutes**	• Introduce homework: Final draft of **Thème** of **Écriture** [5] **5 minutes**	19
• Student pairs confirm understanding of assessment content & grading rubric [10] **10 minutes**	**Assessment** **Lesson Test: 40 minutes**		20

D'accord! 1A Index of Cultural References

Architecture
Art Nouveau (French-born art movement), 127
château de Chenonceau (France), 82
opéra Garnier (opera house, Paris, France), 126

Arts
Cinema
    Bardot, Brigitte (actress, France), 83
    Béart, Emmanuelle (actress, France), 126
    Besson, Luc (filmmaker, France), 83
    Deneuve, Catherine (actress, France), 83
    Depardieu, Gérard (actor, France), 115
    Depardieu, Guillaume (actor, France), 115
    Depardieu, Julie (actress, France), 115
    Lumière, Auguste and Louis (inventors of cinematography, France), 83
    Martinez, Olivier (actor, France), 83
    Reno, Jean (actor, France), 38
    Tautou, Audrey (actress, France), 83
    Renoir, Jean (filmmaker, writer, France), 83
    Sembène, Ousmane (filmmaker, writer, Senegal), 38
    Truffaut, François (filmmaker, France), 83
Music
    Debussy, Claude (composer, musician, France), 82
    Dion, Céline (singer, Quebec, Canada), 38
    opéra Garnier (opera house, Paris, France), 126
    Piaf, Édith (singer, France), 126
Painters
    Cézanne, Paul (France), 9
    Magritte, René (France), 38
    Monet, Claude (painter, France), 171
    Renoir, Auguste (France), 82
Sculptors
    Claudel, Camille (France), 82
    Rodin, Auguste (sculptor, France), 126

Business and Industry
Airbus (aerospace, France), 83
Citroën (automobile, France), 83
Électricité de France (nuclear power, France), 83
INPES (nutrition and health), 19
Pages d'Or (telephone directory, France), 107
Peugeot (automobile, France), 83
Renault (automobile, France), 83
Swiss International Airlines (air carrier, Switzerland), 151
Université de Moncton (Canada), 63

Celebrations and Festivals
Aix en Musique (music, Aix-en-Provence, France), 9
Father's Day and Mother's Day, 97
Festival International d'Art Lyrique (music, France), 9
Heiva (annual festival, Papeete, Tahiti), 38
Journée internationale de la Francophonie, 39

Countries and Regions
Algeria, 26, 39
Bretagne (France), 170–171
Cambodia, 26
ethnicities in France, 26
France (geographical data), 82
Laos, 26
Louisiana (USA), 39
Morocco, 26
Normandie (France), 170–171
Québec, Canada, 39
Senegal, 26
Vietnam, 26

Education
Académie française, 82
Association sportive scolaire, 52
bac, 52, 68, 70
études supérieures, 71
grandes écoles, 71
lycée, 52–53
secondary education in Francophone countries, 53
université, 71

Fashion and attire
beret, 26, 27
Dior, Christian (fashion designer, France), 170

Food
Cajun cuisine, 39
camembert, 171
coffee, 158
crêpes, 171
French cafés, 158
galettes, 171
maquis (restaurant type, West Africa), 141
North African cafés, 159
Procope (first café in France), 158
Prudhomme, Paul (chef), 39
snacks and lighter fare in Francophone countries, 159
tangana (restaurant type, Senegal), 141

French Language
Académie française, 82
Basque, Breton, and Provençal dialects, 26
Francophone countries, 26, 38
Francophone national mottos (les devises), 27
friendship, words describing, 114
official languages of Francophone countries (Switzerland, Belgium, Morocco), 27

History
Anne de Bretagne (queen of France 1477–1514), 170
Bonaparte, Napoléon (emperor of France), 39
Cartier, Jacques (explorer, France), 170
Jeanne d'Arc (military leader, martyr, France), 82
Louis XIV (king of France), 39
pont du Gard (ruins, France), 82

Literature
Baudelaire, Charles (poet, France), 126
comtesse de Ségur (writer, France), 170
de Beauvoir, Simone (writer, France), 126
de Maupassant, Guy (writer, France), 170
Dumas, Alexandre (writer, France), 50
Hugo, Victor (writer, activist, France), 126
Superdupont (comic strip), 27
Zola, Émile (writer, France), 82

Places of Interest
catacombs (Paris, France), 126
Giverny, France, 171
Mont-Saint-Michel (France), 170
pont du Gard (ruins, France), 82
Seine (river, France), 82
Cities and Towns
    Aix-en-Provence (France), 9
    Capital Cities of Francophone countries, 38
    Deauville (resort village, France), 171
    Giverny (France), 171
    Paris (France) 126–127
Monuments
    Arc de Triomphe (Paris, France), 126
    menhirs and dolmens (megaliths, France), 171
    tour Eiffel (Paris, France), 127

Recreation and Leisure
free time in France, 140
parc Astérix (amusement park, Picardie, France), 141
Paris-Plage (beach along the Seine, Paris, France), 127

Science and Technology
André-Deshays, Claudie (doctor, first female French astronaut, France), 82
Curie, Marie (scientist, France), 38
Lumière, Auguste and Louis (inventors of cinematography, France), 83
Train à Grande Vitesse (high speed train, France), 83

Sports
Association sportive scolaire, 52
Hinault, Bernard (cyclist, France), 170
Noah, Joakim (basketball player, United States), 97
Noah, Yannick (tennis player, France), 97
Noah, Zacharie (soccer player, Cameroun), 97
Pérec, Marie-José (athlete, Guadelupe), 38

D'accord! 1A

LANGUE ET CULTURE DU MONDE FRANCOPHONE

VISTA
HIGHER LEARNING

Boston, Massachusetts

Cover photos: clockwise from top left: characters from the **D'ACCORD!** **Roman-photo** video program in Aix-en-Provence, France; honey shop, Provence, France; artichokes at a local market, Paris, France; Mont Saint Michel, Normandy, France

Publisher: José A. Blanco
Vice President, Editorial Director: Amy Baron
Executive Editor: Sharla Zwirek
Senior National Language Consultant: Norah Lulich Jones
Editorial Development: Diego García
Rights Management: Jorgensen Fernandez, Annie Pickert Fuller, Caitlin O'Brien
Technology Production: Paola Ríos Schaaf, Erica Solari
Design: Mark James, Andrés Vanegas
Production: Manuela Arango, Oscar Díez, Jennifer López

Copyright © 2016 by Vista Higher Learning, Inc.

All rights reserved.

No part of this work may be reproduced or distributed in any form or by any means, electronic or mechanical, including photocopying and recording, or by any information storage or retrieval system without prior written permission from Vista Higher Learning, 500 Boylston Street, Suite 620, Boston, MA 02116-3736.

Student Text ISBN: 978-1-68004-105-7
Printed in the United States of America.
Library of Congress Control Number: 2014955376

1 2 3 4 5 6 7 8 9 WC 20 19 18 17 16 15

D'accord! 1A

LANGUE ET CULTURE DU MONDE FRANCOPHONE

TABLE OF CONTENTS

	contextes	roman-photo	culture

UNITÉ 1
Salut!

Leçon 1A
- **Contextes**: Ça va?...................2
- **Les sons et les lettres**: The French alphabet..........5

- Au café......................6

- **Culture à la loupe**: La poignée de main ou la bise?...8
- **Portrait**: Aix-en-Provence: ville d'eau, ville d'art..........9

Leçon 1B
- **Contextes**: En classe..................20
- **Les sons et les lettres**: Silent letters..............23

- Les copains................24

- **Culture à la loupe**: Qu'est-ce qu'un Français typique?...........26
- **Portrait**: Superdupont..............27

UNITÉ 2
Au lycée

Leçon 2A
- **Contextes**: Les cours..................46
- **Les sons et les lettres**: Liaisons..................49

- Trop de devoirs!..............50

- **Culture à la loupe**: Au lycée...................52
- **Portrait**: Immersion française au Canada..53

Leçon 2B
- **Contextes**: Une semaine au lycée........64
- **Les sons et les lettres**: The letter **r**................67

- On trouve une solution.........68

- **Culture à la loupe**: Le bac....................70
- **Portrait**: Les études supérieures en France..................71

UNITÉ 3
La famille et les copains

Leçon 3A
- **Contextes**: La famille de Marie Laval......90
- **Les sons et les lettres**: L'accent aigu and l'accent grave............93

- L'album de photos............94

- **Culture à la loupe**: La famille en France.........96
- **Portrait**: Les Noah..................97

Leçon 3B
- **Contextes**: Comment sont-ils?.........108
- **Les sons et les lettres**: L'accent circonflexe, la cédille, and le tréma.....111

- On travaille chez moi!.......112

- **Culture à la loupe**: L'amitié..................114
- **Portrait**: Les Depardieu.............115

structures	synthèse	savoir-faire
1A.1 Nouns and articles ....10 1A.2 Numbers 0–60 14	Révision ....18 Le Zapping: *Le sucre n'est pas toujour où on le pense*.......19	**Panorama:** *Le monde francophone* .... 38 **Lecture:** *Carnet d'adresses* ..... 40 **Écriture** 42
1B.1 Subject pronouns and the verb **être** ....28 1B.2 Adjective agreement 32	Révision ....36 À l'écoute.................37	
2A.1 Present tense of regular **–er** verbs ....54 2A.2 Forming questions and expressing negation 58	Révision ....62 Le Zapping: *Vie étudiante Université de Moncton*.......63	**Panorama:** *La France* ....82 **Lecture:** *École de français (pour étrangers) de Lille* .....84 **Écriture** 86
2B.1 Present tense of **avoir** ......72 2B.2 Telling time 76	Révision ....80 À l'écoute.................81	
3A.1 Descriptive adjectives ......98 3A.2 Possessive adjectives 102	Révision ....106 Le Zapping: *Pages d'Or*........107	**Panorama:** *Paris* ....126 **Lecture:** *Fido en famille* ....128 **Écriture** 130
3B.1 Numbers 61–100 ....116 3B.2 Prepositions of location and disjunctive pronouns 120	Révision ....124 À l'écoute.................125	

TABLE OF CONTENTS

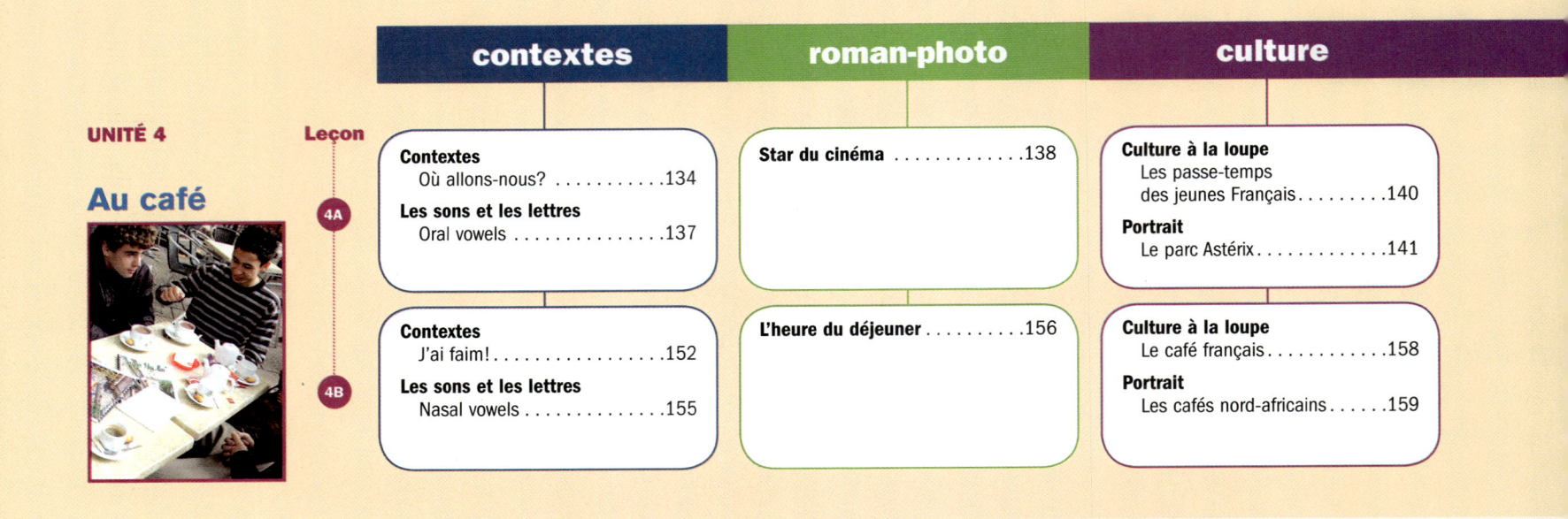

	contextes	roman-photo	culture

UNITÉ 4

Au café

Leçon 4A

Contextes
Où allons-nous? 134
Les sons et les lettres
Oral vowels 137

Star du cinéma 138

Culture à la loupe
Les passe-temps des jeunes Français.........140
Portrait
Le parc Astérix............141

Leçon 4B

Contextes
J'ai faim!................152
Les sons et les lettres
Nasal vowels 155

L'heure du déjeuner 156

Culture à la loupe
Le café français............158
Portrait
Les cafés nord-africains......159

Appendices

Appendice A
The *impératif*; Glossary of Grammatical Terms. .178
Appendice B
Verb Conjugation Tables................182
Vocabulaire
French–English 193
English–French 214

structures	synthèse	savoir-faire
4A.1 The verb **aller** ....142 4A.2 Interrogative words 146	Révision ....150 Le Zapping: *Swiss* 151	**Panorama:** *La Normandie et La Bretagne*...............170
4B.1 The verbs **prendre** and **boire**; Partitives.........160 4B.2 Regular **-ir** verbs 164	Révision ....168 À l'écoute.................169	**Lecture:** *Cybercafé Le connecté*..172 **Écriture** 174

Supplementary Vocabulary..............232
Index................................236
Credits..............................237

MAPS

Le monde francophone

- LE GROENLAND
- L'OCÉAN ARCTIQUE
- LE CANADA
- Le Québec
- Saint-Pierre-et-Miquelon (*France*)
- LES ÉTATS-UNIS
- La Louisiane
- L'OCÉAN ATLANTIQUE
- LE MEXIQUE
- LE BELIZE
- CUBA
- HAÏTI
- Les Antilles françaises
- LE GUATEMALA
- LE SALVADOR
- LE HONDURAS
- LE NICARAGUA
- LE COSTA RICA
- LE PANAMÁ
- LA JAMAÏQUE
- LE VENEZUELA
- LA COLOMBIE
- LE GUYANA
- LE SURINAME
- La Guyane française
- L'ÉQUATEUR
- L'OCÉAN PACIFIQUE
- LE PÉROU
- LE BRÉSIL
- LA BOLIVIE
- LE PARAGUAY
- LE CHILI
- L'ARGENTINE
- L'URUGUAY
- Wallis-et-Futuna
- TUVALU
- KIRIBATI
- VANUATU
- LES SAMOA
- La Polynésie française
- FIDJI
- TONGA
- La Nouvelle-Calédonie
- LA NOUVELLE-ZÉLANDE

Pays et régions francophones

0 — 3,000 miles
0 — 3,000 kilomètres

L'OCÉAN ARCTIQUE

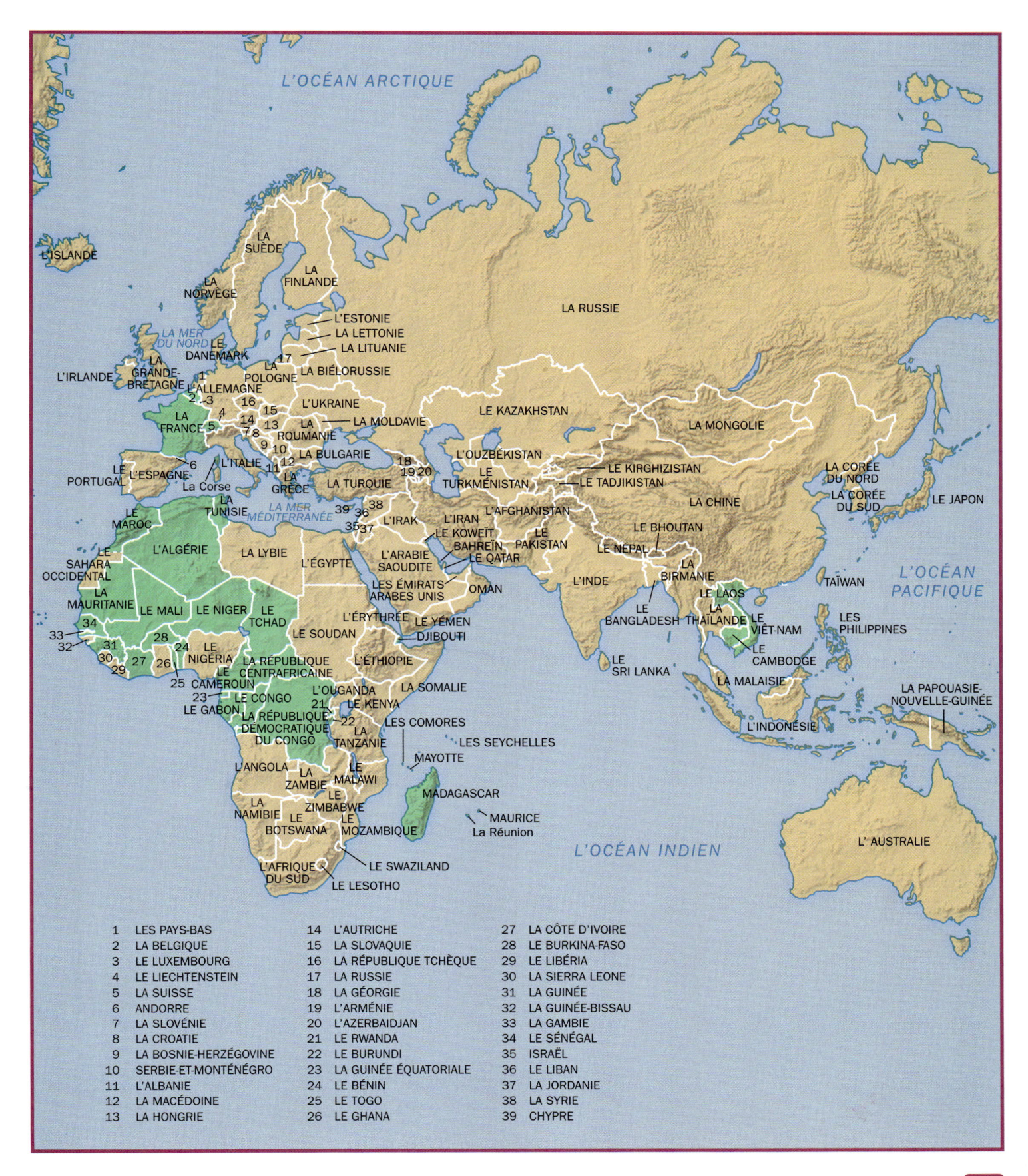

- L'ISLANDE
- LA SUÈDE
- LA NORVÈGE
- LA FINLANDE
- L'ESTONIE
- LA LETTONIE
- LA LITUANIE
- LA RUSSIE
- LA MER DU NORD
- LE DANEMARK
- L'IRLANDE
- LA GRANDE-BRETAGNE
- LA POLOGNE
- L'ALLEMAGNE
- LA BIÉLORUSSIE
- L'UKRAINE
- LA MOLDAVIE
- LE KAZAKHSTAN
- LA FRANCE
- LA ROUMANIE
- LA MONGOLIE
- LA BULGARIE
- L'OUZBÉKISTAN
- LE PORTUGAL
- L'ESPAGNE
- L'ITALIE
- La Corse
- LA GRÈCE
- LA TURQUIE
- LE TURKMÉNISTAN
- LE KIRGHIZISTAN
- LE TADJIKISTAN
- LA CORÉE DU NORD
- LE MAROC
- LA TUNISIE
- LA MER MÉDITERRANÉE
- L'IRAK
- L'IRAN
- L'AFGHANISTAN
- LA CHINE
- LA CORÉE DU SUD
- LE JAPON
- LE SAHARA OCCIDENTAL
- L'ALGÉRIE
- LA LYBIE
- L'ÉGYPTE
- L'ARABIE SAOUDITE
- LE KOWEÏT
- BAHREÏN
- LE QATAR
- LE PAKISTAN
- LE NÉPAL
- LE BHOUTAN
- LA MAURITANIE
- LE MALI
- LE NIGER
- LE TCHAD
- LES ÉMIRATS ARABES UNIS
- OMAN
- L'INDE
- LA BIRMANIE
- TAÏWAN
- L'OCÉAN PACIFIQUE
- LE NIGÉRIA
- LA RÉPUBLIQUE CENTRAFRICAINE
- L'ÉRYTHRÉE
- LE YÉMEN
- LE SOUDAN
- DJIBOUTI
- LE BANGLADESH
- LA THAÏLANDE
- LE LAOS
- LE VIÊT-NAM
- LES PHILIPPINES
- LE CAMEROUN
- L'ÉTHIOPIE
- LE SRI LANKA
- LE CAMBODGE
- LE CONGO
- L'OUGANDA
- LE KENYA
- LA MALAISIE
- LE GABON
- LA RÉPUBLIQUE DÉMOCRATIQUE DU CONGO
- LA TANZANIE
- LES COMORES
- LES SEYCHELLES
- LA PAPOUASIE-NOUVELLE-GUINÉE
- L'INDONÉSIE
- MAYOTTE
- L'ANGOLA
- LA ZAMBIE
- LE MALAWI
- MADAGASCAR
- MAURICE
- La Réunion
- LA NAMIBIE
- LE ZIMBABWE
- LE BOTSWANA
- LE MOZAMBIQUE
- L'OCÉAN INDIEN
- L'AUSTRALIE
- L'AFRIQUE DU SUD
- LE SWAZILAND
- LE LESOTHO

#		#		#	
1	LES PAYS-BAS	14	L'AUTRICHE	27	LA CÔTE D'IVOIRE
2	LA BELGIQUE	15	LA SLOVAQUIE	28	LE BURKINA-FASO
3	LE LUXEMBOURG	16	LA RÉPUBLIQUE TCHÈQUE	29	LE LIBÉRIA
4	LE LIECHTENSTEIN	17	LA RUSSIE	30	LA SIERRA LEONE
5	LA SUISSE	18	LA GÉORGIE	31	LA GUINÉE
6	ANDORRE	19	L'ARMÉNIE	32	LA GUINÉE-BISSAU
7	LA SLOVÉNIE	20	L'AZERBAIDJAN	33	LA GAMBIE
8	LA CROATIE	21	LE RWANDA	34	LE SÉNÉGAL
9	LA BOSNIE-HERZÉGOVINE	22	LE BURUNDI	35	ISRAËL
10	SERBIE-ET-MONTÉNÉGRO	23	LA GUINÉE ÉQUATORIALE	36	LE LIBAN
11	L'ALBANIE	24	LE BÉNIN	37	LA JORDANIE
12	LA MACÉDOINE	25	LE TOGO	38	LA SYRIE
13	LA HONGRIE	26	LE GHANA	39	CHYPRE

MAPS

L'Amérique du Nord et du Sud

Régions francophones

L'OCÉAN ARCTIQUE
LE GROENLAND
L'Alaska
Le Nunavut
Le Yukon
Les Territoires du Nord-Ouest
La Colombie-Britannique
LE CANADA
L'Alberta
Le Manitoba
La Saskatchewan
L'Ontario
Le Québec
Terre-Neuve-et-Labrador
Le Nouveau-Brunswick
Québec
Montréal
Ottawa
Saint-Pierre-et-Miquelon (*France*)
La Nouvelle-Écosse
L'Île-du-Prince-Édouard
LES ÉTATS-UNIS
Washington
L'OCÉAN ATLANTIQUE
L'OCÉAN PACIFIQUE
La Louisiane
LE MEXIQUE
LA JAMAÏQUE
HAÏTI
LE BELIZE
CUBA
Mexico
Belmopan
Tegucigalpa
Les Antilles françaises
LE GUATEMALA
Guatemala
LE HONDURAS
San Salvador
LE NICARAGUA
LE SALVADOR
Managua
Panamá
Caracás
LE COSTA RICA
LE VENEZUELA
Georgetown
Paramaribo
LE PANAMÁ
Bogotá
Cayenne
La Guyane française
Quito
LA COLOMBIE
LE GUYANA
LE SURINAME
L'ÉQUATEUR
LE PÉROU
Lima
LE BRÉSIL
LA BOLIVIE
La Paz
Sucre
Brasília
LE PARAGUAY
LE CHILI
Asunción
L'ARGENTINE
L'URUGUAY
Santiago
Buenos Aires
Montevideo

PORTO RICO
HAÏTI
LA RÉPUBLIQUE DOMINICAINE
Port-au-Prince
Saint-Domingue
San Juan
LA MER DES ANTILLES
La Guadeloupe
Pointe-à-Pitre
DOMINIQUE
Fort-de-France
La Martinique
SAINTE-LUCIE

2,000 miles
2,000 kilomètres
500 miles
500 kilomètres

La France

MAPS

L'Europe

L'Afrique

USING D'ACCORD!

ROMAN-PHOTO VIDEO PROGRAM

Fully integrated with your textbook, the **Roman-photo** video series contains 36 dramatic episodes—one for each lesson in Levels 1 and 2, and 6 episodes in the **Reprise** chapter in Level 3. The episodes present the adventures of four college students who are studying in the south of France at the Université Aix-Marseille. They live in apartments above and near Le P'tit Bistrot, a café owned by Valérie Forestier. The videos tell their story and the story of Madame Forestier and her teenage son, Stéphane.

The **Roman-photo** dialogues in the printed textbook are an abbreviated version of the dramatic version of the video episodes. Therefore, each **Roman-photo** section in the text can used as a preparation before you view the corresponding video episode, as post-viewing reinforcement, or as a stand-alone section.

Each episode in Levels 1 and 2 feature the characters using the vocabulary and grammar you are studying, as well as previously taught language. Each episode ends with a **Reprise** segment, which features the key language functions and grammar points used in the episode. The first four episodes in the Level 3 **Reprise** chapter review the topics and structures from Levels 1 and 2. The final two episodes bring you up-to-date on the lives of the characters.

THE CAST
Here are the main characters you will meet when you watch **Roman-photo**:

Of Senegalese heritage
Amina Mbaye

From Washington, D.C.
David Duchesne

From Paris
Sandrine Aubry

From Aix-en-Provence
Valérie Forestier

Of Algerian heritage
Rachid Kahlid

And, also from Aix-en-Provence
Stéphane Forestier

FLASH CULTURE VIDEO PROGRAM

For one lesson in each chapter, a **Flash culture** segment allows you to experience the sights and sounds of the French-speaking world and the daily life of French speakers. Each segment is from two-to-three minutes long and is correlated to your textbook in one **Culture** section in each unit.

Hosted by narrators Csilla and Benjamin, these segments of specially shot footage transport you to a variety of venues: schools, parks, public squares, cafés, stores, cinemas, outdoor markets, city streets, festivals, and more. They also incorporate mini-interviews with French speakers in various walks of life: for example, family members, friends, students, and people in different professions.

The footage was filmed taking special care to capture rich, vibrant images that will expand your cultural perspectives with information directly related to the content of your textbook. In addition, the narrations were carefully written to reflect the vocabulary and grammar covered in **D'ACCORD!**

USING D'ACCORD!

Supersite

Each section of your textbook comes with activities on the **D'ACCORD!** Supersite, many of which are auto-graded with immediate feedback. Plus, the Supersite is iPad®-friendly, so it can be accessed on the go! Visit **vhlcentral.com** to explore the wealth of exciting resources.

Audio:
Vocabulary Practice
My Vocabulary

> **CONTEXTES**
> Listen to the audio recording of the vocabulary, and practice using Flashcards, My Vocabulary, and activities that give you immediate feedback.

Audio: Explanation
Record and Compare

> **LES SONS ET LES LETTRES**
> Improve your accent by listening to native speakers, then recording your voice and comparing it to the samples provided.

Video: *Roman-photo*
Record and Compare

> **ROMAN-PHOTO**
> Travel with David to Aix-en-Provence, France, and meet a group of students living there. Watch the video again at home to see the characters use the vocabulary in a real context.

Reading
Video: *Flash culture*

> **CULTURE**
> Experience the sights and sounds of the Francophone world. Watch the **Flash culture** video to expand your cultural perspectives by listening to a variety of native speakers of French. Explore cultural topics through the **Sur Internet** activity.

Presentation
Tutorial

> **STRUCTURES**
> Watch an animated, interactive tutorial or review the presentation.

Video: TV Clip
Audio: Activities

> **SYNTHÈSE**
> Watch the **Le Zapping** video again outside of class so that you can pause and repeat to really understand what you hear. Practice listening strategies with the online audio activities for **À l'écoute**.

Audio: Synced Reading
Interactive Map
Reading

> **SAVOIR-FAIRE**
> Listen along with the Audio-Synced Reading. Use the Interactive Map to explore the places you might want to visit. There's a lot of additional practice, including Internet searches and auto-graded activities.

Audio: Vocabulary
Flashcards
My Vocabulary

> **VOCABULAIRE**
> Just what you need to get ready for the test! Review the vocabulary with audio and Flashcards.

Icons

Familiarize yourself with these icons that appear throughout **D'ACCORD!**

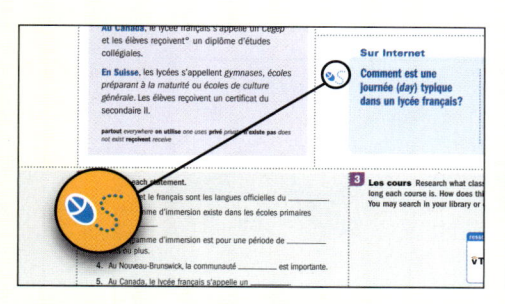

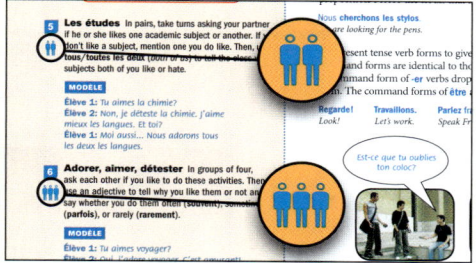

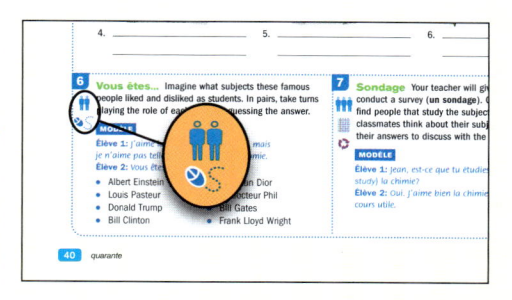

Activity Online
The mouse icon indicates when an activity is also available on the Supersite.

Pair/Group Activities
Two faces indicate a pair activity, and three indicate a group activity.

Partner Chat/Virtual Chat Activities
Pair and mouse icons together indicate that the activity may be assigned as a Partner Chat or Virtual Chat video or audio activity on the Supersite.

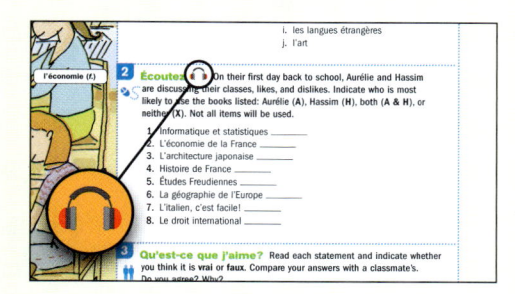

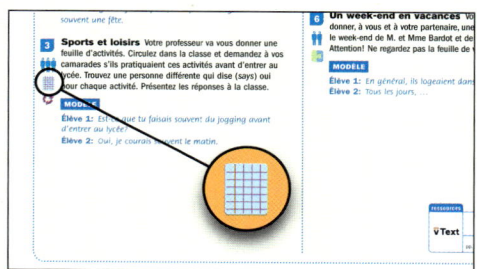

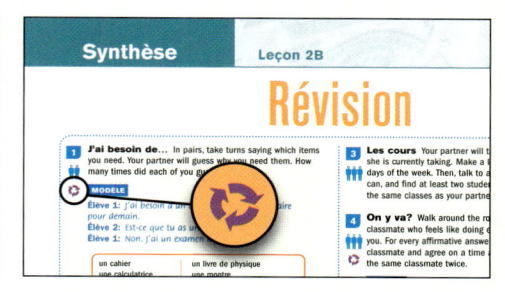

Listening
The headphones icon indicates that audio is available. You will see it in the lesson's **Contextes**, **Les sons et les lettres**, **À l'écoute**, and **Vocabulaire** sections, as well as with all activities that require audio.

Handout
The activities marked with these icons require handouts that your teacher will give you to help you complete the activities.

Recycle
The recycling icon indicates that you will need to use vocabulary and grammar learned in previous lessons.

Resources

Ressources boxes let you know exactly which print and technology ancillaries you can use to reinforce and expand on every section of the lessons in your textbook. They even include page numbers when applicable.

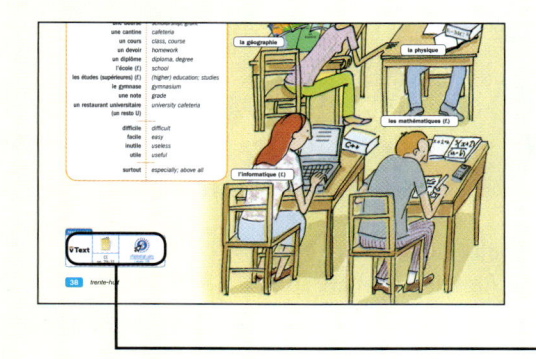

vText
Materials also available in the interactive online textbook

Cahier de l'élève
All-in-one workbook with additional vocabulary and grammar practice; audio activities; and pre-, while-, and post-viewing activities for the video programs

Supersite
Additional practice on the Supersite, not included in the textbook

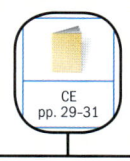

xvii

STUDYING FRENCH

The French-speaking World

Do you know someone who speaks French? Chances are you do! French is the fourth most commonly spoken language in the U.S., after English, Spanish, and Mandarin, and is the second most common language in some states. More than 1 million Americans speak French at home. It is the official language of more than twenty-five countries and an official language of the European Union and United Nations. English and French are the only two languages that are spoken on every continent of the world.

The French-speaking World

Speakers of French
(approx. 200 million worldwide)
- America and the Caribbean: 7%
- Asia and Oceania: 1%
- Europe: 42%
- North Africa and the Middle-East: 11%
- Sub-Saharan Africa and the Indian Ocean: 39%

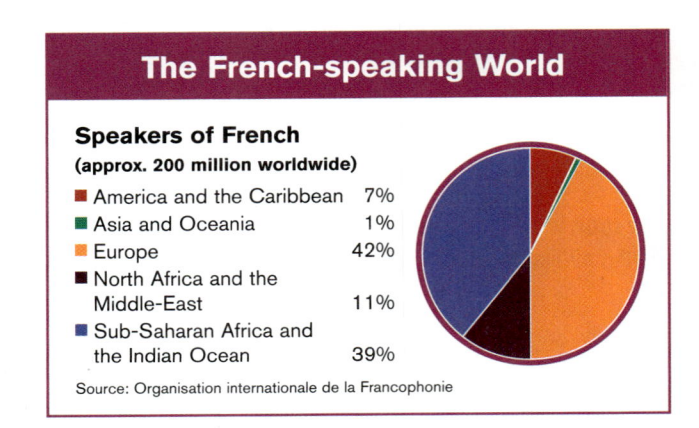

Source: Organisation internationale de la Francophonie

The Growth of French

Have you ever heard someone say that French is a Romance language? This doesn't mean it's romantic—although some say it is the language of love!—but that it is derived from Latin, the language of the Romans. Gaul, a country largely made up of what is now France and Belgium, was absorbed into the Roman Empire after the Romans invaded Gaul in 58 B.C. Most Gauls began speaking Latin. In the third century, Germanic tribes including the Franks invaded the Roman territories of Western Europe. Their language also influenced the Gauls. As the Roman empire collapsed in the fifth century, people in outlying regions and frontiers were cut off from Rome. The Latin spoken by each group was modified more and more over time. Eventually, the language that was spoken in Paris became the standard for modern-day French.

French in the United States

1500 — **1600** — **1700**

1534
Jacques Cartier claims territories for France as he explores the St. Lawrence river, and the French establish fur-trading posts.

1600s
French exploration continues in the Great Lakes and the Mississippi Valley. La Salle takes the colony of Louisiana for France in 1682.

1685–1755
The Huguenots (French Protestants) form communities in America. French Acadians leave Nova Scotia and settle in northern New England and Louisiana.

French in the United States

French came to North America in the 16th and 17th centuries when French explorers and fur traders traveled through what is now America's heartland. French-speaking communities grew rapidly when the French Acadians were forced out of their Canadian settlement in 1755 and settled in New England and Louisiana. Then, in 1803, France sold the Louisiana territory to the United States for 80 million francs, or about 15 million dollars. Overnight, thousands of French people became citizens of the United States, bringing with them their rich history, language, and traditions.

This heritage, combined with that of the other French populations that have immigrated to the United States over the years, as well as U.S. relations with France in World Wars I and II, has led to the remarkable growth of French around the country. After English and Spanish, it is the third most commonly spoken language in the nation. Louisiana, Maine, New Hampshire, and Vermont claim French as the second most commonly spoken language after English.

You've made a popular choice by choosing to take French in school; it is the second most commonly taught foreign language in classrooms throughout the country! Have you heard people speaking French in your community? Chances are that you've come across an advertisement, menu, or magazine that is in French. If you look around, you'll find that French can be found in some pretty common places. Depending on where you live, you may see French on grocery items such as juice cartons and cereal boxes. In some large cities, you can see French language television broadcasts on stations such as TV5Monde. When you listen to the radio or download music from the Internet, some of the most popular choices are French artists who perform in French. In fact, French music sales to the United States have more than doubled since 2004. French and English are the only two official languages of the Olympic Games. More than 20,000 words in the English language are of French origin. Learning French can create opportunities within your everyday life.

1800 — 1900 — 2000

1803
The United States purchases Louisiana, where Cajun French is widely spoken.

1980s
Nearly all high schools, colleges, and universities in the United States offer courses in French as a foreign language. It is the second most commonly studied language.

2009
French is the fourth most commonly spoken language in the U.S., with 1.3 million speakers.

STUDYING FRENCH

Why Study French?

Connect with the World

Learning French can change how you view the world. While you learn French, you will also explore and learn about the origins, customs, art, music, and literature of people all around the world. When you travel to a French-speaking country, you'll be able to converse freely with the people you meet. And whether here in the U.S. or abroad, you'll find that speaking to people in their native language is the best way to bridge any culture gap.

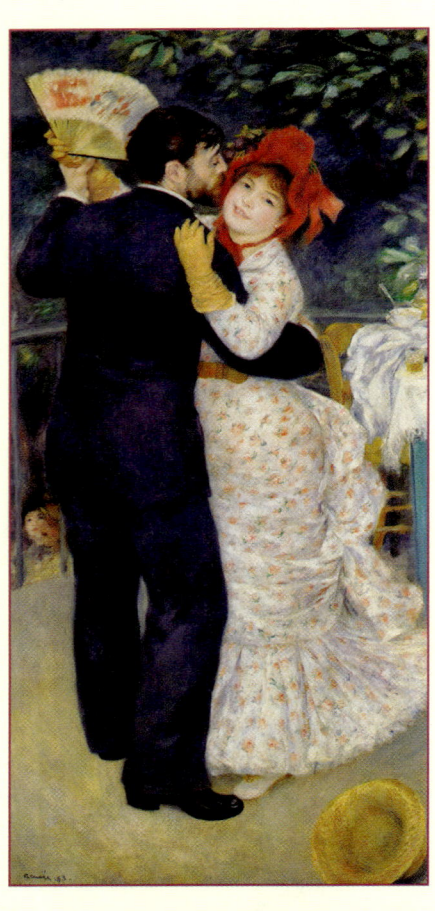

Learn an International Language

There are many reasons for learning French, a language that has spread to many parts of the world and has along the way embraced words and sounds of languages as diverse as Latin, Arabic, German, and Celtic. The French language, standardized and preserved by the **Académie française** since 1634, is now among the most commonly spoken languages in the world. It is the second language of choice among people who study languages other than English in North America.

Understand the World Around You

Knowing French can also open doors to communities within the United States, and it can broaden your understanding of the nation's history and geography. The very names Delaware, Oregon, and Vermont are French in origin. Just knowing their meanings can give you some insight into, of all things, the history and landscapes for which the states are known. Oregon is derived from a word that means "hurricane," which tells you about the windiness of the Columbia River; and Vermont

City Name	Meaning in French
Bel Air, California	"good air"
Boise, Idaho	"wooded"
Des Moines, Iowa	"river of the monks"
Montclair, New Jersey	"clear mountain"

comes from a phrase meaning "green mountain," which is why its official nickname is The Green Mountain State. You've already been speaking French whenever you talk about these states!

Explore Your Future

How many of you are already planning your future careers? Employers in today's global economy look for workers who know different languages and understand other cultures. Your knowledge of French will make you a valuable candidate for careers abroad as well as in the United States. Doctors, nurses, social workers, hotel managers, journalists, businesspeople, pilots, flight attendants, and many other kinds of professionals need to know French or another foreign language to do their jobs well.

Expand Your Skills

Studying a foreign language can improve your ability to analyze and interpret information and help you succeed in many other subject areas. When you begin learning French, much of your studies will focus on reading, writing, grammar, listening, and speaking skills. You'll be amazed at how the skills involved with learning how a language works can help you succeed in other areas of study. Many people who study a foreign language claim that they gained a better understanding of English and the structures it uses. French can even help you understand the origins of many English words and expand your own vocabulary in English. Knowing French can also help you pick up other related languages, such as Portuguese, Spanish, and Italian. French can really open doors for learning many other skills in your school career.

STUDYING FRENCH

How to Learn French

Start with the Basics!
As with anything you want to learn, start with the basics and remember that learning takes time!

Vocabulary Every new word you learn in French will expand your vocabulary and ability to communicate. The more words you know, the better you can express yourself. Focus on sounds and think about ways to remember words. Use your knowledge of English and other languages to figure out the meaning of and memorize words like **téléphone, l'orchestre,** and **mystérieux.**

Grammar Grammar helps you put your new vocabulary together. By learning the rules of grammar, you can use new words correctly and speak in complete sentences. As you learn verbs and tenses, you will be able to speak about the past, present, or future; express yourself with clarity; and be able to persuade others with your opinions. Pay attention to structures and use your knowledge of English grammar to make connections with French grammar.

Culture Culture provides you with a framework for what you may say or do. As you learn about the culture of French-speaking communities, you'll improve your knowledge of French. Think about a word like **cuisine** and how it relates to a type of food as well as the kitchen itself. Think about and explore customs observed at **le Réveillon de la Saint-Sylvestre** (New Year's Eve) or **le Carnaval** (or **Mardi Gras,** "fat Tuesday") and how they are similar to celebrations you are familiar with. Observe customs. Watch people greet each other or say good-bye. Listen for sayings that capture the spirit of what you want to communicate!

Listen, Speak, Read, and Write

Listening Listen for sounds and for words you can recognize. Listen for inflections and watch for key words that signal a question such as **comment** (how), **où** (where), or **qui** (who). Get used to the sound of French. Play French pop songs or watch French movies. Borrow books on CD from your local library, or try to attend a meeting with a French language group in your community. Download a podcast in French or watch a French newscast online. Don't worry if you don't understand every single word. If you focus on key words and phrases, you'll get the main idea. The more you listen, the more you'll understand!

Speaking Practice speaking French as often as you can. As you talk, work on your pronunciation, and read aloud texts so that words and sentences flow more easily. Don't worry if you don't sound like a native speaker, or if you make some mistakes. Time and practice will help you get there. Participate actively in French class. Try to speak French with classmates, especially native speakers (if you know any), as often as you can.

Reading Pick up a French-language newspaper or a magazine on your way to school, read the lyrics of a song as you listen to it, or read books you've already read in English translated into French. Use reading strategies that you know to understand the meaning of a text that looks unfamiliar. Look for cognates, or words that are related in English and French, to guess the meaning of some words. Read as often as you can, and remember to read for fun!

Writing It's easy to write in French if you put your mind to it. Memorize the basic rules of how letters and sounds are related, practice the use of diacritical marks, and soon you can probably become an expert speller in French! Write for fun—make up poems or songs, write e-mails or instant messages to friends, or start a journal or blog in French.

STUDYING FRENCH

Tips for Learning French

- **Listen** to French radio shows, often available online. Write down words you can't recognize or don't know and look up the meaning.
- **Watch** French TV shows or movies. Read subtitles to help you grasp the content.
- **Read** French-language newspapers, magazines, Websites, or blogs.
- **Listen** to French songs that you like—anything from a best-selling pop song by Shy'm to an old French ballad by Edith Piaf. Sing along and concentrate on your pronunciation.
- **Seek** out French speakers. Look for neighborhoods, markets, or cultural centers where French might be spoken in your community. Greet people, ask for directions, or order from a menu at a French restaurant in French.
- **Pursue** language exchange opportunities in your school or community. Try to join language clubs or cultural societies, and explore opportunities for studying abroad or hosting a student from a French-speaking country in your home or school.

> **Practice, practice, practice!**
> Seize every opportunity you find to listen, speak, read, or write French. Think of it like a sport or learning a musical instrument—the more you practice, the more you will become comfortable with the language and how it works. You'll marvel at how quickly you can begin speaking French and how the world that it transports you to can change your life forever!

- **Connect** your learning to everyday experiences. Think about naming the ingredients of your favorite dish in French. Think about the origins of French place names in the U.S., like Baton Rouge and Fond du Lac, or of common English words and phrases like **café, en route, fiancé, matinée, papier mâché, petite,** and **souvenir.**
- **Use** mnemonics, or a memorizing device, to help you remember words. Make up a saying in English to remember the order of the days of the week in French (L, M, M, J, V, S, D).
- **Visualize** words. Try to associate words with images to help you remember meanings. For example, think of a **pâté** or **terrine** as you learn the names of different types of meats and vegetables. Imagine a national park and create mental pictures of the landscape as you learn names of animals, plants, and habitats.
- **Enjoy** yourself! Try to have as much fun as you can learning French. Take your knowledge beyond the classroom and find ways to make your learning experience your very own.

GETTING STARTED

Common Names

Get started learning French by using a French name in class. You can choose from the lists on these pages, or you can find one yourself. How about learning the French equivalent of your name? The most popular French female names are Marie, Jeanne, Françoise, Monique, and Catherine. The most popular male names in French are Jean, Pierre, Michel, André, and Philippe. Is your name, or that of someone you know, in the French top five?

The top five names for boys:	The top five names for girls:
Jean	Marie
Michel	Jeanne
Pierre	Françoise
André	Monique
Philippe	Catherine

More Boys Names	More Girls Names
Thomas	Léa
Lucas	Manon
Théo	Chloé
Hugo	Emma
Maxime	Camille
Alexandre	Océane
Antoine	Marie
Enzo	Sarah
Quentin	Clara
Clément	Inès
Nicolas	Laura
Alexis	Julie
Romain	Mathilde
Louis	Lucie
Valentin	Anaïs
Léo	Pauline
Julien	Marine
Paul	Lisa
Baptiste	Eva
Tom	Justine
Nathan	Maéva
Arthur	Jade
Benjamin	Juliette
Florian	Charlotte
Mathis	Émilie

GETTING STARTED

Useful French Expressions

The following expressions will be very useful in getting you started learning French. You can use them in class to check your understanding, and to ask and answer questions about the lessons. Learn these ahead of time to help you understand direction lines in French, as well as your teacher's instructions. Remember to practice your French as often as you can!

Expressions utiles	Useful expressions
Allez à la page 2.	Go to page 2.
Alternez les rôles.	Switch roles.
À tour de rôle…	Take turns…
À voix haute	Aloud
À votre/ton avis	In your opinion
Après une deuxième écoute…	After a second listening…
Articulez.	Enunciate.; Pronounce carefully.
Au sujet de, À propos de	Regarding/about
Avec un(e) partenaire/ un(e) camarade de classe	With a partner/a classmate
Avez-vous/As-tu des questions?	Do you have any questions?
Avez-vous/As-tu fini/ terminé?	Are you done?/Have you finished?
Chassez l'intrus.	Choose the item that doesn't belong.
Choisissez le bon mot.	Choose the right word.
Circulez dans la classe.	Walk around the classroom.
Comment dit-on _____ en français?	How do you say _____ in French?
Comment écrit-on _____ en français?	How do you spell _____ in French?

Expressions utiles	Useful expressions
Corrigez les phrases fausses	Correct the false statements.
Créez/Formez des phrases…	Create/Form sentences…
D'après vous/Selon vous…	According to you…
Décrivez les images/ dessins…	Describe the images/ drawings…
Désolé(e), j'ai oublié.	I'm sorry, I forgot.
Déterminez si…	Decide whether…
Dites si vous êtes/Dis si tu es d'accord ou non.	Say if you agree or not.
Écrivez une lettre/une phrase.	Write a letter/a sentence.
Employez les verbes de la liste.	Use the verbs from the list.
En utilisant…	Using…
Est-ce que vous pouvez/ tu peux choisir un(e) autre partenaire/ quelqu'un d'autre?	Can you please choose another partner/ someone else?
Êtes vous prêt(e)?/ Es-tu prêt(e)?	Are you ready?
Excusez-moi, je suis en retard.	Excuse me for being late.
Faites correspondre…	Match…
Faites les accords nécessaires.	Make the necessary agreements.

Expressions utiles	*Useful expressions*
Félicitations!	Congratulations!
Indiquez le mot qui ne va pas avec les autres.	Indicate the word that doesn't belong.
Indiquez qui a dit…	Indicate who said…
J'ai gagné!/Nous avons gagné!	I won!/We won!
Je n'ai pas/Nous n'avons pas encore fini.	I/We have not finished yet.
Je ne comprends pas.	I don't understand.
Je ne sais pas.	I don't know.
Je ne serai pas là demain.	I won't be here tomorrow.
Je peux continuer?	May I continue?
Jouez le rôle de…/ la scène…	Play the role of…/ the scene…
Lentement, s'il vous plaît.	Slowly, please.
Lisez…	Read…
Mettez dans l'ordre…	Put in order…
Ouvrez/Fermez votre livre.	Open/Close your books.
Par groupes de trois/ quatre…	In groups of three/four…
Partagez vos résultats…	Share your results…
Posez-vous les questions suivantes.	Ask each other the following questions.
Pour demain, faites…	For tomorrow, do…

Expressions utiles	*Useful expressions*
Pour demain, vous allez/ tu vas faire…	For tomorrow you are going to do…
Prononcez.	Pronounce.
Qu'est-ce que ____ veut dire?	What does ____ mean?
Que pensez-vous/ penses-tu de…	What do you think about…
Qui a gagné?	Who won?
…qui convient le mieux.	…that best completes/is the most appropriate.
Rejoignez un autre groupe.	Get together with another group.
Remplissez les espaces.	Fill in the blanks.
Répondez aux questions suivantes.	Answer the following questions.
Soyez prêt(e)s à…	Be ready to…
Venez/Viens au tableau.	Come to the board.
Vous comprenez?/ Tu comprends?	Do you understand?
Vous pouvez nous expliquer/m'expliquer encore une fois, s'il vous plaît?	Could you explain again, please?
Vous pouvez répéter, s'il vous plaît?	Could you repeat that, please?
Vrai ou faux?	True or false?

ACKNOWLEDGMENTS

On behalf of its authors and editors, Vista Higher Learning expresses its sincere appreciation to the many educators nationwide who reviewed materials from **D'ACCORD!**. Their input and suggestions were vitally helpful in forming and shaping the program in its final, published form.

We also extend a special thank you to Stephen Adamson and Séverine Champeny, whose hard work was central to bringing **D'ACCORD!** to fruition.

We are especially grateful to our Senior National Language Consultant, Norah Jones, for her continued support and feedback regarding all aspects of the text.

Reviewers

Campbell Ainsworth
  The White Mountain School
  Bethlehem, NH

Nancy Aykanian
  Westwood High School
  Westwood, MA

Maureen Mahany Berger
  Moses Brown School
  Providence, RI

Joyce Besserer
  Brookfield Academy
  Brookfield, WI

Liette Brisebois
  New Trier High School
  Winnetka, IL

Susan Brown
  Gaston Day School
  Gastonia, NC

Felice Carr
  Kingswood Regional High School
  Wolfeboro, NH

Allégra Clément-Bayard
  John Burroughs School
  St. Louis, MO

Ann Clogan
  Strake Jesuit College Preparatory
  Houston, TX

Wynne M. Curry
  The Seven Hills School
  Cincinnati, OH

Dr. Sherry Denney
  Truman Middle School
  St. Louis, MO

Gissele Drpich
  Burlington High School
  Burlington, VT

Pamela S. Dykes
  Notre Dame de Sion High School
  Kansas City, MO

Dagmar Ebaugh
  Woodward Academy
  College Park, GA

Lou Ann Erikson
  Deerfield High School
  Deerfield, IL

Morganne C. Freeborn
  New Hampton School
  New Hampton, NH

Kim Frisinger
  West Ottawa High School
  Hollana, MI

Julie Frye
  Lexington High School
  Lexington, OH

Walter Giorgis-Blessent
  The Bronx High School of Science
  Bronx, NY

Andreea Gorodea
  Marion L. Steele High School
  Amherst, OH

Holly Hammerle
  Bloomfield Hills High School
  Bloomfield Hills, MI

Dalila Hannouche
  Professional Children's School
  New York, NY

Michael Houston
  Montclair Kimberley Academy
  Montclair, NJ

Luciana Jeler
  Academy of the Sacred Heart
  Bloomfield Hills, MI

Cathy Kendrigan
  Loyola Academy
  Wilmette, IL

Emily Kunzeman
  Boston Trinity Academy
  Boston, MA

Jennifer L. Lange
: Jefferson High School
: Cedar Rapids, IA

Julie LaRocque
: Assumption High School
: Louisville, KY

Sharon Lawrence
: The Knox School
: St. James, NY

Laura Longacre
: Cheshire Academy
: Cheshire, CT

Véronique Lynch
: Parkway South High School
: Manchester, MO

Rachel M. Martin
: Cheney High School
: Cheney, WA

Irene Marxsen
: First Presbyterian Day School
: Macon, GA

Mindy Orrison
: Centennial High School
: Champaign, IL

Margharita Sandillo Reiter
: Ranney School
: Tinton Falls, NJ

Rebecca Richardson
: Sage Hill School
: Newport Coast, CA

Caroline M. Ridenour
: Heritage Christian School
: North Hills, CA

Sonya Rotman
: Horace Mann School
: Bronx, NY

Renee Saylor
: Walcott Intermediate School
: Davenport, IA

Laura Schmuck
: Carl Sandburg High School
: Orland Park, IL

Lisa Slyman
: Sperreng Middle School
: St. Louis, MO

Christine Stafford
: Holy Innocents' Episcopal School
: Atlanta, GA

Claudia S. Travers
: Ross School
: East Hampton, NY

Nitya Viswanath
: Amos Alonzo Stagg High School
: Palos Hills, IL

Michelle Webster
: Watertown High School
: Watertown, WI

Abigail Wilder
: Champaign Centennial High School
: Champaign, IL

Jason R. Wyckoff
: Brunswick High School
: Brunswick, OH

Valerie N. Yoshimura
: The Archer School for Girls
: Los Angeles, CA

Salut!

Unité 1

Leçon 1A

CONTEXTES .... pages 2–5
- Greetings and good-byes
- Introductions and expressions of courtesy
- The French alphabet

ROMAN-PHOTO ... pages 6–7
- **Au café**

CULTURE .... pages 8–9
- Greetings and manners
- **Flash culture**

STRUCTURES .... pages 10–17
- Nouns and articles
- Numbers 0–60

SYNTHÈSE ...... pages 18–19
- **Révision**
- **Le Zapping**

Leçon 1B

CONTEXTES ..... pages 20–23
- People and things around a classroom
- Silent letters

ROMAN-PHOTO . pages 24–25
- **Les copains**

CULTURE .... pages 26–27
- **French diversity**

STRUCTURES .... pages 28–35
- Subject pronouns and the verb **être**
- Adjective agreement

SYNTHÈSE ...... pages 36–37
- **Révision**
- **À l'écoute**

Savoir-faire ... pages 38–43
- **Panorama:** Le monde francophone
- **Lecture:** Read an address book.
- **Écriture:** Write a list of important numbers and addresses.

Pour commencer
- What are these people saying?
  a. Excusez-moi. b. Bonjour! c. Merci.
- How many people are in the foreground of the photo?
  a. une personne b. deux personnes c. trois personnes
- What do you think is an appropriate title for the person on the left?
  a. Monsieur b. Madame c. Mademoiselle

Unit Goals

Leçon 1A
In this lesson, students will learn:
- terms for greetings, farewells, and introductions
- expressions of courtesy
- the French alphabet and the names of accent marks
- about shaking hands and **bises**
- more about greetings and farewells through specially shot video footage
- gender of nouns
- articles (definite and indefinite)
- the numbers 0–60
- the expression **il y a**
- about the **Institut national de prévention et d'éducation pour la santé**

Leçon 1B
In this lesson, students will learn:
- terms to identify people
- terms for objects in the classroom
- rules for silent letters
- about France's multicultural society
- subject pronouns
- the present tense of **être**
- **c'est** and **il/elle est**
- adjective agreement
- some descriptive adjectives and adjectives of nationality
- to listen for familiar words

Savoir-faire
In this section, students will learn:
- cultural, linguistic, and historical information about the Francophone world
- to recognize cognates
- strategies for writing in French
- to write a telephone/address book

21ST CENTURY SKILLS
Initiative and Self-Direction
Students can monitor their progress online using the Supersite activities and assessments.

Pour commencer
- b. Bonjour!
- b. deux personnes
- a. Monsieur

INSTRUCTIONAL RESOURCES

Student Resources
Print: Student Book, Workbook (*Cahier de l'élève*)
Supersite: vhlcentral.com, **vText**, *eCahier*, Audio, Video, Practice

Teacher Resources
Print: Teacher's Edition, Answer Keys, Testing Program
Technology: Audio MP3s on CD (Textbook, Testing Program, Audio Program), Video Program DVD (*Roman-photo, Flash culture*)

Supersite: vhlcentral.com, Activity Pack, Middle School Activity Pack, Lesson Plans, Grammar Tutorials, Grammar Slides, Testing Program, Audio and Video Scripts, Answer Key, Audio MP3s, Streaming Video (*Roman-photo, Flash culture, Le Zapping*), Digital Image Bank, Learning Management System (Gradebook, Assignments)

Voice boards on the Supersite allow you and your students to record and share up to five minutes of audio. Use voice boards for presentations, oral assessments, discussions, directions, etc.

Section Goals

In this section, students will learn and practice vocabulary related to:
- basic greetings and farewells
- introductions
- courtesy expressions

Key Standards

1.1, 1.2, 4.1

Student Resources
Cahier de l'élève, pp. 1–3; Supersite: Activities, eCahier

Teacher Resources
Answer Keys; Digital Image Bank; Audio Script; Textbook & Audio Activity MP3s/CD; Testing program: Vocabulary Quiz

Suggestions

- To familiarize students with the meanings of headings used in the lessons and important vocabulary for classroom interactions, point students to the frontmatter in their textbooks.
- For complete lesson plans, go to **vhlcentral.com** to access the teacher's part of the **D'accord!** companion Supersite.
- With books closed, write a few greetings, farewells, and courtesy expressions on the board, explain their meaning, and model their pronunciation. Circulate around the room, greeting students, making introductions, and encouraging responses. Then, have students open their books to pages 2–3. Ask them to identify which conversations are exchanges between friends and which seem more formal. Then point out the use of **vous** vs. **tu** in each conversation. Give examples of different situations in which each form would be appropriate.

Successful Language Learning Encourage students to make flash cards to help them memorize or review vocabulary.

Contextes — Leçon 1A

You will learn how to...
- greet people in French
- say good-bye

Audio: Vocabulary Practice
My Vocabulary

Ça va?

Vocabulaire

Bonsoir.	Good evening.; Hello.
À bientôt.	See you soon.
À demain.	See you tomorrow.
Bonne journée!	Have a good day!
Au revoir.	Good-bye.
Comme ci, comme ça.	So-so.
Je vais bien/mal.	I am doing well/badly.
Moi aussi.	Me too.
Comment t'appelles-tu? (*fam.*)	What is your name?
Je vous/te présente... (*form./fam.*)	I would like to introduce (name) to you.
De rien.	You're welcome.
Excusez-moi. (*form.*)	Excuse me.
Excuse-moi. (*fam.*)	Excuse me.
Merci beaucoup.	Thanks a lot.
Pardon.	Pardon (me).
S'il vous plaît. (*form.*)	Please.
S'il te plaît. (*fam.*)	Please.
Je vous/t'en prie. (*form./fam.*)	You're welcome.; It's nothing.
Monsieur (M.)	Sir (Mr.)
Madame (Mme)	Ma'am (Mrs.)
Mademoiselle (Mlle)	Miss
ici	here
là	there
là-bas	over there

GEORGES Ça va, Henri?
HENRI Oui, ça va très bien, merci. Et vous, comment allez-vous?
GEORGES Je vais bien, merci.

PAUL Merci!
JEAN Il n'y a pas de quoi.

MARIE À plus tard, Guillaume!
GUILLAUME À tout à l'heure, Marie!

JACQUES Bonjour, Monsieur Boniface. Je vous présente Thérèse Lemaire.
M. BONIFACE Bonjour, Mademoiselle.
THÉRÈSE Enchantée.

ressources
vText
CE pp. 1–3
vhlcentral.com Leçon 1A

2 deux

EXPANSION

Language Notes Point out that **Salut** and **À plus**, the shortened form of **À plus tard**, are familiar expressions. Explain that the translation of **Je vais bien/mal** is not literal. **Je vais** means *I go*, but **je vais bien** means *I am doing well*.

TEACHING OPTIONS

Using Games Divide the class into two teams. Create sentences and questions based on the **Vocabulaire** and the illustrated conversations. Choose one person at a time, alternating between teams. Tell students to respond logically to your statement or question. Award a point for each correct response. The team with the most points at the end of the game wins.

Salut! — Unité 1

Mise en pratique

Attention!
In French, people can be addressed formally or informally. Use the **tu/toi** forms with close friends, family, or children. Use the **vous** forms with groups, a boss, adults, or someone you do not know, unless they ask you to use **tu**.

1. Chassez l'intrus
Circle the word or expression that does not belong.

1. a. Bonjour.
   b. Bonsoir.
   c. Salut.
   d. (Pardon.)
2. a. Bien.
   b. Très bien.
   c. (De rien.)
   d. Comme ci, comme ça.
3. a. À bientôt.
   b. À demain.
   c. À tout à l'heure.
   d. (Enchanté.)
4. a. Comment allez-vous?
   b. (Comment vous appelez-vous?)
   c. Ça va?
   d. Comment vas-tu?
5. a. (Pas mal.)
   b. Excuse-moi.
   c. Je vous en prie.
   d. Il n'y a pas de quoi.
6. a. Comment vous appelez-vous?
   b. Je vous présente Dominique.
   c. Enchanté.
   d. (Comment allez-vous?)
7. a. Pas mal.
   b. Très bien.
   c. Mal.
   d. (Et vous?)
8. a. Comment allez-vous?
   b. Comment vous appelez-vous?
   c. (Et toi?)
   d. Je vous en prie.

2. Écoutez
Listen to each of these questions or statements and select the most appropriate response.

#	Option A		Option B	
1.	Enchanté.	☐	Je m'appelle Thérèse.	✓
2.	Merci beaucoup.	☐	Je vous en prie.	✓
3.	Comme ci, comme ça.	✓	De rien.	☐
4.	Bonsoir, Monsieur.	✓	Moi aussi.	☐
5.	Enchanté.	✓	Et toi?	☐
6.	Bonjour.	☐	À demain.	✓
7.	Pas mal.	✓	Pardon.	☐
8.	Il n'y a pas de quoi.	✓	Moi aussi.	☐
9.	Enchanté.	☐	Très bien. Et vous?	✓
10.	À bientôt.	✓	Mal.	☐

3. Conversez
Madeleine is introducing her classmate Khaled to Libby, an American exchange student. Complete their conversation, using a different expression from **CONTEXTES** in each blank. *Answers will vary.*

MADELEINE (1) _____!
KHALED Salut, Madeleine. (2) _____?
MADELEINE Pas mal. (3) _____?
KHALED (4) _____, merci.
MADELEINE (5) _____ Libby. Elle est de (*She is from*) Boston.
KHALED (6) _____ Libby. (7) _____ Khaled.
(8) _____?
LIBBY (9) _____, merci.
KHALED Oh, là, là. Je vais rater (*I am going to miss*) le bus. À bientôt.
MADELEINE (10) _____.
LIBBY (11) _____.

MARC Bonjour, je m'appelle Marc, et vous, comment vous appelez-vous?
ANNIE Je m'appelle Annie.
MARC Enchanté.

SOPHIE Bonjour, Catherine!
CATHERINE Salut, Sophie!
SOPHIE Ça va?
CATHERINE Oui, ça va bien, merci. Et toi, comment vas-tu?
SOPHIE Pas mal.

---

1 Suggestion Go over the answers with the class and have students explain why each expression does not belong.

2 Script
1. Comment vous appelez-vous?
2. Excusez-moi.
3. Comment allez-vous?
4. Bonsoir, Mademoiselle.
5. Je te présente Thérèse.
6. À bientôt.
7. Comment vas-tu?
8. Merci.
9. Bonjour, comment allez-vous?
10. Au revoir.
(On Textbook Audio)

2 Suggestion Before students listen, tell them to read the possible responses provided and write down the questions or statements that they think would elicit each response. After completing the listening activity, go over the answers to check whether students' predictions were accurate.

3 Suggestion Have students work in groups of three on the activity. Tell them to choose a role and complete the conversation. Then ask groups to act out their conversation for the class.

trois **3**

EXPANSION
Scrambled Conversations Have students work in pairs. Tell them to write an original conversation with six to eight lines. After completing this task, they should rewrite the conversation and scramble the order of the sentences. Have pairs exchange their scrambled conversations and put them in a logical order. Remind students that they should verify the answers.

PRE-AP®
Interpersonal Speaking Have small groups role-play a conversation in which adults, children, and high school-age people interact. Remind students to use formal and informal expressions in the appropriate situations. Give them time to prepare, and then have a few groups present their conversations to the class.

Contextes — Leçon 1A

Communication

4 Discutez With a partner, complete these conversations. Then act them out. *Answers will vary.*

Conversation 1
Salut! Je m'appelle François. Et toi, comment t'appelles-tu?
_____
Ça va?
_____

Conversation 2
_____
Comme ci, comme ça. Et vous?
_____
Bon (*Well*), à demain.
_____

Conversation 3
Bonsoir, je vous présente Mademoiselle Barnard.
_____
Enchanté(e).
_____
Très bien, merci. Et vous?
_____

5 C'est à vous! How would you greet these people, ask them for their names, and ask them how they are doing? With a partner, write a short dialogue for each item and act it out. Pay attention to the use of **tu** and **vous**. *Answers will vary.*

1. Madame Colombier
2. Mademoiselle Estèves 
3. Monsieur Marchand 
4. Marie, Guillaume et Geneviève 

6 Présentations Form groups of three. Introduce yourself, and ask your partners their names and how they are doing. Then, join another group and take turns introducing your partners. *Answers will vary.*

MODÈLE
Élève 1: *Bonjour. Je m'appelle Fatima. Et vous?*
Élève 2: *Je m'appelle Fabienne.*
Élève 3: *Et moi, je m'appelle Antoine. Ça va?*
Élève 1: *Ça va bien, merci. Et toi?*
Élève 3: *Comme ci, comme ça.*

Suggestions (Activity 4)
- Before beginning the activity, encourage students to use as many different words and expressions as they can from the **Vocabulaire** on page 2 rather than repeating the same expressions in each conversation.
- Have a few volunteers write their conversations on the board. Ask the class to identify, correct, and explain any errors.

Virtual Chat (Activity 4)
You can also assign Activity 4 on the Supersite. Students record individual responses that appear in your gradebook.

Expansions (Activity 4)
- Have students look at the photo, identify the conversation it most likely corresponds to (**Conversation 1**), and explain their reasoning. Point out that nearly all formal greetings are accompanied by a handshake. Tell the class that they will learn more about gestures used in greetings in the **Culture** section of this lesson.
- Have students rewrite **Conversation 1** in the formal register, and **Conversations 2** and **3** in the informal register.

Suggestions (Activity 5)
- Before beginning this activity, ask students if they would use **tu** or **vous** in each situation.
- If class time is limited, assign a specific situation to each pair.
- Call on volunteers to act out their conversations for the class.

Suggestion (Activity 6)
Have two volunteers read the **modèle** aloud. Remind students to use **vous** when addressing more than one classmate at a time.

EXPANSION

Using Categories Read some sentences to the class and ask if they would use them with another student of the same age or an older person they do not know. Examples: **1. Je te présente Guillaume.** (student) **2. Merci beaucoup, Monsieur.** (older person) **3. Comment vas-tu?** (student) **4. Bonjour, professeur ____.** (older person) **5. Comment vous appelez-vous?** (older person)

TEACHING OPTIONS

Mini-conversations Have students circulate around the classroom and conduct mini-conversations in French with other students, using the words and expressions they learned on pages 2–3. As students are carrying out the activity, move around the room, monitoring their work and offering assistance if requested.

Salut! **Unité 1**

Les sons et les lettres
Audio: Explanation Record & Compare

The French alphabet

The French alphabet is made up of the same 26 letters as the English alphabet. While they look the same, some letters are pronounced differently. They also sound different when you spell.

lettre	exemple	lettre	exemple	lettre	exemple
a	(a)	**a**dresse	j	(ji)	**j**ustice	s	(esse)	**s**pécial
b	(bé)	**b**anane	k	(ka)	**k**ilomètre	t	(té)	**t**able
c	(cé)	**c**arotte	l	(elle)	**l**ion	u	(u)	**u**nique
d	(dé)	**d**essert	m	(emme)	**m**ariage	v	(vé)	**v**idéo
e	(e)	r**e**belle	n	(enne)	**n**ature	w	(double vé)	**w**agon
f	(effe)	**f**ragile	o	(o)	**o**live	x	(iks)	**x**ylophone
g	(gé)	**g**enre	p	(pé)	**p**ersonne	y	(i grec)	**y**oga
h	(hache)	**h**éritage	q	(ku)	**q**uiche	z	(zède)	**z**éro
i	(i)	**i**nnocent	r	(erre)	**r**adio			

Notice that some letters in French words have accents. You'll learn how they influence pronunciation in later lessons. Whenever you spell a word in French, include the name of the accent after the letter. For double letters, use **deux**: ss = deux s.

accent	nom	exemple	orthographe
´	accent aigu	identit**é**	I-D-E-N-T-I-T-E-accent aigu
`	accent grave	probl**è**me	P-R-O-B-L-E-accent grave-M-E
^	accent circonflexe	h**ô**pital	H-O-accent circonflexe-P-I-T-A-L
¨	tréma	na**ï**ve	N-A-I-tréma-V-E
¸	cédille	**ç**a	C-cédille-A

L'alphabet Practice saying the French alphabet and example words aloud.

Ça s'écrit comment? Spell these words aloud in French.

1. judo
2. yacht
3. forêt
4. zèbre
5. existe
6. clown
7. numéro
8. français
9. musique
10. favorite
11. kangourou
12. parachute
13. différence
14. intelligent
15. dictionnaire
16. alphabet

Dictons Practice reading these sayings aloud.

Grande invitation, petites portions.¹

Tout est bien qui finit bien.²

¹ Great boast, small roast.
² All's well that ends well.

Lundi   Mardi

ressources
vText
CE p. 4
vhlcentral.com Leçon 1A

cinq 5

Section Goals
In this section, students will learn functional phrases for making introductions and speaking on the telephone through comprehensible input.

Key Standards
1.2, 2.1, 2.2, 4.1, 4.2

Student Resources
Cahier de l'élève, 5–6; Supersite: Activities, eCahier

Teacher Resources
Answer Keys; Video Script & Translation; *Roman-photo* video

Video Synopsis Sandrine buys a magazine at Monsieur Hulot's newsstand. At **Le P'tit Bistrot**, Rachid introduces David, his American friend, to Sandrine and Amina. Madame Forestier (Valérie), who owns the café, gets a phone call from her son's high school French teacher because he didn't do well on his French exam. Stéphane tells Rachid to introduce David to his mother so he can avoid talking to her.

Suggestions
- Have students cover the French captions and guess the plot based only on the video stills. Write their predictions on the board.
- Have students volunteer to read the characters' parts in the **Roman-photo** aloud. Then have them get together in groups of eight to act out the episode.
- After students have read the **Roman-photo**, quickly review their predictions, and ask them which ones were correct.
- Point out that 100 centimes = 1 euro, the monetary unit of the European Union, which includes France.

Roman-photo Leçon 1A

Au café
Video: *Roman-photo*
Record & Compare

PERSONNAGES

Amina
David 
Monsieur Hulot 
Michèle 
Rachid 
Sandrine 
Stéphane 
Valérie 

Au kiosque...
SANDRINE Bonjour, Monsieur Hulot!
M. HULOT Bonjour, Mademoiselle Aubry! Comment allez-vous?
SANDRINE Très bien, merci! Et vous?
M. HULOT Euh, ça va. Voici 45 (quarante-cinq) centimes. Bonne journée!
SANDRINE Merci, au revoir!

À la terrasse du café...
AMINA Salut!
SANDRINE Bonjour, Amina. Ça va?
AMINA Ben... ça va. Et toi?
SANDRINE Oui, je vais bien, merci.
AMINA Regarde! Voilà Rachid et... un ami?

RACHID Bonjour!
AMINA ET SANDRINE Salut!
RACHID Je vous présente un ami, David Duchesne.
SANDRINE Je m'appelle Sandrine.
DAVID Enchanté.

STÉPHANE Oh, non! Madame Richard! Le professeur de français!
DAVID Il y a un problème?

STÉPHANE Oui! L'examen de français! Présentez-vous, je vous en prie!

VALÉRIE Oh... l'examen de français! Oui, merci, merci Madame Richard, merci beaucoup! De rien, au revoir!

ACTIVITÉS

1 Vrai ou faux? Decide whether each statement is **vrai** or **faux**. Correct the false statements. *Answers may vary.*

1. Sandrine va (*is doing*) bien. Vrai.
2. Sandrine et Amina sont (*are*) amies. Vrai.
3. David est français. Faux. David est américain.
4. David est de Washington. Vrai.
5. Rachid présente son frère (*his brother*) David à Sandrine et Amina. Faux. Rachid présente son ami David à Sandrine et à Amina.
6. Stéphane est étudiant à l'université. Faux. Stéphane est au lycée.
7. Il y a un problème avec l'examen de sciences politiques. Faux. Il y a un problème avec l'examen de français.
8. Amina, Rachid et Sandrine sont (*are*) à Paris. Faux. Amina, Rachid et Sandrine sont à Aix-en-Provence.
9. Michèle est au P'tit Bistrot. Vrai.
10. Madame Richard est le professeur de Stéphane. Vrai.
11. Valérie va mal. Vrai.
12. Rachid a (*has*) cours de français dans 30 minutes. Faux. Rachid a cours de sciences politiques dans 30 minutes.

Practice more at vhlcentral.com.

6 *six*

TEACHING OPTIONS

Au café Before showing the video episode, have students brainstorm greetings and other expressions that they might hear in an episode in which some of the characters meet each other for the first time.

EXPANSION

Extra Practice Play the episode once and tell the class to listen for basic greetings. After the video is over, have students recall the greetings they heard and write them on the board. Show the episode again and ask the class to write down all of the courtesy expressions that they hear, including ways to say *pleased to meet you*.

Salut! **Unité 1**

Les étudiants se retrouvent (*meet*) au café.

DAVID Et toi..., comment t'appelles-tu?
AMINA Je m'appelle Amina.
RACHID David est un étudiant américain. Il est de Washington, la capitale des États-Unis.
AMINA Ah, oui! Bienvenue à Aix-en-Provence.
RACHID Bon..., à tout à l'heure.
SANDRINE À bientôt, David.

À l'intérieur (inside) du café...
MICHÈLE Allô. Le P'tit Bistrot. Oui, un moment, s'il vous plaît. Madame Forestier! Le lycée de Stéphane.
VALÉRIE Allô. Oui. Bonjour, Madame Richard. Oui. Oui. Stéphane? Il y a un problème au lycée?

RACHID Bonjour, Madame Forestier. Comment allez-vous?
VALÉRIE Ah, ça va mal.
RACHID Oui? Moi, je vais bien. Je vous présente David Duchesne, étudiant américain de Washington.

DAVID Bonjour, Madame. Enchanté!
RACHID Ah, j'ai cours de sciences politiques dans 30 (trente) minutes. Au revoir, Madame Forestier. À tout à l'heure, David.

Expressions utiles

Introductions
- **David est un étudiant américain. Il est de Washington.**
  David is an American student. He's from Washington.
- **Présentez-vous, je vous en prie!**
  Introduce yourselves, please!
- **Il/Elle s'appelle...**
  His/Her name is...
- **Bienvenue à Aix-en-Provence.**
  Welcome to Aix-en-Provence.

Speaking on the telephone
- **Allô.**
  Hello.
- **Un moment, s'il vous plaît.**
  One moment, please.

Additional vocabulary
- **Regarde! Voilà Rachid et... un ami?**
  Look! There's Rachid and... a friend?
- **J'ai cours de sciences politiques dans 30 (trente) minutes.**
  I have political science class in thirty minutes.
- **Il y a un problème au lycée?**
  Is there a problem at the high school?
- **Il y a...** — **euh**
  There is/are... — *um*
- **Il/Elle est** — **bon**
  He/She is... — *well; good*
- **Voici...** — **centimes**
  Here's... — *cents*
- **Voilà...**
  There's...

2 Complétez Fill in the blanks with the words from the list. Refer to the video scenes as necessary.

ai	est
bienvenue	voici
capitale	

1. _Bienvenue_ à Aix-en-Provence.
2. Il est de Washington, la _capitale_ des États-Unis.
3. _Voici_ 45 (quarante-cinq) centimes. Bonne journée!
4. J'_ai_ cours de sciences politiques.
5. David _est_ un étudiant américain.

3 Conversez In groups of three, write a conversation where you introduce an exchange student to a friend. Be prepared to present your conversation to the class.

sept **7**

Section Goals

In this section, students will:
- learn about gestures used with greetings
- learn some familiar greetings and farewells
- learn some tips about good manners in different Francophone countries
- read about Aix-en-Provence
- view authentic cultural footage

21st CENTURY SKILLS

Global Awareness
Students will gain perspectives on the Francophone world to develop respect and openness to other cultures.

Key Standards
2.1, 2.2, 3.1, 3.2, 4.2

Student Resources
Cahier de l'élève, 7–8;
Supersite: Activities, eCahier
Teacher Resources
Answer Keys; Video Script & Translation; *Flash culture* video

Culture à la loupe

Avant la lecture Ask students how they greet their friends, family members, fellow students, and people they meet for the first time. Ask them for some examples of regional variations in greetings in the United States (e.g., Howdy, Hiya, Yo).

Lecture
- Ask students what information the map on this page shows. (It shows the number of kisses traditionally given by region.)
- Explain that **faire la bise** does not actually mean to kiss another's cheek, but rather to kiss parallel to the other person's face, so that physical contact is limited to a grazing of cheeks.

Après la lecture Have students compare French and American greetings or any other method of greeting with which they are familiar.

1 Expansion Have students work in pairs. Tell them to role-play the situations in items 1–6. Example: 1. Students give each other four kisses because they are in northwestern France.

8 Unit 1 • Lesson 1A

Culture — Leçon 1A

Reading Video: *Flash culture*

CULTURE À LA LOUPE

La poignée de main ou la bise?

French friends and relatives usually exchange a kiss (**la bise**) on alternating cheeks whenever they meet and again when they say good-bye. Friends of friends may also kiss when introduced, even though they have just met. This is particularly true among students and young adults. It is normal for men of the same family to exchange **la bise**; otherwise, men generally greet one another with a handshake (**la poignée de main**). As the map shows, the number of kisses varies from place to place in France. In some regions, two kisses (one on each cheek) is the standard while in others, people may exchange as many as four kisses. Whatever the number, each kiss is accompanied by a slight kissing sound.

Unless they are also friends, business acquaintances and coworkers usually shake hands each time they meet and do so again upon leaving. A French handshake is brief and firm, with a single downward motion.

Combien de *How many*

Coup de main
If you are not sure whether you should shake hands or kiss someone, or if you don't know which side to start on, you can always follow the other person's lead.

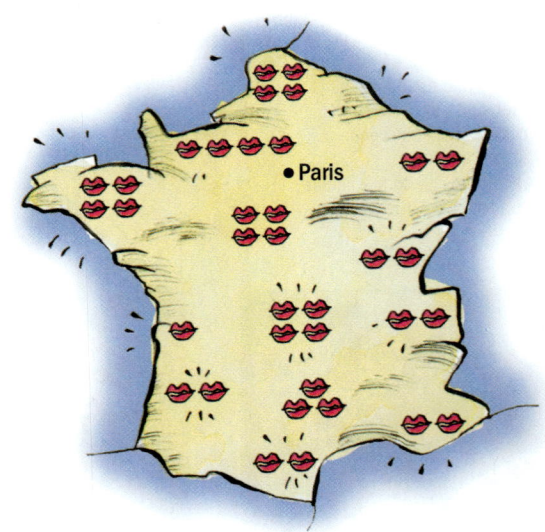

Combien de° bises?

ACTIVITÉS

1 Vrai ou faux? Indicate whether each statement is **vrai** or **faux**. Correct any false statements.

1. In northwestern France, giving four kisses is common.   Vrai.
2. Business acquaintances usually kiss one another on the cheek.   Faux. They usually shake hands.
3. French people may give someone they've just met **la bise**.   Vrai.
4. Bises exchanged between French men at a family gathering are common.   Vrai.
5. In a business setting, French people often shake hands when they meet each day and again when they leave.   Vrai.
6. When shaking hands, French people prefer a long and soft handshake.   Faux. A French handshake is brief and firm.
7. The number of kisses given can vary from one region to another.   Vrai.
8. It is customary for kisses to be given silently.   Faux. Each kiss is accompanied by a slight kissing sound.

Practice more at **vhlcentral.com**.

8 huit

EXPANSION

La bise Tell students that, although people in some social circles in the United States commonly kiss each other on the cheek once, this is not common practice in France. It could be considered impolite to give only one **bise** since the other person would be waiting for the second kiss. In some regions of France and Switzerland, people may even give three **bises**, but just one is rare.

TEACHING OPTIONS

Using Games Divide the class into two teams. Indicate one team member at a time, alternating teams. Give situations in which people greet each other. Students should say if the people should greet each other with **la poignée de main** or **la bise**. Examples: female friends (**la bise**); male and female business associates (**la poignée de main**). Give a point for each correct answer. The team with the most points at the end wins.

Salut! **Unité 1**

LE FRANÇAIS QUOTIDIEN

Les salutations

À la prochaine!	Until next time!
À plus!	See you later!
Ciao!	Bye!
Coucou!	Hi there!/Hey!
Pas grand-chose.	Nothing much.
Quoi de neuf?	What's new?
Rien de nouveau.	Nothing new.

LE MONDE FRANCOPHONE

Les bonnes manières

In any country, an effort to speak the native language is appreciated. Using titles of respect and a few polite expressions, such as **excusez-moi**, **merci**, and **s'il vous plaît**, can take you a long way when conversing with native Francophones.

Dos and don'ts in the francophone world:

France Always greet shopkeepers upon entering a store and say good-bye upon leaving.

Northern Africa Use your right hand when handing items to others.

Quebec Province Make eye contact when shaking hands.

Sub-Saharan Africa Do not show the soles of your feet when sitting.

Switzerland Do not litter or jaywalk.

PORTRAIT

Aix-en-Provence: ville d'eau, ville d'art°

Aix-en-Provence is a vibrant university town that welcomes international students. Its main boulevard, **le cours Mirabeau**, is great for people-watching or just relaxing in a sidewalk café. One can see many beautiful fountains, traditional and ethnic restaurants, and the daily vegetable and flower market among the winding, narrow streets of **la vieille ville** (old town).

Aix is also renowned for its dedication to the arts, hosting numerous cultural festivals every year such as **le Festival International d'Art Lyrique**, and **Aix en Musique**. For centuries, artists have been drawn to Provence for its natural beauty and its unique quality of light. Paul Cézanne, artist and native son of Provence, spent his days painting the surrounding countryside.

ville d'eau, ville d'art *city of water, city of art*

Sur Internet

What behaviors are socially unacceptable in French-speaking countries?

Go to vhlcentral.com to find more information related to this **Culture** section. Then watch the corresponding **Flash culture**.

---

2 **Les bonnes manières** In which places might these behaviors be particularly offensive?

1. littering
   Switzerland
2. offering a business card with your left hand
   Northern Africa
3. sitting with the bottom of your foot facing your host
   Sub-Saharan Africa
4. failing to greet a salesperson
   France
5. looking away when shaking hand
   Quebec Province

3 **À vous** With a partner, practice meeting and greeting people in French in various social situations.

1. Your good friend from Provence introduces you to her close friend.
2. You walk into your neighborhood bakery.
3. You arrive for an interview with a prospective employer.

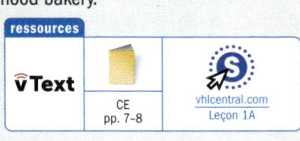

ressources
vText — CE pp. 7–8
vhlcentral.com — Leçon 1A

neuf **9**

Section Goals

In this section, students will learn:
- gender and number of nouns
- definite and indefinite articles

Key Standards
4.1, 5.1

Student Resources
Cahier de l'élève, 9–11; Supersite: Activities, *eCahier*, Grammar Tutorials
Teacher Resources
Answer Keys; Audio Script; Audio Activity MP3s/CD; Activity Pack; Testing program: Grammar Quiz

Suggestions
- Explain what a noun is by giving examples of people (**professeur**), places (**café**), things (**examen**), and ideas (**problème**). Then write these nouns on the board: **ami, amie, cours, télévision**. Point out the gender of each noun. Explain that nouns for male beings are usually masculine, and nouns for female beings are usually feminine. All other nouns can be either masculine or feminine. Tell students that they should memorize the gender of a noun along with the word.
- Explain that **étudiant(e)** usually refers to a college student, while **élève**, which students will learn in **Leçon 1B**, refers more commonly to students of high school age or younger.
- Write these words on the board: **professeur, professeurs, étudiante, étudiantes**. Ask students to point out the singular and plural nouns and to explain why. Then have students pronounce the words. Point out that the **-s** is not pronounced in French.
- Write **bureau** and **bureaux** on the board. Explain that words ending in **-eau** add **-x** to form the plural.

Structures — Leçon 1A

1A.1 Nouns and articles
Presentation Tutorial

Point de départ A noun designates a person, place, or thing. As in English, nouns in French have number (singular or plural). However, French nouns also have gender (masculine or feminine).

masculine singular	masculine plural	feminine singular	feminine plural
le café	**les cafés**	**la bibliothèque**	**les bibliothèques**
the café	the cafés	the library	the libraries

- Nouns that designate a male are usually masculine. Nouns that designate a female are usually feminine.

masculine		feminine	
l'acteur	the actor	l'actrice	the actress
l'ami	the (male) friend	l'amie	the (female) friend
le chanteur	the (male) singer	la chanteuse	the (female) singer
l'étudiant	the (male) student	l'étudiante	the (female) student
le petit ami	the boyfriend	la petite amie	the girlfriend

- Some nouns can designate either a male or a female regardless of their grammatical gender; in other words, whether the word itself is masculine or feminine.

un professeur — a (male or female) teacher, professor
une personne — a (male or female) person

- Nouns for objects that have no natural gender can be either masculine or feminine.

masculine		feminine	
le bureau	the office; desk	la chose	the thing
le lycée	the high school	la différence	the difference
l'examen	the test, exam	la faculté	the faculty
l'objet	the object	la littérature	literature
l'ordinateur	the computer	la sociologie	sociology
le problème	the problem	l'université	the university

Boîte à outils
As you learn new nouns, study them with their corresponding articles. This will help you remember their gender.

Boîte à outils
The final **–s** in the plural form of a noun is not pronounced. Therefore **ami** and **amis** sound the same. You can determine whether the word you're hearing is singular or plural by the article that comes before it.

- You can usually form the plural of a noun by adding **-s**.

	singular		plural	
typical masculine noun	l'objet	the object	les objets	the objects
typical feminine noun	la télévision	the television	les télévisions	the televisions

- However, in the case of words that end in **-eau** in the singular, add **-x** to the end to form the plural. For most nouns ending in **-al**, drop the **-al** and add **-aux**.

le bureau → **les bureaux**
the office — the offices

l'animal → **les animaux**
the animal — the animals

EXPANSION

Rapid Drill Write ten singular nouns on the board. In a rapid-response drill, call on students to give the appropriate gender. Examples: **bureau** (masculine), **télévision** (feminine). You may also do this activity without writing the words on the board.

TEACHING OPTIONS

Using Games Divide the class into groups of three to four students. Bring in photos or magazine pictures, point to various objects or people, and say the French word without saying the article. Call on groups to indicate the person's or object's gender. Give a point for each correct answer. Deduct a point for each wrong answer. The group with the most points at the end wins.

Salut! Unité 1

- When you have a group composed of males and females, use the masculine plural noun to refer to it.

  les amis
  the (male and female) friends

  les étudiants
  the (male and female) students

- The English definite article *the* never varies with number or gender of the noun it modifies. However, in French the definite article takes four different forms depending on the gender and number of the noun that it accompanies: **le, la, l'** or **les**.

	singular noun beginning with a consonant		singular noun beginning with a vowel sound		plural noun	
masculine	le tableau	*the painting/ blackboard*	l'ami	*the (male) friend*	les cafés	*the cafés*
feminine	la librairie	*the bookstore*	l'université	*the university*	les télévisions	*the televisions*

- In English, the singular indefinite article is *a/an*, and the plural indefinite article is *some*. In French, the singular indefinite articles are **un** and **une**, and the plural indefinite article is **des**. Unlike in English, the indefinite article **des** cannot be omitted in French.

	singular		plural	
masculine	un instrument	*an instrument*	des instruments	*(some) instruments*
feminine	une table	*a table*	des tables	*(some) tables*

Il y a **un ordinateur** ici.
There's a computer here.

Il y a **des ordinateurs** ici.
There are (some) computers here.

Il y a **une université** ici.
There's a university here.

Il y a **des universités** ici.
There are (some) universities here.

- Use **c'est** followed by a singular article and noun or **ce sont** followed by a plural article and noun to identify people and objects.

  Qu'est-ce que **c'est**?
  What is that?

  C'est une librairie.
  It's a bookstore.

  Ce sont des bureaux.
  Those are offices.

Boîte à outils

In English, you sometimes omit the definite article when making general statements.

I love French.
Literature is difficult.

In French, you must always use the definite article in such cases.

J'adore le français.
La littérature est difficile.

Essayez! Select the correct article for each noun.

le, la, l' ou les?
1. _le_ café
2. _la_ bibliothèque
3. _l'_ acteur
4. _l'_ amie
5. _les_ problèmes
6. _le_ lycée
7. _les_ examens
8. _la_ littérature

un, une ou des?
1. _un_ bureau
2. _une_ différence
3. _un_ objet
4. _des_ amis
5. _des_ amies
6. _une_ université
7. _un_ ordinateur
8. _des_ tableaux

onze 11

Suggestions
- Write these words on the board: **le café, les cafés, l'ami, les amis, la personne, les personnes**. Explain the use of the definite article. Point out that singular nouns beginning with a vowel or silent **h** use **l'**.
- Follow the same procedure for indefinite articles using these words: **un café, des cafés, un ami, des amis, une personne, des personnes**. Point out that the **-n** of **un** is pronounced before a vowel.
- Model how to pronounce **les** and **des** before words beginning with a consonant and a vowel.
- Consider giving your students some pointers to help them guess the gender of a noun. Words ending in **-al, -age, -eau, -et, -isme** or in a consonant are often masculine while those ending in **-ence, -ance,** or **-ie** are often feminine. However, be sure to caution your students that these are only general guidelines and there are always exceptions. Have students find words they have learned in this lesson that fit these guidelines and also find any exceptions.
- Tell students they will learn more about **c'est/ce sont** in **1B.1**.

Essayez! Have students change the singular nouns and articles to the plural and vice versa.

DIFFERENTIATION

For Kinesthetic Learners Distribute cards preprinted with articles and nouns to each of four students. Then line up ten students, each of whom is assigned a noun. Include a mix of masculine, feminine, singular, and plural nouns. Say one of the nouns (without the article), and that student must step forward. The student assigned the corresponding article has five seconds to join the student with the noun.

TEACHING OPTIONS

Using Video Show the video episode again to offer more input on singular and plural nouns and their articles. With their books closed, have students write down every noun and article that they hear. After viewing the video, ask volunteers to list the nouns and articles they heard.

Structures — Leçon 1A

Mise en pratique

1 **Les singuliers et les pluriels** Make the singular nouns plural, and vice versa.

1. l'actrice — les actrices
2. les lycées — le lycée
3. les différences — la différence
4. la chose — les choses
5. le bureau — les bureaux
6. le café — les cafés
7. les librairies — la librairie
8. la faculté — les facultés
9. les acteurs — l'acteur
10. l'ami — les amis
11. l'université — les universités
12. les tableaux — le tableau
13. le problème — les problèmes
14. les bibliothèques — la bibliothèque

2 **L'université** Complete the sentences with an appropriate word from the list. Don't forget to provide the missing articles. *Answers may slightly vary. Suggested answers below.*

| bibliothèque | examen | ordinateurs | sociologie |
| bureau | faculté | petit ami | |

1. À (a) __la faculté__, les tableaux et (b) __les ordinateurs__ sont (*are*) modernes.
2. Marc, c'est (c) __le petit ami__ de (*of*) Marie. Marc étudie (*studies*) la littérature.
3. Marie étudie (d) __la sociologie__. Elle (*She*) est à (e) __la bibliothèque__ de l'université.
4. Sylvie étudie pour (*for*) (f) __l'examen__ de français.

3 **Les mots** Find ten words (**mots**) hidden in this word jumble. Then, provide the corresponding indefinite articles. *une amie; des bureaux; un café; une chose; une faculté; un lycée; des objets; des ordinateurs; une librairie; un tableau*

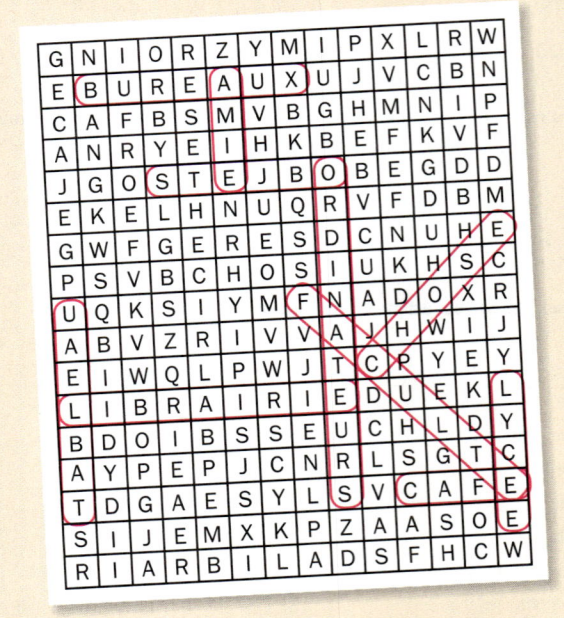

Sidebar suggestions:

1 Suggestion To check students' answers, have volunteers write them on the board or spell out the nouns orally.

2 Suggestion Have volunteers read the words in the list aloud. Tell students to read all four items before attempting to start filling in blanks.

3 Suggestion This activity can also be done in pairs or groups.

EXPANSION

Rapid Drill Do Activity 1 orally. Have students close their books. Tell them to change the plural nouns they hear to the singular and vice versa. Then randomly give them the answers to the items in the activity.

EXPANSION

Jumble Have students create their own word jumbles with words they know. Then, have them exchange jumbles with a partner and find the hidden words.

Salut! Unité 1

Communication

4 Qu'est-ce que c'est? In pairs, take turns identifying the item(s) in each image.

MODÈLE
Élève 1: Qu'est-ce que c'est?
Élève 2: C'est un ordinateur.

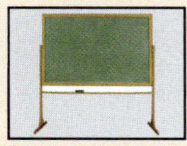

1. Ce sont des tables.
2. Ce sont des étudiants.
3. C'est un tableau.
4. C'est une télévision.
5. C'est une bibliothèque.
6. C'est un café. / Ce sont des cafés.

5 Identifiez In pairs, take turns providing a category for each item.

MODÈLE
Michigan, UCLA, Rutgers, Duke
Ce sont des universités.

1. saxophone — C'est un instrument.
2. Ross, Rachel, Joey, Monica, Chandler, Phoebe — Ce sont des amis.
3. SAT — C'est un examen.
4. Library of Congress — C'est une bibliothèque.
5. Sharon Stone, Debra Messing, Catherine Deneuve — Ce sont des actrices.
6. Céline Dion, Bruce Springsteen — Ce sont des chanteurs.

6 Le français Your partner gets French words mixed up. Correct your partner as he or she points to various people and objects in the illustration and names them. When you're done, switch roles. *Answers will vary.*

MODÈLE
Élève 1: C'est une personne.
Élève 2: Non, c'est un objet.

7 Pictogrammes In groups of four, someone draws a person, object, or concept for the others to guess. Whoever guesses correctly draws next. Continue until everyone has drawn at least once. *Answers will vary.*

treize 13

---

4 Suggestion Before beginning this activity, have students identify the items in the photos. Then read the **modèle** aloud with a volunteer. Remind them that **Ce sont** is used with plural nouns.

5 Expansion Have students work in pairs. Tell them to write two more items for the activity. Example: PSAT, ACT (**Ce sont des examens.**) Then have volunteers read their items aloud, while the rest of the class guesses the category.

5 Virtual Chat You can also assign activity 5 on the Supersite. Students record individual responses that appear in your gradebook.

7 Suggestions
- Before beginning the activity, remind students that they must choose something the class knows how to say in French, and that to guess what the picture is, they should say: **C'est un(e) ____?** or **Ce sont des ____?**
- Tell students they will learn more about **c'est/ce sont** later in the unit.

TEACHING OPTIONS

Pairs Have pairs jot down a mix of ten singular and plural nouns, without their articles. Have them exchange their lists with another pair. Each pair then has to write down the appropriate definite and indefinite articles for each item. After pairs have finished, have them exchange lists and correct them.

EXPANSION

Extra Practice To challenge students, slowly read aloud a short passage from a novel, story, poem or newspaper article written in French, preferably one with a large number of nouns and articles. As a listening exercise, have students write down every noun and article they hear, even unfamiliar ones.

13

Section Goals

In this section, students will learn:
- the numbers 0–60
- the expression **il y a**

Key Standards
4.1, 5.1

Student Resources
Cahier de l'élève, 12–14; Supersite: Activities, eCahier, Grammar Tutorials

Teacher Resources
Answer Keys; Audio Script; Audio Activity MP3s/CD; Testing program: Grammar Quiz

Suggestions

- Introduce numbers by asking students how many of them can count to ten in French. Hold up varying numbers of fingers and ask students to shout out the corresponding number in French.
- Consider demonstrating how the French count numbers on their fingers, starting with the thumb for *one*; the thumb and index finger for *two*; the thumb, index, and middle fingers for *three*; and so on. Ask if other cultures have a different way of counting with their fingers.
- Go through the numbers, modeling the pronunciation of each. Write individual numbers on the board and call on students at random to say each number as you point to it.

Structures — Leçon 1A

1A.2 Numbers 0–60 — Presentation Tutorial

Point de départ Numbers in French follow patterns, as they do in English. First, learn the numbers **0–30**. The patterns they follow will help you learn the numbers **31–60**.

Numbers 0–30

0–10		11–20		21–30	
0	zéro				
1	un	11	onze	21	vingt et un
2	deux	12	douze	22	vingt-deux
3	trois	13	treize	23	vingt-trois
4	quatre	14	quatorze	24	vingt-quatre
5	cinq	15	quinze	25	vingt-cinq
6	six	16	seize	26	vingt-six
7	sept	17	dix-sept	27	vingt-sept
8	huit	18	dix-huit	28	vingt-huit
9	neuf	19	dix-neuf	29	vingt-neuf
10	dix	20	vingt	30	trente

- When counting a series of numbers, use **un** for *one*.

    un, deux, trois, quatre…
    one, two, three, four…

- When *one* is followed by a noun, use **un** or **une** depending on whether the noun is masculine or feminine.

    un objet — *an/one object*
    une télévision — *a/one television*

- Note that the number **21** (**vingt et un**) follows a different pattern than the numbers **22–30**. When **vingt et un** precedes a feminine noun, add **-e** to the end of it: **vingt et une**.

    vingt et un objets — *twenty-one objects*
    vingt et une choses — *twenty-one things*

- Notice that the numbers **31–39, 41–49,** and **51–59** follow the same pattern as the numbers **21–29**.

Numbers 31–60

31–34		35–38		39, 40, 50, 60	
31	trente et un	35	trente-cinq	39	trente-neuf
32	trente-deux	36	trente-six	40	quarante
33	trente-trois	37	trente-sept	50	cinquante
34	trente-quatre	38	trente-huit	60	soixante

- As with the number **21**, to indicate a count of **31, 41,** or **51** for a feminine noun, change the **un** to **une**.

    trente et **un** objets — *thirty-one objects*
    trente et **une** choses — *thirty-one things*

    cinquante et **un** objets — *fifty-one objects*
    cinquante et **une** choses — *fifty-one things*

14 *quatorze*

DIFFERENTIATION

For Kinesthetic Learners Assign ten students a number from 0–60 and line them up in front of the class. Call out one of the numbers at random and have the student assigned to that number take a step forward. When two students have stepped forward, ask them to repeat their numbers. Then ask individuals to add (say: **plus**) or subtract (say: **moins**) the two numbers.

EXPANSION

Using Games Hand out Bingo cards with B-I-N-G-O across the top of five columns. The 25 squares underneath will contain random numbers. From a hat, draw letters and numbers and call them out in French. The first student that can fill in a number in each one of the lettered columns yells "Bingo!" and wins.

Salut! **Unité 1**

- Use **il y a** to say *there is* or *there are* in French. This expression doesn't change, even if the noun that follows it is plural.

  Il y a un ordinateur dans le bureau.
  There is a computer in the office.

  Il y a des tables dans le café.
  There are tables in the café.

  Il y a une table dans le café.
  There is one table in the café.

  Il y a dix-huit objets sur le bureau.
  There are eighteen objects on the desk.

  Il y a deux amies.

  Il y a trois étudiants.

- In most cases, the indefinite article (**un**, **une**, or **des**) is used with **il y a**, rather than the definite article (**le**, **la**, **l'**, or **les**).

  Il y a un professeur de biologie américain.
  There's an American biology teacher.

  Il y a des étudiants français et anglais.
  There are French and English students.

- Use the expression **il n'y a pas de/d'** followed by a noun to express *there isn't a…* or *there aren't any….* Note that no article (definite or indefinite) is used in this case. Use **de** before a consonant sound and **d'** before a vowel sound.

  before a consonant

  before a vowel sound

  Il n'y a pas de tables dans le café.
  There aren't any tables in the café.

  Il n'y a pas d'ordinateur dans le bureau.
  There isn't a computer in the office.

- Use **combien de/d'** to ask how many of something there are.

  Il y a combien de tables?
  How many tables are there?

  Il y a combien d'ordinateurs?
  How many computers are there?

  Il y a combien de librairies?
  How many bookstores are there?

  Il y a combien d'étudiants?
  How many students are there?

Essayez! Write out or say the French word for each number below.

1. 15 _quinze_
2. 6 _six_
3. 22 _vingt-deux_
4. 5 _cinq_
5. 12 _douze_
6. 8 _huit_
7. 30 _trente_
8. 21 _vingt et un_
9. 1 _un_
10. 17 _dix-sept_
11. 44 _quarante-quatre_
12. 14 _quatorze_
13. 38 _trente-huit_
14. 56 _cinquante-six_
15. 19 _dix-neuf_

Suggestions
- Assign each student a number at random that they must remember. When finished, have the student assigned **un** say his or her number aloud, then **deux**, **trois**, etc. Help anyone who struggles with his or her number.
- Emphasize the variable forms of **un** and **une**, **vingt et un**, and **vingt et une**, giving examples of each. Examples: **vingt et un étudiants, vingt et une personnes**.
- Ask questions like the following: **Il y a combien d'élèves dans la classe?** (**Il y a seize élèves dans la classe.**)

Essayez! Have students write four more numbers from 0–60. Tell them to exchange papers with a classmate and write the numbers as words.

DIFFERENTIATION

For Kinesthetic Learners Give ten students a card with a number from 0–60. (You may want to assign numbers in fives to simplify the activity.) The card must be visible to the other students. Then call out simple math problems (addition or subtraction) involving the assigned numbers. When the first two numbers are called, each student steps forward. The student whose assigned number completes the math problem has five seconds to join them.

EXPANSION

My School Ask questions about your school and the town or city in which it is located. Examples: **Il y a combien de professeurs de français? Il y a combien de professeurs d'anglais? Il y a combien de bibliothèques à ____?** Encourage students to guess the number if they don't know it.

Structures — Leçon 1A

Mise en pratique

1 Logique Provide the number that completes each series. Then, write out the number in French.

MODÈLE

2, 4, __6__, 8, 10; __six__

1. 9, 12, __15__, 18, 21; __quinze__
2. 15, 20, __25__, 30, 35; __vingt-cinq__
3. 2, 9, __16__, 23, 30; __seize__
4. 0, 10, 20, __30__, 40; __trente__
5. 15, __17__, 19, 21, 23; __dix-sept__
6. 29, 26, __23__, 20, 17; __vingt-trois__
7. 2, 5, 9, __14__, 20, 27; __quatorze__
8. 30, 22, 16, 12, __10__; __dix__

2 Il y a combien de…? Provide the number that you associate with these pairs of words.

MODÈLE

lettres: l'alphabet vingt-six

1. mois (*months*): année (*year*) douze
2. états (*states*): USA cinquante
3. semaines (*weeks*): année cinquante-deux
4. jours (*days*): octobre trente et un
5. âge: le vote dix-huit
6. Noël: décembre vingt-cinq

3 Numéros de téléphone Your mother left behind a list of phone numbers to call today. Now she calls you and asks you to read them off. (Note that French phone numbers are read as double, not single, digits.)

MODÈLE

Le bureau, c'est le zéro un, vingt-trois, quarante-cinq, vingt-six, dix-neuf.

1. bureau: 01.23.45.26.19
2. bibliothèque: 01.47.15.54.17
   La bibliothèque, c'est le zéro un, quarante-sept, quinze, cinquante-quatre, dix-sept.
3. café: 01.41.38.16.29
   Le café, c'est le zéro un, quarante et un, trente-huit, seize, vingt-neuf.
4. librairie: 01.10.13.60.23
   La librairie, c'est le zéro un, dix, treize, soixante, vingt-trois.
5. lycée: 01.58.36.14.12
   Le lycée, c'est le zéro un, cinquante-huit, trente-six, quatorze, douze.

16 *seize*

Practice more at **vhlcentral.com**.

---

1 Suggestion Once students have filled in the missing numbers, have volunteers read each series aloud.

1 Expansion Ask the class to list the prime numbers (**les nombres premiers**) up to 30. Explain that a prime number is any number that can only be divided by itself and 1. Prime numbers to 30 are: 1, 2, 3, 5, 7, 11, 13, 17, 19, 23, 29.

2 Suggestion Have students form complete sentences using **Il y a** when answering. Example: **Il y a douze mois dans une année.**

2 Expansion For additional practice, give students these items. **7. jours: semaine (sept) 8. jours: novembre (trente) 9. minutes: heure** (*hour*) **(soixante) 10. saisons** (*seasons*)**: année (quatre)**

3 Expansion Write on the board three more telephone numbers for real places in town with their area codes, using double digits as in the activity. Call on volunteers to read the numbers aloud. Permit students to say the digits one by one if the numbers exceed 60.

EXPANSION

Rapid Drill Say numbers aloud at random and have students hold up the appropriate number of fingers. Then reverse the drill; hold up varying numbers of fingers at random and ask students to shout out the corresponding number in French.

DIFFERENTIATION

For Visual Learners Hold up or point to classroom objects and ask how many there are. Since students will not know the names of many items, a simple number will suffice to signal comprehension. Ex. **Il y a combien de dictionnaires? Deux.**

Communication

4 Contradiction Thierry is describing the new Internet café in the neighborhood, but Paul is in a bad mood and contradicts everything he says. In pairs, act out the roles using words from the list. Be sure to pay attention to whether the word is singular (use **un/une**) or plural (use **des**). *Answers will vary.*

MODÈLE

Élève 1: *Dans (In) le café, il y a des tables.*
Élève 2: *Non, il n'y a pas de tables.*

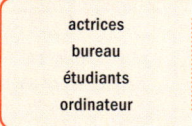

actrices	professeurs
bureau	tableau
étudiants	tables
ordinateur	télévision

5 Sur le campus Nathalie's little brother wants to know everything about her new campus. In pairs, take turns acting out the roles.

MODÈLE

bibliothèques: 3
Élève 1: *Il y a combien de bibliothèques?*
Élève 2: *Il y a trois bibliothèques.*

1. professeurs de littérature: 22   *Il y a vingt-deux professeurs de littérature.*
2. étudiants dans (*in*) la classe de français: 15   *Il y a quinze étudiants dans la classe de français.*
3. télévision dans la classe de sociologie: 0   *Il n'y a pas de télévision dans la classe de sociologie.*
4. ordinateurs dans le café: 8   *Il y a huit ordinateurs dans le café.*
5. employés dans la librairie: 51   *Il y a cinquante et un employés dans la librairie.*
6. tables dans le café: 21   *Il y a vingt et une tables dans le café.*
7. tableaux dans la bibliothèque: 47   *Il y a quarante-sept tableaux dans la bibliothèque.*
8. personne dans le bureau: 1   *Il y a une personne dans le bureau.*

6 Choses et personnes In groups of three, make a list of ten things or people that you see or don't see in the classroom. Use **il y a** and **il n'y a pas de**, and specify the number of items you can find. Then, compare your list with that of another group.   *Answers will vary.*

MODÈLE

Élève 1: *Il y a un étudiant français.*
Élève 2: *Il n'y a pas de télévision.*
Élève 3: *Il y a...*

---

4 Suggestion Have two volunteers read the **modèle** aloud. Remind students that they shouldn't use any article (definite or indefinite) after **Il n'y a pas de/d'**.

4 Partner Chat You can also assign Activity 4 on the Supersite. Students work in pairs to record the activity online. The pair's recorded conversation will appear in your gradebook.

5 Suggestion Have two volunteers read the **modèle** aloud. Remind students to use **combien d'** before a noun that begins with a vowel sound.

6 Expansion After groups have compared their answers, convert the statements into questions. Example: **Il y a combien d'étudiants?**

EXPANSION

Extra Practice Ask questions about your school and the town or city in which it is located. Examples: **Il y a combien de professeurs de français? Il y a combien de professeurs d'anglais? Il y a combien de bibliothèques? Il y a combien de lycées à ____?** Encourage students to guess the number if they don't know it.

DIFFERENTIATION

For Visual Learners Divide the class into pairs. Give half of the pairs magazine pictures that contain images of familiar words or cognates. Give the other half written descriptions of the pictures, using **il y a**. Ex. **Il y a deux instruments sur la photo.** Have pairs circulate around the room to match the descriptions with the corresponding pictures.

Synthèse — Leçon 1A

Révision

1 Des lettres In pairs, take turns choosing nouns. One partner chooses only masculine nouns, while the other chooses only feminine. Slowly spell each noun for your partner, who will guess the word. Find out who can give the quickest answers. *Answers will vary.*

2 Le pendu In groups of four, play hangman (**le pendu**). Form two teams of two partners each. Take turns choosing a French word or expression you learned in this lesson for the other team to guess. Continue to play until your team guesses at least one word or expression from each category. *Answers will vary.*

1. un nom féminin
2. un nom masculin
3. un nombre entre (*number between*) 0 et 30
4. un nombre entre 31 et 60
5. une expression

3 C'est… Ce sont… Doug is spending a week in Paris with his French e-mail pal, Marc. As Doug points out what he sees, Marc corrects him sometimes. In pairs, act out the roles. Doug should be right half the time. *Answers will vary.*

MODÈLE
Élève 1: *C'est une bibliothèque?*
Élève 2: *Non, c'est une librairie.*

1. C'est une bibliothèque./ Ce sont des élèves/étudiants.
2. C'est un café. 
3. C'est une actrice. 
4. Ce sont des acteurs.
5. C'est un professeur. / Ce sont des élèves/étudiants. 
6. Ce sont des amies. 

4 Les présentations In pairs, introduce yourselves. Together, meet another pair. One person per pair should introduce him or herself and his or her partner. Use the items from the list in your conversations. Switch roles until you have met all of the other pairs in the class. *Answers will vary.*

ami	élève
c'est	ami(e)
ce sont	professeur

5 S'il te plaît You need help finding your way and so you ask your partner for assistance. He or she gives you the building (**le bâtiment**) and room (**la salle**) number and you thank him or her. Then, switch roles and repeat with another place from the list. *Answers will vary.*

MODÈLE
Élève 1: *Pardon… l'examen de sociologie, s'il te plaît?*
Élève 2: *Ah oui… bâtiment E, salle dix-sept.*
Élève 1: *Merci beaucoup!*
Élève 2: *De rien.*

Bibliothèque	Bâtiment C Salle 11
Bureau de Mme Girard	Bâtiment A Salle 35
Bureau de M. Brachet	Bâtiment J Salle 42
Bureau de M. Grondin	Bâtiment H Salle 59
Examen de français	Bâtiment B Salle 46
Examen d'anglais	Bâtiment E Salle 24
Examen de sociologie	Bâtiment E Salle 17
Salle de télévision	Bâtiment F Salle 33
Salle des ordinateurs	Bâtiment D Salle 40

6 Mots mélangés You and a partner each have half the words of a wordsearch (**des mots mélangés**). Pick a number and a letter and say them to your partner, who must tell you if he or she has a letter in the corresponding space. Do not look at each other's worksheet. *Answers will vary.*

Key Standards
1.1

Suggestion Tell students that this section reviews and recycles the lesson vocabulary and grammar points.

Student Resources
Supersite: Activities, eCahier

Teacher Resources
Answer Keys; Activity Pack; Testing Program: Lesson Test (Testing Program Audio MP3s/CD)

1 Suggestion Before beginning this activity, you may wish to review the alphabet and how to say the accent marks.

2 Suggestion Tell students not to accept a guess if the letter is not pronounced correctly in French.

3 Virtual Chat You can also assign Activity 3 on the Supersite. Students record individual responses that appear in your gradebook.

3 Suggestion Before beginning the activity, have two volunteers read the **modèle** aloud.

PRE-AP®

4 Interpersonal Speaking Remind students to use appropriate gestures and encourage them to add information to the introduction, such as the person's hometown.

5 Suggestions
- Before beginning this activity, quickly review the numbers 0–60. Hold up cards with various numbers, and have the class or individuals say them in French.
- Read the **modèle** aloud with a volunteer.

6 Suggestion Divide the class into pairs and distribute the Info Gap Handouts from the Activity Pack. Give students ten minutes to complete the activity.

DIFFERENTIATION

For Visual Learners Bring in pictures from newspapers, magazines, or the Internet representing vocabulary items that students have learned, and ask them to identify the people or objects. Examples: **C'est un(e) ____? Ce sont des ____? Qu'est-ce que c'est?** You might also ask how many people or objects are in the picture if there are more than one. Example: **Il y a combien de (d') ____?**

DIFFERENTIATION

For Visual Learners Bring in family photos or magazine pictures showing people greeting or introducing each other in different situations. Assign a photo to each group or allow them to choose one. Tell students to write a brief conversation based on the photo. Remind the class to use formal and informal expressions as appropriate.

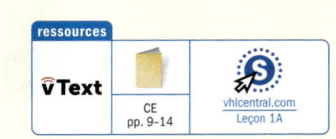

18 dix-huit

ressources
vText
CE pp. 9–14
vhlcentral.com Leçon 1A

Salut! Unité 1

Video: TV Clip

Le Zapping

Attention au sucre°!

In 2001, the **INPES** or **Institut national de prévention et d'éducation pour la santé°** in France started a program to educate the public about good nutrition and a healthy lifestyle. Their website, **manger-bouger°.fr,** explains how we can all become healthier eaters and why we should exercise more. One of their campaigns also raises public awareness about eating excess fat, salt, or sugar. To get the message across, the ads present foods that are rich in one of these ingredients in a new and surprising context. This particular commercial starts when two friends meet in a coffee shop. Focus on the words and phrases you are already familiar with—how the friends greet each other and how they order from the waiter—and on their body language to understand the gist of the scene.

LE SUCRE N'EST PAS TOUJOURS LÀ OÙ ON LE PENSE

Oui, et toi?

Tu veux° du sucre?

Compréhension Answer these questions. *Answers will vary.*

1. Which definite and indefinite articles did you hear in the ad? Provide at least two examples. la, des, un, l', le
2. How many coffees did these friends order? deux

Discussion In groups of three, discuss the answers to these questions. Use as much French as you can. *Answers will vary.*

1. What does the waiter bring with the coffees? What does the ketchup stand for? Can you explain why?
2. Beside the ketchup, what else seems out of place in this scene?
3. Would you say that these two women are close friends? Justify your opinion.

sucre *sugar* **santé** *health* **manger-bouger** *eat-move* **veux** *want*

Practice more at vhlcentral.com.

dix-neuf 19

Section Goals
In this section, students will:
- read about a program to educate the public about good nutrition and healthy lifestyles
- watch an ad designed to raise awareness about high sugar content in foods
- answer questions about the ad

Key Standards
1.2, 2.2, 4.2, 5.2

Student Resources
Supersite: Video, Activities
Teacher Resources
Video Script & Translation;
Supersite: Video

Introduction
To check comprehension, ask these questions.
1. What is the goal of the program started by the **INPES** in 2001? (Its goal is to educate the public about good nutrition and healthy lifestyles.)
2. What type of information is found on the website **manger-bouger.fr**? (The website gives information on how to become a healthier eater and on the importance of regular exercise.)
3. What three ingredients is the **INPES** trying to raise awareness about? (Fat, salt, and sugar.)

PRE-AP®

Audiovisual Interpretive Communication Previewing Strategy
- Have students look at the video stills, read the captions, and describe the scene and the characters featured in the ad.
- Before showing the video, explain to students that they do not need to understand every word they hear. Tell them to listen for numbers, articles, and cognates.

Compréhension Ask students if they can give an example of a definite or indefinite article that they did not hear. Example: **une, les**

Discussion Have students imagine that a third person, who is a good friend of one woman but not the other, arrives and joins them. Have groups of three prepare and role-play the scene. The first woman should greet the newcomer and introduce him or her to the second woman.

EXPANSION

Manger-bouger.fr The website **manger-bouger.fr** contains a wealth of information about good nutrition and exercise habits. It features a questionnaire to help people determine whether they engage in enough physical activity, tips on healthy eating habits, and a list of activities and events one can search by area.

The website also offers the option to sign up to receive sample healthy menus and recipes via email, as well as an application to organize and manage grocery lists. Encourage students to explore the website and report back to the class.

19

Section Goals

In this section, students will learn and practice vocabulary related to:
- objects in the classroom
- identifying people

Key Standards
1.1, 1.2, 4.1

Student Resources
Cahier de l'élève, pp. 15–17; Supersite: Activities, *eCahier*

Teacher Resources
Answer Keys; Digital Image Bank; Audio Script; Textbook & Audio Activity MP3s/CD; Activity Pack; Testing program: Vocabulary Quiz

Suggestions

- Introduce vocabulary for classroom objects, such as **un cahier, une carte, un dictionnaire, un stylo**. Hold up or point to an object and say: **C'est un stylo.**
- Hold up or point to an object and ask either/or questions. Examples: **C'est un crayon ou un stylo? C'est une porte ou une fenêtre?**
- Using either objects in the classroom or the digital image for this page, point to items or people and ask questions, such as **Qu'est-ce que c'est? Qui est-ce? C'est un stylo? C'est un professeur?**
- Have students pick up or point out objects you name. You might want to teach them the expression **Montrez-moi un/une ____.**

Contextes   Leçon 1B

You will learn how to...
- identify yourself and others
- ask yes/no questions

Audio: Vocabulary Practice
My Vocabulary

En classe

Vocabulaire

Qui est-ce?	Who is it?
Quoi?	What?
une calculatrice	calculator
une montre	watch
une porte	door
un résultat	result
une salle de classe	classroom
un(e) camarade de chambre	roommate
un(e) camarade de classe	classmate
une classe	class (group of students)
un copain/ une copine (fam.)	friend
un(e) élève	pupil, student
une femme	woman
une fille	girl
un garçon	boy
un homme	man

Labels: une horloge, un crayon, un sac à dos, une fenêtre, un livre, un cahier, un dictionnaire, un stylo, une feuille (de papier), une corbeille (à papier)

ressources
vText — CE pp. 15–17 — vhlcentral.com Leçon 1B

20 vingt

EXPANSION

Making Lists Have students work in pairs and take an inventory of all the people and items in the classroom. Tell them to write their list in French using the expression **Il y a ____**. After students have finished, tell them to compare their list with another pair's list to see if they are the same.

TEACHING OPTIONS

Using Games Divide the class into teams. Then, in English, say the name of a classroom object and ask one of the teams to provide the French equivalent. If the team provides the correct term, it gets a point. If not, the second team gets a chance to give the correct term. Alternate giving items to the two teams. The team with the most points at the end of the game wins.

Salut! Unité 1

Mise en pratique

1 Chassez l'intrus Circle the word that does not belong.

1. étudiants, élèves, (professeur)
2. un stylo, un crayon, (un cahier)
3. un livre, un dictionnaire, (un stylo)
4. un homme, (un crayon,) un garçon
5. une copine, (une carte,) une femme
6. une porte, une fenêtre, (une chaise)
7. une chaise, (un professeur,) une fenêtre
8. (un crayon,) une feuille de papier, un cahier
9. une calculatrice, une montre, (une copine)
10. une fille, (un sac à dos,) un garçon

2 Écoutez Listen to Madame Arnaud as she describes her French classroom, then check the items she mentions.

1. une porte ☐
2. un professeur ☐
3. une feuille de papier ☐
4. un dictionnaire ☑
5. une carte ☑
6. vingt-quatre cahiers ☐
7. une calculatrice ☐
8. vingt-sept chaises ☑
9. une corbeille à papier ☑
10. un stylo ☑

3 C'est… Work with a partner to identify the items you see in the image.

MODÈLE
Élève 1: *Qu'est-ce que c'est?*
Élève 2: *C'est un tableau.*

1. un tableau
2. une porte
3. un crayon/stylo
4. un livre
5. une calculatrice
6. un stylo/crayon
7. une feuille (de papier)
8. un bureau
9. un dictionnaire
10. une corbeille à papier
11. une chaise
12. un professeur

Practice more at vhlcentral.com.

vingt et un **21**

1 Suggestion Have students compare their answers in pairs or small groups. Tell them to explain why a word does not belong if they don't have the same answer.

1 Expansion For additional practice, read these items aloud or write them on the board.
11. une calculatrice, un élève, un professeur (une calculatrice)
12. une femme, un garçon, une fille (un garçon)
13. un cahier, un copain, un camarade de classe (un cahier)

2 Script Bonjour! Dans la salle de classe, il y a beaucoup de choses! Il y a trois fenêtres, une porte, une carte, un tableau, vingt-sept chaises et une corbeille à papier. Il y a aussi vingt-quatre étudiants et vingt-quatre sacs à dos. Dans les sacs à dos, il y a généralement un cahier, un crayon ou un stylo, un livre et un dictionnaire pour le cours de français.
(On Textbook Audio)

2 Suggestion Have students check their answers by going over **Activité 2** with the whole class. Repeat any sections of the recording that the students missed or did not understand.

3 Suggestion Remind students to use the appropriate form of the indefinite article when doing this activity.

3 Expansion In pairs, tell students to take turns pointing to the items in the drawing and asking: **C'est un(e) ____?** If it's correct, the other person says: **Oui, c'est un(e) ____.** If it is not correct, the person says: **Non, c'est un(e) ____.**

DIFFERENTIATION

For Visual Learners Review numbers and practice vocabulary for classroom objects using printouts of advertisements in French from stores that sell school supplies, such as Monoprix. Make sure the ads include prices. As you show the pictures, ask students about the prices. Examples: **La corbeille à papier est à 15 euros ou à 20 euros? C'est combien, la calculatrice?**

EXPANSION

Using Games Have the class do a chain activity in which the first student says a word in French, for example, **chaise**. The next student has to think of a word that begins with the last letter of the first person's word, such as **élève**. If a student can't think of a word, he or she is out of the game, and it's the next person's turn. The last student left in the game is the winner.

Contextes — Leçon 1B

Communication

4 Expansion For additional practice, point to different students' desks that have objects on them and ask: **Qu'est ce qu'il y a sur le bureau de ____?** You might also ask: **Qu'est-ce qu'il y a sur mon bureau?**

5 Suggestion Before beginning the activity, have a few volunteers demonstrate what students should do using the **modèle**.

6 Suggestion Before beginning the activity, remind students that to guess what the drawing represents, they should say: **C'est un(e) ____?** or **Ce sont des ____?**

7 Suggestions
- Divide the class into pairs and distribute the Info Gap Handouts from the Activity Pack. Give students ten minutes to complete the activity.
- Have two volunteers read the **modèle** aloud.

7 Expansion Have students describe the people and objects in the photo using **Il y a**.

Successful Language Learning Remind the class that errors are a natural part of language learning. Point out that it is impossible to speak "perfectly" in any language. Emphasize that their spoken and written French will improve if they make an effort to practice.

---

4 Qu'est-ce qu'il y a dans mon sac à dos? Make a list of six different items that you have in your backpack, then work with a partner to compare your answers. *Answers will vary.*

Dans mon (*my*) sac à dos, il y a...
1. _____
2. _____
3. _____
4. _____
5. _____
6. _____

Dans le sac à dos de ___nom___, il y a...
1. _____
2. _____
3. _____
4. _____
5. _____
6. _____

5 Qu'est-ce que c'est? Point at eight different items around the classroom and ask a classmate to identify them. Write your partner's responses on the spaces provided below. *Answers will vary.*

MODÈLE
Élève 1: *Qu'est-ce que c'est?*
Élève 2: *C'est un stylo.*

1. _____
2. _____
3. _____
4. _____
5. _____
6. _____
7. _____
8. _____

6 Pictogrammes Play pictionary as a class. *Answers will vary.*
- Take turns going to the board and drawing words you learned on pp. 16–17.
- The person drawing may not speak and may not write any letters or numbers.
- The person who guesses correctly in French what the **grand(e) artiste** is drawing will go next.
- Your teacher will time each turn and tell you if your time runs out.

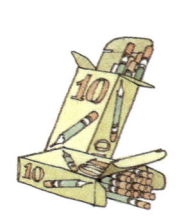

7 Sept différences Your teacher will give you and a partner two different drawings of a classroom. Do not look at each other's worksheet. Find seven differences between your picture and your partner's by asking each other questions and describing what you see.

MODÈLE
Élève 1: *Il y a une fenêtre dans ma (my) salle de classe.*
Élève 2: *Oh! Il n'y a pas de fenêtre dans ma salle de classe.*

22 *vingt-deux*

TEACHING OPTIONS

Using Games Divide the class into two teams. Put labels of classroom vocabulary in a box. Alternating between teams, one person picks a label out of the box without showing it to anyone. This person must place the label on the correct person or object in the classroom and say the word aloud. Each player is allowed only 15 seconds and one guess per turn. Award a point for a correct response. If a player is incorrect, the next player on the opposing team may "steal" the point by placing the label on the correct person or object. The team with the most points at the end of the game wins.

Salut! Unité 1

Les sons et les lettres
Audio: Explanation Record & Compare

Silent letters

Final consonants of French words are usually silent.

| françai~~s~~ | spor~~t~~ | vou~~s~~ | salu~~t~~ |

An unaccented **-e** (or **-es**) at the end of a word is silent, but the preceding consonant is pronounced.

| français~~e~~ | américain~~e~~ | orang~~es~~ | japonais~~es~~ |

The consonants **-c**, **-r**, **-f**, and **-l** are usually pronounced at the ends of words. To remember these exceptions, think of the consonants in the word **careful**.

| par**c** | bonjou**r** | acti**f** | anima**l** |
| la**c** | professeu**r** | naï**f** | ma**l** |

Prononcez Practice saying these words aloud.

1. traditionnel
2. étudiante
3. généreuse
4. téléphones
5. chocolat
6. Monsieur
7. journalistes
8. hôtel
9. sac
10. concert
11. timide
12. sénégalais
13. objet
14. normal
15. importante

Articulez Practice saying these sentences aloud.

1. Au revoir, Paul. À plus tard!
2. Je vais très bien. Et vous, Monsieur Dubois?
3. Qu'est-ce que c'est? C'est une calculatrice.
4. Il y a un ordinateur, une table et une chaise.
5. Frédéric et Chantal, je vous présente Michel et Éric.
6. Voici un sac à dos, des crayons et des feuilles de papier.

Dictons Practice reading these sayings aloud.

Mieux vaut tard que jamais.[1]

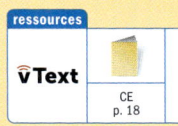

Aussitôt dit, aussitôt fait.[2]

[1] Better late than never.
[2] No sooner said than done.

ressources
vText CE p. 18
vhlcentral.com Leçon 1B

vingt-trois 23

Section Goals
In this section, students will learn about:
- silent letters
- a strategy for remembering which consonants are pronounced at the end of words

Key Standards
4.1

Student Resources
Cahier de l'élève, p. 18;
Supersite: Activities,
eCahier

Teacher Resources
Answer Keys; Audio Script;
Textbook & Audio Activity
MP3s/CD

Suggestions
- Write the sentences below on the board or a transparency. Then say each sentence and ask students which letters are silent. Draw a slash through the silent letters as students say them.
  Qui est-ce? C'est Gilbert. Il est français.
  Qu'est-ce que c'est? C'est un éléphant.
- Work through the example words. Model the pronunciation of each word and have students repeat after you.
- Tell students that the final consonants of a few words that end in **c**, **r**, **f**, or **l** are silent. Examples: **porc** (*pork*), **blanc** (*white*), **nerf** (*nerve*), and **gentil** (*nice*).
- Point out that the letters **-er** at the end of a word are pronounced like the vowel sound in the English word *say*. Examples: **cahier** and **papier**.
- Explain that numbers are exceptions to pronunciation rules. When counting, some final consonants are pronounced. Have students compare the pronunciation of the following: **six**, **sept**, **huit**; **six cahiers**, **sept stylos**, **huit crayons**.
- Tell students that the final consonants of words borrowed from other languages are often pronounced. Examples: **snob**, **autobus**, and **club**.
- The explanations and exercises are recorded on the Textbook MP3s CD-ROM and are available on the **D'ACCORD!** Supersite. You may want to play them in class so students hear French speakers other than yourself.

EXPANSION

Pronunciation Write on the board or an overhead transparency a list of words that have silent letters. Call on volunteers to spell each word in French and then pronounce it. Examples: **art**, **comment**, **sont**, **est**, **intelligent**, **sac à dos**, and **résultat**.

TEACHING OPTIONS

Reading Aloud Working in groups of three or four, have students practice pronunciation by reading the vocabulary words aloud on pages 20–21. Circulate among the groups and model correct pronunciation as needed. When they have finished, ask them if they discovered any exceptions to the pronunciation rules. (**cahier, papier**)

23

Section Goals
In this section, students will learn functional phrases for describing people's character traits and talking about their nationalities through comprehensible input.

Key Standards
1.2, 2.1, 2.2, 4.1, 4.2

Student Resources
Cahier de l'élève, pp. 19–20; Supersite: Activities, *eCahier*

Teacher Resources
Answer Keys; Video Script & Translation; *Roman-photo* video

Video Recap: Leçon 1A
Before doing this **Roman-photo**, review the previous one. Write the names of the main characters on the board and ask students with whom they associate the following people, places, or objects.
1. un étudiant américain (David)
2. Le P'tit Bistrot (Valérie et Stéphane)
3. un magazine (Sandrine)
4. un examen de français (Stéphane)
5. un cours de sciences politiques (Rachid)
6. le lycée (Stéphane)

Video Synopsis
At the café, Valérie waits on some tourists. Valérie argues with Stéphane about his failed math test. While Michèle and Valérie prepare the tourists' orders, Michèle advises Valérie to be patient with her son. At another table, David asks Amina about herself, Rachid, and Sandrine. David repeats his questions about the others to Valérie, who warns him not to get involved with Sandrine because she is seeing Pascal.

Suggestions
- Have students scan the captions and find six adjectives of nationality plus five phrases that describe people's personality or character. Call on volunteers to read the adjectives or phrases they found aloud.
- Have students volunteer to read the characters' parts in the **Roman-photo** aloud.

Roman-photo — Leçon 1B

Les copains
Video: *Roman-photo* Record & Compare

PERSONNAGES
Amina 
David  
Michèle 
Stéphane 
Touriste 
Valérie 

À la terrasse du café...
VALÉRIE Alors, un croissant, une crêpe et trois cafés.
TOURISTE Merci, Madame.
VALÉRIE Ah, vous êtes... américain?
TOURISTE Um, non, je suis anglais. Il est canadien et elle est italienne.
VALÉRIE Moi, je suis française.

À l'intérieur du café...
VALÉRIE Stéphane!!!
STÉPHANE Quoi?! Qu'est-ce que c'est?
VALÉRIE Qu'est-ce que c'est! Qu'est-ce que c'est! Une feuille de papier! C'est l'examen de maths! Qu'est-ce que c'est?
STÉPHANE Oui, euh, les maths, c'est difficile.

VALÉRIE Stéphane, tu es intelligent, mais tu n'es pas brillant! En classe, on fait attention au professeur, au cahier et au livre! Pas aux fenêtres. Et pas aux filles!
STÉPHANE Oh, oh, ça va!!

À la table d'Amina et de David...
DAVID Et Rachid, mon colocataire? Comment est-il?
AMINA Il est agréable et très poli... plutôt réservé mais c'est un étudiant brillant. Il est d'origine algérienne.

DAVID Et toi, Amina. Tu es de quelle origine?
AMINA D'origine sénégalaise.
DAVID Et Sandrine?

AMINA Sandrine? Elle est française.
DAVID Mais non... Comment est-elle?
AMINA Bon, elle est chanteuse, alors elle est un peu égoïste. Mais elle est très sociable. Et charmante. Mais attention! Elle est avec Pascal.
DAVID Pfft, Pascal, Pascal...

ACTIVITÉS

1 Identifiez Indicate which character would make each statement: Amina (A), David (D), Michèle (M), Sandrine (S), Stéphane (St), or Valérie (V).

1. Les maths, c'est difficile. St
2. En classe, on fait attention au professeur! V
3. Michèle, les trois cafés sont pour les trois touristes. V
4. Ah, Madame, du calme! M
5. Ma mère est très impatiente! St
6. J'ai (*I have*) de la famille au Sénégal. A
7. Je suis une grande chanteuse! S
8. Mon colocataire est très poli et intelligent. D
9. Pfft, Pascal, Pascal... D
10. Attention, David! Sandrine est avec Pascal. A/V

Practice more at **vhlcentral.com**.

vingt-quatre

TEACHING OPTIONS

Les copains Before showing the video episode, have students brainstorm the type of information they might give when describing people.

EXPANSION

Extra Practice Show the video episode and have students give you a play-by-play description of the action. Write their descriptions on the board. Then show the episode a second time so students can add details if necessary, or simply consolidate information. Finally, discuss the material on the board and call attention to any incorrect information. Help students prepare a brief plot summary.

Salut! **Unité 1**

Amina, David et Stéphane passent la matinée (*spend the morning*) au café.

Au bar...
VALÉRIE Le croissant, c'est pour l'Anglais, et la crêpe, c'est pour l'Italienne.
MICHÈLE Mais, Madame. Ça va? Qu'est-ce qu'il y a?
VALÉRIE Ben, c'est Stéphane. Des résultats d'examens, des professeurs... des problèmes!

MICHÈLE Ah, Madame, du calme! Je suis optimiste. C'est un garçon intelligent. Et vous, êtes-vous une femme patiente?
VALÉRIE Oui... oui, je suis patiente. Mais le Canadien, l'Anglais et l'Italienne sont impatients. Allez! Vite!

VALÉRIE Alors, ça va bien?
AMINA Ah, oui, merci.
DAVID Amina est une fille élégante et sincère.
VALÉRIE Oui! Elle est charmante.
DAVID Et Rachid, comment est-il?
VALÉRIE Oh! Rachid! C'est un ange! Il est intelligent, poli et modeste. Un excellent camarade de chambre.

DAVID Et Sandrine? Comment est-elle?
VALÉRIE Sandrine?! Oh, là, là. Non, non, non. Elle est avec Pascal.

Expressions utiles

Describing people
- **Vous êtes/Tu es américain?**
  You're American?
- **Je suis anglais. Il est canadien et elle est italienne.**
  I'm English. He's Canadian, and she's Italian.
- **Et Rachid, mon colocataire? Comment est-il?**
  And Rachid, my roommate (in an apartment)? What's he like?
- **Il est agréable et très poli... plutôt réservé mais c'est un étudiant brillant.**
  He's nice and polite... rather reserved, but a brilliant student.
- **Tu es de quelle origine?**
  What's your heritage?
- **Je suis d'origine algérienne/sénégalaise.**
  I'm of Algerian/Senegalese heritage.
- **Elle est avec Pascal.**
  She's with (dating) Pascal.
- **Rachid! C'est un ange!**
  Rachid! He's an angel!

Asking questions
- **Ça va? Qu'est-ce qu'il y a?**
  Are you OK? What is it?/What's wrong?

Additional vocabulary
- **Ah, Madame, du calme!**
  Oh, ma'am, calm down!
- **On fait attention à...**
  One pays attention to...
- **Mais attention!** — **alors** *so*
  But watch out!
- **Allez! Vite!** — **mais** *but*
  Go! Quickly!
- **Mais non...** — **un peu** *a little*
  Of course not...

Expressions utiles
- Model the pronunciation of the **Expressions utiles** and have students repeat after you.
- Point out forms of the verb **être** and adjective agreement in the captions and in the **Expressions utiles**. Tell students that this material will be formally presented in the **Structures** section.
- Ask a few questions based on the **Expressions utiles**. Examples: Et _____, vous êtes américain(e) [canadien(ne)/ italien(ne)]? Ça va? Qu'est-ce qu'il y a?

1 Expansion For additional practice, read these items aloud or write them on the board.
11. Je suis optimiste. (Michèle)
12. Je suis anglais. (le touriste)
13. Rachid! C'est un ange! (Valérie)

2 Expansion Write the following adjectives on the board and ask students which video character they describe.
1. sénégalais(e) (Amina)
2. algérien(ne) (Rachid)
3. français(e) (Sandrine, Stéphane, Valérie, Michèle)
4. charmant(e) (Sandrine)
5. réservé (Rachid)

2 Complétez Use words from the list to describe these people in French. Refer to the video scenes and a dictionary as necessary.
1. Michèle always looks on the bright side. _**optimiste**_
2. Rachid gets great grades. _**intelligent**_
3. Amina is very honest. _**sincère**_
4. Sandrine thinks about herself a lot. _**égoïste**_
5. Sandrine has a lot of friends. _**sociable**_

égoïste / intelligent / optimiste / sincère / sociable

3 Conversez In pairs, choose the words from this list you would use to describe yourselves. What personality traits do you have in common? Be prepared to share your answers with the class.

brillant / charmant / égoïste / élégant / intelligent / modeste / optimiste / patient / sincère / sociable

ressources
vText
CE pp. 19–20
vhlcentral.com Leçon 1B

vingt-cinq **25**

EXPANSION

Mini-dictée Choose four or five lines of the **Roman-photo** to use as a dictation. Read each line twice, pausing after each line so that students have time to write. Have students check their own work by comparing it with the **Roman-photo** text.

EXPANSION

Practicing Improvisation Have students work in pairs. Tell them to look at video stills 2–3 and 6–8, and choose a situation to ad-lib. Assure them that it is not necessary to follow or memorize the **Roman-photo** word for word. Students should be creative while getting the general meaning across with the vocabulary and expressions they know.

Section Goals

In this section, students will:
- learn about France's multicultural society
- learn some familiar terms for identifying people
- read about official languages in some Francophone countries
- read about **Superdupont**, a popular comic-strip character

Key Standards
2.1, 2.2, 3.1, 3.2, 4.2

21ST CENTURY SKILLS

Global Awareness
Students will gain perspectives on the Francophone world to develop respect and openness to other cultures.

Student Resources
Supersite: Activities
Teacher Resources
Answer Keys

Culture à la loupe

Avant la lecture Have students discuss what their idea of a typical French person is.

Lecture
- Point out the regions where Provençal (**Provence**), Breton (**Bretagne**), and Basque (**Pays basque**) are spoken on the map of France in the frontmatter.
- Explain that there are other regional languages not mentioned in the text: Alsatian, Caribbean Creole, Catalan, Corsican, Dutch, Gascon, Lorraine German dialect, and Occitan.

Après la lecture Ask students what facts in this reading are interesting or surprising to them.

1 Expansion For additional practice, give students these items. 11. There are several official languages in France. (**Faux.** French is the only official language.) 12. South Africans represent a significant immigrant population in France. (**Faux.** North and West Africans represent significant immigrant populations.) 13. There are more immigrants in France from both Italy and Spain than from Tunisia. (**Vrai.**)

Culture Leçon 1B

Reading

CULTURE À LA LOUPE

Qu'est-ce qu'un Français typique?

What is your idea of a typical Frenchman? Do you picture a man wearing a **béret**? How about French women? Are they all fashionable and stylish? Do you picture what is shown in these photos? While real French people fitting one aspect or another of these cultural stereotypes do exist, rarely do you find individuals who fit all aspects.

France is a multicultural society with no single, national ethnicity. While the majority of French people are of Celtic or Latin descent, France has significant North and West African (e.g., Algeria, Morocco, Senegal) and Asian (e.g., Vietnam, Laos, Cambodia) populations as well. Long a **terre d'accueil°**, France today has over eleven million foreigners and immigrants. Even as France has maintained a strong concept of its culture through the preservation of its language, history, and traditions, French culture has been ultimately enriched by the contributions of its immigrant populations. Each region of the country also has its own traditions, folklore, and, often, its own language. Regional languages, such as Provençal, Breton, and Basque, are still spoken in some areas, but the official language is, of course, French.

Immigrants in France, by country of birth

COUNTRY NAME	NUMBER OF PEOPLE
Other European countries	712,377
Algeria	702,811
Morocco	645,695
Sub-Saharan Africa	644,049
Portugal	576,084
Other Asian countries	339,260
Italy	323,809
Spain	262,883
Turkey	234,540
Tunisia	231,062
Cambodia, Laos, Vietnam	162,063
UK	142,949

terre d'accueil *a land welcoming of newcomers*

ACTIVITÉS

1 Vrai ou faux? Indicate whether each statement is **vrai** or **faux**. Correct the false statements.

1. Cultural stereotypes are generally true for most people in France. Faux. Rarely do you find individuals who fit all aspects of a stereotype.
2. People in France no longer speak regional languages. Faux. Regional languages are still spoken in some areas.
3. Many immigrants from North Africa live in France. Vrai.
4. More immigrants in France come from Portugal than from Morocco. Faux. More immigrants come from Morocco.
5. Algerians and Moroccans represent the largest immigrant populations in France. Vrai.
6. Immigrant cultures have little impact on French culture. Faux. French culture has been enriched by immigrant cultures.
7. Because of immigration, France is losing its cultural identity. Faux. France has maintained its culture.
8. French culture differs from region to region. Vrai.
9. Most French people are of Anglo-Saxon heritage. Faux. The majority of French people are of Celtic or Latin descent.
10. For many years, France has received immigrants from many countries. Vrai.

Practice more at vhlcentral.com.

26 vingt-six

EXPANSION

Cultural Activity Ask students what stereotypical ideas a French person might have of Americans. If students have difficulty answering, then give them a few examples of American stereotypes and ask them if they are true or valid. Examples: Americans are loud and obnoxious. Americans only speak English. Americans are overweight.

TEACHING OPTIONS

Brainstorming Divide the class into groups of three or four. Give groups five minutes to brainstorm names of cities, states, lakes, rivers, mountain ranges, and so forth in the United States that have French origins. One member of each group should write down the names. Then have groups share their lists with the class.

Salut! **Unité 1**

LE FRANÇAIS QUOTIDIEN

Les gens

ado (*m./f.*)	adolescent, teen
bonhomme (*m.*)	fellow
gars (*m.*)	guy
mec (*m.*)	guy
minette (*f.*)	young woman, sweetie
nana (*f.*)	young woman, girl
pote (*m.*)	buddy
type (*m.*)	guy

LE MONDE FRANCOPHONE

Les langues

Many francophone countries are multilingual, some with several official languages.

Switzerland German, French, Italian, and Romansh are all official languages. German is spoken by about 74% of the population and French by about 21%. Italian and Romansh speakers together account for about 5% of the country's population.

Belgium There are three official languages: French, Dutch, and German. Wallon, the local variety of French, is used by one-third of the population. Flemish, spoken primarily in the north, is used by roughly two-thirds of Belgians.

Morocco Classical Arabic is the official language, but most people speak the Moroccan dialect of Arabic. Berber is spoken by about 10 million people, and French remains Morocco's unofficial third language.

PORTRAIT

Superdupont

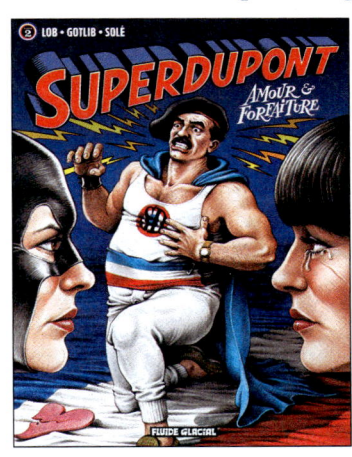

Superdupont is an ultra-French superhero in a popular comic strip parodying French nationalism. The protector of all things French, he battles the secret enemy organization **Anti-France**, whose agents speak **anti-français**, a mixture of English, Spanish, Italian, Russian, and German. *Superdupont* embodies just about every French stereotype imaginable. For example, the name Dupont, much like Smith in the United States, is extremely common in France. In addition to his **béret** and moustache, he wears a blue, white, and red belt around his waist representing **le drapeau français** (*the French flag*). Physically, he is overweight and has a red nose—signs that he appreciates rich French food and wine. Finally, on his arm is **un coq** (*a rooster*), the national symbol of France. The Latin word for rooster (*gallus*) also means "inhabitant of Gaul," as France used to be called.

Extrait de Superdupont - Tome 2 © Solé/Fluide Glacial

Sur Internet

What countries are former French colonies?

Go to vhlcentral.com to find more information related to this **Culture** section.

---

2 Complétez Provide responses to these questions.
1. France is often symbolized by this bird: _____ the rooster
2. Blue, white, and red are the colors of the French flag.
3. France was once named _____ Gaul.
4. The French term _____ ado refers to a person aged 15 or 16.
5. Flemish is spoken by roughly two-thirds of Belgians.

3 Et les Américains? What might a comic-book character based on a "typical American" be like? With a partner, brainstorm a list of stereotypes to create a profile for such a character. Compare the profile you create with your classmates'. Do they fairly represent Americans? Why or why not?

ressources: vText, vhlcentral.com, Leçon 1B

vingt-sept **27**

Le français quotidien
- Point out that this vocabulary is very familiar. These words are usually used in informal conversations among young people.
- Model the pronunciation of each term and have students repeat.

Portrait
- Explain that this political comic strip is not unique and that **la bande dessinée (B.D.)** represents serious reading for young and old alike in France. An international comic-book festival takes place every year in the small town of Angoulême, France.
- Ask students why they think *Superdupont* is so popular in France.

Le monde francophone
- Have students locate the countries listed here on the world map in **Appendice A**.
- To check comprehension, ask these questions. 1. How many official languages does Switzerland have? What are they? (Four: German, French, Italian, and Romansh) 2. What is the name of the local variety of French spoken in Belgium? (Wallon) 3. What percentage of Swiss people speak French? (About 21%) 4. What is the official language of Morocco? (Classical Arabic) 5. Besides French, which language is spoken in both Switzerland and Belgium? (German) 6. Which language is spoken by about 10 million people in Morocco? (Berber)

2 Expansion Have students write four more fill-in-the-blank statements. Then tell them to exchange papers with a classmate and complete the activity.

3 Expansion Have students draw a picture of their comic-book character to illustrate the character's profile.

21ST CENTURY SKILLS

Information and Media Literacy: Sur Internet
Students access and critically evaluate information from the Internet.

EXPANSION

Cultural Comparison Have students compare *Superdupont* to American comic-book superheroes, such as Superman, Batman, and Wonder Woman. Bring in pictures of these comic-book characters, if possible, to facilitate the discussion. Have students discuss the following aspects: their clothing and general appearance, the reason for their existence or purpose, what they represent, and why they are so popular.

EXPANSION

Les langues Have students research official and non-official languages in other Francophone countries or areas, and report on their findings.

27

Section Goals

In this section, students will learn:
- subject pronouns
- the verb **être**
- **c'est** and **il/elle est**

Key Standards
4.1, 5.1

Student Resources
Cahier de l'élève, pp. 21–23; Supersite: Activities, *eCahier*, Grammar Tutorials

Teacher Resources
Answer Keys; Audio Script; Audio Activity MP3s/CD; Testing program: Grammar Quiz

Suggestions
- Point to yourself and say: **Je suis professeur.** Then walk up to a student and say: **Tu es…** The student should say: **élève.** Once the pattern has been established, include other subject pronouns and forms of **être** while pointing to other students. Examples: **Il est élève. Elle est élève. Elles sont élèves.**
- Ask students a few simple questions and tell them to respond **Oui** or **Non**. Examples: **Brad Pitt est acteur? Angelina Jolie est chanteuse?**
- Point out that in French you do not use an article before a profession after **il/elle est** and **ils/elles sont**. You say: **Il est acteur**, not **Il est un acteur.**
- Remind students that in **Leçon 1A**, they learned that the noun **personne** is always feminine regardless of the gender of the subject. So **une/la personne** will be replaced by the pronoun **elle** even though it might refer to a male.

Structures — Leçon 1B

1B.1 Subject pronouns and the verb *être*

Presentation Grammar Tutorial

Point de départ In French, as in English, the subject of a sentence is the person or thing that performs the action. The verb expresses the action.

SUBJECT ⟷ VERB
Le professeur parle français.
The teacher speaks French.

Subject pronouns

- Subject pronouns replace a noun that is the subject of a sentence.

SUBJECT PRONOUN ⟷ VERB
Il parle français.
He speaks French.

Boîte à outils
In English, you sometimes use the pronoun *it* to replace certain nouns.
The exam is long.
It is long.

In French, there is no equivalent neuter pronoun. You must use **il** or **elle** depending on the gender of the noun it is replacing.
L'examen est long.
Il est long.

French subject pronouns				
	singular		**plural**	
first person	je	*I*	nous	*we*
second person	tu	*you*	vous	*you*
third person	il	*he/it (masc.)*	ils	*they (masc.)*
	elle	*she/it (fem.)*	elles	*they (fem.)*
	on	*one*		

- Subject pronouns in French show number (singular vs. plural) and gender (masculine vs. feminine). When a subject consists of both males and females, use the masculine form of the pronoun to replace it.

Rémy et Marie dansent très bien.
Ils dansent très bien.
They dance very well.

M. et Mme Diop sont de Dakar.
Ils sont de Dakar.
They are from Dakar.

- Use **tu** for informal address and **vous** for formal. **Vous** is also the plural form of *you*, both informal and formal.

Comment vas-**tu**?
How's it going?

Comment allez-**vous**?
How are you?

Comment t'appelles-**tu**?
What's your name?

Comment vous appelez-**vous**?
What is/What are your name(s)?

- The subject pronoun **on** refers to people in general, just as the English subject pronouns *one*, *they*, or *you* sometimes do. **On** can also mean *we* in casual speech. **On** always takes the same verb form as **il** and **elle**.

En France, **on** parle français.
In France, they speak French.

On est au café.
We are at the coffee shop.

28 *vingt-huit*

EXPANSION

Extra Practice As a rapid-response drill, call out subject pronouns and have students respond with the correct form of **être**. Examples: **tu** (**es**) and **vous** (**êtes**). Then reverse the drill; say the forms of **être** and have students give the subject pronouns. Accept multiple answers for **est** and **sont**.

EXPANSION

Extra Practice Ask students to indicate whether the following people would be addressed as **vous** or **tu**. Examples: a classmate, a friend's grandmother, a doctor, and a neighbor's child.

28 Unit 1 • Lesson 1B

Salut! | Unité 1

The verb *être*

- **Être** (*to be*) is an irregular verb; its conjugation (set of forms for different subjects) does not follow a pattern. The form **être** is called the infinitive; it does not correspond to any particular subject.

être (to be)			
je suis	I am	nous sommes	we are
tu es	you are	vous êtes	you are
il/elle est	he/she/it is	ils/elles sont	they are
on est	one is		

- Note that the **-s** of the subject pronoun **vous** is pronounced as an English *z* in the phrase **vous êtes**.

    Vous êtes à Paris.
    You are in Paris.

    Vous êtes M. Leclerc? Enchantée.
    Are you Mr. Leclerc? Pleased to meet you.

C'est and il/elle est

- Use **c'est** or its plural form **ce sont** plus a noun to identify who or what someone or something is. Remember to use an article before the noun.

    C'est un téléphone.
    That's a phone.

    Ce sont des photos.
    Those are pictures.

- When the expressions **c'est** and **ce sont** are followed by proper names, don't use an article before the names.

    C'est Amina.
    That's Amina.

    Ce sont Amélie et Anne.
    That's Amélie and Anne.

- Use **il/elle est** and **ils/elles sont** to refer to someone or something previously mentioned.

    La bibliothèque? Elle est moderne.
    The library? It's modern.

    Nathalie et Félix? Ils sont intelligents.
    Nathalie and Félix? They are intelligent.

- Use the phrases **il/elle est** and **ils/elles sont** to tell someone's profession. Note that in French, you do not use the article before the profession.

    Voilà M. Richard. Il est acteur.
    There's Mr. Richard. He's an actor.

    Elles sont chanteuses.
    They are singers.

> **Boîte à outils**
>
> Use **c'est** or **ce sont** instead of **il/elle est** and **ils/elles sont** when you have an adjective qualifying the noun that follows:
>
> **C'est un professeur intelligent.**
> *He is an intelligent teacher.*
>
> **Ce sont des actrices élégantes.**
> *Those are elegant actresses.*

Essayez! Fill in the blanks with the correct forms of the verb *être*.

1. Je __suis__ ici.
2. Ils __sont__ intelligents.
3. Tu __es__ étudiante.
4. Nous __sommes__ à Québec.
5. Vous __êtes__ Mme Lacroix?
6. Marie __est__ chanteuse.

Suggestions
- Ask students to give examples of situations in which they would use the **tu** and **vous** forms of **être**.
- Give examples of how **on** can mean *we* in casual conversation: **On est copains.** *We are friends.*
- Point out the liaison in **vous êtes**. Also point out that the **-n** in **on est** is pronounced. Have students practice pronouncing these phrases.
- When teaching the difference between **c'est/ce sont** and **il(s)/elle(s) est/sont**, explain that **c'est/ce sont** is most often followed by a noun and **il(s)/elle(s) est/sont** is most often followed by an adjective. Point out the exceptions: **C'est très bien. Elle est chanteuse.**
- Tell students that the term **une photo**, which appears in the example **Ce sont des photos**, comes from the word **une photographie**.

Essayez! Have students create additional simple sentences using the verb **être**.

EXPANSION

Video Replay the video episode, having students focus on subject pronouns and the verb **être**. Ask them to write down as many examples of sentences that use forms of **être** as they can. Stop the video where appropriate to ask comprehension questions about what the characters said.

EXPANSION

Extra Practice Have pairs of students introduce each other to the class. They should begin by saying **C'est... Il/Elle est...** Assist them with unfamiliar vocabulary as necessary.

Structures — Leçon 1B

Mise en pratique

1. Pascal répète Pascal repeats everything his older sister Odile says. Give his response after each statement, using subject pronouns.

MODÈLE

Chantal est étudiante.
Elle est étudiante.

1. Les professeurs sont en Tunisie. Ils sont en Tunisie.
2. Mon (*My*) petit ami Charles n'est pas ici. Il n'est pas ici.
3. Moi, je suis chanteuse. Tu es chanteuse.
4. Nadège et moi, nous sommes au lycée. Vous êtes au lycée.
5. Tu es un ami. Je suis un ami.
6. L'ordinateur est dans (*in*) la chambre. Il est dans la chambre.
7. Claude et Charles sont là. Ils sont là.
8. Lucien et toi (*you*), vous êtes copains. Nous sommes copains.

2. Où sont-ils? Thérèse wants to know where all her friends are. Tell her by completing the sentences with the appropriate subject pronouns and the correct forms of être.

MODÈLE

Sylvie / au café
Elle est au café.

1. Georges / à la faculté de médecine Il est à la faculté de médecine.
2. Marie et moi / dans (*in*) la salle de classe Nous sommes dans la salle de classe.
3. Christine et Anne / à la bibliothèque Elles sont à la bibliothèque.
4. Richard et Vincent / là-bas Ils sont là-bas.
5. Véronique, Marc et Anne / à la librairie Ils sont à la librairie.
6. Jeanne / au bureau Elle est au bureau.
7. Hugo et Isabelle / au lycée Ils sont au lycée.
8. Martin / au bureau Il est au bureau.

3. Identifiez Describe these photos using **c'est, ce sont, il/elle est,** or **ils/elles sont.**

1. _C'est_ un acteur.
2. _Il est_ ici. 
3. _Elles sont_ copines. 
4. _Elle est_ chanteuse. 
5. _Elle est_ là. 
6. _Ce sont_ des montres.

Salut! — Unité 1

Communication

4 Assemblez In pairs, take turns using the verb **être** to combine elements from both columns. Talk about yourselves and people you know.

A	B
Singulier:	
Je	agréable
Tu	d'origine française
Mon (*My,* masc.) prof	difficile
Mon/Ma (*My,* fem.) camarade de classe	élève
	sincère
Mon cours	sociable
Pluriel:	
Nous	agréables
Mes (*My*) profs	copains/copines
Mes camarades de classe	difficiles
	élèves
Mes cours	sincères

5 Qui est-ce? In pairs, identify who or what is in each picture. If possible, use **il/elle est** or **ils/elles sont** to add something else about each person or place. *Answers will vary.*

▶ **MODÈLE**
C'est Céline Dion. Elle est chanteuse.

1. _____ 2. _____
3. _____ 4. _____ 5. _____ 6. _____

6 On est comment? In pairs, take turns describing these famous people using the phrases **C'est, Ce sont, Il/Elle est,** or **Ils/Elles sont** and words from the box.

professeur(s)	actrice(s)	chanteuse(s)
chanteur(s)	adorable(s)	pessimiste(s)
optimiste(s)	timide(s)	acteur(s)

1. Justin Bieber
2. Rihanna et Gwen Stefani
3. Barack Obama
4. Johnny Depp
5. Lucille Ball et Desi Arnaz
6. Meryl Streep

7 Enchanté You and your brother are in a local bookstore. You run into one of his classmates, whom you've never met. In a brief conversation, introduce yourselves, ask one another how you are, and say something about yourselves using a form of **être**. *Answers will vary.*

trente et un **31**

---

4 Suggestion Tell students to add two questions of their own to the list and to jot down notes during their interviews.

5 Suggestion Tell students to write down their descriptions. After they have completed the activity, call on volunteers to read their descriptions.

6 Partner Chat You can also assign activity 6 on the Supersite. Students work in pairs to record the activity online. The pair's recorded conversation will appear in your gradebook.

7 Suggestion Have volunteers act out their conversations for the class.

TEACHING OPTIONS

Small Groups Working in small groups, have students invent a story about the people in the photos for **Activité 5**. Tell them to include who the people are, where they are from, and what they do in the story. Circulate around the room and assist with unfamiliar vocabulary as necessary, but encourage students to use terms they already know.

EXPANSION

Extra Practice Bring in pictures of people and objects and ask students to describe them using **c'est, ce sont, il/elle est,** or **ils/elles sont**.

31

Section Goals

In this section, students will learn:
- forms, agreement, and position of adjectives
- some descriptive adjectives
- adjectives of nationality

Key Standards

4.1, 5.1

Student Resources
Cahier de l'élève, pp. 24–26; Supersite: Activities, *eCahier*, Grammar Tutorials

Teacher Resources
Answer Keys; Audio Script; Audio Activity MP3s/CD; Testing program: Grammar Quiz

Suggestions

- Write these adjectives on the board: **impatient, impatiente, impatients, impatientes**. Model each adjective in a sentence and ask volunteers to tell you whether it is masculine or feminine and singular or plural.
- Model the pronunciation of adjectives of nationality and have students repeat them. Point out that the feminine forms ending in **-ienne**.

Structures | Leçon 1B

1B.2 Adjective agreement

Presentation Grammar Tutorial

Point de départ Adjectives are words that describe people, places, and things. In French, adjectives are often used with the verb **être** to point out the qualities of nouns or pronouns.

Le cours est difficile.

Je suis optimiste.

- Many adjectives in French are cognates; that is, they have the same or similar spellings and meanings in French and English.

Cognate descriptive adjectives

agréable	pleasant	intelligent(e)	intelligent
amusant(e)	fun	intéressant(e)	interesting
brillant(e)	brilliant	occupé(e)	busy
charmant(e)	charming	optimiste	optimistic
désagréable	unpleasant	patient(e)	patient
différent(e)	different	pessimiste	pessimistic
difficile	difficult	poli(e)	polite
égoïste	selfish	réservé(e)	reserved
élégant(e)	elegant	sincère	sincere
impatient(e)	impatient	sociable	sociable
important(e)	important	sympathique (sympa)	nice
indépendant(e)	independent	timide	shy

Boîte à outils

Use the masculine plural form of an adjective to describe a group composed of masculine and feminine nouns: **Henri et Patricia sont élégants.**

- In French, most adjectives agree in number and gender with the nouns they describe. Most adjectives form the feminine by adding a silent **-e** (no accent) to the end of the masculine form. Adding a silent **-s** to the end of masculine and feminine forms gives you the plural forms of both.

	masculine	feminine
singular	patient	patiente
plural	patients	patientes

Henri est élégant.
Henri is elegant.

Claire et Lise sont élégantes.
Claire and Lise are elegant.

- If the masculine form of the adjective already ends in an unaccented **–e**, do not add another one for the feminine form.

MASCULINE SINGULAR	NO CHANGE	FEMININE SINGULAR
optimiste	⟷	optimiste

EXPANSION

Extra Practice Have pairs of students write sentences using adjectives such as **intelligent(e), optimiste, sociable**. When they have finished, ask volunteers to dictate their sentences to you while you write them on the board. After you have written a sentence and corrected any errors, ask volunteers to suggest a sentence that uses the antonym of the adjective.

TEACHING OPTIONS

TPR Divide the class into two teams and have them line up. Point to a member from each team and give a certain form of an adjective (Ex: **patients**). Then name another form that you want students to provide (Ex: feminine singular) and have them race to the board. The first student who writes the correct form earns one point for his or her team. Deduct one point for each wrong answer. The team with the most points at the end wins.

Salut! **Unité 1**

- French adjectives are usually placed after the noun they modify when they don't directly follow a form of **être**.

  Ce sont des **élèves brillantes**.
  They're brilliant students.

  Bernard est un homme **agréable et poli**.
  Bernard is a pleasant and polite man.

- Here are some adjectives of nationality. Note that the **-n** of adjectives that end in **-ien** doubles before the final **-e** of the feminine form: **algérienne, canadienne, italienne, vietnamienne**.

Adjectives of nationality

algérien(ne)	Algerian	japonais(e)	Japanese
allemand(e)	German	marocain(e)	Moroccan
anglais(e)	English	martiniquais(e)	from Martinique
américain(e)	American	mexicain(e)	Mexican
canadien(ne)	Canadian	québécois(e)	from Quebec
espagnol(e)	Spanish	sénégalais(e)	Senegalese
français(e)	French	suisse	Swiss
italien(ne)	Italian	vietnamien(ne)	Vietnamese

- The first letter of adjectives of nationality is not capitalized.

  Il est américain. **Elle est française.**

- An adjective whose masculine singular form already ends in **-s** keeps the identical form in the masculine plural.

  Pierre est **un ami sénégalais**.
  Pierre is a Senegalese friend.

  Pierre et Yves sont **des amis sénégalais**.
  Pierre and Yves are Senegalese friends.

- To ask someone's nationality or heritage, use **Quelle est ta/votre nationalité?** or **Tu es/Vous êtes de quelle origine?**

  Quelle est votre nationalité?
  What is your nationality?

  Je suis de nationalité canadienne.
  I'm Canadian.

  Tu es de quelle origine?
  What is your heritage?

  Je suis d'origine italienne.
  I'm of Italian heritage.

Essayez! Write in the correct forms of the adjectives.

1. Marc est _timide_ (timide).
2. Ils sont _anglais_ (anglais).
3. Elle adore la littérature _française_ (français).
4. Ce sont des actrices _suisses_ (suisse).
5. Marie n'est pas _mexicaine_ (mexicain).
6. Les actrices sont _impatientes_ (impatient).
7. Elles sont _réservées_ (réservé).
8. Il y a des universités _importantes_ (important).
9. Christelle est _amusante_ (amusant).
10. Les élèves sont _polis_ (poli) en cours.
11. Mme Castillion est très _occupée_ (occupé).
12. Luc et moi, nous sommes _sincères_ (sincère).

trente-trois **33**

Suggestions
- Go around the room asking **Quelle est votre nationalité?** Also have a few students ask each other their nationalities.
- Use pictures and the names of celebrities to practice other adjectives of nationality. Examples: **Le prince William est-il canadien? (Non, il est anglais.) Julia Roberts est-elle française? (Non, elle est américaine.)**
- Explain that adjectives of nationality can be used as nouns as well. Examples: **La femme anglaise est réservée. L'Anglaise est réservée.** Point out that nouns of nationality are capitalized, while adjectives of nationality are not.
- Point out that in English most adjectives are placed before the noun, but in French they are placed after the noun. Write the following example on the board, circle the adjective, and draw an arrow pointing to the noun. Example: **C'est un examen difficile.**
- At this point you may want to present the adjectives in the **Vocabulaire supplémentaire** on the Supersite.

EXPANSION

Extra Practice Have students collect several interesting pictures of people from magazines or newspapers. Have them prepare a description of one of the pictures ahead of time. Invite them to show the pictures to the class and then give their descriptions orally without indicating which picture they are talking about. The class will guess which of the pictures is being described.

EXPANSION

Extra Practice Do a quick class survey to find out how many nationalities are represented in your class. As students respond, write the nationality and number of students on the board. Ask: **Combien d'élèves sont d'origine américaine? Mexicaine? Vietnamienne?** If students ask, clarify that the gender of the adjective of nationality agrees with the word **origine**, which is feminine.

Structures Leçon 1B

Mise en pratique

1 Nous aussi! Jean-Paul is bragging about himself, but his younger sisters Stéphanie and Gisèle believe they possess the same attributes. Provide their responses.

MODÈLE
Je suis amusant.
Nous aussi, nous sommes amusantes.

1. Je suis intelligent. Nous aussi, nous sommes intelligentes.
2. Je suis sincère. Nous aussi, nous sommes sincères.
3. Je suis élégant. Nous aussi, nous sommes élégantes.
4. Je suis patient. Nous aussi, nous sommes patientes.
5. Je suis sociable. Nous aussi, nous sommes sociables.
6. Je suis poli. Nous aussi, nous sommes polies.
7. Je suis charmant. Nous aussi, nous sommes charmantes.
8. Je suis optimiste. Nous aussi, nous sommes optimistes.

2 Les nationalités You are with a group of students from all over the world. Indicate their nationalities according to the cities they come from.

MODÈLE
Monique est de (*from*) Paris.
Elle est française.

1. Les amies Fumiko et Keiko sont de Tokyo. Elles sont japonaises.
2. Hans est de Berlin. Il est allemand.
3. Juan et Pablo sont de Guadalajara. Ils sont mexicains.
4. Wendy est de Londres. Elle est anglaise.
5. Jared est de San Francisco. Il est américain.
6. Francesca est de Rome. Elle est italienne.
7. Aboud et Moustafa sont de Casablanca. Ils sont marocains.
8. Jean-Pierre et Mario sont de Québec. Ils sont québécois.

3 Voilà Mme... Your parents are having a party and you point out different people to your friend. Use one of the adjectives you just learned each time. Answers will vary.

MODÈLE
Voilà M. Duval. Il est sénégalais.
C'est un ami.

M. Duval — Catherine et Jeanne — M. Forestier — Georges et Denise — Mme Malbon

34 trente-quatre

Practice more at **vhlcentral.com**.

---

1 Suggestion Before beginning the activity, make sure students understand that they should use feminine plural forms of the adjectives. For each item, call on one student to read the sentence in the book and another student to respond.

2 Expansion For additional practice, change the subject of the sentence and have students restate or write the sentences. Examples: **1. Kazumi est de Tokyo. (Il est japonais.) 2. Gerta et Katarina sont de Berlin. (Elles sont allemandes.) 3. Carmen est de Guadalajara. (Elle est mexicaine.) 4. Tom et Susan sont de Londres. (Ils sont anglais.) 5. Linda est de San Francisco. (Elle est américaine.) 6. Luciano et Gino sont de Rome. (Ils sont italiens.) 7. Fatima est de Casablanca. (Elle est marocaine.) 8. Denise et Monique sont de Québec. (Elles sont canadiennes/québécoises.)**

EXPANSION

Extra Practice Have students write brief descriptions of themselves: where they are from, their personalities, and what they look like. Collect the descriptions, shuffle them, and read a few of them to the class. Have the class guess who wrote each description.

EXPANSION

Extra Practice Research zodiac signs on the Internet and prepare a simple personality description for each sign, using cognates and adjectives from this lesson. Divide the class into pairs and distribute the descriptions. Have students describe their partner's sign: **Il est lion. Il est indépendant et optimiste.**

Salut! Unité 1

Communication

4 Interview Interview someone to see what he or she is like. In pairs, play both roles. Are you compatible as friends? *Answers will vary.*

MODÈLE
pessimiste
Élève 1: *Tu es pessimiste?*
Élève 2: *Non, je suis optimiste.*

1. impatient
2. modeste
3. timide
4. sincère
5. égoïste
6. sociable
7. indépendant
8. amusant

5 Ils sont comment? In pairs, take turns describing each item below. Tell your partner whether you agree (**C'est vrai**) or disagree (**C'est faux**) with the descriptions. *Answers will vary.*

MODÈLE
Johnny Depp
Élève 1: *C'est un acteur désagréable.*
Élève 2: *C'est faux. Il est charmant.*

1. Beyoncé et Céline Dion
2. les étudiants de Harvard
3. Usher
4. la classe de français
5. le président des États-Unis (*United States*)
6. Tom Hanks et Gérard Depardieu
7. le prof de français
8. Steven Spielberg
9. notre (*our*) lycée
10. Kate Winslet et Julia Roberts

6 Au café You and two classmates are talking about your new teachers, each of whom is very different from the other two. In groups of three, create a dialogue in which you greet one another and describe your teachers. *Answers will vary.*

trente-cinq **35**

---

4 Suggestions
- Have students add two more qualities to the list that are important to them.
- After students have completed the activity, ask them if they are compatible and to explain why or why not.

4 Virtual Chat You can also assign Activity 4 on the Supersite. Students record individual responses that appear in your gradebook.

5 Suggestion Have two volunteers read the **modèle** aloud.

5 Expansion Have small groups brainstorm names of famous people, places, and things not found in the activity and write them in a list. Tell them to include some plural items. Then ask the groups to exchange lists and describe the people, places, and things on that list.

6 Suggestion Encourage students to ask each other questions about their teachers during the conversation.

EXPANSION

Extra Practice Write each descriptive adjective in Activity 4 on two cards or slips of paper and put them in two separate piles in random order. Hand out one card to each student. Tell students they have to find the person who has the same adjective as they do. Example: **Élève 1: Tu es optimiste? Élève 2: Oui, je suis optimiste./Non, je suis sociable**. For variation, this activity can also be used to practice adjectives of nationality.

EXPANSION

Extra Practice As a rapid-response drill, say the name of a country and have students respond with the appropriate adjective of nationality. For variation, have students write the adjective on the board or tell them to spell the adjective after they say it.

Synthèse Leçon 1B

Révision

1 Festival francophone
With a partner, choose two characters from the list and act out a conversation between them. The people are meeting for the first time at a francophone festival. Then, change characters and repeat. *Answers will vary.*

- Angélique, Sénégal
- Abdel, Algérie
- Laurent, Martinique
- Sylvain, Suisse
- Hélène, Canada
- Daniel, France
- Mai, Viêt-Nam
- Nora, Maroc

2 Tu ou vous?
How would the conversations between the characters in **Activité 1** differ if they were all 19-year-old students at a university orientation? Write out what you would have said differently. Then, exchange papers with a new partner and make corrections. Return the paper to your partner and act out the conversation using a new character. *Answers will vary.*

3 En commun
In pairs, tell your partner the name of a friend. Use adjectives to say what you both (**tous/toutes les deux**) have in common. Then, share with the class what you learned about your partner and his or her friend. *Answers will vary.*

MODÈLE

Charles est un ami. Nous sommes tous les deux amusants. Nous sommes patients aussi.

4 Comment es-tu?
Your teacher will give you a worksheet. Survey as many classmates as possible to ask if they would use the adjectives listed to describe themselves. Then, decide which two students in the class are most similar. *Answers will vary.*

MODÈLE

Élève 1: Tu es timide?
Élève 2: Non. Je suis sociable.

Adjectifs	Noms
1. timide	Éric
2. impatient(e)	
3. optimiste	
4. réservé(e)	
5. charmant(e)	
6. poli(e)	
7. agréable	
8. amusant(e)	

5 Mes camarades de classe
Write a brief description of the students in your French class. What are their names? What are their personalities like? What is their heritage? Use all the French you have learned so far. Your paragraph should be at least eight sentences long. Remember, be complimentary! *Answers will vary.*

6 Les descriptions
Your teacher will give you one set of drawings of eight people and a different set to your partner. Each person in your drawings has something in common with a person in your partner's drawings. Find out what it is without looking at your partner's sheet. *Answers will vary.*

MODÈLE

Élève 1: Jean est à la bibliothèque.
Élève 2: Gina est à la bibliothèque.
Élève 1: Jean et Gina sont à la bibliothèque.

ressources
vText
CE pp. 21–26
vhlcentral.com
Leçon 1B

36 trente-six

Salut! Unité 1

À l'écoute 🔊 Audio: Activities

STRATÉGIE

Listening for words you know

You can get the gist of a conversation by listening for words and phrases you already know.

🎧 To help you practice this strategy, listen to this sentence and make a list of the words you have already learned.

_____ _____
_____ _____

Préparation

Look at the photograph. Where are these people? What are they doing? In your opinion, do they know one another? Why or why not? What do you think they're talking about?

À vous d'écouter 🎧

As you listen, circle the items you associate with Hervé and those you associate with Laure and Lucas.

HERVÉ	LAURE ET LUCAS
(la littérature)	(le café)
(l'examen)	la littérature
le bureau	la sociologie
le café	la librairie
la bibliothèque	le lycée
(la librairie)	l'examen
le tableau	(l'université)

Compréhension

Vrai ou faux? 🔊 Based on the conversation you heard, indicate whether each of the following statements is **vrai** or **faux**.

	Vrai	Faux
1. Lucas and Hervé are good friends.	☐	☑
2. Hervé is preparing for an exam.	☑	☐
3. Laure and Lucas know each other from school.	☑	☐
4. Hervé is on his way to the library.	☐	☑
5. Lucas and Laure are going to a café.	☑	☐
6. Lucas studies literature.	☐	☑
7. Laure is in high school.	☐	☑
8. Laure is not feeling well today.	☐	☑

Présentations 👥 It's your turn to get to know your classmates. Using the conversation you heard as a model, select a partner you do not know and introduce yourself to him or her in French. Follow the steps below.

- Greet your partner.
- Find out his or her name.
- Ask how he or she is doing.
- Introduce your partner to another student.
- Say good-bye.

Practice more at vhlcentral.com.

ressources: vText | vhlcentral.com Leçon 1B

trente-sept **37**

Section Goals
In this section, students will:
- learn to listen for known vocabulary
- listen to sentences containing familiar and unfamiliar vocabulary
- listen to a conversation and complete several activities

Key Standards
1.2, 2.1

21ST CENTURY SKILLS

Critical Thinking and Problem Solving
Students practice aural comprehension as a tool to negotiate meaning in French.

Student Resources
Supersite: Activities, Audio
Teacher Resources
Answer Keys; Audio Script; Audio Activity MP3s/CD

Stratégie
Script Je vous présente une amie, Juliette Lenormand. Elle étudie la sociologie à la faculté.

Successful Language Learning Tell your students that many people feel nervous about their ability to comprehend what they learn in a foreign language. Tell them that they will probably feel less anxious if they follow the advice for increasing listening comprehension in the **Stratégie** sections.

Préparation Have students look at the photo and describe what they see. Ask them to justify their responses based on the visual clues.

À vous d'écouter
Script
HERVÉ: Salut, Laure! Ça va?
LAURE: Bonjour, Hervé. Ça va bien. Et toi?
HERVÉ: Pas mal, merci.
LAURE: Je te présente un copain de l'université. Lucas, Hervé. Hervé, Lucas.
LUCAS: Enchanté.
H: Bonjour, Lucas. Comment vas-tu?
LU: Très bien, merci.
LA: Qu'est-ce que tu fais, Hervé?
H: Je vais à la librairie pour acheter un livre sur la littérature.
LA: Pour un examen?
H: Oui, pour un examen. Et vous?
LA: Nous, on va au café.
H: Alors, à plus tard.
LA: Oui, salut.
LU: Au revoir, Hervé.
H: À bientôt.

Section Goals

In this section, students will:
- read statistics and cultural information about the French language and the Francophone world
- learn historical and cultural information about Quebec, Louisiana, and Algeria

Key Standards
2.2, 3.1, 3.2, 5.1

21ST CENTURY SKILLS

Global Awareness
Students will gain perspectives on the Francophone world to develop respect and openness to others and to interact appropriately and effectively with citizens of Francophone cultures.

Student Resources
Cahier de l'élève, pp. 27–28;
Supersite: Activities,
eCahier

Teacher Resources
Answer Keys;
Digital Image Bank

Carte du monde francophone
Have students look at the map or use the digital image for this page. Ask them to identify the continents where French is spoken. Then ask them to make inferences about why French is spoken in these regions.

Les pays en chiffres
- Call on volunteers to read the sections. Point out cognates and clarify unfamiliar words.
- Have students locate the capitals of the countries listed in **Villes capitales** on the maps in the frontmatter.
- After reading **Francophones célèbres**, ask students if they know any additional information about these people.
- Ask students if they know of other Francophone celebrities, e.g. Édith Piaf, Chopin, Jacques Brel.

Incroyable mais vrai!
French is one of the official languages of UNESCO, which is the United Nations Educational Scientific and Cultural Organization. UNESCO not only builds classrooms in impoverished countries, but it also brings nations together on social issues.

Savoir-faire

Panorama

Interactive Map Reading

Le monde francophone

Les pays en chiffres°
- **Nombre de pays° où le français est langue° officielle:** 28
- **Nombre de pays où le français est parlé°:** *plus de°* 60
- **Nombre de francophones dans le monde°:** 200.000.000 (deux cents millions)

SOURCE: Organisation internationale de la Francophonie

Villes capitales
- **Algérie:** Alger
- **Cameroun:** Yaoundé
- **France:** Paris
- **Guinée:** Conakry
- **Haïti:** Port-au-Prince
- **Laos:** Vientiane
- **Mali:** Bamako
- **Rwanda:** Kigali
- **Seychelles:** Victoria
- **Suisse:** Berne

Francophones célèbres
- **Marie Curie,** Pologne, scientifique, prix Nobel en chimie et physique (1867–1934)
- **René Magritte,** Belgique, peintre° (1898–1967) 
- **Ousmane Sembène,** Sénégal, cinéaste° et écrivain° (1923–2007) 
- **Jean Reno,** France, acteur (1948–)
- **Céline Dion,** Québec, chanteuse° (1968–) 
- **Marie-José Pérec,** Guadeloupe (France), athlète (1968–)

chiffres numbers *pays* countries *langue* language *parlé* spoken *plus de* more than *monde* world *peintre* painter *cinéaste* filmmaker *écrivain* writer *chanteuse* singer *sur* on *comme* such as *l'OTAN* NATO *Jeux* Games *deuxième* second *enseignée* taught *Heiva* an annual Tahitian festival

38 trente-huit

Heiva°, Papeete, Tahiti

L'AMÉRIQUE DU NORD
L'EUROPE
LA FRANCE
L'ASIE
L'OCÉAN ATLANTIQUE
L'AFRIQUE
L'OCÉAN PACIFIQUE
L'AMÉRIQUE DU SUD
L'OCÉAN INDIEN

PAYS FRANCOPHONES EN ASIE
- LE LAOS
- LE CAMBODGE
- LE VIÊT-NAM

L'OCÉAN INDIEN

la mosquée de la plage de Ouakam, Dakar, Sénégal

0 3,000 miles
0 3,000 kilomètres

■ Pays et régions francophones

Incroyable mais vrai!
La langue française est une des rares langues à être parlées sur° cinq continents. C'est aussi la langue officielle de beaucoup d'organisations internationales comme° l'OTAN°, les Nations unies, l'Union européenne, et aussi les Jeux° Olympiques! Le français est la deuxième° langue enseignée° dans le monde, après l'anglais.

EXPANSION

Francophones célèbres **Marie Curie** received Nobel Prizes for the discovery of radioactivity and the isolation of radium. **René Magritte** was one of the most prominent surrealist painters. **Ousmane Sembène** is considered one of the founders of the African realist tradition and the first African to produce a film. **Jean Reno** has played a variety of roles in French and American films. **Céline Dion** has received Grammy awards in the U.S., Juno and Felix awards in Canada, and World Music Awards in Europe for her vocal talents. **Marie-José Pérec** is the first sprinter to win consecutive gold medals in the 400-meter dash.

Unit 1

Salut! **Unité 1**

La société
Le français au Québec

Au Québec, province du Canada, le français est la langue officielle, parlée par° 80% (quatre-vingts pour cent) de la population. Les Québécois, pour° préserver l'usage de la langue, ont° une loi° qui oblige l'affichage° en français dans les lieux° publics. Le français est aussi la langue co-officielle du Canada: les employés du gouvernement doivent° être bilingues.

Les gens
Les francophones d'Algérie

Depuis° 1830 (mille huit cent trente), date de l'acquisition de l'Algérie par la France, l'influence culturelle française y° est très importante. À présent ancienne° colonie, l'Algérie est un des plus grands° pays francophones au monde. L'arabe est la langue officielle, mais le français est la deuxième langue parlée et est compris° par la majorité de la population algérienne.

Les destinations
La Louisiane

Ce territoire au sud° des États-Unis a été nommé «Louisiane» en l'honneur du Roi° de France Louis XIV. En 1803 (mille huit cent trois), Napoléon Bonaparte vend° la colonie aux États-Unis pour 15 millions de dollars, pour empêcher° son acquisition par les Britanniques. Aujourd'hui° en Louisiane, 200.000 (deux cent mille) personnes parlent° le français cajun. La Louisiane est connue° pour sa° cuisine cajun, comme° le jambalaya, ici sur° la photo avec le chef Paul Prudhomme.

Les traditions
La Journée internationale de la Francophonie

Chaque année°, l'Organisation internationale de la Francophonie (O.I.F.) coordonne la Journée internationale de la Francophonie. Dans plus de° 100 (cent) pays et sur cinq continents, on célèbre la langue française et la diversité culturelle francophone avec des festivals de musique, de gastronomie, de théâtre, de danse et de cinéma. Le rôle principal de l'O.I.F. est la promotion de la langue française et la défense de la diversité culturelle et linguistique du monde francophone.

Qu'est-ce que vous avez appris? Complete the sentences.

1. _Ousmane Sembène_ est un cinéaste africain.
2. _200 millions_ de personnes parlent français dans le monde.
3. _L'Organisation internationale de la Francophonie_ est responsable de la promotion de la diversité culturelle francophone.
4. Les employés du gouvernement du Canada parlent _anglais et français_.
5. En Algérie, la langue officielle est _l'arabe_.
6. Une majorité d'Algériens comprend (*understands*) _le français_.
7. Le nom «Louisiane» vient du (*comes from the*) nom de _Louis XIV_.
8. Plus de 100 pays célèbrent _la Journée internationale de la Francophonie_.
9. Le français est parlé sur _cinq_ continents.
10. En 1803, Napoléon Bonaparte vend _la Louisiane_ aux États-Unis.

Sur Internet

1. Les États-Unis célèbrent la Journée internationale de la Francophonie. Faites (*Make*) une liste de trois événements (*events*) et dites (*say*) où ils ont lieu (*take place*).
2. Trouvez des informations sur un(e) chanteur/chanteuse francophone célèbre aux États-Unis. Citez (*Cite*) trois titres de chanson (*song titles*).

Practice more at **vhlcentral.com**.

parlée par spoken by **pour** in order to **ont** have **loi** law **affichage** posting **lieux** places **doivent** must **Depuis** Since **y** there **ancienne** former **un des plus grands** one of the largest **compris** understood **au sud** in the South **a été nommé** was named **Roi** King **vend** sells **empêcher** to prevent **Aujourd'hui** Today **parlent** speak **connue** known **sa** its **comme** such as **sur** in **Chaque année** Each year **Dans plus de** In more than

trente-neuf 39

Le français au Québec Since Jacques Cartier first arrived in Gaspé and claimed the land for the French king in 1534, the people of Quebec have maintained their language and culture, despite being outnumbered and surrounded by English speakers. French became an official language of Canada in 1867.

Les francophones d'Algérie Algeria gained its independence from France in 1962, but French is still taught from primary school through high school. French is principally used in business relations, some social situations, and in the information industries. Some newspapers, as well as several television and radio broadcasts, are produced in French.

La Louisiane The early settlers of Louisiana came from France and Acadia (now Nova Scotia and adjacent areas) during the seventeenth and eighteenth centuries. The Acadian settlers were descendents of French Canadians who were exiled from Acadia by the English and eventually settled in the bayou region. Cajun French evolved over time borrowing terms from American Indian, German, English, African, and Spanish speakers.

La Journée internationale de la Francophonie
- The members of **l'Organisation internationale de la Francophonie** comprise 63 states and governments (notice the organization's symbol on page 38). The celebrations in the various Francophone regions take place throughout the month of March. The date **20 mars** was chosen to commemorate the signature of a treaty which created **l'Agence intergouvernementale de la Francophonie**.

21st CENTURY SKILLS

Information and Media Literacy: Sur Internet
Students access and critically evaluate information from the Internet.

EXPANSION

Using Maps Have students work in pairs. Tell them to look at the maps in the frontmatter and make a list of the Francophone countries and capitals that do not appear in the section **Villes capitales**. Point out that they need to find eighteen countries.

Cultural Comparison Ask students if they know of any places in the United States where people speak two languages or they can see bilingual signs.

EXPANSION

Cultural Comparison In groups of three, have students compare **la Journée internationale de la Francophonie** to a cultural celebration held in their town, city, or country. Tell them to discuss the purpose of each celebration, the reasons why people attend them, and the types of events or activities that are part of the celebration.

Section Goals

In this section, students will:
- learn to recognize cognates
- use context to guess the meaning of new words
- read some pages from an address book in French

Key Standards

1.3, 3.1, 5.1

PRE-AP®

**Interpretive reading:
Stratégie** Tell students that cognates are words in one language that have identical or similar counterparts in another language. True cognates are close in meaning, so recognizing French words that are cognates of English words can help them read French. To help students recognize cognates, write these common correspondences between French and English on the board: **-ie** = *-y* (**sociologie**); **-ique** = *-ic* (**fantastique**); **-if(-ive)** = *-ive* (**active**).

Successful Language Learning Tell students that reading in French will be less anxiety provoking if they follow the advice in the **Stratégie** sections, which are designed to reinforce and improve reading comprehension skills.

Examinez le texte Ask students to tell you what type of text this is and how they can tell. (It's an excerpt from an address book. You can tell because it contains names and telephone numbers.)

Mots apparentés
- Check to see if students found all of the cognates from the **Stratégie** box in the reading: **pharmacie, dentiste, télévision, médecin, banque,** and **restaurant**.
- If students are having trouble finding other cognates, point out a few to get them started: **route** (*route*), **avenue** (*avenue*), **boulevard** (*boulevard*), **théâtre** (*theater*), **comédie** (*comedy*), **dîner** (*dinner*), and **municipale** (*municipal*).

Devinez Check if students were able to guess the meanings correctly: **horaires** (*schedule [hours open]*), **lundi** (*Monday*), **ouvert** (*open*), **soirs** (*evenings; nights*), and **tous** (*all; every*).

40 Unit 1

Savoir-faire

Lecture 🎧 Audio: Synced Reading

Avant la lecture

STRATÉGIE

Recognizing cognates

Cognates are words that share similar meanings and spellings in two or more languages. When reading in French, it's helpful to look for cognates and use them to guess the meaning of what you're reading. However, watch out for false cognates. For example, **librairie** means *bookstore*, not *library*, and **coin** means *corner*, not *coin*. Look at this list of French words. Can you guess the meaning of each word?

important	banque
pharmacie	culture
intelligent	actif
dentiste	sociologie
décision	fantastique
télévision	restaurant
médecine	police

Examinez le texte
Briefly look at the document. What kind of information is listed? In what order is it listed? Where do you usually find such information? Can you guess what this document is?

Mots apparentés
Read the list of cognates in the **Stratégie** box again. How many cognates can you find in the reading selection? Are there additional cognates in the reading? Which ones? Can you guess their English equivalents?

Devinez
In addition to using cognates and words you already know, you can also use context to guess the meaning of words you do not know. Find the following words in the reading selection and try to guess what they mean. Compare your answers with those of a classmate.

horaires   lundi   ouvert   soirs   tous

40   quarante

Carnet d'adresses

Carnet d'adresses

Recherche ▶

A B C D E F G H I J K

✓ ✉ **DAMERY Jean-Claude**
dentiste
18, rue des Lilas   02 38 23 45 46
45000 Orléans

☐ ✉ **Café de la Poste**
Ouvert° tous les jours°, de 7h00° à 22h00
25, place de la Poste   02 38 27 18 00
45000 Orléans

☐ ✉ **Librairie Balzac**
Horaires: 9h00–12h00 et 14h00–18h00
18, route de Lorient   02 38 18 60 36
45000 Orléans

☐ ✉ **DANTEC Pierre-Henri**
médecin généraliste
23, rue du Lac   02 38 47 34 20
45000 Orléans

✓ ✉ **Banque du Centre**
Ouvert de 9h00 à 17h00 du lundi° au vendredi°
17, boulevard Giroud   02 38 58 35 00
45000 Orléans

📝 Dîner vendredi 8h00
Restaurant du Chat qui dort

EXPANSION

Cognates Write these words on the board and have students guess the English meaning: **un agent** (*agent*), **un concert** (*concert*), **la géographie** (*geography*), **une guitare** (*guitar*), **la musique** (*music*), **un réfrigérateur** (*refrigerator*), **confortable** (*comfortable*), **courageux** (*courageous*), **riche** (*rich*), and **typique** (*typical*). Then have them look at the **Vocabulaire** on page 44 and identify all the cognates they have learned.

TEACHING OPTIONS

Using Lists Have students work in groups of three or four. Assign four letters of the alphabet to each group. (Adjust the number of letters according to your class size so that the entire alphabet is covered.) Tell students to use a French-English dictionary and make a list of all the cognates they find beginning with their assigned letters. Have groups read their list of cognates to the rest of the class.

Salut! Unité 1

Après la lecture

Où aller? Tell where each of these people should go based on what they need or want to do.

MODÈLE
Camille's daughter is starting high school.
Lycée Molière

1. Mrs. Leroy needs to deposit her paycheck.
   Banque du Centre
2. Laurent would like to take his girlfriend out for a special dinner.
   Restaurant du Chat qui dort
3. Marc has a toothache.
   DAMERY Jean-Claude, dentiste
4. Céleste would like to go see a play tonight.
   Théâtre de la Comédie
5. Pauline's computer is broken.
   Messier et fils, Réparations ordinateurs et télévisions
6. Mr. Duchemin needs to buy some aspirin for his son.
   Pharmacie Vidal
7. Jean-Marie needs a book on French history but he doesn't want to buy one.
   Bibliothèque municipale
8. Noémie thinks she has the flu.
   DANTEC Pierre-Henri, médecin généraliste
9. Mr. and Mrs. Prudhomme want to go out for breakfast this morning.
   Café de la Poste
10. Jonathan wants to buy a new book for his sister's birthday.
    Librairie Balzac

Notre annuaire With a classmate, select three of the listings from the reading and use them as models to create similar listings in French advertising places or services in your area.

MODÈLE
Restaurant du Chat qui dort
Ouvert tous les soirs pour le dîner
Horaires: 19h00 à 23h00
29, avenue des Rosiers
45000 Orléans
02 38 45 35 08

Always Good Eats Restaurant
Ouvert tous les jours
Horaires: 6h00 à 19h00
1250 9th Avenue
San Diego, CA 92108
224-0932

Messier et fils°
Réparations ordinateurs et télévisions
56, boulevard Henri IV   02 38 44 42 59
45000 Orléans

Théâtre de la Comédie
11, place de la Comédie   02 38 45 32 11
45000 Orléans

Pharmacie Vidal
45, rue des Acacias   02 38 13 57 53
45000 Orléans

Restaurant du Chat qui dort°
Ouvert tous les soirs pour le dîner / Horaires: 19h00 à 23h00
29, avenue des Rosiers   02 38 45 35 08
45000 Orléans

Bibliothèque municipale
Place de la gare   02 38 56 43 22
45000 Orléans

Lycée Molière
15, rue Molière   02 38 29 23 04
45000 Orléans

*Ouvert Open **tous les jours** every day **7h00 (sept heures)** 7:00 **lundi** Monday **vendredi** Friday **fils** son(s) **Chat qui dort** Sleeping cat*

quarante et un 41

Où aller? Go over the activity with the class. If students have trouble inferring the answer to any question, help them identify the cognate or provide additional context clues.

Notre annuaire
- Before beginning the activity, have students brainstorm places and services in the area, and write a list on the board. You might also want to bring in a few local telephone books for students to use as references for addresses and phone numbers.
- You may wish to have students include e-mail addresses (**les adresses e-mail**) in their lists.

21st CENTURY SKILLS

Creativity and Innovation
Ask students to research and prepare a presentation on ten common false cognates in French, inspired by the information on these two pages. Challenge them to provide examples in full sentences.

EXPANSION

Addresses To review numbers 0–60, have students work in pairs and take turns asking each other the phone numbers and addresses of the people and places listed in the reading. Example: **Élève 1:** Le numéro de téléphone du dentiste Jean-Claude DAMERY? **Élève 2:** C'est le zéro deux, trente-huit, vingt-trois, quarante-cinq, quarante-six. **Élève 1:** Et l'adresse? **Élève 2:** Dix-huit, rue des Lilas, Orléans.

TEACHING OPTIONS

Reading Aloud Have several students select one of the three listings they created for the **Notre annuaire** activity to read aloud. Instruct the rest of the class to write down the information they hear. To check students' work, have the students who read the listings write the information on the board.

Section Goals

In this section, students will:
- learn strategies for writing in French
- learn to write a telephone/address book in French
- integrate vocabulary and structures taught in **Leçons 1A–1B**

Key Standards

1.3, 3.1, 5.1

PRE-AP®

**Interpersonal Writing:
Stratégie** Have students focus on the final point under the "Do" section. Ask them to think about the types of writing that most interests them as readers. Why? Is it that the writer supplies vivid detail? Interesting anecdotes? An easy-to-read style? Is it simply that the subject is important to them? This shows the value of putting themselves in their reader's place.

Thème Introduce students to standard headings used in a telephone/address list: **Nom**, **Adresse**, **Numéro de téléphone**, **Numéro de portable**, and **Adresse e-mail**. Students may wish to add notes pertaining to home (**Numéro de domicile**) or office (**Numéro de bureau**) telephone numbers, fax numbers (**Numéro de fax**), or office hours (**Horaires de bureau**).

Savoir-faire

Écriture

STRATÉGIE

Writing in French

Why do we write? All writing has a purpose. For example, we may write a poem to reveal our innermost feelings, a letter to impart information, or an essay to persuade others to accept a point of view. Proficient writers are not born, however. Writing requires time, thought, effort, and a lot of practice. Here are some tips to help you write more effectively in French.

DO

- ▶ Write your ideas in French.
- ▶ Make an outline of your ideas.
- ▶ Decide what the purpose of your writing will be.
- ▶ Use the grammar and vocabulary that you know.
- ▶ Use your textbook for examples of style, format, and expressions in French.
- ▶ Use your imagination and creativity to make your writing more interesting.
- ▶ Put yourself in your reader's place to determine if your writing is interesting.

DON'T

- ▶ Translate your ideas from English to French.
- ▶ Repeat what is in the textbook or on a web page.
- ▶ Use a bilingual dictionary until you have learned how to use one effectively.

Thème

Faites une liste!

Avant l'écriture

1. Imagine that several students from a French-speaking country will be spending a year at your school. You've been asked to put together a list of people and places that might be useful and of interest to them. Your list should include:

   - Your name, address, phone number(s) (home and/or cell), and e-mail address
   - The names of four other students in your French class, their addresses, phone numbers, and e-mail addresses
   - Your French teacher's name, office and/or cell phone number(s), and e-mail address
   - Your school library's phone number and hours
   - The names, addresses, and phone numbers of three places near your school where students like to go

2. Write down the names of the classmates you want to include.

3. Interview your classmates and your teacher to find out the information you need to include. Use the following questions and write down their responses.

Informal	Formal
Comment t'appelles-tu?	Comment vous appelez-vous?
Quel est ton numéro de téléphone?	Quel est votre numéro de téléphone?
Quelle est ton adresse e-mail?	Quelle est votre adresse e-mail?

quarante-deux

EXPANSION

Stratégie Review the **Do** list with students. Ask them if they have tried any of these tips. Tell them that they should refer back to this list as they complete the **Écriture** tasks in each lesson. Students may also find it helpful to keep track of which tips work best for them.

EXPANSION

Avant l'écriture Before students begin writing, brainstorm a list of popular places where students frequently go. Group them by name in different categories, such as **bibliothèques, cafés, restaurants, magasins, théâtres, parcs, libraries**, and so on. Encourage students to incorporate these category headings into their lists, along with the specific names of different businesses that fall into the categories.

Salut! Unité 1

4. Think of three places in your community that a group of students from a French-speaking country would enjoy visiting. They could be a library, a bookstore, a coffee shop, a restaurant, a theater, or a park. Find out their addresses, telephone numbers, and e-mail addresses/URLs and write them down.

5. Go online and do a search for two websites that promote your town or area's history, culture, and attractions. Write down their URLs.

Écriture

Write your complete list, making sure it includes all the relevant information. It should include at least five people (with their phone numbers and e-mail addresses), four places (with phone numbers and addresses), and two websites (with URLs). Avoid using a dictionary and just write what you can in French.

Après l'écriture

1. Exchange your list with a partner's. Comment on his or her work by answering these questions.
   - Did your partner include the correct number of people, places, and websites?
   - Did your partner include the pertinent information for each?

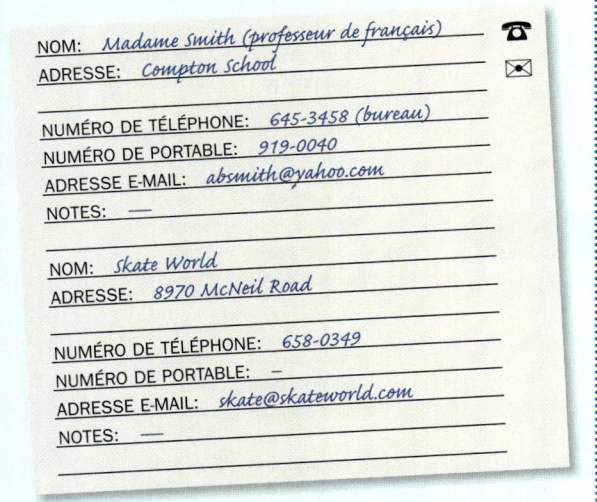

   NOM: Madame Smith (professeur de français)
   ADRESSE: Compton School
   NUMÉRO DE TÉLÉPHONE: 645-3458 (bureau)
   NUMÉRO DE PORTABLE: 919-0040
   ADRESSE E-MAIL: absmith@yahoo.com
   NOTES: —

   NOM: Skate World
   ADRESSE: 8970 McNeil Road
   NUMÉRO DE TÉLÉPHONE: 658-0349
   NUMÉRO DE PORTABLE: —
   ADRESSE E-MAIL: skate@skateworld.com
   NOTES: —

2. Edit your partner's work, pointing out any spelling or content errors. Notice the use of these editing symbols:

   - ⌒ delete
   - ∧ insert letter or word(s) written in margin
   - | replace letter or word(s) with one(s) in margin
   - ≡ change to uppercase
   - / change to lowercase
   - ∾ transpose indicated letters or words

   Now look at this model of what an edited draft looks like:

   o Nm: Sally Wagner
   é Télephone: 655-8888
      Adresse e-mali: sally@uru.edu
      Nom: Madamed Nancy smith
   Téléphone: 655-8090
      Adresse e-mail: nsmith@uru.edu

3. Revise your list according to your partner's comments and corrections. After writing the final version, read it one more time to eliminate these kinds of problems:
   - spelling errors
   - punctuation errors
   - capitalization errors
   - use of incorrect verb forms
   - use of incorrect adjective agreement
   - use of incorrect definite and indefinite articles

quarante-trois 43

EVALUATION

Criteria

Content Includes all the information mentioned in the five parts of the task description.
Scale: 1 2 3 4 5

Organization Organizes the list similarly to the model provided.
Scale: 1 2 3 4 5

Accuracy Spells the French words used to designate the list categories correctly, including correct accentuation.
Scale: 1 2 3 4 5

Creativity Includes extra information (such as home, office, and fax numbers), more than three students, more than three places.
Scale: 1 2 3 4 5

Scoring

Excellent	18–20 points
Good	14–17 points
Satisfactory	10–13 points
Unsatisfactory	< 10 points

21st CENTURY SKILLS

Productivity and Accountability
Provide the rubric to students before they hand their work in for grading. Ask students to make sure they have met the highest standard possible on the rubric before submitting their work.

EXPANSION

Après l'écriture Share the evaluation rubric with students before they begin writing. Tell them that you will use these criteria to evaluate their work. Be sure you do this for each **Écriture** task in subsequent units so students will have a clear understanding of your expectations for their work before they undertake the writing task.

EXPANSION

Using Categories Ask the class to come up with other categories, such as **postes, banques, docteurs, pharmacies**. Then have them complete their address book list with new items falling into these categories.

Vocabulaire — Unité 1

Key Standards
4.1

Teacher Resources
Vocabulary MP3s/CD

Suggestions
- Tell students that this is active vocabulary for which they are responsible and that it will appear on tests and exams.
- Tell them that an easy way to study from **Vocabulaire** is to cover up the French half of each section, leaving only the English equivalents exposed. They can then quiz themselves on the French items. To focus on the English equivalents of the French entries, they simply reverse this process.

21st CENTURY SKILLS
Creativity and Innovation
Ask students to prepare a list of three products or perspectives they learned about in this unit to share with the class. Consider asking them to focus on the **Culture** and **Panorama** sections.

21st CENTURY SKILLS
Leadership and Responsibility: Extension Project
If you have access to students in a Francophone country, have students decide on three questions they want to ask the partner class related to this unit's topic. Based on the responses they receive, work as a class to explain to the partner class one aspect of their responses that surprised the class and why.

En classe
une bibliothèque	library
un café	café
une faculté	university; faculty
une librairie	bookstore
un lycée	high school
une salle de classe	classroom
une université	university
un dictionnaire	dictionary
une différence	difference
un examen	exam, test
la littérature	literature
un livre	book
un problème	problem
un résultat	result
la sociologie	sociology
un bureau	desk; office
une carte	map
une chaise	chair
une fenêtre	window
une horloge	clock
un ordinateur	computer
une porte	door
une table	table
un tableau	blackboard; picture
la télévision	television
un cahier	notebook
une calculatrice	calculator
une chose	thing
une corbeille (à papier)	wastebasket
un crayon	pencil
une feuille (de papier)	sheet of paper
un instrument	instrument
une montre	watch
un objet	object
un sac à dos	backpack
un stylo	pen

Les personnes
un(e) ami(e)	friend
un(e) camarade de chambre	roommate
un(e) camarade de classe	classmate
une classe	class (group of students)
un copain/une copine (fam.)	friend
un(e) élève	pupil, student
un(e) étudiant(e)	student
un(e) petit(e) ami(e)	boyfriend/girlfriend
une femme	woman
une fille	girl
un garçon	boy
un homme	man
une personne	person
un acteur/une actrice	actor
un chanteur/une chanteuse	singer
un professeur	teacher, professor

Les présentations
Comment vous appelez-vous? (form.)	What is your name?
Comment t'appelles-tu? (fam.)	What is your name?
Enchanté(e).	Delighted.
Et vous/toi? (form./fam.)	And you?
Je m'appelle…	My name is…
Je vous/te présente… (form./fam.)	I would like to introduce (name) to you.

Identifier
c'est/ce sont	it's/they are
Combien…?	How much/many…?
ici	here
Il y a…	There is/are…
là	there
là-bas	over there
Qu'est-ce que c'est?	What is it?
Qui est-ce?	Who is it?
Quoi?	What?
voici	here is/are
voilà	there is/are

Bonjour et au revoir
À bientôt.	See you soon.
À demain.	See you tomorrow.
À plus tard.	See you later.
À tout à l'heure.	See you later.
Au revoir.	Good-bye.
Bonne journée!	Have a good day!
Bonjour.	Good morning.; Hello.
Bonsoir.	Good evening.; Hello.
Salut!	Hi!; Bye!

Comment ça va?
Ça va?	What's up?; How are things?
Comment allez-vous? (form.)	How are you?
Comment vas-tu? (fam.)	How are you?
Comme ci, comme ça.	So-so.
Je vais bien/mal.	I am doing well/badly.
Moi aussi.	Me too.
Pas mal.	Not badly.
Très bien.	Very well.

Expressions de politesse
De rien.	You're welcome.
Excusez-moi. (form.)	Excuse me.
Excuse-moi. (fam.)	Excuse me.
Il n'y a pas de quoi.	You're welcome.
Je vous/t'en prie. (form./fam.)	You're welcome.; It's nothing.
Merci beaucoup.	Thank you very much.
Monsieur (M.)	Sir (Mr.)
Madame (Mme)	Ma'am (Mrs.)
Mademoiselle (Mlle)	Miss
Pardon.	Pardon (me).
S'il vous plaît. (form.)	Please.
S'il te plaît. (fam.)	Please.

Expressions utiles	See pp. 7 and 25.
Numbers 0–60	See p. 14.
Subject pronouns	See p. 28.
être	See p. 29.
Descriptive adjectives	See p. 32.
Adjectives of nationality	See p. 33.

quarante-quatre

Au lycée

Unité 2

Leçon 2A

CONTEXTES ..... pages 46–49
- Academic life
- Liaisons

ROMAN-PHOTO . pages 50–51
- Trop de devoirs!

CULTURE .... pages 52–53
- Au lycée
- Flash culture

STRUCTURES .... pages 54–61
- Present tense of regular -er verbs
- Forming questions and expressing negation

SYNTHÈSE ...... pages 62–63
- Révision
- Le Zapping

Leçon 2B

CONTEXTES ..... pages 64–67
- Everyday activities
- The letter r

ROMAN-PHOTO . pages 68–69
- On trouve une solution.

CULTURE .... pages 70–71
- Le bac

STRUCTURES .... pages 72–79
- Present tense of avoir
- Telling time

SYNTHÈSE ...... pages 80–81
- Révision
- À l'écoute

Savoir-faire ... pages 82–87
- **Panorama:** La France
- **Lecture:** Read an academic brochure.
- **Écriture:** Write a description of yourself.

Pour commencer
- Which room at school is pictured?
  a. la bibliothèque b. la salle de classe c. le café
- What are the students looking at?
  a. un cahier b. un professeur c. un livre
- How do the students look in this photo?
  a. intelligents b. sociables c. sérieux
- Which item is not visible in the photo?
  a. une table b. une fenêtre c. un ordinateur

Unit Goals

Leçon 2A
In this lesson, students will learn:
- terms for academic subjects
- to express likes and dislikes
- about liaisons
- about French high schools and the Canadian French immersion program
- the present tense of regular -er verbs
- about spelling changes in -cer and -ger verbs
- to ask questions and express negation
- about the University of Moncton

Leçon 2B
In this lesson, students will learn:
- terms for talking about schedules and when things happen
- to pronounce the French r
- about le bac and higher education in France
- more about university life through specially shot video footage
- the present tense of avoir
- some expressions with avoir
- to tell time
- to listen for cognates

Savoir-faire
In this section, students will learn:
- cultural, economic, geographical, and historical information about France
- to use text formats to predict content
- to brainstorm before writing
- to write a personal description

21st CENTURY SKILLS
Initiative and Self-Direction
Students can monitor their progress online using the Supersite activities and assessments.

Pour commencer
- b. la salle de classe
- b. un professeur
- a. intelligents
- b. une fenêtre

INSTRUCTIONAL RESOURCES

Student Materials
Print: Student Book, Workbook (Cahier de l'élève)
Technology: vText, eCahier
Supersite: vhlcentral.com Audio, Video, Practice

Teacher Materials
Print: Teacher's Edition, Answer Keys, Testing Program
Technology: Audio MP3s on CD (Textbook, Testing Program, Audio Program), Video Program DVD (Roman-photo, Flash culture)

Supersite: vhlcentral.com Activity Pack, Middle School Activity Pack, Lesson Plans, Grammar Tutorials, Grammar Slides, Testing Program, Audio and Video Scripts, Answer Key, Audio MP3s, Streaming Video (Roman-photo, Flash culture, Le Zapping), Digital Image Bank, Learning Management System (Gradebook, Assignments)

VOICE BOARD Voice boards on the Supersite allow you and your students to record and share up to five minutes of audio. Use voice boards for presentations, oral assessments, discussions, directions, etc.

Section Goals
In this section, students will learn and practice vocabulary related to:
- academic subjects
- places around school
- expressing likes and dislikes

Key Standards
1.1, 1.2, 4.1

Student Resources
Cahier de l'élève, pp. 29–31; Supersite: Activities, eCahier

Teacher Resources
Answer Keys; Digital Image Bank; Audio Script; Textbook & Audio Activity MP3s/CD; Activity Pack; Testing program: Vocabulary Quiz

Suggestions
- Have students look at the new vocabulary and identify cognates. Say the words and have students guess the meaning. Point out that the words **lettres** and **note** are **faux amis** in this context.
- Call students' attention to the pronunciation of **ps** in **psychologie**.
- Point out that abbreviations such as **sciences po** are common. For more examples, see **Le français quotidien** on page 53.
- To review classroom objects and practice new vocabulary, show items and ask what courses they might be used for. Example: **Un dictionnaire, c'est pour quel cours?**
- Explain that many of the adjectives students learned for nationalities in **Leçon 1B** are also used for languages and language classes. Examples: **le cours de français (d'anglais, d'italien, d'espagnol)**
- Introduce vocabulary for expressing likes and dislikes by talking about your own. Use facial and hand gestures to convey meaning. Examples: **J'adore la littérature française. J'aime bien l'histoire. Je n'aime pas tellement la biologie. Je déteste l'informatique.**

Contextes — Leçon 2A

You will learn how to...
- talk about your classes
- ask questions and express negation

Audio: Vocabulary Practice
My Vocabulary

Les cours

Vocabulaire

J'aime bien...	I like...
Je n'aime pas tellement...	I don't like... very much
être reçu(e) à un examen	to pass an exam
l'architecture (f.)	architecture
l'art (m.)	art
le droit	law
l'éducation physique (f.)	physical education
la gestion	business administration
les lettres (f.)	humanities
la philosophie	philosophy
les sciences (politiques / po) (f.)	(political) science
le stylisme	fashion design
une bourse	scholarship, grant
une cantine	cafeteria
un cours	class, course
un devoir	homework
un diplôme	diploma, degree
l'école (f.)	school
les études (supérieures) (f.)	(higher) education; studies
le gymnase	gymnasium
une note	grade
un restaurant universitaire (un resto U)	university cafeteria
difficile	difficult
facile	easy
inutile	useless
utile	useful
surtout	especially; above all

la biologie
la chimie
Je déteste la physique! (détester)
J'adore la géographie! (adorer)
la géographie
la physique
les mathématiques (f.)
l'informatique (f.)

ressources
vText
CE pp. 29–31
vhlcentral.com
Leçon 2A

46 quarante-six

TEACHING OPTIONS

Oral Practice Ask students questions using the new vocabulary words. Examples: **La physique, c'est facile ou difficile? L'informatique, c'est utile ou inutile?**

Brainstorming Have them brainstorm adjectives that can describe their courses and write them: **facile, difficile, utile, intéressant, amusant, agréable,** and **important**. Ask students to describe various courses. Example: **Le cours de chimie est difficile.**

EXPANSION

Using Games Divide the class into teams. Say the name of a course in English and ask one team to say it in French. If the team is correct, it gets a point. If not, the other team gets a chance to say it and "steal" the point. Alternate giving words to the two teams.

Au lycée — Unité 2

Mise en pratique

1 Associez Which classes, activities, or places do you associate with these words? Not all items in the second column will be used.

_d_ 1. manger
_e_ 2. un ordinateur
_i_ 3. le français
_a_ 4. une calculatrice
_f_ 5. le sport
_h_ 6. Socrate
_b_ 7. E=MC²
_c_ 8. Napoléon

a. les mathématiques
b. la physique
c. l'histoire
d. une cantine
e. l'informatique
f. l'éducation physique
g. la biologie
h. la philosophie
i. les langues étrangères
j. l'art

2 Écoutez On their first day back to school, Aurélie and Hassim are discussing their classes, likes, and dislikes. Indicate who is most likely to use the books listed: Aurélie (**A**), Hassim (**H**), both (**A & H**), or neither (**X**). Not all items will be used.

1. Informatique et statistiques _A & H_
2. L'économie de la France _A_
3. L'architecture japonaise _X_
4. Histoire de France _H_
5. Études psychologiques _H_
6. La géographie de l'Europe _H_
7. L'italien, c'est facile! _A & H_
8. Le droit international _A_

3 Qu'est-ce que j'aime? Read each statement and indicate whether you think it is **vrai** or **faux**. Compare your answers with a classmate's. Do you agree? Why? Answers will vary.

	Vrai	Faux
1. C'est facile d'être reçu à l'examen de mathématiques.	☐	☐
2. Je déteste manger à la cantine.	☐	☐
3. Je vais recevoir (receive) une bourse; c'est très utile.	☐	☐
4. Le stylisme, c'est inutile.	☐	☐
5. Avoir un diplôme de l'université, c'est facile.	☐	☐
6. La chimie, c'est un cours difficile.	☐	☐
7. Je déteste les lettres.	☐	☐
8. Les notes sont très importantes.	☐	☐
9. Je n'aime pas tellement les études.	☐	☐
10. J'adore les langues étrangères.	☐	☐

Practice more at **vhlcentral.com**.

quarante-sept 47

Labels in illustration: les langues étrangères (f.); l'économie (f.); l'histoire (f.); la psychologie

---

1 Expansions
- Items g. and j. were not used. Ask the class what words they associate with **la biologie** and **l'art**.
- Have students brainstorm a list of famous people that they associate with the following fields: **la physique** (Isaac Newton, Albert Einstein); **l'informatique** (Bill Gates, Mark Zuckerberg); and **la gestion** (Donald Trump, Marissa Mayer). Then have the class guess the field associated with each of the following people: Louis Pasteur (**la biologie**), Ben Bernanke (**l'économie**).

2 Script AURÉLIE: Bonjour, Hassim. Comment ça va?
HASSIM: Bien. Et toi?
A: Pas mal, merci.
H: Tu aimes le cours d'informatique?
A: Oui, j'adore et j'aime bien l'économie et le droit aussi.
H: Moi, je n'aime pas tellement l'informatique, c'est difficile. J'aime l'histoire, la géographie et la psychologie. C'est très intéressant.
A: Tu aimes la gestion?
H: Ah non, je déteste!
A: Mais c'est très utile!
H: Mais non! Les langues, oui, sont utiles. J'aime bien l'italien.
A: Oui, j'adore l'italien, moi aussi!
H: Bon, à tout à l'heure, Aurélie!
A: Oui, à bientôt!
(On Textbook Audio)

2 Expansion Play the recording again and give students these true/false statements or write them on the board. **1. Aurélie n'aime pas le cours d'économie.** (Faux.) **2. Hassim déteste le cours de gestion.** (Vrai.) **3. Pour Hassim, le cours d'informatique est facile.** (Faux.) **4. Hassim aime la psychologie et la géographie.** (Vrai.) **5. Aurélie et Hassim aiment bien l'italien.** (Vrai.)

3 Expansion Take a class survey of students' responses to each question and tally the results on the board. Ask students which questions are most controversial. Then ask them on which questions they agree. You might want to introduce the expression **être d'accord**, which will be presented in the **Roman-photo** later in this lesson.

TEACHING OPTIONS

Categories Write the names of different fields of study across the board (for example, **les langues**, **les sciences naturelles**, **les sciences humaines**, **les cours techniques**). Working in groups of three or four, have students list the courses under the appropriate category.

DIFFERENTIATION

For Visual Learners Using the digital image for this page, point to various people in the drawing and ask general questions about them. Examples: **Les élèves sont à la cantine? Il aime la physique?**

Contextes — Leçon 2A

Communication

4 **Conversez** In pairs, fill in the blanks according to your own situations. Then, act out the conversation for the class. *Answers will vary.*

- Élève A: _____, comment ça va?
- Élève B: _____. Et toi?
- Élève A: _____ merci.
- Élève B: Est-ce que tu aimes le cours de _____?
- Élève A: J'adore le cours de _____.
- Élève B: Moi aussi. Tu aimes _____?
- Élève A: Non, j'aime mieux (*better*) _____.
- Élève B: Bon, à bientôt.
- Élève A: À _____.

5 **Qu'est-ce que c'est?** Write a caption for each image, stating where the students are and how they feel about the classes they are attending. Then, in pairs, take turns reading your captions for your partner to guess about whom you are talking. *Answers will vary. Suggested answers.*

MODÈLE
C'est le cours de français. Le français, c'est facile.

1. C'est le cours d'informatique. Je déteste l'informatique.
2. Être reçu à l'examen / Avoir le diplôme de l'université, c'est difficile. 
3. C'est la philosophie. J'adore la philosophie. 
4. C'est le cours de chimie. La chimie, c'est facile. 
5. C'est le cours d'éducation physique / la cantine. Je n'aime pas tellement... 
6. C'est un devoir d'architecture / de stylisme. J'aime bien... 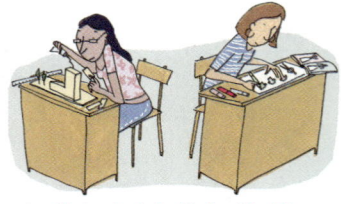

6 **Vous êtes...** Imagine what subjects these famous people liked and disliked as students. In pairs, take turns playing the role of each one and guessing the answer. *Answers will vary.*

MODÈLE
Élève 1: J'aime la physique et la chimie, mais je n'aime pas tellement les cours d'économie.
Élève 2: Vous êtes Albert Einstein!

- Albert Einstein
- Louis Pasteur
- Donald Trump
- Bill Clinton
- Christian Dior
- Le docteur Phil
- Bill Gates
- Frank Lloyd Wright

7 **Sondage** Your teacher will give you a worksheet to conduct a survey (**un sondage**). Go around the room to find people that study the subjects listed. Ask what your classmates think about their subjects. Keep a record of their answers to discuss with the class. *Answers will vary.*

MODÈLE
Élève 1: Jean, est-ce que tu étudies (*do you study*) la chimie?
Élève 2: Oui. J'aime bien la chimie. C'est un cours utile.

quarante-huit

---

4 Suggestion Before doing this activity, complete a similar exchange; scramble the order of the sentences and write them on the board or on a transparency. Tell students to put the sentences in order to make a logical conversation.

5 Suggestion Have several volunteers write their captions on the board.

6 Suggestion For more practice, come up with other names.

6 Partner Chat You can also assign Activity 6 on the Supersite. Students work in pairs to record the activity online. The pair's recorded conversation will appear in your gradebook.

PRE-AP®

6 Interpersonal speaking For additional practice, have students ask each celebrity one or two questions, such as **Comment allez-vous, Monsieur Einstein?** or **Quelle est votre nationalité?**

7 Suggestions
- Read the **modèle** aloud with a volunteer. Then distribute the **Feuilles d'activités** from the Activity Pack.
- Have volunteers share their findings with the class.

21ST CENTURY SKILLS

7 Collaboration If you have access to students in a Francophone country, ask them to conduct a similar survey to find out about their opinions on the subjects they study in school. Then, ask groups of students to read their counterparts' answers and prepare a comparison of the preferences of both classes.

EXPANSION

Using Games Divide the class into two teams. Write names of courses or people on index cards and tape them face down on the board. Play a game of Concentration in which students match courses with an expert in the field. Examples: **le stylisme/**Jean-Paul Gaultier, **l'art/**Claude Monet, and **la philosophie/**Jean-Paul Sartre. As students turn over a card, they must read it aloud. If a player has a match, that player's team collects those cards. When all the cards have been matched, the team with the most cards wins.

TEACHING OPTIONS

Oral Practice To practice expressing likes and dislikes, ask students yes/no and either/or questions. Examples: **Vous aimez bien la psychologie? Vous détestez la géographie? Vous adorez les lettres ou les sciences?**

Les sons et les lettres

Liaisons

Consonants at the end of French words are generally silent but are usually pronounced when the word that follows begins with a vowel sound. This linking of sounds is called a liaison.

À tout à l'heure!   Comment allez-vous?

An **s** or an **x** in a liaison sounds like the letter **z**.

les étudiants   trois élèves   six élèves   deux hommes

Always make a liaison between a subject pronoun and a verb that begins with a vowel sound; always make a liaison between an article and a noun that begins with a vowel sound.

nous aimons   ils ont   un étudiant   les ordinateurs

Always make a liaison between **est** (a form of **être**) and a word that begins with a vowel or a vowel sound. Never make a liaison with the final consonant of a proper name.

Robert est anglais.   Paris est exceptionnelle.

Never make a liaison with the conjunction **et** (*and*).

Carole et Hélène   Jacques et Antoinette

Never make a liaison between a singular noun and an adjective that follows it.

un cours horrible   un instrument élégant

Prononcez Practice saying these words and expressions aloud.

1. un examen
2. des étudiants
3. les hôtels
4. dix acteurs
5. Paul et Yvette
6. cours important
7. des informations
8. les études
9. deux hommes
10. Bernard aime
11. chocolat italien
12. Louis est

Articulez Practice saying these sentences aloud.

1. Nous aimons les arts.
2. Albert habite à Paris.
3. C'est un objet intéressant.
4. Sylvie est avec Anne.
5. Ils adorent les deux universités.

Dictons Practice reading these sayings aloud.

Les amis de nos amis sont nos amis.[1]

Un hôte non invité doit apporter son siège.[2]

[1] Friends of our friends are our friends.
[2] An uninvited guest must bring his own chair.

quarante-neuf 49

Section Goals
In this section, students will learn functional phrases for talking about their courses.

Key Standards
1.2, 2.1, 2.2, 4.1, 4.2

Student Resources
Cahier de l'élève, pp. 33–34; Supersite: Activities, *eCahier*

Teacher Resources
Answer Keys; Video Script & Translation; *Roman-photo* video

Video Recap: Leçon 1B
Before doing this **Roman-photo**, review the previous one.
1. Le cours d'histoire est difficile pour Stéphane, n'est-ce pas? (Non, les maths et le français sont difficiles pour Stéphane.)
2. Comment est Sandrine? (égoïste, sociable et charmante)
3. De quelle origine est Amina? (sénégalaise) Et Rachid? (algérienne)
4. Comment est Amina? (charmante, sincère et élégante)
5. Comment est Rachid? (intelligent, poli, modeste, réservé et brillant)

Video Synopsis Rachid and Antoine discuss their political science class. As they are walking, David joins them, and Rachid introduces him. Then Antoine leaves. When the two roommates get to Rachid's car, Sandrine and Amina are waiting for them. The girls ask David about school and his classes. Later, at **Le P'tit Bistrot**, Stéphane joins the four friends and they continue their discussion about classes. Stéphane hates all of his courses.

Suggestions
- Have students predict what they think the episode will be about. Record predictions on the board.
- Have students work in groups of six. Tell them to choose a role and read the **Roman-photo** conversation aloud. Ask one or two groups to act out the conversation for the class.
- After students have read the **Roman-photo**, review their predictions and ask which ones were correct. Then ask a few questions to guide them in summarizing this episode.

50 Unit 2 • Lesson 2A

Roman-photo   Leçon 2A

Trop de devoirs!
Video: Roman-photo Record & Compare

PERSONNAGES
Amina
Antoine
David
Rachid
Sandrine
Stéphane

1.
ANTOINE Je déteste le cours de sciences po.
RACHID Oh? Mais pourquoi? Je n'aime pas tellement le prof, Monsieur Dupré, mais c'est un cours intéressant et utile!
ANTOINE Tu crois? Moi, je pense que c'est très difficile, et il y a beaucoup de devoirs. Avec Dupré, je travaille, mais je n'ai pas de bons résultats.

2.
RACHID Si on est optimiste et si on travaille, on est reçu à l'examen.
ANTOINE Toi, oui, mais pas moi! Toi, tu es un étudiant brillant! Mais moi, les études, oh là là.
DAVID Eh! Rachid! Oh! Est-ce que tu oublies ton coloc?

3.
RACHID Pas du tout, pas du tout. Antoine, voilà, je te présente David, mon colocataire américain.
DAVID Nous partageons un des appartements du P'tit Bistrot.
ANTOINE Le P'tit Bistrot? Sympa!

6.
SANDRINE Salut! Alors, ça va l'université française?
DAVID Bien, oui. C'est différent de l'université américaine, mais c'est intéressant.
AMINA Tu aimes les cours?
DAVID J'aime bien les cours de littérature et d'histoire françaises. Demain, on étudie *Les Trois Mousquetaires* d'Alexandre Dumas.

7.
SANDRINE J'adore Dumas. Mon livre préféré, c'est *Le Comte de Monte-Cristo*.
RACHID Sandrine! S'il te plaît! *Le Comte de Monte-Cristo*?
SANDRINE Pourquoi pas? Je suis chanteuse, mais j'adore les classiques de la littérature.
DAVID Donne-moi le sac à dos, Sandrine.

8.
Au P'tit Bistrot...
RACHID Moi, j'aime le cours de sciences po, mais Antoine n'aime pas Dupré. Il pense qu'il donne trop de devoirs.

1 Vrai ou faux?
Choose whether each statement is **vrai** or **faux**. Correct the false statements.
Answers may vary slightly.
1. Rachid et Antoine n'aiment pas le professeur Dupré.   Vrai.
2. Antoine aime bien le cours de sciences po.
   Faux. Antoine déteste le cours de sciences po.
3. Rachid et Antoine partagent (*share*) un appartement.
   Faux. Rachid et David partagent un appartement.
4. David et Rachid cherchent (*look for*) Amina et Sandrine après (*after*) les cours.   Vrai.
5. Le livre préféré de Sandrine est *Le Comte de Monte-Cristo*.   Vrai.
6. L'université française est très différente de l'université américaine.   Vrai.
7. Stéphane aime la chimie.
   Faux. Stéphane n'aime pas la chimie.
8. Monsieur Dupré est professeur de maths.
   Faux. Monsieur Dupré est professeur de sciences po.
9. Antoine a (*has*) beaucoup de devoirs.   Vrai.
10. Stéphane adore l'anglais.   Faux. Stéphane déteste l'anglais.

Practice more at **vhlcentral.com**.

50   cinquante

TEACHING OPTIONS

Trop de devoirs! Before showing the video episode, have students brainstorm some expressions people might use when talking about their classes and teachers.

TEACHING OPTIONS

Regarder la vidéo Download and print the videoscript and white out ten words or expressions in order to create a master for a cloze activity. Hand out the photocopies and tell students to fill in the missing words as they watch the video episode. You may want to show the episode twice if students have difficulty with the activity. Then have students compare their answers in small groups.

Au lycée   Unité 2

Antoine, David, Rachid et Stéphane parlent (*talk*) de leurs (*their*) cours.

RACHID Ah… on a rendez-vous avec Amina et Sandrine. On y va?
DAVID Ah, oui, bon, ben, salut, Antoine!
ANTOINE Salut, David. À demain, Rachid!

SANDRINE Bon, Pascal, au revoir, chéri.
RACHID Bonjour, chérie. Comme j'adore parler avec toi au téléphone! Comme j'adore penser à toi!

Expressions utiles

Talking about classes

- **Tu aimes les cours?**
  Do you like the classes?
- **Antoine n'aime pas Dupré.**
  Antoine doesn't like Dupré.
- **Il pense qu'il donne trop de devoirs.**
  He thinks he gives too much homework.
- **Tu crois? Mais pourquoi?**
  You think? But why?
- **Avec Dupré, je travaille, mais je n'ai pas de bons résultats.**
  With Dupré, I work, but I don't get good results (grades).
- **Demain, on étudie *Les Trois Mousquetaires*.**
  Tomorrow we're studying The Three Musketeers.
- **C'est mon livre préféré.**
  It's my favorite book.

Additional vocabulary

- **On a rendez-vous (avec des ami(e)s).**
  We're meeting (friends).
- **Comme j'adore…**
  How I love…
- **parler au téléphone**
  to talk on the phone
- **C'est une blague.**
  It's a joke.
- **Si, malheureusement!**
  Yes, unfortunately!
- **On y va? / On y va.**
  Are you ready? / Let's go.
- **Eh!**
  Hey!
- **pas du tout**
  not at all
- **chéri(e)**
  darling

STÉPHANE Dupré? Ha! C'est Madame Richard, mon prof de français. Elle, elle donne trop de devoirs.
AMINA Bonjour, comment ça va?
STÉPHANE Plutôt mal. Je n'aime pas Madame Richard. Je déteste les maths. La chimie n'est pas intéressante. L'histoire-géo, c'est l'horreur. Les études, c'est le désastre!

DAVID Le français, les maths, la chimie, l'histoire-géo… mais on n'étudie pas les langues étrangères au lycée en France?
STÉPHANE Si, malheureusement! Moi, j'étudie l'anglais. C'est une langue très désagréable! Oh, non, non, ha, ha, c'est une blague, ha, ha. L'anglais, j'adore l'anglais. C'est une langue charmante….

2 Complétez Match the people in the second column with the verbs in the first. Refer to a dictionary, the dialogue, and the video stills as necessary. Use each option once.

b/e 1. travailler   a. Sandrine is very forgetful.
_c_ 2. partager   b. Rachid is very studious.
_a_ 3. oublier   c. David can't afford his own apartment.
b/e 4. étudier   d. Amina is very generous.
_d_ 5. donner   e. Stéphane needs to get good grades.

3 Conversez In this episode, Rachid, Antoine, David, and Stéphane talk about the subjects they are studying. Get together with a partner. Do any of the characters' complaints or preferences remind you of your own? Whose opinions do you agree with? Whom do you disagree with?

ressources
vText
CE pp. 33–34
vhlcentral.com
Leçon 2A

cinquante et un 51

Culture
Leçon 2A

Reading Video: *Flash culture*

CULTURE À LA LOUPE

Au lycée

What is high school like in France? At the end of middle school (**le collège**), French students begin three years of high-school study at the **lycée**. Beginning in **seconde** (10th grade), students pass into **première** (11th grade) and end with **la terminale** (12th grade).

The **lycée** experience is quite different from American high school. For example, the days are much longer: often from 8:00 am until 5:00 pm. On Wednesdays, classes typically end at noon. Students in some **lycées** may also have class on Saturday morning. French schools do not offer organized sports, like American schools do, but students who want to play an organized sport can join **l'Association sportive scolaire.** Every public **lycée** must offer this option to its students. All such extra-curricular activities take place after school hours or on Wednesday afternoons.

Grades are based on a 20-point scale, with 10 being the average grade. As students advance in their studies, it becomes harder for them to achieve a grade of 16/20 or even 14/20. A student can receive a below-average score in one or more courses and still advance to the next level as long as their overall grade average is at least 10/20.

Another important difference is that French students must begin a specialization while in high school, at the end of the **classe de seconde.** That choice is likely to influence the rest of their studies and, later, their job choice. While they can change their mind after the first trimester of **première,** by then students are already set on a course towards the **baccalauréat** or **bac,** the terminal exam that concludes their **lycée** studies.

Système français de notation

NOTE FRANÇAISE	NOTE AMÉRICAINE	%	NOTE FRANÇAISE	NOTE AMÉRICAINE	%
0	F	0	11	B-	82
2	F	3	12	B+	88
3	F	8	13	A-	93
4	F	18	14	A	95
5	F	28	15	A	96
6	F	38	16	A+	98
7	D-	60	17	A+	98
8	D-	65	18	A+	99
9	D+	68	19	A+	99
10	C	75	20	A+	100

ACTIVITÉS

1 Vrai ou faux? Indicate whether each statement is **vrai** or **faux.**

1. The **lycée** comes after **collège**.
   Vrai.
2. It takes 4 years to complete **lycée**.
   Faux. It takes three years.
3. The grade order in the **lycée** is **terminale, première,** and lastly **seconde.**
   Faux. The order is seconde, première, terminale.
4. **Lycées** never have classes on Saturday.
   Faux. Some lycées have classes Saturday mornings.
5. French students have class from Monday to Friday all day long.
   Faux. Wednesdays are typically half days.
6. French students have to specialize in a field of study while in high school.
   Vrai.
7. French students begin their specialization in **première.**
   Vrai.
8. The French grading system resembles the US grading system.
   Faux. The American grading system is based on 100 points.
9. The highest grade that a French student can get is 20/20.
   Vrai.
10. To obtain a grade of 20/20 is common in France.
    Faux. A grade of 20/20 is very rare.

Practice more at **vhlcentral.com.**

52 cinquante-deux

Au lycée — Unité 2

LE FRANÇAIS QUOTIDIEN

Les cours

être fort(e) en...	to be good at
être nul(le) en...	to stink at
sécher un cours	to skip a class
potasser	to cram
piger	to get it
l'emploi du temps	class schedule
l'histoire-géo	history-geography
les maths	math
la philo	philosophy
le prof	teacher
la récré(ation)	recess

LE MONDE FRANCOPHONE

Le lycée

Le «lycée» n'existe pas partout°.

En Afrique francophone, on utilise° les termes de *lycée* et de *baccalauréat*.

En Belgique, le lycée public s'appelle une *école secondaire* ou un *athénée*. Un lycée privé° s'appelle un *collège*. Le bac n'existe pas°.

En Suisse, les lycées s'appellent *gymnases, écoles préparant à la maturité* ou *écoles de culture générale*. Les élèves reçoivent° un certificat du secondaire II.

partout *everywhere* on utilise *one uses* privé *private* n'existe pas *does not exist* reçoivent *receive*

PORTRAIT

Immersion française au Canada

Au Canada, l'anglais et le français sont les langues officielles, mais les provinces ne sont pas nécessairement bilingues — le Nouveau-Brunswick est la seule province officiellement bilingue. Seulement 17,4% des Canadiens parlent le français et l'anglais. Pourtant°, il existe un programme d'immersion française qui encourage le bilinguisme: certains élèves d'école primaire ou secondaire (lycée) choisissent de suivre leurs cours° en français. Pendant° trois années ou plus, les élèves ont tous° les cours uniquement en français. Au Nouveau-Brunswick, 32% des élèves y sont inscrits°. Au Québec, province majoritairement francophone, mais avec une communauté anglophone importante, 22% des élèves sont inscrits dans le programme d'immersion française.

Pourtant However **suivre leurs cours** take their classes **Pendant** For **ont tous** take all **inscrits** enrolled

Coup de main

To read decimal places in French, use the French word *virgule* (*comma*) where you would normally say *point* in English. To say *percent*, use **pour cent**.

17,4% dix-sept virgule quatre pour cent
seventeen point four percent

Sur Internet

Comment est une journée (*day*) typique dans un lycée français?

Go to **vhlcentral.com** to find more information related to this **Cultura** section.

---

2 Complete each statement.

1. L'anglais et le français sont les langues officielles du ___Canada___.
2. Le programme d'immersion existe dans les écoles primaires et ___secondaires___.
3. Le programme d'immersion est pour une période de ___trois___ ans ou plus.
4. Au Nouveau-Brunswick, la communauté ___francophone___ est importante.
5. En Suisse, les lycées s'appellent ___gymnases___.

3 Les cours Research what classes are taught in the **lycée** and how long each course is. How does this compare to your class schedule? You may search in your library or online.

ressources: vText, CE pp. 35–36, vhlcentral.com Leçon 2A

cinquante-trois 53

Section Goals
In this section, students will learn:
- the present tense of regular -er verbs
- spelling changes in -cer and -ger verbs

Key Standards
4.1, 5.1

Student Resources
Cahier de l'élève, pp. 37–39;
Supersite: Activities,
eCahier
Grammar Tutorials
Teacher Resources
Answer Keys; Audio Script;
Audio Activity MP3s/CD; Testing
program: Grammar Quiz

Suggestions
- Point out that students have been using verbs from the start: **Comment t'appelles-tu?, il y a**, forms of **être**, etc. Ask the class: **Quels cours aimez-vous?** Model the response **J'aime….** Ask a student: **____ aime quels cours?** Model **Il/Elle aime….** Give other subjects.
- Introduce the idea of a "boot verb." Write the conjugation of a common -er verb on the board with the singular forms in the first column and the plural forms in the second column. Draw a line around **je, tu, il/elle/on,** and **ils/elles**, forming the shape of a boot. The four verb forms inside the "boot" are pronounced alike.
- Model the pronunciation of each infinitive, having students repeat. Create sentences with **j'aime…** and **j'adore…** followed by infinitives. Stress that **je** changes to **j'** before verbs starting with a vowel and most verbs starting with **h**. Ask if students like some of the activities. Example: **Vous aimez voyager?**
- Consider explaining to students that the adverb **assez** can also mean *rather* when placed before an adjective.

Structures — Leçon 2A

2A.1 Present tense of regular -er verbs

Presentation Grammar Tutorial

- The infinitives of most French verbs end in **-er**. To form the present tense of regular **-er** verbs, drop the **-er** from the infinitive and add the corresponding endings for the different subject pronouns. This chart demonstrates how to conjugate regular **-er** verbs.

parler (to speak)			
je parl**e**	I speak	nous parl**ons**	we speak
tu parl**es**	you speak	vous parl**ez**	you speak
il/elle/on parl**e**	he/she/it/one speaks	ils/elles parl**ent**	they speak

- Here are some other verbs that are conjugated the same way as **parler**.

Common -er verbs			
adorer	to love; to adore	habiter (à)	to live (in)
aimer	to like; to love	manger	to eat
aimer mieux	to prefer (to like better)	oublier	to forget
arriver	to arrive	partager	to share
chercher	to look for	penser (que/qu'…)	to think (that…)
commencer	to begin, to start	regarder	to look (at)
dessiner	to draw; to design	rencontrer	to meet
détester	to hate	retrouver	to meet up with; to find (again)
donner	to give	travailler	to work
étudier	to study	voyager	to travel

- Note that **je** becomes **j'** when it appears before a verb that begins with a vowel sound.

  J'habite à Bruxelles.   **J'étudie** la psychologie.
  I live in Brussels.   I study psychology.

- With the verbs **adorer**, **aimer**, and **détester**, use the definite article before a noun to tell what someone loves, likes, prefers, or hates.

  J'aime mieux **l'**art.   Marine déteste **les** devoirs.
  I prefer art.   Marine hates homework.

- Use infinitive forms after the verbs **adorer**, **aimer**, and **détester** to say that you like (or hate, etc.) to do something. Only the first verb should be conjugated.

  Ils **adorent travailler** ici.   Ils **détestent étudier** ensemble.
  They love working here.   They hate to study together.

- The present tense in French can be translated in different ways in English. The English equivalent for a sentence depends on its context.

  Éric et Nadine **étudient** la physique.   Nous **travaillons** à Paris.
  Éric and Nadine study physics.   We work in Paris.
  Éric and Nadine are studying physics.   We are working in Paris.
  Éric and Nadine do study physics.   We do work in Paris.

- Sometimes the present tense can be used to indicate an event in the near future, in which case it can be translated using *will* in English.

  Je **retrouve** le professeur demain.   Elles **arrivent** à Dijon demain.
  I will meet up with the teacher tomorrow.   They will arrive in Dijon tomorrow.

Boîte à outils
To express yourself with greater accuracy, use these adverbs: **assez** (*enough*), **d'habitude** (*usually*), **de temps en temps** (*from time to time*), **parfois** (*sometimes*), **quelquefois** (*sometimes*), **rarement** (*rarely*), **souvent** (*often*), **toujours** (*always*).

54   cinquante-quatre

EXPANSION

Questions Ask students questions, using **étudier, manger,** and **parler**. Students should answer in complete sentences.
Ex: —____, tu étudies le français? —Oui, j'étudie le français.
—Vous mangez beaucoup? —Qui mange plus?

EXPANSION

Pairs Ask students to create a two-column chart with the heads **J'adore…** and **Je déteste…** Have them complete the chart with five things they love and hate doing. Ex: **J'adore manger des pizzas. Je déteste dessiner.** Assist them with unfamiliar vocabulary as necessary. Have students share their sentences with the class.

Au lycée — Unité 2

- Verbs ending in **-ger** (**manger**, **partager**, **voyager**) and **-cer** (**commencer**) have a spelling change in the **nous** form. All the other forms are the same as regular **-er** verbs.

manger	commencer
je mange	je commence
tu manges	tu commences
il/elle/on mange	il/elle/on commence
nous mang**e**ons	nous commen**ç**ons
vous mangez	vous commencez
ils/elles mangent	ils/elles commencent

Nous **voyageons** avec une amie.
We are traveling with a friend.

Nous **commençons** les devoirs.
We're starting our homework.

> Est-ce que tu oublies ton coloc?

> Nous partageons un des appartements du P'tit Bistrot.

Boîte à outils
The spelling change in the **nous** form is made in order to maintain the same sound that the **c** and the **g** make in the infinitives **commencer** and **manger**.

- Unlike the English *to look for*, the French **chercher** requires no preposition before the noun that follows it.

Nous **cherchons les stylos**.
We're looking for the pens.

Vous **cherchez la montre**?
Are you looking for the watch?

- The **nous** and **vous** command forms are identical to those of the present tense. The **tu** command form of **-er** verbs drops the **-s** from the present tense form. The command forms of **être** are irregular: **sois, soyons, soyez**.

Regarde!	**Travaillons.**	**Parlez** français.	**Sois** patiente!
Look!	*Let's work.*	*Speak French.*	*Be patient!*

Essayez!
Complete the sentences with the correct present tense forms of the verbs.

1. Je __parle__ (parler) français en classe.
2. Nous __habitons__ (habiter) près de (*near*) l'école.
3. Ils __aiment__ (aimer) le cours de sciences politiques.
4. Vous __mangez__ (manger) en classe?!
5. Le cours __commence__ (commencer) à huit heures (*at eight o'clock*).
6. Marie-Claire __cherche__ (chercher) un stylo.
7. Nous __partageons__ (partager) un crayon en cours de maths.
8. Tu __étudies__ (étudier) l'économie.
9. Les élèves __voyagent__ (voyager) en France.
10. Nous __adorons__ (adorer) le prof d'anglais.

Structures
Leçon 2A

Mise en pratique

1 **Complétez** Complete the conversation with the correct forms of the verbs.

ARTHUR Tu (1) _parles_ (parler) bien français!

OLIVIER Mon ami Marc et moi, nous (2) _retrouvons_ (retrouver) un professeur de français et nous (3) _étudions_ (étudier) ensemble. Et toi, tu (4) _travailles_ (travailler)?

ARTHUR Non, j' (5) _étudie_ (étudier) l'art et l'économie. Je (6) _dessine_ (dessiner) bien et j' (7) _aime_ (aimer) beaucoup l'art moderne. Marc et toi, vous (8) _habitez_ (habiter) à Paris?

2 **Phrases** Form sentences using the words provided. Conjugate the verbs and add any necessary words.

1. je / oublier / devoir de littérature   J'oublie le devoir de littérature.
2. nous / commencer / études supérieures   Nous commençons des études supérieures.
3. vous / rencontrer / amis / au / lycée   Vous rencontrez des amis au lycée.
4. Hélène / détester / travailler   Hélène déteste travailler.
5. tu / chercher / cours / facile   Tu cherches un cours facile.
6. élèves / arriver / avec / dictionnaires   Les élèves arrivent avec des dictionnaires.

3 **Après l'école** Say what Stéphanie and her friends are doing after (après) school. Answers may vary.

▶ **MODÈLE**
Nathalie cherche un livre.

1. André _travaille_ à la bibliothèque.
2. Édouard _retrouve_ Caroline au café. 
3. Jérôme et moi, nous _dessinons_. 
4. Julien et Audrey _parlent_ avec Simon. 
5. Robin et toi, vous _voyagez_ avec la classe. 
6. Je _mange_. 

4 **Le verbe logique** Complete the following sentences logically with the correct form of an –er verb. Suggested answers.

1. La chimie, c'est très difficile. Je _déteste_ !
2. Qu'est-ce que tu _cherches_ dans le sac à dos?
3. Nous _mangeons_ souvent à la cantine.
4. Tristan et Irène _oublient_ toujours les clés (keys).
5. Le film _commence_ dans dix minutes.
6. Yves et toi, vous _pensez_ que Martine est charmante?
7. M. et Mme Legrand _habitent_ à Paris.
8. On n'aime pas _regarder_ la télévision.

56   cinquante-six

Practice more at vhlcentral.com.

---

1 Suggestion Go over the answers quickly in class, then ask several pairs of students to act out the conversation and add at least two lines of their own at the end.

2 Suggestion To check students' answers, have volunteers write the sentences on the board and read them aloud.

2 Expansion For additional practice, change the subjects of the sentences and have students restate or write the sentences. Examples: **1. Tu (Tu oublies le devoir de littérature.) 2. Chantal (Chantal commence des études supérieures.) 3. Je (Je rencontre des amis au lycée.) 4. Les élèves (Les élèves détestent travailler.) 5. Nous (Nous cherchons un cours facile.) 6. Pascale (Pascale arrive avec des dictionnaires.)**

3 Expansion Have students add additional sentences to the captions below the drawings. Example: **1. Il étudie l'histoire. Il y a un examen.**

3 Expansion Have students redo the activity using **aimer** + [*infinitive*] to tell what Stéphanie's friends like to do after school. Ex.: **Nathalie aime aller à la bibliothèque.**

EXPANSION

Pairs Ask student pairs to write eight sentences, using verbs presented in this section. Point out that students can use vocabulary words from **Contextes**. Have pairs share their sentences with the class.

TEACHING OPTIONS

Extra Practice Have individual students write five dehydrated sentences (like those in Activity 2 on this page) and exchange them with a partner, who will recreate them. After pairs have completed the activity, ask volunteers to share some of their dehydrated sentences. Write them on the board and have the class "rehydrate" them.

56   Unit 2 • Lesson 2A

Au lycée   Unité 2

Communication

5 Activités In pairs, tell your partner which of these activities you and your best friend both do. Then, share your partner's answers with the class. Later, get together with a second partner and report to the class again. *Answers will vary.*

MODÈLE

To your partner: *Nous parlons au téléphone, nous...*
To the class: *Ils/Elles parlent au téléphone, ils/elles...*
To your partner: *Nous travaillons, nous...*
To the class: *Ils/Elles travaillent, ils/elles...*

manger à la cantine	étudier une langue étrangère
oublier les devoirs	commencer les devoirs
retrouver des amis au café	arriver en classe
travailler	voyager

6 Les études In pairs, take turns asking your partner if he or she likes one academic subject or another. If you don't like a subject, mention one you do like. Then, use **tous** (*m.*)/**toutes** (*f.*) **les deux** (*both of us*) to tell the class what subjects both of you like or hate. *Answers will vary.*

MODÈLE

Élève 1: *Tu aimes la chimie?*
Élève 2: *Non, je déteste la chimie. J'aime mieux les langues.*
Élève 1: *Moi aussi... Nous adorons tous/toutes les deux les langues.*

7 Un sondage In groups of three, survey your partners to find out how frequently they do certain activities. First, prepare a chart with a list of eight activities. Then take turns asking your partners how often they do each one, and record each person's response.

MODÈLE

Élève 1: *Moi, je dessine rarement. Et toi?*
Élève 2: *Moi aussi, je dessine rarement.*
Élève 3: *Moi, je dessine parfois.*

Activité	souvent	parfois	rarement
dessiner		Sara	David, Clara
voyager	Clara, David, Sara		

8 Adorer, aimer, détester In groups of four, ask each other if you like to do these activities. Then, use an adjective to tell why you like them or not and say whether you do them often (**souvent**), sometimes (**parfois**), or rarely (**rarement**). *Answers will vary.*

MODÈLE

Élève 1: *Tu aimes voyager?*
Élève 2: *Oui, j'adore voyager. C'est amusant! Je voyage souvent.*
Élève 3: *Moi, je déteste voyager. C'est désagréable! Je voyage rarement.*

dessiner	partager une chambre
étudier le week-end	retrouver des amis
manger au restaurant	travailler à la bibliothèque
oublier les devoirs	voyager
parler avec les professeurs	

cinquante-sept 57

5 Suggestion Encourage students to personalize the information and to add additional information. Examples: **étudier** *a different subject*, **travailler dans** *a place*, and **regarder la télé**.

5 Partner Chat You can also assign Activity 5 on the Supersite. Students work in pairs to record the activity online. The pair's recorded conversation will appear in your gradebook.

6 Suggestion Before beginning the activity, tell students to jot down a list of academic subjects that they can ask their partner about and to note their partner's responses. Examples: **Il/Elle aime** or **Il/Elle déteste**.

7 Expansion Have students share with the class which activity most people in their group do often and which one most do rarely.

8 Suggestion Before beginning the activity, have students brainstorm adjectives they can use and write them on the board.

EXPANSION

Game Divide the class into two teams. Choose one team member at a time to go to the board, alternating between teams. Say an infinitive and a subject pronoun. The person at the board must write and say the correct present tense form. Example: **parler: vous (vous parlez)**. Give a point for each correct answer. The team with the most points at the end of the game wins.

EXPANSION

Questions Prepare eight questions. Write their answers on the board in random order. Then read your questions aloud, having students match the question to the appropriate answer. Make sure that only one of the possible answers corresponds logically to the question you ask. Example: **Pourquoi déteste-t-il les maths? (Le prof est désagréable.)**

Section Goals

In this section, students will learn:
- to form questions
- to express negation
- expressions for agreeing and disagreeing

Key Standards
4.1, 5.1

Student Resources
Cahier de l'élève, pp. 40–42; Supersite: Activities, eCahier
Grammar Tutorials

Teacher Resources
Answer Keys; Audio Script; Audio Activity MP3s/CD; Testing program: Grammar Quiz

Suggestions

- Model the pronunciation and intonation of the different types of example questions. Point out that most of the questions on page 58 elicit yes-no responses.
- Explain how to form inverted questions. Point out that inversion is usually used in written and formal language. Inversion with **je** is rare in spoken French, but seen in literary language, especially questions. Examples: **Ai-je le droit? Qui suis-je?**

Structures — Leçon 2A

2A.2 Forming questions and expressing negation

Presentation Grammar Tutorial

Forming questions

- There are four principal ways to ask a question in French. The first and simplest way is to make a statement but with rising intonation. In writing, simply put a question mark at the end. This method is considered informal.

  Vous habitez à Bordeaux?
  You live in Bordeaux?

  Tu aimes le cours de français?
  You like French class?

- A second way is to place the phrase **Est-ce que...** directly before a statement. This turns it into a question. If the next word begins with a vowel sound, use **Est-ce qu'**. Questions with **est-ce que** are somewhat formal.

  Est-ce que vous parlez français?
  Do you speak French?

  Est-ce qu'il aime dessiner?
  Does he like to draw?

- A third way is to end a statement with a tag question, such as **n'est-ce pas?** (*isn't that right?*) or **d'accord?** (*OK?*). This method can be formal or informal.

  Nous mangeons à midi, **n'est-ce pas**?
  We eat at noon, don't we?

  On commence à deux heures, **d'accord**?
  We're starting at two o'clock, OK?

- A fourth way is to invert the order of the subject pronoun and the verb and place a hyphen between them. If the verb ends in a vowel and the subject pronoun begins with one (e.g., **il**, **elle**, or **on**), insert **-t-** between the verb and the pronoun to make pronunciation easier. Inversion is considered more formal.

  Parlez-vous français?
  Do you speak French?

  Mange-t-il à midi?
  Does he eat at noon?

  Est-elle élève?
  Is she a student?

- If the subject is a noun rather than a pronoun, place the noun at the beginning of the question followed by the inverted verb and pronoun.

  Le professeur parle-t-il français?
  Does the teacher speak French?

  Nina arrive-t-elle demain?
  Does Nina arrive tomorrow?

  Les élèves mangent-ils à la cantine?
  Do the students eat at the cafeteria?

  Rachid et toi étudiez-vous l'économie?
  Do you and Rachid study Economics?

- The inverted form of **il y a** is **y a-t-il**. **C'est** becomes **est-ce**.

  Y a-t-il une horloge dans la classe?
  Is there a clock in the class?

  Est-ce le professeur de lettres?
  Is he the humanities professor?

- Use **pourquoi** to ask *why?* Use **parce que** (**parce qu'** before a vowel sound) to answer *because*.

  Pourquoi retrouves-tu Sophie ici?
  Why are you meeting Sophie here?

  Parce qu'elle habite près d'ici.
  Because she lives near here.

- You can use **est-ce que** after **pourquoi** or any question word to form a question. With **est-ce que**, you don't use inversion.

  Pourquoi détestes-tu la chimie?
  Why do you hate Chemistry?

  Pourquoi est-ce que tu détestes la chimie?
  Why do you hate Chemistry?

  Où habitez-vous?
  Where do you live?

  Où est-ce que vous habitez?
  Where do you live?

Boîte à outils

Note the statements that correspond to the questions on the right:

Vous habitez à Bordeaux.
Tu aimes le cours de français.

Boîte à outils

Note the statements that correspond to the questions on the right:

Vous parlez français.
Il mange à midi.
Elle est élève.

Boîte à outils

Note the statements that correspond to the questions on the right:

Le professeur parle français.
Nina arrive demain.
Les élèves mangent à la cantine.
Rachid et toi, vous étudiez l'économie.

---

58 *cinquante-huit*

DIFFERENTIATION

For Auditory Learners To add a listening aspect to this grammar presentation, read aloud a series of statements and questions, including tag questions. Have students raise their right hand when they hear a statement or their left hand when they hear a question.

EXPANSION

Extra Practice Have students go back to the **Roman-photo** on pages 50-51 and write as many questions as they can about what they see in the photos. Ask volunteers to share their questions as you write them on the board. Then call on individual students to answer them.

58 Unit 2 • Lesson 2A

Au lycée Unité 2

Expressing negation

- To make a sentence negative in French, place **ne** (**n'** before a vowel sound) before the conjugated verb and **pas** after it.

    Je **ne** dessine **pas** bien.
    I don't draw well.

    Elles **n'**étudient **pas** la chimie.
    They don't study chemistry.

- In the construction [*conjugated verb + infinitive*], **ne** (**n'**) comes before the conjugated verb and **pas** after it.

    Abdel **n'**aime **pas** étudier.
    Abdel doesn't like to study.

    Vous **ne** détestez **pas** travailler?
    You don't hate to work?

- In questions with inversion, place **ne** before the inversion and **pas** after it.

    Abdel **n'**aime-t-il **pas** étudier?
    Doesn't Abdel like to study?

    Ne détestez-vous **pas** travailler?
    Don't you hate to work?

- Use these expressions to respond to a statement or a question that requires a *yes* or *no* answer.

Boîte à outils

Note the affirmative statements that correspond to the negative ones on the left:
Je dessine bien.
Elles étudient la chimie.

Expressions of agreement and disagreement

oui	*yes*	(mais) non	*no (but of course not)*
bien sûr	*of course*	pas du tout	*not at all*
moi/toi non plus	*me/you neither*	peut-être	*maybe, perhaps*

Vous aimez manger à la cantine?
Do you like to eat in the cafeteria?

Non, pas du tout.
No, not at all.

- Use **si** instead of **oui** to contradict a negative question.

    Parles-tu à Daniel?
    Are you talking to Daniel?

    Oui.
    Yes.

    Ne parles-tu pas à Daniel?
    Aren't you talking to Daniel?

    Si!
    Yes (I am)!

Essayez!

Make questions out of these statements. Use **est-ce que/qu'** in items 1–6 and inversion in 7–12.

Statement	Question
1. Vous mangez à la cantine.	Est-ce que vous mangez à la cantine?
2. Ils adorent les devoirs.	Est-ce qu'ils adorent les devoirs?
3. La biologie est difficile.	Est-ce que la biologie est difficile?
4. Tu travailles.	Est-ce que tu travailles?
5. Elles cherchent le prof.	Est-ce qu'elles cherchent le prof?
6. Aude voyage beaucoup.	Est-ce qu'Aude voyage beaucoup?
7. Vous arrivez demain.	Arrivez-vous demain?
8. L'élève oublie le livre.	L'élève oublie-t-il/elle le livre?
9. La physique est utile.	La physique est-elle utile?
10. Il y a deux salles de classe.	Y a-t-il deux salles de classe?
11. Ils n'habitent pas à Québec.	N'habitent-ils pas à Québec?
12. C'est le professeur d'art.	Est-ce le professeur d'art?

cinquante-neuf 59

Suggestions

- Explain the positions of **ne** (**n'**) and **pas** in negative phrases and in inverted questions. If an infinitive follows a conjugated verb, **ne** (**n'**) and **pas** surround the conjugated verb. Example: **Tu n'aimes pas regarder la vidéo?**
- Tell students that **ne** (**n'**) in negative sentences is sometimes dropped in informal speech.
- Model the expressions indicating agreement and disagreement. Show how **mais** can precede **oui** as well as **non** if you want to say yes or no more emphatically.
- Make sure students grasp when to say **si** instead of **oui** by asking questions like these: **Tu n'étudies pas le français?** (**Si, j'étudie le français.**) **Je ne suis pas le professeur?** (**Si, vous êtes le professeur.**) Choose two students that are friends and ask: _____ et _____, vous n'êtes pas copains/copines? (**Si, nous sommes copains/copines.**) Tell students to say, **Mais si!** if they want to contradict a negative question more forcefully.
- Consider further practicing the concept of **oui** versus **si** by asking students affirmative and negative questions and having them respond appropriately.

Essayez! Have students repeat using inversion for items 1–6 and **est-ce que/qu'** in 7–12.

TEACHING OPTIONS

Pairs Write ten statements on the board or a transparency. Have students work in pairs. Tell them to convert the statements into questions by inverting the subject and verb. When they have finished writing the questions, call on volunteers to read their questions aloud. This activity can also be done orally with the class.

EXPANSION

Extra Practice Using the same ten statements from the previous activity, ask students to form tag questions. Encourage them to use both **d'accord?** and **n'est-ce pas?** Have students answer some of the questions. Then add a few negative statements so that students will have to respond with **si**.

Structures — Leçon 2A

Mise en pratique

1 **L'inversion** Restate the questions using inversion.

1. Est-ce que vous parlez espagnol? *Parlez-vous espagnol?*
2. Est-ce qu'il étudie à Paris? *Étudie-t-il à Paris?*
3. Est-ce qu'ils voyagent avec des amis? *Voyagent-ils avec des amis?*
4. Est-ce que tu aimes les cours de langues? *Aimes-tu les cours de langues?*
5. Est-ce que le professeur parle anglais? *Le professeur parle-t-il anglais?*
6. Est-ce que les élèves aiment dessiner? *Les élèves aiment-ils dessiner?*

2 **Les questions** Ask the questions that correspond to the answers. Use **est-ce que/qu'** and inversion for each item.

MODÈLE
Nous habitons loin (*far away*).
Est-ce que vous habitez loin? / Habitez-vous loin?

1. Il mange à la cantine. *Est-ce qu'il mange à la cantine? / Mange-t-il à la cantine?*
2. J'oublie les examens. *Est-ce que tu oublies les examens? / Oublies-tu les examens?*
3. François déteste les maths. *Est-ce que François déteste les maths? / François déteste-t-il les maths?*
4. Nous adorons voyager. *Est-ce que vous adorez voyager? / Adorez-vous voyager?*
5. Les cours ne commencent pas demain. *Est-ce que les cours ne commencent pas demain? / Les cours ne commencent-ils pas demain?*
6. Les élèves arrivent en classe. *Est-ce que les élèves arrivent en classe? / Les élèves arrivent-ils/elles en classe?*

3 **Complétez** Complete the conversation with the correct questions for the answers given. Act it out with a partner. *Suggested answers*

MYLÈNE Salut, Arnaud. Ça va?
ARNAUD Oui, ça va. Alors (*So*)... (1) _Tu aimes les cours?_
MYLÈNE J'adore le cours de sciences po, mais je déteste l'informatique.
ARNAUD (2) _Pourquoi est-ce que tu détestes l'informatique?_
MYLÈNE Parce que le prof est très strict.
ARNAUD (3) _Il y a des élèves sympathiques, n'est-ce pas?_
MYLÈNE Oui, il y a des élèves sympathiques... Et demain? (4) _Tu retrouves Béatrice?_
ARNAUD Peut-être, mais demain je retrouve aussi Dominique.
MYLÈNE (5) _Tu cherches une petite amie?_
ARNAUD Pas du tout!

---

1 Expansion Have students work in pairs, and take turns asking and answering the questions in the negative.

2 Expansion Have students write two additional statements. Tell them to exchange papers with a partner who will ask the questions that would elicit those statements.

3 Expansion Have pairs of students create a similar conversation, replacing the answers and some of the questions with information that is true for them. Then have volunteers act out their conversations for the class.

TEACHING OPTIONS

Large Groups Divide the class into two groups, A and B. Give each member of group A a strip of paper with a question on it, and each member of group B an appropriate answer. Ex A: **André adore la biologie?** Ex B: **Oui, il adore la biologie.** Have students find their partners. Be sure that each question has only one possible answer.

EXPANSION

Interview Have pairs of students write a questionnaire of about 5-6 items and practice interviewing a classmate. For example: **Tu habites à _____? Est-ce que tu parles français?** The interviewee should respond with complete sentences. For example: **Oui, j'habite à _____. Oui, je parle français/Non, je ne parle pas français.** Students should be ready to perform their interviews in front of the class.

Communication

4 Au café In pairs, take turns asking each other questions about the drawing. Use verbs from the list. *Answers will vary.*

MODÈLE

Élève 1: *Monsieur Laurent parle à Madame Martin, n'est-ce pas?*
Élève 2: *Mais non. Il déteste parler!*

arriver	dessiner	manger	partager
chercher	étudier	oublier	rencontrer

Anne et Sylvie — Didier — André — Madame Martin — Monsieur Laurent

5 Questions You and your partner want to get to know each other better. Take turns asking each other questions. Modify or add elements as needed. *Some answers will vary.*

MODÈLE aimer / l'art
Élève 1: *Est-ce que tu aimes l'art?*
Élève 2: *Oui, j'adore l'art.*

1. détester / devoirs   *Est-ce que tu détestes les devoirs?*
2. étudier / avec / amis   *Est-ce que tu étudies avec des amis?*
3. penser qu'il y a / cours / intéressant / au lycée   *Est-ce que tu penses qu'il y a des cours intéressants au lycée?*
4. cours de sciences / être / facile   *Est-ce que les cours de sciences sont faciles?*
5. aimer mieux / biologie / ou / physique   *Est-ce que tu aimes mieux la biologie ou la physique?*
6. retrouver / copains / à la cantine   *Est-ce que tu retrouves des copains à la cantine?*

6 Confirmez In groups of three, confirm whether the statements are true of your school. Correct any untrue statements by making them negative. *Answers will vary.*

MODÈLE

Les profs sont désagréables.
Pas du tout, les profs ne sont pas désagréables.

1. Les cours d'informatique sont inutiles.
2. Il y a des élèves de nationalité allemande.
3. Nous mangeons une cuisine excellente à la cantine.
4. Tous (*All*) les élèves étudient à la bibliothèque.
5. Le cours de chimie est facile.
6. Nous adorons le gymnase.

soixante et un **61**

---

4 Suggestion Tell students to vary the method of asking questions instead of always using a tag question as in the **modèle**.

5 Suggestions
- Have two volunteers read the **modèle** aloud.
- After students have completed the activity, ask volunteers to report what they learned about their partner.

6 Suggestion Encourage students to use as many expressions indicating agreement or disagreement as they can.

6 Expansion Have groups write three additional true/false statements about your school. Ask several groups to read their statements and have the class respond to them. Encourage students to respond with **Mais oui!** or **Mais non!** where appropriate.

EXPANSION

Have students write six sentences containing two parts connected by the word **mais** (*but*). The first part of the sentence should be affirmative and the second part negative. Ex. **J'aime la biologie mais je n'aime pas les maths.** Encourage students to share their sentences in small groups.

EXPANSION

Video Replay the video episode, having students focus on the different forms of questions used. Tell them to write down each question they hear. Stop the video where suitable to give students time to write and to discuss what was heard.

Synthèse — Leçon 2A

Révision

1 Des styles différents In pairs, compare these two very different classes. Then, tell your partner which class you prefer and why. *Answers will vary.*

2 Les activités In pairs, discuss whether these expressions apply to both of you. React to every answer you hear. *Answers will vary.*

MODÈLE

Élève 1: Est-ce que tu étudies le week-end?
Élève 2: Non! Je n'aime pas étudier le week-end.
Élève 1: Moi non plus. J'aime mieux étudier le soir.

1. adorer la cantine
2. aimer le cours d'art
3. étudier à la bibliothèque
4. manger souvent (*often*) des sushis
5. oublier les devoirs
6. parler espagnol
7. travailler le soir
8. voyager souvent

3 Le lycée In pairs, prepare ten questions inspired by the list and what you know about your school. Together, survey as many classmates as possible to find out what they like and dislike. *Answers will vary.*

MODÈLE

Élève 1: Est-ce que tu aimes étudier à la bibliothèque?
Élève 2: Non, pas trop. J'aime mieux étudier…

bibliothèque	élève	cantine
bureau	gymnase	salle de classe
cours	librairie	salle d'ordinateurs

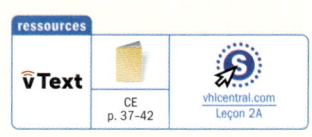

ressources
vText
CE p. 37–42
vhlcentral.com
Leçon 2A

4 Pourquoi? Survey as many classmates as possible to find out if they like these subjects and why. Ask what adjective they would pick to describe them. Tally the most popular answers for each subject. *Answers will vary.*

MODÈLE

Élève 1: Est-ce que tu aimes la philosophie?
Élève 2: Pas tellement.
Élève 1: Pourquoi?
Élève 2: Parce que c'est trop difficile.

1. la biologie
2. la chimie
3. l'histoire
4. l'éducation physique
5. l'informatique
6. les langues
7. les mathématiques
8. la psychologie

a. agréable
b. amusant
c. désagréable
d. difficile
e. facile
f. important
g. inutile
h. utile

5 Les conversations In pairs, act out a short conversation between the people shown in each drawing. They should greet each other, describe what they are doing, and discuss their likes or dislikes. Choose your favorite skit and role-play it for another pair. *Answers will vary.*

MODÈLE

Élève 1: Bonjour, Aurélie.
Élève 2: Salut! Tu travailles, n'est-ce pas?

6 Les portraits Your teacher will give you and a partner a set of drawings showing the likes and dislikes of eight people. Discuss each person's tastes. Do not look at each other's worksheet. *Answers will vary.*

MODÈLE

Élève 1: Sarah n'aime pas travailler.
Élève 2: Mais elle adore manger.

soixante-deux

Au lycée — Unité 2

Le Zapping
Video: TV Clip

À vos marques, prêts°... étudiez!

The University of Moncton was founded in 1963 and is the largest French-speaking university in Canada outside Quebec. Its three campuses of Edmunston, Moncton, and Shippagan are located in New Brunswick. Students come from the local Francophone region of Acadia, from other Canadian provinces, and from countries around the world such as Guinea, Haiti, and Morocco.

The mission of the University of Moncton is not only to foster the academic development of these students but also to offer them a nurturing environment that will encourage their personal and social growth.

On n'apprend° pas seulement° dans les classes.

Mon université.

Compréhension Answer these questions. *Answers will vary.*

1. What are the three kinds of activities offered at the University of Moncton?
   Suggested answer: social activities, cultural activities, and sports.
2. Give examples of each type of activity. *Answers will vary.*
3. Where does learning take place at the University of Moncton?
   Suggested answer: in class, in labs, and in the field.
4. Do students receive a lot of attention from their professors? Explain.
   Suggested answer: The professors use a personalized approach and spend a lot of time working with their students.

Discussion In pairs, discuss the answers to these questions. *Answers will vary.*

1. What are the University of Moncton's strengths?
2. Would you like to study there once you graduate from high school? Explain.

À vos marques, prêts *Ready, set* apprend *learn* seulement *only*

Practice more at vhlcentral.com.

soixante-trois 63

Section Goals
In this section, students will:
- read about the University of Moncton
- watch a video about the University of Moncton
- answer questions about the University of Moncton

Key Standards
1.2, 2.2, 4.2, 5.2

Student Resources
Supersite: Video, Activities
Teacher Resources
Video Script & Translation; Supersite: Video

Introduction
To check students' comprehension, ask these questions.
1. How is the University of Moncton described? (It is a welcoming and dynamic environment that fosters success.)
2. What are students able to do at the University of Moncton? (They are able to put what they learn into practice thanks to modern labs and equipment.)
3. Do students enjoy their experience at the University of Moncton? (Yes, they describe it as one of their best memories.)

PRE-AP®

Audiovisual Interpretive Communication Previewing Strategy
- Have students look at the video stills, read the captions, and predict what will be featured in the video.
- Before showing the video, explain to students that they do not need to understand every word they hear. Tell them to listen for cognates and school-related vocabulary.

Compréhension Have pairs come up with a slogan for the University of Moncton and share it with the class.

Discussion Have students compare the University of Moncton to a typical university in your area and make a list of differences and/or similarities between the two institutions. Examples: À l'université de Moncton, il y a... et ils étudient... Ici, à [name of school in your area], il n'y a pas... mais il y a... Les étudiants n'étudient pas... mais ils étudient...

EXPANSION

L'Université de Moncton The University of Moncton is Canada's largest French-language university in New Brunswick. It offers 160 programs in a variety of fields, such as education, engineering, administration, nursing, social work, law, and sciences.

There are over 6,200 students enrolled at the University of Moncton, which is known for its high-quality personalized teaching style.

63

Contextes

Leçon 2B

You will learn how to...
- say when things happen
- discuss your schedule

🔊 **Audio:** Vocabulary Practice
My Vocabulary

Une semaine au lycée

Vocabulaire

demander	to ask
échouer	to fail
écouter	to listen (to)
enseigner	to teach
expliquer	to explain
trouver	to find; to think
Quel jour sommes-nous?	What day is it?
un an	year
une/cette année	one/this year
après	after
après-demain	day after tomorrow
un/cet après-midi	an/this afternoon
aujourd'hui	today
demain (matin/ après-midi/soir)	tomorrow (morning/ afternoon/evening)
un jour	day
une journée	day
un/ce matin	a/this morning
la matinée	morning
un mois/ce mois-ci	month/this month
une/cette nuit	a/this night
une/cette semaine	a/this week
un/ce soir	an/this evening
une soirée	evening
un/le/ce week-end	a/the/this weekend
dernier/dernière	last
premier/première	first
prochain(e)	next

semaine

lundi | mardi | mercredi | jeudi | vendredi

matin — après-midi — soir

- assister au cours d'économie
- passer l'examen de maths
- téléphoner à Marc
- préparer l'examen de maths
- dîner en famille

ressources

vText
CE pp. 43–45

vhlcentral.com
Leçon 2B

64 soixante-quatre

Section Goals
In this section, students will learn and practice vocabulary related to:
- talking about schedules
- the days of the week
- sequencing events

Key Standards
1.1, 1.2, 4.1

Student Resources
Cahier de l'élève, pp. 43–45;
Supersite: Activities,
eCahier

Teacher Resources
Answer Keys; Digital Image Bank; Audio Script; Textbook & Audio Activity MP3s/CD; Activity Pack; Testing program: Vocabulary Quiz

Suggestions
- Write days of the week across the board and present them like this: **Aujourd'hui, c'est ____. Demain, c'est ____. Après-demain, c'est ____?**
- Write the following questions and answers on the board, explaining their meaning:
  —**Quel jour sommes-nous?**
  —**Nous sommes ____.**
  —**C'est quel jour demain?**
  —**Demain, c'est ____.**
  —**C'est quand l'examen?**
  —**L'examen est ____.**
  Ask students the questions.
- Tell students Monday is the first day of the week in France.
- Point out that days of the week are masculine and lowercase.
- Explain the differences between **le matin/la matinée, le soir/la soirée,** and **le jour/ la journée.**
- Introduce new vocabulary using the digital image for this page. Give the student a name, for example, Henri. Ask students picture-based questions. Examples: **Quel jour Henri assiste-t-il au cours d'économie? Il assiste au cours d'économie le matin ou le soir? Quels jours visite-t-il Paris avec Annette?**
- Point out that **visiter** is used with places, not people.

EXPANSION

Categories Write **le matin, l'après-midi,** and **le soir** on the board or a transparency. Have your students tell when they do various activities, such as **préparer les cours, assister aux cours, téléphoner à des amis, écouter de la musique, regarder la télévision, rentrer à la maison,** and **dîner.**

TEACHING OPTIONS

Brainstorming Have the class brainstorm a list of nouns associated with verbs from **Contextes**. For example, for the verb **regarder**, students might think of **télévision** or **vidéo**. Write the verbs and nouns on the board as students say them. Then have students work in pairs. Give them five minutes to write original sentences using these words. Ask volunteers to write their sentences on the board.

64 Unit 2 • Lesson 2B

Au lycée — Unité 2

Mise en pratique

1 **Écoutez** You will hear Lorraine describing her schedule. Listen carefully and indicate whether the statements are **vrai** or **faux**.

	Vrai	Faux
1. Lorraine étudie à l'université le soir.	☐	☑
2. Elle trouve le cours de mathématiques facile.	☐	☑
3. Elle étudie le week-end.	☐	☑
4. Lorraine étudie la chimie le mardi et le jeudi matin.	☐	☑
5. Le professeur de mathématiques explique bien.	☐	☑
6. Lorraine regarde la télévision, écoute de la musique ou téléphone à Claire et Anne le soir.	☑	☐
7. Lorraine travaille dans (*in*) une librairie.	☐	☑
8. Elle étudie l'histoire le mardi et le jeudi matin.	☑	☐
9. Lorraine adore dîner avec sa famille le week-end.	☑	☐
10. Lorraine rentre à la maison le soir.	☐	☑

2 **La classe de Mme Arnaud** Complete this paragraph by selecting the correct verb from the list below. Make sure to conjugate the verb. Some verbs will not be used.

demander	expliquer	rentrer
écouter	passer un examen	travailler
enseigner	préparer	trouver
étudier	regarder	visiter

Madame Arnaud (1) _travaille_ au lycée. Elle (2) _enseigne_ le français. Elle (3) _explique_ les verbes et la grammaire aux élèves. Le vendredi, en classe, les élèves (4) _regardent_ une vidéo en français ou (*or*) (5) _écoutent_ de la musique française. Ce week-end, ils (6) _étudient/travaillent_ pour (*for*) (7) _préparer_ l'examen très difficile de lundi matin. Je/J' (8) _travaille/étudie_ beaucoup pour ce cours, mais mes (*my*) amis et moi, nous (9) _trouvons_ la classe sympa.

3 **Quel jour sommes-nous?** Complete each statement with the correct day of the week.

1. Aujourd'hui, c'est _Answers will vary._
2. Demain, c'est _Answers will vary._
3. Après-demain, c'est _Answers will vary._
4. Le week-end, c'est _le samedi et le dimanche_.
5. Le premier jour de la semaine en France, c'est _le lundi_.
6. Les jours du cours de français sont _Answers will vary._
7. Mon (*My*) jour préféré de la semaine, c'est _Answers will vary._
8. Je travaille à la bibliothèque _Answers will vary._

Attention!
Use the masculine definite article **le** + [day of the week] when an activity is done on a weekly basis. Omit **le** when it is done on a specific day.
Le prof enseigne le lundi.
The teacher teaches on Mondays.
Je passe un examen lundi.
I'm taking a test on Monday.

Contextes — Leçon 2B

Communication

4 Conversez Interview a classmate. *Answers will vary.*
1. Quel jour sommes-nous?
2. Quand (*When*) est le prochain cours de français?
3. Quand rentres-tu à la maison?
4. Est-ce que tu prépares un examen cette année?
5. Est-ce que tu écoutes la radio? Quel genre de musique aimes-tu?
6. Quand téléphones-tu à des amis?
7. Est-ce que tu regardes la télévision l'après-midi ou (*or*) le soir?
8. Est-ce que tu dînes dans un restaurant ce mois-ci?

5 Le premier jour You make a new friend in your French class and want to know what his or her class schedule is like this semester. With a partner, prepare a conversation to perform for the class where you: *Answers will vary.*
- ask his or her name
- ask what classes he or she is taking
- ask on which days of the week he or she has French class
- ask at which times of day (morning or afternoon) he or she has English and History classes

6 Bataille navale Your teacher will give you a worksheet. Choose four spaces on your chart and mark them with a battleship. In pairs, formulate questions by using the subjects in the first column and the verbs in the first row to find out where your partner has placed his or her battleships. Whoever "sinks" the most battleships wins. *Answers will vary.*

MODÈLE
Élève 1: *Est-ce que Luc et Sabine téléphonent à Jérôme?*
Élève 2: *Oui, ils téléphonent à Jérôme.*
(if you marked that square)
Non, ils ne téléphonent pas à Jérôme.
(if you didn't mark that square)

	enseigner	téléphoner
Marie		
Luc et Sabine		🚢

7 Le week-end Write a schedule to show what you do during a typical weekend. Use the verbs you know. Compare your schedule with a classmate's, and talk about the different activities that you do and when. Be prepared to discuss your results with the class. *Answers will vary.*

	Moi	Nom
Le vendredi soir 🌙		
Le samedi matin ☀		
Le samedi après-midi ☀		
Le samedi soir 🌙		
Le dimanche matin ☀		
Le dimanche après-midi ☀		
Le dimanche soir 🌙		

soixante-six

---

4 Suggestion Before doing this activity, you may want to write a short list of musical genres on the board for item 5. Also tell students that **quand** means *when*.

4 Expansions
- Have volunteers report what they learned about their classmate.
- To practice the **nous** forms, ask students what they have in common with their partner.

4 Virtual Chat You can assign Activity 4 on the Supersite. Students record individual responses that appear in your gradebook.

5 Suggestion Tell students to switch roles after completing the conversation so that both students have the opportunity to ask and answer questions.

6 Suggestions
- Have two volunteers read the **modèle** aloud. Make sure students understand the directions. Then distribute the **Feuilles d'activités** from the Activity Pack.
- Have students repeat the activity with a different partner.

7 Suggestion To save time in class, assign the written part of this activity the day before as homework.

EXPANSION

Using Games Play a memory game in which the first player says one activity he or she does on a particular day of the week. The next player repeats what the first person said, then adds what he or she does on the following day. The third player must remember what the first two people said before saying what he or she does on the next day. Continue until the end of a week. If someone makes a mistake, then choose another student to continue.

TEACHING OPTIONS

Oral Practice Have students work in groups of three. Tell them to take turns asking and answering what days of the week different TV shows are on. Example: **Quel(s) jour(s) est la série *CSI*?**

Au lycée Unité 2

Les sons et les lettres

🎧 **The letter r**

Audio: Explanation
Record & Compare

The French **r** is very different from the English *r*. The English *r* is pronounced by placing the tongue in the middle and toward the front of the mouth. The French **r** is pronounced in the throat. You have seen that an **-er** at the end of a word is usually pronounced *-ay*, as in the English word *way*, but without the glide sound.

| chant**er** | mang**er** | expliqu**er** | aim**er** |

In most other cases, the French **r** has a very different sound. Pronunciation of the French **r** varies according to its position in a word. Note the different ways the **r** is pronounced in these words.

| ri**v**iè**r**e | litté**r**ature | o**r**dinateu**r** | devoi**r** |

If an **r** falls between two vowels or before a vowel, it is pronounced with slightly more friction.

| **r**a**r**e | ga**r**age | Eu**r**ope | **r**ose |

An **r** sound before a consonant or at the end of a word is pronounced with slightly less friction.

| po**r**te | bou**r**se | ado**r**e | jou**r** |

Prononcez Practice saying these words aloud.

1. crayon
2. professeur
3. plaisir
4. différent
5. terrible
6. architecture
7. trouver
8. restaurant
9. rentrer
10. regarder
11. lettres
12. réservé
13. être
14. dernière
15. arriver
16. après

Articulez Practice saying these sentences aloud.

1. Au revoir, Professeur Colbert!
2. Rose arrive en retard mardi.
3. Mercredi, c'est le dernier jour des cours.
4. Robert et Roger adorent écouter la radio.
5. La corbeille à papier, c'est quarante-quatre euros!
6. Les parents de Richard sont brillants et très agréables.

Dictons Practice reading these sayings aloud.

Qui ne risque rien n'a rien.[1]

Quand le renard prêche, gare aux oies.[2]

[1] Nothing ventured, nothing gained.
[2] When the fox preaches, watch your geese.

soixante-sept 67

Section Goals

In this section, students will learn functional phrases for talking about their schedules and classes and telling time.

Key Standards

1.2, 2.1, 2.2, 4.1, 4.2

Student Resources
Cahier de l'élève, pp. 47–48; Supersite: Activities, *eCahier*

Teacher Resources
Answer Keys; Video Script & Translation; *Roman-photo* video

Video Recap: Leçon 2A
Before doing this **Roman-photo**, review the previous one with this activity.

1. **Comment est-ce que Rachid trouve le cours de sciences po?** (intéressant et utile)
2. **Comment s'appelle le colocataire de Rachid?** (David)
3. **Comment est-ce que David trouve l'université française?** (C'est différent de l'université américaine, mais c'est intéressant.)
4. **Quels cours est-ce que David aime?** (littérature et histoire françaises)
5. **Stéphane a des problèmes dans quels cours?** (français, maths, chimie et histoire-géo)

Video Synopsis
At **Le P'tit Bistrot**, Rachid, Sandrine, Amina and David discuss their schedules. Astrid arrives; she is supposed to study with Stéphane. While she waits, Astrid talks about **le bac** and how Stéphane never does his homework. Rachid and Astrid decide to go to the park because they think Stéphane is there. At the park, Astrid and Stéphane argue. When Stéphane complains about his problems at school, Rachid offers to help him study.

Suggestions
- Have volunteers play the roles of Rachid, Sandrine, Amina, David, and Astrid in the scenes that match video stills 1–5.
- Have the class predict what will happen in scenes 6–10. Write predictions on the board.
- Read remaining scenes correcting the predictions. Ask questions to help students summarize this episode.

Unit 2 • Lesson 2B

Roman-photo — Leçon 2B

On trouve une solution

Video: *Roman-photo*
Record & Compare

PERSONNAGES

Amina
Astrid
David
Rachid
Sandrine
Stéphane

À la terrasse du café...
RACHID Alors, on a rendez-vous avec David demain à cinq heures moins le quart pour rentrer chez nous.
SANDRINE Aujourd'hui, c'est mercredi. Demain... jeudi. Le mardi et le jeudi, j'ai cours de chant de trois heures vingt à quatre heures et demie. C'est parfait!
AMINA Pas de problème. J'ai cours de stylisme...

AMINA Salut, Astrid!
ASTRID Bonjour.
RACHID Astrid, je te présente David, mon (*my*) coloc américain.
DAVID Alors, cette année, tu as des cours très difficiles, n'est-ce pas?

ASTRID Oui? Pourquoi?
DAVID Ben, Stéphane pense que les cours sont très difficiles.
ASTRID Ouais, Stéphane, il assiste au cours, mais... il ne fait pas ses (*his*) devoirs et il n'écoute pas les profs. Cette année est très importante, parce que nous avons le bac...
DAVID Ah, le bac...

Au parc...
ASTRID Stéphane! Quelle heure est-il? Tu n'as pas de montre?
STÉPHANE Oh, Astrid, excuse-moi! Le mercredi, je travaille avec Astrid au café sur le cours de maths...
ASTRID Et le mercredi après-midi, il oublie! Tu n'as pas peur du bac, toi!

STÉPHANE Tu as tort, j'ai très peur du bac! Mais je n'ai pas envie de passer mes (*my*) journées, mes soirées et mes week-ends avec des livres!
ASTRID Je suis d'accord avec toi, Stéphane! J'ai envie de passer les week-ends avec mes copains... des copains qui n'oublient pas les rendez-vous!

RACHID Écoute, Stéphane, tu as des problèmes avec ta (*your*) mère, avec Astrid aussi.
STÉPHANE Oui, et j'ai d'énormes problèmes au lycée. Je déteste le bac.
RACHID Il n'est pas tard pour commencer à travailler pour être reçu au bac.
STÉPHANE Tu crois, Rachid?

A C T I V I T É S

1 Vrai ou faux? Choose whether each statement is **vrai** or **faux**. Correct the false statements.
Answers may vary slightly.

1. Le mardi et le mercredi, Sandrine a (*has*) cours de chant. Faux. Sandrine a cours de chant le mardi et le jeudi.
2. Le jeudi, Amina a cours de stylisme. Vrai.
3. Astrid pense qu'il est impossible de réussir (*pass*) le bac. Faux. Astrid pense que ce n'est pas impossible.
4. La famille de David est allemande. Faux. La famille de David est française.
5. Le mercredi, Stéphane travaille avec Astrid au café sur le cours de maths. Vrai.
6. Stéphane a beaucoup de problèmes. Vrai.
7. Rachid est optimiste. Vrai.
8. Stéphane dîne chez Rachid samedi. Faux. Stéphane dîne chez Rachid dimanche.
9. Le sport est très important pour Stéphane. Vrai.
10. Astrid est fâchée (*angry*) contre Stéphane. Vrai.

Practice more at vhlcentral.com.

68 soixante-huit

TEACHING OPTIONS

On trouve une solution Write the title **On trouve une solution** on the board. Ask the class: Who has a problem in the video? What is it? Then ask the class to predict how the problem will be solved.

TEACHING OPTIONS

Regarder la vidéo Show the video episode and have students give you a play-by-play description of the action. Write their descriptions on the board. Then show the episode again so students can add more details to the description.

Au lycée — Unité 2

Les amis organisent des rendez-vous.

RACHID C'est un examen très important que les élèves français passent la dernière année de lycée pour continuer en études supérieures.
DAVID Euh, n'oublie pas, je suis de famille française.
ASTRID Oui, et c'est difficile, mais ce n'est pas impossible. Stéphane trouve que les études ne sont pas intéressantes. Le sport, oui, mais pas les études.

RACHID Le sport? Tu cherches Stéphane, n'est-ce pas? On trouve Stéphane au parc! Allons-y, Astrid.
ASTRID D'accord. À demain!

RACHID Oui. Mais le sport, c'est la dernière des priorités. Écoute, dimanche prochain, tu dînes chez moi et on trouve une solution.
STÉPHANE Rachid, tu n'as pas envie de donner des cours à un lycéen nul comme moi!
RACHID Mais si, j'ai très envie d'enseigner les maths...

STÉPHANE Bon, j'accepte. Merci, Rachid. C'est sympa.
RACHID De rien. À plus tard!

Expressions utiles

Talking about your schedule

- Alors, on a rendez-vous demain à cinq heures moins le quart pour rentrer chez nous.
  So, we're meeting tomorrow at quarter to five to go home (our home).
- J'ai cours de chant de trois heures vingt à quatre heures et demie.
  I have voice (singing) class from three-twenty to four-thirty.
- J'ai cours de stylisme de deux heures à quatre heures vingt.
  I have fashion design class from two o'clock to four-twenty.
- Quelle heure est-il?   • Tu n'as pas de montre?
  What time is it?   You don't have a watch?

Talking about school

- Nous avons le bac.
  We have the bac.
- Il ne fait pas ses devoirs.
  He doesn't do his homework.
- Tu n'as pas peur du bac!
  You're not afraid of the bac!
- Tu as tort, j'ai très peur du bac!
  You're wrong, I'm very afraid of the bac!
- Je suis d'accord avec toi.
  I agree with you.
- J'ai d'énormes problèmes.
  I have big/enormous problems.
- Tu n'as pas envie de donner des cours à un(e) lycéen(ne) nul(le) comme moi.
  You don't want to teach a high school student as bad as myself.

Useful expressions

- C'est parfait!   • Ouais.
  That's perfect!   Yeah.
- Allons-y!   • C'est sympa.
  Let's go!   That's nice/fun.
- D'accord.
  OK./All right.

ACTIVITÉS

2 Répondez Answer these questions. Refer to the video scenes and use a dictionary as necessary. You do not have to answer in complete sentences. *Answers will vary.*

1. Où est-ce que tu as envie de voyager?
2. Est-ce que tu as peur de quelque chose? De quoi?
3. Qu'est-ce que tu dis (*say*) quand tu as tort?

3 À vous! With a partner, describe someone you know whose personality, likes, or dislikes resemble those of Rachid or Stéphane.

MODÈLE
Paul est comme (*like*) Rachid... il est sérieux.

ressources: vText • CE pp. 47–48 • vhlcentral.com Leçon 2B

soixante-neuf **69**

Culture

Lecon 2B

CULTURE À LA LOUPE

Le bac

The three years of lycée **culminate in a high-stakes exam called the** baccalauréat **or** bac. Students begin preparing for this exam by the end of **seconde** (10th grade), when they must decide the type of **bac** they will take. This choice determines their coursework during the last two years of **lycée**; for example, a student who plans to take the **bac S** will study mainly physics, chemistry, and math. Most students take **le bac économique et social (ES), le bac littéraire (L),** or **le bac scientifique (S)**. Others, though, choose to follow a more technical path, for example **le bac sciences et technologies de l'industrie et du développement durable (STI2D) le bac sciences et technologies de la santé et du social (ST2S),** or **le bac sciences et technologies du management et de la gestion (STMG)** There is even a **bac technique** for hotel management, and music/dance!

The **bac** has both oral and written sections, which are weighted differently according to the type of **bac**. This means that, for example, a bad grade on the math section would lower a student's grade significantly on a **bac S** but to a lesser degree on a **bac L**. In all cases the highest possible grade is 20/20. If a student's overall score on the **bac** is below 10/20 (the minimum passing grade) but above 8/20, he/she can take the **rattrapage**, or make-up exam. If the student fails again, then he/she can **redoubler**, or repeat the school year and take the **bac** again.

Students usually go to find out their results with friends and classmates just a few days after they take the exam. This yearly ritual is full of emotion: it's common to see groups of students frantically looking for their results posted on bulletin boards at the **lycée**. Over 80% of students successfully pass the **bac** every year, granting them access to France's higher education system.

Students can pass the bac with:

18/20 - 20/20	mention Très bien et félicitations du jury
16/20 - 18/20	mention Très bien
14/20 - 16/20	mention Bien
12/20 - 14/20	mention Assez bien
10/20 - 12/20	no special mention

Coup de main

In French, a superscript -e following a numeral tells you that it is an ordinal number. It is the equivalent of a -th after a numeral in English: 10e (dixième) = 10th.

1 Vrai ou faux? Indicate whether each statement is **vrai** or **faux**.

1. The **bac** is an exam that students take at the end of **terminale**.
   Vrai.
2. The **bac** has only oral exams.
   Faux. It also has written exams.
3. The highest possible grade on the **bac** is 20/20.
   Vrai.
4. Students decide which **bac** they will take at the beginning of **terminale**.
   Faux. Students must decide which bac they will take by the end of seconde.
5. Most students take the **bac technique**.
   Faux. Most students take le bac ES, le bac L, or le bac S.
6. All the grades of the **bac** are weighted equally.
   Faux. The different sections are weighted differently in each bac.
7. A student with an average grade of 14.5 on the **bac** receives his diploma with **mention bien**.
   Vrai.
8. A student who fails the **bac** but has an overall grade of 8/20 can take a make-up exam.
   Vrai.
9. A student who fails the **bac** and the **rattrapage** cannot repeat the year.
   Faux. He can repeat the year and attempt the bac again.
10. Passing the **bac** enables students to register for college or to apply for the **grandes écoles**.
    Vrai.

Practice more at **vhlcentral.com.**

70 soixante-dix

Au lycée Unité 2

LE FRANÇAIS QUOTIDIEN

Les examens

assurer/cartonner (à un examen)	to ace (an exam)
bachoter	to cram for the *bac*
bosser	to work hard
une moyenne	an average
rater (un examen)	to fail (an exam)
réviser	to study, to review
un(e) surveillant(e)	a proctor
tricher	to cheat

LE MONDE FRANCOPHONE

Le français langue étrangère

Voici quelques° écoles du monde francophone où vous pouvez étudier° le français.

En Belgique Université de Liège

En France Université de Franche-Comté–Centre de linguistique appliquée, Université de Grenoble, Université de Paris IV-Sorbonne

À la Martinique Institut Supérieur d'Études Francophones, à Schoelcher

En Nouvelle-Calédonie Centre de Rencontres et d'Échanges Internationaux du Pacifique, à Nouméa

Au Québec Université Laval, Université de Montréal

Aux îles Saint-Pierre et Miquelon Le FrancoForum, à Saint-Pierre

En Suisse Université Populaire de Lausanne, Université de Neuchâtel

quelques some   *où vous pouvez étudier* where you can study

PORTRAIT

Les études supérieures en France

Après qu'ils passent le bac, les étudiants français ont le choix° de plusieurs° types d'étude: les meilleurs° entrent en classe préparatoire pour passer les concours d'entrée aux° grandes écoles. Les grandes écoles forment l'élite de l'enseignement supérieur en France. Les plus connues° sont l'ENA (école nationale d'administration), Polytechnique, HEC (école des hautes études commerciales) et Sciences Po (institut des sciences politiques). Certains étudiants choisissent° une école spécialisée, comme une école de commerce ou de journalisme. Ces écoles proposent une formation° et un diplôme très spécifiques. L'autre° possibilité est l'entrée à l'université. Les étudiants d'université se spécialisent dans un domaine dès° la première année. Les études universitaires durent° trois ou quatre ans en général, et plus pour un doctorat.

choix choice *plusieurs* several *meilleurs* best *concours d'entrée aux* entrance tests to the *plus connues* most well known *choisissent* choose *formation* education *autre* other *dès* starting in *durent* last

Sur Internet

Quel (*Which*) bac aimeriez-vous (*would you like*) passer?

Go to vhlcentral.com to find more information related to this **Culture** section.

---

2 Les études supérieures en France What kind of higher education might these students seek?

1. Une future journaliste   une école spécialisée
2. Un élève exceptionnel   une grande école
3. Une étudiante en anglais   l'université
4. Un étudiant en affaires   une école spécialisée
5. Un étudiant de chimie   l'université

3 Et les cours? In French, name two courses you might take in preparation for each of these **baccalauréat** exams.   *Answers will vary. Possible answers shown.*

1. un bac L   le français et la philosophie
2. un bac STMG   la biologie et la psychologie
3. un bac ES   l'économie et la sociologie
4. un bac STI2D   la physique et les maths

soixante et onze 71

Section Goals

In this section, students will learn:
- the verb **avoir**
- some common expressions with **avoir**

Key Standards

4.1, 5.1

Student Resources
Cahier de l'élève, pp. 49–51; Supersite: Activities, *eCahier* Grammar Tutorials

Teacher Resources
Answer Keys; Audio Script; Audio Activity MP3s/ CD; Activity Pack; Testing program: Grammar Quiz

Suggestions

- Model **avoir** by asking questions such as: **Avez-vous un examen cette semaine? Avez-vous une calculatrice? ____ a-t-il/elle une calculatrice?** Point out that forms of **avoir** were in the **Roman-photo**.
- Explain that **avoir** is irregular and must be memorized. Begin a paradigm for **avoir** by writing **j'ai** on the board and asking volunteers questions that elicit **j'ai**. Examples: **J'ai un stylo. Qui a un crayon?**
- Add **tu as** and **il/elle/on a** to the paradigm on the board. Point out that **as** and **a** are pronounced alike. Tell students that **avoir** has no real stem apart from the letter **a**.
- Write **nous avons** and **vous avez**. Point out that **-ons** and **-ez** are the same endings as in **-er** verbs. Add **ils/elles ont**.
- Remind students of liaisons in the plural forms of **avoir** and have them pronounce these forms.

Structures — Leçon 2B

2B.1 Present tense of *avoir*

Presentation Grammar Tutorial

Point de départ The verb **avoir** (*to have*) is used frequently. You will have to memorize each of its present tense forms because they are irregular.

Present tense of *avoir*

j'ai	I have		nous avons	we have
tu as	you have		vous avez	you have
il/elle/on a	he/she/it/one has		ils/elles ont	they have

On a rendez-vous avec David demain.

Cette année, nous avons le bac.

- Liaison is required between the final consonants of **on**, **nous**, **vous**, **ils**, and **elles** and the first vowel of forms of **avoir** that follow them. When the final consonant is an **-s**, pronounce it as a z before the verb forms.

  On a un prof sympa.
  We have a nice teacher.

  Nous avons un cours d'art.
  We have an art class.

  Vous avez deux stylos.
  You have two pens.

  Elles ont un examen de psychologie.
  They have a Psychology exam.

- Keep in mind that an indefinite article, whether singular or plural, usually becomes **de/d'** after a negation.

  J'ai **un** cours difficile.
  I have a difficult class.

  Je n'ai pas **de** cours difficile.
  I don't have a difficult class.

  Il a **des** examens.
  He has exams.

  Il n'a pas **d'**examens.
  He does not have exams.

72 *soixante-douze*

EXPANSION

Inventory Have students write a list of items they have in their backpacks and share the list with a classmate. Ex. **J'ai un dictionnaire, j'ai un livre...** Then have them tell the class what their classmates have: **Il/Elle a un stylo, Il/Elle a un cahier...** They should also draw conclusions on the objects they have in common. Ex. **Nous avons des livres. Nous avons trois stylos...**

TEACHING OPTIONS

Extra Practice Write eight sentences containing liaisons on the board and model their pronunciation for students. Then, have them repeat the sentences after you out loud. Ex. **Nous avons froid. Ils ont des crayons.** Finally, ask students to write similar sentences and exchange them with one of their classmates for them to practice liaisons. Ask them to read some of their sentences out loud and correct their pronunciation.

72 Unit 2 • Lesson 2B

Au lycée — Unité 2

- The verb **avoir** is used in certain idiomatic or set expressions where English generally uses *to be* or *to feel*.

Expressions with *avoir*

avoir... ans	to be... years old	avoir froid	to be cold
avoir besoin (de)	to need	avoir honte (de)	to be ashamed (of)
avoir de la chance	to be lucky	avoir l'air	to look like, to seem
avoir chaud	to be hot	avoir peur (de)	to be afraid (of)
avoir envie (de)	to feel like	avoir raison	to be right
		avoir sommeil	to be sleepy
		avoir tort	to be wrong

Boîte à outils

In the expression **avoir l'air** + [*adjective*], the adjective does not change to agree with the subject. It is always masculine singular, because it agrees with **air**. Examples:

Elle a l'air charmant.
She looks charming.

Ils ont l'air content.
They look happy.

Il a chaud. Ils ont froid.

Elle a sommeil. Il a de la chance.

- The expressions **avoir besoin de**, **avoir honte de**, **avoir peur de**, and **avoir envie de** can be followed by either a noun or a verb.

  J'**ai besoin d'**une calculatrice. J'**ai besoin d'**étudier.
  I need a calculator. *I need to study.*

- The command forms of **avoir** are irregular: **aie**, **ayons**, **ayez**.

  Aie un peu de patience. N'**ayez** pas peur.
  Be a little patient. *Don't be afraid.*

Essayez! Complete the sentences with the correct forms of *avoir*.

1. La température est de 35 degrés Celsius. Nous _avons_ chaud.
2. En Alaska, en décembre, vous _avez_ froid.
3. Martine _a_ envie de danser.
4. Ils _ont_ besoin d'une calculatrice pour le devoir.
5. Est-ce que tu _as_ peur des insectes?
6. Sébastien pense que je travaille aujourd'hui. Il _a_ raison.
7. J' _ai_ cours d'économie le lundi.
8. Mes amis voyagent beaucoup. Ils _ont_ de la chance.
9. Mohammed _a_ deux cousins à Marseille.
10. Vous _avez_ un grand appartement.

soixante-treize 73

Structures
Leçon 2B

Mise en pratique

1 **On a...** Use the correct forms of **avoir** to form questions from these elements. Use inversion and provide an affirmative or negative answer as indicated.

MODÈLE

tu / bourse (oui)
As-tu une bourse? Oui, j'ai une bourse.

1. nous / dictionnaire (oui)   *Avons-nous un dictionnaire? Oui, nous avons un dictionnaire.*
2. Luc / diplôme (non)   *Luc a-t-il un diplôme? Non, il n'a pas de diplôme.*
3. elles / montres (non)   *Ont-elles des montres? Non, elles n'ont pas de montres.*
4. vous / copains (oui)   *Avez-vous des copains? Oui, j'ai/nous avons des copains.*
5. Thérèse / téléphone (oui)   *Thérèse a-t-elle un téléphone? Oui, elle a un téléphone.*
6. Charles et Jacques / calculatrice (non)   *Charles et Jacques ont-ils une calculatrice? Non, ils n'ont pas de calculatrice.*
7. on / examen (non)   *A-t-on un examen? Non, on n'a pas d'examen.*
8. tu / livres de français (non)   *As-tu des livres de français? Non, je n'ai pas de livres de français.*

2 **C'est évident** Describe these people using expressions with **avoir**.

1. J' _ai besoin d'_ étudier.
2. Vous _avez froid_.
3. Tu _as honte_.
4. Elles _ont sommeil_.

3 **Assemblez** Use the verb avoir and combine elements from the two columns to create sentences about yourself, your class, and your school. Make any necessary changes or additions. *Answers will vary.*

A	B
Je	cours utiles
Le lycée	bonnes notes
Les profs	professeurs brillants
Mon (*My*) petit ami	ami(e) mexicain(e) / anglais(e)
Ma (*My*) petite amie	/ canadien(ne) / vietnamien(ne)
Nous	élèves intéressants
	cantine agréable
	cours d'informatique

1 Suggestion This activity can be done in pairs. Tell students to alternate asking and answering the questions.

2 Expansion For each drawing, ask students how many people there are, their names, and their ages. Example: **Combien de personnes y a-t-il sur le dessin numéro 1? Comment s'appellent les personnes sur le dessin numéro 2? Quel âge a ____?**

3 Suggestion This activity can be done orally or in writing, in pairs or groups.

DIFFERENTIATION

For Visual Learners Bring in magazine photos or illustrations showing people in different conditions with **avoir** (cold, warm, sleepy, lucky, etc.). Distribute slips of paper with sentences describing the photos. When you show a photo, the students holding the corresponding slip of paper should stand up. Ask one of them to read the description out loud.

TEACHING OPTIONS

Small Groups Have students work in groups of three. Tell them to write nine sentences, each of which uses a different expression with **avoir**. Call on volunteers to write some of their group's best sentences on the board. Have the class read the sentences aloud and correct any errors.

Au lycée   Unité 2

Communication

4 Besoins Your teacher will give you a worksheet. Ask different classmates if they need to do these activities. Find at least one person to answer **Oui** and at least one to answer **Non** for each item. *Answers will vary.*

MODÈLE

regarder la télé
Élève 1: *Tu as besoin de regarder la télé?*
Élève 2: *Oui, j'ai besoin de regarder la télé.*
Élève 3: *Non, je n'ai pas besoin de regarder la télé.*

Activités	Oui	Non
1. regarder la télé	Anne	Louis
2. étudier ce soir		
3. passer un examen cette semaine		
4. retrouver des amis demain		
5. travailler à la bibliothèque		
6. commencer un devoir important		
7. téléphoner à un(e) copain/copine ce week-end		
8. parler avec le professeur		

5 C'est vrai? Interview a classmate by transforming each of these statements into a question. Be prepared to report the results of your interview to the class.

MODÈLE J'ai deux ordinateurs.
Élève 1: *Tu as deux ordinateurs?*
Élève 2: *Non, je n'ai pas deux ordinateurs.*

1. J'ai peur des examens.
2. J'ai seize ans.
3. J'ai envie de visiter Montréal.
4. J'ai un cours de biologie.
5. J'ai sommeil le lundi matin.
6. J'ai un(e) petit(e) ami(e) égoïste.

6 Interview You are talking to a college admissions advisor. Answer his or her questions. In pairs, practice the scene and role-play it for the class. *Answers will vary.*

1. Qu'est-ce que (*What*) vous avez envie d'étudier?
2. Est-ce que vous avez d'excellentes notes?
3. Est-ce que vous avez envie de partager une chambre?
4. Est-ce que vous mangez à la cantine?
5. Est-ce que vous avez un ordinateur?
6. Est-ce que vous retrouvez des amis au lycée?
7. Est-ce que vous écoutez de la musique?
8. Est-ce que vous avez des cours le matin?
9. Est-ce que vous avez envie d'habiter sur le campus?

soixante-quinze 75

---

4 Suggestions
- Have three volunteers read the **modèle** aloud. Then distribute the **Feuilles d'activités**, found in the Activity Pack on the Supersite.
- Have students add at least two activities of their own.

5 Suggestion Have two volunteers read the **modèle** aloud. Remind students that an indefinite article becomes **de (d')** if it follows **avoir** in the negative.

5 Virtual Chat You can assign Activity 5 on the Supersite. Students record individual responses that appear in your gradebook.

6 Suggestions
- Remind students to do the interview twice so each person asks and answers the questions.
- Ask volunteers to summarize their partners' responses. Record the responses on the board as a survey (**un sondage**) about the class' characteristics. Then ask questions like this: **Combien d'élèves dans la classe ont envie d'étudier la physique?**

6 Virtual Chat You can assign Activity 6 on the Supersite. Students record individual responses that appear in your gradebook.

EXPANSION

Game Divide the class into two teams. Choose one team member at a time to go to the board, alternating between teams. Say a subject pronoun. The person at the board must write and say the correct form of **avoir**. Example: **elle** (**elle a**). Give a point for each correct answer. The team with the most points at the end of the game wins.

TEACHING OPTIONS

For Visual Learners Bring in magazine photos or illustrations showing people holding different items. As you show the images, ask students to raise their hands and say what the people in the images are holding. Ex. **Il a un café, elle a un livre.**

75

Section Goals

In this section, students will learn:
- to tell time
- some time expressions
- the 24-hour system of telling time

Student Resources
Cahier de l'élève, pp. 52–54; Supersite: Activities, eCahier Grammar Tutorials

Teacher Resources
Answer Keys; Digital Image Bank; Audio Script; Audio Activity MP3s/CD; Testing program: Grammar Quiz

Suggestions

- To prepare for telling time, review the meanings of **il est** and numbers 0–60.
- Introduce: **Il est sept heures (huit heures, neuf heures…).**
- Explain to students that **heures** refers to *hours* when telling time, but can also mean *o'clock*.
- Introduce: **Il est ____ heure(s) cinq, dix, et quart,** and **et demie.**
- Using a paper plate clock, display various times on the hour. Ask: **Quelle heure est-il?**
- Introduce and explain: **Il est ____ heure(s) moins cinq, moins dix, moins le quart,** and **moins vingt.** Repeat the procedure above using your movable-hands clock.
- Explain that the French view times of day differently from Americans. In France, they say «**bonjour**» until about 4:00 or 5:00 p.m. After that, they use the greeting «**bonsoir**». They say «**bonne nuit**» only when going to sleep.

Structures | Leçon 2B

2B.2 Telling time
Presentation Grammar Tutorial

Point de départ Use the verb être with numbers to tell time.

- There are two ways to ask what time it is.

  Quelle heure est-il?
  What time is it?

  Quelle heure avez-vous/as-tu?
  What time do you have?

- Use **heures** by itself to express time on the hour. Use **une heure** for one o'clock.

  Il est **six heures**.    Il est **une heure**.

Boîte à outils

In English, you often leave out the word *o'clock* when telling time. You might say "The class starts at eleven" or "I arrive at seven." In French, however, you must always include the word **heure(s)**.

- Express time from the hour to the half-hour by stating the number of minutes it is past the hour.

  Il est quatre heures **cinq**.    Il est onze heures **vingt**.

- Use **et quart** to say that it is fifteen minutes past the hour.
  Use **et demie** to say that it is thirty minutes past the hour.

  Il est une heure **et quart**.    Il est sept heures **et demie**.

- To express time from the half hour to the hour, subtract the number of minutes or the portion of an hour from the next hour.

  Il est trois heures **moins dix**.    Il est une heure **moins le quart**.

- To express at what time something happens, use the preposition **à**.

  Le cours commence **à neuf heures moins vingt**.
  The class starts at 8:40.

  Nous avons un examen **à une heure**.
  We have a test at one o'clock.

76 soixante-seize

EXPANSION

Extra Practice Give half the class slips of paper with clock faces depicting certain times. Give the corresponding times written out in French to the other half of the class. Have students circulate around the room to match their times. To increase difficulty, include duplicates of each time with **du matin** or **du soir** on the written-out times and a sun or a moon on the clock faces.

TEACHING OPTIONS

Game Divide the class into two teams. Write two city names on the board. (Ex: **Detroit** and **Des Moines**) Check that students know the time difference and then list a time underneath the first city. (Ex: **7:30 a.m.**) Point to the first member of each team and ask: **Il est sept heures et demie à Detroit. Quelle heure est-il à Des Moines?** The first student to write the correct time in French earns a point for his or her team.

76 Unit 2 • Lesson 2B

Au lycée — Unité 2

- In French, the hour and minutes are separated by the letter **h**, which stands for **heure**, whereas in English a colon is used.

   3:25 = **3h25**   11:10 = **11h10**   5:15 = **5h15**

- **Liaison** occurs between numbers and the word **heure(s)**. Final **-s** and **-x** in **deux**, **trois**, **six**, and **dix** are pronounced like a z. The final **-f** of **neuf** is pronounced like a v.

   Il est **deux heures**. Il est **neuf heures** et quart.
   It's two o'clock. *It's 9:15.*

- You do not usually make a **liaison** between the verb form **est** and a following number that starts with a vowel sound.

   Il est onze heures. Il est une heure vingt. Il est huit heures et demie.
   It's eleven o'clock. *It's 1:20.* *It's 8:30.*

Expressions for telling time

À quelle heure?	(At) what time/ When?	midi	noon
de l'après-midi	in the afternoon	minuit	midnight
du matin	in the morning	pile	sharp, on the dot
du soir	in the evening	presque	almost
en avance	early	tard	late
en retard	late	tôt	early
		vers	about

Il est **minuit** à Paris. Il est **six heures du soir** à New York.
It's midnight in Paris. *It's six o'clock in the evening in New York.*

Boîte à outils
In French, there are no words for *a.m.* and *p.m.* You can use **du matin** for *a.m.*, **de l'après-midi** from noon until about 6 p.m., and **du soir** from about 6 p.m. until midnight. When you use the 24-hour clock, it becomes obvious whether you're referring to *a.m.* or *p.m.*

- The 24-hour clock is often used to express official time. Departure times, movie times, and store hours are expressed in this fashion. Only numbers are used to tell time this way. Expressions like **et demie**, **moins le quart**, etc. are not used.

   Le train arrive à **dix-sept heures six**. Le film est à **vingt-deux heures trente-sept**.
   The train arrives at 5:06 p.m. *The film is at 10:37 p.m.*

À noter
As you learned in **Leçon 1A**, when you say 21, 31, 41, etc. in French, the *one* agrees with the gender of the noun that follows. Therefore, **21h00** is **vingt et une heures**.

J'ai cours de trois heures vingt à quatre heures et demie.

Stéphane! Quelle heure est-il?

Essayez! Complete the sentences by writing out the correct times according to the cues.

1. (1:00 a.m.) Il est _une heure_ du matin.
2. (2:50 a.m.) Il est _trois heures moins dix_ du matin.
3. (8:30 p.m.) Il est _huit heures et demie_ du soir.
4. (10:08 a.m.) Il est _dix heures huit_ du matin.
5. (7:15 p.m.) Il est _sept heures et quart_ du soir.
6. (12:00 p.m.) Il est _midi_.
7. (4:05 p.m.) Il est _quatre heures cinq_ de l'après-midi.
8. (4:45 a.m.) Il est _cinq heures moins le quart_ du matin.
9. (3:20 a.m.) Il est _trois heures vingt_ du matin.
10. (12:00 a.m.) Il est _minuit_.

soixante-dix-sept **77**

Suggestions
- Explain the use of the 24-hour clock. Have students practice saying times this way by adding 12.
- Model the pronunciation of the time expressions in the box and have students repeat. Point out that a.m. and p.m. are not used in France or most Francophone regions. Instead, they use **du matin**, **de l'après midi**, and **du soir**.
- Tell students that **et demi(e)** agrees in gender with the noun it follows, but not in number. After **midi** and **minuit**, both **et demi** and **et demie** are accepted.

Essayez! For additional practice, give students these items.
11. 6:20 p.m.   12. 9:10 a.m.
13. 2:15 p.m.   14. 10:35 a.m.
15. 11:15 a.m. 16. 9:55 p.m.

EXPANSION

Extra Practice Draw a large clock face on the board with its numbers but without the hands. Say a time and ask a volunteer to come up and draw the hands to indicate that time. The rest of the class verifies whether or not the person has written the correct time, saying: **Il/Elle a raison/tort**. Repeat this procedure a number of times.

TEACHING OPTIONS

Video Play the video episode again to give students additional input on telling time and the verb **avoir**. Pause the video where appropriate to discuss how time or **avoir** were used and to ask comprehension questions. Example: **Est-ce que Stéphane a peur de parler à Astrid? (Mais non, il a peur du bac.)**

Structures | Leçon 2B

1 Expansion At random, say the times shown and have students say the number of the clock or watch described. Example: **Il est sept heures cinq. (C'est le numéro six.)**

2 Suggestion Read the **modèle** aloud with a volunteer. Working in pairs, have students take turns asking and answering the questions.

3 Expansion Create a train schedule and write it on the board or use photocopies of a real one. Ask students questions based on the schedule. Example: **À quelle heure est le train Paris-Bordeaux le vendredi soir?**

Mise en pratique

1 Quelle heure est-il? Give the time shown on each clock or watch.

MODÈLE
Il est quatre heures et quart de l'après-midi.

1. Il est midi/minuit et demi(e).
2. Il est une heure du matin.
3. Il est huit heures dix.
4. Il est onze heures moins le quart.
5. Il est deux heures douze.
6. Il est sept heures cinq.
7. Il est quatre heures moins cinq.
8. Il est minuit moins vingt-cinq.

2 À quelle heure? Find out when you and your friends are going to do certain things.

MODÈLE
À quelle heure est-ce qu'on étudie? (about 8 p.m.)
On étudie vers huit heures du soir.

À quelle heure...
1. ...est-ce qu'on arrive au café? (at 10:30 a.m.)   On arrive au café à dix heures et demie du matin.
2. ...est-ce que vous parlez avec le professeur? (at noon)   Nous parlons avec le professeur à midi.
3. ...est-ce que tu travailles? (late, at 11:15 p.m.)   Je travaille tard, à onze heures et quart du soir.
4. ...est-ce qu'on regarde la télé? (at 9:00 p.m.)   On regarde la télé à neuf heures du soir.
5. ...est-ce que Marlène et Nadine mangent? (around 1:45 p.m.)   Elles mangent vers deux heures moins le quart de l'après-midi.
6. ...est-ce que le cours commence? (very early, at 8:20 a.m.)   Il commence très tôt, à huit heures vingt du matin.

3 Départ à... Tell what each of these times would be on a 24-hour clock.

MODÈLE
Il est trois heures vingt de l'après-midi.
Il est quinze heures vingt.

1. Il est dix heures et demie du soir.   Il est vingt-deux heures trente.
2. Il est deux heures de l'après-midi.   Il est quatorze heures.
3. Il est huit heures et quart du soir.   Il est vingt heures quinze.
4. Il est minuit moins le quart.   Il est vingt-trois heures quarante-cinq.
5. Il est six heures vingt-cinq du soir.   Il est dix-huit heures vingt-cinq.
6. Il est trois heures moins cinq du matin.   Il est deux heures cinquante-cinq.
7. Il est six heures moins le quart de l'après-midi.   Il est dix-sept heures quarante-cinq.
8. Il est une heure et quart de l'après-midi.   Il est treize heures quinze.
9. Il est neuf heures dix du soir.   Il est vingt et une heures dix.
10. Il est sept heures quarante du soir.   Il est dix-neuf heures quarante.

EXPANSION

Pairs Have student pairs take turns telling each other what time their classes are this semester/trimester/term. Example: **J'ai un cours à ____ heures**.... For each time given, the other student draws a clock face with the corresponding time. The first student verifies if the clock is correct.

EXPANSION

Pairs Have students work with a partner to create an original conversation in which they: (1) greet each other appropriately, (2) ask for the time, (3) ask what time a particular class is, and (4) say goodbye. Have pairs role-play their conversations for the class.

Au lycée — Unité 2

Communication

4 Télémonde Look at this French TV guide. In pairs, ask questions about program start times. *Answers will vary.*

MODÈLE

Élève 1: À quelle heure commence Télé-ciné sur Antenne 4?
Élève 2: Télé-ciné commence à dix heures dix du soir.

dessins animés	cartoons
feuilleton télévisé	soap opera
film policier	detective film
informations	news
jeu télévisé	game show

VENDREDI

Antenne 2	Antenne 4	Antenne 5
15h30 Pomme d'Api (dessins animés)	**14h00** Football: match France-Italie	**18h25** Montréal: une ville à visiter
17h35 Reportage spécial: le sport dans les lycées	**19h45** Les informations	**19h30** Des chiffres et des lettres (jeu télévisé)
20h15 La famille Menet (feuilleton télévisé)	**20h30** Concert: orchestre de Nice	**21h05** Reportage spécial: les Sénégalais
21h35 Télé-ciné: L'inspecteur Duval (film policier)	**22h10** Télé-ciné: Une chose difficile (comédie dramatique)	**22h05** Les informations

5 Où es-tu? In pairs, take turns asking where (**où**) your partner usually is on these days at these times. Choose from the places listed. *Answers will vary.*

au lit (*bed*)	chez moi (*at home*)
à la cantine	chez mes copains
à la bibliothèque	au lycée
en ville (*town*)	au restaurant
au parc	
en cours	

1. Le samedi: à 8h00 du matin; à midi; à minuit
2. En semaine: à 9h00 du matin; à 3h00 de l'après-midi; à 7h00 du soir
3. Le dimanche: à 4h00 de l'après-midi; à 6h30 du soir; à 10h00 du soir
4. Le vendredi: à 11h00 du matin; à 5h00 de l'après-midi; à 11h00 du soir

6 Le suspect A student at your school is a suspect in a crime. You and a partner are detectives. Keeping a log of the student's activities, use the 24-hour clock to say what he or she is doing when. *Answers will vary.*

MODÈLE

À vingt-deux heures trente-trois, il parle au téléphone.

soixante-dix-neuf 79

Key Standards
1.1

Student Resources
Supersite: Activities, eCahier

Teacher Resources
Answer Keys; Activity Pack; Testing Program: Lesson Test (Testing Program Audio MP3s/CD)

1 Suggestion Have two volunteers read the **modèle** aloud. Encourage students to add other items to the list.

2 Suggestion Before beginning the activity, tell students to choose two language classes, a science class, and an elective in the list. Then read the **modèle** aloud with a volunteer.

3 Expansion Have volunteers report their findings to the class. Then do a quick class survey to find out how many students are taking the same courses. Example: **Combien d'élèves ont éducation physique ce semestre?**

4 Suggestion Before doing the activity, point out the use of the construction **avoir envie de** + *infinitive*. Encourage students to add activities to the list. Examples: **regarder un film, manger/partager une pizza, parler au téléphone,** and **voyager en France/Europe.**

5 Suggestion Ask what expressions are used to talk about likes and dislikes, and write them on the board before assigning this activity.

6 Suggestions
- Divide the class into pairs and distribute the Info Gap Handouts from the Activity Pack. Have two volunteers read the **modèle**. Give students ten minutes to complete the activity.
- After completing the activity, ask students what activities Patrick would like to do this weekend.

80 Unit 2 • Lesson 2B

Synthèse — Leçon 2B

Révision

1 J'ai besoin de... In pairs, take turns saying which items you need. Your partner will guess why you need them. How many times did each of you guess correctly? *Answers will vary.*

MODÈLE
Élève 1: *J'ai besoin d'un cahier et d'un dictionnaire pour demain.*
Élève 2: *Est-ce que tu as un cours de français?*
Élève 1: *Non. J'ai un examen d'anglais.*

un cahier	un livre de physique
une calculatrice	une montre
une carte	un ordinateur
un dictionnaire	un stylo
une feuille de papier	un téléphone

2 À la fac Imagine you're attending college. To complete your degree, you need two language classes, a science class, and an elective of your choice. Take turns deciding what classes you need or want to take. Your partner will tell you the days and times so you can set up your schedule. *Answers will vary.*

MODÈLE
Élève 1: *J'ai besoin d'un cours de maths, peut-être «Initiation aux maths».*
Élève 2: *C'est le mardi et le jeudi après-midi, de deux heures à trois heures et demie.*
Élève 1: *J'ai aussi besoin d'un cours de langue...*

Les cours	Jours et heures
Allemand	mardi, jeudi; 14h00-15h30
Biologie II	mardi, jeudi; 9h00-10h30
Chimie générale	lundi, mercredi; 11h00-12h30
Espagnol	lundi, mercredi; 11h00-12h30
Gestion	mercredi; 13h00-14h30
Histoire des États-Unis	jeudi; 12h15-14h15
Initiation à la physique	lundi, mercredi; 12h00-13h30
Initiation aux maths	mardi, jeudi; 14h00-15h30
Italien	lundi, mercredi; 12h00-13h30
Japonais	mardi, jeudi; 9h00-10h30
Les philosophes grecs	lundi; 15h15-16h45
Littérature moderne	mardi; 10h15-11h15

3 Les cours Your partner will tell you what classes he or she is currently taking. Make a list, including the times and days of the week. Then, talk to as many classmates as you can, and find at least two students who take at least two of the same classes as your partner. *Answers will vary.*

4 On y va? Walk around the room and find at least one classmate who feels like doing each of these activities with you. For every affirmative answer, record the name of your classmate and agree on a time and date. Do not speak to the same classmate twice. *Answers will vary.*

MODÈLE
Élève 1: *Tu as envie de retrouver des amis avec moi?*
Élève 2: *Oui, pourquoi pas? Samedi, à huit heures du soir, peut-être?*
Élève 1: *D'accord!*

chercher un café sympa	regarder la télé française
manger à la cantine	retrouver des amis
écouter de la musique	travailler à la bibliothèque
étudier le français cette semaine	visiter un musée

5 Au téléphone Two former high school friends are attending different universities. In pairs, imagine a conversation where they discuss the time, their classes, and likes or dislikes about campus life. Then, role-play the conversation for the class and vote for the best skit. *Answers will vary.*

MODÈLE
Élève 1: *J'ai cours de chimie à dix heures et demie.*
Élève 2: *Je n'ai pas de cours de chimie cette année.*
Élève 1: *N'aimes-tu pas les sciences?*
Élève 2: *Si, mais...*

6 La semaine de Patrick Your teacher will give you and a partner different incomplete pages from Patrick's day planner. Do not look at each other's worksheet while you complete your own. *Answers will vary.*

MODÈLE
Élève 1: *Lundi matin, Patrick a cours de géographie à dix heures et demie.*
Élève 2: *Lundi, il a cours de sciences po à deux heures de l'après-midi.*

ressources
vText — CE pp. 49-54 — vhlcentral.com Leçon 2B

TEACHING OPTIONS

Skits Working in groups of three or four, have students create a short skit similar to the scene in video still 1 of the **Roman-photo**. Tell them that they have to decide on a day, time, and place to meet for a study session in order to prepare for the next French test. Have groups perform their skits for the class.

TEACHING OPTIONS

Oral Practice Have students make a list of six items that students normally carry in their backpacks to class. Then tell them to circulate around the room asking their classmates if they have those items in their backpacks. Also tell them to ask how many they have. Example: **As-tu un cahier dans le sac à dos? Combien de cahiers as-tu?**

Au lycée — Unité 2

À l'écoute

Audio: Activities

STRATÉGIE

Listening for cognates

You already know that cognates are words that have similar spellings and meanings in two or more languages: for example *group* and **groupe** or *activity* and **activité**. Listen for cognates to increase your comprehension of spoken French.

> To help you practice this strategy, you will listen to two sentences. Make a list of all the cognates you hear.

Préparation

Based on the photograph, who and where do you think Marie-France and Dominique are? Do you think they know each other well? Where are they probably going this morning? What do you think they are talking about?

À vous d'écouter

Listen to the conversation and list any cognates you hear. Listen again and complete the highlighted portions of Marie-France's schedule.

28 OCTOBRE	lundi		
8H00	*jogging*	14H00	psychologie
8H30		14H30	
9H00		15H00	
9H30	biologie	15H30	physique
10H00		16H00	
10H30		16H30	
11H00	chimie	17H00	
11H30		17H30	*étudier*
12H00	resto U	18H00	
12H30		18H30	
13H00	*bibliothèque*	19H00	*téléphoner à papa*
13H30		19H30	*Sophie:* restaurant vietnamien

ressources
vText
vhlcentral.com
Leçon 2B

Practice more at vhlcentral.com.

Compréhension

Vrai ou faux? Indicate whether each statement is **vrai** or **faux**. Then correct the false statements.

1. D'après Marie-France, la biologie est facile.
   Vrai.

2. Marie-France adore la chimie.
   Faux. Elle déteste la chimie.

3. Marie-France et Dominique mangent au restaurant vietnamien à midi.
   Faux. Ils mangent au restaurante vietnamien à sept heures et demie du soir.

4. Dominique aime son cours de sciences politiques.
   Fax. Il aime son cours d'informatique.

5. Monsieur Meyer est professeur de physique.
   Vrai.

6. Monsieur Meyer donne des devoirs faciles.
   Faux. Il donne des devoirs très difficiles.

7. Le lundi après-midi, Marie-France a psychologie et physique.
   Vrai.

8. Aujourd'hui, Dominique mange au resto U.
   Faux. Aujourd'hui, Marie-France mange au resto U.

Votre emploi du temps With a partner, discuss the classes you're taking. Be sure to say when you have each one, and give your opinion of at least three courses.

quatre-vingt-un 81

Section Goals
In this section, students will:
- learn to listen for cognates
- listen to sentences containing familiar and unfamiliar vocabulary
- listen to a conversation, complete a schedule, and answer true/false questions

Key Standards
1.2, 2.1

Student Resources
Supersite: Activities, Audio
Teacher Resources
Answer Keys; Audio Script; Audio Activity MP3s/CD

Stratégie
Script 1. Dans certaines institutions d'études supérieures, les étudiants reçoivent un salaire. 2. Ma cousine étudie la médecine vétérinaire. C'est sa passion!

Préparation Have students describe the photo. Ask them to justify their descriptions based on the visual clues.

Suggestion To check answers for the **À vous d'écouter** activity, have students work in pairs and take turns asking questions about Marie-France's schedule. Example: **Est-ce que Marie-France a cours de biologie à 14h00? (Non, elle a cours de biologie à 9h30.)**

À vous d'écouter
Script DOMINIQUE: Tiens, bonjour, Marie-France. Comment ça va?
MARIE-FRANCE: Salut, Dominique. Ça va bien. Et toi?
D: Très bien, merci. Tu vas en cours?
M: Oui, j'ai cours toute la journée, le lundi. Ce matin, j'ai biologie à neuf heures et demie.
D: Tu aimes la biologie?
M: Oui, j'aime bien. C'est facile. Après, à onze heures, j'ai chimie. Ça, je déteste! C'est difficile! À midi, je mange au resto U avec des copains.
D: Et cet après-midi?
M: Alors, à deux heures, j'ai psychologie et à trois heures et demie, j'ai physique.
D: Est-ce que tu aimes ça, la physique?
M: Oui, mais cette année, le prof n'est pas très intéressant.

D: Ah bon? Qui est-ce?
M: Monsieur Meyer.
D: Ah oui! Tu as raison. Il n'est pas très intéressant. Et il donne des devoirs et des examens très difficiles.
M: C'est vrai. Et toi, tu aimes tes cours cette année?
D: Oui, beaucoup. J'adore l'informatique. Le prof est amusant et il explique bien.

M: Tu as de la chance! Dis, est-ce que tu as envie de dîner au restaurant avec Sophie et moi ce soir? On va au restaurant vietnamien près de l'université.
D: Oui, avec plaisir. À quelle heure?
M: À sept heures et demie.
D: Bon, d'accord. À ce soir.
M: Salut.

81

Section Goals
In this section, students will learn historical, cultural, and geographical information about France.

Key Standards
2.2, 3.1, 3.2, 5.1

21st CENTURY SKILLS
Global Awareness
Students will gain perspectives on the Francophone world to develop respect and openness to others and to interact appropriately and effectively with citizens of Francophone cultures.

Student Resources
Cahier de l'élève, pp. 55–56;
Supersite: Activities,
eCahier
Teacher Resources
Answer Keys;
Digital Image Bank

Carte de la France
- Have students look at the map of France or use the digital image for this page. Ask volunteers to read the cities' names aloud.
- Have students identify the location of the place or object in each photo.

Le pays en chiffres
- Have students read the section headings. Point out the type of information contained in each section and clarify unfamiliar words.
- Have volunteers read the sections aloud. After each section, ask questions about the content.
- Ask students to share any additional information they might know about the people in **Français célèbres**.

Incroyable mais vrai!
L'Académie française was founded by Cardinal Richelieu during the reign of Louis XIII. In the beginning, the Academy's primary role was to standardize the language for French-speaking people by establishing rules to make it pure, eloquent, and capable of dealing with the arts and sciences.

Savoir-faire

Panorama

Interactive Map Reading

La France

Le pays en chiffres

▶ **Superficie:** 549.000 km²
(cinq cent quarante-neuf mille kilomètres carrés°)
▶ **Population:** 62.106.000 (soixante-deux millions cent six mille)
SOURCE: INSEE
▶ **Industries principales:** agro-alimentaires°, assurance°, banques, énergie, produits pharmaceutiques, produits de luxe, télécommunications, tourisme, transports

La France est le pays° le plus° visité du monde° avec plus de° 60 millions de touristes chaque° année. Son histoire, sa culture et ses monuments–plus de 12.000 (douze mille)–et musées–plus de 1.200 (mille deux cents)–attirent° des touristes d'Europe et de partout° dans le monde.

▶ **Villes principales:** Paris, Lille, Lyon, Marseille, Toulouse
▶ **Monnaie°:** l'euro

La France est un pays membre de l'Union européenne et, en 2002, l'euro a remplacé° le franc français comme° monnaie nationale.

Français célèbres

▶ **Jeanne d'Arc,** héroïne française (1412–1431)
▶ **Émile Zola,** écrivain° (1840–1902)
▶ **Auguste Renoir,** peintre° (1841–1919)
▶ **Claude Debussy,** compositeur et musicien (1862–1918)
▶ **Camille Claudel,** femme sculpteur (1864–1943)
▶ **Claudie André-Deshays,** médecin, première astronaute française (1957–)

carrés square *agro-alimentaires* food processing *assurance* insurance *pays* country *le plus* the most *monde* world *plus de* more than *chaque* each *attirent* attract *partout* everywhere *Monnaie* Currency *a remplacé* replaced *comme* as *écrivain* writer *peintre* painter *élus à vie* elected for life *Depuis* Since *mots* words *courrier* mail *pont* bridge

82   quatre-vingt-deux

un bateau-mouche sur la Seine

LE ROYAUME-UNI · LA MER DU NORD · LA MANCHE · LA BELGIQUE · L'ALLEMAGNE · LE LUXEMBOURG · LES ARDENNES · Lille · Rouen · Le Havre · Caen · la Seine · la Marne · Versailles · Paris · Strasbourg · LES VOSGES · le Rhin · le Mont-St-Michel · Rennes · Nantes · la Loire · Bourges · Poitiers · la Saône · LE JURA · LA SUISSE · L'OCÉAN ATLANTIQUE · Limoges · Clermont-Ferrand · LE MASSIF CENTRAL · Lyon · L'ITALIE · Bordeaux · la Garonne · le Rhône · LES ALPES · Toulouse · Nîmes · Aix-en-Provence · MONACO · Marseille · LES PYRÉNÉES · LA CORSE · ANDORRE · L'ESPAGNE · LA MER MÉDITERRANÉE

le château de Chenonceau

le pont° du Gard

Incroyable mais vrai!
Être «immortel», c'est réguler et défendre le bon usage du français! Les académiciens de l'Académie française sont élus à vie° et s'appellent les «Immortels». Depuis° 1635 (mille six cent trente-cinq), ils décident de l'orthographe correcte des mots° et publient un dictionnaire. Attention, c'est «courrier° électronique», pas «e-mail»!

EXPANSION

Le pays en chiffres France is the third largest country in Europe. It is divided into 22 **régions** (*regions*), which include **la Corse** (*Corsica*). The **régions** are divided into 95 **départements** (*departments*). France also has four overseas **Départements et régions d'outre-mer (DROM): la Guadeloupe, la Guyane française, la Réunion,** and **la Martinique**. Using the map of France on **p. xiii** that shows the **régions** and **départements**, have students locate various cities as you say the names. Example: **Marseille (C'est dans le département des Bouches-du-Rhône.)**

EXPANSION

Oral Presentation If a student has visited France (preferably outside Paris), ask him or her to prepare a short presentation about his or her experiences there. Encourage the student to bring in photos and souvenirs of France.

82   Unit 2

Au lycée Unité 2

La géographie

L'Hexagone

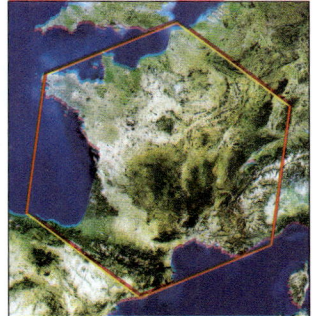

Surnommé° «Hexagone» à cause de° sa forme géométrique, le territoire français a trois fronts maritimes: l'océan Atlantique, la mer° Méditerranée et la Manche°; et quatre frontières° naturelles: les Pyrénées, les Ardennes, les Alpes et le Jura. À l'intérieur du pays°, le Massif central et les Vosges ponctuent° un relief composé de vastes plaines et de forêts. La Loire, la Seine, la Garonne, le Rhin et le Rhône sont les fleuves° principaux de l'Hexagone.

La technologie

Le Train à Grande Vitesse

Le chemin de fer° existe en France depuis° 1827 (mille huit cent vingt-sept). Aujourd'hui, la SNCF (Société nationale des chemins de fer français) offre la possibilité aux voyageurs de se déplacer° dans tout° le pays et propose des tarifs° avantageux aux élèves et aux moins de 25 ans°. Le TGV (Train à Grande Vitesse°) roule° à plus de 300 (trois cents) km/h (kilomètres/heure) et emmène° les voyageurs jusqu'à° Londres et Bruxelles.

Les arts

Le cinéma, le 7ᵉ art!

L'invention du cinématographe par les frères° Lumière en 1895 (mille huit cent quatre-vingt-quinze) marque le début° du «7ᵉ (septième) art». Le cinéma français donne naissance° aux prestigieux César° en 1976 (mille neuf cent soixante-seize), à des cinéastes talentueux comme° Jean Renoir, François Truffaut et Luc Besson, et à des acteurs mémorables comme Brigitte Bardot, Catherine Deneuve, Olivier Martinez et Audrey Tautou.

L'économie

L'industrie

Avec la richesse de la culture française, il est facile d'oublier que l'économie en France n'est pas limitée à l'artisanat°, à la gastronomie ou à la haute couture°. En fait°, la France est une véritable puissance° industrielle et se classe° parmi° les économies les plus° importantes du monde. Ses° activités dans des secteurs comme la construction automobile (Peugeot, Citroën, Renault), l'industrie aérospatiale (Airbus) et l'énergie nucléaire (Électricité de France) sont considérables.

Qu'est-ce que vous avez appris? Complete these sentences.

1. _Camille Claudel_ est une femme sculpteur française.
2. Les Académiciens sont élus _à vie_.
3. Pour «e-mail», on utilise aussi l'expression _courrier électronique_.
4. À cause de sa forme, la France s'appelle aussi _l'Hexagone_.
5. La _SNCF_ offre la possibilité de voyager dans tout le pays.
6. Avec le _TGV_, on voyage de Paris à Londres.
7. Les _frères Lumière_ sont les inventeurs du cinéma.
8. _Answers will vary. Possible answer: Jean Renoir_ est un grand cinéaste français.
9. La France est une grande puissance _industrielle_.
10. Électricité de France produit (*produces*) _l'énergie nucléaire_.

Sur Internet

1. Cherchez des informations sur l'Académie française. Faites (*Make*) une liste de mots ajoutés à la dernière édition du dictionnaire de l'Académie française.
2. Cherchez des informations sur l'actrice Catherine Deneuve. Quand a-t-elle commencé (*did she begin*) sa (*her*) carrière? Trouvez ses (*her*) trois derniers films.

Practice more at vhlcentral.com.

Surnommé Nicknamed **à cause de** because of **mer** sea **Manche** English Channel **frontières** borders **pays** country **ponctuent** punctuate **fleuves** rivers **chemin de fer** railroad **depuis** since **se déplacer** travel **dans tout** throughout **tarifs** fares **moins de 25 ans** people under 25 **Train à Grande Vitesse** high speed train **roule** rolls, travels **emmène** takes **jusqu'à** all the way to **frères** brothers **début** beginning **donne naissance** gives birth **César** equivalent of the Oscars in France **comme** such as **artisanat** craft industry **haute couture** high fashion **En fait** In fact **puissance** power **se classe** ranks **parmi** among **les plus** the most **Ses** Its

quatre-vingt-trois 83

Section Goals

In this section, students will:
- learn to use text formats to predict content
- read a brochure for a French language school

Key Standards
1.2, 2.1, 3.2, 5.2

PRE-AP®

Interpretive Reading
Ask students to discuss these questions in small groups: What clues can the format of a document provide about what content you can expect? What kind of document does this reading present? What can you predict about this reading from its format?

Stratégie
Tell students that many documents have easily identifiable formats that can help them predict the content. Have them look at the document in the **Stratégie** box and ask them to identify the recognizable elements:
- days of the week
- times
- classes

Ask what kind of document it is. (a student's weekly schedule)

Examinez le texte Have students look at the headings and ask them what type of information is contained in **École de français (pour étrangers) de Lille**. (lists of courses by level and specialization, a list of supplementary activities, and a list of types of housing available) Then ask students what types of documents contain these elements. (brochures)

Mots apparentés
- In pairs, have students scan the brochure, identify cognates, and guess their meanings.
- Ask students what this document is and its purpose. (It's a brochure. It's advertising a French language and culture immersion program. Its purpose is to attract students.)

Savoir-faire

Lecture
Audio: Synced Reading

Avant la lecture

STRATÉGIE

Predicting content through formats

Recognizing the format of a document can help you to predict its content. For instance, invitations, greeting cards, and classified ads follow an easily identifiable format, which usually gives you a general idea of the information they contain. Look at the text and identify it based on its format.

	lundi	mardi	mercredi	jeudi	vendredi
8h30	biologie	littérature	biologie	littérature	biologie
9h00					
9h30	anglais	anglais	anglais	anglais	anglais
10h00					
10h30	maths	histoire	maths	histoire	maths
11h00					
11h30	français		français		français
12h00					
12h30					
1h00	art	économie	art	économie	art

If you guessed that this is a page from a student's schedule, you are correct. You can now infer that the document contains information about a student's weekly schedule, including days, times, and activities.

Examinez le texte
Briefly look at the document. What is its format? What kind of information is given? How is it organized? Are there any visuals? What kind? What type(s) of documents usually contain these elements?

Mots apparentés
As you have already learned, in addition to format, you can use cognates to help you predict the content of a document. With a classmate, make a list of all the cognates you find in the reading selection. Based on these cognates and the format of the document, can you guess what this document is and what it's for?

84 quatre-vingt-quatre

ÉCOLE DE FRANÇAIS
(pour étrangers°) DE LILLE

COURS DE FRANÇAIS POUR TOUS°	COURS DE SPÉCIALISATION
Niveau° débutant°	Français pour enfants°
Niveau élémentaire	Français des affaires°
Niveau intermédiaire	Droit° français
Niveau avancé	Français pour le tourisme
Conversation	Culture et civilisation
Grammaire française	Histoire de France
	Art et littérature
	Arts culinaires

26, place d'Arsonval • 59000 Lille
Tél. 03.20.52.48.17 • Fax. 03.20.52.48.18 • www.efpelille.fr

EXPANSION

Schedules Have students write a friend's or family member's weekly schedule as homework. Tell them to label the days of the week in French and add notes for that person's appointments and activities. In class, ask students questions about the schedules they wrote. Examples: **Quel cours est-ce que ____ a aujourd'hui? Combien de jours est-ce que ____ travaille cette semaine?**

EXPANSION

Cultural Activity Ask students what aspects of this school they find appealing or interesting: **Qu'est-ce que vous trouvez intéressant à l'école?** Jot down their responses on the board. Then do a quick class survey to find out which aspect is the most appealing.

Au lycée — Unité 2

Programmes de 2 à 8 semaines,
4 à 8 heures par jour
Immersion totale
Professeurs diplômés

le Musée des Beaux-Arts, Lille

GRAND CHOIX° D'ACTIVITÉS SUPPLÉMENTAIRES
- Excursions à la journée dans la région
- Visites de monuments et autres sites touristiques
- Sorties° culturelles (théâtre, concert, opéra et autres spectacles°)
- Sports et autres activités de loisir°

HÉBERGEMENT°
- En cité universitaire°
- Dans° une famille française
- À l'hôtel

pour étrangers for foreigners **tous** *all* **Niveau** *Level* **débutant** *beginner* **enfants** *children* **affaires** *business* **Droit** *Law* **choix** *choice* **Sorties** *Outings* **spectacles** *shows* **loisir** *leisure* **hébergement** *lodging* **cité universitaire** *university dormitories (on campus)* **Dans** *In*

Après la lecture

Répondez Select the correct response or completion to each question or statement, based on the reading selection.

1. C'est une brochure pour...
   a. des cours de français pour étrangers. ✓
   b. une université française.
   c. des études supérieures en Belgique.

2. «Histoire de France» est...
   a. un cours pour les professeurs diplômés.
   b. un cours de spécialisation. ✓
   c. un cours pour les enfants.

3. Le cours de «Français pour le tourisme» est utile pour...
   a. une étudiante qui (*who*) étudie les sciences po.
   b. une femme qui travaille dans un hôtel de luxe. ✓
   c. un professeur d'administration des affaires.

4. Un étudiant étranger qui commence le français assiste probablement à quel (*which*) cours?
   a. Cours de français pour tous, Niveau avancé
   b. Cours de spécialisation, Art et littérature
   c. Cours de français pour tous, Niveau débutant ✓

5. Quel cours est utile pour un homme qui parle assez bien français et qui travaille dans l'économie?
   a. Cours de spécialisation, Français des affaires ✓
   b. Cours de spécialisation, Arts culinaires
   c. Cours de spécialisation, Culture et civilisation

6. Le week-end, les étudiants...
   a. passent des examens.
   b. travaillent dans des hôtels.
   c. visitent la ville et la région. ✓

7. Les étudiants qui habitent dans une famille...
   a. ont envie de rencontrer des Français. ✓
   b. ont des bourses.
   c. ne sont pas reçus aux examens.

8. Un étudiant en architecture va aimer...
   a. le cours de droit français.
   b. les visites de monuments et de sites touristiques. ✓
   c. les activités sportives.

Complétez Complete these sentences.

1. Le numéro de téléphone est le ___03.20.52.48.17___.
2. Le numéro de fax est le ___03.20.52.48.18___.
3. L'adresse de l'école est ___26, place d'Arsonval, 59000 Lille___.
4. L'école offre des programmes de français de ___2 à 8___ semaines et de ___4 à 8 heures___ par jour.

ressources
vText
vhlcentral.com
Leçon 2B

quatre-vingt-cinq 85

Répondez Go over the answers with the whole class or have students check their answers in pairs.

Complétez For additional practice, give these items.
5. L'école est à ____. (Lille)
6. L'adresse Internet de l'école est ____. (www.efpelille.fr)
7. «Grammaire française» est un cours de ____. (français pour tous)
8. Les professeurs de l'école sont ____. (diplômés)
9. On habite en cité universitaire, ____ ou à l'hôtel. (dans une famille française)

Suggestion Encourage students to record unfamiliar words and phrases that they learn in **Lecture** in their notebooks.

21st CENTURY SKILLS

Creativity and Innovation
Ask students to prepare a presentation on the ideal language school inspired by the information on these two pages.

DIFFERENTIATION

For Visual Learners Provide students with magazines and newspapers in French. Have groups of three or four students work together to look for documents in French with easily recognizable formats, such as classified ads or other advertisements. Ask them to use cognates and other context clues to predict the content. Then have groups present their examples and findings to the class.

EXPANSION

Oral Presentation Invite a student who has studied abroad to come and speak to the class about the school he or she attended, the classes, and any interesting experiences he or she had there. Encourage the class to ask questions.

Savoir-faire

Écriture

STRATÉGIE

Brainstorming

How do you find ideas to write about? In the early stages of writing, brainstorming can help you generate ideas on a specific topic. You should spend ten to fifteen minutes brainstorming and jotting down any ideas about the topic that occur to you. Whenever possible, try to write down your ideas in French. Express your ideas in single words or phrases, and jot them down in any order. While brainstorming, do not worry about whether your ideas are good or bad. Selecting and organizing ideas should be the second stage of your writing. Remember that the more ideas you write down while brainstorming, the more options you will have to choose from later when you start to organize your ideas.

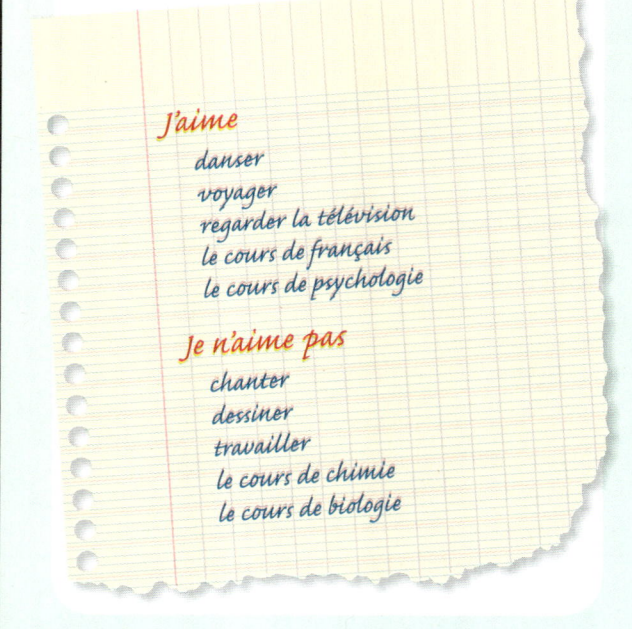

J'aime
- danser
- voyager
- regarder la télévision
- le cours de français
- le cours de psychologie

Je n'aime pas
- chanter
- dessiner
- travailler
- le cours de chimie
- le cours de biologie

Thème

Une description personnelle

Avant l'écriture

1. Write a description of yourself to post on a website in order to find a francophone e-pal. Your description should include:

   - your name and where you are from
   - the name of your school and where it is located
   - the courses you are currently taking and your opinion of each one
   - some of your likes and dislikes
   - where you work if you have a job
   - any other information you would like to include

   Use a chart like this one to brainstorm information about your likes and dislikes.

J'aime	Je n'aime pas

86 *quatre-vingt-six*

Au lycée — Unité 2

2. Now take the information about your likes and dislikes and fill out this new chart to help you organize the content of your description.

Je m'appelle...	(name).
Je suis de...	(where you are from).
J'étudie...	(names of classes) à/au/à la (name of school).
Je ne travaille pas./ Je travaille à/au/ à la/chez...	(place where you work).
J'aime...	(activities you like).
Je n'aime pas...	(activities you dislike).

Écriture

Use the information from the second chart to write a paragraph describing yourself. Make sure you include all the information from the chart in your paragraph. Use the structures provided for each topic.

Bonjour!

Je m'appelle Stacy Adams. Je suis américaine. J'étudie au lycée à New York. Je travaille à la bibliothèque le samedi. J'aime parler avec des amis, lire (*read*), écouter de la musique et voyager, parce que j'aime rencontrer des gens. Par contre, je n'aime pas le sport...

Après l'écriture

1. Exchange a rough draft of your description with a partner. Comment on his or her work by answering these questions:

   - Did your partner include all the necessary information (at least six facts)?
   - Did your partner use the structures provided in the chart?
   - Did your partner use the vocabulary of the unit?
   - Did your partner use the grammar of the unit?

2. Revise your description according to your partner's comments. After writing the final version, read it one more time to eliminate these kinds of problems:

   - spelling errors
   - punctuation errors
   - capitalization errors
   - use of incorrect verb forms
   - use of incorrect adjective agreement
   - use of incorrect definite and indefinite articles

ressources
vText
vhlcentral.com
Leçon 2B

quatre-vingt-sept 87

EVALUATION

Criteria

Content Includes all the information mentioned in the six bulleted items in the description of the task.
Scale: 1 2 3 4 5

Organization Organizes the description similarly to the model provided.
Scale: 1 2 3 4 5

Accuracy Uses **j'aime/je n'aime pas**, regular **-er** verbs, and negation patterns correctly. Words are spelled correctly and adjectives agree with the nouns they modify.
Scale: 1 2 3 4 5

Creativity Includes additional information that is not specified in the task and makes an effort to create longer sentences with a number of items.
Scale: 1 2 3 4 5

Scoring
Excellent   18–20 points
Good   14–17 points
Satisfactory   10–13 points
Unsatisfactory   < 10 points

21ST CENTURY SKILLS

Social and Cross-cultural skills
Remind your students their description will be read by someone from a different culture so it is important to offer specific details on issues such as geographic location, schedules, or leisure activities.

EXPANSION

Écriture Before students begin writing, give them some transition words they may want to incorporate into their descriptions. Words and expressions such as **mais**, **parce que**, **alors**, **pourtant**, **par contre**, **ou**, and **et** can be used to make sentences longer and to make transitions between them.

TEACHING OPTIONS

Après l'écriture Once students have written their descriptions, choose several among those and ask the authors for their permission to read them aloud. As you read each one, see if the class can guess whom it is describing, based on the likes, dislikes, and other information included.

87

Vocabulaire — Unité 2

Key Standards
4.1

Teacher Resources
Vocabulary MP3s/CD

Suggestion Tell students that an easy way to study from **Vocabulaire** is to cover up the French half of each section, leaving only the English equivalents exposed. They can then quiz themselves on the French items. To focus on the English equivalents of the French entries, they simply reverse this process.

21st CENTURY SKILLS
Creativity and Innovation
Ask students to prepare a list of three products or perspectives they learned about in this unit to share with the class. Consider asking them to focus on the **Culture** and **Panorama** sections.

21st CENTURY SKILLS
Leadership and Responsibility Extension Project
If you have access to students in a Francophone country, have students decide on three questions they want to ask the partner class related to this unit's topic. Based on the responses they receive, work as a class to explain to the partner class one aspect of their responses that surprised the class and why.

Verbes

adorer	to love
aimer	to like; to love
aimer mieux	to prefer
arriver	to arrive
chercher	to look for
commencer	to begin, to start
dessiner	to draw
détester	to hate
donner	to give
étudier	to study
habiter (à/en)	to live in
manger	to eat
oublier	to forget
parler (au téléphone)	to speak (on the phone)
partager	to share
penser (que/qu')	to think (that)
regarder	to look (at), to watch
rencontrer	to meet
retrouver	to meet up with; to find (again)
travailler	to work
voyager	to travel

Vocabulaire supplémentaire

J'adore...	I love...
J'aime bien...	I like...
Je n'aime pas tellement...	I don't like... very much.
Je déteste...	I hate...
être reçu(e) à un examen	to pass an exam

Des questions et des opinions

bien sûr	of course
d'accord	OK, all right
Est-ce que/qu'...?	question phrase
(mais) non	no (but of course not)
moi/toi non plus	me/you neither
ne... pas	no, not
n'est-ce pas?	isn't that right?
oui/si	yes
parce que	because
pas du tout	not at all
peut-être	maybe, perhaps
pourquoi?	why?

Les cours

assister	to attend
demander	to ask
dîner	to have dinner
échouer	to fail
écouter	to listen (to)
enseigner	to teach
expliquer	to explain
passer un examen	to take an exam
préparer	to prepare (for)
rentrer (à la maison)	to return (home)
téléphoner à	to telephone
trouver	to find; to think
visiter	to visit (a place)
l'architecture (f.)	architecture
l'art (m.)	art
la biologie	biology
la chimie	chemistry
le droit	law
l'économie (f.)	economics
l'éducation physique (f.)	physical education
la géographie	geography
la gestion	business administration
l'histoire (f.)	history
l'informatique (f.)	computer science
les langues (étrangères) (f.)	(foreign) languages
les lettres (f.)	humanities
les mathématiques (maths) (f.)	mathematics
la philosophie	philosophy
la physique	physics
la psychologie	psychology
les sciences (politiques/po) (f.)	(political) science
le stylisme	fashion design
une bourse	scholarship, grant
une cantine	cafeteria
un cours	class, course
un devoir	homework
un diplôme	diploma, degree
l'école (f.)	school
les études (supérieures) (f.)	(higher) education; studies
le gymnase	gymnasium
une note	grade
un restaurant universitaire (un resto U)	university cafeteria

Expressions utiles	See pp. 51 and 69.
Telling time	See pp. 76–77.

Expressions de temps

Quel jour sommes-nous?	What day is it?
un an	year
une/cette année	one/this year
après	after
après-demain	day after tomorrow
un/cet après-midi	an/this afternoon
aujourd'hui	today
demain (matin/après-midi/soir)	tomorrow (morning/afternoon/evening)
un jour	day
une journée	day
(le) lundi, mardi, mercredi, jeudi, vendredi, samedi, dimanche	(on) Monday(s), Tuesday(s), Wednesday(s), Thursday(s), Friday(s), Saturday(s), Sunday(s)
un/ce matin	a/this morning
la matinée	morning
un mois/ce mois-ci	a month/this month
une/cette nuit	a/this night
une/cette semaine	a/this week
un/ce soir	an/this evening
une soirée	evening
un/le/ce week-end	a/the/this weekend
dernier/dernière	last
premier/première	first
prochain(e)	next

Adjectifs et adverbes

difficile	difficult
facile	easy
inutile	useless
utile	useful
surtout	especially; above all

Expressions avec avoir

avoir	to have
avoir... ans	to be... years old
avoir besoin (de)	to need
avoir chaud	to be hot
avoir de la chance	to be lucky
avoir envie (de)	to feel like
avoir froid	to be cold
avoir honte (de)	to be ashamed (of)
avoir l'air	to look like
avoir peur (de)	to be afraid (of)
avoir raison	to be right
avoir sommeil	to be sleepy
avoir tort	to be wrong

quatre-vingt-huit

La famille et les copains

Unité 3

Pour commencer
- Combien de personnes y a-t-il sur la photo?
  a. deux b. trois c. quatre
- Où sont ces personnes?
  a. à la maison b. en ville c. dans un magasin
- Que font ces amis?
  a. Ils mangent. b. Ils étudient. c. Ils parlent et ils s'amusent.

Leçon 3A

CONTEXTES .... pages 90–93
- Family, friends, and pets
- L'accent aigu and l'accent grave

ROMAN-PHOTO . pages 94–95
- L'album de photos

CULTURE .... pages 96–97
- The family in France
- Flash culture

STRUCTURES... pages 98–105
- Descriptive adjectives
- Possessive adjectives

SYNTHÈSE .... pages 106–107
- Révision
- Le Zapping

Leçon 3B

CONTEXTES ... pages 108–111
- More descriptive adjectives
- Professions and occupations
- L'accent circonflexe, la cédille, and le tréma

ROMAN-PHOTO .pages 112–113
- On travaille chez moi!

CULTURE ...... pages 114–115
- Relationships

STRUCTURES.. pages 116–123
- Numbers 61–100
- Prepositions of location and disjunctive pronouns

SYNTHÈSE .... pages 124–125
- Révision
- À l'écoute

Savoir-faire . pages 126–131
- Panorama: Paris
- Lecture: Read a short article about pets.
- Écriture: Write a letter to a friend.

Unit Goals
Leçon 3A
In this lesson, students will learn:
- words for family members and marital status
- some words for pets
- usage of l'accent aigu and l'accent grave
- about the French family
- more about families and friends through specially shot video footage
- descriptive adjectives
- possessive adjectives
- about the Belgian company Pages d'Or

Leçon 3B
In this lesson, students will learn:
- words for some professions and occupations
- more descriptive adjectives
- usage of l'accent circonflexe, la cédille, and le tréma
- about different types of friendships and relationships
- the numbers 61–100
- some prepositions of location
- disjunctive pronouns
- to ask for repetition in oral communication

Savoir-faire
In this section, students will learn:
- historical and cultural information about Paris
- to use visuals and graphic elements to predict content
- to use idea maps to organize information
- to write an informal letter

21st CENTURY SKILLS
Initiative and Self-Direction
Students can monitor their progress online using the Supersite activities and assessments.

Pour commencer
- c. quatre
- b. en ville
- c. Ils parlent et ils s'amusent.

INSTRUCTIONAL RESOURCES

Student Resources
Print: Student Book, Workbook (*Cahier de l'élève*)
Supersite: vhlcentral.com, vText, eCahier, Audio, Video, Practice

Teacher Resources
Print: Teacher's Edition, Answer Keys, Testing Program
Technology: Audio MP3s on CD (Textbook, Testing Program, Audio Program), Video Program DVD (*Roman-photo, Flash culture*)

Supersite: vhlcentral.com, Activity Pack, Middle School Activity Pack, Lesson Plans, Grammar Tutorials, Grammar Slides, Testing Program, Audio and Video Scripts, Answer Key, Audio MP3s, Streaming Video (*Roman-photo, Flash culture, Le Zapping*), Digital Image Bank, Learning Management System (Gradebook, Assignments)

VOICE BOARD Voice boards on the Supersite allow you and your students to record and share up to five minutes of audio. Use voice boards for presentations, oral assessments, discussions, directions, etc.

Section Goals

In this section, students will learn and practice vocabulary related to:
- family members
- some pets
- marital status

Key Standards
1.1, 1.2, 4.1

Student Resources
Cahier de l'élève, pp. 57–59; Supersite: Activities, *eCahier*

Teacher Resources
Answer Keys; Digital Image Bank; Audio Script; Textbook & Audio Activity MP3s/CD; Activity Pack; Testing program: Vocabulary Quiz

Suggestions
- Introduce active lesson vocabulary with questions and gestures. Ask: **Comment s'appelle votre frère?** Ask a different student: **Comment s'appelle le frère de ____?** Work your way through various family relationships.
- Point out the meanings of plural family terms so students understand that the masculine plural forms can refer to mixed groups of males and females:
  les enfants *male children; male and female children*
  les cousins *male cousins; male and female cousins*
  les petits-enfants *male grandchildren; male and female grandchildren*
- Point out the difference in meaning between the noun **mari** (*husband*) and the adjective **marié(e)** (*married*).
- Use the digital image for this page. Point out that the family tree is drawn from the point of view of Marie Laval. Have students refer to the family tree to answer your questions about it. Example: **Comment s'appelle la mère de Marie?**

Contextes — Leçon 3A

**Audio: Vocabulary Practice
My Vocabulary**

You will learn how to...
- discuss family, friends, and pets
- express ownership

La famille de Marie Laval

Luc Garneau — mon grand-père

Juliette Laval — ma mère, fille de Luc et d'Hélène
Robert Laval — mon père, mari de Juliette

Véronique Laval — ma belle-sœur, femme de mon frère
Guillaume Laval — mon frère
Marie Laval — moi, Marie Laval, fille de Juliette et de Robert

Matthieu Laval — mon neveu
Émilie Laval — ma nièce

petits-enfants de mes parents

Vocabulaire

divorcer	to divorce
épouser	to marry
aîné(e)	elder
cadet(te)	younger
un beau-frère	brother-in-law
un beau-père	father-in-law; stepfather
une belle-mère	mother-in-law; stepmother
un demi-frère	half-brother; stepbrother
une demi-sœur	half-sister; stepsister
les enfants (*m., f.*)	children
un(e) époux/épouse	husband/wife
une famille	family
une femme	wife; woman
une fille	daughter; girl
les grands-parents (*m.*)	grandparents
les parents (*m.*)	parents
un(e) voisin(e)	neighbor
un chat	cat
un oiseau	bird
un poisson	fish
célibataire	single
divorcé(e)	divorced
fiancé(e)	engaged
marié(e)	married
séparé(e)	separated
veuf/veuve	widowed

ressources
vText
CE p. 57–59
vhlcentral.com Leçon 3A

90 *quatre-vingt-dix*

EXPANSION

Family Tree Draw your own family tree on a transparency or the board and label it with names. Ask students questions about it. Examples: **Est-ce que ____ est ma sœur ou ma tante? Comment s'appelle ma grand-mère? ____ est le neveu ou le frère de ____ ? Qui est le grand-père de ____ ?** Help them identify the relationships between members. Then invite them to ask you questions.

EXPANSION

Les noms de famille français Ask for a show of hands to see if any students' last names are French in origin. Examples: names that begin with **Le____** or **La____** such as **Leblanc** or **Larose**, or even names such as **Fitzgerald** or **Fitzpatrick** (**Fitz-** = **fils de**). Ask these students what they know about their French heritage or family history.

La famille et les copains — Unité 3

Mise en pratique

Hélène Garneau — ma grand-mère

Sophie Garneau — ma tante, femme de Marc
Marc Garneau — mon oncle, fils de Luc et d'Hélène

Jean Garneau — mon cousin, petit-fils de Luc et d'Hélène
Isabelle Garneau — ma cousine, sœur de Jean et de Virginie, petite-fille de Luc et d'Hélène
Virginie Garneau — ma cousine, sœur de Jean et d'Isabelle, petite-fille de Luc et d'Hélène

Bambou — le chien de mes cousins

1 Qui est-ce?
Match the definition in the first list with the correct item from the second list. Not all the items will be used.

1. __d__ le frère de ma cousine
2. __g__ le père de mon cousin
3. __a__ le mari de ma grand-mère
4. __e__ le fils de mon frère
5. __c__ la fille de mon grand-père
6. __i__ le fils de ma mère
7. __h__ la fille de mon fils
8. __f__ le fils de ma belle-mère

a. mon grand-père
b. ma sœur
c. ma tante
d. mon cousin
e. mon neveu
f. mon demi-frère
g. mon oncle
h. ma petite-fille
i. mon frère

2 Choisissez
Fill in the blank by selecting the most appropriate answer.

1. Voici le frère de mon père. C'est mon __oncle__ (oncle, neveu, fiancé).
2. Voici la mère de ma cousine. C'est ma __tante__ (grand-mère, voisine, tante).
3. Voici la petite-fille de ma grand-mère. C'est ma __cousine__ (cousine, nièce, épouse).
4. Voici le père de ma mère. C'est mon __grand-père__ (grand-père, oncle, cousin).
5. Voici le fils de mon père, mais ce n'est pas le fils de ma mère. C'est mon __demi-frère__ (petit-fils, demi-frère, voisin).

3 Complétez
Complete each sentence with the appropriate word.

1. Voici ma nièce. C'est la __petite-fille__ de ma mère.
2. Voici la mère de ma tante. C'est ma __grand-mère__.
3. Voici la sœur de mon oncle. C'est ma __tante__.
4. Voici la fille de mon père, mais pas de ma mère. C'est ma __demi-sœur__.
5. Voici le mari de ma mère, mais ce n'est pas mon père. C'est mon __beau-père__.

4 Écoutez
Listen to each statement made by Marie Laval. Based on her family tree, indicate whether it is **vrai** or **faux**.

	Vrai	Faux		Vrai	Faux
1.	✓		6.		✓
2.		✓	7.		✓
3.	✓		8.	✓	
4.		✓	9.	✓	
5.		✓	10.	✓	

Practice more at vhlcentral.com.

quatre-vingt-onze 91

Successful Language Learning
Tell students that it isn't necessary to understand every word they hear in French. They will feel less anxious if they listen for general meaning.

1 Suggestion Mention that adjectives such as **beau** and **petit** in hyphenated family terms must agree in gender. Exceptions: **la grand-mère, la demi-sœur.**

2 & 3 Expansion Have students provide additional examples for the class to identify.

4 Script
1. Marc est mon oncle.
2. Émilie est la nièce de Véronique.
3. Jean est le petit-fils d'Hélène.
4. Robert est mon grand-père.
5. Luc est le père de Sophie.
6. Isabelle est ma tante.
7. Matthieu est le fils de Jean.
8. Émilie est la fille de Guillaume.
9. Juliette est ma mère.
10. Virginie est ma cousine.
(On Textbook Audio)

4 Expansion Play Marie's statements again, stopping at the end of each. Where the statements are true, have students repeat. Where the statements are false, have students correct them by referring to Marie Laval's family tree.

EXPANSION

Using Games As a class or group activity, have students state the relationship between people on Marie Laval's family tree. Their classmates will guess which person on the family tree they are describing. Example: **C'est la sœur de Jean et la fille de Sophie. (Isabelle ou Virginie)** Take turns until each member of the class or group has had a chance to state a relationship.

EXPANSION

My Family Tree Have students draw their own family tree as homework. Tell them to label each position on the tree with the appropriate French term and the person's name. Also tell them to write five fill-in-the-blank statements based on their family tree. Examples: **Je suis la fille de ____. Mon frère s'appelle ____.** In the next class, have students exchange papers with a classmate and complete the activity.

91

Contextes   Leçon 3A

Communication

5 🧑‍🤝‍🧑 **L'arbre généalogique** With a classmate, identify the members of the family by asking how each one is related to Anne Durand. *Answers will vary.*

MODÈLE

Élève 1: *Qui est Louis Durand?*
Élève 2: *C'est le grand-père d'Anne.*

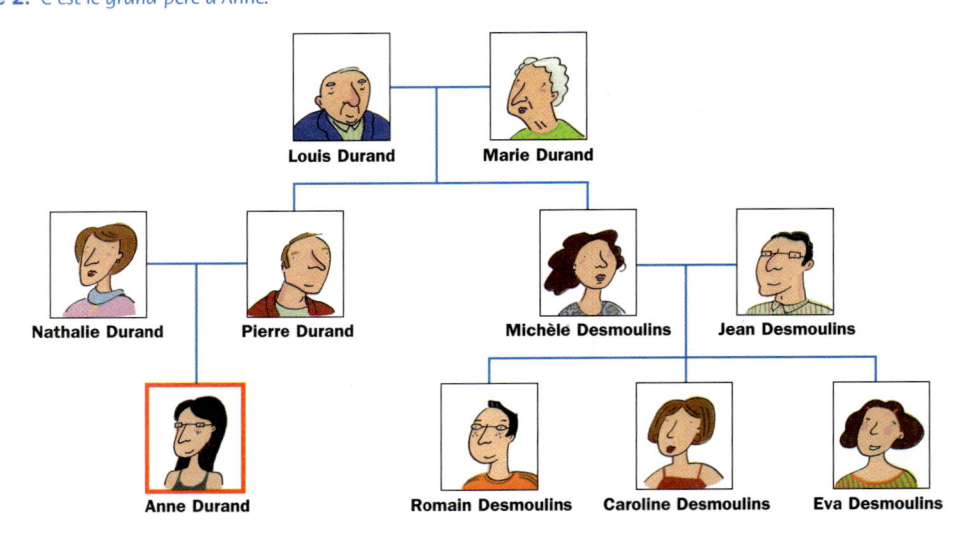

Louis Durand — Marie Durand

Nathalie Durand Pierre Durand Michèle Desmoulins Jean Desmoulins

Anne Durand   Romain Desmoulins Caroline Desmoulins Eva Desmoulins

6 🧑‍🤝‍🧑 **Entrevue** With a classmate, take turns asking each other these questions. *Answers will vary.*

1. Combien de personnes y a-t-il dans ta famille?
2. Comment s'appellent tes parents?
3. As-tu des frères et sœurs?
4. Combien de cousins/cousines as-tu? Comment s'appellent-ils/elles? Où habitent-ils/elles?
5. Quel(le) (*Which*) est ton cousin préféré/ta cousine préférée?
6. As-tu des neveux/des nièces?
7. Comment s'appellent tes grands-parents? Où habitent-ils?
8. Combien de petits-enfants ont tes grands-parents?

Coup de main

Use these words to help you complete this activity.

ton *your (m.)* → mon *my (m.)*
ta *your (f.)* → ma *my (f.)*
tes *your (pl.)* → mes *my (pl.)*

7 👥 **Qui suis-je?** Your teacher will give you a worksheet. Walk around the class and ask your classmates questions about their families. When a classmate gives one of the answers on the worksheet, write his or her name in the corresponding space. Be prepared to discuss the results with the class. *Answers will vary.*

MODÈLE *J'ai un chien.*

Élève 1: *Est-ce que tu as un chien?*
Élève 2: *Oui, j'ai un chien (You write the student's name.)/Non, je n'ai pas de chien. (You ask another classmate.)*

92   *quatre-vingt-douze*

La famille et les copains — Unité 3

Les sons et les lettres
Audio: Explanation Record & Compare

L'accent aigu and l'accent grave

In French, diacritical marks (*accents*) are an essential part of a word's spelling. They indicate how vowels are pronounced or distinguish between words with similar spellings but different meanings. **L'accent aigu** (´) appears only over the vowel **e**. It indicates that the **e** is pronounced similarly to the vowel *a* in the English word *cake*, but shorter and crisper.

| étudier | réservé | élégant | téléphone |

L'accent aigu also signals some similarities between French and English words. Often, an **e** with **l'accent aigu** at the beginning of a French word marks the place where the letter *s* would appear at the beginning of the English equivalent.

| éponge | épouse | état | étudiante |
| sponge | spouse | state | student |

L'accent grave (`) appears only over the vowels **a**, **e**, and **u**. Over the vowel **e**, it indicates that the **e** is pronounced like the vowel *e* in the English word *pet*.

| très | après | mère | nièce |

Although **l'accent grave** does not change the pronunciation of the vowels **a** or **u**, it distinguishes words that have a similar spelling but different meanings.

| la | là | ou | où |
| the | there | or | where |

Prononcez Practice saying these words aloud.
1. agréable
2. sincère
3. voilà
4. faculté
5. frère
6. à
7. déjà
8. éléphant
9. lycée
10. poème
11. là
12. élève

Articulez Practice saying these sentences aloud.
1. À tout à l'heure!
2. Thérèse, je te présente Michèle.
3. Hélène est très sérieuse et réservée.
4. Voilà mon père, Frédéric, et ma mère, Ségolène.
5. Tu préfères étudier à la fac demain après-midi?

Dictons Practice reading these sayings aloud.

Tel père, tel fils.¹

À vieille mule, frein doré.²

¹ Like father, like son.
² For an old mule, a golden bit.

quatre-vingt-treize 93

Section Goals
In this section, students will learn about:
- l'accent aigu
- l'accent grave
- a strategy for recognizing cognates

Key Standards
4.1

Student Resources
Cahier de l'élève, p. 60;
Supersite: Activities, eCahier

Teacher Resources
Answer Keys; Audio Script; Textbook & Audio Activity MP3s/CD

Suggestions
- Write **é** on the board. Tell students to watch your mouth as you pronounce the sound. Explain that when **é** appears at the beginning of a word, the corners of your mouth are slightly turned up and your tongue is low behind your bottom teeth. Have students repeat **é** after you several times.
- Write words and/or French names from the Laval family with **l'accent aigu** on the board. Pronounce each word as you point to it and have students repeat it after you. Examples: **époux, célibataire, fiancé, séparé, Émilie,** and **Véronique**.
- Give students some sample sentences with **la, là, ou,** or **où** and ask them what the words mean to demonstrate how context clarifies meaning. Examples: 1. **Où est la fille?** 2. **La fille est là.** 3. **Est-ce que Sophie est la tante ou la grand-mère de Marie Laval?**
- Ask students to provide more examples of words they know with these accents.
- The explanation and exercises are available on the Supersite. You may want to play them in class so students hear French speakers besides yourself.

Dictons Explain to students that the saying «**À vieille mule, frein doré**» applies to a situation in which someone tries to sell something old by dressing it up or decorating it. For example, to have a better chance at selling an old car, give it a new paint job.

EXPANSION
Mini-dictée Here are additional sentences to use for extra practice with **l'accent aigu** and **l'accent grave**. 1. Étienne est mon frère préféré. 2. Ma sœur aînée est très occupée avec les études. 3. André et Geneviève sont séparés. 4. Vous êtes marié ou célibataire? 5. Éric et Sabine sont fiancés.

TEACHING OPTIONS
Using Games Have a spelling bee using words with **l'accent aigu** and/or **l'accent grave** from Leçon 3A or previous lessons. Divide the class into two teams. Call on one team member at a time, alternating between teams. Give a point for each correct answer. The team with the most points at the end of the game wins. Before students begin, remind them that they must indicate the accent marks in the words. Give them an example: **très** T-R-E accent grave-S.

93

Section Goals
In this section, students will learn functional phrases for talking about their families and describing people through comprehensible input.

Key Standards
1.2, 2.1, 2.2, 4.1, 4.2

Student Resources
Cahier de l'élève, pp. 61–62; Supersite: Activities, *eCahier*

Teacher Resources
Answer Keys; Video Script & Translation; *Roman-photo* video

Video Recap: Leçon 2B
Before doing this **Roman-photo**, review the previous one with this activity.
1. Comment s'appelle la copine de Stéphane? (Astrid)
2. Qu'est-ce qu'elle pense de Stéphane? (Answers will vary. **Elle pense qu'il n'est pas sérieux, qu'il ne fait pas ses devoirs et qu'il n'écoute pas en classe.**)
3. Qui téléphone à Sandrine? (Pascal)
4. Comment Stéphane prépare-t-il le bac? (Il étudie les maths avec Rachid.)

Video Synopsis
Michèle wants to know what Amina's friend, Cyberhomme, looks like. Valérie describes her brother's family as she, Stéphane, and Amina look at their photos. Valérie keeps pointing out all the people who have their **bac** because she thinks Stéphane is not studying enough to pass his **bac**. To ease his mother's mind, Stéphane finally tells her that Rachid is helping him study.

Suggestions
- Ask students to read the title, glance at the video stills, and predict what they think the episode will be about. Record their predictions.
- Have students work in groups of four. Tell them to choose a role and read the **Roman-photo** conversation aloud.
- After students have read the **Roman-photo**, quickly review their predictions and ask them which ones were correct. Then ask a few questions to help guide students in summarizing this episode.

Roman-photo — Leçon 3A

L'album de photos
Video: Roman-photo
Record & Compare

PERSONNAGES
Amina
Michèle
Stéphane
Valérie

MICHÈLE Mais, qui c'est? C'est ta sœur? Tes parents?
AMINA C'est mon ami Cyberhomme.
MICHÈLE Comment est-il? Est-ce qu'il est beau? Il a les yeux de quelle couleur? Marron ou bleue? Et ses cheveux? Ils sont blonds ou châtains?
AMINA Je ne sais pas.
MICHÈLE Toi, tu es timide.

VALÉRIE Stéphane, tu as dix-sept ans. Cette année, tu passes le bac, mais tu ne travailles pas!
STÉPHANE Écoute, ce n'est pas vrai, je déteste mes cours, mais je travaille beaucoup. Regarde, mon cahier de chimie, mes livres de français, ma calculatrice pour le cours de maths, mon dictionnaire anglais-français…

STÉPHANE Oh, et qu'est-ce que c'est? Ah, oui, les photos de tante Françoise.
VALÉRIE Des photos? Mais où?
STÉPHANE Ici! Amina, on peut regarder des photos de ma tante sur ton ordinateur, s'il te plaît?

AMINA Ah, et ça, c'est toute la famille, n'est-ce pas?
VALÉRIE Oui, ça, c'est Henri, sa femme, Françoise, et leurs enfants: le fils aîné, Bernard, et puis son frère, Charles, sa sœur, Sophie, et leur chien, Socrate.
STÉPHANE J'aime bien Socrate. Il est vieux, mais il est amusant!

VALÉRIE Ah! Et Bernard, il a son bac aussi et sa mère est très heureuse.
STÉPHANE Moi, j'ai envie d'habiter avec oncle Henri et tante Françoise. Comme ça, pas de problème pour le bac!

STÉPHANE Pardon, maman. Je suis très heureux ici, avec toi. Ah, au fait, Rachid travaille avec moi pour préparer le bac.
VALÉRIE Ah, bon? Rachid est très intelligent… un étudiant sérieux.

---

1 Vrai ou faux? Are these sentences **vrai** or **faux**? Correct the false ones.

1. Amina communique avec sa (*her*) tante par ordinateur. Faux. Elle communique avec Cyberhomme.
2. Stéphane n'aime pas ses (*his*) cours au lycée. Vrai.
3. Ils regardent des photos de vacances. Faux. Ils regardent les photos de tante Françoise.
4. Henri est le frère aîné de Valérie. Vrai.
5. Bernard est le cousin de Stéphane. Vrai.
6. Charles a déjà son bac. Vrai.
7. La tante de Stéphane s'appelle Françoise. Vrai.
8. Stéphane travaille avec Amina pour préparer le bac. Faux. Il travaille avec Rachid.
9. Socrate est le fils d'Henri et de Françoise. Faux. C'est le chien d'Henri et de Françoise.
10. Rachid n'est pas un bon étudiant. Faux. C'est un étudiant sérieux.

Practice more at **vhlcentral.com**.

94 *quatre-vingt-quatorze*

TEACHING OPTIONS

L'album de photos Before students view the video episode **L'album de photos**, ask them to brainstorm a list of things someone might say when describing his or her family photos.

TEACHING OPTIONS

Extra Practice Play the first half of the video episode and have students describe what happened. Write their observations on the board. Then ask them to guess what will happen in the second half of the episode. Write their ideas on the board. Play the entire video episode; then help the class summarize the plot.

La famille et les copains — Unité 3

Stéphane et Valérie regardent des photos de famille avec Amina.

À la table d'Amina...
AMINA Alors, voilà vos photos. Qui est-ce?
VALÉRIE Oh, c'est Henri, mon frère aîné!
AMINA Quel âge a-t-il?
VALÉRIE Il a cinquante ans. Il est très sociable et c'est un très bon père.

VALÉRIE Ah! Et ça, c'est ma nièce Sophie et mon neveu Charles! Regarde, Stéphane, tes cousins!
STÉPHANE Je n'aime pas Charles. Il est tellement sérieux.
VALÉRIE Il est peut-être trop sérieux, mais, lui, il a son bac!
AMINA Et Sophie, qu'elle est jolie!
VALÉRIE ... et elle a déjà son bac.

AMINA Ça, oui, préparer le bac avec Rachid, c'est une idée géniale!

VALÉRIE Oui, c'est vrai. En théorie, c'est une excellente idée. Mais tu prépares le bac avec Rachid, hein? Pas le prochain match de foot!

Expressions utiles

Talking about your family
- C'est ta sœur? Ce sont tes parents?
  Is that your sister? Are those your parents?
- C'est mon ami.
  That's my friend.
- Ça, c'est Henri, sa femme, Françoise, et leurs enfants.
  That's Henri, his wife, Françoise, and their kids.

Describing people
- Il a les yeux de quelle couleur? Marron ou bleue?
  What color are his eyes? Brown or blue?
- Il a les yeux bleus.
  He has blue eyes.
- Et ses cheveux? Ils sont blonds ou châtains? Frisés ou raides?
  And his hair? Is it blond or brown? Curly or straight?
- Il a les cheveux châtains et frisés.
  He has curly brown hair.

Additional vocabulary
- On peut regarder des photos de ma tante sur ton ordinateur?
  Can/May we look at some photos from my aunt on your computer?
- C'est toute la famille, n'est-ce pas?
  That's the whole family, right?
- Je ne sais pas (encore).
  I (still) don't know.
- Alors... — *So...*
- vrai — *true*
- une photo(graphie) — *a photograph*
- une idée — *an idea*
- peut-être — *maybe*
- au fait — *by the way*
- Hein? — *Right?*
- déjà — *already*

Activités

2 Vocabulaire Choose the adjective that describes how Stéphane would feel on these occasions. Refer to a dictionary as necessary.

1. on his 87th birthday ___vieux___
2. after finding 20€ ___heureux___
3. while taking the bac ___sérieux___
4. after getting a good grade ___heureux___
5. after dressing for a party ___beau___

beau / heureux / sérieux / vieux

3 Conversez In pairs, describe which member of your family is most like Stéphane. How are they alike? Do they both like sports? Do they take similar courses? How do they like school? How are their personalities? Be prepared to describe your partner's "Stéphane" to the class.

ressources: vText, CE pp. 61–62, vhlcentral.com Leçon 3A

quatre-vingt-quinze 95

Expressions utiles
- Point out the various forms of possessive adjectives and descriptive adjectives in the captions and the **Expressions utiles**. Tell students that this material will be formally presented in the **Structures** section. Do not expect students to produce the forms correctly at this time.
- Model the pronunciation of the **Expressions utiles** and have students repeat them.
- To practice new vocabulary, ask students to describe their classmates' eyes and hair. Examples: ____ a les yeux de quelle couleur? Marron ou bleue? Avez-vous les yeux bleus? ____ a-t-il/elle les cheveux blonds ou châtains? Qui a les cheveux blonds/châtains dans la classe? Est-ce que les cheveux de ____ sont frisés ou raides?

1 Suggestion Have students correct the false statements.

1 Expansion For additional practice, give students these items. 11. Valérie n'aime pas son frère, Henri. (Faux.) 12. Stéphane aime les gens très sérieux. (Faux.) 13. Socrate est un chien. (Vrai.) 14. Stéphane et Rachid préparent le prochain match de foot. (Faux.)

2 Suggestion Before students begin the activity, you might want to introduce the adjectives in the word list using pictures or people in the video stills, rather than having students look them up in the dictionary.

2 Expansion Have students describe Rachid, Charles, and Henri using the adjectives in the word list. At this point, avoid asking students to describe people that would require a feminine or plural form of these adjectives.

3 Suggestion If time is limited, this activity may be assigned as a written composition for homework.

3 Partner Chat You can also assign Activity 3 on the Supersite. Students work in pairs to record the activity online. The pair's recorded conversation will appear in your gradebook.

EXPANSION

Valérie's Family Tree Working in pairs, have students draw a family tree based on Valérie's description of her brother's family. Tell them to use the family tree on pages 90–91 as a model. Remind them to include Valérie and Stéphane. Then have them get together with another pair of students and compare their drawings.

EXPANSION

Writing Questions Have students write four questions about Henri's family based on the conversation and video still #6. Then have them get together in groups of three and take turns asking and answering each other's questions. Examples: **Combien de personnes y a-t-il dans la famille d'Henri? Comment s'appelle le fils aîné? Combien de frères a Sophie?**

Culture
Leçon 3A

CULTURE À LA LOUPE

La famille en France

Les nombres° de personnes divorcées et de personnes célibataires augmentent chaque° année.

La structure familiale traditionnelle existe toujours en France, mais il y a des structures moins traditionnelles, comme les familles monoparentales, où° l'unique parent est divorcé, séparé ou veuf. Il y a aussi des familles recomposées, c'est-à-dire qui combinent deux familles, avec un beau-père, une belle-mère, des demi-frères et des demi-sœurs. Certains couples choisissent° le Pacte Civil de Solidarité (PACS), qui offre certains droits° et protections aux couples non-mariés.

Comment est la famille française? Est-elle différente de la famille américaine? La majorité des Français sont-ils mariés, divorcés ou célibataires?

Il n'y a pas de réponse simple à ces questions. Les familles françaises sont très diverses. Le mariage est toujours° très populaire: la majorité des hommes et des femmes sont mariés. Mais attention!

Géographiquement, les membres d'une famille d'immigrés peuvent° habiter près ou loin° les uns des autres°. Mais en général, ils préfèrent habiter les uns près des autres parce que l'intégration est parfois° difficile. Il existe aussi des familles d'immigrés séparées entre° la France et le pays d'origine.

Alors, oubliez les stéréotypes des familles en France. Elles sont grandes et petites, traditionnelles et non-conventionnelles; elles changent et sont toujours les mêmes°.

La situation familiale des Français
(par tranche° d'âge)

ÂGE	CÉLIBATAIRE	EN COUPLE SANS ENFANTS	EN COUPLE AVEC ENFANTS	PARENT D'UNE FAMILLE MONOPARENTALE
< 25 ans	3,6%	2,8%	1%	0,3%
25–29 ans	16,7%	26,5%	26,2%	2,6%
30–44 ans	10,9%	9,8%	64,3%	6,2%
45–59 ans	11,7%	29,9%	47,2%	5,9%
> 60 ans	20,3%	59,2%	11,7%	2,9%

SOURCE: INSEE

toujours still **nombres** numbers **chaque** each **où** where **choisissent** choose **droits** rights **peuvent** can **près ou loin** near or far from **les uns des autres** one another **parfois** sometimes **entre** between **mêmes** same **tranche** bracket

Coup de main

Remember to read decimal places in French using the French word **virgule** (*comma*) where you would normally say *point* in English. To say *percent*, use **pour cent**.

64,3% soixante-quatre virgule trois pour cent

sixty-four point three percent

---

1 Complétez Provide logical answers, based on the reading.

1. Si on regarde la population française d'aujourd'hui, on observe que les familles françaises sont très ___diverses___.
2. Le ___mariage___ est toujours très populaire en France.
3. La majorité des hommes et des femmes sont ___mariés___.
4. Le nombre de Français qui sont ___célibataires___ augmente.
5. Dans les familles ___monoparentales___, l'unique parent est divorcé, séparé ou veuf.
6. Il y a des familles qui combinent ___deux___ familles.
7. Le ___PACS___ offre certains droits et protections aux couples qui ne sont pas mariés.
8. Les immigrés aiment ___habiter___ les uns près des autres.
9. Oubliez les ___stéréotypes___ des familles en France.
10. Les familles changent et sont toujours ___les mêmes___.

Practice more at **vhlcentral.com**.

La famille et les copains — Unité 3

LE FRANÇAIS QUOTIDIEN

La famille

un frangin	brother
une frangine	sister
maman	Mom
mamie	Nana, Grandma
un minou	kitty
papa	Dad
papi	Grandpa
tata	Auntie
tonton	Uncle
un toutou	doggy

LE MONDE FRANCOPHONE

Les fêtes et la famille

Les États-Unis ont quelques fêtes° en commun avec le monde francophone, mais les dates et les traditions de ces fêtes diffèrent d'un pays° à l'autre°. Voici deux fêtes associées à la famille.

La Fête des mères
En France le dernier° dimanche de mai ou le premier° dimanche de juin
En Belgique le deuxième° dimanche de mai
À l'île Maurice le dernier dimanche de mai
Au Canada le deuxième dimanche de mai

La Fête des pères
En France le troisième° dimanche de juin
En Belgique le deuxième dimanche de juin
Au Canada le troisième dimanche de juin

quelques fêtes some holidays **pays** country **autre** other
dernier last **premier** first **deuxième** second **troisième** third

PORTRAIT

Les Noah

Dans° la famille Noah, le sport est héréditaire. À chacun son° sport: pour° Yannick, né° en France, c'est le tennis; pour son père, Zacharie, né à Yaoundé, au Cameroun, c'est le football°; pour son fils, Joakim, né aux États-Unis, c'est le basket-ball. Yannick est champion junior à Wimbledon en 1977 et participe aux championnats° du Grand Chelem° dans les années 1980. Son fils, Joakim, est un joueur° de basket-ball aux États-Unis. Il gagne° la finale du *Final Four NCAA* en 2006 et en 2007 avec les Florida Gators. Il est aujourd'hui joueur professionnel avec les Chicago Bulls. Le sport est dans le sang° chez les Noah!

Dans In **À chacun son** To everybody his **pour** for **né** born **football** soccer **championnats** championships **Chelem** Slam **joueur** player **gagne** wins **sang** blood

Sur Internet

Yannick Noah: célébrité du tennis et... de la chanson?°

Go to vhlcentral.com to find more cultural information related to this **Culture** section. Then watch the corresponding **Flash culture**.

ACTIVITÉS

2 Vrai ou faux? Indicate if these statements are **vrai** or **faux**.
1. Le tennis est héréditaire chez les Noah. *Faux. Le sport est héréditaire chez les Noah.*
2. Zacharie Noah est né au Cameroun. *Vrai.*
3. Zacharie Noah était (*was*) un joueur de basket-ball. *Faux. Zacharie Noah était un joueur de football.*
4. Yannick gagne à l'US Open. *Faux. Yannick gagne à Wimbledon.*
5. Joakim joue (*plays*) pour les Lakers. *Faux. Joakim joue pour les Chicago Bulls.*
6. Le deuxième dimanche de mai, c'est la Fête des mères en Belgique et au Canada. *Vrai.*

3 À vous... With a partner, write six sentences describing another celebrity family whose members all share a common field or profession. Be prepared to share your sentences with the class.

ressources
vText
CE pp. 63–64
vhlcentral.com Leçon 3A

quatre-vingt-dix-sept 97

Teacher's notes

Le français quotidien Point out that these words are commonly used in informal conversations with family members, children, and close friends.

Portrait Show the class a photo of Yannick Noah. Ask: **Qui est-ce? Comment s'appelle-t-il?** Ask students what they know about him. Explain that thanks to his active involvement in charity work, Noah is often referred to as **Tonton Yannick**.

Le monde francophone Explain that Mother's Day and Father's Day did not originate in France. The first **Journée des mères** took place in France in 1926; it became an official holiday, **la Fête des mères**, in 1950.

2 Suggestion Have students correct the false statements.

2 Expansion Have students write three more true/false statements based on **Portrait** and **Le monde francophone**. Then have them work in groups of three and take turns reading their statements while the other group members respond **vrai** or **faux**.

3 Expansion Have students work in pairs to create a brief conversation in which they talk about their families and pets, using vocabulary in **Le français quotidien**. Example: **Est-ce que tu as un minou? Non, mais ma tata, elle a des minous.** Remind students that this level of language is only appropriate in informal conversations.

Flash culture Tell students that they will learn more about family and friends by watching a variety of real-life images narrated by Csilla. Show the video segment, then have students jot down in French at least three examples of people or things they saw. You can also use the activities in the video manual in class to reinforce this **Flash culture** or assign them as homework.

21st CENTURY SKILLS

Information and Media Literacy: Sur Internet
Students access and critically evaluate information from the Internet.

EXPANSION

Les fêtes et la famille Explain to students that many countries around the world have a special day to honor mothers. **La Fête des mères** and **la Fête des pères** are celebrated somewhat similarly in France, Belgium, and Canada to the way Mother's Day and Father's Day are celebrated in the United States. Children create cards, write poems, and make handicrafts in school to give to their parents on these holidays. Older sons and daughters often give a small gift. On **l'Île Maurice**, they do not officially celebrate Father's Day. In other Francophone regions, such as North and West Africa, there is no official holiday for either Mother's or Father's Day.

Section Goals

In this section, students will learn:
- forms, agreement, and position of adjectives
- high-frequency descriptive adjectives and some irregular adjectives

Key Standards

4.1, 5.1

Student Resources
Cahier de l'élève, pp. 65–67; Supersite: Activities, *eCahier*, *Grammar Tutorials*

Teacher Resources
Answer Keys; Audio Script; Audio Activity MP3s/CD; Testing program: Grammar Quiz

Suggestions

- Consider reviewing previously learned adjectives by calling out names of celebrities or school subjects and having students give a sentence to describe them. Examples: **Léonard de Vinci: Il est italien. La biologie: C'est facile.**
- Write these adjectives on the board: **américain, amusant, intelligent, timide, aînée.** Say each word and ask students if it is masculine or feminine. Model one of the adjectives in a sentence and ask volunteers to use the others in sentences.
- Work through the discussion of adjective forms point by point, writing examples on the board. Remind students that grammatical gender doesn't necessarily reflect the actual gender. Example: **Charles est une personne nerveuse.**
- Use magazine pictures and the names of celebrities to teach or practice descriptive adjectives in semantic pairs. Use either/or questions, yes/no questions, or a combination. Examples: **Tiger Woods est-il grand ou petit? (Il est grand.) Jessica Simpson est-elle brune? (Non, elle est blonde.)**
- Point out the adjectives that have the same masculine and feminine form.

Language Note Point out that the adjective **châtain** comes from the noun **une châtaigne**, which is a type of sweet chestnut. The adjective **marron** is also a noun; **un marron** means horse chestnut.

Structures   Leçon 3A

3A.1 Descriptive adjectives *Presentation Grammar Tutorial*

Point de départ As you learned in **Leçon 1B**, adjectives describe people, places, and things. In French, unlike English, the forms of most adjectives will vary depending on whether the nouns they describe are masculine or feminine, singular or plural. Furthermore, French adjectives are usually placed after the noun they modify when they don't directly follow a form of **être**.

SINGULAR MASCULINE NOUN ⟷ SINGULAR MASCULINE ADJECTIVE

Le **père** est **américain**.
The father is American.

PLURAL MASCULINE NOUN ⟷ PLURAL MASCULINE ADJECTIVE

As-tu des **cours faciles**?
Do you have easy classes?

- You've already learned several adjectives of nationality and some adjectives to describe your classes. Here are some adjectives used to describe physical characteristics.

Adjectives of physical description

bleu(e)	blue	joli(e)	pretty
blond(e)	blond	laid(e)	ugly
brun(e)	dark (hair)	marron	brown (not for hair)
châtain	brown (hair)	noir(e)	black
court(e)	short	petit(e)	small, short (stature)
grand(e)	tall, big	raide	straight (hair)
jeune	young	vert(e)	green

- Notice that, in the examples below, the adjectives agree in gender (masculine or feminine) and number (singular or plural) with the subjects. In general, add **-e** to make an adjective feminine. If an adjective already ends in an unaccented **-e**, add nothing. In general, to make an adjective plural, add **-s.** If an adjective already ends in an **-s,** add nothing.

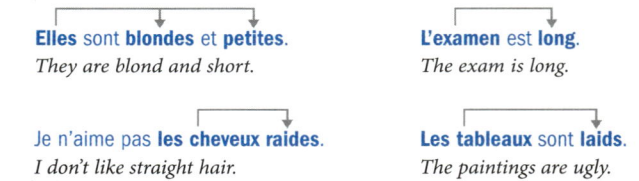

Elles sont **blondes** et **petites**.
They are blond and short.

L'examen est **long**.
The exam is long.

Je n'aime pas **les cheveux raides**.
I don't like straight hair.

Les tableaux sont **laids**.
The paintings are ugly.

- Use the expression **de taille moyenne** to describe someone or something of medium size.

Victor est un homme **de taille moyenne**.
Victor is a man of medium height.

C'est une université **de taille moyenne**.
It's a medium-sized university.

- The adjective **marron** is invariable; in other words, it does not agree in gender and number with the noun it modifies. The adjective **châtain** is almost exclusively used to describe hair color.

Mon neveu a les **yeux marron**.
My nephew has brown eyes.

Ma nièce a les **cheveux châtains**.
My niece has brown hair.

quatre-vingt-dix-huit

EXPANSION

Extra Practice Ask students to draw a chart with three columns on a piece of paper with the following heads: **Sujet**, **Être**, and **Adjectif**. Ask students to populate column 1 with a variety of subjects, and column 3 with a list of adjectives from this lesson. Ask them to exchange their charts with a classmate and write sentences combining the three columns. Warn them to pay attention to gender and number variations.

DIFFERENTIATION

For Visual Learners Bring in magazine photos or illustrations showing a variety of people (tall, short, blond, etc.). As you show each image to the class, ask your students to describe the characters as fully as possible by using adjectives they have learned in this lesson. Write their responses on the board.

98   Unit 3 • Lesson 3A

La famille et les copains — Unité 3

Some irregular adjectives

masculine singular	feminine singular	masculine plural	feminine plural	
beau	belle	beaux	belles	beautiful; handsome
bon	bonne	bons	bonnes	good; kind
fier	fière	fiers	fières	proud
gros	grosse	gros	grosses	fat
heureux	heureuse	heureux	heureuses	happy
intellectuel	intellectuelle	intellectuels	intellectuelles	intellectual
long	longue	longs	longues	long
naïf	naïve	naïfs	naïves	naive
roux	rousse	roux	rousses	red-haired
vieux	vieille	vieux	vieilles	old

À noter

In **Leçon 1B**, you learned that if the masculine singular form of an adjective already ends in **-s (sénégalais)**, you don't add another one to form the plural. The same is also true for words that end in **-x (roux, vieux)**.

- The forms of the adjective **nouveau** (*new*) follow the same pattern as those of **beau**.

  MASCULINE PLURAL
  J'ai trois **nouveaux** stylos.
  I have three new pens.

  FEMININE SINGULAR
  Tu aimes la **nouvelle** horloge?
  Do you like the new clock?

- Other adjectives that follow the pattern of **heureux** are **curieux** (*curious*), **malheureux** (*unhappy*), **nerveux** (*nervous*), and **sérieux** (*serious*).

Position of certain adjectives

- Certain adjectives are usually placed *before* the noun they modify. These include: **beau**, **bon**, **grand**, **gros**, **jeune**, **joli**, **long**, **nouveau**, **petit**, and **vieux**.

  J'aime bien les **grandes familles**.
  I like large families.

  Joël est un **vieux copain**.
  Joël is an old friend.

- Other adjectives that are also generally placed before a noun are: **mauvais(e)** (*bad*), **pauvre** (*poor as in unfortunate*), **vrai(e)** (*true, real*).

  Ça, c'est un **pauvre** homme.
  That is an unfortunate man.

  C'est une **vraie** catastrophe!
  This is a real disaster!

Boîte à outils

When **pauvre** and **vrai(e)** are placed after the noun, they have a slightly different meaning: **pauvre** means *poor* as in *not rich*, and **vrai(e)** means *true*.

Ça, c'est un homme **pauvre**.
That is a poor man.

C'est une histoire **vraie**.
This is a true story.

- When placed before a *masculine singular noun that begins with a vowel sound*, these adjectives have a special form.

beau	bel	un **bel** appartement
vieux	vieil	un **vieil** homme
nouveau	nouvel	un **nouvel** ami

- The plural indefinite article **des** changes to **de** when the adjective comes before the noun.

  ADJECTIVE BEFORE NOUN
  J'habite avec **de bons amis**.
  I live with good friends.

  ADJECTIVE AFTER NOUN
  J'habite avec **des amis sympathiques**.
  I live with nice friends.

Essayez! Provide all four forms of the adjectives.

1. grand — grand, grande, grands, grandes
2. nerveux — nerveux, nerveuse, nerveux, nerveuses
3. roux — roux, rousse, roux, rousses
4. bleu — bleu, bleue, bleus, bleues
5. naïf — naïf, naïve, naïfs, naïves
6. gros — gros, grosse, gros, grosses
7. long — long, longue, longs, longues
8. fier — fier, fière, fiers, fières

Structures   Leçon 3A

Mise en pratique

1 Ressemblances Family members often look and behave alike. Describe these family members.

MODÈLE
Caroline est intelligente. Elle a un frère.
Il est intelligent aussi.

1. Jean est curieux. Il a une sœur. Elle est curieuse aussi.
2. Carole est blonde. Elle a un cousin. Il est blond aussi.
3. Albert est gros. Il a trois tantes. Elles sont grosses aussi.
4. Sylvie est fière et heureuse. Elle a un fils. Il est fier et heureux aussi.
5. Christophe est vieux. Il a une demi-sœur. Elle est vieille aussi.
6. Martin est laid. Il a une petite-fille. Elle est laide aussi.
7. Sophie est intellectuelle. Elle a deux grands-pères. Ils sont intellectuels aussi.
8. Céline est naïve. Elle a deux frères. Ils sont naïfs aussi.
9. Anne est belle. Elle a cinq neveux. Ils sont beaux aussi.
10. Anissa est rousse. Elle a un mari. Il est roux aussi.

2 Une femme heureuse Complete these sentences about Christine. Remember: some adjectives precede and some follow the nouns they modify.

MODÈLE
Christine / avoir / trois enfants (beau)
Christine a trois beaux enfants.

1. Elle / avoir / des amis (sympathique)
   Elle a des amis sympathiques.
2. Elle / habiter / dans un appartement (nouveau)
   Elle habite dans un nouvel appartement.
3. Son *(Her)* mari / avoir / un travail (bon)
   Son mari a un bon travail.
4. Ses *(Her)* filles / être / des étudiantes (sérieux)
   Ses filles sont des étudiantes sérieuses.
5. Christine / être / une femme (heureux)
   Christine est une femme heureuse.
6. Son mari / être / un homme (beau)
   Son mari est un bel homme.
7. Elle / avoir / des collègues amusant(e)s
   Elle a des collègues amusant(e)s.
8. Sa *(Her)* secrétaire / être / une fille (jeune/intellectuel)
   Sa secrétaire est une jeune fille intellectuelle.
9. Elle / avoir / des chiens (bon)
   Elle a de bons chiens.
10. Ses voisins / être (poli)
    Ses voisins sont polis.

---

1 Expansion Have students restate the answers, except #3, #7, #8 and #9, using the phrase **les deux** to practice plural forms. Example: 1. **Les deux sont curieux.**

2 Suggestion To check students' work, have volunteers write their sentences on the board and read them aloud.

2 Expansion For additional practice, change the adjective(s) and have students restate or write the sentences. Examples: **1. bon (Elle a de bons amis.) 2. beau (Elle habite dans un bel appartement.) 3. agréable (Son mari a un travail agréable.) 4. bon (Ses filles sont de bonnes étudiantes.) 5. indépendant/élégant (Christine est indépendante et élégante.) 6. fier (Son mari est un homme fier.) 7. poli (Elle a des collègues polis.) 8. joli/intelligent (Sa secrétaire est une jolie fille intelligente.) 9. beau (Elle a de beaux chiens.) 10. américain (Ses voisins sont américains.)**

EXPANSION

Extra Practice Have students create an imaginary character like Christine in Activity 2 on this page. They should use adjectives to describe their character and his/her friends and relatives. Encourage students to share their descriptions with a classmate.

EXPANSION

Extra Practice Have students write brief descriptions of themselves: what they study, their personalities, and what they look like. Collect the descriptions, shuffle them, and read a few of them to the class. Have the class guess who wrote each description.

La famille et les copains — Unité 3

Communication

3 Descriptions In pairs, take turns describing these people and things using the expressions **C'est** or **Ce sont**. *Answers will vary.*

MODÈLE
C'est un cours difficile.

1. _____
2. _____ 
3. _____ 
4. _____ 
5. _____ 
6. _____ 

4 Comparaisons In pairs, take turns comparing these brothers and their sister. Make as many comparisons as possible, then share them with the class to find out which pair is most perceptive. *Answers will vary.*

MODÈLE
Géraldine et Jean-Paul sont grands mais Tristan est petit.

Jean-Paul   Tristan   Géraldine

5 Qui est-ce? Choose the name of a classmate. Your partner must guess the person by asking up to 10 **oui** or **non** questions. Then, switch roles. *Answers will vary.*

MODÈLE
Élève 1: C'est un homme?
Élève 2: Oui.
Élève 1: Il est de taille moyenne?
Élève 2: Non.

6 Les bons copains Interview two classmates to learn about one of their friends, using these questions. Your partners' answers will incorporate descriptive adjectives. Be prepared to report to the class what you learned. *Answers will vary.*

- Est-ce que tu as un(e) bon(ne) copain/copine?
- Comment est-ce qu'il/elle s'appelle?
- Quel âge est-ce qu'il/elle a?
- Comment est-ce qu'il/elle est?
- Il/Elle est de quelle origine?
- Quels cours est-ce qu'il/elle aime?
- Quels cours est-ce qu'il/elle déteste?

cent un 101

---

3 Expansion Students could also describe an image and have their partner guess which one they are describing. Example: **Élève 1:** Elles sont belles. **Élève 2:** C'est la photo numéro un!

4 Expansion To practice negation, have students say what the people in the drawings are not. Example: **Géraldine et Jean-Paul ne sont pas petits.**

4 Partner Chat You can also assign Activity 4 on the Supersite. Students work in pairs to record the activity online. The pair's recorded conversation will appear in your gradebook.

5 Suggestion This activity can also be done in small groups or with the whole class.

6 Suggestions
- To model this activity, have students respond as you ask the interview questions. Tell them to invent answers, where necessary.
- Tell students to add two questions of their own to the list and to take notes during their interviews.
- If time is limited, have students write a description of one of their classmates' friends as written homework.

EXPANSION

Extra Practice Prepare short descriptions of five easily recognizable people. Write their names on the board in random order. Tell students to write your descriptions as you dictate them. Then have them match the description to the appropriate name. Example: **Elle est jeune, brune, athlétique et intellectuelle. (Serena Williams)**

TEACHING OPTIONS

Game Divide the class into two teams. Call on one team member at a time, alternating between teams. Give a certain form of an adjective and name another form that the person must say and write on the board. Example: **beau**; feminine plural (**belles**). Give a point for each correct answer. The team with the most points at the end of the game wins.

Section Goals

In this section, students will learn:
- possessive adjectives
- to express possession and relationships with **de**

Key Standards
4.1, 5.1

Student Resources
Cahier de l'élève, pp. 68–70;
Supersite: Activities, eCahier, Grammar Tutorials

Teacher Resources
Answer Keys; Audio Script; Audio Activity MP3s/CD; Testing program: Grammar Quiz

Suggestions

- Introduce the concept of possessive adjectives. Ask volunteers questions, such as: **Est-ce que votre mère est heureuse? Comment est votre oncle préféré?** Point out the possessive adjectives in questions and responses.
- List the possessive adjectives on the board. Use each with a noun to illustrate agreement. Point out that all possessive adjectives agree in number with the noun they modify, but that all singular possessives must agree in gender and number. Examples: **son cousin, sa cousine, ses cousin(e)s; leur cousin, leur cousine, leurs cousin(e)s**. Also point out that **mon, ton,** and **son** are used before feminine singular nouns beginning with a vowel sound or silent **h**. Examples: **mon épouse, ton idée, son université**.
- Have students give the plural or singular of possessive adjectives with nouns. Say: **Donnez le pluriel: mon élève, ton examen, notre cours.** Say: **Donnez le singulier: mes sœurs, nos frères, leurs chiens, ses enfants.**

Structures   Leçon 3A

3A.2 Possessive adjectives
Presentation Grammar Tutorial

Point de départ In both English and French, possessive adjectives express ownership or possession.

Boîte à outils

In **Contextes**, you learned a few possessive adjectives with family vocabulary: **mon grand-père, ma sœur, mes cousins**.

Possessive adjectives

masculine singular	feminine singular	plural	
mon	ma	mes	my
ton	ta	tes	your (fam. and sing.)
son	sa	ses	his, her, its
notre	notre	nos	our
votre	votre	vos	your (form. or pl.)
leur	leur	leurs	their

C'est ta sœur? Tes parents?

Voilà vos photos.

- Possessive adjectives are always placed before the nouns they modify.

  C'est **ton** père?   Non, c'est **mon** oncle.
  Is that your father?   *No, that's my uncle.*

  Voici **notre** mère.   Ce sont **tes** livres?
  Here's our mother.   *Are these your books?*

- In French, unlike English, possessive adjectives agree in gender and number with the nouns they modify.

  mon frère   **ma** sœur   **mes** grands-parents
  my brother   *my sister*   *my grandparents*

  ton chat   **ta** nièce   **tes** chiens
  your cat   *your niece*   *your dogs*

- Note that the forms **notre, votre,** and **leur** are the same for both masculine and feminine nouns. They only change to indicate whether the noun is singular or plural.

  notre neveu   **notre** famille   **nos** enfants
  our nephew   *our family*   *our children*

  leur cousin   **leur** cousine   **leurs** cousins
  their cousin   *their cousin*   *their cousins*

Boîte à outils

You already know that there are two ways to express *you* in French: **tu** (informal and singular) and **vous** (formal or plural). Remember that the possessive adjective must always correspond to the form of *you* that is used.

Tu parles à **tes** amis?

Vous parlez à **vos** amis?

- The masculine singular forms **mon, ton,** and **son** are used with all singular nouns that begin with a vowel *even if they are feminine.*

  mon amie   **ton** école   **son** histoire
  my friend   *your school*   *his story*

102   cent deux

TEACHING OPTIONS

Video Replay the video episode, having students focus on possessive adjectives. Tell them to write down each one they hear with the noun it modifies. Afterward, ask the class to describe Valérie and Stéphane's family. Remind them to use definite articles and **de** if necessary.

DIFFERENTIATION

For Visual Learners Ask students to bring photos of their families (including pets) to the class. In small groups, each student will describe his/her family members (pointing at the photos) using both possessive and descriptive adjectives. Bring your own photos and visit the small groups to share with your students and check their work.

La famille et les copains — Unité 3

- In English, the possessor's gender is indicated by the use of the possessive adjectives *his* or *her*. In French however, the choice of **son**, **sa**, and **ses** depends on the gender and number of the noun possessed, *not* the gender and number of the possessor.

    son frère = *his/her brother*   **sa** sœur = *his/her sister*   **ses** parents = *his/her parents*

    Context will usually help to clarify the meaning of the possessive adjective.

    J'aime **Nadine** mais je n'aime pas **son** frère.   **Rémy** et **son** frère sont trop sérieux.
    I like Nadine but I don't like her brother.   *Rémy and his brother are too serious.*

Possession with *de*

- In English, you use *'s* to express relationships or ownership. In French, use **de (d')** + [*the noun or proper name*] instead.

    C'est le petit ami **d'Élisabeth**.   C'est le petit ami **de ma sœur**.
    That's Élisabeth's boyfriend.   *That's my sister's boyfriend.*

    Tu aimes la cousine **de Thierry**?   J'ai l'adresse **de ses parents**.
    Do you like Thierry's cousin?   *I have his parents' address.*

- When the preposition **de** is followed by the definite articles **le** and **les**, they contract to form **du** and **des**, respectively. There is no contraction when **de** is followed by **la** and **l'**.

    de + le ▶ du   de + les ▶ des

    L'opinion **du** grand-père est importante.   La fille **des** voisins a les cheveux châtains.
    The grandfather's opinion is important.   *The neighbors' daughter has brown hair.*

    Le nom **de l'**oiseau, c'est Lulu.   J'ai le nouvel album **de la** chanteuse française.
    The bird's name is Lulu.   *I have the French singer's new album.*

> On peut regarder des photos de ma tante?

> Elle a déjà son bac.

Essayez! Provide the appropriate form of each possessive adjective.

mon, ma, mes
1. _mon_ livre
2. _ma_ librairie
3. _mes_ professeurs

ton, ta, tes
4. _tes_ ordinateurs
5. _ta_ télévision
6. _ton_ stylo

son, sa, ses
7. _sa_ table
8. _ses_ problèmes
9. _son_ école

notre, nos
10. _notre_ cahier
11. _nos_ études
12. _notre_ bourse

votre, vos
13. _vos_ soirées
14. _votre_ lycée
15. _vos_ devoirs

leur, leurs
16. _leur_ résultat
17. _leur_ classe
18. _leurs_ notes

Suggestions
- Point out that all possessive adjectives agree in number with the noun they modify, but that all singular possessives must agree in gender and number.
- To introduce possession with **de**, write the following phrases in a list on the board: **l'ordinateur de Monique, l'ordinateur d'Alain, l'ordinateur du professeur, les ordinateurs des professeurs.** Explain the use of the contractions **d'**, **du (de + le)**, and **des (de + les)**.
- Ask students these questions. **C'est mon stylo? C'est votre amie? Ce sont leurs devoirs? C'est sa feuille de papier? Ce sont nos livres de français? C'est l'ordinateur de ____? C'est le sac à dos de ____?**

Essayez! Have students create sentences using these phrases. Examples: **C'est mon livre. Mes professeurs sont patients.**

EXPANSION

Pairs To practice plural possessive adjectives, have pairs describe the family on pages 90-91 from the point of view of Luc and Hélène Garneau. Encourage them to include descriptive adjectives and be creative in their sentences. You might want to introduce the term **les arrière-petits-enfants** (*great-grandchildren*) for this activity. Examples: **Juliette et Marc sont nos enfants. Juliette est blonde, mais Marc est brun. Juliette et son époux, Robert, ont trois enfants. Leurs enfants s'appellent Véronique, Guillaume et Marie.**

Structures
Leçon 3A

Mise en pratique

1 Complétez Complete the sentences with the correct possessive adjectives.

MODÈLE
Karine et Léo, vous avez __vos__ (your) stylos?

1. __Ma__ (My) sœur est très patiente.
2. Marc et Julien adorent __leurs__ (their) cours de philosophie et de maths.
3. Nadine et Gisèle, qui est __votre__ (your) amie?
4. C'est une belle photo de __leur__ (their) grand-mère.
5. Nous voyageons en France avec __nos__ (our) enfants.
6. Est-ce que tu travailles beaucoup sur __ton__ (your) ordinateur?
7. __Ses__ (Her) cousins habitent à Paris.

2 Identifiez Identify the owner of each object.

MODÈLE
Ce sont les cahiers de Sophie.

Sophie

Christophe
1. C'est la télévision de Christophe.

Paul
2. C'est l'ordinateur de Paul.

Stéphanie
3. C'est la calculatrice de Stéphanie.

Georgette
4. Ce sont les stylos de Georgette.

Jacqueline
5. C'est l'université/la bibliothèque/le lycée de Jacqueline.

Christine
6. Ce sont les dictionnaires de Christine.

3 Qui est-ce? Look at the Mercier family tree and explain the relationships between these people.

MODÈLE
Hubert → Marie et Fabien
C'est leur père.

1. Marie → Guy C'est sa femme.
2. Agnès et Hubert → Thomas et Mégane Ce sont leurs grands-parents.
3. Thomas et Daniel → Yvette Ce sont ses fils.
4. Fabien → Guy C'est son beau-frère.
5. Claire → Thomas et Daniel C'est leur cousine.
6. Thomas → Marie C'est son neveu.

---

1 Suggestion To check answers, call on volunteers to read the completed sentences aloud.

1 Expansion For additional practice, give students these items. **8. Est-ce que ____** (*your, form.*) **famille est française?** (votre) **9. ____** (*My*) **femme est italienne.** (Ma) **10. ____** (*Our*) **professeur est américain.** (Notre) **11. Est-ce que ____** (*her*) **cousins sont espagnols?** (ses) **12. ____** (*Their*) **parents sont canadiens.** (Leurs) **13. ____** (*Your, fam.*) **amis sont anglais?** (Tes)

2 Suggestion Have students work in pairs. Tell them to take turns identifying the owners of the items.

2 Expansion To reinforce the relationship between possessive adjectives and possession with **de**, have students restate the answers using **son**, **sa**, or **ses**. Example: **C'est sa télévision.**

3 Expansion Have students come up with more combinations of family members and have volunteers tell the relationships between them.

DIFFERENTIATION

For Visual Learners Collect personal items from your students and bring them to your desk. Make sure to remember who the owner of each item is. Pick one item at a time saying who it belongs to. Your students are to say whether you are right or wrong. Ex. —**C'est la montre de Paul.** / (the class:) —**Non, c'est la montre de Tom.** / (Tom:) —**Oui, c'est ma montre.**

EXPANSION

Extra Practice Have students work in small groups to prepare a description of a famous person, such as a politician, a movie star, or a sports figure, and his or her extended family. Tell them to feel free to invent family members as necessary. Have groups present their descriptions to the class.

La famille et les copains   Unité 3

Communication

4 Ma famille Use these cues to interview as many classmates as you can to learn about their family members. Then, tell the class what you found out. *Answers will vary.*

MODÈLE

mère / parler / espagnol
Élève 1: *Est-ce que ta mère parle espagnol?*
Élève 2: *Oui, ma mère parle espagnol.*

1. sœur / travailler / en Californie
2. frère / être / célibataire
3. cousins / avoir / un chien
4. cousin / voyager / beaucoup
5. père / adorer / les ordinateurs
6. parents / être / divorcés
7. tante / avoir / les yeux marron
8. grands-parents / habiter / en Floride

5 Tu connais? In pairs, take turns telling your partner if someone among your family or friends has these characteristics. Be sure to use a possessive adjective or **de** in your responses. *Answers will vary.*

MODÈLE

français
Mes cousins sont français.

1. naïf
2. beau
3. petit
4. sympathique
5. optimiste
6. grand
7. blond
8. mauvais
9. curieux
10. vieux
11. roux
12. intellectuel

6 Portrait de famille In groups of three, take turns describing your family. Listen carefully to your partners' descriptions without taking notes. After everyone has spoken, two of you describe the other's family to see how well you remember. *Answers will vary.*

MODÈLE

Élève 1: *Sa mère est sociable.*
Élève 2: *Sa mère est blonde.*
Élève 3: *Mais non! Ma mère est timide et elle a les cheveux châtains.*

cent cinq **105**

---

4 Suggestion Have two volunteers read the **modèle**. Explain to students that they use the cues to create the questions.

4 Expansion To practice asking questions with the formal *you* forms, tell students that they are going to interview a French teacher about his or her family. Then have students restate the questions.

5 Expansion Have students take notes on what their partner says and share them with the rest of the class. Example:
Élève 1: Mon cousin est beau.
Élève 2: Son cousin est beau.

5 Virtual Chat You can also assign Activity 5 on the Supersite. Students record individual responses that appear in your gradebook.

6 Suggestion Before students begin the activity, tell them to make a list of the family members they plan to describe. Call on three volunteers to read the **modèle**. Explain that one student will describe his or her own family (using **mon**, **ma**, **mes**) and then the other two will describe the first student's family (using **son**, **sa**, **ses**).

TEACHING OPTIONS

Small Groups Give small groups three minutes to brainstorm how many words they can associate with the phrases **notre lycée** and **notre cours de français**. Have them model their responses on **Dans notre cours, nous avons un(e)/des** _____ and **Notre lycée est** _____. Have the groups share their associations with the rest of the class.

EXPANSION

Extra Practice To practice **votre** and **vos**, have students ask you questions about your family. Examples: **Comment s'appellent vos parents? Est-ce que vous avez des enfants? Comment s'appellent-ils? Est-ce que vous avez des neveux ou des nièces? Comment s'appellent-ils?**

105

Synthèse — Leçon 3A

Révision

Key Standards
1.1

Student Resources
Supersite: Activities, eCahier

Teacher Resources
Answer Keys; Activity Pack; Testing Program: Lesson Test (Testing Program Audio MP3s/CD)

1 Suggestion You may also do this activity with the whole class using the digital image for the **Leçon 3A Contextes** section. Have two students do the **modèle** beforehand. The first student will read **Élève 1**. The second student [**Élève 2**] will point to the people on the digital image as he or she states the relationship.

2 Suggestion Have students brainstorm a list of adjectives that describe personality traits and write them on the board.

3 Suggestion Before students begin the activity, show them pictures of the families listed for identification purposes. You might also wish to add a few names. Examples: **la famille Noah, la famille Bush, la famille Clinton, la famille Soprano, la famille Skywalker,** or **la famille Barone.**

4 Expansion Do a class survey to find out what students think is an ideal family size. Ask: **La famille idéale est grande? Petite? Combien d'enfants a la famille idéale? Un? Deux? Trois? Plus?** Tally the results.

5 Suggestion Before students begin the activity, make sure they understand that **Élève 1** is the agent and **Élève 2** is the casting director. Then ask students to describe the family in the comedy. Example: **Comment est le fils? (Il a les cheveux châtains et il est grand.)**

5 Partner Chat You can also assign Activity 5 on the Supersite. Students work in pairs to record the activity online. The pair's recorded conversation will appear in your gradebook.

6 Suggestion Divide the class into pairs and distribute the Info Gap Handouts from the Activity Pack for this activity.

Unit 3 • Lesson 3A

---

1 Expliquez In pairs, take turns randomly calling out one person from column A and one from column B. Your partner will explain how they are related. *Answers will vary.*

MODÈLE
Élève 1: *ta sœur et ta mère*
Élève 2: *Ma sœur est la fille de ma mère.*

A	B
1. sœur	a. cousine
2. tante	b. mère
3. cousins	c. grand-père
4. frère	d. neveux
5. père	e. oncle

2 Les yeux de ma mère List seven physical or personality traits that you share with other members of your family. Be specific. Then, in pairs, compare your lists and be ready to present your partner's list to the class. *Answers will vary.*

MODÈLE
Élève 1: *J'ai les yeux bleus de mon père et je suis fier/fière comme mon grand-père.*
Élève 2: *Moi, je suis impatient(e) comme ma mère.*

3 Les familles célèbres In groups of four, play a guessing game. Imagine that you belong to one of these famous families or one of your choice. Start describing your new family to your partners. The first person who guesses which family you are describing and where you fit in is the winner. He or she should describe another family. *Answers will vary.*

> La famille Adams
> La famille Griswold
> La famille Kennedy
> La famille Osborne
> La famille Simpson

4 La famille idéale Walk around the room to survey your classmates. Ask them to describe their ideal family. Record their answers. Then, in pairs, compare your results. *Answers will vary.*

MODÈLE
Élève 1: *Comment est ta famille idéale?*
Élève 2: *Ma famille idéale est petite, avec deux enfants et beaucoup de chiens et de chats.*

106   cent six

---

5 Le casting A casting director is on the phone with an agent to find actors for a new comedy about a strange family. In pairs, act out their conversation and find an actor to play each character, based on these illustrations. *Answers will vary.*

MODÈLE
Élève 1 (**agent**): *Pour la mère, il y a Émilie. Elle est rousse et elle a les cheveux courts.*
Élève 2 (**casting director**): *Ah, non. La mère est brune et elle a les cheveux longs. Avez-vous une actrice brune?*

La famille
le fils   la fille   le père   la mère   le cousin

Les acteurs et les actrices
Julie   Annick   Michelle   Patrick   Laurent   Émilie   Stéphane   Robert

6 Les différences Your teacher will give you and a partner each a similar drawing of a family. Identify and name the six differences between your picture and your partner's.

MODÈLE
Élève 1: *La mère est blonde.*
Élève 2: *Non, la mère est brune.*

ressources
vText
CE pp. 65–70
vhlcentral.com
Leçon 3A

EXPANSION

Mini-dictée Use this paragraph as a dictation. Read each sentence twice, pausing to give students time to write. **Ma famille est très grande. Mes parents sont divorcés. Mon beau-père a une fille. La mère de mon demi-frère cadet est française. Leur père est américain. Leurs enfants sont franco-américains. Ma demi-sœur et son frère sont blonds, grands et beaux. Il y a aussi ma sœur aînée. Elle est jolie et de taille moyenne. Notre mère est très fière.**

Call on volunteers to write the sentences on the board. Then ask students to draw a family tree based on this description. You can also ask a few comprehension questions. Examples: **Combien de filles a son beau-père? (Il a une fille.) Qui est franco-américain? (la demi-sœur et le demi-frère)**

La famille et les copains — Unité 3

Le Zapping

Video: TV Clip

Pages d'Or

The **Pages d'Or** (*Golden Pages*) of Belgium offer a range of services that connect businesses with potential customers. In addition to the traditional printed telephone book, the **Pages d'Or** use technology to reach a wide customer base. The **Pages d'Or** website, listings on CD-ROM or DVD, and digital television allow consumers to find businesses quickly for the services they need.

Pages d'Or
www.pagesdor.be

—Papa, combien tu m'aimes?

—Pour toi, je décrocherais° la Lune°.

Compréhension Answer these questions. *Some answers will vary.*

1. Qui (*Who*) sont les deux personnes dans la publicité (*ad*)? C'est un père et son fils.
2. Pourquoi l'homme téléphone-t-il pour obtenir une grue (*crane*)? Il aime beaucoup son fils.
3. Comment trouve-t-il le numéro de téléphone? Il cherche dans les Pages d'Or.

Discussion In groups of three, discuss the answers to these questions. *Answers will vary.*

1. Pourquoi est-il facile de trouver un numéro de téléphone aujourd'hui? Comment le faites-vous?
2. Employez le vocabulaire de cette leçon pour décrire les parents idéaux.

décrocherais *would take down* **Lune** *Moon*

Practice more at vhlcentral.com.

cent sept 107

Section Goals

In this section, students will:
- read about the **Pages d'Or** of Belgium
- watch a commercial for their information services
- answer questions about the commercial and the **Pages d'Or**

Key Standards
1.2, 2.2, 4.2, 5.2

Student Resources
Supersite: Video, Activities
Teacher Resources
Video Script & Translation; Supersite: Video

Introduction
Have students compare and contrast the **Pages d'Or** to the Yellow Pages. Have them visit each company's website and ask them to compare the range of services each offers.

PRE-AP®

Audiovisual Interpretive Communication Previewing Strategy
- Have students look at the video stills, read the captions, and predict what is happening in the commercial for each visual. (1. Le petit garçon parle à son père. Le père écoute son fils. 2. Le garçon regarde la Lune. Il est heureux.)
- Before showing the video, explain to students that they do not need to understand every word they hear. Tell them to listen for the text in the captions and for cognates or any familiar words from this lesson.

Compréhension
Have students work in pairs or groups for this activity. Tell them to write their answers. Then show the video again so that they can check their answers and add any missing information.

Discussion
- Ask volunteers to share their group's answers to the first item with the class.
- Write on the board the students' descriptions of the ideal parents. Determine the three most common answers and discuss why it is so important for a good parent to have these particular skills.

EXPANSION

Les Pages d'Or Obtaining a business telephone listing has come a long way since the printed phone book. The **Pages d'Or** website offers customers an attractive and user-friendly interface for finding a specific number, of course. However, its services go a great deal beyond that. Depending on the time of year, for instance, the site might provide lists of seasonal tasks that people typically need to accomplish around that time. A selection of categories not only reminds the user that it is spring and time to plant a new garden, but also provides links to business throughout Belgium for starting the job.

Contextes

Leçon 3B

You will learn how to...
- describe people
- talk about occupations

Comment sont-ils?

Ils sont paresseux.

Il est rapide.

Il est fort.

Il est travailleur.

discrète (discret m.)

fatiguée (fatigué m.)

jaloux (jalouse f.)

inquiète (inquiet m.)

triste

Vocabulaire

actif/active	active
antipathique	unpleasant
courageux/courageuse	courageous, brave
cruel(le)	cruel
doux/douce	sweet; soft
ennuyeux/ennuyeuse	boring
étranger/étrangère	foreign
faible	weak
favori(te)	favorite
fou/folle	crazy
généreux/généreuse	generous
génial(e) (géniaux pl.)	great
gentil(le)	nice
lent(e)	slow
méchant(e)	mean
modeste	modest, humble
pénible	tiresome
prêt(e)	ready
sportif/sportive	athletic
un(e) architecte	architect
un(e) artiste	artist
un(e) athlète	athlete
un(e) avocat(e)	lawyer
un(e) dentiste	dentist
un homme/une femme d'affaires	businessman/woman
un ingénieur	engineer
un(e) journaliste	journalist
un médecin	doctor

108 cent huit

La famille et les copains — Unité 3

Mise en pratique

1 Les célébrités Match these famous people with their professions. Not all of the professions will be used.

h	1. Donald Trump	a. médecin
e	2. Claude Monet	b. journaliste
d	3. Paul Mitchell	c. musicien(ne)
a	4. Dr. Phil C. McGraw	d. coiffeur/coiffeuse
i	5. Serena Williams	e. artiste
b	6. Katie Couric	f. architecte
c	7. Beethoven	g. avocat(e)
f	8. Frank Lloyd Wright	h. homme/femme d'affaires
		i. athlète
		j. dentiste

2 Les contraires Complete each sentence with the opposite adjective.

1. Ma grand-mère n'est pas cruelle, elle est _douce/gentille_.
2. Mon frère n'est pas travailleur, il est _paresseux_.
3. Mes cousines ne sont pas faibles, elles sont _fortes_.
4. Ma tante n'est pas drôle, elle est _ennuyeuse_.
5. Mon oncle est un bon athlète. Il n'est pas lent, il est _rapide_.
6. Ma famille et moi, nous ne sommes pas antipathiques, nous sommes _sympathiques_.
7. Mes parents ne sont pas méchants, ils sont _gentils/doux_.
8. Mon oncle n'est pas heureux, il est _triste_.

3 Écoutez You will hear descriptions of three people. Listen carefully and indicate whether the statements about them are **vrai** or **faux**.

Nora — Ahmed — Françoise

	Vrai	Faux
1. L'architecte aime le sport.		✓
2. L'artiste est paresseuse.		✓
3. L'artiste aime son travail.	✓	
4. Ahmed est médecin.		✓
5. Françoise est gentille.	✓	
6. Nora est avocate.		✓
7. Nora habite au Québec.		✓
8. Ahmed est travailleur.	✓	
9. Françoise est mère de famille.	✓	
10. Ahmed habite avec sa femme.		✓

Practice more at vhlcentral.com.

la coiffeuse (coiffeur m.)
Il est drôle.
un musicien (musicienne f.)

Contextes — Leçon 3B

Communication

4 Les professions In pairs, say what the real professions of these people are. Alternate reading and answering the questions.

MODÈLE
Élève 1: Est-ce que Sabine et Sarah sont femmes d'affaires?
Élève 2: Non, elles sont avocates.

1. Est-ce que Louis est architecte?
   Non, il est dentiste.
2. Est-ce que Jean est professeur? 
   Non, il est coiffeur.
3. Est-ce que Juliette est ingénieur? 
   Non, elle est journaliste.
4. Est-ce que Charles est médecin? 
   Non, il est homme d'affaires.
5. Est-ce que Pauline est musicienne? 
   Non, elle est architecte.
6. Est-ce que Jacques et Brigitte sont avocats? 
   Non, ils sont athlètes.
7. Est-ce qu'Édouard est dentiste? 
   Non, il est artiste.
8. Est-ce que Martine et Sophie sont dentistes? 
   Non, elles sont musiciennes.

5 Conversez Interview a classmate. Your partner should answer **pourquoi** questions with **parce que** (because). Answers will vary.

1. Quel âge ont tes parents? Comment sont-ils?
2. Quelle est la profession de tes parents?
3. Qui est ton/ta cousin(e) préféré(e)? Pourquoi?
4. Qui n'est pas ton/ta cousin(e) préféré(e)? Pourquoi?
5. As-tu des animaux de compagnie (*pets*)? Quel est ton animal de compagnie favori? Pourquoi?
6. Qui est ton professeur préféré? Pourquoi?
7. Qui est gentil dans la classe?
8. Quelles professions aimes-tu?

6 Les petites annonces Write a **petite annonce** (*personal ad*) where you describe yourself and your ideal significant other. Include details such as profession, age, physical characteristics, and personality, both for yourself and for the person you hope reads the ad. Your teacher will post the ads. In groups, take turns reading them and then vote for the most interesting one. Answers will vary.

7 Quelle surprise! You run into your best friend from high school ten years after you graduated and want to know what his or her life is like today. With a partner, prepare a conversation where you: Answers will vary.

- greet each other
- ask each other's ages
- ask what each other's professions are
- ask about marital status and for a description of your significant others
- ask if either of you have children, and if so, for a description of them

110 cent dix

PRE-AP®

Presentational Writing For homework, have students write a short composition about a person they admire. Tell them to include the reasons why they admire that person. Provide them with the opening statement: **J'admire ____ parce que...** On the following day, ask a few volunteers to read their compositions aloud to the class.

EXPANSION

Using Games Play a game of **Dix questions**. Have a volunteer think of a profession and have the class take turns asking yes/no questions until someone guesses the profession. Limit attempts to ten questions per item instead of twenty.

---

4 Expansion Ask the class questions about the photos. Examples: **Qui est artiste?** (Édouard est artiste.) **Qui travaille avec un ordinateur?** (Charles travaille avec un ordinateur.) **Qui est coiffeur?** (Jean est coiffeur.) **Est-il un bon coiffeur?** (Oui, il est un bon coiffeur./Non, il est un mauvais coiffeur.) **Qui est actif?** (Jacques et Brigitte sont actifs.)

5 Suggestions
- Tell students to add at least two more questions to the list and to jot down their partner's responses.
- After completing the interviews, have volunteers report to the class what their partner said.

5 Virtual Chat You can also assign Activity 5 on the Supersite. Students record individual responses that appear in your gradebook.

6 Suggestions
- Provide students with a few models by passing out copies of authentic French personal ads or using transparencies of personal ads.
- Have students divide a sheet of paper into two columns, labeling one **Moi** and the other **Mon petit ami idéal/Ma petite amie idéale**. Have them brainstorm French adjectives for each column. Ask them to rank each adjective in the second column in terms of its importance to them.

7 Suggestions
- Give pairs a few minutes to decide which role they are going to play and to plan what they are going to say. Have them role-play their conversation and then change partners and repeat.
- Ask a few pairs to present their conversations to the class.

7 Partner Chat You can also assign Activity 7 on the Supersite. Students work in pairs to record the activity online. The pair's recorded conversation will appear in your gradebook.

110 Unit 3 • Lesson 3B

La famille et les copains — Unité 3

Les sons et les lettres
Audio: Explanation Record & Compare

L'accent circonflexe, la cédille, and le tréma

L'accent circonflexe (^) can appear over any vowel.

| pâté | prêt | aîné | drôle | croûton |

L'accent circonflexe is also used to distinguish between words with similar spellings but different meanings.

| mûr | mur | sûr | sur |
| ripe | wall | sure | on |

L'accent circonflexe indicates that a letter, frequently an **s**, has been dropped from an older spelling. For this reason, l'accent circonflexe can be used to identify French cognates of English words.

hospital → hôpital forest → forêt

La cédille (¸) is only used with the letter **c**. A **c** with a **cédille** is pronounced with a soft **c** sound, like the s in the English word *yes*. Use a **cédille** to retain the soft **c** sound before an **a**, **o**, or **u**. Before an **e** or an **i**, the letter **c** is always soft, so a **cédille** is not necessary.

| garçon | français | ça | leçon |

Le tréma (¨) is used to indicate that two vowel sounds are pronounced separately. It is always placed over the second vowel.

| égoïste | naïve | Noël | Haïti |

Prononcez Practice saying these words aloud.

1. naïf
2. reçu
3. châtain
4. âge
5. français
6. fenêtre
7. théâtre
8. garçon
9. égoïste
10. château

Articulez Practice saying these sentences aloud.

1. Comment ça va?
2. Comme ci, comme ça.
3. Vous êtes française, Madame?
4. C'est un garçon cruel et égoïste.
5. J'ai besoin d'être reçu à l'examen.
6. Caroline, ma sœur aînée, est très drôle.

Dictons Practice reading these sayings aloud.

Impossible n'est pas français.[1]

Plus ça change, plus c'est la même chose.[2]

[1] There's no such thing as "can't". (lit. Impossible is not French.)
[2] The more things change, the more they stay the same.

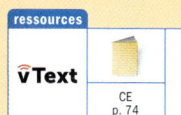

cent onze 111

Section Goals

In this section, students will learn through comprehensible input functional phrases for making complaints, expressing location, and reading numbers.

Key Standards

1.2, 2.1, 2.2, 4.1, 4.2

Student Resources
Cahier de l'élève, pp. 75–76;
Supersite: Activities,
eCahier

Teacher Resources
Answer Keys; Video Script & Translation; *Roman-photo* video

Video Recap: Leçon 3A

Before doing this **Roman-photo**, review the previous one with this activity.
1. **Qui a un ami Cyberhomme sur Internet?** (Amina)
2. **Pourquoi est-ce que Valérie est très inquiète?** (Parce que Stéphane ne travaille pas pour le bac.)
3. **Qu'est-ce que Stéphane, Valérie et Amina regardent sur l'ordinateur portable?** (les photos de la famille de Valérie et de Stéphane)
4. **Qui travaille avec Stéphane pour préparer le bac?** (Rachid)

Video Synopsis
In the café, Sandrine searches frantically for her ringing cell phone, only to find that Stéphane is playing a joke on her. Rachid and Stéphane leave to go study. At Rachid's and David's apartment, Stéphane and Rachid complain about how tiresome it is to hear David constantly talk about Sandrine. They also look at photos of Rachid's parents. Finally, they start studying math. Stéphane says he wants to be an architect.

Suggestions
- Have students scan the captions under the video stills and find four phrases with descriptive adjectives and two that mention professions.
- Have the class read through the scenes that correspond to video stills 1–4 with volunteers playing character roles. Then have small groups read scenes 5–10.
- Have students locate **Algérie** on the world map in **Appendice A**.

Roman-photo Leçon 3B

On travaille chez moi!

Video: Roman-photo
Record & Compare

PERSONNAGES

Amina
David 
Rachid 
Sandrine 
Stéphane 
Valérie 

SANDRINE Alors, Rachid, où est David?
Un portable sonne (a cell phone rings)...
VALÉRIE Allô.
RACHID Allô.
AMINA Allô.

SANDRINE C'est Pascal! Je ne trouve pas mon téléphone!
AMINA Il n'est pas dans ton sac à dos?
SANDRINE Non!
RACHID Ben, il est sous tes cahiers.
SANDRINE Non plus!
AMINA Il est peut-être derrière ton livre... ou à gauche.

SANDRINE Mais non! Pas derrière! Pas à gauche! Pas à droite! Et pas devant!
RACHID Non! Il est là... sur la table. Mais non! La table à côté de la porte.
SANDRINE Ce n'est pas vrai! Ce n'est pas Pascal! Numéro de téléphone 06.62.70.94.87. Mais qui est-ce?

DAVID Sandrine? Elle est au café?
RACHID Oui... pourquoi?
DAVID Ben, j'ai besoin d'un bon café, oui, d'un café très fort. D'un espresso! À plus tard!
RACHID Tu sais, David, lui aussi, est pénible. Il parle de Sandrine. Sandrine, Sandrine, Sandrine.
RACHID ET STÉPHANE C'est barbant!

STÉPHANE C'est ta famille? C'est où?
RACHID En Algérie, l'année dernière chez mes grands-parents. Le reste de ma famille — mes parents, mes sœurs et mon frère, habitent à Marseille.
STÉPHANE C'est ton père, là?
RACHID Oui. Il est médecin. Il travaille beaucoup.

RACHID Et là, c'est ma mère. Elle, elle est avocate. Elle est très active... et très travailleuse aussi.

ACTIVITÉS

1 Identifiez Indicate which character would make each statement. The names may be used more than once. Write **D** for David, **R** for Rachid, **S** for Sandrine, and **St** for Stéphane.

1. J'ai envie d'être architecte. ___St___
2. Numéro de téléphone 06.62.70.94.87. ___S___
3. David est un colocataire pénible. ___R___
4. Stéphane! Tu n'es pas drôle! ___S___
5. Que c'est ennuyeux! ___St___
6. On travaille chez moi! ___R___
7. Sandrine, elle est tellement pénible. ___St___
8. Sandrine? Elle est au café? ___D___
9. J'ai besoin d'un café très fort. ___D___
10. C'est pour ça qu'on prépare le bac. ___R___

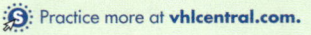

Practice more at **vhlcentral.com**.

112 *cent douze*

TEACHING OPTIONS

On travaille chez moi! Write the episode title **On travaille chez moi!** on the board and have students guess its meaning. Then ask them to predict who might say this phrase in the video and to explain their reasons. Also ask them to guess in what context or situation the person might say this phrase.

EXPANSION

Extra Practice Show the video episode and have students give you a play-by-play description of the action. Write their descriptions on the board. Then show the episode again so students can add more details to the description.

La famille et les copains — Unité 3

Sandrine perd (*loses*) son téléphone.
Rachid aide Stéphane à préparer le bac.

STÉPHANE Qui est-ce? C'est moi!
SANDRINE Stéphane! Tu n'es pas drôle!
AMINA Oui, Stéphane. C'est cruel.
STÉPHANE C'est génial...
RACHID Bon, tu es prêt? On travaille chez moi!

À l'appartement de Rachid et de David...
STÉPHANE Sandrine, elle est tellement pénible. Elle parle de Pascal, elle téléphone à Pascal... Pascal, Pascal, Pascal! Que c'est ennuyeux!
RACHID Moi aussi, j'en ai marre.

STÉPHANE Avocate? Moi, j'ai envie d'être architecte.
RACHID Architecte? Alors, c'est pour ça qu'on prépare le bac.

Rachid et Stéphane au travail...
RACHID Allez, si *x* égale 83 et *y* égale 90, la réponse, c'est...
STÉPHANE Euh... 100?
RACHID Oui! Bravo!

Expressions utiles

Making complaints
- Sandrine, elle est tellement pénible.
  Sandrine is so tiresome.
- J'en ai marre.
  I'm fed up.
- Tu sais, David, lui aussi, est pénible.
  You know, David, he's tiresome, too.
- C'est barbant!/C'est la barbe!
  What a drag!

Reading numbers
- Numéro de téléphone 06.62.70.94.87 (zéro six, soixante-deux, soixante-dix, quatre-vingt-quatorze, quatre-vingt-sept).
  Phone number 06.62.70.94.87.
- Si *x* égale 83 (quatre-vingt-trois) et *y* égale 90 (quatre-vingt-dix)...
  If x equals 83 and y equals 90...
- La réponse, c'est 100 (cent).
  The answer is 100.

Expressing location
- Où est le téléphone de Sandrine?
  Where is Sandrine's telephone?
- Il n'est pas dans son sac à dos.
  It's not in her backpack.
- Il est sous ses cahiers.
  It's under her notebooks.
- Il est derrière son livre, pas devant.
  It's behind her book, not in front.
- Il est à droite ou à gauche?
  Is it to the right or to the left?
- Il est sur la table à côté de la porte.
  It's on the table next to the door.

---

2 Vocabulaire Refer to the video stills and dialogues to match these people and objects with their locations.

- _a/c/e_ 1. sur la table   a. le téléphone de Sandrine
- _a_ 2. pas sous les cahiers   b. Sandrine
- _b/c/e_ 3. devant Rachid   c. l'ordinateur de Rachid
- _b_ 4. au café   d. la famille de Rachid
- _a/f_ 5. à côté de la porte   e. le café de Rachid
- _d_ 6. en Algérie   f. la table

3 Écrivez In pairs, write a brief description in French of one of the video characters. Do not mention the character's name. Describe his or her personality traits, physical characteristics, and career path. Be prepared to read your description aloud to your classmates, who will guess the identity of the character.

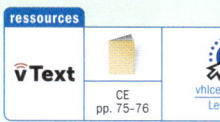

ressources
vText
CE pp. 75–76
vhlcentral.com Leçon 3B

cent treize **113**

Expressions utiles
- Point out any numbers between 61–100 and prepositions of location in the captions in the **Expressions utiles**. Tell students that this material will be formally presented in the **Structures** section.
- Model the pronunciation of the **Expressions utiles** and have students repeat after you. If available, use a cell phone to model the phrases that express location.
- To practice expressing location, point to different objects in the room and ask students where they are located. Examples: **Le livre de ____ est-il sur ou sous le bureau? Où est le sac à dos de ____?**

1 Expansion Give students these additional items: **11. Ce n'est pas Pascal! (Sandrine) 12. Elle est avocate. (Rachid) 13. Si *x* égale 83 et *y* égale 90, la réponse, c'est... (Rachid)**

2 Suggestion To check students' answers, have them form complete sentences using **être**. Examples: **Le téléphone de Sandrine est sur la table. L'ordinateur de Rachid est sur la table.**

3 Suggestions
- Tell pairs to choose a video character and brainstorm a list of adjectives that describe the person before they begin to write their descriptions. Remind them that they can include information from previous episodes.
- Have volunteers read their descriptions and ask the class to guess who it is. Alternatively, you can have students read their descriptions in small groups.

DIFFERENTIATION

For Visual Learners To practice the terms **à droite** and **à gauche**, ask students to describe the people's positions in reference to each other in the video stills of the **Roman-photo**. Example: **1. Amina est à droite de Sandrine.**

PRE-AP®

Interpersonal Speaking Have groups create a short skit similar to the scenes in video stills 1–4 in which someone is searching for a lost object. Provide suggestions for objects. Examples: a notebook (**un cahier**), their homework (**leurs devoirs**), a calculator (**une calculatrice**), a dictionary (**un dictionnaire**), a pen (**un stylo**), and a pencil (**un crayon**). Give students ten minutes to prepare, then call on groups to act out their skits for the class.

Culture — Leçon 3B

Section Goals
In this section, students will:
- learn to distinguish between different types of friendships
- learn some commonly used adjectives to describe people
- learn about marriage in the Francophone world
- read about the Depardieu family

Key Standards
2.1, 2.2, 3.1, 3.2, 4.2

21ST CENTURY SKILLS
Global Awareness
Students will gain perspectives on the Francophone world to develop respect and openness to other cultures.

Student Resources
Supersite: Activities
Teacher Resources
Answer Keys

Culture à la loupe
Avant la lecture
- Introduce the reading topic by asking: **Avez-vous beaucoup de copains? Combien d'amis avez-vous? De quoi parlez-vous avec vos copains? Et avec vos amis?**
- Have students look at the photos and describe the people.
- Tell students to scan the reading, identify the cognates, and guess their meanings.

Lecture
- Point out that **un(e) petit(e) ami(e)** is the main term for boyfriend and girlfriend, but **mon ami(e)** or **mon copain/ma copine** alone without **petit(e)** can also imply a romantic relationship.
- Tell students that it is not uncommon to hear people describe their significant others as **fiancé(e)** even if they are not officially engaged.

Après la lecture Have students identify some differences in French and American dating customs.

1 Expansion Have students write two more true/false statements. Then tell them to exchange their papers with a classmate and complete the activity.

CULTURE À LA LOUPE

L'amitié

Quelle est la différence entre un copain et un ami? Un petit ami, qu'est-ce que c'est? Avoir plus de copains que° d'amis, c'est normal. Des copains sont des personnes qu'on voit assez souvent°, comme° des gens de l'école ou du travail°, et avec qui on parle de sujets ordinaires. L'amitié° entre copains est souvent éphémère et n'est pas très profonde. D'habitude°, ils ne parlent pas de problèmes très personnels.

Par contre°, des amis parlent de choses plus importantes et plus intimes. L'amitié est plus profonde, solide et stable, même si° on ne voit pas ses amis très souvent. Un ami, c'est une personne très proche° qui vous écoute quand vous avez un problème.

Un(e) petit(e) ami(e) est une personne avec qui on a une relation très intime et établie°, basée sur l'amour. Les jeunes couples français sortent° souvent en groupe avec d'autres° couples plutôt que° seuls; même si un jeune homme et une jeune femme sortent ensemble°, normalement chaque personne paie sa part.

plus de... que *more... than* voit assez souvent *sees rather often* comme *such as* du travail *from work* L'amitié *Friendship* D'habitude *Usually* Par contre *On the other hand* même si *even if* proche *close* établie *established* sortent *go out* d'autres *other* plutôt que *rather than* ensemble *together*

> **Coup de main**
>
> To ask *what is* or *what are*, you can use **quel** and a form of the verb **être**. The different forms of **quel** agree in gender and number with the nouns to which they refer:
>
> **Quel/Quelle est...?**
> *What is...?*
>
> **Quels/Quelles sont...?**
> *What are...?*

---

1 Vrai ou faux? Are these statements **vrai** or **faux**? Correct the false statements.

1. D'habitude, on a plus d'amis que de copains. *Faux. On a plus de copains que d'amis.*
2. Un copain est une personne qu'on ne voit pas souvent. *Faux. C'est une personne qu'on voit souvent.*
3. On parle de sujets intimes avec un copain. *Faux. On parle de sujets ordinaires.*
4. Un ami est une personne avec qui on a une relation très solide. *Vrai.*
5. Normalement, on ne parle pas de ses problèmes personnels avec ses copains. *Vrai.*
6. Un ami vous écoute quand vous avez un problème. *Vrai.*
7. L'amitié entre amis est plus profonde que l'amitié entre copains. *Vrai.*
8. En général, les jeunes couples français vont au café ou au cinéma en groupe. *Vrai.*
9. Un petit ami est comme un copain. *Faux. Un petit ami est une personne avec qui on a une relation intime.*
10. En France, les femmes ne paient pas quand elles sortent. *Faux. Chaque personne paie sa part.*

Practice more at **vhlcentral.com**.

TEACHING OPTIONS

Using Categories In small groups, have students draw a chart with three columns. Tell them to label the columns with the three main types of relationships between people: fellow students or coworkers (**les copains, les collègues**); intimate, platonic friends (**les amis**); and people that are boyfriend and girlfriend (**un[e] petit[e] ami[e]**). Then have students list at least five adjectives in each column in French that apply to the people in that type of relationship. Tell them that they can use adjectives from the reading or others that they know. Examples: **normal, ordinaire, intime, personnel, établi, profond, stable, solide,** and **éphémère**. When students have finished, ask different groups to read their lists of adjectives and compile the results on the board.

Unité 3 — La famille et les copains

LE FRANÇAIS QUOTIDIEN

Pour décrire les gens

bête	stupid
borné(e)	narrow-minded
canon	good-looking
coincé(e)	inhibited
cool	relaxed
dingue	crazy
malin/maligne	clever
marrant(e)	funny
mignon(ne)	cute
zarbi	weird

LE MONDE FRANCOPHONE

Le mariage: Qu'est-ce qui est différent?

En France Les mariages sont toujours à la mairie°, en général le samedi après-midi. Beaucoup de couples vont° à l'église° juste après. Il y a un grand dîner le soir. Tous les amis et la famille sont invités.

Au Maroc Les amis de la mariée lui appliquent° du henné sur les mains°.

En Suisse Il n'y a pas de *bridesmaids* comme aux États-Unis mais il y a deux témoins°. En Suisse romande, la partie francophone du pays°, les traditions pour le mariage sont assez° similaires aux traditions en France.

mairie *city hall* vont *go* église *church* lui appliquent *apply* henné sur les mains *henna to the hands* témoins *witnesses* pays *country* assez *rather*

PORTRAIT

Les Depardieu

Les Depardieu sont une famille d'acteurs français. Gérard, le père, est l'acteur le plus célèbre° de France. Lauréat° de deux César°, un pour *Le Dernier Métro*° et l'autre° pour *Cyrano de Bergerac*, et d'un Golden Globe pour le film américain *Green Card*, il joue depuis plus de trente ans° et a tourné dans° plus de 120 (cent vingt) films. Sa fille, Julie, a aussi du succès dans la profession: elle a déjà° deux César et a joué° dans *Un long dimanche de fiançailles*°. Son fils, Guillaume (1971–2008), a joué dans beaucoup de films dont° *Tous les matins du monde*° avec son père. Les deux enfants ont joué avec leur père dans *Le Comte de Monte-Cristo*.

Gérard

Guillaume

Julie

le plus célèbre *most famous* Lauréat *Winner* César *César awards (the equivalent of the Oscars in France)* Le Dernier Métro *The Last Metro* l'autre *the other* il joue depuis plus de trente ans *he has been acting for more than thirty years* a tourné dans *has been in* déjà *already* a joué *has acted* Un long dimanche de fiançailles *A Very Long Engagement* dont *including* Tous les matins du monde *All the Mornings of the World*

Sur Internet

Quand ils sortent (*go out*), où vont (*go*) les jeunes couples français?

Go to vhlcentral.com to find more cultural information related to this **Culture** section.

ACTIVITÉS

2. Les Depardieu Complete these statements with the correct information.

1. Gérard Depardieu a joué dans plus de _____120_____ films.
2. Guillaume était (*was*) _____le fils_____ de Gérard Depardieu.
3. Julie est _____la fille_____ de Gérard Depardieu.
4. Julie joue avec Gérard dans _____*Le Comte de Monte-Cristo*_____.
5. Guillaume a joué avec Gérard dans _____*Tous les matins du monde*/*Le Comte de Monte-Cristo*_____.
6. Julie a déjà _____deux_____ César.

3. Comment sont-ils? Look at the photos of the Depardieu family. With a partner, take turns describing each person in detail in French. How old do you think they are? What do you think their personalities are like? Do you see any family resemblances?

cent quinze **115**

Section Goals

In this section, students will learn numbers 61–100.

Key Standards

4.1, 5.1

Student Resources
Cahier de l'élève, pp. 77–79; Supersite: Activities, eCahier, Grammar Tutorials

Teacher Resources
Answer Keys; Audio Script; Audio Activity MP3s/CD; Testing program: Grammar Quiz

Suggestions
- Review numbers 0–20 by having the class count with you. Then have them count by tens to 60.
- Model the pronunciation of numbers 61–100 and have students repeat them.
- Explain that the numbers 70–99 follow a slightly different pattern than the numbers 21–69. Point out that 61 and 71 use the conjunction **et**, while 81 and 91 need hyphens.
- Write a few numbers on the board, such as 68, 72, 85, and 99. Have students say each number in French as you point to it. Then have students count by fives from 60–100.

Essayez! Have students write five more numbers between 61–100. Then tell them to get together with a classmate and take turns dictating their numbers to each other and writing them down. Remind students to check each other's answers.

Structures — Leçon 3B

3B.1 Numbers 61–100
Presentation Grammar Tutorial

Boîte à outils

Study tip: To say numbers 70–99, remember the arithmetic behind them. For example, **quatre-vingt-douze (92)** is **4 (quatre) × 20 (vingt) + 12 (douze)**.

Numbers 61–100

61–69	80–89
61 soixante et un	80 quatre-vingts
62 soixante-deux	81 quatre-vingt-un
63 soixante-trois	82 quatre-vingt-deux
64 soixante-quatre	83 quatre-vingt-trois
65 soixante-cinq	84 quatre-vingt-quatre
66 soixante-six	85 quatre-vingt-cinq
67 soixante-sept	86 quatre-vingt-six
68 soixante-huit	87 quatre-vingt-sept
69 soixante-neuf	88 quatre-vingt-huit
	89 quatre-vingt-neuf

70–79	90–100
70 soixante-dix	90 quatre-vingt-dix
71 soixante et onze	91 quatre-vingt-onze
72 soixante-douze	92 quatre-vingt-douze
73 soixante-treize	93 quatre-vingt-treize
74 soixante-quatorze	94 quatre-vingt-quatorze
75 soixante-quinze	95 quatre-vingt-quinze
76 soixante-seize	96 quatre-vingt-seize
77 soixante-dix-sept	97 quatre-vingt-dix-sept
78 soixante-dix-huit	98 quatre-vingt-dix-huit
79 soixante-dix-neuf	99 quatre-vingt-dix-neuf
	100 cent

- Numbers that end in the digit **1** are not usually hyphenated. They use the conjunction **et** instead.

  (trente et un)   (cinquante et un)   (soixante et un)

- Note that **81** and **91** are exceptions:

  (quatre-vingt-un)   (quatre-vingt-onze)

- The number **quatre-vingts** ends in **-s**, but there is no **-s** when it is followed by another number.

  (quatre-vingts)   (quatre-vingt-cinq)   (quatre-vingt-dix-huit)

Essayez! What are these numbers in French?

1. 67 _soixante-sept_
2. 75 _soixante-quinze_
3. 99 _quatre-vingt-dix-neuf_
4. 70 _soixante-dix_
5. 82 _quatre-vingt-deux_
6. 91 _quatre-vingt-onze_
7. 66 _soixante-six_
8. 87 _quatre-vingt-sept_
9. 52 _cinquante-deux_
10. 60 _soixante_

116 *cent seize*

EXPANSION

Extra Practice Give simple math problems (addition and subtraction) with numbers 61 and higher. Include numbers 0–60 as well, for a balanced review. Remind students that **plus, et** = *plus*, **moins** = *minus*, and **égale, font, ça fait** = *equals*.

Game Ask students to form a circle. One student starts by saying a number between 10 and 100, then calls the name of another student who should reverse the digits. Example: Student 1 says: "36 (**trente-six**), Steve." Steve says: "63 (**soixante-trois**)." Then Student 2 (Steve) says a new number and the name of another student in the class, who should reverse the digits of this new number. Students who make mistakes should sit down. The last two students standing win the game.

TEACHING OPTIONS

La famille et les copains — Unité 3

Le français vivant

As-tu envie d'être ingénieur, musicien, architecte, professeur?

- le sac à dos 70€
- le bureau 96€
- la chaise 82€
- la calculatrice 61€

Tu as besoin d'une calculatrice intelligente, d'un beau bureau, d'une chaise confortable et d'un bon sac à dos.

Tu trouves tout dans le Catalogue AAZ!

Identifiez Scan this catalogue page, and identify the instances where the numbers 61–100 are used. *Answers will vary.*

Questions *Answers will vary.*
1. Qui sont les personnes sur la photo?
2. Où est-ce qu'elles habitent?
3. Qu'est-ce qu'elles ont dans leur maison?
4. Quels autres *(other)* objets trouve-t-on dans le Catalogue AAZ? (Imaginez.)
5. Quels sont leurs prix *(prices)*?

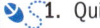

cent dix-sept 117

Le français vivant
- Call on a volunteer to read the catalogue page aloud. Point out the prices in euros.
- Ask students: **Combien d'objets y a-t-il sur la photo?**

TEACHING OPTIONS

Game Ask for two volunteers and station them at opposite ends of the board so neither one can see what the other is writing. Say a number from 0–100 and tell them to write it on the board. If both students are correct, continue to give numbers until one writes an incorrect number. The winner continues on to play against another student.

DIFFERENTIATION

For Kinesthetic Learners Assign ten students a number from 0–100 and line them up in front of the class. As you call out a number at random, that student should take a step forward. When two students have stepped forward, ask them to repeat their numbers. Then ask volunteers to add or subtract the two numbers given. Make sure the resulting sum is not greater than 100.

Structures   Leçon 3B

Mise en pratique

1 Les numéros de téléphone Write down these phone numbers, then read them aloud in French.

MODÈLE

C'est le zéro un, quarante-trois, soixante-quinze, quatre-vingt-trois, seize.
01.43.75.83.16

1. C'est le zéro deux, soixante-cinq, trente-trois, quatre-vingt-quinze, zéro six.
   02.65.33.95.06
2. C'est le zéro un, quatre-vingt-dix-neuf, soixante-quatorze, quinze, vingt-cinq.
   01.99.74.15.25
3. C'est le zéro cinq, soixante-cinq, onze, zéro huit, quatre-vingts.
   05.65.11.08.80
4. C'est le zéro trois, quatre-vingt-dix-sept, soixante-dix-neuf, cinquante-quatre, vingt-sept.
   03.97.79.54.27
5. C'est le zéro quatre, quatre-vingt-cinq, soixante-neuf, quatre-vingt-dix-neuf, quatre-vingt-onze.
   04.85.69.99.91
6. C'est le zéro un, vingt-quatre, quatre-vingt-trois, zéro un, quatre-vingt-neuf.
   01.24.83.01.89
7. C'est le zéro deux, quarante et un, soixante et onze, douze, soixante.
   02.41.71.12.60
8. C'est le zéro quatre, cinquante-huit, zéro neuf, quatre-vingt-dix-sept, treize.
   04.58.09.97.13

2 Les maths Read these math problems aloud, then write out each answer in words.

MODÈLE

65 + 3 = _soixante-huit_
Soixante-cinq plus trois font (equals) soixante-huit.

1. 70 + 15 = quatre-vingt-cinq
2. 82 + 10 = quatre-vingt-douze
3. 76 + 3 = soixante-dix-neuf
4. 88 + 12 = cent
5. 40 + 27 = soixante-sept
6. 67 + 6 = soixante-treize
7. 43 + 54 = quatre-vingt-dix-sept
8. 78 + 5 = quatre-vingt-trois
9. 70 + 20 = quatre-vingt-dix
10. 64 + 16 = quatre-vingts

3 Comptez Read the following numbers aloud in French, then follow the pattern to provide the missing numbers.

1. 60, 62, 64, … 80   66, 68, 70, 72, 74, 76, 78
2. 76, 80, 84, … 100   88, 92, 96
3. 10, 20, 30, … 90   40, 50, 60, 70, 80
4. 81, 83, 85, … 99   87, 89, 91, 93, 95, 97
5. 62, 63, 65, 68, … 98   72, 77, 83, 90
6. 55, 57, 59, … 73   61, 63, 65, 67, 69, 71
7. 100, 95, 90, … 60   85, 80, 75, 70, 65
8. 99, 96, 93, … 69   90, 87, 84, 81, 78, 75, 72

cent dix-huit

Practice more at **vhlcentral.com**.

---

1 Expansions
- Model the question: **Quel est ton numéro de téléphone?** Then have students circulate around the room asking each other their phone numbers. Tell them to write the person's number next to his or her name and have the person verify it.
- Dictate actual phone numbers to the class and tell them to write the numerals. Examples: your office number, the school's number, etc.

2 Expansion Have each student write five more addition or subtraction problems. Then have students work in pairs and take turns reading their problems aloud while the other person says the answer.

3 Expansion Tell students to write three additional series of numbers. Then have them exchange papers with a classmate and take turns reading the series and filling in the numbers.

DIFFERENTIATION

For Kinesthetic Learners Write number patterns on cards (one number per card) and distribute them among the class. Begin a number chain by calling out **the first three numbers in the pattern**. Ex: **vingt-cinq, cinquante, soixante-quinze**. The students holding these cards have five seconds to get up and stand in front of the class. The rest of the class continues by calling out the numbers in the pattern for the students to join the chain. Continue until the chain is broken or complete; then begin a new pattern.

EXPANSION

Extra Practice Write the beginning of a series of numbers on the board and have students continue the sequence out loud. Ex: **50, 55, 60…** or **77, 80, 83, 86…**

La famille et les copains — Unité 3

Communication

4 Questions indiscrètes With a partner, take turns asking how old these people are. *Answers will vary.*

M. Hubert — Mme Hubert — M. Moreau — Mme Moreau — M. Durand — Mme Durand

MODÈLE
Élève 1: *Madame Hubert a quel âge?*
Élève 2: *Elle a 70 ans.*

5 Qui est-ce? Interview as many classmates as you can in five minutes to find out the name, relationship, and age of their oldest family member. Identify the student with the oldest family member to the class. *Answers will vary.*

MODÈLE
Élève 1: *Qui est le plus vieux (the oldest) dans ta famille?*
Élève 2: *C'est ma tante Julie. Elle a soixante-dix ans.*

6 Fournitures scolaires Take turns playing the role of a store employee ordering the school supplies (**fournitures scolaires**) below. Tell how many of each item you need. Your partner will write down the number of items ordered. Switch roles when you're done.

MODÈLE
Élève 1: *Vous avez besoin de combien de crayons?*
Élève 2: *J'ai besoin de soixante-dix crayons.*

1. _____ 2. _____ 3. _____ 4. _____
5. _____ 6. _____ 7. _____ 8. _____

cent dix-neuf **119**

---

4 Expansion To review descriptive adjectives, have students describe the people in the drawing.

4 Virtual Chat You can also assign Activity 4 on the Supersite. Students record individual responses that appear in your gradebook.

5 Suggestions
- Have two volunteers read the **modèle**.
- You may wish to provide a few supplementary terms for family members, such as **l'arrière-grand-mère** and **l'arrière-grand-père**.
- Ask various students to identify the person who has the oldest family member from their interviews. Continue until students identify the oldest person among all the families.

EXPANSION

Extra Practice Ask students to write down their phone numbers on a slip of paper. Collect the papers. Tell students to say «**C'est mon numéro de téléphone!**» when they hear their number. Then proceed to read the numbers aloud at random.

TEACHING OPTIONS

Game Play a game of Bingo. Have students draw a square on a sheet of paper with three horizontal and three vertical rows. Tell them to write nine different numbers between 61–100 in the boxes. Explain that they should cross out the numbers as they hear them and that they should say "Bingo!" if they have three numbers in a horizontal, vertical, or diagonal row. Then call out numbers at random and write them down to verify.

119

Section Goals

In this section, students will learn:
- prepositions of location
- disjunctive pronouns

Key Standards

4.1, 5.1

Student Resources
Cahier de l'élève, pp. 80–82; Supersite: Activities, *eCahier*, Grammar Tutorials

Teacher Resources
Answer Keys; Audio Script; Audio Activity MP3s/CD; Testing program: Grammar Quiz

Suggestions

- Explain that prepositions typically indicate where one thing or person is in relation to another: *near, far, on, between, under*. Model the pronunciation of the prepositions and have students repeat.
- Remind students that they may need to use the contractions **du** and **des**.
- Take a book or other object and place it in various locations in relation to your desk or a student's desk as you ask individual students about its location. Examples: **Où est le livre? Est-ce qu'il est derrière le bureau? Quel objet est à côté du livre?** Work through various locations, eliciting all prepositions of location.

Structures   Leçon 3B

3B.2 Prepositions of location and disjunctive pronouns

Presentation Grammar Tutorial

Point de départ You have already learned expressions in French containing prepositions like **à**, **de**, and **en**. Prepositions of location describe the location of something or someone in relation to something or someone else.

- Use the preposition **à** before the name of any city to express *in*, *to*. The preposition that accompanies the name of a country varies, but you can use **en** in many cases.

  Il étudie **à Nice**.
  He studies in Nice.

  Je voyage **en France** et **en Belgique**.
  I'm traveling to France and Belgium.

Prepositions of location

à côté de	next to	en face de	facing, across from
à droite de	to the right of	entre	between
à gauche de	to the left of	loin de	far from
dans	in	par	by
derrière	behind	près de	close to, near
devant	in front of	sous	under
en	in	sur	on

- Use the forms **du, de la, de l'** and **des** in prepositional expressions when they are appropriate.

  La cantine est **à côté du** gymnase.
  The cafeteria is next to the gym.

  Notre chien aime manger **près des** fenêtres.
  Our dog likes to eat near the windows.

  Ils sont **devant** la bibliothèque.
  They're in front of the library.

  Le café est **à droite de** l'hôtel.
  The café is to the right of the hotel.

- You can further modify prepositions of location by using intensifiers such as **tout** (*very, really*) and **juste** (*just, right*).

  Ma sœur habite **juste en face de** l'université.
  My sister lives right across from the university.

  Le lycée est **juste derrière** son appartement.
  The high school is just behind his apartment.

  Eva travaille **tout près de** la fac.
  Eva works really close to (the university) campus.

  La librairie est **tout à côté du** café.
  The bookstore is right next to the café.

- You may use a preposition without the word **de** if it is not followed by a noun.

  Ma sœur habite **juste à côté**.
  My sister lives right next door.

  Elle travaille **tout près**.
  She works really close by.

Boîte à outils

You can also use the prepositions **derrière** and **devant** without a following noun.

Le chien habite derrière.
The dog lives out back.

However, a noun must always follow the prepositions **dans**, **en**, **entre**, **par**, **sous**, and **sur**.

Il n'est pas sous les cahiers.

Pas derrière! Pas à droite!

120   *cent vingt*

EXPANSION

Extra Practice Ask where different students are in relation to one another. Example: ___ , où est ___? (Il/Elle est à côté de [à droite de, à gauche de, derrière] ___.)

TEACHING OPTIONS

For Kinesthetic Learners On the board, write a number of prepositions, such as **à droite de, derrière,** and **entre**. Have students pass around an object. Each time the object gets moved, ask a volunteer to describe where it is using a preposition. Ex. **Le livre est à droite de Marie. Le livre est entre le stylo et le dictionnaire.**

La famille et les copains — Unité 3

- The preposition **chez** has no exact English equivalent. It expresses the idea of *at* or *to someone's house* or *place*.

    Louise n'aime pas étudier **chez Arnaud** parce qu'il parle beaucoup.
    Louise doesn't like studying at Arnaud's because he talks a lot.

    Ce matin, elle n'étudie pas parce qu'elle est **chez sa cousine**.
    This morning she's not studying because she's at her cousin's.

- The preposition **chez** is also used to express the idea of *at* or *to a professional's office* or *business*.

    chez le docteur
    at the doctor's

    chez la coiffeuse
    to the hairdresser's

    On travaille chez moi!

    Stéphane est chez Rachid.

- When you want to use a pronoun that refers to a person after any type of preposition, you don't use a subject pronoun. Instead, you use what are called disjunctive pronouns.

Disjunctive pronouns

singular		plural	
je → moi		nous → nous	
tu → toi		vous → vous	
il → lui		ils → eux	
elle → elle		elles → elles	

Maryse travaille **à côté de moi**.
Maryse is working next to me.

J'aime mieux dîner **chez vous**.
I prefer to have dinner at your house.

Nous pensons **à toi**.
We're thinking about you.

Voilà ma cousine Lise, **devant nous**.
There's my cousin Lise, in front of us.

Tu as besoin **d'elle** aujourd'hui?
Do you need her today?

Vous n'avez pas peur **d'eux**.
You're not afraid of them.

Essayez! Complete each sentence with the equivalent of the expression in parentheses.

1. La librairie est _derrière_ (*behind*) la cantine.
2. J'habite _près de_ (*close to*) leur lycée.
3. Le laboratoire est _à côté de_ (*next to*) ma résidence.
4. Tu retournes _chez_ (*to the house of*) tes parents ce week-end?
5. La fenêtre est _en face de_ (*across from*) la porte.
6. Mon sac à dos est _sous_ (*under*) la chaise.
7. Ses crayons sont _sur_ (*on*) la table.
8. Votre ordinateur est _dans_ (*in*) la corbeille!
9. Il n'y a pas de secrets _entre_ (*between*) amis.
10. Le professeur est _devant_ (*in front of*) les élèves.

cent vingt et un **121**

Suggestions
- Model the pronunciation of the disjunctive pronouns and have students repeat them. Explain that these pronouns are used in prepositional phrases. Examples: 1. **Ma famille vient** (*comes*) **souvent chez moi.** 2. **Je suis en face de toi.** Then ask volunteers for examples.
- Write the following in a column on the board and explain each usage of **chez**: **chez** + *person's name or person* (**chez Rachid, chez des amis**); **chez** + *professional's office or business* (**chez le docteur**); and **chez** + *disjunctive pronoun* (**chez toi**).
- Compare sentences with subject pronouns and disjunctive pronouns to help students understand when to use each. On the board, write: **Mon ami est français. ____ parle français. Je travaille chez ____ le week-end.** Ask students to fill in the blanks. Highlight that the first blank, which precedes a verb, requires a subject pronoun while the second, which follows a preposition, must be filled with a disjunctive pronoun. Give other examples.

Essayez! Have students write three more fill-in-the-blank sentences describing where certain objects are located in their family's house or apartment. Then tell them to exchange papers with a classmate and complete the sentences.

DIFFERENTIATION

For Kinesthetic Learners Have one student start with a small beanbag or rubber ball. You call out another student identified only by his or her location with reference to other students. Example: **C'est la personne derrière ___.** The student with the beanbag or ball has to throw it to the student identified. The latter student must then throw the object to the next person you identify.

EXPANSION

Video Show the video episode again to give students more input using prepositions and disjunctive pronouns. Stop the video where appropriate to discuss how the prepositions of location and disjunctive pronouns were used. Ask comprehension questions.

121

Structures   Leçon 3B

Mise en pratique

1 Où est ma montre? Claude has lost her watch. Choose the appropriate prepositions to complete her friend Pauline's questions.

MODÈLE

Elle est (*à gauche du* / entre le) livre?

1. Elle est (sur / entre) le bureau? sur
2. Elle est (par / derrière) la télévision? derrière
3. Elle est (entre / dans) le lit et la table? entre
4. Elle est (en / sous) la chaise? sous
5. Elle est (sur / à côté de) la fenêtre? à côté de
6. Elle est (près du / entre le) sac à dos? près du
7. Elle est (devant / sur) la porte? devant
8. Elle est (dans / sous) la corbeille? dans

2 Complétez Look at the drawing, and complete these sentences with the appropriate prepositions. Suggested answers

MODÈLE

Nous sommes _chez_ nos cousins.

1. Nous sommes _devant_ la maison de notre tante.
2. Michel est _loin de_ Béatrice.
3. _Entre_ Jasmine et Laure, il y a le petit cousin, Adrien.
4. Béatrice est _à côté de_ Jasmine.
5. Jasmine est tout _près de_ Béatrice.
6. Michel est _derrière_ Laure.
7. Un oiseau est _sur_ la maison.
8. Laure est _à gauche d'_ Adrien.

Michel   Béatrice
Laure Adrien Jasmine

3 Où est-on? Tell where these people, animals, and things are in relation to each other. Replace the second noun or pronoun with the appropriate disjunctive pronoun. Suggested answers

MODÈLE

Alex / Anne
Alex est à droite d'elle.

1. l'oiseau / je L'oiseau est loin de moi.
2. le chien / Gabrielle et Emma Le chien est entre elles.
3. le monument / tu Le monument est en face de toi.
4. l'ordinateur / Ousmane L'ordinateur est devant lui.
5. Mme Fleury / Max et Élodie Mme Fleury est derrière eux.
6. les enfants / la grand-mère Les enfants sont près d'elle.

122 cent vingt-deux

La famille et les copains — Unité 3

Communication

4 Où est l'objet? In pairs, take turns asking where these items are in the classroom. Use prepositions of location. *Answers will vary.*

MODÈLE la carte

Élève 1: *Où est la carte?*
Élève 2: *Elle est devant la classe.*

1. l'horloge
2. l'ordinateur
3. le tableau
4. la fenêtre
5. le bureau du professeur
6. ton livre de français
7. la corbeille
8. la porte

5 Qui est-ce? Choose someone in the room. The rest of the class will guess whom you chose by asking yes/no questions that use prepositions of location. *Answers will vary.*

MODÈLE

Est-ce qu'il/elle est derrière Dominique?
Est-ce qu'il/elle est entre Jean-Pierre et Suzanne?

6 S'il vous plaît…? A tourist stops someone on the street to ask where certain places are located. In pairs, play these roles using the map to locate the places. *Answers will vary.*

MODÈLE

Élève 1: *La banque, s'il vous plaît?*
Élève 2: *Elle est en face de l'hôpital.*

1. le cinéma Ambassadeur
2. le restaurant Chez Marlène
3. la librairie Antoine
4. le lycée Camus
5. l'hôtel Royal
6. le café de la Place

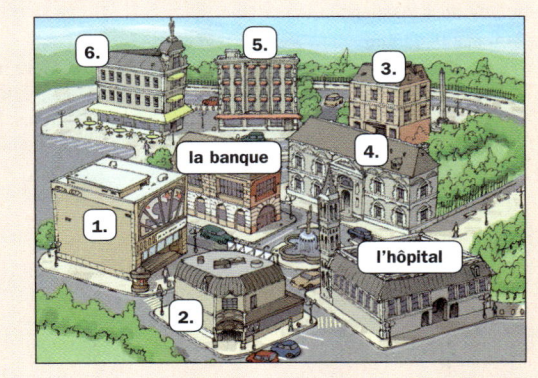

7 Ma ville In pairs, take turns telling your partner where the places below are located in your town or neighborhood. You may use your school as a reference point. Correct your partner when you disagree. *Answers will vary.*

MODÈLE

la banque
La banque est tout près du lycée.

1. le café
2. la librairie
3. l'université
4. le gymnase
5. l'hôtel
6. la bibliothèque
7. l'hôpital
8. le restaurant italien

cent vingt-trois **123**

---

4 Suggestion Have two volunteers read the **modèle** aloud. Remind students to pay attention to the gender of the nouns when responding.

4 Expansion For additional practice, give students these items if they are present in the classroom. **9. le dictionnaire de français 10. la calculatrice 11. les examens**

5 Suggestion To continue this activity, allow the student who guessed the correct person to choose another person and have the class ask the student yes/no questions.

6 Suggestion Before students begin this activity, make sure they understand that the numbers on the illustration correspond to the places on the list. Have two volunteers read the **modèle** aloud.

6 Virtual Chat You can also assign Activity 6 on the Supersite. Students record individual responses that appear in your gradebook.

7 Suggestion Students could even draw a rough map of the town based on their partner's description. They should first situate your school before they draw the other places.

TEACHING OPTIONS

Small Groups In groups of three or four, have students think of a city or town within a 100-mile radius of your school. They need to figure out how many miles away it is and what other cities or towns are nearby (**La ville est près de…**). Then have them get together with another group and read their descriptions. The other group has to guess which city or town is being described.

EXPANSION

Extra Practice Have students look at the world maps in the frontmatter at the beginning of this book, or use the digital images. Make true/false statements about the locations of various countries. Examples: **1. La Chine est près des États-Unis. (Faux.) 2. Le Luxembourg est entre la France et l'Allemagne. (Vrai.)** For variation, you can make statements or ask true/false questions about the location of various cities in France.

123

Synthèse Leçon 3B

Révision

1 Le basket These basketball rivals are competing for the title. In pairs, predict the missing playoff scores. Then, compare your predictions with those of another pair. Be prepared to share your predictions with the class. *Answers will vary.*

1. Ohio State 76, Michigan _____
2. Florida _____, Florida State 84
3. Stanford _____, UCLA 79
4. Purdue 81, Indiana _____
5. Duke 100, Virginia _____
6. Kansas 95, Colorado _____
7. Texas _____, Oklahoma 88
8. Kentucky 98, Tennessee _____

2 La famille d'Édouard In pairs, take turns guessing how the members of Édouard's family are related to him and to each other by describing their locations in the photo. Compare your answers with those of another pair. *Answers will vary.*

MODÈLE
Son père est derrière sa mère.

Édouard

3 La ville In pairs, take turns describing the location of a building (**un bâtiment**) somewhere in your town or city. Your partner must guess which building you are describing in three tries. Keep score to determine the winner after several rounds. *Answers will vary.*

MODÈLE
Élève 1: *C'est un bâtiment entre la banque et le lycée.*
Élève 2: *C'est l'hôpital?*
Élève 1: *C'est ça!*

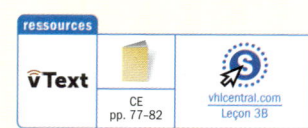

ressources
vText
CE pp. 77–82
vhlcentral.com
Leçon 3B

4 C'est quel numéro? What courses would you take if you were studying at a French university? Take turns deciding and having your partner give you the phone number for enrollment information. *Answers will vary.*

MODÈLE
Élève 1: *Je cherche un cours de philosophie.*
Élève 2: *C'est le zéro quatre...*

Département	Numéro de téléphone
Architecture	04.76.65.74.92
Biologie	04.76.72.63.85
Chimie	04.76.84.79.64
Littérature anglaise	04.76.99.90.82
Mathématiques	04.76.86.66.93
Philosophie	04.76.75.99.80
Psychologie	04.76.61.88.91
Sciences politiques	04.76.68.96.81
Sociologie	04.76.70.83.97

5 À la librairie In pairs, role-play a customer at a bookstore and a clerk who points out where supplies are located. Then, switch roles. Each turn, the customer picks four items from the list. Use the drawing to find the supplies. *Answers will vary.*

MODÈLE
Élève 1: *Je cherche des stylos.*
Élève 2: *Ils sont à côté des cahiers.*

des cahiers	un dictionnaire
une calculatrice	un iPhone®
une carte	du papier
des crayons	un sac à dos

6 Trouvez Your teacher will give you and your partner each a drawing of a family picnic. Ask each other questions to find out where all of the family members are located. *Answers will vary.*

MODÈLE
Élève 1: *Qui est à côté du père?*
Élève 2: *Le neveu est à côté du père.*

124 cent vingt-quatre

La famille et les copains — Unité 3

À l'écoute

Audio: Activities

STRATÉGIE

Asking for repetition / Replaying the recording

Sometimes it is difficult to understand what people say, especially in a noisy environment. During a conversation, you can ask someone to repeat by asking **Comment?** (*What?*) or **Pardon?** (*Pardon me?*). In class, you can ask your teacher to repeat by saying, **Répétez, s'il vous plaît** (*Repeat, please*). If you don't understand a recorded activity, you can simply replay it.

🎧 To help you practice this strategy, you will listen to a short paragraph. Ask your teacher to repeat it or replay the recording, and then summarize what you heard.

Préparation

Based on the photograph, where do you think Suzanne and Diane are? What do you think they are talking about?

À vous d'écouter 🎧

Now you are going to hear Suzanne and Diane's conversation. Use **R** to indicate adjectives that describe Suzanne's boyfriend, Robert. Use **E** for adjectives that describe Diane's boyfriend, Édouard. Some adjectives will not be used.

- _E_ brun
- ___ laid
- _E_ grand
- _E_ intéressant
- _E_ gentil
- _R_ drôle
- _R_ optimiste
- _E_ intelligent
- ___ blond
- _E_ beau
- _R_ sympathique
- _R_ patient

ressources
vText — vhlcentral.com — Leçon 3B

Practice more at vhlcentral.com.

Compréhension

Identifiez-les Whom do these statements describe?

1. Elle a un problème avec un garçon. _Diane_
2. Il ne parle pas à Diane. _Édouard_
3. Elle a de la chance. _Suzanne_
4. Ils parlent souvent. _Suzanne et Robert_
5. Il est sympa. _Robert_
6. Il est timide. _Édouard_

Vrai ou faux? Indicate whether each sentence is **vrai** or **faux**, then correct any false statements.

1. Édouard est un garçon très patient et optimiste.
   Faux. Robert est très patient et optimiste.
2. Diane pense que Suzanne a de la chance.
   Vrai.
3. Suzanne et son petit ami parlent de tout.
   Vrai.
4. Édouard parle souvent à Diane.
   Faux. Édouard ne parle pas à Diane.
5. Robert est peut-être un peu timide.
   Faux. Édouard est peut-être un peu timide.
6. Suzanne parle de beaucoup de choses avec Robert.
   Vrai.

cent vingt-cinq **125**

Section Goals
In this section, students will:
- learn to ask for repetition in oral communication
- listen to and summarize a short paragraph
- listen to a conversation and complete several activities

Key Standards
1.2, 2.1

21st CENTURY SKILLS
Critical Thinking and Problem Solving
Students practice aural comprehension as a tool to negotiate meaning in French.

Student Resources
Supersite: Activities, Audio
Teacher Resources
Answer Keys; Audio Script; Audio Activity MP3s/CD

Stratégie
Script Bonjour, je m'appelle Christine Dupont. Je suis médecin et mère de famille. Mon mari, Richard, est ingénieur. Il est intelligent et très drôle aussi. Nous avons trois enfants charmants: deux fils et une fille. Les garçons sont roux et notre fille est blonde. Notre fils aîné, Marc, a 17 ans. Le cadet, Pascal, a 15 ans. Leur petite sœur, Véronique, a 12 ans.

Préparation Before students do the activity, tell them to look at the photo and describe what they see. Ask students to justify their responses based on visual clues in the photo.

Suggestion To check students' answers for the **À vous d'écouter** activity, have them work in pairs and take turns asking and answering questions using the adjectives listed. Example: **Est-ce que Robert est brun? Non, Édouard est brun**.

À vous d'écouter
Script
SUZANNE: Salut, Diane. Est-ce que ça va?
DIANE: Oh, comme ci, comme ça. J'ai un petit problème. Ce n'est pas grand-chose, mais…
S: Quel genre de problème?
D: Tu sais que j'aime bien Édouard.
S: Oui.
D: Le problème, c'est qu'il ne me parle pas!
S: Il t'aime bien aussi. Il est peut-être un peu timide?
D: Tu crois? …Il est si beau! Grand, brun… Et puis, il est gentil, très intelligent et aussi très intéressant. Et Robert et toi, comment ça va?
S: Euh… plutôt bien. Robert est sympa. Je l'aime beaucoup. Il est patient, optimiste et très drôle.
D: Vous parlez souvent?
S: Oui. Nous parlons deux à trois heures par jour. Nous parlons de beaucoup de choses! De nos cours, de nos amis, de nos familles… de tout.
D: C'est super! Tu as de la chance.

125

Section Goals
In this section, students will learn historical and cultural information about the city of Paris.

Key Standards
2.2, 3.1, 3.2, 5.1

21ST CENTURY SKILLS
Global Awareness
Students will gain perspectives on the Francophone world to develop respect and openness to other cultures.

Student Resources
Cahier de l'élève, pp. 83–84;
Supersite: Activities,
eCahier

Teacher Resources
Answer Keys;
Digital Image Bank

Plan de Paris
- Have students look at the map of Paris or use the Digital Image Bank. Point out that **Paris** and its surrounding areas (**la banlieue**) are called **l'Île-de-France**. This area is also known as **la Région parisienne**. Ask students to locate places mentioned in the **Panorama** on the map. Examples: **le musée du Louvre, le musée d'Orsay, l'Arc de Triomphe,** and **la tour Eiffel.**
- Point out that the Seine River (**la Seine**) divides Paris into two parts: the left bank (**la rive gauche**) and the right bank (**la rive droite**).

La ville en chiffres
- Point out the city's coat of arms.
- Point out that the population figure for Paris includes the city and the surrounding areas.
- Tell students that there is a Rodin Museum in Paris and one in Philadelphia. If possible, show students pictures of two of Rodin's most famous sculptures: *The Kiss* (**le Baiser**) and *The Thinker* (**le Penseur**).

Incroyable mais vrai!
The miles of tunnels and catacombs under Paris used to be quarries; the city was built with much of the stone dug from them. Some of these quarries date back to Roman times. The skeletons in the catacombs are Parisians who were moved from overcrowded cemeteries in the late 1700s.

126 Unit 3

Savoir-faire

Interactive Map Reading

Panorama

Paris

La ville en chiffres

- **Superficie:** 105 km² (cent cinq kilomètres carrés°)
- **Population:** plus de° 9.828.000 (neuf millions huit cent vingt-huit mille)
  SOURCE: Population Division, UN Secretariat

Paris est la capitale de la France. On a l'impression que Paris est une grande ville—et c'est vrai si on compte° ses environs°. Néanmoins°, Paris mesure moins de° 10 kilomètres de l'est à l'ouest°. On peut ainsi° très facilement visiter la ville à pied°. Paris est divisée en 20 arrondissements°. Chaque° arrondissement a son propre maire° et son propre caractère.

- **Industries principales:** haute couture, finances, transports, technologie, tourisme
- **Musées:** plus de 150 (cent cinquante): le musée° du Louvre, le musée d'Orsay, le centre Georges Pompidou et le musée Rodin

Parisiens célèbres

- **Victor Hugo,** écrivain° et activiste (1802–1885)
- **Charles Baudelaire,** poète (1821–1867)
- **Auguste Rodin,** sculpteur (1840–1917)
- **Jean-Paul Sartre,** philosophe (1905–1980)
- **Simone de Beauvoir,** écrivain (1908–1986)
- **Édith Piaf,** chanteuse (1915–1963)
- **Emmanuelle Béart,** actrice (1965–)

l'Arc de Triomphe

l'opéra Garnier

une terrasse de café

Incroyable mais vrai!

Sous les rues° de Paris, il y a une autre ville: les catacombes. Ici reposent° les squelettes d'environ 7.000.000 (sept millions) de personnes provenant° d'anciens cimetières de Paris et de ses environs. Plus de 250.000 (deux cent cinquante mille) touristes par an visitent cette ville de repos° éternel.

carrés square **plus de** more than **si on compte** if one counts **environs** surrounding areas **Néanmoins** Nevertheless **moins de** less than **de l'est à l'ouest** from east to west **ainsi** in this way **à pied** on foot **arrondissements** districts **Chaque** Each **son propre maire** its own mayor **musée** museum **écrivain** writer **rues** streets **reposent** lie; rest **provenant** from **repos** rest

126 cent vingt-six

PRE-AP®
Presentational Speaking with Cultural Comparison If a student has visited Paris, ask the person to prepare a short presentation about his or her experiences there. Encourage the student to bring in photos and souvenirs. Tell the presenter to include what his or her favorite place or activity is in Paris and to explain why. Also, ask him or her to talk about any cultural differences observed during the visit.

EXPANSION
Parisiens célèbres **Jean-Paul Sartre** and **Simone de Beauvoir** had a personal and professional relationship. Sartre became famous as the leader of a group of intellectuals who used to gather regularly at the **Café de Flore**. This group included Simone de Beauvoir and **Albert Camus**. Ask students to name some works they may have read or heard of by Sartre, de Beauvoir, or Camus.

La famille et les copains — Unité 3

Les monuments
La tour Eiffel

La tour Eiffel a été construite° en 1889 (mille huit cent quatre-vingt-neuf) pour l'Exposition universelle, à l'occasion du centenaire° de la Révolution française. Elle mesure 324 (trois cent vingt-quatre) mètres de haut et pèse° 10.100 (dix mille cent) tonnes. La tour attire près de° 7.000.000 (sept millions) de visiteurs par an°.

Les gens
Paris-Plages

Pour les Parisiens qui ne voyagent pas pendant l'été°, la ville de Paris a créé° Paris-Plages pour apporter la plage° aux Parisiens! Inauguré en 2001 et installé sur les quais° de la Seine, Paris-Plages consiste en trois kilomètres de sable et d'herbe°, plein° d'activités comme la natation° et le volley. Ouvert en° juillet et en août, près de 4.000.000 (quatre millions) de personnes visitent Paris-Plages chaque° année.

Les musées
Le musée du Louvre

Ancien° palais royal, le musée du Louvre est aujourd'hui un des plus grands musées du monde° avec sa vaste collection de peintures°, de sculptures et d'antiquités orientales, égyptiennes, grecques et romaines. L'œuvre° la plus célèbre de la collection est La Joconde° de Léonard de Vinci. La pyramide de verre°, créée par l'architecte américain I.M. Pei, marque l'entrée° principale du musée.

Les transports
Le métro

L'architecte Hector Guimard a commencé à réaliser° des entrées du métro de Paris en 1898 (mille huit cent quatre-vingt-dix-huit). Ces entrées sont construites dans le style Art Nouveau: en forme de plantes et de fleurs°. Le métro est aujourd'hui un système très efficace° qui permet aux passagers de traverser° Paris rapidement.

Qu'est-ce que vous avez appris? Complétez les phrases.

1. La ville de Paris est divisée en vingt __arrondissements__.
2. Chaque arrondissement a ses propres __maire__ et __caractère__.
3. Charles Baudelaire est le nom d'un __poète__ français.
4. Édith Piaf est une __chanteuse__ française.
5. Plus de 250.000 personnes par an visitent __les catacombes__ sous les rues de Paris.
6. La tour Eiffel mesure __324__ mètres de haut.
7. En 2001, la ville de Paris a créé __Paris-Plages__ au bord (banks) de la Seine.
8. Le musée du Louvre est un ancien __palais__.
9. __La pyramide de verre__ est une création de I.M. Pei.
10. Certaines entrées du métro sont de style __Art Nouveau__.

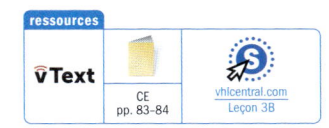

Sur Internet

1. Quels sont les monuments les plus importants à Paris? Qu'est-ce qu'on peut faire (can do) dans la ville?
2. Trouvez des informations sur un des musées de Paris.
3. Recherchez la vie (Research the life) d'un(e) Parisien(ne) célèbre.
4. Cherchez un plan du métro de Paris et trouvez comment aller du Louvre à la tour Eiffel.

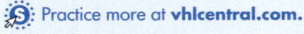

Practice more at vhlcentral.com.

construite built **centenaire** 100-year anniversary **pèse** weighs **attire près de** attracts nearly **par an** per year **pendant l'été** during the summer **a créé** created **apporter la plage** bring the beach **quais** banks **de sable et d'herbe** of sand and grass **plein** full **natation** swimming **Ouvert en** Open in **chaque** each **Ancien** Former **monde** world **peintures** paintings **L'œuvre** The work (of art) **La Joconde** The Mona Lisa **verre** glass **entrée** entrance **a commencé à réaliser** began to create **fleurs** flowers **efficace** efficient **traverser** to cross

Savoir-faire

Lecture

🔊 Audio: Synced Reading

Avant la lecture

STRATÉGIE

Predicting content from visuals

When you are reading in French, be sure to look for visual clues that will orient you as to the content and purpose of what you are reading. Photos and illustrations, for example, will often give you a good idea of the main points that the reading covers. You may also encounter helpful visuals that summarize large amounts of data in a way that is easy to comprehend; these visuals include bar graphs, pie charts, flow charts, lists of percentages, and other diagrams.

Le Top 10 des chiens de race°	
% DE FOYERS° POSSESSEURS	
les caniches°	9,3%
les labradors	7,8%
les yorkshires	5,6%
les épagneuls bretons°	4,6%
les bergers allemands°	4,1%
les autres bergers	3,3%
les bichons	2,7%
les cockers/fox-terriers	2,2%
les boxers	2%
les colleys	1,6%

Examinez le texte

Take a quick look at the visual elements of the article in order to generate a list of ideas about its content. Then, compare your list with a classmate's. Are your lists the same or are they different? Discuss your lists and make any changes needed to produce a final list of ideas.

ressources
vText
vhlcentral.com
Leçon 3B

race *breed* foyers *households* caniches *poodles*
épagneuls bretons *Brittany Spaniels* bergers
allemands *German Shepherds*

128 cent vingt-huit

Fido

Les Français adorent les animaux. Plus de la moitié° des foyers en France ont un chien, un chat ou un autre animal de compagnie°. Les chiens sont particulièrement appréciés et intégrés dans la famille et la société françaises.

Qui possède un chien en France et pourquoi? Souvent°, la présence d'un chien en famille suit l'arrivée° d'enfants, parce que les parents pensent qu'un chien contribue positivement à leur développement. Il est aussi commun de trouver deux chiens ou plus dans le même° foyer.

Les chiens sont d'excellents compagnons. Leurs maîtres° sont moins seuls° et déclarent avoir moins de stress. Certaines personnes possèdent un chien pour avoir plus d'exercice

en famille

physique. Et il y a aussi des personnes qui possèdent un chien parce qu'elles en ont toujours eu un° et n'imaginent pas une vie° sans° chien.

Les chiens ont parfois° les mêmes droits° que les autres membres de la famille, et parfois des droits spéciaux. Bien sûr, ils accompagnent leurs maîtres pour les courses en ville° et les promenades dans le parc, et ils entrent même dans certains magasins°. Ne trouvez-vous pas parfois un caniche ou un labrador, les deux races les plus° populaires en France, avec son maître dans un restaurant?

En France, il n'est pas difficile d'observer que les chiens ont une place privilégiée au sein de° la famille.

Pourquoi avoir un animal de compagnie?

RAISON	CHIENS	CHATS	OISEAUX	POISSONS
Pour l'amour des animaux	61,4%	60,5%	61%	33%
Pour avoir de la compagnie	43,5%	38,2%	37%	10%
Pour s'occuper*	40,4%	37,7%	0%	0%
Parce que j'en ai toujours eu un*	31,8%	28,9%	0%	0%
Pour le bien-être* personnel	29,2%	26,2%	0%	0%
Pour les enfants	23,7%	21,3%	30%	48%

Plus de la moitié *More than half* **animal de compagnie** *pet* **Souvent** *Often* **suit l'arrivée** *follows the arrival* **même** *same* **maîtres** *owners* **moins seuls** *less lonely* **en ont toujours eu un** *have always had one* **vie** *life* **sans** *without* **parfois** *sometimes* **droits** *rights* **courses en ville** *errands in town* **magasins** *stores* **les plus** *the most* **au sein de** *in the heart of* **s'occuper** *keep busy* **Parce que j'en ai toujours eu un** *Because I've always had one* **bien-être** *well-being*

La famille et les copains — Unité 3

Après la lecture

Vrai ou faux? Indicate whether these items are **vrai** or **faux**, based on the reading. Correct the false ones.

	Vrai	Faux
1. Les chiens accompagnent leurs maîtres pour les promenades dans le parc.	✓	
2. Parfois, les chiens accompagnent leurs maîtres dans les restaurants.	✓	
3. Le chat n'est pas un animal apprécié en France. *En France, plus de la moitié des foyers ont un chien, un chat ou un autre animal de compagnie.*		✓
4. Certaines personnes déclarent posséder un chien pour avoir plus d'exercice physique.	✓	
5. Certaines personnes déclarent posséder un chien pour avoir plus de stress. *Certaines personnes déclarent avoir moins de stress avec un chien.*		✓
6. En France, les familles avec enfants n'ont pas de chien. *Souvent, la présence d'un chien dans une famille suit l'arrivée d'enfants.*		✓

Fido en famille Choose the correct response according to the article.

1. Combien de foyers en France ont au moins (*at least*) un animal de compagnie?
   a. 20%–25%
   b. 40%–45%
   c. 50%–55%

2. Pourquoi est-ce une bonne idée d'avoir un chien?
   a. pour plus de compagnie et plus de stress
   b. pour l'exercice physique et être seul
   c. pour la compagnie et le développement des enfants

3. Que pensent les familles françaises de leurs chiens?
   a. Les chiens sont plus importants que les enfants.
   b. Les chiens font partie (*are part*) de la famille et participent aux activités quotidiennes (*daily*).
   c. Le rôle des chiens est limité aux promenades.

4. Quelles races de chien les Français préfèrent-ils?
   a. les caniches et les oiseaux
   b. les labradors et les bergers allemands
   c. les caniches et les labradors

5. Y a-t-il des familles avec plus d'un chien?
   a. non
   b. oui
   c. les caniches et les labradors

Mes animaux In groups of three, say why you own or someone you know owns a pet. Give one of the reasons listed in the table on the left or a different one. Use the verb **avoir** and possessive adjectives.

MODÈLE
Mon grand-père a un chien pour son bien-être personnel.

cent vingt-neuf 129

Section Goals

In this section, students will:
- learn to use idea maps to organize information
- learn to write an informal letter in French

Key Standards

1.3, 3.1, 5.1

Stratégie Tell students that they might find it helpful to use note cards to create idea maps. Writing each detail on a separate card will allow them to rearrange ideas and experiment with organization. Remind students to write their ideas in French, since they may not have the vocabulary or structures for some English terms they generate.

PRE-AP®

Interpersonal Writing Introduce the common salutations and closings used in informal letters in French. Point out the difference between **cher** (masculine) and **chère** (feminine). Model the pronunciation to show students that the two words sound the same.

Savoir-faire

Écriture

STRATÉGIE

Using idea maps

How do you organize ideas for a first draft? Often, the organization of ideas represents the most challenging part of the writing process. Idea maps are useful for organizing pertinent information. Here is an example of an idea map you can use when writing.

SCHÉMA D'IDÉES

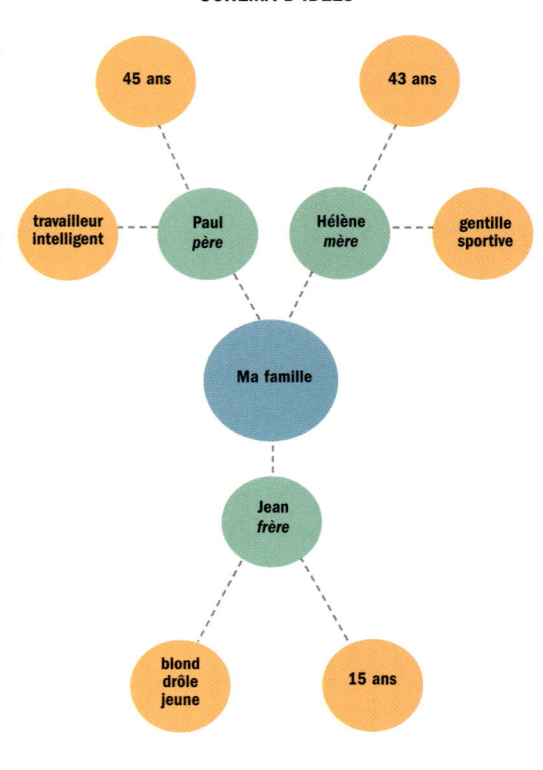

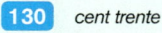

- 45 ans — Paul *père* — travailleur, intelligent
- 43 ans — Hélène *mère* — gentille, sportive
- Ma famille
- Jean *frère*
- blond, drôle, jeune
- 15 ans

Thème

Écrivez une lettre

Avant l'écriture

1. A French-speaking friend wants to know about your family. Using some of the verbs and adjectives you learned in this lesson, write a brief letter describing your own family or an imaginary one. Be sure to include information from each of these categories for each family member:

   - Names, ages, and relationships
   - Physical characteristics
   - Hobbies and interests

   Before you begin, create an idea map like the one on the left, with a circle for each member of your family.

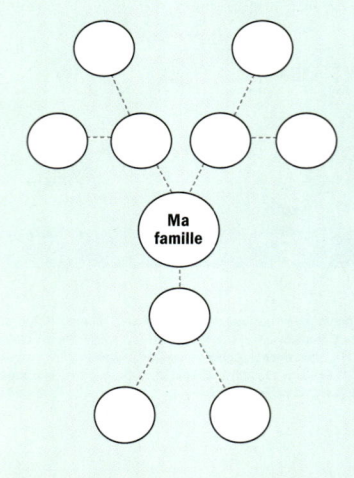

130 cent trente

EXPANSION

Avant l'écriture Remind students that they used a word web to brainstorm ideas in Unit 2. Tell them that an idea map is similar, but that it links various ideas to a central topic and breaks those ideas down into smaller categories. Point out the colors used in the idea map on page 130 and how they are used to group similar levels of information.

Help students create an outline for a typical letter: a salutation, an introductory paragraph, a second paragraph with the family description, a third paragraph with a request for a response, a closing, and a signature. Tell students their introductory paragraph should include an inquiry into how the person is doing, along with a similar comment about themselves.

La famille et les copains — Unité 3

2. Once you have completed your idea map, compare it with the one created by a classmate. Did you both include the same kind of information? Did you list all your family members? Did you include information from each of the three categories for each person?

3. Here are some useful expressions for writing a letter in French:

Salutations

Cher Fabien,	Dear Fabien,
Chère Joëlle,	Dear Joëlle,

Asking for a response

Réponds-moi vite.	Write back soon.
Donne-moi de tes nouvelles.	Tell me all your news.

Closings

Grosses bises!	Big kisses!
Je t'embrasse!	Kisses!
Bisous!	Kisses!
À bientôt!	See you soon!
Amitiés,	In friendship,
Cordialement,	Cordially,
À plus (tard),	Until later,

Écriture

Use your idea map and the list of letter-writing expressions to write a letter that describes your family to a friend. Be sure to include some of the verbs and adjectives you have learned in this lesson.

Cher Christophe,

Mon père s'appelle Gabriel. Il a 42 ans. Il est grand, a les cheveux châtains et les yeux marron. Il est architecte et travaille à Paris. Il aime dessiner, lire (to read) et voyager. Ma mère, Nicole, a 37 ans. Elle est petite, blonde et a les yeux bleus. Elle est professeur d'anglais à l'université. Comme mon père, elle aime voyager. Elle aime aussi faire (to do) du sport. Ma sœur, Élodie, a 17 ans. Elle est grande, a les cheveux châtains et les yeux verts. Elle est encore au lycée. Elle adore écouter de la musique et aller au (to go to) cinéma. Mon oncle, …
Et ta famille, comment est-elle? Donne-moi vite de tes nouvelles!
À bientôt!
Caroline

Après l'écriture

1. Exchange rough drafts with a partner. Comment on his or her work by answering these questions:

   - Did your partner make the adjectives agree with the person described?
   - Did your partner include the age, family relationship, physical characteristics, and hobbies and interests of each family member?
   - Did your partner use verb forms correctly?
   - Did your partner use the letter-writing expressions correctly?

2. Revise your description according to your partner's comments. After writing the final version, read it once more to eliminate these kinds of problems:

   - spelling errors
   - punctuation errors
   - capitalization errors
   - use of incorrect verb forms
   - adjectives that do not agree with the nouns they modify

EVALUATION

Criteria

Content Includes all the information mentioned in the three bulleted items in the task description as well as some of the expressions in the list of salutations, requests for response, and closings.
Scale: 1 2 3 4 5

Organization Organizes the letter into a salutation, a family description, a request for a response, and a closing.
Scale: 1 2 3 4 5

Accuracy Uses possessive and descriptive adjectives and modifies them accordingly. Spells words and conjugates verbs correctly throughout.
Scale: 1 2 3 4 5

Creativity Includes additional information that is not included in the task and/or provides detailed information about numerous family members.
Scale: 1 2 3 4 5

Scoring

Excellent	18–20 points
Good	14–17 points
Satisfactory	10–13 points
Unsatisfactory	< 10 points

21st CENTURY SKILLS

Productivity and Accountability
Provide the rubric to students before they hand their work in for grading. Ask students to make sure they have met the highest standard possible on the rubric before submitting their work.

PRE-AP®

Interpersonal Writing Remind students of the **-er** verbs that they can use to talk about family members' hobbies and interests: **adorer**, **aimer**, and **détester**. Encourage them to go beyond the task to talk about what their family members dislike as well. Brainstorm a list of possible interests and hobbies that students can draw upon as they write.

Clarify the cultural differences among the closing expressions shown. **Grosses bises**, **Bisous**, and **À plus** are used with close friends. Where the relationship is informal but the person is not a close friend, **À plus tard** is a better choice. **Amitiés** and **Cordialement** are more formal and often used when addressing an older person or a business associate.

Vocabulaire — Unité 3

Flashcards
Audio: Vocabulary
My Vocabulary

Key Standards
4.1

Teacher Resources
Vocabulary MP3s/CD

Suggestion Tell students that an easy way to study from **Vocabulaire** is to cover up the French half of each section, leaving only the English equivalents exposed. They can then quiz themselves on the French items. To focus on the English equivalents of the French entries, they simply reverse this process.

21st CENTURY SKILLS

Creativity and Innovation
Ask students to prepare a list of three products or perspectives they learned about in this unit to share with the class. Consider asking them to focus on the **Culture** and **Panorama** sections.

21st CENTURY SKILLS

Leadership and Responsibility Extension Project
If you have access to students in a Francophone country, have students decide on three questions they want to ask the partner class related to this unit's topic. Based on the responses they receive, work as a class to explain to the partner class one aspect of their responses that surprised the class and why.

La famille

aîné(e)	elder
cadet(te)	younger
un beau-frère	brother-in-law
un beau-père	father-in-law; stepfather
une belle-mère	mother-in-law; stepmother
une belle-sœur	sister-in-law
un(e) cousin(e)	cousin
un demi-frère	half-brother; stepbrother
une demi-sœur	half-sister; stepsister
les enfants (m., f.)	children
un époux/ une épouse	spouse
une famille	family
une femme	wife; woman
une fille	daughter; girl
un fils	son
un frère	brother
une grand-mère	grandmother
un grand-père	grandfather
les grands-parents (m.)	grandparents
un mari	husband
une mère	mother
un neveu	nephew
une nièce	niece
un oncle	uncle
les parents (m.)	parents
un père	father
une petite-fille	granddaughter
un petit-fils	grandson
les petits-enfants (m.)	grandchildren
une sœur	sister
une tante	aunt
un chat	cat
un chien	dog
un oiseau	bird
un poisson	fish

Adjectifs descriptifs

antipathique	unpleasant
bleu(e)	blue
blond(e)	blond
brun(e)	dark (hair)
court(e)	short
drôle	funny
faible	weak
fatigué(e)	tired
fort(e)	strong
frisé(e)	curly
génial(e) (géniaux pl.)	great
grand(e)	big; tall
jeune	young
joli(e)	pretty
laid(e)	ugly
lent(e)	slow
mauvais(e)	bad
méchant(e)	mean
modeste	modest, humble
noir(e)	black
pauvre	poor, unfortunate
pénible	tiresome
petit(e)	small, short (stature)
prêt(e)	ready
raide	straight
rapide	fast
triste	sad
vert(e)	green
vrai(e)	true; real

Vocabulaire supplémentaire

divorcer	to divorce
épouser	to marry
célibataire	single
divorcé(e)	divorced
fiancé(e)	engaged
marié(e)	married
séparé(e)	separated
veuf/veuve	widowed
un(e) voisin(e)	neighbor

Expressions utiles	See pp. 95 and 113.
Possessive adjectives	See p. 102.
Numbers 61–100	See p. 116.
Prepositions of location	See p. 120.

Professions et occupations

un(e) architecte	architect
un(e) artiste	artist
un(e) athlète	athlete
un(e) avocat(e)	lawyer
un coiffeur/ une coiffeuse	hairdresser
un(e) dentiste	dentist
un homme/une femme d'affaires	businessman/ woman
un ingénieur	engineer
un(e) journaliste	journalist
un médecin	doctor
un(e) musicien(ne)	musician

Adjectifs irréguliers

actif/active	active
beau/belle	beautiful; handsome
bon(ne)	kind; good
châtain	brown (hair)
courageux/ courageuse	courageous, brave
cruel(le)	cruel
curieux/curieuse	curious
discret/discrète	discreet; unassuming
doux/douce	sweet; soft
ennuyeux/ennuyeuse	boring
étranger/étrangère	foreign
favori(te)	favorite
fier/fière	proud
fou/folle	crazy
généreux/généreuse	generous
gentil(le)	nice
gros(se)	fat
inquiet/inquiète	worried
intellectuel(le)	intellectual
jaloux/jalouse	jealous
long(ue)	long
(mal)heureux/ (mal)heureuse	(un)happy
marron	brown
naïf/naïve	naive
nerveux/nerveuse	nervous
nouveau/nouvelle	new
paresseux/paresseuse	lazy
roux/rousse	red-haired
sérieux/sérieuse	serious
sportif/sportive	athletic
travailleur/ travailleuse	hard-working
vieux/vieille	old

132 *cent trente-deux*

Au café

Unité 4

Leçon 4A

CONTEXTES . . . pages 134–137
- Places and activities around town
- Oral vowels

ROMAN-PHOTO . pages 138–139
- Star du cinéma

CULTURE . . . . . . pages 140–141
- Popular leisure activities

STRUCTURES. . pages 142–149
- The verb **aller**
- Interrogative words

SYNTHÈSE . . . . pages 150–151
- Révision
- Le Zapping

Leçon 4B

CONTEXTES . . . pages 152–155
- Going to a café
- Nasal vowels

ROMAN-PHOTO . pages 156–157
- L'heure du déjeuner

CULTURE . . . . . . pages 158–159
- Café culture
- Flash culture

STRUCTURES. . pages 160–167
- The verbs **prendre** and **boire**; Partitives
- Regular -ir verbs

SYNTHÈSE . . . . pages 168–169
- Révision
- À l'écoute

Savoir-faire . pages 170–175
- **Panorama:** La Normandie and La Bretagne
- **Lecture:** Read a cybercafé brochure.
- **Écriture:** Write a note to explain plans.

Pour commencer
- Quelle heure est-il, à votre avis?
  a. neuf heures du matin b. midi
  c. dix heures du soir
- Qu'est-ce qu'il y a sur la table?
  a. des sandwiches b. des boissons
  c. de la soupe
- Qu'est-ce que ces garçons ont envie de faire?
  a. boire b. manger c. partager

Unit Goals

Leçon 4A
In this lesson, students will learn:
- names for places around town
- terms for activities around town
- to pronounce oral vowels
- about pastimes of young French people and **le verlan**
- the verb **aller** and to express future actions with it
- the preposition **à** and contractions with it
- interrogative words
- about the Swiss national airline

Leçon 4B
In this lesson, students will learn:
- terms for food items at a café
- expressions of quantity
- to pronounce nasal vowels
- about the role of the café in France and the cafés of North Africa
- more about cafés and food items through specially shot video footage
- the present tense of **prendre** and **boire**
- the formation and use of partitive articles
- regular **-ir** verbs
- to listen for the gist in oral communication

Savoir-faire
In this section, students will learn:
- cultural and historical information about the French regions of **Normandie** and **Bretagne**
- to scan a text to improve comprehension
- to add details in French to make writing more interesting

21st CENTURY SKILLS
Initiative and Self-Direction
Students can monitor their progress online using the Supersite activities and assessments.

Pour commencer
- a. neuf heures du matin
- b. des boissons
- a. boire

INSTRUCTIONAL RESOURCES

Student Resources
Print: Student Book, Workbook (*Cahier de l'élève*)
Supersite: vhlcentral.com, **vText**, *eCahier*, Audio, Video, Practice

Teacher Resources
Print: Teacher's Edition, Answer Keys, Testing Program
Technology: Audio MP3s on CD (Textbook, Testing Program, Audio Program), Video Program DVD (*Roman-photo, Flash culture*)

Supersite: vhlcentral.com, Activity Pack, Middle School Activity Pack, Lesson Plans, Grammar Tutorials, Grammar Slides, Testing Program, Audio and Video Scripts, Answer Key, Audio MP3s, Streaming Video (*Roman-photo, Flash culture, Le Zapping*), Digital Image Bank, Learning Management System (Gradebook, Assignments)

VOICE BOARD Voice boards on the Supersite allow you and your students to record and share up to five minutes of audio. Use voice boards for presentations, oral assessments, discussions, directions, etc.

Section Goals

In this section, students will learn and practice vocabulary related to:
- places in a city
- pastimes

Key Standards
1.1, 1.2, 4.1

Student Resources
Cahier de l'élève, pp. 85–87;
Supersite: Activities,
eCahier

Teacher Resources
Answer Keys; Digital Image Bank; Audio Script; Textbook & Audio Activity MP3s/CD; Activity Pack; Testing program: Vocabulary Quiz

Suggestions

- Have students look at the new vocabulary and identify the cognates.
- Use the digital image for this page. As you point to different people, describe where they are and what they are doing. Examples: **Ils sont à la terrasse d'un café. Elles bavardent.** Follow up with simple questions based on your narrative.
- Ask students yes/no and either/or questions about their preferences using the new vocabulary. Examples: **Aimez-vous nager? Préférez-vous regarder un film au cinéma ou à la maison?**
- Tell students that proper names of places, like adjectives, usually follow generic nouns. Examples: **le cinéma Rex** and **le parc Monceau.**
- Point out that the term **une boîte de nuit** is familiar and usually used among young people. **Une discothèque** is the more formal word for *nightclub*.
- Point out that **un gymnase** in France generally has a track, exercise equipment, basketball or tennis courts, showers, but no pool.

Contextes — Leçon 4A

Audio: Vocabulary Practice
My Vocabulary

Où allons-nous?

You will learn how to...
- say where you are going
- say what you are going to do

Vocabulaire

danser	to dance
explorer	to explore
fréquenter	to frequent; to visit
inviter	to invite
nager	to swim
patiner	to skate
une banlieue	suburbs
une boîte (de nuit)	nightclub
un bureau	office; desk
un centre commercial	shopping center, mall
un centre-ville	city/town center, downtown
un cinéma (ciné)	movie theater, movies
un endroit	place
un grand magasin	department store
un gymnase	gym
un hôpital	hospital
un lieu	place
un magasin	store
un marché	market
un musée	museum
un parc	park
une piscine	pool
un restaurant	restaurant
une ville	city, town

Image labels: une maison · une montagne · Il passe chez quelqu'un. (passer) · Elle quitte la maison. (quitter) · Ils déjeunent. (déjeuner) · une place · une terrasse de café · Elles bavardent. (bavarder)

ressources
vText
CE pp. 85–87
vhlcentral.com
Leçon 4A

TEACHING OPTIONS

Using Games Divide the class into two teams. Put objects related to different places in a box (for example, movie ticket stubs, sunglasses, and a coffee cup). Without looking, have a student reach into the box and pick out an object. The next player on that person's team has five seconds to name a place associated with the object. If the person cannot do so within the time limit, the other team may "steal" the point by giving a correct response. When the box is empty, the team with the most points wins.

DIFFERENTIATION

For Visual Learners Use magazine photos or clip art from the Internet to make flash cards representing places in and around town. As you show each image, students should say the name of the place and as many activities associated with it as they can think of.

Au café — Unité 4

Mise en pratique

une église

Attention!
Remember that nouns that end in –al have an irregular plural. Replace –al with –aux.
un hôpital → deux hôpitaux

À (to, at) before le or les makes these contractions:
à + le = au   à + les = aux
le musée → au musée
les endroits → aux endroits
À does NOT contract with l' or la.

une épicerie

un kiosque

Il dépense de l'argent (m.). (dépenser)

1 Associez
Quels lieux associez-vous à ces activités?
1. nager _une piscine_
2. danser _une boîte (de nuit)_
3. dîner _un restaurant_
4. travailler _un bureau_
5. habiter _une maison_
6. épouser _une église_
7. voir (to see) un film _un cinéma_
8. acheter (to buy) des fruits _un marché, une épicerie_

2 Écoutez
Djamila parle de sa journée à son amie Samira. Écoutez la conversation et mettez (put) les lieux de la liste dans l'ordre chronologique. Il y a deux lieux en trop (extra).

_3_ a. à l'hôpital
_8_ b. à la maison
_1_ c. à la piscine
_5_ d. au centre commercial
_6_ e. au cinéma
_NA_ f. à l'église
_2_ g. au musée
_7_ h. au bureau
_NA_ i. au parc
_4_ j. au restaurant

Coup de main
Note that the French **Je vais à...** is the equivalent of the English *I am going to...*

3 Logique ou illogique
Lisez chaque phrase et déterminez si l'action est logique ou illogique. Corrigez si nécessaire. *Suggested answers*

	logique	illogique
1. Maxime invite Delphine à une épicerie. *Maxime invite Delphine au musée.*		✓
2. Caroline et Aurélie bavardent au marché.	✓	
3. Nous déjeunons à l'épicerie. *Nous déjeunons au restaurant.*		✓
4. Ils dépensent beaucoup d'argent au centre commercial.	✓	
5. Vous explorez une ville.	✓	
6. Vous escaladez (climb) une montagne.	✓	
7. J'habite en banlieue.	✓	
8. Tu danses dans un marché. *Tu danses dans une boîte (de nuit).*		✓

Practice more at vhlcentral.com.

cent trente-cinq **135**

Contextes   Leçon 4A

Communication

4 **Conversez** Avec un(e) partenaire, échangez vos opinions sur ces activités. Utilisez un élément de chaque colonne dans vos réponses. *Answers will vary.*

MODÈLE
Élève 1: Moi, j'adore bavarder au restaurant, mais je déteste parler au musée.
Élève 2: Moi aussi, j'adore bavarder au restaurant. Je ne déteste pas parler au musée, mais j'aime mieux bavarder au parc.

Opinion	Activité	Lieu
adorer	bavarder	au bureau
aimer (mieux)	danser	au centre commercial
ne pas tellement aimer	déjeuner	au centre-ville
détester	dépenser de l'argent	au cinéma
	étudier	au gymnase
	inviter	au musée
	nager	au parc
	parler	à la piscine
	patiner	au restaurant

5 **La journée d'Anne** Votre professeur va vous donner, à vous et à votre partenaire, une feuille d'activités partiellement illustrée. À tour de rôle, posez-vous des questions pour compléter vos feuilles respectives. Utilisez le vocabulaire de la leçon. Attention! Ne regardez pas la feuille de votre partenaire. *Answers will vary.*

MODÈLE
Élève 1: À 7h30, Anne quitte la maison. Qu'est-ce qu'elle fait ensuite (do next)?
Élève 2: À 8h00, elle…

Anne

6 **Une lettre** Écrivez une lettre à un(e) ami(e) dans laquelle (*in which*) vous décrivez vos activités de la semaine. Utilisez les expressions de la liste. *Answers will vary.*

bavarder	passer chez quelqu'un
déjeuner	travailler
dépenser de l'argent	quitter la maison
étudier	un centre commercial
manger au restaurant	un cinéma

Cher Paul,

Comment vas-tu? Pour (For) moi, tout va bien. Je suis très actif/active. Je travaille beaucoup et j'ai beaucoup d'amis. En général, le samedi, après les cours, je déjeune chez moi et l'après-midi, je bavarde avec mes amis…

---

4 Suggestion Have two volunteers read the **modèle** aloud.

4 Expansion After completing the activity, have students share their partners' opinions with the rest of the class.

5 Suggestion Divide the class into pairs and distribute the Info Gap Handouts from the Activity Pack. Give students ten minutes to complete the activity.

PRE-AP®

6 Interpersonal Writing: Suggestion Tell students that they should use the salutation **chère** if they are writing to a female. Remind them to include expressions of time, such as **le lundi après-midi** and **le samedi soir** in their letters.

Successful Language Learning Remind students that it's important to proofread their work. Have them brainstorm a checklist of potential errors, for example, accents, adjective agreement, and subject-verb agreement. Tell students to add grammar points to their checklists as they learn new structures and make mistakes.

21ˢᵀ CENTURY SKILLS

Technology Literacy Ask students to prepare a digital presentation on an ideal town. They should include a map of the city showing its layout.

DIFFERENTIATION

For Kinesthetic Learners On a sheet of paper, have students write down six places they like to go and what they like to do there. Tell them to circulate around the room trying to find other students who also like to go to those places or do those things. Remind them to jot down the names of people who share something in common with them. Then have them report what they have in common with their classmates.

TEACHING OPTIONS

Ideal Town Have small groups plan and design an ideal town or neighborhood. Have them draw the plan, label each place, and list fun activities to do at each one. One person from each group should present the plan to the class. Hold a secret vote and give prizes for the best plan in various categories, such as **le plus amusant**, **le plus créatif**, and **le plus réaliste**.

Les sons et les lettres

Audio: Explanation Record & Compare

Oral vowels

French has two basic kinds of vowel sounds: oral vowels, the subject of this discussion, and nasal vowels, presented in **Leçon 4B**. Oral vowels are produced by releasing air through the mouth. The pronunciation of French vowels is consistent and predictable.

In short words (usually two-letter words), **e** is pronounced similarly to the *a* in the English word *about*.

l**e**   qu**e**   c**e**   d**e**

The letter **a** alone is pronounced like the *a* in *father*.

l**a**   ç**a**   m**a**   t**a**

The letter **i** by itself and the letter **y** are pronounced like the vowel sound in the word *bee*.

ici   l**i**vre   st**y**lo   l**y**cée

The letter combination **ou** sounds like the vowel sound in the English word *who*.

v**ou**s   n**ou**s   **ou**blier   éc**ou**ter

The French **u** sound does not exist in English. To produce this sound, say *ee* with your lips rounded.

t**u**   d**u**   **u**ne   ét**u**dier

Prononcez Répétez les mots suivants à voix haute.

1. je
2. chat
3. fou
4. ville
5. utile
6. place
7. jour
8. triste
9. mari
10. active
11. Sylvie
12. rapide
13. gymnase
14. antipathique
15. calculatrice
16. piscine

Articulez Répétez les phrases suivantes à voix haute.

1. Salut, Luc. Ça va?
2. La philosophie est difficile.
3. Brigitte est une actrice fantastique.
4. Suzanne va à son cours de physique.
5. Tu trouves le cours de maths facile?
6. Viviane a une bourse universitaire.

Dictons Répétez les dictons à voix haute.

Qui va à la chasse perd sa place.¹

Plus on est de fous, plus on rit.²

¹ He who steps out of line loses his place. ² The more the merrier.

cent trente-sept 137

Roman-photo Leçon 4A

Star du cinéma
Video: Roman-photo Record & Compare

PERSONNAGES

Amina
David
Pascal
Sandrine

À l'épicerie...
DAVID Juliette Binoche? Pas possible! Je vais chercher Sandrine!

Au café...
PASCAL Alors, chérie, tu vas faire quoi de ton week-end?
SANDRINE Euh, demain je vais déjeuner au centre-ville.
PASCAL Bon... et quand est-ce que tu vas rentrer?
SANDRINE Euh, je ne sais pas. Pourquoi?

PASCAL Pour rien. Et demain soir, tu vas danser?
SANDRINE Ça dépend. Je vais passer chez Amina pour bavarder avec elle.
PASCAL Combien d'amis as-tu à Aix-en-Provence?
SANDRINE Oh, Pascal...
PASCAL Bon, moi, je vais continuer à penser à toi jour et nuit.

DAVID Mais l'actrice! Juliette Binoche!
SANDRINE Allons-y! Vite! C'est une de mes actrices préférées! J'adore le film *Chocolat*!
AMINA Et comme elle est chic! C'est une vraie star!
DAVID Elle est à l'épicerie! Ce n'est pas loin d'ici!

Dans la rue...
AMINA Mais elle est où, cette épicerie? Nous allons explorer toute la ville pour rencontrer Juliette Binoche?
SANDRINE C'est là, l'épicerie Pierre Dubois, à côté du cinéma?
DAVID Mais non, elle n'est pas à l'épicerie Pierre Dubois, elle est à l'épicerie près de l'église, en face du parc.

AMINA Et combien d'églises est-ce qu'il y a à Aix?
SANDRINE Il n'y a pas d'église en face du parc!
DAVID Bon, hum, l'église sur la place.
AMINA D'accord, et ton église sur la place, elle est ici au centre-ville ou en banlieue?

ACTIVITÉS

1 Vrai ou faux? Indiquez pour chaque phrase si l'affirmation est vraie ou fausse et corrigez si nécessaire.

1. David va chercher Pascal. *Faux. David va chercher Sandrine.*
2. Sandrine va déjeuner au centre-ville. *Vrai.*
3. Pascal va passer chez Amina. *Faux. Sandrine va passer chez Amina.*
4. Pascal va continuer à penser à Sandrine jour et nuit. *Vrai.*
5. Pascal va bien. *Vrai.*
6. Juliette Binoche est l'actrice préférée de Sandrine. *Vrai.*
7. L'épicerie est loin du café. *Faux. L'épicerie n'est pas loin.*
8. L'épicerie Pierre Dubois est à côté de l'église. *Faux. L'épicerie Pierre Dubois est à côté du cinéma.*
9. Il n'y a pas d'église en face du parc. *Vrai.*
10. Juliette Binoche fréquente le P'tit Bistrot. *Faux. Juliette Binoche ne fréquente pas le P'tit Bistrot.*

Practice more at vhlcentral.com.

cent trente-huit

Au café — Unité 4

David et les filles à la recherche de (*in search of*) leur actrice préférée

SANDRINE Oui. Génial. Au revoir, Pascal.
AMINA Salut, Sandrine. Comment va Pascal?
SANDRINE Il va bien, mais il adore bavarder.

DAVID Elle est là, elle est là!
SANDRINE Mais, qui est là?
AMINA Et c'est où, «là»?
DAVID Juliette Binoche! Mais non, pas ici!
SANDRINE ET AMINA Quoi? Qui? Où?

Devant l'épicerie...
DAVID C'est elle, là! Hé, JULIETTE!
AMINA Oh, elle est belle!
SANDRINE Elle est jolie, élégante!
AMINA Elle est... petite?
DAVID Elle, elle... est... vieille?!?

AMINA Ce n'est pas du tout Juliette Binoche!
SANDRINE David, tu es complètement fou! Juliette Binoche, au centre-ville d'Aix?
AMINA Pourquoi est-ce qu'elle ne fréquente pas le P'tit Bistrot?

Expressions utiles

Talking about your plans

- **Tu vas faire quoi de ton week-end?**
  What are you doing this weekend?
- **Je vais déjeuner au centre-ville.**
  I'm going to have lunch downtown.
- **Quand est-ce que tu vas rentrer?**
  When are you coming back?
- **Je ne sais pas.**
  I don't know.
- **Je vais passer chez Amina.**
  I am going to Amina's (house).
- **Nous allons explorer toute la ville.**
  We're going to explore the whole city.

Additional vocabulary

- **C'est une de mes actrices préférées.**
  She's one of my favorite actresses.
- **Comme elle est chic!**
  She is so chic!
- **Ce n'est pas loin d'ici!**
  It's not far from here!
- **Ce n'est pas du tout...**
  It's not... at all.
- **Ça dépend.**
  It depends.
- **Pour rien.**
  No reason.
- **Vite!**
  Quick!, Hurry!

---

2 Questions À l'aide (*the help*) d'un dictionnaire, choisissez le bon mot pour chaque question.

1. (Avec qui, Quoi) Sandrine parle-t-elle au téléphone?
2. (Où, Parce que) Sandrine va-t-elle déjeuner?
3. (Qui, Pourquoi) Pascal demande-t-il à Sandrine quand elle va rentrer?
4. (Combien, Comment) d'amis Sandrine a-t-elle?
5. (Combien, À qui) Amina demande-t-elle comment va Pascal?
6. (Quand, Où) est Juliette Binoche?

3 Écrivez Pensez à votre acteur ou actrice préféré(e) et préparez un paragraphe où vous décrivez son apparence, sa personnalité et sa carrière. Comment est-il/elle? Dans quel(s) (*which*) film(s) joue-t-il/elle? Si un jour vous rencontrez cet acteur/cette actrice, qu'est-ce que vous allez lui dire (*say to him or her*)?

Culture
Leçon 4A

CULTURE À LA LOUPE

Les passe-temps des jeunes Français

Comment est-ce que les jeunes occupent leur temps libre° en France? Les jeunes de 15 à 25 ans passent beaucoup de temps à regarder la télévision: environ° 12 heures par° semaine. Ils écoutent aussi beaucoup de musique: environ 16 heures par semaine, et surfent souvent° sur Internet (11 heures). Environ 25% des jeunes Français ont même° déjà° un blog sur Internet. Les jeux° vidéo sont aussi très populaires: les jeunes jouent° en moyenne° 15 heures par semaine.

En France, les jeunes aiment également° les activités culturelles, en particulier le cinéma: en moyenne, ils y° vont une fois° par semaine. Ils aiment aussi la littérature et l'art: presque° 50% (pour cent) visitent des musées ou des monuments historiques chaque année et plus de° 40% vont au théâtre ou à des concerts. Un jeune sur cinq° joue d'un instrument de musique ou chante°, et environ 20% d'entre eux° pratiquent une activité artistique, comme la danse, le théâtre, la sculpture, le dessin° ou la peinture°. La photographie et la vidéo sont aussi très appréciées.

Il ne faut pas° oublier de mentionner que les jeunes Français sont aussi très sportifs. Bien sûr, comme tous les jeunes, ils préfèrent parfois° simplement se détendre° et bavarder avec des amis.

Finalement, les passe-temps des jeunes Français sont similaires aux activités des jeunes Américains!

temps libre *free time* **environ** *around* **par** *per* **souvent** *often* **même** *even* **déjà** *already* **jeux** *games* **jouent** *play* **en moyenne** *on average* **également** *also* **y** *there* **fois** *time* **presque** *almost* **plus de** *more than* **Un... sur cinq** *One... in five* **chante** *sings* **d'entre eux** *of them* **dessin** *drawing* **peinture** *painting* **Il ne faut pas** *One must not* **parfois** *sometimes* **se détendre** *relax* **les** *them*

Les activités culturelles des Français
(% des Français qui les° pratiquent)

le dessin	7%
la peinture	4%
le piano	3%
autre instrument de musique	3%
la danse	2%
la guitare	2%
la sculpture	1%
le théâtre	1%

SOURCE: Francoscopie

---

1 Vrai ou faux? Indiquez si les phrases sont **vraies** ou **fausses**. Corrigez les phrases fausses. *Some answers may vary.*

1. Les jeunes Français n'écoutent pas de musique. Faux. Les jeunes Français écoutent de la musique environ 16 heures par semaine.
2. Ils n'utilisent pas Internet. Faux. Ils utilisent Internet 11 heures par semaine.
3. Ils aiment aller au musée. Vrai.
4. Ils n'aiment pas beaucoup les livres. Faux. Ils aiment la littérature.
5. Ils n'aiment pas pratiquer d'activités artistiques. Faux. Possible answer: Ils aiment la danse, le théâtre et le dessin.
6. Les Français entre 15 et 25 ans ne font pas de sport. Faux. Les jeunes Français sont très sportifs.
7. Les passe-temps des jeunes Américains sont similaires aux passe-temps des jeunes Français. Vrai.
8. L'instrument de musique le plus (*the most*) populaire en France est le piano. Vrai.
9. Plus de (*More*) gens pratiquent la peinture que la sculpture. Vrai.
10. Environ 10% des Français pratiquent la sculpture. Faux. 1% des Français pratiquent la sculpture.

Practice more at **vhlcentral.com**.

cent quarante

Au café Unité 4

LE FRANÇAIS QUOTIDIEN

Le verlan

En France, on entend parfois° des jeunes parler en verlan. En verlan, les syllabes des mots sont inversées°:

l'en**vers**° → **vers**-l'en → verlan.

Voici quelques exemples:

français	verlan	anglais
louche	chelou	shady
café	féca	café
mec	keum	guy
femme	meuf	woman

parfois sometimes **inversées** inverted **l'envers** the reverse

PORTRAIT

Le parc Astérix

Situé° à 30 kilomètres de Paris, en Picardie, le parc Astérix est le premier parc à thème français. Le parc d'attractions°, ouvert° en 1989, est basé sur la bande dessinée° française, *Astérix le Gaulois*. Création de René Goscinny et d'Albert Uderzo, Astérix est un guerrier gaulois° qui lutte° contre l'invasion des Romains. Au parc Astérix, il y a des montagnes russes°, des petits trains et des spectacles, tous° basés sur les aventures d'Astérix et de son meilleur ami, Obélix. Une des attractions, *le Tonnerre° de Zeus*, est la plus grande° montagne russe en bois° d'Europe.

Situé Located **parc d'attractions** amusement park **ouvert** opened **bande dessinée** comic strip **guerrier gaulois** Gallic warrior **lutte** fights **montagnes russes** roller coasters **tous** all **Tonnerre** Thunder **la plus grande** the largest **en bois** wooden

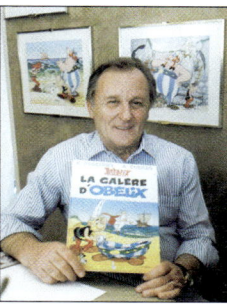

LE MONDE FRANCOPHONE

Où passer le temps

Voici quelques endroits typiques où les jeunes francophones aiment se restaurer° et passer du temps.

En Afrique de l'Ouest
Le maquis Commun dans beaucoup de pays° d'Afrique de l'Ouest°, le maquis est un restaurant où on peut manger à bas prix°. Situé en ville ou en bord de route°, le maquis est typiquement en plein air°.

Au Sénégal
Le tangana Le terme «tang» signifie «chaud» en wolof, une des langues nationales du Sénégal. Le tangana est un lieu populaire pour se restaurer. On trouve souvent les tanganas au coin de la rue°, en plein air, avec des tables et des bancs°.

se restaurer have something to eat **pays** countries **Ouest** West **à bas prix** inexpensively **en bord de route** on the side of the road **en plein air** outdoors **coin de la rue** street corner **bancs** benches

Sur Internet

Comment sont les parcs d'attractions dans les autres pays francophones?

Go to vhlcentral.com to find more information related to this Culture section.

2 Compréhension Complétez les phrases.
1. Le parc Astérix est basé sur Astérix le Gaulois, une **bande dessinée**.
2. Astérix le Gaulois est une **création** de René Goscinny et d'Albert Uderzo.
3. Le parc Astérix est près de la ville de **Paris**.
4. Astérix est un **guerrier** gaulois.
5. En verlan, on peut passer du temps avec ses copains au **féca**.
6. Au Sénégal, on parle aussi le **wolof**.

3 Vos activités préférées Posez des questions à trois ou quatre de vos camarades de classe à propos de leurs activités favorites. Comparez vos résultats avec ceux (*those*) d'un autre groupe.

cent quarante et un 141

Section Goals

In this section, students will learn:
- the verb **aller**
- the **futur proche** with **aller**
- the preposition **à**

Key Standards

4.1, 5.1

Student Resources
Cahier de l'élève, pp. 91–93; Supersite: Activities, *eCahier*, Grammar Tutorials

Teacher Resources
Answer Keys; Audio Script; Audio Activity MP3s/CD; Activity Pack; Testing program: Grammar Quiz

Suggestions

- Write the paradigm of **aller** on the board and model the pronunciation. Ask students what forms of **aller** are irregular.
- Write your next day's schedule on the board using infinitives and nouns. Examples: **8h00: bibliothèque; 10h00: cours de français; 12h00: déjeuner** Explain what you are going to do using the verb **aller**. Examples: **Je vais (aller) à la bibliothèque à huit heures. Je vais déjeuner à midi.** Ask students questions about their schedules using forms of **aller**.
- Ask individual students questions about their future plans using **aller**. Examples: **Allez-vous chez vos grands-parents ce week-end? Allez-vous manger avec des copains vendredi soir?**

Structures — Leçon 4A

4A.1 The verb *aller*

Presentation Grammar Tutorial

Point de départ In **Leçon 1A**, you saw a form of the verb **aller** (*to go*) in the expression **ça va**. Now you will use this verb, first, to talk about going places and, second, to express actions that take place in the immediate future.

aller

je vais	I go	nous allons	we go
tu vas	you go	vous allez	you go
il/elle/on va	he/she/it/one goes	ils/elles vont	they go

- The verb **aller** is irregular. Only the **nous** and **vous** forms resemble the infinitive.

Tu **vas** souvent au cinéma?
Do you go to the movies often?

Nous **allons** au marché le samedi.
We go to the market on Saturdays.

Je **vais** à la piscine.
I'm going to the pool.

Vous **allez** au parc aussi?
Are you going to the park too?

- **Aller** can also be used with another verb to tell what is going to happen. This construction is called **le futur proche** (*the immediate future*). Conjugate **aller** in the present tense and place the other verb's infinitive form directly after it.

Nous **allons déjeuner** sur la terrasse.
We're going to eat lunch on the terrace.

Marc et Julie **vont explorer** le centre-ville.
Marc and Julie are going to explore the city center.

Je **vais partager** la pizza avec ma copine.
I'm going to share the pizza with my friend.

Elles **vont retrouver** Guillaume à la cantine.
They're going to meet Guillaume at the cafeteria.

> *Demain, je vais déjeuner au centre-ville.*

> *Et quand est-ce que tu vas rentrer?*

À noter

In **Leçon 2A**, you learned how to form questions with inversion when you have a conjugated verb + infinitive. Follow the same pattern for **le futur proche**. Example: **Théo va-t-il déjeuner à midi?**

- To negate an expression in **le futur proche**, place **ne/n'** before the conjugated form of **aller** and **pas** after it.

Je **ne vais pas** oublier la date.
I'm not going to forget the date.

Nous **n'allons pas** quitter la maison.
We're not going to leave the house.

Tu **ne vas pas** manger au café?
Aren't you going to eat at the café?

Ousmane **ne va pas** retrouver Salima au parc.
Ousmane is not going to meet Salima at the park.

- Note that **le futur proche** can be used with the infinitive of **aller** to mean *going to go (somewhere)*.

Elle **va aller** à la piscine.
She's going to go to the pool.

Vous **allez aller** au gymnase ce soir?
Are you going to go to the gym tonight?

cent quarante-deux

EXPANSION

Video Show the video episode again to give students additional input on the verb **aller**. Pause the video where appropriate to discuss how **aller** was used and to ask comprehension questions.

EXPANSION

Extra Practice Have student pairs interview each other about what they are doing tonight. Ex. **Je vais regarder la télé.** Then ask them to tell the rest of the class about their partner's plans. Ex. **Il/Elle va regarder la télé. Il/Elle va faire....**

Au café — Unité 4

The preposition à

- The preposition **à** can be translated in various ways in English: *to, in, at*. When followed by the definite article **le** or **les**, the preposition **à** and the definite article contract into one word.

  à + le ▶ au　　　　　　　　**à + les ▶ aux**

  Nous allons **au** magasin.　　　Ils parlent **aux** profs.
  We're going to the store.　　　*They're talking to the teachers.*

- The preposition **à** does not contract with **la** or **l'**.

  à + la ▶ à la　　　　　　　**à + l' ▶ à l'**

  Je rentre **à la** maison.　　　Il va **à l'**épicerie.
  I'm going back home.　　　*He's going to the grocery store.*

- The preposition **à** often indicates a physical location, as with **aller à** and **habiter à**. However, it can have other meanings depending on the verb used.

  Verbs with the preposition à

commencer à + [infinitive]	to start (doing something)	penser à	to think about
parler à	to talk to	téléphoner à	to phone (someone)

  Elle va **parler au** professeur.　　　Il **commence à travailler** demain.
  She's going to talk to the teacher.　*He starts working tomorrow.*

- In general, **à** is used to mean *at* or *in*, whereas **dans** is used to mean *inside* or *within*. When learning a place name in French, learn the preposition that accompanies it.

  Prepositions with place names

à la maison	at home	dans la maison	inside the house
à Paris	in Paris	dans Paris	within Paris
en ville	in town	dans la ville	within the town
sur la place	in the square	à/sur la terrasse	on the terrace

  Tu travailles **à la maison**?　　　On mange **dans la maison**.
  Are you working at home?　　　*We'll eat in the house.*

Essayez! Utilisez la forme correcte du verbe **aller**.

1. Comment ça __va__?
2. Tu __vas__ à la piscine pour nager.
3. Ils __vont__ au centre-ville.
4. Nous __allons__ bavarder au parc.
5. Vous __allez__ aller au restaurant ce soir?
6. Elle __va__ aller à l'église dimanche matin.
7. Ce soir, je __vais__ faire mes devoirs.
8. On ne __va__ pas passer par l'épicerie cet après-midi.

Suggestions
- Bring in pictures of people dressed for different activities. Describe them to the class using the verb **aller**. Example: Showing a picture of a swimmer, say: **Il/Elle va à la piscine.** Then explain the contractions **à + le = au** and **à + les = aux**.
- Tell students that, when followed by another verb (in the infinitive), **penser** doesn't take a preposition. Example: **Je pense aller au parc après les cours**.
- Model the pronunciation of the list of prepositions with places. Tell students that they should memorize these phrases.

Essayez! Have students create a few additional sentences using the verb **aller**.

EXPANSION

Extra Practice Have students make a list of activities for their next school break using the verb **aller**. If they don't have plans yet, they can make something up. Ask them to share their lists with a classmate. Then, each pair should share their classmate's plans with the class. Example: **Il/Elle va voyager en Afrique**. Encourage them to mention activities they have in common so they use **nous**: **Nous allons nager à la piscine**.

DIFFERENTIATION

For Kinesthetic Learners Invent gestures to pantomime some activities taught in **Leçon 4B**. Examples: **nager**: *move arms as if swimming*; **bavarder**: *make talking gestures with hands*; **dépenser de l'argent**: *turn pockets inside out*. Signal individuals to gesture appropriately as you cue activities by saying: **Nous allons…** or **On va…**.

Structures   Leçon 4A

Mise en pratique

1 Suggestion To check students' answers, have a volunteer say the question, then call on another student to answer it.

2 Expansion For additional practice, give students these items. **9. Nous passons chez Martine.** (Samedi prochain aussi, nous allons passer chez Martine.) **10. André travaille le matin.** (… André va travailler le matin.) **11. Je dîne avec un ami.** (… je vais dîner avec un ami.)

3 Suggestion Have students take turns asking where the people in the drawings are going and answering the questions. Example: **Où va Henri?** (Henri va au cinéma.)

3 Expansion Have students redo the activity using **le futur proche** to ask questions about each image. Example: **Henri va-t-il aller au cinéma?**

1 **Questions parentales** Votre père est très curieux. Trouvez les questions qu'il pose.

MODÈLE

tes frères / piscine
Tes frères vont à la piscine?

1. tu / cinéma / ce soir   Tu vas au cinéma ce soir?
2. tes amis et toi, vous / café   Tes amis et toi, vous allez au café?
3. ta mère et moi, nous / ville / vendredi   Ta mère et moi, nous allons en ville vendredi?
4. ton ami(e) / souvent / marché   Ton ami(e) va souvent au marché?
5. je / musée / avec toi / demain   Je vais au musée avec toi demain?
6. tes amis / parc   Tes amis vont au parc?
7. on / église / dimanche   On va à l'église dimanche?
8. tes amis et toi, vous / parfois / gymnase   Tes amis et toi, vous allez parfois au gymnase?

2 **Samedi prochain** Voici ce que (*what*) vous et vos amis faites (*are doing*) aujourd'hui. Indiquez que vous allez faire les mêmes (*same*) choses samedi prochain.

MODÈLE

Je nage.
Samedi prochain aussi, je vais nager.

1. Paul bavarde avec ses copains.   Samedi prochain aussi, Paul va bavarder avec ses copains.
2. Nous dansons.   … nous allons danser.
3. Je dépense de l'argent dans un magasin.   … je vais dépenser de l'argent dans un magasin.
4. Luc et Sylvie déjeunent au restaurant.   … Luc et Sylvie vont déjeuner au restaurant.
5. Vous explorez le centre-ville.   … vous allez explorer le centre-ville.
6. Tu patines.   … tu vas patiner.
7. Amélie nage à la piscine.   … Amélie va nager à la piscine.
8. Lucas et Sabrina téléphonent à leurs grands-parents.   … Lucas et Sabrina vont téléphoner à leurs grands-parents.

3 **Où vont-ils?** Avec un(e) partenaire, indiquez où vont les personnages.   Answers will vary.

MODÈLE

Henri va au cinéma.

Henri

1. tu
2. nous
3. Paul et Luc
4. vous

144   *cent quarante-quatre*

Practice more at **vhlcentral.com**.

TEACHING OPTIONS

Extra Practice Have individual students write five dehydrated sentences (like those in Activity 1 on this page) and exchange them with a partner, who will recreate them. After pairs have recreated their sentences, ask volunteers to share some of their dehydrated sentences. Write them on the board and have the class "rehydrate" them.

TEACHING OPTIONS

Pairs Have students form pairs and tell them they are going somewhere. On paper strips, write varying dollar amounts, ranging from three dollars to five thousand. Have each pair pick a strip of paper at random and tell the class where they will go and what they will do with the money. Encourage creativity. Ex: **Nous avons six dollars. Nous allons manger à McDonald's. Nous avons cinq mille dollars. Nous allons manger à Paris.**

Au café — Unité 4

Communication

4 Activités du week-end Avec un(e) partenaire, assemblez les éléments des colonnes pour poser des questions. Rajoutez (*Add*) d'autres éléments utiles. *Answers will vary.*

MODÈLE
Élève 1: *Est-ce que tu vas déjeuner avec tes copains?*
Élève 2: *Oui, je vais déjeuner avec mes copains.*

A	B	C	D
ta sœur	aller	voyager	professeur
vous		aller	cinéma
tes copains		déjeuner	piscine
nous		bavarder	centre commercial
tu		nager	café
ton petit ami		parler	parents
ta petite amie		inviter	copains
tes grands-parents		téléphoner	petit(e) ami(e)
		visiter	camarades de classe
		patiner	musée
			cousin(e)s

5 Le grand voyage Vous avez gagné (*have won*) un voyage. Par groupes de trois, expliquez à vos camarades ce que vous allez faire pendant (*during*) le voyage. Vos camarades vont deviner (*to guess*) où vous allez. *Answers will vary.*

MODÈLE
Élève 1: *Je vais visiter le musée du Louvre.*
Élève 2: *Est-ce que tu vas aller à Paris?*

6 À Deauville Votre professeur va vous donner, à vous et à votre partenaire, un plan (*map*) de Deauville. Attention! Ne regardez pas la feuille de votre partenaire. *Answers will vary.*

MODÈLE
Élève 1: *Où va Simon?*
Élève 2: *Il va au kiosque.*

---

4 Suggestion Have two volunteers read the **modèle**. Remind students that they can answer in the negative. Encourage them to expand on their answers. Examples: **Oui, je vais déjeuner avec mes copains au Petit Croissant./Non, je ne vais pas déjeuner avec mes copains, mais je vais aller au centre commercial avec ma mère.**

4 Partner Chat You can also assign Activity 4 on the Supersite. Students work in pairs to record the activity online. The pair's recorded conversation will appear in your gradebook.

5 Suggestion Have two volunteers read the **modèle**. Encourage students to choose famous places in the Francophone world.

6 Suggestions
- Tell students that Deauville is a fashionable seaside resort in Normandy frequented by the rich and famous.
- Divide the class into pairs and distribute the Info Gap Handouts found in the Activity Pack on the Supersite. Give students ten minutes to complete the activity.

---

cent quarante-cinq **145**

TEACHING OPTIONS

Extra Practice Do a quick substitution drill to practice **aller**. Write a sentence on the board and have students read it aloud. Then say a new subject and have students repeat the sentence, substituting the new subject. Examples: **1. Tu vas à l'hôpital.** (nous, mon frère, vous, mes parents, je) **2. Il va aller au kiosque.** (je, Claudine, nous, tu, les enfants, vous)

TEACHING OPTIONS

Game Divide the class into four-member teams. Using the immediate future, each team will write a description of tomorrow's events for a well-known fictional character. Teams take turns reading and/or writing the description on the board without giving the character's name. The other teams will guess the identity. Each correct guess earns a point. If a team fools the others, it earns two points. The team with the most points wins.

Section Goals
In this section, students will learn interrogative words.

Key Standards
4.1, 5.1

Student Resources
Cahier de l'élève, pp. 94–96; Supersite: Activities, eCahier, Grammar Tutorials

Teacher Resources
Answer Keys; Audio Script; Audio Activity MP3s/CD; Testing program: Grammar Quiz

Suggestions
- Write the interrogative words on the board. Have students identify the words they know. Examples: **comment?**, **combien?**, **pourquoi?**, **qui?**, and **quel(s)/quelle(s)?** Model the pronunciation of the new words and have students repeat.
- Point out that in informal conversation interrogative words can be placed after the verb. Examples: **Tu vas où? Il s'appelle comment?**
- Remind students that they learned the expressions **Quelle heure est-il?** and **Quelle heure avez-vous/as-tu?** in 2B.2.
- Point out that **que?** and **quoi?** are used to ask about things. A preposition usually precedes **quoi?** or the word appears at the end of an informal question. Examples: **De quoi parlez-vous? Tu manges quoi?**
- Point out that **qui?** is used to ask about people. **Qui?** takes the third person singular verb form. You may also wish to introduce the expression **Qui est-ce qui…?**
- Emphasize to students that ending a question with **quoi** is more common in informal speech.

Structures | Leçon 4A

4A.2 Interrogative words
Presentation Grammar Tutorial

Point de départ In **Leçon 2A**, you learned four ways to formulate yes or no questions in French. However, many questions seek information that can't be provided by a simple yes or no answer.

- Use these words with **est-ce que** or inversion.

Boîte à outils
If a question word is followed immediately by the verb **être**, don't use **est-ce que**.

Où est mon sac à dos?
Where is my backpack?
Comment est ta petite amie?
What's your girlfriend like?

À noter
Refer to **Structures 2A.2** to review how to answer a question with **pourquoi** using **parce que/qu'**.

Interrogative words			
à quelle heure?	at what time?	quand?	when?
combien (de)?	how many?; how much?	que/qu'…?	what?
comment?	how?; what?	quel(le)(s)?	which?; what?
où?	where?	(à/avec/pour) qui?	(to/with/for) who(m)?
pourquoi?	why?	quoi?	what?

À qui le professeur parle-t-il ce matin?
Who is the teacher talking to this morning?

Combien de villes y a-t-il en Suisse?
How many cities are there in Switzerland?

Pourquoi est-ce que tu danses?
Why are you dancing?

Que vas-tu manger?
What are you going to eat?

- When the question word **qui** (*who*) is the subject of a sentence, it is followed directly by a verb. The verb in this case is always in the third person singular.

Qui invite Patrice à dîner?
Who is inviting Patrice to dinner?

Qui n'aime pas danser?
Who doesn't like to dance?

- When the question word **qui** (*whom*) is the object of a sentence, it is followed by **est-ce que** or inversion.

Qui est-ce que tu regardes?
Who are you looking at?

Qui regardes-tu?
Who are you looking at?

- Although **quand?** and **à quelle heure?** can both be translated as *when?*, they are not interchangeable in French. Use **quand** to talk about a day or date, and **à quelle heure** to talk about a specific time of day.

Quand est-ce que le cours commence?
When does the class start?

À quelle heure est-ce qu'il commence?
At what time does it begin?

Il commence **le lundi 28 août**.
It starts Monday, August 28.

Il commence **à dix heures et demie**.
It begins at 10:30.

- Another way to formulate questions with most interrogative words is by placing them after a verb. This kind of formulation is very informal but very common.

Tu t'appelles **comment**?
What's your name?

Tu habites **où**?
Where do you live?

- Note that **quoi?** (*what?*) must immediately follow a preposition in order to be used with **est-ce que** or **inversion**. If no preposition is necessary, place **quoi** after the verb.

À quoi pensez-vous?
What are you thinking about?

Elle étudie **quoi**?
What does she study?

De quoi est-ce qu'il parle?
What is he talking about?

Tu regardes **quoi**?
What are you looking at?

146 cent quarante-six

DIFFERENTIATION

For Kinesthetic Learners Read aloud a series of statements and questions, including tag questions (which were introduced in **Leçon 2A**). Have students raise their right hand when they hear a statement or their left hand when they hear a question.

TEACHING OPTIONS

Pairs Give pairs of students five minutes to write original questions using as many interrogative words as they can. Can any pair come up with questions using all the interrogative words?

Au café — Unité 4

- Use **Comment?** or **Pardon?** to indicate that you don't understand what's being said. You may also use **Quoi?** but only in informal situations with friends.

  Vous allez voyager cette année?
  Are you going to travel this year?

  Comment?
  I beg your pardon?

The interrogative adjective *quel(le)(s)*

- The interrogative adjective **quel** means *what* or *which*. The form of **quel** varies in gender and number with the noun it modifies.

The interrogative adjective *quel(le)(s)*			
	singular		**plural**
masculine	**Quel** *restaurant?*	**Quels** *cours?*
feminine	**Quelle** *montre?*	**Quelles** *filles?*

  Quel restaurant aimes-tu?
  Which restaurant do you like?

  Quels cours commencent à dix heures?
  What classes start at ten o'clock?

  Quelle montre a-t-il?
  What watch does he have?

  Quelles filles vont à la cantine?
  Which girls are going to the cafeteria?

> **Boîte à outils**
> You can also use a form of **quel** as an exclamation.
> **Quel beau garçon!**
> *What a handsome boy!*
> **Quelles grandes maisons!**
> *What big houses!*

- **Qu'est-ce que** and **quel** both mean *what*, but they are used differently. Use a form of **quel** to ask *What is/are...?* if you want to know specific information about a noun. **Quel(le)(s)** may be followed directly by a form of **être** and a noun, in which case the form of **quel(le)(s)** agrees with that noun.

  Quel est ton numéro de téléphone?
  What is your phone number?

  Quels sont tes cours préférés?
  What are your favorite classes?

  Quelles amies invites-tu?
  What friends are you inviting?

  Quelle heure est-il?
  What time is it?

- Use **qu'est-ce que** in most other cases.

  Qu'est-ce que tu vas manger?
  What are you going to eat?

  Qu'est-ce que Sandrine étudie?
  What is Sandrine studying?

Tu es de quelle origine?

Quel jour sommes-nous?

Essayez! Donnez les mots (*words*) interrogatifs.

1. _Comment_ allez-vous?
2. _Qu'_ est-ce que vous allez faire (*do*) après le cours?
3. Le cours de français commence à _quelle_ heure?
4. _Pourquoi_ est-ce que tu ne travailles pas?
5. Avec _qui_ est-ce qu'on va au cinéma ce soir?
6. _Combien_ d'élèves y a-t-il dans la salle de classe?
7. _Quels_ musées vas-tu visiter?
8. _Quand_ est-ce que tes parents arrivent?
9. _Qui_ n'aime pas voyager?
10. _Où_ est-ce qu'on dîne ce soir?

cent quarante-sept 147

Structures | Leçon 4A

Mise en pratique

1 Le français familier Utilisez l'inversion pour reformuler les questions.

MODÈLE
Tu t'appelles comment?
Comment t'appelles-tu?

1. Tu habites où? **Où habites-tu?**
2. Le film commence à quelle heure? **À quelle heure le film commence-t-il?**
3. Il est quelle heure? **Quelle heure est-il?**
4. Tu as combien de frères? **Combien de frères as-tu?**
5. Le prof parle quand? **Quand le prof parle-t-il?**
6. Vous aimez quoi? **Qu'aimez-vous?**
7. Elle téléphone à qui? **À qui téléphone-t-elle?**
8. Il étudie comment? **Comment étudie-t-il?**
9. Il y a combien d'enfants? **Combien d'enfants y a-t-il?**
10. Elle aime qui? **Qui aime-t-elle?**

2 La paire Trouvez la paire et formez des phrases complètes. Utilisez chaque (*each*) option une seule fois (*only once*). Answers may vary.

1. À quelle heure — d
2. Comment — f
3. Combien de — g
4. Avec qui — h
5. Où — b
6. Pourquoi — c
7. Qu' — a
8. Quelle — e

a. est-ce que tu regardes?
b. habitent-ils?
c. est-ce que tu habites dans le centre-ville?
d. est-ce que le cours commence?
e. heure est-il?
f. vous appelez-vous?
g. villes est-ce qu'il y a aux États-Unis?
h. parlez-vous?

3 La question Vous avez les réponses. Quelles sont les questions? Some answers will vary.

MODÈLE
Il est midi.
Quelle heure est-il?

1. Les cours commencent à huit heures. **À quelle heure est-ce que les cours commencent?**
2. Stéphanie habite à Paris. **Où est-ce que Stéphanie habite?**
3. Julien danse avec Caroline. **Avec qui est-ce que Julien danse?**
4. Elle s'appelle Julie. **Comment s'appelle-t-elle?**
5. Laetitia a deux chiens. **Combien de chiens Laetitia a-t-elle?**
6. Elle déjeune dans ce restaurant parce qu'il est à côté de son bureau. **Pourquoi déjeune-t-elle dans ce restaurant?**
7. Nous allons bien, merci. **Comment allez-vous?**
8. Je vais au marché mardi. **Quand est-ce que tu vas au marché?**
9. Simon aime danser. **Qui aime danser?**
10. Brigitte pense à ses études. **À quoi Brigitte pense-t-elle?**

148   cent quarante-huit

---

1 Suggestion Have one student ask the question and call on another student to answer it.

1 Expansion Have students compare their answers with a classmate's.

2 Suggestion Have one student say the question and call on another student to answer it.

3 Suggestion Before beginning the activity, point out that there is more than one way to form some of the questions. Have students work in pairs. Tell them to take turns asking and answering the questions.

DIFFERENTIATION

For Auditory Learners Prepare eight questions and answers. Write only the answers on the board in random order. Then read the questions aloud and have students identify the appropriate answer. Ex: **À quelle heure est le cours de français?** (à neuf heures).

EXPANSION

Pairs Have student pairs script an interview with a famous person, using as many interrogative words as possible. Have them present their interviews to the class. To make sure listeners pay attention and are involved, ask the pair presenting the interview not to say the name of the interviewee so the rest of the class can try to guess who he/she is.

Communication

4 Questions et réponses À tour de rôle, posez une question à un(e) partenaire au sujet de chaque (*each*) thème de la liste. Posez une seconde question basée sur sa réponse. *Answers will vary.*

MODÈLE

Élève 1: Où est-ce que tu habites?
Élève 2: J'habite chez mes parents.
Élève 1: Pourquoi est-ce que tu habites chez tes parents?

Thèmes
- où vous habitez
- ce que vous faites (*do*) le week-end
- à qui vous téléphonez
- combien de frères et sœurs vous avez
- les endroits que vous fréquentez avec vos copains
- comment sont vos camarades de classe
- quels cours vous aimez

5 La montagne Par groupes de quatre, lisez (*read*) avec attention la lettre de Céline. Fermez votre livre. Une personne du groupe va poser une question basée sur l'information donnée. La personne qui répond pose une autre question au groupe, etc. *Answers will vary.*

> Bonjour. Je m'appelle Céline. J'ai 17 ans. Je suis grande, mince et sportive. J'habite à Grenoble dans une maison agréable. Je suis en première. J'adore la montagne.
>
> Tous les week-ends, je vais skier à Chamrousse avec mes trois amis Alain, Catherine et Pascal. Nous skions de midi à cinq heures. À six heures, nous prenons un chocolat chaud à la terrasse d'un café ou nous allons manger des crêpes dans un restaurant. Nous allons au cinéma tous ensemble.

6 Le week-end Avec un(e) partenaire, posez-vous des questions pour savoir (*know*) où vous allez aller ce (*this*) week-end. Utilisez **le futur proche**. Posez beaucoup de questions pour avoir tous les détails sur les projets (*plans*) de votre partenaire.

MODÈLE

Élève 1: Où est-ce que tu vas aller samedi?
Élève 2: Je vais aller au centre commercial.
Élève 1: Avec qui?

cent quarante-neuf **149**

---

4 Suggestion Have two volunteers read the **modèle** aloud. Tell students to jot down their partner's responses.

4 Partner Chat You can also assign Activity 4 on the Supersite. Students work in pairs to record the activity online. The pair's recorded conversation will appear in your gradebook.

5 Suggestion Circulate among the groups, providing help where necessary. You might want to have one person in each group keep the book open to verify answers.

6 Suggestion Tell students to jot down notes on their partner's plans. Have them report to the class what their partners will be doing next weekend in as much detail as possible.

EXPANSION

Extra Practice Tell students to write a simple statement about something they like, love, or hate. Have the first student say the statement. The next student asks **Pourquoi?** and the first student answers. Then the second student says his or her statement, and a third student asks why. Examples: **Élève 1: Je déteste étudier le samedi soir. Élève 2: Pourquoi? Élève 1: Parce que c'est la barbe/barbant!**

EXPANSION

Extra Practice Have students turn to the **Roman-photo** on pages 138-139. Tell them to write as many questions as they can based on the photos. Example: **Où est David? (Il est à l'épicerie.)** Ask volunteers to read their questions aloud and then call other students to answer them. You may also have students ask their questions in pairs.

149

Synthèse — Leçon 4A

Révision

Key Standards
1.1

Student Resources
Supersite: Activities, eCahier

Teacher Resources
Answer Keys; Activity Pack; Testing Program: Lesson Test (Testing Program Audio MP3s/CD)

1 Suggestion Model the activity with a volunteer by asking questions about **le café**. Tell students to jot down notes during the interviews. Encourage them to add other places to the list.

2 Suggestion Photocopy and distribute a page from a French day planner so that students can make a note of the activities in the appropriate place. To review telling time, tell students to say the time at which they do the activities as well as the day.

3 Suggestion Before beginning the activity, have students make a list of possible activities for the weekend.

4 Suggestion Before beginning the activity, give students a few minutes to make a list of possible activities in their hometown to discuss.

4 Partner Chat You can also assign Activity 4 on the Supersite. Students work in pairs to record the activity online. The pair's recorded conversation will appear in your gradebook.

5 Suggestion Have two volunteers read the **modèle** aloud. Then have students brainstorm places they could go and things they could do in each city. Write their suggestions on the board.

5 Partner Chat You can also assign Activity 5 on the Supersite. Students work in pairs to record the activity online.

6 Expansion Call on volunteers to read their descriptions aloud and have the class compare them.

150 Unit 4 • Lesson 4A

---

1 En ville Par groupes de trois, interviewez vos camarades. Où allez-vous en ville? Quand ils mentionnent un endroit de la liste, demandez des détails (quand? avec qui? pourquoi? etc.). Présentez les réponses à la classe. *Answers will vary.*

le centre commercial	le musée
le cinéma	le parc
le gymnase	la piscine
le marché	le restaurant

2 La semaine prochaine Voici votre agenda (*day planner*). Parlez de votre semaine avec un(e) partenaire. Mentionnez trois activités associées au travail et trois activités d'un autre type. Deux des activités doivent (*must*) être des activités de groupe. *Answers will vary.*

MODÈLE
Lundi, je vais préparer un examen, mais samedi, je vais danser en boîte.

	L	M	M	J	V	S	D
8h30							
9h00							
9h30							
10h00							
10h30							
11h00							
11h30							
12h00							
12h30							

3 Le week-end Par groupes de trois, posez-vous des questions sur vos projets (*plans*) pour le week-end prochain. Donnez des détails. Mentionnez aussi des activités faites (*made*) pour deux personnes. *Answers will vary.*

MODÈLE
Élève 1: Quels projets avez-vous pour ce week-end?
Élève 2: Nous allons au marché samedi.
Élève 3: Et nous allons au cinéma dimanche.

4 Ma ville À tour de rôle, vous invitez votre partenaire dans une ville pour une visite d'une semaine. Préparez une liste d'activités variées et proposez-les (*them*) à votre partenaire. Ensuite (*Then*), comparez vos villes et vos projets (*plans*) avec ceux (*those*) d'un autre groupe. *Answers will vary.*

MODÈLE
Élève 1: Samedi, on va au centre-ville.
Élève 2: Nous allons dépenser de l'argent!

5 Où passer un long week-end? Vous et votre partenaire avez la possibilité de passer un long week-end à Montréal ou à La Nouvelle-Orléans, mais vous préférez chacun(e) (*each one*) une ville différente. Jouez la conversation pour la classe. *Answers will vary.*

MODÈLE
Élève 1: À Montréal, on va aller dans les librairies!
Élève 2: Oui, mais à La Nouvelle-Orléans, je vais aller à des concerts de musique cajun!

Montréal
- le jardin (*garden*) botanique
- le musée des Beaux-Arts
- le parc du Mont-Royal
- le Vieux-Montréal

La Nouvelle-Orléans
- le Café du Monde
- la cathédrale Saint-Louis
- la route des plantations
- le vieux carré, quartier (*neighborhood*) français

6 La semaine de Martine Votre professeur va vous donner, à vous et à votre partenaire, des informations sur la semaine de Martine. Attention! Ne regardez pas la feuille de votre partenaire. *Answers will vary.*

MODÈLE
Lundi matin, Martine va dessiner au parc.

ressources
vText — CE pp. 91–96 — vhlcentral.com Leçon 4A

cent cinquante

PRE-AP®

Interpersonal Speaking Invite a native French speaker to class. Before the person arrives, have students prepare a list of questions that they would like to ask this person. For example, they could ask about the person's job, family, leisure-time activities, weekend plans, and the places he or she frequents. Have students use their questions to interview the person.

TEACHING OPTIONS

Writing Practice Give pairs three minutes to write as many questions as they can using interrogative words. Then have them get together with another pair and take turns asking and answering the questions.

Au café Unité 4

Le Zapping

Video: TV Clip

SWISS made

La compagnie Swiss International Air Lines offre à ses passagers une alternative aux compagnies aériennes° contemporaines. En général, le public a une mauvaise opinion des compagnies: les gens° se plaignent° constamment du mauvais service et de la mauvaise cuisine. Voilà pourquoi Swiss International Air Lines propose à ses clients l'élégance et le confort. Sa stratégie de marketing bénéficie de l'excellente réputation des produits et des services suisses, dont° la qualité supérieure est reconnue° dans le monde entier.

—Le ventilateur doucement° murmure...
—Au micro° parle le copilote...

Compréhension Répondez aux questions.

1. Quels endroits d'une ville trouve-t-on dans la publicité (*ad*)? *Dans la publicité, on trouve un parc, un bureau, un restaurant et une piscine.*
2. Quels types de personnes y a-t-il dans la publicité? Pourquoi est-ce important? *Answers will vary.*

Discussion Par groupes de quatre, répondez aux questions. *Answers will vary.*

1. Avez-vous un produit fabriqué en Suisse? Si oui, quel produit? Décrivez sa qualité. Sinon, quel produit suisse avez-vous envie de posséder? Pourquoi?
2. Vous allez fonder une compagnie aérienne différente des autres (*from the others*). Comment est-elle différente? Quelles destinations va-t-elle proposer?

compagnies aériennes *airlines* **les gens** *people* **se plaignent** *complain* **dont** *whose* **reconnue** *recognized* **avion** *plane* **Le ventilateur doucement** *The fan gently* **micro** *microphone*

Practice more at vhlcentral.com.

cent cinquante et un 151

Section Goals

In this section, students will learn and practice vocabulary related to:
- foods and beverages
- eating at a café or restaurant

Key Standards
1.1, 1.2, 4.1

Student Resources
Cahier de l'élève, pp. 97–99;
Supersite: Activities, eCahier

Teacher Resources
Answer Keys; Digital Image Bank; Audio Script; Textbook & Audio Activity MP3s/CD; Activity Pack; Testing program: Vocabulary Quiz

Suggestions
- Use the digital image for this page. Ask students to describe where the scene takes place and what people are doing. Have students identify items they know.
- Have students look at the new vocabulary and identify the cognates.
- Model the pronunciation of the words and have students repeat after you. Then ask students a few questions about the people in the drawing. Examples: **Qui a faim? Que mange l'homme? Qui a soif?**
- Point out the menu in the illustration. Explain the difference between **un menu** and **une carte**. Ask students what **soupe du jour** and **plat du jour** mean. Then ask: **Combien coûte le plat du jour? Et la soupe du jour?**
- Tell students that a 15% tip is usually included in the price of a meal in a café or restaurant. If the service is particularly good, it is customary to leave a little bit extra.

Contextes — Leçon 4B

You will learn how to...
- order food and beverages
- ask for your check

Audio: Vocabulary Practice
My Vocabulary

J'ai faim!

Vocabulaire

apporter	to bring, to carry
coûter	to cost
Combien coûte(nt)...?	How much is/are...?
une baguette	baguette (long, thin loaf of bread)
le beurre	butter
des frites (f.)	French fries
un fromage	cheese
le jambon	ham
un pain (de campagne)	(country-style) bread
un sandwich	sandwich
une boisson (gazeuse)	(soft) (carbonated) drink/beverage
un chocolat (chaud)	(hot) chocolate
une eau (minérale)	(mineral) water
un jus (d'orange, de pomme, etc.)	(orange, apple, etc.) juice
le lait	milk
une limonade	lemon soda
un thé (glacé)	(iced) tea
(pas) assez (de)	(not) enough (of)
beaucoup (de)	a lot (of)
d'autres	others
un morceau (de)	piece, bit (of)
un peu (plus/moins) (de)	a little (more/less) (of)
plusieurs	several
quelque chose	something; anything
quelques	some
tous (m. pl.)	all
tout (m. sing.)	all
tout le/tous les (m.)	all the
toute la/toutes les (f.)	all the
trop (de)	too many/much (of)
un verre (de)	glass (of)

Labels in illustration: un serveur (serveuse f.); le prix; une bouteille d'eau; l'addition (f.); une soupe; les croissants (m.); Elle laisse un pourboire. (laisser); Il a faim.

Menu board: menu du jour / soupe du jour 3,50€ / plat du jour 12€

ressources
vText
CE pp. 97–99
vhlcentral.com Leçon 4B

152 *cent cinquante-deux*

EXPANSION

Food and Drink Write **le matin**, **à midi**, and **le soir** on the board or on a transparency. Then ask students when they prefer to have various foods and beverages. Example: **Préférez-vous manger des frites le matin ou à midi?** Other items you can mention are **un éclair**, **un sandwich**, **une soupe**, and **un croissant**.

EXPANSION

Categories Have students work in pairs. Tell them to classify the foods and drinks under the headings **Manger** and **Boire** (*To drink*). After pairs have completed the activity, tell them to compare their lists with another pair and to resolve any differences.

152 Unit 4 • Lesson 4B

Au café — Unité 4

Mise en pratique

Attention!
To read prices in French, say the number of euros (**euros**) followed by the number of cents (**centimes**). French decimals are marked with a comma, not a period.
8,10€ = huit euros dix (centimes)

1 Chassez l'intrus Trouvez le mot qui ne va pas avec les autres.

1. un croissant, le pain, **le fromage**, une baguette
2. une limonade, un jus de pomme, un jus d'orange, **le beurre**
3. des frites, un sandwich, **le sucre**, le jambon
4. **le jambon**, un éclair, un croissant, une baguette
5. l'eau, la boisson, l'eau minérale, **la soupe**
6. l'addition, **un chocolat**, le pourboire, coûter
7. **apporter**, d'autres, plusieurs, quelques
8. **un morceau**, une bouteille, un verre, une tasse

2 Reliez Choisissez les expressions de quantité qui correspondent le mieux (*the best*) aux produits.

MODÈLE
un morceau de baguette

| une bouteille de | une tasse de |
| un morceau de | un verre de |

1. _un verre d'/une bouteille d'_ eau
2. _un morceau de_ sandwich
3. _un morceau de_ fromage
4. _une tasse de_ chocolat
5. _une tasse de_ café
6. _un verre de/une bouteille de_ jus de pomme
7. _une tasse de_ thé
8. _un verre de_ limonade

3 Écoutez Écoutez la conversation entre André et le serveur du café Gide, et décidez si les phrases sont **vraies** ou **fausses**.

	Vrai	Faux
1. André n'a pas très soif.	✓	
2. André n'a pas faim.		✓
3. Au café, on peut commander (*one may order*) un jus d'orange, une limonade, un café ou une boisson gazeuse.	✓	
4. André commande un sandwich au jambon avec du fromage.		✓
5. André commande une tasse de chocolat.		✓
6. André déteste le lait et le sucre.		✓
7. André n'a pas beaucoup d'argent.	✓	
8. André ne laisse pas de pourboire.	✓	

Practice more at vhlcentral.com.

cent cinquante-trois 153

Image labels: le sucre, le thé, une tasse, Il mange quelque chose. (manger), un café, un éclair, Il a soif.

---

1 Expansion For additional practice, give students these items. 9. beaucoup de, un verre de, assez de, un peu de (un verre de) 10. le café, le jus, le thé, le chocolat chaud (le jus) 11. l'addition, le prix, le serveur, le pourboire (le serveur)

2 Suggestion You may wish to introduce words for other types of containers, such as **une assiette, un bol,** and **un paquet**.

2 Expansion For additional practice, give students these items. 9. lait (une bouteille de/un verre de) 10. beurre (un morceau de)

3 Script SERVEUR: Bonjour, Monsieur! Vous désirez?
ANDRÉ: Bonjour! Combien coûtent les sandwichs?
S: Ça dépend. Un sandwich au jambon coûte 3€, mais un sandwich au jambon avec du fromage et des frites coûte 5,50€.
A: Et combien coûte le café?
S: Une tasse de café coûte 3€ et avec du lait 3,50€.
A: Y a-t-il d'autres boissons?
S: Bien sûr, il y a du jus d'orange, des boissons gazeuses, de la limonade et de l'eau.
A: Je n'ai pas beaucoup d'argent sur moi, mais j'ai très faim. J'ai envie d'un sandwich au jambon. Je n'ai pas très soif, alors une tasse de café au lait avec un peu de sucre, s'il vous plaît.
S: Très bien, Monsieur.
A: Excusez-moi, c'est combien?
S: C'est 6,50€.
A: Voici. Merci et bonne journée!
S: Merci, Monsieur, au revoir. Oh là là! Pas de pourboire!
(On Textbook Audio)

3 Suggestion Have students correct the false items.

TEACHING OPTIONS

Using Games Write these categories on the board: **Boissons froides / chaudes** and **Nourriture froide / chaude**. Toss a beanbag to a student at random and call out a category. The student has four seconds to name a food or beverage that fits the category. He or she then tosses the beanbag to another student and calls out a category. Players who cannot think of an item in time or repeat an item are eliminated. The last person standing wins.

EXPANSION

Oral Practice For additional practice, ask students questions about their food and drink preferences. Examples: **Préférez-vous le thé ou le chocolat? Le lait ou l'eau minérale? Le jus d'orange ou le jus de pomme? Le jambon ou le fromage? Les sandwichs ou les éclairs? La soupe ou les frites? Les baguettes ou les croissants?**

153

Contextes — Leçon 4B

Communication

4 Combien coûte...? Regardez la carte et, à tour de rôle, demandez à votre partenaire combien coûte chaque élément. Répondez par des phrases complètes.

MODÈLE
Élève 1: *Combien coûte un sandwich?*
Élève 2: *Un sandwich coûte 3,50€.*

1. Combien coûtent les frites? Les frites coûtent 2€.
2. Combien coûte une boisson gazeuse? Une boisson gazeuse coûte 2€.
3. Combien coûte une limonade? Une limonade coûte 1,75€.
4. Combien coûte une bouteille d'eau? Une bouteille d'eau coûte 2€.
5. Combien coûte une tasse de café? Une tasse de café coûte 3€.
6. Combien coûte une tasse de thé? Une tasse de thé coûte 2,50€.
7. Combien coûte un croissant? Un croissant coûte 1€.
8. Combien coûte un éclair? Un éclair coûte 1,95€.

5 Conversez Interviewez un(e) camarade de classe. Answers will vary.

1. Qu'est-ce que tu aimes boire (*drink*) quand tu as soif? Quand tu as froid? Quand tu as chaud?
2. Quand tu as faim, est-ce que tu manges un sandwich? Qu'est-ce que tu aimes manger?
3. Est-ce que tu aimes le café ou le thé? Combien de tasses est-ce que tu aimes boire par jour?
4. Comment est-ce que tu aimes le café? Avec du lait? Avec du sucre? Noir (*Black*)?
5. Comment est-ce que tu aimes le thé? Avec du lait? Avec du sucre? Nature (*Black*)?
6. Dans ta famille, qui aime le thé? Et le café?
7. Est-ce que tu aimes les boissons gazeuses ou l'eau minérale?
8. Quand tu manges avec ta famille dans un restaurant, est-ce que vous laissez un pourboire au serveur/à la serveuse?

6 Au restaurant Choisissez deux partenaires et écrivez une conversation entre deux client(e)s et leur serveur/serveuse. Préparez-vous à jouer (*perform*) la scène devant la classe. Answers will vary.

Client(e)s
- Demandez des détails sur le menu et les prix.
- Choisissez des boissons et des plats (*dishes*).
- Demandez l'addition.

Serveur/Serveuse
- Parlez du menu et répondez aux questions.
- Apportez les plats et l'addition.

Coup de main
Vous désirez?
What can I get you?

Je voudrais...
I would like...

C'est combien?
How much is it/this/that?

7 Sept différences Votre professeur va vous donner, à vous et à votre partenaire, deux feuilles d'activités différentes. Attention! Ne regardez pas la feuille de votre partenaire.

MODÈLE
Élève 1: *J'ai deux tasses de café.*
Élève 2: *Oh, j'ai une tasse de thé!*

cent cinquante-quatre

Les sons et les lettres

Nasal vowels

Audio: Explanation Record & Compare

In French, when vowels are followed by an **m** or an **n** in a single syllable, they usually become nasal vowels. Nasal vowels are produced by pushing air through both the mouth and the nose.

The nasal vowel sound you hear in **français** is usually spelled **an** or **en**.

| **an** | fr**an**çais | **en**chanté | **en**f**an**t |

The nasal vowel sound you hear in **bien** may be spelled **en**, **in**, **im**, **ain**, or **aim**. The nasal vowel sound you hear in **brun** may be spelled **un** or **um**.

| exam**en** | améric**ain** | l**un**di | parf**um** |

The nasal vowel sound you hear in **bon** is spelled **on** or **om**.

| t**on** | all**ons** | c**om**bien | **on**cle |

When **m** or **n** is followed by a vowel sound, the preceding vowel is not nasal.

| i**ma**ge | i**nu**tile | a**mi** | a**mou**r |

Prononcez Répétez les mots suivants à voix haute.

1. blond
2. dans
3. faim
4. entre
5. garçon
6. avant
7. maison
8. cinéma
9. quelqu'un
10. différent
11. amusant
12. télévision
13. impatient
14. rencontrer
15. informatique
16. comment

Articulez Répétez les phrases suivantes à voix haute.

1. Mes parents ont cinquante ans.
2. Tu prends une limonade, Martin?
3. Le Printemps est un grand magasin.
4. Lucien va prendre le train à Montauban.
5. Pardon, Monsieur, l'addition s'il vous plaît!
6. Jean-François a les cheveux bruns et les yeux marron.

Dictons Répétez les dictons à voix haute.

L'appétit vient en mangeant.[1]

N'allonge pas ton bras au-delà de ta manche.[2]

[1] Appetite comes from eating.
[2] Don't bite off more than you can chew. (lit. Don't stretch your arm out farther than your sleeve.)

cent cinquante-cinq 155

Section Goals
In this section, students will learn functional phrases for ordering foods and drinks and talking about food through comprehensible input.

Key Standards
1.2, 2.1, 2.2, 4.1, 4.2

Student Resources
Cahier de l'élève, pp. 101–102;
Supersite: Activities, eCahier

Teacher Resources
Answer Keys; Video Script & Translation; *Roman-photo* video

Video Recap: Leçon 4A
Before doing this **Roman-photo**, review the previous one with this activity.
1. David pense qu'il y a une femme célèbre à l'épicerie. Qui est-ce? **(Juliette Binoche)**
2. À qui Sandrine parle-t-elle au téléphone? **(à Pascal)**
3. Les jeunes trouvent-ils facilement l'épicerie? **(non)**
4. Comment est la femme à l'épicerie? **(belle, jolie, élégante, petite et vieille)**
5. En réalité, qui est la femme? **(quelqu'un qui travaille à l'épicerie)**

Video Synopsis
As the four friends approach **Le P'tit Bistrot**, Amina and Sandrine are hungry and want to go eat. Rachid and David decide to go back to their apartment. Valérie tells Amina and Sandrine what she is serving for lunch that day, and they place their order. Michèle makes a mistake on a customer's check, and Valérie serves the wrong food and drinks to Amina and Sandrine.

Suggestions
- Ask students to read the title, glance at the video stills, and predict what the episode will be about. Record their predictions.
- Have students volunteer to read the characters' parts in the **Roman-photo** aloud.
- After reading the **Roman-photo**, review students' predictions and ask them which ones are correct. Then help them summarize this episode.

Roman-photo — Leçon 4B

L'heure du déjeuner
Video: *Roman-photo* Record & Compare

PERSONNAGES
Amina 
David 
Michèle 
Rachid 
Sandrine 
Valérie 

1. *Près du café...*
AMINA J'ai très faim. J'ai envie de manger un sandwich.
SANDRINE Moi aussi, j'ai faim, et puis j'ai soif. J'ai envie d'une bonne boisson. Eh, les garçons, on va au café?

2. **RACHID** Moi, je rentre à l'appartement étudier pour un examen de sciences po. David, tu vas au café avec les filles?
DAVID Non, je rentre avec toi. J'ai envie de dessiner un peu.
AMINA Bon, alors, à tout à l'heure.

3. *Au café...*
VALÉRIE Bonjour, les filles! Alors, ça va, les études?
AMINA Bof, ça va. Qu'est-ce qu'il y a de bon à manger, aujourd'hui?
VALÉRIE Eh bien, j'ai une soupe de poisson maison délicieuse! Il y a aussi des sandwichs jambon-fromage, des frites... Et, comme d'habitude, j'ai des éclairs, euh...

6. **VALÉRIE** Et pour toi, Amina?
AMINA Hmm... Pour moi, un sandwich jambon-fromage avec des frites.
VALÉRIE Très bien, et je vous apporte du pain tout de suite.
SANDRINE ET AMINA Merci!

7. *Au bar...*
VALÉRIE Alors, pour la table d'Amina et Sandrine, une soupe du jour, un sandwich au fromage... Pour la table sept, une limonade, un café, un jus d'orange et trois croissants.
MICHÈLE D'accord! Je prépare ça tout de suite. Mais Madame Forestier, j'ai un problème avec l'addition de la table huit.

8. **VALÉRIE** Ah, bon?
MICHÈLE Le monsieur ne comprend pas pourquoi ça coûte onze euros cinquante. Je ne comprends pas non plus. Regardez.
VALÉRIE Ah, non! Avec tout le travail que nous avons cet après-midi, des problèmes d'addition aussi?!

ACTIVITÉS

1. Identifiez Trouvez à qui correspond chacune (*each*) des phrases. Écrivez **A** pour Amina, **D** pour David, **M** pour Michèle, **R** pour Rachid, **S** pour Sandrine et **V** pour Valérie.

__M__ 1. Je ne comprends pas non plus.
__V__ 2. Vous prenez du jus d'orange uniquement le matin.
__S__ 3. Tu bois de l'eau aussi?
__M__ 4. Je prépare ça tout de suite.
__A__ 5. Je ne bois pas de limonade.
__S__ 6. Je vais apprendre à préparer des éclairs.
__D__ 7. J'ai envie de dessiner un peu.
__V__ 8. Je vous apporte du pain tout de suite.
__R__ 9. Moi, je rentre à l'appartement étudier pour un examen de sciences po.
__A__ 10. Qu'est-ce qu'il y a de bon à manger, aujourd'hui?

Practice more at **vhlcentral.com**.

TEACHING OPTIONS

L'heure du déjeuner Before viewing the video, have students work in pairs and write a list of words and expressions that they might hear in a video episode entitled **L'heure du déjeuner**.

TEACHING OPTIONS

Regarder la vidéo Show the video episode and tell students to check off the words or expressions they hear on their lists. Then show the episode again and have students give you a play-by-play description of the action. Write their descriptions on the board.

Au café — Unité 4

Amina et Sandrine déjeunent au café.

SANDRINE Oh, Madame Forestier, j'adore! Un jour, je vais apprendre à préparer des éclairs. Et une bonne soupe maison. Et beaucoup d'autres choses.
AMINA Mais pas aujourd'hui. J'ai trop faim!
SANDRINE Alors, je choisis la soupe et un sandwich au fromage.

VALÉRIE Et comme boisson?
SANDRINE Une bouteille d'eau minérale, s'il vous plaît. Tu bois de l'eau aussi? Avec deux verres, alors.

VALÉRIE Ah, ça y est! Je comprends! La boisson gazeuse coûte un euro vingt-cinq, pas un euro soixante-quinze. C'est noté, Michèle?
MICHÈLE Merci, Madame Forestier. Excusez-moi. Je vais expliquer ça au monsieur. Et voilà, tout est prêt pour la table d'Amina et Sandrine.
VALÉRIE Merci, Michèle.

À la table des filles...
VALÉRIE Voilà, une limonade, un café, un jus d'orange et trois croissants.
AMINA Oh? Mais Madame Forestier, je ne bois pas de limonade!
VALÉRIE Et vous prenez du jus d'orange uniquement le matin, n'est-ce pas? Ah! Excusez-moi, les filles!

Expressions utiles

Talking about food
- Moi aussi, j'ai faim, et puis j'ai soif.
  Me too, I am hungry, and I am thirsty as well.
- J'ai envie d'une bonne boisson.
  I feel like having a nice drink.
- Qu'est-ce qu'il y a de bon à manger, aujourd'hui?
  What looks good on the menu today?
- Une soupe de poisson maison délicieuse.
  A delicious homemade fish soup.
- Je vais apprendre à préparer des éclairs.
  I am going to learn (how) to prepare éclairs.
- Je choisis la soupe.
  I choose the soup.
- Tu bois de l'eau aussi?
  Are you drinking water too?
- Vous prenez du jus d'orange uniquement le matin.
  You only have orange juice in the morning.

Additional vocabulary
- On va au café?
  Shall we go to the café?
- Bof, ça va.
  So-so.
- comme d'habitude
  as usual
- Le monsieur ne comprend pas pourquoi ça coûte onze euros cinquante.
  The gentleman doesn't understand why this costs 11,50€.
- Je ne comprends pas non plus.
  I don't understand either.
- Je prépare ça tout de suite.
  I am going to prepare this right away.
- Ça y est! Je comprends!
  That's it! I get it!
- C'est noté?
  Understood?/Got it?
- Tout est prêt.
  Everything is ready.

Activités

2 Mettez dans l'ordre Numérotez les phrases suivantes dans l'ordre correspondant à l'histoire.
- 5 a. Michèle a un problème avec l'addition.
- 3 b. Amina prend (*gets*) un sandwich jambon-fromage.
- 1 c. Sandrine dit qu'elle (*says that she*) a soif.
- 2 d. Rachid rentre à l'appartement.
- 4 e. Valérie va chercher du pain.
- 6 f. Tout est prêt pour la table d'Amina et Sandrine.

3 Conversez Au moment où Valérie apporte le plateau (*tray*) de la table sept à Sandrine et Amina, Michèle apporte le plateau de Sandrine et Amina à la table sept. Avec trois partenaires, écrivez la conversation entre Michèle et les client(e)s et jouez-la devant la classe.

ressources: vText, CE pp. 101–102, vhlcentral.com Leçon 4B

cent cinquante-sept 157

Expressions utiles
- Model the pronunciation of the **Expressions utiles** and have students repeat after you.
- As you work through the list, point out the forms of the verbs **prendre** and **boire** and the partitive articles. Tell students that these verbs and the partitive articles will be formally presented in the **Structures** section.
- Ask students questions about foods and beverages using the vocabulary in the **Expressions utiles**. Examples: **Vous prenez du jus d'orange uniquement le matin? Quand est-ce que vous avez envie de boire de l'eau?**

1 Expansion
- For additional practice, give students these items. **11. Le monsieur ne comprend pas pourquoi ça coûte 11,50€. (M) 12. J'ai faim et puis j'ai soif. (S) 13. Mais pas aujourd'hui. J'ai trop faim! (A) 14. Non, je rentre avec toi. (D)**
- Write these adverbial expressions on the board: **non plus**, **aussi**, and **tout de suite**. Have students create sentences with them.

2 Suggestion Have students work in groups of six. Write each sentence on a strip of paper. Make a set of sentences for each group, then distribute them to students. Tell them to read their sentences aloud and arrange them in the proper order.

2 Expansion Have students create sentences to fill in the missing parts of the story.

PRE-AP®

3 Interpersonal Speaking: Suggestion Before doing this activity, have the class brainstorm vocabulary and expressions they might use in this activity and write their ideas on the board.

EXPANSION

Mini-dialogues Have students work in pairs. Tell them to combine sentences in **Expressions utiles** with other words and expressions they know to create mini-dialogues. Example:
—**Qu'est-ce qu'il y a de bon aujourd'hui?**
—**Il y a une soupe de poisson maison délicieuse.**

PRE-AP®

Interpersonal Speaking Ask volunteers to ad-lib the **Roman-photo** episode for the class. Tell them that it is not necessary to memorize the episode or to stick strictly to its content. They should try to get the general meaning across with the vocabulary and expressions they know, and they should also feel free to be creative. Give them time to prepare.

157

Culture Leçon 4B

Reading Video: *Flash culture*

CULTURE À LA LOUPE

Le café français

À Toute Heure

Quiches	3,50€
Pâtisseries	3,50€
Omelettes	5,25€
Thé	1,50€
Glaces	5,50€
Café	1,50€
Cappuccino	2,00€
Chocolat chaud	2,30€

Le premier café français, le Procope, a ouvert° ses portes à Paris en 1686. C'était° un lieu° pour boire du café, qui était une boisson exotique à l'époque°. On pouvait° aussi manger un sorbet dans des tasses en porcelaine. Benjamin Franklin et Napoléon Bonaparte fréquentaient le Procope.

Le café est une partie importante de la culture française. Les Français adorent passer du temps° à la terrasse des cafés. C'est un des symboles de l'art de vivre° à la française.

Le matin, ils y° vont pour prendre un café et un croissant. À midi, pour le déjeuner, ils y vont pour manger un plat du jour° ou un sandwich. Après le travail, ils y vont pour prendre l'apéritif°. L'apéritif, c'est un moment où on boit un verre pour se détendre° avec ses amis. Les élèves et les étudiants se retrouvent souvent° au café, près de leur lycée ou de leur faculté, pour étudier ou prendre un verre.

Il y a de très célèbres cafés à Paris: «Les Deux Magots» ou le «Café de Flore» par exemple, dans le quartier° de Saint-Germain. Ils sont connus° parce que c'était le rendez-vous des intellectuels et des écrivains°, comme Jean-Paul Sartre, Simone de Beauvoir et Albert Camus, après la Deuxième Guerre mondiale°.

a ouvert opened **C'était** It was **lieu** place **à l'époque** at the time **pouvait** could **fréquentaient** used to frequent **passer du temps** spending time **vivre** living **y** there **plat du jour** lunch special **apéritif** before-dinner drink **se détendre** to relax **souvent** often **célèbres** famous **quartier** neighborhood **connus** known **écrivains** writers **Deuxième Guerre mondiale** World War II

ACTIVITÉS

1 Vrai ou faux? Indiquez si les phrases sont vraies ou fausses. Corrigez les phrases fausses.

1. Le premier café parisien date des années 1686. Vrai.
2. Les Français vont au café uniquement le matin. Faux. Les Français vont aussi au café à midi et après le travail.
3. Napoléon Bonaparte et Benjamin Franklin sont d'anciens clients du Procope. Vrai.
4. Le café est une partie importante de la culture française. Vrai.
5. Les Français évitent (avoid) les terrasses des cafés. Faux. Ils adorent passer du temps à la terrasse des cafés.
6. Le matin, les Français prennent du jambon et du fromage. Faux. Ils prennent un café et un croissant.
7. Les Français ne prennent pas leur apéritif au café. Faux. Ils prennent leur apéritif au café après le travail.
8. Les élèves et les étudiants se retrouvent souvent avec leurs amis au café. Vrai.
9. «Les Deux Magots» et le «Café de Flore» sont deux cafés célèbres à Paris. Vrai.
10. Les intellectuels français fréquentent les cafés après la Première Guerre mondiale. Faux. Ils fréquentent les cafés après la Deuxième Guerre mondiale.

Practice more at vhlcentral.com.

158   cent cinquante-huit

Au café Unité 4

LE FRANÇAIS QUOTIDIEN
J'ai faim!

avoir les crocs	to be hungry
avoir un petit creux	to be slightly hungry
boire à petites gorgées	to sip
bouffer	to eat
dévorer	to devour
grignoter	to snack on
mourir de faim	to be starving
siroter	to sip (with pleasure)

LE MONDE FRANCOPHONE
Des spécialités à grignoter

Voici quelques spécialités à grignoter dans les pays et régions francophones.

En Afrique du Nord la merguez (saucisse épicée°) et le makroud (pâtisserie° au miel° et aux dattes)

En Côte d'Ivoire l'aloco (bananes plantains frites°)

En France le pan-bagnat (sandwich avec de la salade, des tomates, des œufs durs° et du thon°) et les crêpes (pâte° cuite° composée de farine°, d'œufs et de lait, de forme ronde)

À la Martinique les accras de morue° (beignets° à la morue)

Au Québec la poutine (frites avec du fromage fondu° et de la sauce)

Au Sénégal le chawarma (de la viande°, des oignons et des tomates dans du pain pita)

saucisse épicée spicy sausage pâtisserie pastry miel honey frites fried œufs durs hard-boiled eggs thon tuna pâte batter cuite cooked farine flour morue cod beignets fritters fondu melted viande meat

PORTRAIT
Les cafés nord-africains

Comme en France, les cafés ont une grande importance culturelle en Afrique du Nord. C'est le lieu où les amis se rencontrent pour discuter° ou pour jouer aux cartes° ou aux dominos. Les cafés ont une variété de boissons, mais ils n'offrent° pas d'alcool. La boisson typique, au café comme à la maison, est le thé à la menthe°. Il a peu de caféine, mais il a des vertus énergisantes et il favorise la digestion. En général, ce sont les hommes qui le° préparent. C'est la boisson qu'on vous sert° quand vous êtes invité, et ce n'est pas poli de refuser!

pour discuter to chat jouer aux cartes play cards offrent offer menthe mint le it on vous sert you are served

Sur Internet

Comment prépare-t-on le thé à la menthe au Maghreb?

Go to vhlcentral.com to find more information related to this **Culture** section. Then watch the corresponding **Flash culture**.

2 Compréhension Complétez les phrases.
1. Quand on a un peu soif, on a tendance à (tends to) boire ___à petites gorgées___.
2. On ne peut pas boire de/d' ___alcool___ dans un café nord-africain.
3. Les hommes préparent ___le thé à la menthe___ en Afrique du Nord.
4. Il n'est pas poli de ___refuser___ une tasse de thé en Afrique du Nord.
5. Si vous aimez les frites, vous allez aimer ___la poutine___ au Québec.

3 Un café francophone
Par groupes de quatre, préparez une liste de suggestions pour un nouveau café francophone: noms pour le café, idées (ideas) pour le menu, prix, heures, etc. Indiquez où le café va être situé et qui va fréquenter ce café.

ressources: vText CE pp. 103–104 vhlcentral.com Leçon 4B

cent cinquante-neuf 159

Section Goals

In this section, students will learn:
- the verbs **prendre**, **apprendre**, and **comprendre**
- the verb **boire**
- partitive articles

Key Standards
4.1, 5.1

Student Resources
Cahier de l'élève, pp. 105–107; Supersite: Activities, eCahier, Grammar Tutorials

Teacher Resources
Answer Keys; Audio Script; Audio Activity MP3s/CD; Activity Pack; Testing program: Grammar Quiz

Suggestions

- Point out that **prendre** means *to have* when saying what one is having to eat or drink, but it cannot be used to express possession. For possession, **avoir** must be used.
- Point out to students that all the singular forms of **prendre** sound the same. Make sure that students pronounce the **n** sound in **prennent**.
- Ask students if they can think of any English words related to **apprendre** (*apprentice*) and **comprendre** (*comprehend*).
- Work through the forms of **boire**, asking students what they drink most often or rarely. Model a response by first saying what you drink: **Je bois souvent ____. Qu'est-ce que vous buvez?**
- Write the conjugation of **boire** on the board with the singular forms in one column and the plural forms in another column. Draw a line around the forms that have **oi**. Tell students that **boire** is a "boot verb."

Structures — Leçon 4B

4B.1 The verbs *prendre* and *boire*; Partitives

Presentation Grammar Tutorial

Point de départ The verbs **prendre** (*to take, to have food or drink*) and **boire** (*to drink*), like **être, avoir,** and **aller,** are irregular.

Je prends la soupe et un sandwich au fromage.

Je ne bois pas de limonade.

prendre

je prends	I take	nous prenons	we take
tu prends	you take	vous prenez	you take
il/elle/on prend	he/she/it/one takes	ils/elles prennent	they take

Brigitte **prend** le métro le soir.
Brigitte takes the subway in the evening.

Nous **prenons** un café chez moi.
We are having a coffee at my house.

- The forms of the verbs **apprendre** (*to learn*) and **comprendre** (*to understand*) follow the same pattern as that of **prendre**.

Tu ne **comprends** pas l'espagnol?
Don't you understand Spanish?

Elles **apprennent** beaucoup.
They're learning a lot.

Boîte à outils

You can use the construction **apprendre à** + [*infinitive*] to mean *to learn to do something*. Example: **J'apprends à** nager. *I'm learning to swim.*

Je ne comprends pas non plus.

Un jour, je vais apprendre à préparer des éclairs.

boire

je bois	I drink	nous buvons	we drink
tu bois	you drink	vous buvez	you drink
il/elle/on boit	he/she/it/one drinks	ils/elles boivent	they drink

Ton père **boit** un jus d'orange.
Your father is drinking an orange juice.

Vous **buvez** un chocolat chaud, M. Dion?
Are you drinking hot chocolate, Mr. Dion?

Je **bois** toujours du lait.
I always drink milk.

Nous ne **buvons** pas de café.
We don't drink coffee.

cent soixante

EXPANSION

Extra Practice On the board, write a list of sentences containing the verbs **prendre** and **boire**, and partitives. Ask your students to say the same sentences out loud using different subjects. Example: **Je prends de la limonade à la cantine** (Nous). (**Nous prenons de la limonade à la cantine**).

EXPANSION

Interview Have pairs of students interview each other about what they eat and drink in certain situations (**le matin, dans un restaurant…**). Ask them to report to the class about their partners. Ex. **Il/Elle boit du chocolat chaud le matin**. They should also mention common habits in order to use **nous**. Ex. **Nous buvons du jus d'orange le matin**.

Au café — Unité 4

Partitives

- Use partitive articles in French to express *some* or *any*. To form the partitive, use the preposition **de** followed by a definite article. Although the words *some* and *any* are often omitted in English, the partitive must always be used in French.

masculine singular	feminine singular	singular noun beginning with a vowel
du thé	**de la** limonade	**de l'**eau

Je bois **du** thé chaud.
I drink (some) hot tea.

Tu bois **de la** limonade?
Are you drinking (any) lemon soda?

Elle prend **de l'**eau?
Is she having (some) water?

- Note that partitive articles are only used with non-count nouns (nouns whose quantity cannot be expressed by a number).

PARTITIVE ARTICLE / NON-COUNT NOUN
Tu prends **du pain** tous les jours.
You have (some) bread every day.

INDEFINITE ARTICLE / COUNT NOUN
Tu prends **une banane**, aussi.
You have a banana, too.

- The article **des** also means *some*, but it is the plural form of the indefinite article, not the partitive.

PARTITIVE ARTICLE
Vous prenez **de la** limonade.
You're having (some) lemon soda.

INDEFINITE ARTICLE
Nous prenons **des** croissants.
We're having (some) croissants.

- As with the indefinite articles, the partitives **du**, **de la** and **de l'** also become **de** (meaning *not any*) in a negative sentence.

Est-ce qu'il y a **du** lait?
Is there (any) milk?

Non, il n'y a pas **de** lait.
No, there isn't (any) milk.

Prends-tu **de la** soupe?
Will you have (some) soup?

Non, je ne prends pas **de** soupe.
No, I'm not having (any) soup.

À noter

The partitives follow the same pattern of contraction as the possessive **de** + [definite article] you learned in **Structures 3A.2: du, de la, de l'**.

Boîte à outils

Partitives are used to say that you want *some* of an item, whereas indefinite articles are used to say that you want *a whole item* or *several whole items*.
Tu prends de la pizza?
(part of a whole pizza)
Tu prends une pizza?
(a whole pizza)

Essayez!

Complétez les phrases. Utilisez la forme correcte du verbe entre parenthèses et l'article qui convient.

1. Ma sœur __prend__ (prendre) __des__ éclairs.
2. Tes parents __boivent__ (boire) __du__ café?
3. Louise ne __boit__ (boire) pas __de__ thé.
4. Est-ce qu'il y __a__ (avoir) __du__ sucre?
5. Nous __buvons__ (boire) __de la__ limonade.
6. Non, merci. Je ne __prends__ (prendre) pas __de__ frites.
7. Vous __prenez__ (prendre) __un__ taxi?
8. Nous __apprenons__ (apprendre) __le__ français.

Structures   Leçon 4B

Mise en pratique

1 Au café Indiquez l'article correct.

MODÈLE

Avez-vous __du__ lait froid?

1. Prenez-vous __du/un__ thé glacé?
2. Je voudrais __une__ baguette, s'il vous plaît.
3. Elle prend __un__ croissant.
4. Nous ne prenons pas __de__ sucre dans le café.
5. Tu ne laisses pas __de__ pourboire?
6. Vous mangez __des__ frites.
7. Zeina commande __une__ boisson gazeuse.
8. Voici __de l'/une__ eau minérale.
9. Nous mangeons __du__ pain.
10. Je ne prends pas __de__ fromage.

2 Des suggestions Laurent est au café avec des amis et il fait (*makes*) des suggestions. Que suggère-t-il?

MODÈLE

On prend du jus d'orange?

1. On prend de la limonade?
2. On prend de l'eau minérale?
3. On prend du thé?
4. On prend des sandwichs?

3 Au restaurant Alain est au restaurant avec toute sa famille. Il note les préférences de tout le monde. Utilisez le verbe indiqué.

MODÈLE

Oncle Lucien aime bien le café. (prendre) *Il prend un café.*

1. Marie-Hélène et papa adorent le thé. (prendre)
   Ils prennent un thé.
2. Tu adores le chocolat chaud. (boire)
   Tu bois un chocolat chaud.
3. Vous aimez bien le jus de pomme. (prendre)
   Vous prenez un jus de pomme.
4. Mes nièces aiment la limonade. (boire)
   Elles boivent une limonade.
5. Tu aimes les boissons gazeuses. (prendre)
   Tu prends une boisson gazeuse.
6. Vous adorez le café. (boire)
   Vous buvez un café.

162   cent soixante-deux

Practice more at vhlcentral.com.

Au café   Unité 4

Communication

4 Échanges Posez les questions à un(e) partenaire. *Answers will vary.*
1. Qu'est-ce que tu bois quand tu as très soif?
2. Qu'est-ce que tu apprends au lycée?
3. Quelles langues est-ce que tes parents comprennent?
4. Est-ce que tu bois beaucoup de café? Pourquoi?
5. Qu'est-ce que tu prends à manger à midi?
6. Quelle langue est-ce que ton/ta meilleur(e) ami(e) apprend?
7. Où est-ce que tu prends tes repas (*meals*)?
8. Qu'est-ce que tu bois le matin? À midi? Le soir?

5 Je bois, je prends Votre professeur va vous donner une feuille d'activités. Circulez dans la classe pour demander à vos camarades s'ils prennent rarement, une fois (*once*) par semaine ou tous les jours la boisson ou le plat (*dish*) indiqués. Écrivez (*Write*) les noms sur la feuille, puis présentez vos réponses à la classe. *Answers will vary.*

MODÈLE

Élève 1: Est-ce que tu bois du café?
Élève 2: Oui, je bois du café une fois par semaine. Et toi?

Boisson ou plat	rarement	une fois par semaine	tous les jours
1. café		Didier	
2. fromage			
3. thé			
4. soupe			
5. chocolat chaud			
6. jambon			

6 Après les cours Des amis se retrouvent au café. Par groupes de quatre, jouez (*play*) les rôles d'un(e) serveur/serveuse et de trois clients. Utilisez les mots de la liste et présentez la scène à la classe. *Answers will vary.*

addition	chocolat chaud	frites
avoir faim	coûter	prix
avoir soif	croissant	sandwich
boisson	eau minérale	soupe
éclair	jambon	limonade

cent soixante-trois   163

4 Virtual Chat You can also assign Activity 4 on the Supersite. Students record individual responses that appear in your gradebook.

5 Suggestion Have two volunteers read the **modèle** aloud. Then distribute the **Feuilles d'activités** found in the Activity Pack on the Supersite.

6 Suggestions
- Bring in a few props, such as cups, bottles, and plates, for students to use in their role-plays.
- Have volunteers perform their role-plays for the class, then vote on the best one.

EXPANSION

Extra Practice Write this activity on the board. Tell students to add the missing words and form complete sentences.
1. Marc / boire / eau / et / prendre / sandwich / jambon
2. Solange / prendre / soupe / et / boire / boisson gazeuse
3. Nous / boire / café / lait / et / prendre / éclairs
4. Henri et Paul / prendre / hot-dogs / et / frites
5. Anne / prendre / soupe / poisson / et / verre / thé glacé

PRE-AP®

Interpersonal Speaking Have students look back at the **Roman photo** on pages 156-157. Have them ask and answer questions about what the characters are eating, drinking, taking and learning. They should use the verbs **prendre**, **apprendre** and **boire**, and partitives.

163

Section Goals
In this section, students will learn regular -ir verbs.

Key Standards
4.1, 5.1

Student Resources
Cahier de l'élève, pp. 108–110; Supersite: Activities, *eCahier*, Grammar Tutorials

Teacher Resources
Answer Keys; Audio Script; Audio Activity MP3s/CD; Testing program: Grammar Quiz

Suggestions
- Model the pronunciation of -ir verbs and have students repeat them.
- Introduce the verbs by saying what time you finish teaching today and asking students what time they finish classes. Examples: **Aujourd'hui, je finis d'enseigner à cinq heures. Et vous, à quelle heure finissez-vous les cours?** Then ask students to ask a classmate: **Et toi, à quelle heure finis-tu, aujourd'hui?**
- Point out that the singular forms of -ir verbs all sound the same.
- Call students' attention to the -iss- in the plural forms of -ir verbs.
- Remind students that -ss- sounds like an *s*, but a single *s* between vowels is pronounced like a *z*.
- Tell students that many -ir verbs are derived from adjectives, such as **grand**, **rouge**, **gros**, or **vieux**.

Essayez! For additional practice, give students these items. 9. Comment _____ (réagir)-vous quand vous avez peur? (réagissez) 10. Vos grands-parents _____ (vieillir) ensemble. (vieillissent)

Structures | Leçon 4B

4B.2 Regular *-ir* verbs

Presentation Grammar Tutorial

Point de départ In **Leçon 2A**, you learned the pattern of **-er** verbs. Verbs that end in **-ir** follow a different pattern.

finir
je fin**is**	nous fin**issons**
tu fin**is**	vous fin**issez**
il/elle/on fin**it**	ils/elles fin**issent**

Je **finis** mes devoirs.
I'm finishing my homework.

Alain et Chloé **finissent** leurs sandwichs.
Alain and Chloé are finishing their sandwiches.

- Here are some other verbs that follow the same pattern as **finir**.

Other regular *-ir* verbs
choisir	to choose	réfléchir (à)	to think (about), to reflect (on)
grandir	to grow		
grossir	to gain weight	réussir (à)	to succeed (in doing something)
maigrir	to lose weight		
obéir (à)	to obey	rougir	to blush
réagir	to react	vieillir	to grow old

Je **choisis** un chocolat chaud.
I choose a hot chocolate.

Vous **réfléchissez** à ma question?
Are you thinking about my question?

🏃 Boîte à outils
Use the constructions **finir de** + [*infinitive*] and **choisir de** + [*infinitive*] to mean *to finish doing* and *to choose to do something*.

Je **finis de manger**.
I'm finishing eating.

Nous **choisissons de rester** ici.
We choose to stay here.

À noter
In **Leçon 2A**, you learned the phrase **être reçu(e) à un examen**. You can also use the phrase **réussir un examen** to mean *to pass a test or exam*.

Une minute... je réfléchis.

Je choisis un sandwich.

- Like for **-er** verbs, use present tense verb forms to give commands.

Réagis vite!
React quickly!

Obéissez-moi.
Obey me.

Réfléchissons bien.
Let's think well.

Ne **rougis** pas.
Don't blush.

Essayez! Complétez les phrases.

1. Quand on ne mange pas beaucoup, on ___maigrit___ (maigrir).
2. Il ___réussit___ (réussir) son examen.
3. Vous ___finissez___ (finir) vos devoirs?
4. Lundi prochain nous ___finissons___ (finir) le livre.
5. Les enfants ___grandissent___ (grandir) très vite (*fast*).
6. Vous ___choisissez___ (choisir) le fromage?
7. Ils n'___obéissent___ (obéir) pas à leur parents.
8. Je ___réfléchis___ (réfléchir) beaucoup à ce problème.

EXPANSION

Video Replay the **Roman-photo**. Have students listen for -ir verbs and write down those they hear. Afterward, write the verbs on the board and ask their meanings. Have students write original sentences using each verb.

EXPANSION

Questions Ask students questions using -ir verbs in the present and also with the **futur proche**. Examples: **Quand allez-vous finir le lycée? Réussissez-vous vos examens?**

Au café — Unité 4

Le français vivant

Café du Marché

Formule petit-déjeuner simple — 5,50€

boisson chaude + croissant + jus de fruits (au choix°) ou
boisson chaude + mini-baguette avec du beurre + jus de fruits (au choix)

✳✳✳

Formule petit-déjeuner complet — 7,50€

boisson chaude + sandwich jambon-fromage + jus de fruits (au choix)

Boissons

Café .... 1,50€	
Café déca .... 1,60€	
Café crème .... 2,00€	Eau minérale .... 2,50€
Chocolat chaud .... 2,20€	Jus de fruits .... 2,80€
Thé .... 2,20€	Limonade .... 2,80€

au choix *your choice of*

Répondez Avec un(e) partenaire, discutez de la carte et de ces (*these*) situations. Utilisez des verbes en **-ir**.

1. Je prends quatre croissants.
2. J'ai très faim.
3. Je ne mange pas beaucoup.
4. Je ne commande pas encore.
5. Je bois toute la bouteille d'eau minérale.

Structures
Leçon 4B

Mise en pratique

1 On fait quoi? Choisissez la forme correcte du verbe en **-ir**.

1. Nous (**finissons** / grandissons) nos devoirs avant le dîner.
2. Ursula (choisis / **choisit**) un croissant.
3. Eva et Léo (rougissent / **réussissent**) à faire un gâteau.
4. Omar (**réfléchit** / réfléchis) à ses problèmes.
5. Nous essayons de ne pas (grandir / **grossir**).
6. Tu manges une salade parce que tu essaies de (vieillir / **maigrir**).

2 Au restaurant Complétez le dialogue avec la forme correcte du verbe entre parenthèses.

SERVEUR Vous désirez?
MARC Nous (1) _réfléchissons_ (réfléchir) encore.
FANNY Je pense savoir ce que je veux (*know what I want*).
SERVEUR Que (2) _choisissez_ (choisir)-vous, Mademoiselle?
FANNY Je (3) _choisis_ (choisir) un hamburger avec des frites. Et toi?
MARC Euh... je (4) _réfléchis_ (réfléchir). La soupe ou la salade, je pense... Oui, je prends la salade.
SERVEUR Très bien. Je vous apporte ça tout de suite (*right away*).
FANNY Tu n'as pas très faim?
MARC Non, pas trop. Et je suis au régime (*on a diet*). J'ai besoin de (5) _maigrir_ (maigrir) un peu.
FANNY Tu (6) _réussis_ (réussir) déjà. Ton jean est trop grand. Tu n'as pas envie de partager mon éclair?
MARC Mais non! Je vais (7) _grossir_ (grossir)!
FANNY Alors, je (8) _finis_ (finir) l'éclair.

3 Complétez Complétez les phrases avec la forme correcte des verbes de la liste. N'utilisez les verbes qu'une seule fois.

choisir	maigrir
finir	obéir
grandir	rougir
grossir	vieillir

1. Nous _choisissons_ l'endroit où nous allons déjeuner.
2. Corinne _rougit_ quand elle a honte.
3. Mes frères cadets _grandissent_ encore. Ils sont déjà (*already*) très grands!
4. Vous ne mangez pas assez et vous _maigrissez_.
5. Nous _obéissons_ aux profs.
6. Sylvie _finit_ ses études cette année.
7. Mes grands-parents _vieillissent_.
8. Quand on mange beaucoup de chocolat, on _grossit_.

Au café Unité 4

Communication

4 Ça, c'est moi! Avec un(e) partenaire, complétez les phrases suivantes pour parler de vous-même.
1. Je ne finis jamais (de)…
2. Je grossis quand…
3. Je maigris quand…
4. Au restaurant, je choisis souvent…
5. Je réfléchis quelquefois (*sometimes*) à…
6. Je réussis toujours (à)…

5 Assemblez Avec un(e) partenaire, assemblez les éléments des trois colonnes pour créer des phrases. Attention! Quelques verbes sont irréguliers. *Answers will vary.*

A	B	C
je	choisir	aujourd'hui
tu	finir	beaucoup
le prof	grandir	cette (this)
mon frère	grossir	année
mes parents	maigrir	cours
ma sœur	réfléchir	devoirs
mon/ma petit(e) ami(e)	réussir	diplôme
	rougir	encore
mes camarades de classe	vieillir	problème
		vite
?		?

6 Votre vie au lycée Posez ces questions à un(e) partenaire puis présentez vos réponses à la classe. *Answers will vary.*
1. Pendant ce semestre, dans quel cours réussis-tu le mieux (*best*)?
2. Comment est-ce que tu choisis un/une ami(e)?
3. En général, est-ce que tu réussis aux examens de français? Comment les trouves-tu?
4. Est-ce que tu maigris ou grossis au lycée? Pourquoi?
5. À quelle heure est-ce que tes cours finissent le vendredi? Que fais-tu après les cours?
6. Que font tes parents pour toi quand tu réussis tes examens?
7. Quand fais-tu tes devoirs? À quelle heure finis-tu tes devoirs?

7 Qui…? Posez (*Ask*) des questions pour trouver une personne dans la classe qui fait ces (*does these*) choses.

MODÈLE
Élève 1: *Est-ce que tu rougis facilement?*
Élève 2: *Non, je ne rougis pas facilement.*

1. rougir facilement (*easily*)
2. réagir vite
3. obéir à ses parents
4. finir toujours ses devoirs
5. choisir bien sa nourriture (*food*)

---

4 Suggestion Call on volunteers to share their information with the rest of the class.

4 Partner Chat You can also assign Activity 4 on the Supersite. Students work in pairs to record the activity online. The pair's recorded conversation will appear in your gradebook.

5 Suggestion Give students five minutes to write as many sentences as they can using –ir verbs. Then have volunteers read some of their sentences aloud or write them on the board.

7 Suggestion Remind students to ask and answer questions using complete sentences. Have them write the name of the person they find for each question. Follow up with questions about what they found out. Example: **Qui finit toujours ses devoirs?**

EXPANSION

Extra Practice Have students restate these sentences using -ir verbs. **1. Mes tantes sont moins jeunes qu'avant (*than before*). 2. Cédric est moins gros qu'avant. 3. Nous sommes plus grands qu'avant. 4. Vous pensez beaucoup. 5. Je termine le lycée**.

EXPANSION

Extra Practice Have students write fill-in-the-blank or dehydrated sentences for each of the -ir verbs. Then tell them to exchange papers with a partner and complete the activity. Remind students to verify their answers.

Synthèse

Leçon 4B

Révision

1 **Ils aiment apprendre** Vous demandez à Sylvie et à Jérôme pourquoi ils aiment apprendre. Un(e) partenaire va poser des questions et l'autre partenaire va jouer les rôles de Jérôme et de Sylvie. Answers will vary.

MODÈLE

Élève 1: *Pourquoi est-ce que tu apprends à travailler sur l'ordinateur?*
Élève 2: *J'apprends parce que j'aime les ordinateurs.*

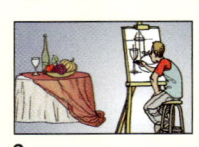

1.
2.
3.
4.
5.
6.

2 **Quelle boisson?** Interviewez une personne de votre classe. Que boit-on dans ces circonstances? Ensuite (*Then*), posez les questions à une personne différente. Utilisez des articles partitifs dans vos réponses. Answers will vary.

1. au café
2. au cinéma
3. en classe
4. le dimanche matin
5. le matin très tôt
6. quand il/elle passe des examens
7. quand il/elle a très soif
8. quand il/elle étudie toute la nuit

3 **Notre café** Vous et votre partenaire allez créer un café français. Choisissez le nom du café et huit boissons. Pour chaque (*each*) boisson, inventez deux prix, un pour le comptoir (*bar*) et un pour la terrasse. Comparez votre café au café d'un autre groupe. Answers will vary.

4 **La terrasse du café** Avec un(e) partenaire, observez les deux dessins et trouvez au minimum quatre différences. Comparez votre liste à la liste d'un autre groupe. Ensuite, écrivez (*write*) un paragraphe sur ces trois personnages en utilisant (*by using*) des verbes en **-ir**. Answers will vary.

MODÈLE

Élève 1: *Mylène prend une limonade.*
Élève 2: *Mylène prend de la soupe.*

Patrick   Mylène   Djamel

5 **Dialogue** Avec un(e) partenaire, créez un dialogue avec les éléments de la liste. Answers will vary.

choisir	du chocolat
grossir	de l'eau minérale
maigrir	un sandwich au jambon
réagir	des frites
réfléchir (à)	de la soupe
réussir (à)	du jus de pomme

6 **La famille Arnal au café** Votre professeur va vous donner, à vous et à votre partenaire, des photos de la famille Arnal. Attention! Ne regardez pas la feuille de votre partenaire. Answers will vary.

MODÈLE

Élève 1: *Qui prend un sandwich?*
Élève 2: *La grand-mère prend un sandwich.*

ressources

vText
CE pp. 105–110
vhlcentral.com
Leçon 4B

À l'écoute

STRATÉGIE

Listening for the gist

Listening for the general idea, or gist, can help you follow what someone is saying even if you can't hear or understand some of the words. When you listen for the gist, you try to capture the essence of what you hear without focusing on individual words.

> To help you practice this strategy, you will listen to three sentences. Jot down a brief summary of what you hear.

Préparation

Regardez la photo. Combien de personnes y a-t-il? Où sont Charles et Gina? Qu'est-ce qu'ils vont manger? Boire? Quelle heure est-il? Qu'est-ce qu'ils vont faire (*to do*) cet après-midi?

À vous d'écouter

Écoutez la conversation entre Charles, Gina et leur serveur. Écoutez une deuxième fois (*a second time*) et indiquez quelles activités ils vont faire.

- ✓ 1. acheter un livre
- ✓ 2. aller à la librairie
- ____ 3. aller à l'église
- ✓ 4. aller chez des grands-parents
- ____ 5. boire un coca
- ✓ 6. danser
- ✓ 7. dépenser de l'argent
- ____ 8. étudier
- ✓ 9. manger au restaurant
- ✓ 10. manger un sandwich

Compréhension

Un résumé Complétez ce résumé (*summary*) de la conversation entre Charles et Gina avec des mots et expressions de la liste.

aller au cinéma	une eau minérale
aller au gymnase	en boîte de nuit
avec son frère	faim
café	un jus d'orange
chez ses grands-parents	manger au restaurant
des copains	du pain
un croissant	soif

Charles et Gina sont au (1) __café__. Charles va boire (2) __une eau minérale__. Gina n'a pas très (3) __faim__. Elle va manger (4) __un croissant__. Cet après-midi, Charles va (5) __aller au gymnase__. Ce soir, il va (6) __manger au restaurant__ avec (7) __des copains__. Cet après-midi, Gina va peut-être (8) __aller au cinéma__. Ce soir, elle va manger (9) __chez ses grands-parents__. À onze heures, elle va aller (10) __en boîte de nuit__ avec Charles.

Et vous? Avec un(e) camarade, discutez de vos projets (*plans*) pour ce week-end. Où est-ce que vous allez aller? Qu'est-ce que vous allez faire (*to do*)?

cent soixante-neuf **169**

Section Goals
In this section, students will learn historical and cultural information about Normandy and Brittany.

Key Standards
2.2, 3.1, 3.2, 5.1

21st CENTURY SKILLS
Global Awareness
Students will gain perspectives on the Francophone world to develop respect and openness to others and to interact appropriately and effectively with citizens of Francophone cultures.

Student Resources
Cahier de l'élève, pp. 111–112;
Supersite: Activities,
eCahier

Teacher Resources
Answer Keys;
Digital Image Bank

Carte de la Normandie et de la Bretagne
- Have students look at the map of Normandy and Brittany or use the digital image for this page. Ask volunteers to read the cities' names aloud.
- Have students read the photo captions and locate the places on the map.

La région en chiffres
- Have volunteers read the sections aloud. After each section, ask questions about the content.
- Have students compare the industries of these two regions.
- Ask students to share any information they might know about the **Personnes célèbres**.

Incroyable mais vrai!
The Abbey of Mont-Saint-Michel was a small chapel in the eighth century. In 966 it became a Benedictine monastery. After the French Revolution, the abbey was a political prison. In 1874, it was declared a national monument, and it presently houses a small monastic community.

Savoir-faire

Panorama

Interactive Map Reading

La Normandie

La région en chiffres
- **Superficie:** 29.906 km² (vingt-neuf mille neuf cent six kilomètres carrés°)
- **Population:** 3.248.000 (trois millions deux cent quarante-huit mille)
  SOURCE: Institut National de la Statistique et des Études Économiques (INSEE)
- **Industries principales:** élevage bovin°, énergie nucléaire, raffinage° du pétrole
- **Villes principales:** Alençon, Caen, Évreux, Le Havre, Rouen

Personnes célèbres
- **la comtesse de Ségur,** femme écrivain° (1799–1874)
- **Guy de Maupassant,** écrivain (1850–1893)
- **Christian Dior,** couturier° (1905–1957)

La Bretagne

La région en chiffres
- **Superficie:** 27.208 km² (vingt-sept mille deux cent huit kilomètres carrés)
- **Population:** 3.011.000 (trois millions onze mille)
- **Industries principales:** agriculture, élevage°, pêche°, tourisme
- **Villes principales:** Brest, Quimper, Rennes, Saint-Brieuc, Vannes

Personnes célèbres
- **Anne de Bretagne,** reine° de France (1477–1514)
- **Jacques Cartier,** explorateur (1491–1557)
- **Bernard Hinault,** cycliste (1954–)

carrés squared élevage bovin cattle raising raffinage refining femme écrivain writer couturier fashion designer élevage livestock raising pêche fishing reine queen les plus grandes marées the highest tides presqu'île peninsula entourée de sables mouvants surrounded by quicksand basse low île island haute high chaque each onzième siècle 11th century pèlerinage pilgrimage falaises cliffs faire make moulin mill

170 cent soixante-dix

les falaises° d'Étretat

l'art de faire° les crêpes

un moulin°

Incroyable mais vrai!
C'est au Mont-Saint-Michel qu'il y a les plus grandes marées° d'Europe. Le Mont-Saint-Michel, presqu'île° entourée de sables mouvants° à marée basse°, est transformé en île° à marée haute°. Trois millions de touristes visitent chaque° année l'église du onzième siècle°, centre de pèlerinage° depuis 1000 (mille) ans.

EXPANSION

Personnes célèbres **La comtesse de Ségur** wrote 25 novels, notably **Les Malheurs de Sophie**. **Guy de Maupassant** published some 300 short stories and 6 novels. His stories present a picture of French life from 1870–1890. **Christian Dior** dominated post-World War II fashion. Today Christian Dior S.A. runs 160 boutiques worldwide. The company also markets lingerie, cosmetics, perfumes, handbags, watches, and accessories under the Dior name. **Anne de Bretagne** was Queen of France twice by marriage. She married Charles VIII in 1491 and Louis XII in 1499. **Jacques Cartier** explored the St. Lawrence River region during his three voyages to North America (1534, 1535, and 1541–1542). France based its claims to that area on Cartier's discoveries. **Bernard Hinault** won the **Tour de France** five times and dominated international cycling from 1977–1987.

Au café — **Unité 4**

La gastronomie
Les crêpes et galettes bretonnes et le camembert normand

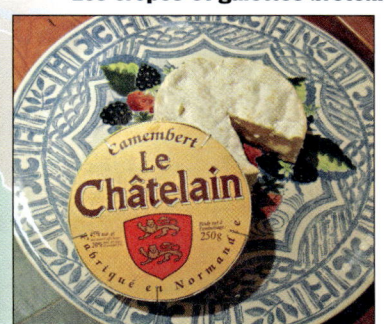

Les crêpes et les galettes sont une des spécialités culinaires de Bretagne; en Normandie, c'est le camembert. Les crêpes sont appréciées sucrées, salées°, flambées... Dans les crêperies°, le menu est complètement composé de galettes et de crêpes! Le camembert normand est un des grands symboles gastronomiques de la France. Il est vendu° dans la fameuse boîte en bois ronde° pour une bonne conservation.

Les arts
Giverny et les impressionnistes

La maison° de Claude Monet, maître du mouvement impressionniste, est à Giverny, en Normandie. Après des rénovations, la résidence et les deux jardins° ont aujourd'hui leur ancienne° splendeur. Le légendaire jardin d'eau est la source d'inspiration pour les célèbres peintures° «Les Nymphéas°» et «Le pont japonais°». Depuis la fin° du dix-neuvième siècle°, beaucoup d'artistes américains, influencés par les techniques impressionnistes, font de la peinture à Giverny.

Les monuments
Les menhirs et les dolmens

À Carnac, en Bretagne, il y a 3.000 (trois mille) menhirs et dolmens. Les menhirs sont d'énormes pierres° verticales. Alignés ou en cercle, ils ont une fonction rituelle associée au culte de la fécondité ou à des cérémonies en l'honneur du soleil°. Les plus anciens° datent de 4.500 (quatre mille cinq cents) ans avant J.-C.° Les dolmens servent de° sépultures° collectives et ont une fonction culturelle comme° le rite funéraire du passage de la vie° à la mort°.

Les destinations
Deauville: station balnéaire de réputation internationale

Deauville, en Normandie, est une station balnéaire° de luxe et un centre de thalassothérapie°. La ville est célèbre pour sa marina, ses courses hippiques°, son casino, ses grands hôtels et son festival du film américain. La clientèle internationale apprécie beaucoup la plage°, le polo et le golf. L'hôtel le Royal Barrière est un palace° du début° du vingtième° siècle.

Compréhension Complétez ces phrases.

1. _Jacques Cartier_ est un explorateur breton.
2. Le Mont-Saint-Michel est une _île_ à marée haute.
3. _Les crêpes/galettes_ sont une spécialité bretonne.
4. Dans _les crêperies_, on mange uniquement des crêpes.
5. _Le camembert_ est vendu dans une boîte en bois ronde.
6. Le _jardin d'eau_ de Monet est la source d'inspiration de beaucoup de peintures.
7. Beaucoup d'artistes _américains_ font de la peinture à Giverny.
8. Les menhirs ont une fonction _rituelle_.
9. Les dolmens servent de _sépultures_.
10. Deauville est une _station balnéaire_ de luxe.

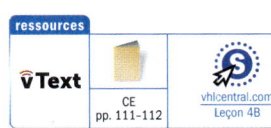

Sur Internet

1. Cherchez des informations sur les marées du Mont-Saint-Michel. À quelle heure est la marée haute aujourd'hui?
2. Cherchez des informations sur deux autres impressionnistes. Trouvez deux peintures que vous aimez et dites (*say*) pourquoi.

Practice more at vhlcentral.com.

---

salées salty **crêperies** crêpes restaurants **vendu** sold **boîte en bois ronde** round, wooden box **maison** house **jardins** gardens **ancienne** former **peintures** paintings **Nymphéas** Waterlilies **pont japonais** Japanese Bridge **Depuis la fin** Since the end **dix-neuvième siècle** 19th century **pierres** stones **soleil** sun **Les plus anciens** The oldest **avant J.-C.** B.C. **servent de** serve as **sépultures** graves **comme** such as **vie** life **mort** death **station balnéaire** seaside resort **thalassothérapie** seawater therapy **courses hippiques** horse races **plage** beach **palace** luxury hotel **début** beginning **vingtième** twentieth

cent soixante et onze 171

Savoir-faire

Lecture
Audio: Synced Reading

Avant la lecture

STRATÉGIE
Scanning

Scanning involves glancing over a document in search of specific information. For example, you can scan a document to identify its format, to find cognates, to locate visual clues about the document's content, or to find specific facts. Scanning allows you to learn a great deal about a text without having to read it word-for-word.

Examinez le texte
Regardez le texte et indiquez huit mots apparentés (*cognates*) que vous trouvez. *Answers may vary.*

1. Chocolat
2. Cybercafé
3. Accès Internet
4. Omelette
5. Salade
6. Tarte
7. Soupe
8. Snack

Trouvez
Regardez le document. Indiquez si les informations suivantes sont présentes dans le texte.

- ✓ 1. une adresse
- ___ 2. le nombre d'ordinateurs
- ___ 3. un plat du jour (*daily special*)
- ✓ 4. une terrasse
- ✓ 5. les noms des propriétaires
- ___ 6. des prix réduits pour les jeunes
- ___ 7. de la musique *live*
- ✓ 8. les heures d'ouverture (*business hours*)
- ✓ 9. un numéro de téléphone
- ___ 10. une librairie à l'intérieur

Décrivez
Regardez les photos. Écrivez un paragraphe succinct pour décrire (*describe*) le cybercafé. Comparez votre paragraphe avec le paragraphe d'un(e) camarade.

172 cent soixante-douze

Cybercafé Le

- Ouvert° du lundi au samedi, de 7h00 à 20h00
- Snack et restauration rapide
- Accès Internet et jeux° vidéo

Cybercafé Le connecté

MENU

PETIT-DÉJEUNER° FRANÇAIS 12,00€	**PETIT-DÉJEUNER ANGLAIS** 15,00€
Café, thé, chocolat chaud ou lait	Café, thé, chocolat chaud ou lait
Pain, beurre et confiture°	Œufs° (au plat° ou brouillés°), bacon, toasts
Orange pressée	Orange pressée
VIENNOISERIES° 3,00€	**DESSERTS**
Croissant, pain au chocolat, brioche°, pain aux raisins	Tarte aux fruits 7,50€
	Banana split 6,40€
SANDWICHS ET SALADES	
Sandwich (jambon ou fromage; baguette ou pain de campagne) 7,50€	**AUTRES SÉLECTIONS CHAUDES**
Croque-monsieur° 7,80€	Frites 4,30€
Salade verte° 6,20€	Soupe à l'oignon 6,40€
	Omelette au fromage 8,50€
BOISSONS CHAUDES	Omelette au jambon 8,50€
Café/Déca 3,80€	
Grand crème 5,50€	**BOISSONS FROIDES**
Chocolat chaud 5,80€	Eau minérale non gazeuse 3,00€
Thé 5,50€	Eau minérale gazeuse 3,50€
Lait chaud 4,80€	Jus de fruits (orange...) 5,80€
	Soda, limonade 5,50€
	Café, thé glacé° 5,20€

Propriétaires: Bernard et Marie-Claude Fouchier

Au café — Unité 4

connecté

- Le connecté, le cybercafé préféré des étudiants
- Ordinateurs disponibles° de 10h00 à 18h00, 1,50€ les 10 minutes

24, place des Terreaux
69001 LYON
Tél. 04.72.45.87.90
www.leconnecte.fr

Situé en face du musée des Beaux-Arts

Ouvert Open **jeux** games **Petit-déjeuner** Breakfast **confiture** jam **Viennoiseries** Breakfast pastries **brioche** a light, slightly-sweet bread **Croque-monsieur** Grilled sandwich with cheese and ham **verte** green **Œufs** Eggs **au plat** fried **brouillés** scrambled **glacé** iced **disponibles** available

Après la lecture

Répondez
Répondez aux questions par des phrases complètes.

1. Combien coûte un sandwich?
   Un sandwich coûte 7,50€.
2. Quand est-ce qu'on peut (can) surfer sur Internet?
   On peut surfer sur Internet de 10h00 à 18h00.
3. Qui adore ce cybercafé?
   Les étudiants adorent ce cybercafé.
4. Quelles sont les deux boissons gazeuses? Combien coûtent-elles?
   L'eau minérale gazeuse coûte 3,50€. Un soda coûte 5,50€.
5. Combien de desserts sont proposés?
   Deux desserts sont proposés.
6. Vous aimez le sucre. Qu'est-ce que vous allez manger? (2 sélections) Answers may vary. Je vais manger... Any two of the following: un croissant, un pain au chocolat, une brioche, un pain aux raisins, une tarte aux fruits, un banana split.

Choisissez
Indiquez qui va prendre quoi. Écrivez des phrases complètes. Answers may vary. Possible answers provided.

MODÈLE
Julie a soif. Elle n'aime pas les boissons gazeuses. Elle a 6 euros.
Julie va prendre un jus d'orange.

1. Lise a froid. Elle a besoin d'une boisson chaude. Elle a 4 euros et 90 centimes.
   Lise va prendre un café.
2. Nathan a faim et soif. Il a 14 euros.
   Nathan va prendre un croque-monsieur et un soda.
3. Julien va prendre un plat chaud. Il a 8 euros et 80 centimes.
   Julien va prendre une omelette au jambon.
4. Annie a chaud et a très soif. Elle a 5 euros et 75 centimes.
   Annie va prendre un thé glacé.
5. Martine va prendre une boisson gazeuse. Elle a 4 euros et 20 centimes.
   Martine va prendre une eau minérale gazeuse.
6. Ève va prendre un dessert. Elle n'aime pas les bananes. Elle a 8 euros.
   Ève va prendre une tarte aux fruits.

L'invitation
Avec un(e) camarade, jouez (play) cette scène: vous invitez un ami à déjeuner au cybercafé Le connecté. Parlez de ce que vous allez manger et boire. Puis (Then), bavardez de vos activités de l'après-midi et du soir.

Répondez Go over the answers with the class. Take a quick class poll to find out what is the most popular food chosen for question 6.

Choisissez Have students write two more situations similar to those in the activity. Then tell them to exchange papers with a partner, write the answers, and verify the answers.

L'invitation Before beginning the activity, tell students that they only have 20€ to spend at the Cybercafé Le connecté.

21st CENTURY SKILLS
Creativity and Innovation
Ask students to prepare a presentation on the ideal cybercafé, inspired by the information on these two pages.

EXPANSION
Cultural Comparison Working in groups of three, have students compare the **Cybercafé Le connecté** menu to a typical menu found at an American Internet café. Tell them to list the similarities and differences in a two-column chart under the headings **Similitudes** and **Différences**. After completing their charts, call on volunteers to read their lists.

PRE-AP
Interpretive Reading: Scanning To practice scanning written material, bring in short, simple French-language magazine or newspaper articles you have read. Have pairs or small groups scan the articles to determine what they are about. Have them write down all the clues that help them. When each group has come to a decision, ask it to present its findings to the class. Confirm the accuracy of the group's inferences.

Section Goals

In this section, students will:
- learn to add informative details
- learn to write an informative note

Key Standards
1.3, 3.1, 5.1

PRE-AP®

Interpersonal Writing: Stratégie Discuss the importance of being informative when writing a note and answering the "W" questions. For example, someone calls while you are out, and your brother or sister answers the phone. If your note has enough information, he or she can answer the person's questions about where you are or when you will return.

Suggestion Have students read the model note in **Écriture** and identify the details. (**aujourd'hui; avec Xavier et Laurent, deux élèves belges du lycée**)

Proofreading Activity Have the class correct these sentences.
1. Ou est-ce que tu va après le cours? 2. Il vont à le magasin cet après-midi. 3. Est-ce que tu prend de le sucre dans le café? 4. Dominique bois de la thé avec le petit-déjeuner.

Savoir-faire

Écriture

STRATÉGIE

Adding details

How can you make your writing more informative or more interesting? You can add details by answering the "W" questions: Who? What? When? Where? Why? The answers to these questions will provide useful and interesting details that can be incorporated into your writing. You can use the same strategy when writing in French. Here are some useful question words that you have already learned:

(À/Avec) Qui?	À quelle heure?
Quoi?	Où?
Quand?	Pourquoi?

Compare these two sentences.

Je vais aller nager.

Aujourd'hui, à quatre heures, je vais aller nager à la piscine du parc avec mon ami Paul, parce que nous avons chaud.

While both sentences give the same basic information (the writer is going to go swimming), the second, with its detail, is much more informative.

Thème

Un petit mot

Avant l'écriture

1. Vous passez un an en France et vous vivez (*are living*) dans une famille d'accueil (*host family*). C'est samedi, et vous allez passer la journée en ville avec des amis. Écrivez un petit mot (*note*) pour informer votre famille de vos projets (*plans*) pour la journée.

2. D'abord (*First*), choisissez (*choose*) cinq activités que vous allez faire (*to do*) avec vos amis aujourd'hui.

Activité 1:

Activité 2:

Activité 3:

Activité 4:

Activité 5:

EXPANSION

Avant l'écriture Discuss the importance of facts when writing a note and answering the "W" questions. Encourage students to identify a note's purpose (to provide specific information and instructions). Point out that if a note is not complete enough, it fails to serve its purpose. Redundancies can also detract from the message.

Demonstrate how the question strategy works by choosing a general topic and then, as a class, asking and answering the questions in the box. Put students in pairs and have them try it out on their own, using the questions provided to narrow their topic and add details while avoiding redundancies.

Au café — Unité 4

3. Ensuite (*Then*), complétez ce tableau (*this chart*) pour organiser vos idées. Répondez à (*Answer*) toutes les questions.

	Activité 1	Activité 2	Activité 3	Activité 4	Activité 5
Qui?					
Quoi?					
Quand?					
Où?					
Comment?					
Pourquoi?					

4. Maintenant (*Now*), comparez votre tableau à celui (*to the one*) d'un(e) partenaire. Avez-vous tous les deux (*both of you*) cinq activités? Avez-vous des informations dans toutes les colonnes? Avez-vous répondu à toutes les questions?

Écriture

Écrivez la note à votre famille d'accueil. Référez-vous au tableau que vous avez créé (*have created*) et incluez toutes les informations. Utilisez les verbes **aller**, **boire** et **prendre**, et le vocabulaire de l'unité. Organisez vos idées de manière logique.

*Chère famille,
Aujourd'hui, je vais visiter la ville avec Xavier et Laurent, deux élèves belges du lycée…*

Après l'écriture

1. Échangez votre tableau et votre note avec ceux (*the ones*) d'un(e) partenaire. Faites des commentaires sur son travail (*work*) d'après (*according to*) ces questions:

   ■ Votre partenaire a-t-il/elle inclus dans la note toutes les informations du tableau?

   ■ A-t-il/elle correctement (*correctly*) utilisé le vocabulaire de l'unité?

   ■ A-t-il/elle utilisé la forme correcte des verbes **aller**, **boire** et **prendre**?

   ■ A-t-il/elle présenté ses informations de manière logique?

2. Corrigez (*Correct*) votre note d'après les commentaires de votre partenaire. Relisez votre travail pour éliminer ces (*these*) problèmes:

   ■ des fautes (*errors*) d'orthographe

   ■ des fautes de ponctuation

   ■ des fautes de conjugaison

   ■ des fautes d'accord (*agreement*) des adjectifs

ressources
vText
vhlcentral.com
Leçon 4B

cent soixante-quinze

EVALUATION

Criteria

Content Contains a greeting, describes the five planned activities, answers the questions: **qui? quoi? quand? où? pourquoi?**, and includes supporting detail without redundancy.
Scale: 1 2 3 4 5

Organization Organizes the note into a salutation, a description, and a signature.
Scale: 1 2 3 4 5

Accuracy Uses forms of **aller** and places in town correctly. Spells words, conjugates verbs, and modifies adjectives correctly throughout. Avoids redundant language.
Scale: 1 2 3 4 5

Creativity Includes additional information that is not included in the task, mentions more than five activities and/or includes a closing (not shown in the model).
Scale: 1 2 3 4 5

Scoring
Excellent	18–20 points
Good	14–17 points
Satisfactory	10–13 points
Unsatisfactory	< 10 points

21st CENTURY SKILLS

Productivity and Accountability
Provide the rubric to students before they hand their work in for grading. Ask students to make sure they have met the highest standard possible on the rubric before submitting their work.

EXPANSION

Écriture Ask for other details that could be added, such as departure and return times, activities in the town, the town's name and the students' ages. Finally, have students analyze these extra details to see which are useful for the note's message and which are extraneous or redundant.

Show students how to avoid redundancies by combining similar sentences. Compare **Je vais en ville**. **Je vais avec mes amis**. **Je vais lundi matin**. with **Je vais en ville avec mes amis lundi matin**. Tell them to look for ways to condense language when they edit their work.

Vocabulaire — Unité 4

Key Standards
4.1

Teacher Resources
Vocabulary MP3s/CD

Suggestion Tell students that an easy way to study from **Vocabulaire** is to cover up the French half of each section, leaving only the English equivalents exposed. They can then quiz themselves on the French items. To focus on the English equivalents of the French entries, they simply reverse this process.

21ST CENTURY SKILLS
Creativity and Innovation
Ask students to prepare a list of three products or perspectives they learned about in this unit to share with the class. Consider asking them to focus on the **Culture** and **Panorama** sections.

21ST CENTURY SKILLS
Leadership and Responsibility: Extension Project
If you have access to students in a Francophone country, have students decide on three questions they want to ask the partner class related to this unit's topic. Based on the responses they receive, work as a class to explain to the partner class one aspect of their responses that surprised the class and why.

Dans la ville

une boîte (de nuit)	nightclub
un bureau	office; desk
un centre commercial	shopping center, mall
un cinéma (ciné)	movie theater, movies
une église	church
une épicerie	grocery store
un grand magasin	department store
un gymnase	gym
un hôpital	hospital
un kiosque	kiosk
un magasin	store
une maison	house
un marché	market
un musée	museum
un parc	park
une piscine	pool
une place	square; place
un restaurant	restaurant
une terrasse de café	café terrace
une banlieue	suburbs
un centre-ville	city/town center, downtown
un endroit	place
un lieu	place
une montagne	mountain
une ville	city, town

Les questions

à quelle heure?	at what time?
à qui?	to whom?
avec qui?	with whom?
combien (de)?	how many?; how much?
comment?	how?; what?
où?	where?
parce que	because
pour qui?	for whom?
pourquoi?	why?
quand?	when?
quel(le)(s)?	which?; what?
que/qu'...?	what?
qui?	who?; whom?
quoi?	what?

À table

avoir faim	to be hungry
avoir soif	to be thirsty
manger quelque chose	to eat something
une baguette	baguette (long, thin loaf of bread)
le beurre	butter
un croissant	croissant (flaky, crescent-shaped roll)
un éclair	éclair (pastry filled with cream)
des frites (f.)	French fries
un fromage	cheese
le jambon	ham
un pain (de campagne)	(country-style) bread
un sandwich	sandwich
une soupe	soup
le sucre	sugar
une boisson (gazeuse)	(soft) (carbonated) drink/beverage
un café	coffee
un chocolat (chaud)	(hot) chocolate
une eau (minérale)	(mineral) water
un jus (d'orange, de pomme, etc.)	(orange, apple, etc.) juice
le lait	milk
une limonade	lemon soda
un thé (glacé)	(iced) tea

Activités

bavarder	to chat
danser	to dance
déjeuner	to eat lunch
dépenser de l'argent (m.)	to spend money
explorer	to explore
fréquenter	to frequent; to visit
inviter	to invite
nager	to swim
passer chez quelqu'un	to stop by someone's house
patiner	to skate
quitter la maison	to leave the house

Expressions utiles	See pp. 139 and 157.
Prepositions	See p. 143.
Partitives	See p. 161.

Expressions de quantité

(pas) assez (de)	(not) enough (of)
beaucoup (de)	a lot (of)
d'autres	others
une bouteille (de)	bottle (of)
un morceau (de)	piece, bit (of)
un peu (plus/moins) (de)	little (more/less) (of)
plusieurs	several
quelque chose	something; anything
quelques	some
une tasse (de)	cup (of)
tous (m. pl.)	all
tout (m. sing.)	all
tout le/tous les (m.)	all the
toute la/toutes les (f.)	all the
trop (de)	too many/much (of)
un verre (de)	glass (of)

Au café

apporter	to bring, to carry
coûter	to cost
laisser un pourboire	to leave a tip
l'addition (f.)	check, bill
Combien coûte(nt)...?	How much is/are...?
un prix	price
un serveur/une serveuse	server

Verbes

aller	to go
apprendre	to learn
boire	to drink
comprendre	to understand
prendre	to take; to have

Verbes réguliers en -ir

choisir	to choose
finir	to finish
grandir	to grow
grossir	to gain weight
maigrir	to lose weight
obéir (à)	to obey
réagir	to react
réfléchir (à)	to think (about), to reflect (on)
réussir (à)	to succeed (in doing something)
rougir	to blush
vieillir	to grow old

cent soixante-seize

Appendices

Appendice A
The *impératif*	178
Glossary of Grammatical Terms	178

Appendice B
Verb Conjugation Tables	182

Vocabulaire
French–English	193
English–French	214
Vocabulaire Supplémentaire	232

Index
236

Credits
237

Appendice A

The *impératif*

Point de départ The **impératif** is the form of a verb that is used to give commands or to offer directions, hints, and suggestions. With command forms, you do not use subject pronouns.

- Form the **tu** command of **-er** verbs by dropping the **-s** from the present tense form. Note that **aller** also follows this pattern.

  Réserve deux chambres.   **Ne travaille pas.**   **Va** au marché.
  Reserve two rooms.   *Don't work.*   *Go to the market.*

- The **nous** and **vous** command forms of **-er** verbs are the same as the present tense forms.

  Nettoyez votre chambre.   **Mangeons** au restaurant ce soir.
  Clean your room.   *Let's eat at the restaurant tonight.*

- For **-ir** verbs, **-re** verbs, and most irregular verbs, the command forms are identical to the present tense forms.

  Finis la salade.   **Attendez** dix minutes.   **Faisons** du yoga.
  Finish the salad.   *Wait ten minutes.*   *Let's do some yoga.*

The *impératif* of *avoir* and *être*

	avoir	être
(tu)	aie	sois
(nous)	ayons	soyons
(vous)	ayez	soyez

- The forms of **avoir** and **être** in the **impératif** are irregular.

  Aie confiance.   Ne **soyons** pas en retard.
  Have confidence.   *Let's not be late.*

- An object pronoun can be added to the end of an affirmative command. Use a hyphen to separate them. Use **moi** and **toi** for the first- and second-person object pronouns.

  Permettez-moi de vous aider.   Achète le dictionnaire et **utilise-le**.
  Allow me to help you.   *Buy the dictionary and use it.*

- In negative commands, place object pronouns between **ne** and the verb. Use **me** and **te** for the first- and second-person object pronouns.

  Ne **me** montre pas les réponses, s'il te plaît.   Cette photo est fragile. Ne **la** touchez pas.
  Please don't show me the answers.   *That picture is fragile. Don't touch it.*

Glossary of Grammatical Terms

ADJECTIVE A word that modifies, or describes, a noun or pronoun.

des livres **amusants**   une **jolie** fleur
*some **funny** books*   *a **pretty** flower*

Demonstrative adjective An adjective that specifies which noun a speaker is referring to.

cette chemise   **ce** placard
this shirt   *this closet*

cet hôtel   **ces** boîtes
this hotel   *these boxes.*

Possessive adjective An adjective that indicates ownership or possession.

ma belle montre   C'est **son** cousin.
my beautiful watch   *This is **his/her** cousin.*

tes crayons   Ce sont **leurs** tantes.
your pencils   *Those are **their** aunts.*

ADVERB A word that modifies, or describes, a verb, adjective, or other adverb.

Michael parle **couramment** français.
*Michael speaks French **fluently**.*

Elle lui parle **très** franchement.
*She speaks to him **very** candidly.*

ARTICLE A word that points out a noun in either a specific or a non-specific way.

Definite article An article that points out a noun in a specific way.

le marché   **la** valise
the market   *the suitcase*

les dictionnaires   **les** mots
the dictionaries   *the words*

Indefinite article An article that points out a noun in a general, non-specific way.

un vélo   **une** fille
a bike   *a girl*

des oiseaux   **des** affiches
some birds   *some posters*

CLAUSE A group of words that contains both a conjugated verb and a subject, either expressed or implied.

Main (or Independent) clause A clause that can stand alone as a complete sentence.

J'ai un manteau vert.
I have a green coat.

Glossary of Grammatical Terms

Subordinate (or Dependent) clause A clause that does not express a complete thought and therefore cannot stand alone as a sentence.

Je travaille dans un restaurant **parce que j'ai besoin d'argent**.
*I work in a restaurant **because I need money**.*

COMPARATIVE A construction used with an adjective or adverb to express a comparison between two people, places, or things.

Thomas est **plus petit** qu'Adrien.
*Thomas is **shorter than** Adrien.*

En Corse, il pleut **moins souvent qu'**en Alsace.
*In Corsica, it rains **less often than** in Alsace.*

Cette maison n'a pas **autant de fenêtres** que l'autre.
*This house does not have **as many windows as** the other one.*

CONJUGATION A set of the forms of a verb for a specific tense or mood, or the process by which these verb forms are presented.

Imparfait conjugation of **chanter**:
je chant**ais**	nous chant**ions**
tu chant**ais**	vous chant**iez**
il/elle chant**ait**	ils/elles chant**aient**

CONJUNCTION A word used to connect words, clauses, or phrases.

Suzanne **et** Pierre habitent en Suisse.
*Suzanne **and** Pierre live in Switzerland.*

Je ne dessine pas très bien, **mais** j'aime les cours de dessin.
*I don't draw very well, **but** I like art classes.*

CONTRACTION The joining of two words into one. In French, the contractions are **au**, **aux**, **du**, and **des**.

Ma sœur est allée **au** concert hier soir.
*My sister went **to a** concert last night.*

Il a parlé **aux** voisins cet après-midi.
*He talked **to the** neighbors this afternoon.*

Je retire de l'argent **du** distributeur automatique.
*I withdraw money **from the** ATM machine.*

Nous avons campé près **du** village.
*We camped **near the** village.*

DIRECT OBJECT A noun or pronoun that directly receives the action of the verb.

Thomas lit **un livre**.   Je **l'**ai vu hier.
*Thomas reads **a book**.   I saw **him** yesterday.*

GENDER The grammatical categorizing of certain kinds of words, such as nouns and pronouns, as masculine, feminine, or neuter.

Masculine
articles **le, un**
pronouns **il, lui, le, celui-ci, celui-là, lequel**
adjective **élégant**

Feminine
articles **la, une**
pronouns **elle, la, celle-ci, celle-là, laquelle**
adjective **élégante**

IMPERSONAL EXPRESSION A third-person expression with no expressed or specific subject.

Il pleut.   **C'est** très important.
It's raining.   *It's very important.*

INDIRECT OBJECT A noun or pronoun that receives the action of the verb indirectly; the object, often a living being, to or for whom an action is performed.

Éric donne un livre **à Linda**.
*Éric gave a book **to Linda**.*

Le professeur **m'**a donné une bonne note.
*The teacher gave **me** a good mark.*

INFINITIVE The basic form of a verb. Infinitives in French end in **-er**, **-ir**, **-oir**, or **-re**.

parler	**finir**	**savoir**	**prendre**
to speak	*to finish*	*to know*	*to take*

INTERROGATIVE An adjective or pronoun used to ask a question.

Qui parle?
Who *is speaking?*

Combien de biscuits as-tu achetés?
How many *cookies did you buy?*

Que penses-tu faire aujourd'hui?
What *do you plan to do today?*

INVERSION Changing the word order of a sentence, often to form a question.

Statement: Elle a vendu sa voiture.

Inversion: A-t-elle vendu sa voiture?

MOOD A grammatical distinction of verbs that indicates whether the verb is intended to make a statement or command or to express a doubt, emotion, or condition contrary to fact.

cent soixante-dix-neuf **179**

Glossary of Grammatical Terms

Conditional mood Verb forms used to express what would be done or what would happen under certain circumstances, or to make a polite request, soften a demand, express what someone could or should do, or to state a contrary-to-fact situation.

Il **irait** se promener s'il avait le temps.
He would go for a walk if he had the time.

Pourrais-tu éteindre la lumière, s'il te plaît?
Would you turn off the light, please?

Je **devrais** lui parler gentiment.
I should talk to her nicely.

Imperative mood Verb forms used to make commands or suggestions.

Parle lentement.   **Venez** avec moi.
Speak slowly.   *Come with me.*

Indicative mood Verb forms used to state facts, actions, and states considered to be real.

Je sais qu'**il a** un chat.
I know that he has a cat.

Subjunctive mood Verb forms used principally in subordinate (dependent) clauses to express wishes, desires, emotions, doubts, and certain conditions, such as contrary-to-fact situations.

Il est important que **tu finisses** tes devoirs.
It's important that you finish your homework.

Je doute que **Louis ait** assez d'argent.
I doubt that Louis has enough money.

NOUN A word that identifies people, animals, places, things, and ideas.

homme	chat	Belgique
man	*cat*	*Belgium*
maison	livre	amitié
house	*book*	*friendship*

NUMBER A grammatical term that refers to singular or plural. Nouns in French and English have number. Other parts of a sentence, such as adjectives, articles, and verbs, can also have number.

Singular	Plural
une chose	**des** choses
a thing	*some things*
le professeur	**les** professeurs
the teacher	*the teachers*
the professor	*the professors*

NUMBERS Words that represent amounts.

Cardinal numbers Words that show specific amounts.

cinq minutes   l'année **deux mille six**
five minutes   *the year 2006*

Ordinal numbers Words that indicate the order of a noun in a series.

le **quatrième** joueur   la **dixième** fois
the fourth player   *the tenth time*

PAST PARTICIPLE A past form of the verb used in compound tenses. The past participle may also be used as an adjective, but it must then agree in number and gender with the word it modifies.

Ils ont beaucoup **marché**.
They have walked a lot.

Je n'ai pas **préparé** mon examen.
I haven't prepared for my exam.

Il y a une fenêtre **ouverte** dans le salon.
There is an open window in the living room.

PERSON The form of the verb or pronoun that indicates the speaker, the one spoken to, or the one spoken about. In French, as in English, there are three persons: first, second, and third.

Person	Singular		Plural	
1st	**je**	*I*	**nous**	*we*
2nd	**tu**	*you*	**vous**	*you*
3rd	**il/elle**	*he/she/it*	**ils/elles**	*they*
	on	*one*		

PREPOSITION A word or words that describe(s) the relationship, most often in time or space, between two other words.

Annie habite **loin de** Paris.
Annie lives far from Paris.

Le blouson est **dans** la voiture.
The jacket is in the car.

Martine s'est coiffée **avant de** sortir.
Martine combed her hair before going out.

PRONOUN A word that takes the place of a noun or nouns.

Demonstrative pronoun A pronoun that takes the place of a specific noun.

Je veux **celui-ci**.
I want this one.

Marc préférait **ceux-là**.
Marc preferred those.

Glossary of Grammatical Terms

Object pronoun A pronoun that functions as a direct or indirect object of the verb.

Elle **lui** donne un cadeau.
She gives **him** a present.

Frédéric **me l'**a apporté.
Frédéric brought **it** to **me**.

Reflexive pronoun A pronoun that indicates that the action of a verb is performed by the subject on itself. These pronouns are often expressed in English with -*self*: *myself*, *yourself*, etc.

Je **me lave** avant de sortir.
I **wash (myself)** before going out.

Marie **s'est couchée** à onze heures et demie.
Marie **went to bed** at eleven-thirty.

Relative pronoun A pronoun that connects a subordinate clause to a main clause.

Le garçon **qui** nous a écrit vient nous voir demain.
The boy **who** wrote us is coming to visit tomorrow.

Je sais **que** nous avons beaucoup de choses à faire.
I know **that** we have a lot of things to do.

Subject pronoun A pronoun that replaces the name or title of a person or thing, and acts as the subject of a verb.

Tu vas partir.
You are going to leave.

Il arrive demain.
He arrives tomorrow.

SUBJECT A noun or pronoun that performs the action of a verb and is often implied by the verb.

Marine va au supermarché.
Marine goes to the supermarket.

Ils travaillent beaucoup.
They work a lot.

Ces livres sont très chers.
Those books are very expensive.

SUPERLATIVE A word or construction used with an adjective, adverb or a noun to express the highest or lowest degree of a specific quality among three or more people, places, or things.

Le cours de français est **le plus intéressant**.
The French class is **the most interesting**.

Romain court **le moins rapidement**.
Romain runs **the least fast**.

C'est son jardin qui a **le plus d'arbres**.
It is her garden that has **the most trees**.

TENSE A set of verb forms that indicates the time of an action or state: past, present, or future

Compound tense A two-word tense made up of an auxiliary verb and a present or past participle. In French, there are two auxiliary verbs: **être** and **avoir**.

Le colis n'**est** pas encore **arrivé**.
The package **has** not **arrived** yet.

Elle **a réussi** son examen.
She **has passed** her exam.

Simple tense A tense expressed by a single verb form.

Timothée **jouait** au volley-ball pendant les vacances.
Timothée **played** volleyball during his vacation.

Joëlle **parlera** à sa mère demain.
Joëlle **will speak** with her mom tomorrow.

VERB A word that expresses actions or states-of-being.

Auxiliary verb A verb used with a present or past participle to form a compound tense. **Avoir** is the most commonly used auxiliary verb in French.

Ils **ont** vu les éléphants.
They **have** seen the elephants.

J'espère que tu **as** mangé.
I hope you **have** eaten.

Reflexive verb A verb that describes an action performed by the subject on itself and is always used with a reflexive pronoun.

Je **me suis acheté** une voiture neuve.
I **bought myself** a new car.

Pierre et Adeline **se lèvent** très tôt.
Pierre and Adeline **get (themselves) up** very early.

Spelling-change verb A verb that undergoes a predictable change in spelling in the various conjugations.

acheter	e → è	nous achetons	j'achète
espérer	é → è	nous espérons	j'espère
appeler	l → ll	nous appelons	j'appelle
envoyer	y → i	nous envoyons	j'envoie
essayer	y → i	nous essayons	j'essaie/ j'essaye

Appendice B

Verb Conjugation Tables

Each verb in this list is followed by a model verb conjugated according to the same pattern. The number in parentheses indicates where in the verb tables you can find the conjugated forms of the model verb. Reminder: All reflexive (pronominal) verbs use **être** as their auxiliary verb in the **passé composé**. The infinitives of reflexive verbs begin with **se** (**s'**).

* = This verb, unlike its model, takes **être** in the **passé composé**.
† = This verb, unlike its model, takes **avoir** in the **passé composé**.

In the tables you will find the infinitive, past participles, and all the forms of each model verb you have learned.

abolir like finir (2)
aborder like parler (1)
abriter like parler (1)
accepter like parler (1)
accompagner like parler (1)
accueillir like ouvrir (31)
acheter (7)
adorer like parler (1)
afficher like parler (1)
aider like parler (1)
aimer like parler (1)
aller (13) p.c. with être
allumer like parler (1)
améliorer like parler (1)
amener like acheter (7)
animer like parler (1)
apercevoir like recevoir (36)
appeler (8)
applaudir like finir (2)
apporter like parler (1)
apprendre like prendre (35)
arrêter like parler (1)
arriver* like parler (1)
assister like parler (1)
attacher like parler (1)
attendre like vendre (3)
attirer like parler (1)
avoir (4)
balayer like essayer (10)
bavarder like parler (1)
boire (15)
bricoler like parler (1)
bronzer like parler (1)
célébrer like préférer (12)
chanter like parler (1)
chasser like parler (1)

chercher like parler (1)
choisir like finir (2)
classer like parler (1)
commander like parler (1)
commencer (9)
composer like parler (1)
comprendre like prendre (35)
compter like parler (1)
conduire (16)
connaître (17)
consacrer like parler (1)
considérer like préférer (12)
construire like conduire (16)
continuer like parler (1)
courir (18)
coûter like parler (1)
couvrir like ouvrir (31)
croire (19)
cuisiner like parler (1)
danser like parler (1)
débarrasser like parler (1)
décider like parler (1)
découvrir like ouvrir (31)
décrire like écrire (22)
décrocher like parler (1)
déjeuner like parler (1)
demander like parler (1)
démarrer like parler (1)
déménager like manger (11)
démissionner like parler (1)
dépasser like parler (1)
dépendre like vendre (3)
dépenser like parler (1)
déposer like parler (1)
descendre* like vendre (3)
désirer like parler (1)

dessiner like parler (1)
détester like parler (1)
détruire like conduire (16)
développer like parler (1)
devenir like venir (41)
devoir (20)
dîner like parler (1)
dire (21)
diriger like parler (1)
discuter like parler (1)
divorcer like commencer (9)
donner like parler (1)
dormir† like partir (32)
douter like parler (1)
durer like parler (1)
échapper like parler (1)
échouer like parler (1)
écouter like parler (1)
écrire (22)
effacer like commencer (9)
embaucher like parler (1)
emménager like manger (11)
emmener like acheter (7)
employer like essayer (10)
emprunter like parler (1)
enfermer like parler (1)
enlever like acheter (7)
enregistrer like parler (1)
enseigner like parler (1)
entendre like vendre (3)
entourer like parler (1)
entrer* like parler (1)
entretenir like tenir (40)
envahir like finir (2)
envoyer like essayer (10)
épouser like parler (1)

espérer like préférer (12)
essayer (10)
essuyer like essayer (10)
éteindre (24)
éternuer like parler (1)
étrangler like parler (1)
être (5)
étudier like parler (1)
éviter like parler (1)
exiger like manger (11)
expliquer like parler (1)
explorer like parler (1)
faire (25)
falloir (26)
fermer like parler (1)
fêter like parler (1)
finir (2)
fonctionner like parler (1)
fonder like parler (1)
freiner like parler (1)
fréquenter like parler (1)
fumer like parler (1)
gagner like parler (1)
garder like parler (1)
garer like parler (1)
gaspiller like parler (1)
enfler like parler (1)
goûter like parler (1)
graver like parler (1)
grossir like finir (2)
guérir like finir (2)
habiter like parler (1)
imprimer like parler (1)
indiquer like parler (1)
interdire like dire (21)
inviter like parler (1)

Verb Conjugation Tables

jeter like appeler (8)
jouer like parler (1)
laisser like parler (1)
laver like parler (1)
lire (27)
loger like manger (11)
louer like parler (1)
lutter like parler (1)
maigrir like finir (2)
maintenir like tenir (40)
manger (11)
marcher like parler (1)
mêler like préférer (12)
mener like parler (1)
mettre (28)
monter* like parler (1)
montrer like parler (1)
mourir (29); **p.c.** with **être**
nager like manger (11)
naître (30); **p.c.** with **être**
nettoyer like essayer (10)
noter like parler (1)
obtenir like tenir (40)
offrir like ouvrir (31)
organiser like parler (1)
oublier like parler (1)
ouvrir (31)
parler (1)
partager like manger (11)
partir (32); **p.c.** with **être**
passer like parler (1)
patienter like parler (1)
patiner like parler (1)
payer like essayer (10)
penser like parler (1)
perdre like vendre (3)
permettre like mettre (28)
pleuvoir (33)
plonger like manger (11)
polluer like parler (1)
porter like parler (1)
poser like parler (1)
posséder like préférer (12)
poster like parler (1)
pouvoir (34)
pratiquer like parler (1)
préférer (12)

prélever like parler (1)
prendre (35)
préparer like parler (1)
présenter like parler (1)
préserver like parler (1)
prêter like parler (1)
prévenir like tenir (40)
produire like conduire (16)
profiter like parler (1)
promettre like mettre (28)
proposer like parler (1)
protéger like préférer (12)
provenir like venir (41)
publier like parler (1)
quitter like parler (1)
raccrocher like parler (1)
ranger like manger (11)
réaliser like parler (1)
recevoir (36)
recommander like parler (1)
reconnaître like connaître (17)
recycler like parler (1)
réduire like conduire (16)
réfléchir like finir (2)
regarder like parler (1)
régner like préférer (12)
remplacer like parler (1)
remplir like finir (2)
rencontrer like parler (1)
rendre like vendre (3)
rentrer* like parler (1)
renvoyer like essayer (10)
réparer like parler (1)
repasser like parler (1)
répéter like préférer (12)
repeupler like parler (1)
répondre like vendre (3)
réserver like parler (1)
rester* like parler (1)
retenir like tenir (40)
retirer like parler (1)
retourner* like parler (1)
retrouver like parler (1)
réussir like finir (2)
revenir like venir (41)

revoir like voir (42)
rire (37)
rouler like parler (1)
salir like finir (2)
s'amuser like se laver (6)
s'asseoir (14)
sauvegarder like parler (1)
sauver like parler (1)
savoir (38)
se brosser like se laver (6)
se coiffer like se laver (6)
se composer like se laver (6)
se connecter like se laver (6)
se coucher like se laver (6)
se croiser like se laver (6)
se dépêcher like se laver (6)
se déplacer* like commencer (9)
se déshabiller like se laver (6)
se détendre* like vendre (3)
se disputer like se laver (6)
s'embrasser like se laver (6)
s'endormir like partir (32)
s'énerver like se laver (6)
s'ennuyer* like essayer (10)
s'excuser like se laver (6)
se fouler like se laver (6)
s'installer like se laver (6)
se laver (6)
se lever* like acheter (7)
se maquiller like se laver (6)
se marier like se laver (6)
se promener* like acheter (7)
se rappeler* like appeler (8)
se raser like se laver (6)
se rebeller like se laver (6)
se réconcilier like se laver (6)
se relever* like acheter (7)
se reposer like se laver (6)
se réveiller like se laver (6)

servir† like partir (32)
se sécher* like préférer (12)
se souvenir like venir (41)
se tromper like se laver (6)
s'habiller like se laver (6)
sentir† like partir (32)
signer like parler (1)
s'inquiéter* like préférer (12)
s'intéresser like se laver (6)
skier like parler (1)
s'occuper like se laver (6)
sonner like parler (1)
s'orienter like se laver (6)
sortir like partir (32)
sourire like rire (37)
souffrir like ouvrir (31)
souhaiter like parler (1)
subvenir† like venir (41)
suffire like lire (27)
suggérer like préférer (12)
suivre (39)
surfer like parler (1)
surprendre like prendre (35)
télécharger like parler (1)
téléphoner like parler (1)
tenir (40)
tomber* like parler (1)
tourner like parler (1)
tousser like parler (1)
traduire like conduire (16)
travailler like parler (1)
traverser like parler (1)
trouver like parler (1)
tuer like parler (1)
utiliser like parler (1)
valoir like falloir (26)
vendre (3)
venir (41); **p.c.** with **être**
vérifier like parler (1)
visiter like parler (1)
vivre like suivre (39)
voir (42)
vouloir (43)
voyager like manger (11)

Verb Conjugation Tables

Regular verbs

Infinitive / Past participle	Subject Pronouns	INDICATIVE Present	INDICATIVE Passé composé	INDICATIVE Imperfect	INDICATIVE Future	CONDITIONAL Present	SUBJUNCTIVE Present	IMPERATIVE
1 parler *(to speak)* parlé	je (j')	parle	ai parlé	parlais	parlerai	parlerais	parle	
	tu	parles	as parlé	parlais	parleras	parlerais	parles	parle
	il/elle/on	parle	a parlé	parlait	parlera	parlerait	parle	
	nous	parlons	avons parlé	parlions	parlerons	parlerions	parlions	parlons
	vous	parlez	avez parlé	parliez	parlerez	parleriez	parliez	parlez
	ils/elles	parlent	ont parlé	parlaient	parleront	parleraient	parlent	
2 finir *(to finish)* fini	je (j')	finis	ai fini	finissais	finirai	finirais	finisse	
	tu	finis	as fini	finissais	finiras	finirais	finisses	finis
	il/elle/on	finit	a fini	finissait	finira	finirait	finisse	
	nous	finissons	avons fini	finissions	finirons	finirions	finissions	finissons
	vous	finissez	avez fini	finissiez	finirez	finiriez	finissiez	finissez
	ils/elles	finissent	ont fini	finissaient	finiront	finiraient	finissent	
3 vendre *(to sell)* vendu	je (j')	vends	ai vendu	vendais	vendrai	vendrais	vende	
	tu	vends	as vendu	vendais	vendras	vendrais	vendes	vends
	il/elle/on	vend	a vendu	vendait	vendra	vendrait	vende	
	nous	vendons	avons vendu	vendions	vendrons	vendrions	vendions	vendons
	vous	vendez	avez vendu	vendiez	vendrez	vendriez	vendiez	vendez
	ils/elles	vendent	ont vendu	vendaient	vendront	vendraient	vendent	

Verb Conjugation Tables

Auxiliary verbs: *avoir* and *être*

4

| Infinitive | Subject Pronouns | INDICATIVE | | | | CONDITIONAL | SUBJUNCTIVE | IMPERATIVE |
Past participle		Present	Passé composé	Imperfect	Future	Present	Present	
avoir	j'	ai	ai eu	avais	aurai	aurais	aie	
(*to have*)	tu	as	as eu	avais	auras	aurais	aies	aie
	il/elle/on	a	a eu	avait	aura	aurait	ait	
eu	nous	avons	avons eu	avions	aurons	aurions	ayons	ayons
	vous	avez	avez eu	aviez	aurez	auriez	ayez	ayez
	ils/elles	ont	ont eu	avaient	auront	auraient	aient	

5

| Infinitive | Subject Pronouns | INDICATIVE | | | | CONDITIONAL | SUBJUNCTIVE | IMPERATIVE |
Past participle		Present	Passé composé	Imperfect	Future	Present	Present	
être	je (j')	suis	ai été	étais	serai	serais	sois	
(*to be*)	tu	es	as été	étais	seras	serais	sois	sois
	il/elle/on	est	a été	était	sera	serait	soit	
été	nous	sommes	avons été	étions	serons	serions	soyons	soyons
	vous	êtes	avez été	étiez	serez	seriez	soyez	soyez
	ils/elles	sont	ont été	étaient	seront	seraient	soient	

Reflexive (Pronominal)

6

| Infinitive | Subject Pronouns | INDICATIVE | | | | CONDITIONAL | SUBJUNCTIVE | IMPERATIVE |
Past participle		Present	Passé composé	Imperfect	Future	Present	Present	
se laver	je	me lave	me suis lavé(e)	me lavais	me laverai	me laverais	me lave	
(*to wash oneself*)	tu	te laves	t'es lavé(e)	te lavais	te laveras	te laverais	te laves	lave-toi
	il/elle/on	se lave	s'est lavé(e)	se lavait	se lavera	se laverait	se lave	
lavé	nous	nous lavons	nous sommes lavé(e)s	nous lavions	nous laverons	nous laverions	nous lavions	lavons-nous
	vous	vous lavez	vous êtes lavé(e)s	vous laviez	vous laverez	vous laveriez	vous laviez	lavez-vous
	ils/elles	se lavent	se sont lavé(e)s	se lavaient	se laveront	se laveraient	se lavent	

Verb Conjugation Tables

Verbs with spelling changes

	Infinitive / Past participle	Subject Pronouns	INDICATIVE Present	INDICATIVE Passé composé	INDICATIVE Imperfect	INDICATIVE Future	CONDITIONAL Present	SUBJUNCTIVE Present	IMPERATIVE
7	acheter (to buy) / acheté	j'	achète	ai acheté	achetais	achèterai	achèterais	achète	
		tu	achètes	as acheté	achetais	achèteras	achèterais	achètes	achète
		il/elle/on	achète	a acheté	achetait	achètera	achèterait	achète	
		nous	achetons	avons acheté	achetions	achèterons	achèterions	achetions	achetons
		vous	achetez	avez acheté	achetiez	achèterez	achèteriez	achetiez	achetez
		ils/elles	achètent	ont acheté	achetaient	achèteront	achèteraient	achètent	
8	appeler (to call) / appelé	j'	appelle	ai appelé	appelais	appellerai	appellerais	appelle	
		tu	appelles	as appelé	appelais	appelleras	appellerais	appelles	appelle
		il/elle/on	appelle	a appelé	appelait	appellera	appellerait	appelle	
		nous	appelons	avons appelé	appelions	appellerons	appellerions	appelions	appelons
		vous	appelez	avez appelé	appeliez	appellerez	appelleriez	appeliez	appelez
		ils/elles	appellent	ont appelé	appelaient	appelleront	appelleraient	appellent	
9	commencer (to begin) / commencé	je (j')	commence	ai commencé	commençais	commencerai	commencerais	commence	
		tu	commences	as commencé	commençais	commenceras	commencerais	commences	commence
		il/elle/on	commence	a commencé	commençait	commencera	commencerait	commence	
		nous	commençons	avons commencé	commencions	commencerons	commencerions	commencions	commençons
		vous	commencez	avez commencé	commenciez	commencerez	commenceriez	commenciez	commencez
		ils/elles	commencent	ont commencé	commençaient	commenceront	commenceraient	commencent	
10	essayer (to try) / essayé	j'	essaie	ai essayé	essayais	essaierai	essaierais	essaie	
		tu	essaies	as essayé	essayais	essaieras	essaierais	essaies	essaie
		il/elle/on	essaie	a essayé	essayait	essaiera	essaierait	essaie	
		nous	essayons	avons essayé	essayions	essaierons	essaierions	essayions	essayons
		vous	essayez	avez essayé	essayiez	essaierez	essaieriez	essayiez	essayez
		ils/elles	essayent	ont essayé	essayaient	essaieront	essaieraient	essaient	
11	manger (to eat) / mangé	je (j')	mange	ai mangé	mangeais	mangerai	mangerais	mange	
		tu	manges	as mangé	mangeais	mangeras	mangerais	manges	mange
		il/elle/on	mange	a mangé	mangeait	mangera	mangerait	mange	
		nous	mangeons	avons mangé	mangions	mangerons	mangerions	mangions	mangeons
		vous	mangez	avez mangé	mangiez	mangerez	mangeriez	mangiez	mangez
		ils/elles	mangent	ont mangé	mangeaient	mangeront	mangeraient	mangent	

Verb Conjugation Tables

		INDICATIVE				CONDITIONAL	SUBJUNCTIVE	IMPERATIVE
Infinitive	Subject Pronouns	Present	Passé composé	Imperfect	Future	Present	Present	
Past participle								
12 préférer *(to prefer)*	je (j')	préfère	ai préféré	préférais	préférerai	préférerais	préfère	
	tu	préfères	as préféré	préférais	préféreras	préférerais	préfères	préfère
	il/elle/on	préfère	a préféré	préférait	préférera	préférerait	préfère	
préféré	nous	préférons	avons préféré	préférions	préférerons	préférerions	préférions	préférons
	vous	préférez	avez préféré	préfériez	préférerez	préféreriez	préfériez	préférez
	ils/elles	préfèrent	ont préféré	préféraient	préféreront	préféreraient	préfèrent	

Irregular verbs

		INDICATIVE				CONDITIONAL	SUBJUNCTIVE	IMPERATIVE
Infinitive	Subject Pronouns	Present	Passé composé	Imperfect	Future	Present	Present	
Past participle								
13 aller *(to go)*	je (j')	vais	suis allé(e)	allais	irai	irais	aille	
	tu	vas	es allé(e)	allais	iras	irais	ailles	va
	il/elle/on	va	est allé(e)	allait	ira	irait	aille	
allé	nous	allons	sommes allé(e)s	allions	irons	irions	allions	allons
	vous	allez	êtes allé(e)s	alliez	irez	iriez	alliez	allez
	ils/elles	vont	sont allé(e)s	allaient	iront	iraient	aillent	
14 s'asseoir *(to sit down, to be seated)*	je	m'assieds	me suis assis(e)	m'asseyais	m'assiérai	m'assiérais	m'asseye	
	tu	t'assieds	t'es assis(e)	t'asseyais	t'assiéras	t'assiérais	t'asseyes	assieds-toi
	il/elle/on	s'assied	s'est assis(e)	s'asseyait	s'assiéra	s'assiérait	s'asseye	
assis	nous	nous asseyons	nous sommes assis(e)s	nous asseyions	nous assiérons	nous assiérions	nous asseyions	asseyons-nous
	vous	vous asseyez	vous êtes assis(e)s	vous asseyiez	vous assiérez	vous assiériez	vous asseyiez	asseyez-vous
	ils/elles	s'asseyent	se sont assis(e)s	s'asseyaient	s'assiéront	s'assiéraient	s'asseyent	
15 boire *(to drink)*	je (j')	bois	ai bu	buvais	boirai	boirais	boive	
	tu	bois	as bu	buvais	boiras	boirais	boives	bois
	il/elle/on	boit	a bu	buvait	boira	boirait	boive	
bu	nous	buvons	avons bu	buvions	boirons	boirions	buvions	buvons
	vous	buvez	avez bu	buviez	boirez	boiriez	buviez	buvez
	ils/elles	boivent	ont bu	buvaient	boiront	boiraient	boivent	

Verb Conjugation Tables

| Infinitive | Subject Pronouns | INDICATIVE | | | | | CONDITIONAL | SUBJUNCTIVE | IMPERATIVE |
Past participle		Present	Passé composé	Imperfect	Future		Present	Present	
16 conduire	je (j')	conduis	ai conduit	conduisais	conduirai		conduirais	conduise	
(to drive; to lead)	tu	conduis	as conduit	conduisais	conduiras		conduirais	conduises	conduis
	il/elle/on	conduit	a conduit	conduisait	conduira		conduirait	conduise	
conduit	nous	conduisons	avons conduit	conduisions	conduirons		conduirions	conduisions	conduisons
	vous	conduisez	avez conduit	conduisiez	conduirez		conduiriez	conduisiez	conduisez
	ils/elles	conduisent	ont conduit	conduisaient	conduiront		conduiraient	conduisent	
17 connaître	je (j')	connais	ai connu	connaissais	connaîtrai		connaîtrais	connaisse	
(to know, to be acquainted with)	tu	connais	as connu	connaissais	connaîtras		connaîtrais	connaisses	connais
	il/elle/on	connaît	a connu	connaissait	connaîtra		connaîtrait	connaisse	
connu	nous	connaissons	avons connu	connaissions	connaîtrons		connaîtrions	connaissions	connaissons
	vous	connaissez	avez connu	connaissiez	connaîtrez		connaîtriez	connaissiez	connaissez
	ils/elles	connaissent	ont connu	connaissaient	connaîtront		connaîtraient	connaissent	
18 courir	je (j')	cours	ai couru	courais	courrai		courrais	coure	
(to run)	tu	cours	as couru	courais	courras		courrais	coures	cours
	il/elle/on	court	a couru	courait	courra		courrait	coure	
couru	nous	courons	avons couru	courions	courrons		courrions	courions	courons
	vous	courez	avez couru	couriez	courrez		courriez	couriez	courez
	ils/elles	courent	ont couru	couraient	courront		courraient	courent	
19 croire	je (j')	crois	ai cru	croyais	croirai		croirais	croie	
(to believe)	tu	crois	as cru	croyais	croiras		croirais	croies	crois
	il/elle/on	croit	a cru	croyait	croira		croirait	croie	
cru	nous	croyons	avons cru	croyions	croirons		croirions	croyions	croyons
	vous	croyez	avez cru	croyiez	croirez		croiriez	croyiez	croyez
	ils/elles	croient	ont cru	croyaient	croiront		croiraient	croient	
20 devoir	je (j')	dois	ai dû	devais	devrai		devrais	doive	
(to have to; to owe)	tu	dois	as dû	devais	devras		devrais	doives	dois
	il/elle/on	doit	a dû	devait	devra		devrait	doive	
dû	nous	devons	avons dû	devions	devrons		devrions	devions	devons
	vous	devez	avez dû	deviez	devrez		devriez	deviez	devez
	ils/elles	doivent	ont dû	devaient	devront		devraient	doivent	

Verb Conjugation Tables

	Infinitive / Past participle	Subject Pronouns	INDICATIVE Present	INDICATIVE Passé composé	INDICATIVE Imperfect	INDICATIVE Future	CONDITIONAL Present	SUBJUNCTIVE Present	IMPERATIVE
21	dire (to say, to tell) dit	je (j')	dis	ai dit	disais	dirai	dirais	dise	
		tu	dis	as dit	disais	diras	dirais	dises	dis
		il/elle/on	dit	a dit	disait	dira	dirait	dise	
		nous	disons	avons dit	disions	dirons	dirions	disions	disons
		vous	dites	avez dit	disiez	direz	diriez	disiez	dites
		ils/elles	disent	ont dit	disaient	diront	diraient	disent	
22	écrire (to write) écrit	j'	écris	ai écrit	écrivais	écrirai	écrirais	écrive	
		tu	écris	as écrit	écrivais	écriras	écrirais	écrives	écris
		il/elle/on	écrit	a écrit	écrivait	écrira	écrirait	écrive	
		nous	écrivons	avons écrit	écrivions	écrirons	écririons	écrivions	écrivons
		vous	écrivez	avez écrit	écriviez	écrirez	écririez	écriviez	écrivez
		ils/elles	écrivent	ont écrit	écrivaient	écriront	écriraient	écrivent	
23	envoyer (to send) envoyé	j'	envoie	ai envoyé	envoyais	enverrai	enverrais	envoie	
		tu	envoies	as envoyé	envoyais	enverras	enverrais	envoies	envoie
		il/elle/on	envoie	a envoyé	envoyait	enverra	enverrait	envoie	
		nous	envoyons	avons envoyé	envoyions	enverrons	enverrions	envoyions	envoyons
		vous	envoyez	avez envoyé	envoyiez	enverrez	enverriez	envoyiez	envoyez
		ils/elles	envoient	ont envoyé	envoyaient	enverront	enverraient	envoient	
24	éteindre (to turn off) éteint	j'	éteins	ai éteint	éteignais	éteindrai	éteindrais	éteigne	
		tu	éteins	as éteint	éteignais	éteindras	éteindrais	éteignes	éteins
		il/elle/on	éteint	a éteint	éteignait	éteindra	éteindrait	éteigne	
		nous	éteignons	avons éteint	éteignions	éteindrons	éteindrions	éteignions	éteignons
		vous	éteignez	avez éteint	éteigniez	éteindrez	éteindriez	éteigniez	éteignez
		ils/elles	éteignent	ont éteint	éteignaient	éteindront	éteindraient	éteignent	
25	faire (to do; to make) fait	je (j')	fais	ai fait	faisais	ferai	ferais	fasse	
		tu	fais	as fait	faisais	feras	ferais	fasses	fais
		il/elle/on	fait	a fait	faisait	fera	ferait	fasse	
		nous	faisons	avons fait	faisions	ferons	ferions	fassions	faisons
		vous	faites	avez fait	faisiez	ferez	feriez	fassiez	faites
		ils/elles	font	ont fait	faisaient	feront	feraient	fassent	
26	falloir (to be necessary) fallu	il	faut	a fallu	fallait	faudra	faudrait	faille	

Verb Conjugation Tables

			INDICATIVE				CONDITIONAL	SUBJUNCTIVE	IMPERATIVE
Infinitive / Past participle	Subject Pronouns	Present	Passé composé	Imperfect	Future	Present	Present	
27 lire *(to read)* lu	je (j')	lis	ai lu	lisais	lirai	lirais	lise	
	tu	lis	as lu	lisais	liras	lirais	lises	lis
	il/elle/on	lit	a lu	lisait	lira	lirait	lise	
	nous	lisons	avons lu	lisions	lirons	lirions	lisions	lisons
	vous	lisez	avez lu	lisiez	lirez	liriez	lisiez	lisez
	ils/elles	lisent	ont lu	lisaient	liront	liraient	lisent	
28 mettre *(to put)* mis	je (j')	mets	ai mis	mettais	mettrai	mettrais	mette	
	tu	mets	as mis	mettais	mettras	mettrais	mettes	mets
	il/elle/on	met	a mis	mettait	mettra	mettrait	mette	
	nous	mettons	avons mis	mettions	mettrons	mettrions	mettions	mettons
	vous	mettez	avez mis	mettiez	mettrez	mettriez	mettiez	mettez
	ils/elles	mettent	ont mis	mettaient	mettront	mettraient	mettent	
29 mourir *(to die)* mort	je	meurs	suis mort(e)	mourais	mourrai	mourrais	meure	
	tu	meurs	es mort(e)	mourais	mourras	mourrais	meures	meurs
	il/elle/on	meurt	est mort(e)	mourait	mourra	mourrait	meure	
	nous	mourons	sommes mort(e)s	mourions	mourrons	mourrions	mourions	mourons
	vous	mourez	êtes mort(e)s	mouriez	mourrez	mourriez	mouriez	mourez
	ils/elles	meurent	sont mort(e)s	mouraient	mourront	mourraient	meurent	
30 naître *(to be born)* né	je	nais	suis né(e)	naissais	naîtrai	naîtrais	naisse	
	tu	nais	es né(e)	naissais	naîtras	naîtrais	naisses	nais
	il/elle/on	naît	est né(e)	naissait	naîtra	naîtrait	naisse	
	nous	naissons	sommes né(e)s	naissions	naîtrons	naîtrions	naissions	naissons
	vous	naissez	êtes né(e)s	naissiez	naîtrez	naîtriez	naissiez	naissez
	ils/elles	naissent	sont né(e)s	naissaient	naîtront	naîtraient	naissent	
31 ouvrir *(to open)* ouvert	j'	ouvre	ai ouvert	ouvrais	ouvrirai	ouvrirais	ouvre	
	tu	ouvres	as ouvert	ouvrais	ouvriras	ouvrirais	ouvres	ouvre
	il/elle/on	ouvre	a ouvert	ouvrait	ouvrira	ouvrirait	ouvre	
	nous	ouvrons	avons ouvert	ouvrions	ouvrirons	ouvririons	ouvrions	ouvrons
	vous	ouvrez	avez ouvert	ouvriez	ouvrirez	ouvririez	ouvriez	ouvrez
	ils/elles	ouvrent	ont ouvert	ouvraient	ouvriront	ouvriraient	ouvrent	

Verb Conjugation Tables

| | Infinitive | Subject Pronouns | INDICATIVE | | | | CONDITIONAL | SUBJUNCTIVE | IMPERATIVE |
	Past participle		Present	Passé composé	Imperfect	Future	Present	Present	
32	partir *(to leave)* parti	je tu il/elle/on nous vous ils/elles	pars pars part partons partez partent	suis parti(e) es parti(e) est parti(e) sommes parti(e)s êtes parti(e)(s) sont parti(e)s	partais partais partait partions partiez partaient	partirai partiras partira partirons partirez partiront	partirais partirais partirait partirions partiriez partiraient	parte partes parte partions partiez partent	pars partons partez
33	pleuvoir *(to rain)* plu	il	pleut	a plu	pleuvait	pleuvra	pleuvrait	pleuve	
34	pouvoir *(to be able)* pu	je (j') tu il/elle/on nous vous ils/elles	peux peux peut pouvons pouvez peuvent	ai pu as pu a pu avons pu avez pu ont pu	pouvais pouvais pouvait pouvions pouviez pouvaient	pourrai pourras pourra pourrons pourrez pourront	pourrais pourrais pourrait pourrions pourriez pourraient	puisse puisses puisse puissions puissiez puissent	
35	prendre *(to take)* pris	je (j') tu il/elle/on nous vous ils/elles	prends prends prend prenons prenez prennent	ai pris as pris a pris avons pris avez pris ont pris	prenais prenais prenait prenions preniez prenaient	prendrai prendras prendra prendrons prendrez prendront	prendrais prendrais prendrait prendrions prendriez prendraient	prenne prennes prenne prenions preniez prennent	prends prenons prenez
36	recevoir *(to receive)* reçu	je (j') tu il/elle/on nous vous ils/elles	reçois reçois reçoit recevons recevez reçoivent	ai reçu as reçu a reçu avons reçu avez reçu ont reçu	recevais recevais recevait recevions receviez recevaient	recevrai recevras recevra recevrons recevrez recevront	recevrais recevrais recevrait recevrions recevriez recevraient	reçoive reçoives reçoive recevions receviez reçoivent	reçois recevons recevez
37	rire *(to laugh)* ri	je (j') tu il/elle/on nous vous ils/elles	ris ris rit rions riez rient	ai ri as ri a ri avons ri avez ri ont ri	riais riais riait riions riiez riaient	rirai riras rira rirons rirez riront	rirais rirais rirait ririons ririez riraient	rie ries rie riions riiez rient	ris rions riez

Verb Conjugation Tables

	Infinitive / Past participle	Subject Pronouns	INDICATIVE Present	INDICATIVE Passé composé	INDICATIVE Imperfect	INDICATIVE Future	CONDITIONAL Present	SUBJUNCTIVE Present	IMPERATIVE
38	savoir (to know) / su	je (j') tu il/elle/on nous vous ils/elles	sais sais sait savons savez savent	ai su as su a su avons su avez su ont su	savais savais savait savions saviez savaient	saurai sauras saura saurons saurez sauront	saurais saurais saurait saurions sauriez sauraient	sache saches sache sachions sachiez sachent	sache sachons sachez
39	suivre (to follow) / suivi	je (j') tu il/elle/on nous vous ils/elles	suis suis suit suivons suivez suivent	ai suivi as suivi a suivi avons suivi avez suivi ont suivi	suivais suivais suivait suivions suiviez suivaient	suivrai suivras suivra suivrons suivrez suivront	suivrais suivrais suivrait suivrions suivriez suivraient	suive suives suive suivions suiviez suivent	suis suivons suivez
40	tenir (to hold) / tenu	je (j') tu il/elle/on nous vous ils/elles	tiens tiens tient tenons tenez tiennent	ai tenu as tenu a tenu avons tenu avez tenu ont tenu	tenais tenais tenait tenions teniez tenaient	tiendrai tiendras tiendra tiendrons tiendrez tiendront	tiendrais tiendrais tiendrait tiendrions tiendriez tiendraient	tienne tiennes tienne tenions teniez tiennent	tiens tenons tenez
41	venir (to come) / venu	je tu il/elle/on nous vous ils/elles	viens viens vient venons venez viennent	suis venu(e) es venu(e) est venu(e) sommes venu(e)s êtes venu(e)(s) sont venu(e)s	venais venais venait venions veniez venaient	viendrai viendras viendra viendrons viendrez viendront	viendrais viendrais viendrait viendrions viendriez viendraient	vienne viennes vienne venions veniez viennent	viens venons venez
42	voir (to see) / vu	je (j') tu il/elle/on nous vous ils/elles	vois vois voit voyons voyez voient	ai vu as vu a vu avons vu avez vu ont vu	voyais voyais voyait voyions voyiez voyaient	verrai verras verra verrons verrez verront	verrais verrais verrait verrions verriez verraient	voie voies voie voyions voyiez voient	vois voyons voyez
43	vouloir (to want, to wish) / voulu	je (j') tu il/elle/on nous vous ils/elles	veux veux veut voulons voulez veulent	ai voulu as voulu a voulu avons voulu avez voulu ont voulu	voulais voulais voulait voulions vouliez voulaient	voudrai voudras voudra voudrons voudrez voudront	voudrais voudrais voudrait voudrions voudriez voudraient	veuille veuilles veuille voulions vouliez veuillent	veuille veuillons veuillez

Vocabulaire

Guide to Vocabulary

This glossary contains the words and expressions listed on the **Vocabulaire** page found at the end of each unit in **D'ACCORD!** Levels 1 & 2. The number following an entry indicates the **D'ACCORD!** level and unit where the term was introduced. For example, the first entry in the glossary, **à**, was introduced in **D'ACCORD!** Level 1, Unit 4. Note that II–P refers to the **Unité Préliminaire** in **D'ACCORD!** Level 2.

Abbreviations used in this glossary

adj.	adjective	*f.*	feminine	*i.o.*	indirect object	*prep.*	preposition
adv.	adverb	*fam.*	familiar	*m.*	masculine	*pron.*	pronoun
art.	article	*form.*	formal	*n.*	noun	*refl.*	reflexive
comp.	comparative	*imp.*	imperative	*obj.*	object	*rel.*	relative
conj.	conjunction	*indef.*	indefinite	*part.*	partitive	*sing.*	singular
def.	definite	*interj.*	interjection	*p.p.*	past participle	*sub.*	subject
dem.	demonstrative	*interr.*	interrogative	*pl.*	plural	*super.*	superlative
disj.	disjunctive	*inv.*	invariable	*poss.*	possessive	*v.*	verb
d.o.	direct object						

French-English

A

à *prep.* at; in; to I-4
  À bientôt. See you soon. I-1
  à condition que on the condition that, provided that II-7
  à côté de *prep.* next to I-3
  À demain. See you tomorrow. I-1
  à droite (de) *prep.* to the right (of) I-3
  à gauche (de) *prep.* to the left (of) I-3
  à … heure(s) at … (o'clock) I-4
  à la radio on the radio II-7
  à la télé(vision) on television II-7
  à l'étranger abroad, overseas I-7
  à mi-temps half-time (*job*) II-5
  à moins que unless II-7
  à plein temps full-time (*job*) II-5
  À plus tard. See you later. I-1
  À quelle heure? What time?; When? I-2
  À qui? To whom? I-4
  À table! Let's eat! Food is on! II-1
  à temps partiel part-time (*job*) II-5
  À tout à l'heure. See you later. I-1
  au bout (de) *prep.* at the end (of) II-4
  au contraire on the contrary II-7
  au fait by the way I-3
  au printemps in the spring I-5
  Au revoir. Good-bye. I-1
  au secours help II-3
  au sujet de on the subject of, about II-6
abolir *v.* to abolish II-6
absolument *adv.* absolutely I-8, II-P
accident *m.* accident II-3
  avoir un accident to have/to be in an accident II-3
accompagner *v.* to accompany II-4
acheter *v.* to buy I-5
acteur *m.* actor I-1
actif/active *adj.* active I-3
activement *adv.* actively I-8, II-P
actrice *f.* actress I-1
addition *f.* check, bill I-4
adieu farewell II-6
adolescence *f.* adolescence I-6
adorer *v.* to love I-2
  J'adore… I love… I-2
adresse *f.* address II-4
aérobic *m.* aerobics I-5
  faire de l'aérobic *v.* to do aerobics I-5
aéroport *m.* airport I-7
affaires *f., pl.* business I-3
affiche *f.* poster I-8, II-P
afficher *v.* to post II-5
âge *m.* age I-6
  âge adulte *m.* adulthood I-6
agence de voyages *f.* travel agency I-7
agent *m.* officer; agent II-3
agent de police *m.* police officer II-3
agent de voyages *m.* travel agent I-7
agent immobilier *m.* real estate agent II-5
agréable *adj.* pleasant I-1
agriculteur/agricultrice *m., f.* farmer II-5
aider (à) *v.* to help (*to do something*) I-5
aie (avoir) *imp. v.* have I-7
ail *m.* garlic II-1
aimer *v.* to like I-2
  aimer mieux to prefer I-2
  aimer que… to like that… II-6
  J'aime bien… I really like… I-2
  Je n'aime pas tellement… I don't like … very much. I-2
aîné(e) *adj.* elder I-3
algérien(ne) *adj.* Algerian I-1
aliment *m.* food item; a food II-1
Allemagne *f.* Germany I-7
allemand(e) *adj.* German I-1
aller *v.* to go I-4
  aller à la pêche to go fishing I-5
  aller aux urgences to go to the emergency room II-2
  aller avec to go with I-6
  aller-retour *adj.* round-trip I-7
  billet aller-retour *m.* round-trip ticket I-7
Allons-y! Let's go! I-2
Ça va? What's up?; How are things? I-1
Comment allez-vous? *form.* How are you? I-1
Comment vas-tu? *fam.* How are you? I-1

cent quatre-vingt-treize 193

Vocabulaire

French-English

Je m'en vais. I'm leaving. I-8, II-P
Je vais bien/mal. I am doing well/badly. I-1
J'y vais. I'm going/coming. I-8, II-P
Nous y allons. We're going/coming. II-1
allergie *f.* allergy II-2
Allez. Come on. I-5
allô *(on the phone)* hello I-1
allumer *v.* to turn on II-3
alors *adv.* so, then; at that moment I-2
améliorer *v.* to improve II-5
amende *f.* fine II-3
amener *v.* to bring *(someone)* I-5
américain(e) *adj.* American I-1
    football américain *m.* football I-5
ami(e) *m., f.* friend I-1
    petit(e) ami(e) *m., f.* boyfriend/girlfriend I-1
amitié *f.* friendship I-6
amour *m.* love I-6
amoureux/amoureuse *adj.* in love I-6
    tomber amoureux/amoureuse *v.* to fall in love I-6
amusant(e) *adj.* fun I-1
an *m.* year I-2
ancien(ne) *adj.* ancient, old; former II-7
ange *m.* angel I-1
anglais(e) *adj.* English I-1
angle *m.* corner II-4
Angleterre *f.* England I-7
animal *m.* animal II-6
année *f.* year I-2
    cette année this year I-2
anniversaire *m.* birthday I-5
    C'est quand l'anniversaire de ... ? When is ...'s birthday? I-5
    C'est quand ton/votre anniversaire? When is your birthday? I-5
annuler (une réservation) *v.* to cancel (a reservation) I-7
anorak *m.* ski jacket, parka I-6
antipathique *adj.* unpleasant I-3
août *m.* August I-5
apercevoir *v.* to see, to catch sight of II-4
aperçu (apercevoir) *p.p.* seen, caught sight of II-4
appareil *m.* (on the phone) telephone II-5
    appareil (électrique/ménager) *m.* (electrical/household) appliance I-8, II-P

appareil photo (numérique) *m.* (digital) camera II-3
    C'est M./Mme/Mlle ... à l'appareil. It's Mr./Mrs./Miss ... on the phone. II-5
    Qui est à l'appareil? Who's calling, please? II-5
appartement *m.* apartment II-7
appeler *v.* to call I-7
applaudir *v.* to applaud II-7
applaudissement *m.* applause II-7
apporter *v.* to bring, to carry *(something)* I-4
apprendre (à) *v.* to teach; to learn *(to do something)* I-4
appris (apprendre) *p.p., adj.* learned I-6
après (que) *adv.* after I-2
après-demain *adv.* day after tomorrow I-2
après-midi *m.* afternoon I-2
    cet après-midi this afternoon I-2
    de l'après-midi in the afternoon I-2
    demain après-midi *adv.* tomorrow afternoon I-2
    hier après-midi *adv.* yesterday afternoon I-7
arbre *m.* tree II-6
architecte *m., f.* architect I-3
architecture *f.* architecture I-2
argent *m.* money II-4
    dépenser de l'argent *v.* to spend money I-4
    déposer de l'argent *v.* to deposit money II-4
    retirer de l'argent *v.* to withdraw money II-4
armoire *f.* armoire, wardrobe I-8, II-P
arrêt d'autobus (de bus) *m.* bus stop I-7
arrêter (de faire quelque chose) *v.* to stop (doing something) II-3
arrivée *f.* arrival I-7
arriver (à) *v.* to arrive; to manage *(to do something)* I-2
art *m.* art I-2
    beaux-arts *m., pl.* fine arts II-7
artiste *m., f.* artist I-3
ascenseur *m.* elevator I-7
aspirateur *m.* vacuum cleaner I-8, II-P
    passer l'aspirateur to vacuum I-8, II-P
aspirine *f.* aspirin II-2
Asseyez-vous! (s'asseoir) *imp. v.* Have a seat! II-2
assez *adv.* (before adjective or adverb) pretty; quite I-8, II-P

assez (de) (before noun) enough (of) I-4
    pas assez (de) not enough (of) I-4
assiette *f.* plate II-1
assis (s'asseoir) *p.p., adj.* (used as past participle) sat down; (used as adjective) sitting, seated II-2
assister *v.* to attend I-2
assurance (maladie/vie) *f.* (health/life) insurance II-5
athlète *m., f.* athlete I-3
attacher *v.* to attach II-3
    attacher sa ceinture de sécurité to buckle one's seatbelt II-3
attendre *v.* to wait I-6
attention *f.* attention I-5
    faire attention (à) *v.* to pay attention (to) I-5
au (à + le) *prep.* to/at the I-4
auberge de jeunesse *f.* youth hostel I-7
aucun(e) *adj.* no; *pron.* none II-2
    ne... aucun(e) none, not any II-4
augmentation (de salaire) *f.* raise (in salary) II-5
aujourd'hui *adv.* today I-2
auquel (à + lequel) *pron., m., sing.* which one II-5
aussi *adv.* too, as well; as I-1
    Moi aussi. Me too. I-1
    aussi ... que (used with an adjective) as ... as II-1
autant de ... que *adv.* (used with noun to express quantity) as much/as many ... as II-6
auteur/femme auteur *m., f.* author II-7
autobus *m.* bus I-7
    arrêt d'autobus (de bus) *m.* bus stop I-7
    prendre un autobus to take a bus I-7
automne *m.* fall I-5
    à l'automne in the fall I-5
autoroute *f.* highway II-3
autour (de) *prep.* around II-4
autrefois *adv.* in the past I-8, II-P
aux (à + les) to/at the I-4
auxquelles (à + lesquelles) *pron., f., pl.* which ones II-5
auxquels (à + lesquels) *pron., m., pl.* which ones II-5
avance *f.* advance I-2
    en avance *adv.* early I-2
avant (de/que) *adv.* before I-7
avant-hier *adv.* day before yesterday I-7
avec *prep.* with I-1

Vocabulaire
French-English

Avec qui? With whom? I-4
aventure *f.* adventure II-7
  film d'aventures *m.* adventure film II-7
avenue *f.* avenue II-4
avion *m.* airplane I-7
  prendre un avion *v.* to take a plane I-7
avocat(e) *m., f.* lawyer I-3
avoir *v.* to have I-2
  aie *imp. v.* have I-2
  avoir besoin (de) to need (*something*) I-2
  avoir chaud to be hot I-2
  avoir de la chance to be lucky I-2
  avoir envie (de) to feel like (*doing something*) I-2
  avoir faim to be hungry I-4
  avoir froid to be cold I-2
  avoir honte (de) to be ashamed (of) I-2
  avoir mal to have an ache II-2
  avoir mal au cœur to feel nauseated II-2
  avoir peur (de/que) to be afraid (of/that) I-2
  avoir raison to be right I-2
  avoir soif to be thirsty I-4
  avoir sommeil to be sleepy I-2
  avoir tort to be wrong I-2
  avoir un accident to have/to be in an accident II-3
  avoir un compte bancaire to have a bank account II-4
  en avoir marre to be fed up I-3
avril *m.* April I-5
ayez (avoir) *imp. v.* have I-7
ayons (avoir) *imp. v.* let's have I-7

B

bac(alauréat) *m.* an important exam taken by high-school students in France I-2
baguette *f.* baguette I-4
baignoire *f.* bathtub I-8, II-P
bain *m.* bath I-6
  salle de bains *f.* bathroom I-8, II-P
balai *m.* broom I-8, II-P
balayer *v.* to sweep I-8, II-P
balcon *m.* balcony I-8, II-P
banane *f.* banana II-1
banc *m.* bench II-4
bancaire *adj.* banking II-4
  avoir un compte bancaire *v.* to have a bank account II-4
bande dessinée (B.D.) *f.* comic strip I-5
banlieue *f.* suburbs I-4
banque *f.* bank II-4
banquier/banquière *m., f.* banker II-5
barbant *adj.*, **barbe** *f.* drag I-3
baseball *m.* baseball I-5
basket(-ball) *m.* basketball I-5
baskets *f., pl.* tennis shoes I-6
bateau *m.* boat I-7
  prendre un bateau *v.* to take a boat I-7
bateau-mouche *m.* riverboat I-7
bâtiment *m.* building II-4
batterie *f.* drums II-7
bavarder *v.* to chat I-4
beau (belle) *adj.* handsome; beautiful I-3
  faire quelque chose de beau *v.* to be up to something interesting II-4
  Il fait beau. The weather is nice. I-5
beaucoup (de) *adv.* a lot (of) 4
  Merci (beaucoup). Thank you (very much). I-1
beau-frère *m.* brother-in-law I-3
beau-père *m.* father-in-law; stepfather I-3
beaux-arts *m., pl.* fine arts II-7
belge *adj.* Belgian I-7
Belgique *f.* Belgium I-7
belle *adj., f.* (*feminine form of* **beau**) beautiful I-3
belle-mère *f.* mother-in-law; stepmother I-3
belle-sœur *f.* sister-in-law I-3
besoin *m.* need I-2
  avoir besoin (de) to need (*something*) I-2
beurre *m.* butter 4
bibliothèque *f.* library I-1
bien *adv.* well I-7
  bien sûr *adv.* of course I-2
  Je vais bien. I am doing well. I-1
  Très bien. Very well. I-1
bientôt *adv.* soon I-1
  À bientôt. See you soon. I-1
bienvenu(e) *adj.* welcome I-1
bière *f.* beer I-6
bijouterie *f.* jewelry store II-4
billet *m.* (*travel*) ticket I-7; (*money*) bills, notes II-4
  billet aller-retour *m.* round-trip ticket I-7
biologie *f.* biology I-2
biscuit *m.* cookie I-6
blague *f.* joke I-2
blanc(he) *adj.* white I-6
blessure *f.* injury, wound II-2
bleu(e) *adj.* blue I-3
blond(e) *adj.* blonde I-3
blouson *m.* jacket I-6
bœuf *m.* beef II-1
boire *v.* to drink I-4
bois *m.* wood II-6
boisson (gazeuse) *f.* (carbonated) drink/beverage I-4
boîte *f.* box; can II-1
  boîte aux lettres *f.* mailbox II-4
  boîte de conserve *f.* can (of food) II-1
  boîte de nuit *f.* nightclub I-4
bol *m.* bowl II-1
bon(ne) *adj.* kind; good I-3
  bon marché *adj.* inexpensive I-6
  Il fait bon. The weather is good/warm. I-5
bonbon *m.* candy I-6
bonheur *m.* happiness I-6
Bonjour. Good morning.; Hello. I-1
Bonsoir. Good evening.; Hello. I-1
bouche *f.* mouth II-2
boucherie *f.* butcher's shop II-1
boulangerie *f.* bread shop, bakery II-1
boulevard *m.* boulevard II-4
  suivre un boulevard *v.* to follow a boulevard II-4
bourse *f.* scholarship, grant I-2
bout *m.* end II-4
  au bout (de) *prep.* at the end (of) II-4
bouteille (de) *f.* bottle (of) I-4
boutique *f.* boutique, store II-4
bras *m.* arm II-2
brasserie *f.* café; restaurant II-4
Brésil *m.* Brazil II-2
brésilien(ne) *adj.* Brazilian I-7
bricoler *v.* to tinker; to do odd jobs I-5
brillant(e) *adj.* bright I-1
bronzer *v.* to tan I-6
brosse (à cheveux/à dents) *f.* (hair/tooth)brush II-2
brun(e) *adj.* (*hair*) dark I-3
bu (boire) *p.p.* drunk I-6
bureau *m.* desk; office I-1
  bureau de poste *m.* post office II-4
bus *m.* bus I-7
  arrêt d'autobus (de bus) *m.* bus stop I-7
  prendre un bus *v.* to take a bus I-7

C

ça *pron.* that; this; it I-1
  Ça dépend. It depends. I-4
  Ça ne nous regarde pas. That has nothing to do with us.; That is none of our business. II-6

Vocabulaire — French-English

Ça suffit. That's enough. I-5
Ça te dit? Does that appeal to you? II-6
Ça va? What's up?; How are things? I-1
ça veut dire that is to say II-2
Comme ci, comme ça. So-so. I-1
cabine téléphonique *f.* phone booth II-4
cadeau *m.* gift I-6
  paquet cadeau wrapped gift I-6
cadet(te) *adj.* younger I-3
cadre/femme cadre *m., f.* executive II-5
café *m.* café; coffee I-1
  terrasse de café *f.* café terrace I-4
  cuillère à café *f.* teaspoon II-1
cafetière *f.* coffeemaker I-8, II-P
cahier *m.* notebook I-1
calculatrice *f.* calculator I-1
calme *adj.* calm I-1; *m.* calm I-1
camarade *m., f.* friend I-1
  camarade de chambre *m., f.* roommate I-1
  camarade de classe *m., f.* classmate I-1
caméra vidéo *f.* camcorder II-3
caméscope *m.* camcorder II-3
campagne *f.* country(side) I-7
  pain de campagne *m.* country-style bread I-4
  pâté (de campagne) *m.* pâté, meat spread II-1
camping *m.* camping I-5
  faire du camping *v.* to go camping I-5
Canada *m.* Canada I-7
canadien(ne) *adj.* Canadian I-1
canapé *m.* couch I-8, II-P
candidat(e) *m., f.* candidate; applicant II-5
cantine *f.* (school) cafeteria II-1
capitale *f.* capital I-7
capot *m.* hood II-3
carafe (d'eau) *f.* pitcher (of water) II-1
carotte *f.* carrot II-1
carrefour *m.* intersection II-4
carrière *f.* career II-5
carte *f.* map I-1; menu II-1; card II-4
  payer avec une carte de crédit to pay with a credit card II-4
  carte postale *f.* postcard II-4
  cartes *f. pl.* (*playing*) cards I-5

casquette *f.* (baseball) cap I-6
cassette vidéo *f.* videotape II-3
catastrophe *f.* catastrophe II-6
cave *f.* basement, cellar I-8, II-P
CD *m.* CD(s) II-3
ce *dem. adj., m., sing.* this; that I-6
  ce matin this morning I-2
  ce mois-ci this month I-2
  Ce n'est pas grave. It's no big deal. I-6
  ce soir this evening I-2
  ce sont… those are… I-1
  ce week-end this weekend I-2
ceinture *f.* belt I-6
  attacher sa ceinture de sécurité *v.* to buckle one's seatbelt II-3
célèbre *adj.* famous II-7
célébrer *v.* to celebrate I-5
célibataire *adj.* single I-3
celle *pron., f., sing.* this one; that one; the one II-6
celles *pron., f., pl.* these; those; the ones II-6
celui *pron., m., sing.* this one; that one; the one II-6
cent *m.* one hundred I-3
  cent mille *m.* one hundred thousand I-5
  cent un *m.* one hundred one I-5
  cinq cents *m.* five hundred I-5
centième *adj.* hundredth I-7
centrale nucléaire *f.* nuclear plant II-6
centre commercial *m.* shopping center, mall I-4
centre-ville *m.* city/town center, downtown I-4
certain(e) *adj.* certain II-1
  Il est certain que… It is certain that… II-7
  Il n'est pas certain que… It is uncertain that… II-7
ces *dem. adj., m., f., pl.* these; those I-6
c'est… it/that is… I-1
  C'est de la part de qui? On behalf of whom? II-5
  C'est le 1ᵉʳ (premier) octobre. It is October first. I-5
  C'est M./Mme/Mlle … (à l'appareil). It's Mr./Mrs./Miss … (on the phone). II-5
  C'est quand l'anniversaire de… ? When is …'s birthday? I-5
  C'est quand ton/votre anniversaire? When is your birthday? I-5

  Qu'est-ce que c'est? What is it? I-1
cet *dem. adj., m., sing.* this; that I-6
  cet après-midi this afternoon I-2
cette *dem. adj., f., sing.* this; that I-6
  cette année this year I-2
  cette semaine this week I-2
ceux *pron., m., pl.* these; those; the ones II-6
chaîne (de télévision) *f.* (television) channel II-3
chaîne stéréo *f.* stereo system I-3
chaise *f.* chair I-1
chambre *f.* bedroom I-8, II-P
  chambre (individuelle) *f.* (single) room I-7
  camarade de chambre *m., f.* roommate I-1
champ *m.* field II-6
champagne *m.* champagne I-6
champignon *m.* mushroom II-1
chance *f.* luck I-2
  avoir de la chance *v.* to be lucky I-2
chanson *f.* song II-7
chanter *v.* to sing I-5
chanteur/chanteuse *m., f.* singer I-1
chapeau *m.* hat I-6
chaque *adj.* each I-6
charcuterie *f.* delicatessen II-1
charmant(e) *adj.* charming I-1
chasse *f.* hunt II-6
chasser *v.* to hunt II-6
chat *m.* cat I-3
châtain *adj.* (*hair*) brown I-3
chaud *m.* heat I-2
  avoir chaud *v.* to be hot I-2
  Il fait chaud. (*weather*) It is hot. I-5
chauffeur de taxi/de camion *m.* taxi/truck driver II-5
chaussette *f.* sock I-6
chaussure *f.* shoe I-6
chef d'entreprise *m.* head of a company II-5
chef-d'œuvre *m.* masterpiece II-7
chemin *m.* path; way II-4
  suivre un chemin *v.* to follow a path II-4
chemise (à manches courtes/ longues) *f.* (short-/long-sleeved) shirt I-6
chemisier *m.* blouse I-6
chèque *m.* check II-4
  compte-chèques *m.* checking account II-4
  payer par chèque *v.* to pay by check II-4

Vocabulaire — French-English

cher/chère *adj.* expensive I-6
chercher *v.* to look for I-2
  chercher un/du travail to look for work II-4
chercheur/chercheuse *m., f.* researcher II-5
chéri(e) *adj.* dear, beloved, darling I-2
cheval *m.* horse I-5
  faire du cheval *v.* to go horseback riding I-5
cheveux *m., pl.* hair II-1
  brosse à cheveux *f.* hairbrush II-2
  cheveux blonds blond hair I-3
  cheveux châtains brown hair I-3
  se brosser les cheveux *v.* to brush one's hair II-1
cheville *f.* ankle II-2
  se fouler la cheville *v.* to twist/sprain one's ankle II-2
chez *prep.* at (*someone's*) house I-3, at (*a place*) I-3
  passer chez quelqu'un *v.* to stop by someone's house I-4
chic *adj.* chic I-4
chien *m.* dog I-3
chimie *f.* chemistry I-2
Chine *f.* China I-7
chinois(e) *adj.* Chinese 7
chocolat (chaud) *m.* (hot) chocolate I-4
chœur *m.* choir, chorus II-7
choisir *v.* to choose I-4
chômage *m.* unemployment II-5
  être au chômage *v.* to be unemployed II-5
chômeur/chômeuse *m., f.* unemployed person II-5
chose *f.* thing I-1
  quelque chose *m.* something; anything I-4
chrysanthèmes *m., pl.* chrysanthemums II-1
chut shh II-7
-ci (*used with demonstrative adjective* **ce** *and noun or with demonstrative pronoun* **celui**) here I-6
  ce mois-ci this month I-2
ciel *m.* sky II-6
cinéma (ciné) *m.* movie theater, movies I-4
cinq *m.* five I-1
cinquante *m.* fifty I-1
cinquième *adj.* fifth 7
circulation *f.* traffic II-3
clair(e) *adj.* clear II-7
  Il est clair que… It is clear that… II-7
classe *f.* (*group of students*) class I-1

camarade de classe *m., f.* classmate I-1
  salle de classe *f.* classroom I-1
clavier *m.* keyboard II-3
clé *f.* key I-7
client(e) *m., f.* client; guest I-7
cœur *m.* heart II-2
  avoir mal au cœur to feel nauseated II-2
coffre *m.* trunk II-3
coiffeur/coiffeuse *m., f.* hairdresser I-3
coin *m.* corner II-4
colis *m.* package II-4
colocataire *m., f.* roommate (*in an apartment*) I-1
Combien (de)… ? *adv.* How much/many… ? I-1
  Combien coûte… ? How much is… ? I-4
combiné *m.* receiver II-5
comédie (musicale) *f.* comedy (musical) II-7
commander *v.* to order II-1
comme *adv.* how; like, as I-2
  Comme ci, comme ça. So-so. I-1
commencer (à) *v.* to begin (*to do something*) I-2
comment *adv.* how I-4
  Comment? *adv.* What? I-4
  Comment allez-vous?, *form.* How are you? I-1
  Comment t'appelles-tu? *fam.* What is your name? I-1
  Comment vas-tu? *fam.* How are you? I-1
  Comment vous appelez-vous? *form.* What is your name? I-1
commerçant(e) *m., f.* shopkeeper II-1
commissariat de police *m.* police station II-4
commode *f.* dresser, chest of drawers I-8, II-P
compact disque *m.* compact disc II-3
complet (complète) *adj.* full (no vacancies) I-7
composer (un numéro) *v.* to dial (a number) II-3
compositeur *m.* composer II-7
comprendre *v.* to understand I-4
compris (comprendre) *p.p., adj.* understood; included I-6
comptable *m., f.* accountant II-5
compte *m.* account (*at a bank*) II-4
  avoir un compte bancaire *v.* to have a bank account II-4
  compte de chèques *m.* checking account II-4

compte d'épargne *m.* savings account II-4
  se rendre compte *v.* to realize II-2
compter sur quelqu'un *v.* to count on someone I-8, II-P
concert *m.* concert II-7
condition *f.* condition II-7
  à condition que on the condition that…, provided that… II-7
conduire *v.* to drive I-6
conduit (conduire) *p.p., adj.* driven I-6
confiture *f.* jam II-1
congé *m.* day off I-7
  jour de congé *m.* day off I-7
  prendre un congé *v.* to take time off II-5
congélateur *m.* freezer I-8, II-P
connaissance *f.* acquaintance I-5
  faire la connaissance de *v.* to meet (*someone*) I-5
connaître *v.* to know, to be familiar with I-8, II-P
connecté(e) *adj.* connected II-3
  être connecté(e) avec quelqu'un *v.* to be online with someone I-7, II-3
connu (connaître) *p.p., adj.* known; famous I-8, II-P
conseil *m.* advice II-5
conseiller/conseillère *m., f.* consultant; advisor II-5
considérer *v.* to consider I-5
constamment *adv.* constantly I-8, II-P
construire *v.* to build, to construct I-6
conte *m.* tale II-7
content(e) *adj.* happy II-5
  être content(e) que… *v.* to be happy that… II-6
continuer (à) *v.* to continue (*doing something*) II-4
contraire *adj.* contrary II-7
  au contraire on the contrary II-7
copain/copine *m., f.* friend I-1
corbeille (à papier) *f.* wastebasket I-1
corps *m.* body II-2
costume *m.* (*man's*) suit I-6
côte *f.* coast II-6
coton *m.* cotton II-4
cou *m.* neck II-2
couche d'ozone *f.* ozone layer II-6
  trou dans la couche d'ozone *m.* hole in the ozone layer II-6
couleur *f.* color 6
  De quelle couleur… ? What color… ? I-6

Vocabulaire — French-English

couloir *m.* hallway I-8, II-P
couple *m.* couple I-6
courage *m.* courage II-5
courageux/courageuse *adj.* courageous, brave I-3
couramment *adv.* fluently I-8, II-P
courir *v.* to run I-5
courrier *m.* mail II-4
cours *m.* class, course I-2
course *f.* errand II-1
   faire les courses *v.* to go (grocery) shopping II-1
court(e) *adj.* short I-3
   chemise à manches courtes *f.* short-sleeved shirt I-6
couru (courir) *p.p.* run I-6
cousin(e) *m., f.* cousin I-3
couteau *m.* knife II-1
coûter *v.* to cost I-4
   Combien coûte... ? How much is... ? I-4
couvert (couvrir) *p.p.* covered II-3
couverture *f.* blanket I-8, II-P
couvrir *v.* to cover II-3
covoiturage *m.* carpooling II-6
cravate *f.* tie I-6
crayon *m.* pencil I-1
crème *f.* cream II-1
   crème à raser *f.* shaving cream II-2
crêpe *f.* crêpe I-5
crevé(e) *adj.* deflated; blown up II-3
   pneu crevé *m.* flat tire II-3
critique *f.* review; criticism II-7
croire (que) *v.* to believe (that) II-7
   ne pas croire que... to not believe that... II-7
croissant *m.* croissant I-4
croissant(e) *adj.* growing II-6
   population croissante *f.* growing population II-6
cru (croire) *p.p.* believed II-7
cruel/cruelle *adj.* cruel I-3
cuillère (à soupe/à café) *f.* (soup/tea)spoon II-1
cuir *m.* leather II-4
cuisine *f.* cooking; kitchen 5
   faire la cuisine *v.* to cook 5
cuisiner *v.* to cook II-1
cuisinier/cuisinière *m., f.* cook II-5
cuisinière *f.* stove I-8, II-P
curieux/curieuse *adj.* curious I-3
curriculum vitæ (C.V.) *m.* résumé II-5
cybercafé *m.* cybercafé II-4

D

d'abord *adv.* first I-7
d'accord *(tag question)* all right? I-2; *(in statement)* okay I-2
   être d'accord to be in agreement I-2
d'autres *m., f.* others I-4
d'habitude *adv.* usually I-8, II-P
danger *m.* danger, threat II-6
dangereux/dangereuse *adj.* dangerous II-3
dans *prep.* in I-3
danse *f.* dance II-7
danser *v.* to dance I-4
danseur/danseuse *m., f.* dancer II-7
date *f.* date I-5
   Quelle est la date? What is the date? I-5
de/d' *prep.* of I-3; from I-1
   de l'après-midi in the afternoon I-2
   de laquelle *pron., f., sing.* which one II-5
   De quelle couleur... ? What color... ? I-6
   De rien. You're welcome. I-1
   de taille moyenne of medium height I-3
   de temps en temps *adv.* from time to time I-8, II-P
débarrasser la table *v.* to clear the table I-8, II-P
déboisement *m.* deforestation II-6
début *m.* beginning; debut II-7
décembre *m.* December I-5
déchets toxiques *m., pl.* toxic waste II-6
décider (de) *v.* to decide (to do something) II-3
découvert (découvrir) *p.p.* discovered II-3
découvrir *v.* to discover II-3
décrire *v.* to describe I-7
décrocher *v.* to pick up II-5
décrit (décrire) *p.p., adj.* described I-7
degrés *m., pl.* (temperature) degrees I-5
   Il fait ... degrés. *(to describe weather)* It is ... degrees. I-5
déjà *adv.* already I-5
déjeuner *m.* lunch II-1; *v.* to eat lunch I-4
de l' *part. art., m., f., sing.* some I-4
de la *part. art., f., sing.* some I-4
délicieux/délicieuse delicious I-8, II-P
demain *adv.* tomorrow I-2

À demain. See you tomorrow. I-1
après-demain *adv.* day after tomorrow I-2
demain matin/après-midi/soir *adv.* tomorrow morning/afternoon/evening I-2
demander (à) *v.* to ask (someone), to make a request (of someone) I-6
demander que... *v.* to ask that... II-6
démarrer *v.* to start up II-3
déménager *v.* to move out I-8, II-P
demie half I-2
   et demie half past ... (o'clock) I-2
demi-frère *m.* half-brother, stepbrother I-3
demi-sœur *f.* half-sister, stepsister I-3
démissionner *v.* to resign II-5
dent *f.* tooth II-1
   brosse à dents *f.* toothbrush II-2
   se brosser les dents *v.* to brush one's teeth II-1
dentifrice *m.* toothpaste II-2
dentiste *m., f.* dentist I-3
départ *m.* departure I-7
dépasser *v.* to go over; to pass II-3
dépense *f.* expenditure, expense II-4
dépenser *v.* to spend I-4
   dépenser de l'argent *v.* to spend money I-4
déposer de l'argent *v.* to deposit money II-4
déprimé(e) *adj.* depressed II-2
depuis *adv.* since; for II-1
dernier/dernière *adj.* last I-2
dernièrement *adv.* lastly, finally I-8, II-P
derrière *prep.* behind I-3
des *part. art., m., f., pl.* some I-4
des (de + les) *m., f., pl.* of the I-3
dès que *adv.* as soon as II-5
désagréable *adj.* unpleasant I-1
descendre (de) *v.* to go downstairs; to get off; to take down I-6
désert *m.* desert II-6
désirer (que) *v.* to want (that) I-5
désolé(e) *adj.* sorry I-6
   être désolé(e) que... to be sorry that... II-6
desquelles (de + lesquelles) *pron., f., pl.* which ones II-5
desquels (de + lesquels) *pron., m., pl.* which ones II-5

Vocabulaire — French-English

dessert *m.* dessert I-6
dessin animé *m.* cartoon II-7
dessiner *v.* to draw I-2
détester *v.* to hate I-2
  Je déteste… I hate… I-2
détruire *v.* to destroy I-6
détruit (détruire) *p.p., adj.* destroyed I-6
deux *m.* two I-1
deuxième *adj.* second I-7
devant *prep.* in front of I-3
développer *v.* to develop II-6
devenir *v.* to become II-1
devoir *m.* homework I-2; *v.* to have to, must II-1
dictionnaire *m.* dictionary I-1
différemment *adv.* differently I-8, II-P
différence *f.* difference I-1
différent(e) *adj.* different I-1
difficile *adj.* difficult I-1
dimanche *m.* Sunday I-2
dîner *m.* dinner II-1; *v.* to have dinner I-2
diplôme *m.* diploma, degree I-2
dire *v.* to say I-7
  Ça te dit? Does that appeal to you? II-6
  ça veut dire that is to say II-2
  veut dire *v.* means, signifies II-1
diriger *v.* to manage II-5
discret/discrète *adj.* discreet; unassuming I-3
discuter *v.* discuss I-6
disque *m.* disk II-3
  compact disque *m.* compact disc II-3
  disque dur *m.* hard drive II-3
dissertation *f.* essay II-3
distributeur automatique/de billets *m.* ATM II-4
dit (dire) *p.p., adj.* said I-7
divorce *m.* divorce I-6
divorcé(e) *adj.* divorced I-3
divorcer *v.* to divorce I-3
dix *m.* ten I-1
dix-huit *m.* eighteen I-1
dixième *adj.* tenth I-7
dix-neuf *m.* nineteen I-1
dix-sept *m.* seventeen I-1
documentaire *m.* documentary II-7
doigt *m.* finger II-2
doigt de pied *m.* toe II-2
domaine *m.* field II-5
dommage *m.* harm II-6
  Il est dommage que… It's a shame that… II-6
donc *conj.* therefore I-7
donner (à) *v.* to give (*to someone*) I-2

dont *rel. pron.* of which; of whom; that II-3
dormir *v.* to sleep I-5
dos *m.* back II-2
  sac à dos *m.* backpack I-1
douane *f.* customs I-7
douche *f.* shower I-8, II-P
  prendre une douche *v.* to take a shower II-2
doué(e) *adj.* talented, gifted II-7
douleur *f.* pain II-2
douter (que) *v.* to doubt (that) II-7
douteux/douteuse *adj.* doubtful II-7
  Il est douteux que… It is doubtful that… II-7
doux/douce *adj.* sweet; soft I-3
douze *m.* twelve I-1
dramaturge *m.* playwright II-7
drame (psychologique) *m.* (psychological) drama II-7
draps *m., pl.* sheets I-8, II-P
droit *m.* law I-2
droite *f.* the right (side) I-3
  à droite de *prep.* to the right of I-3
drôle *adj.* funny I-3
du *part. art., m., sing.* some I-4
du (de + le) *m., sing.* of the I-3
dû (devoir) *p.p., adj.* (*used with infinitive*) had to; (*used with noun*) due, owed II-1
duquel (de + lequel) *pron., m., sing.* which one II-5

E

eau (minérale) *f.* (mineral) water I-4
  carafe d'eau *f.* pitcher of water II-1
écharpe *f.* scarf I-6
échecs *m., pl.* chess I-5
échouer *v.* to fail I-2
éclair *m.* éclair I-4
école *f.* school I-2
écologie *f.* ecology II-6
écologique *adj.* ecological II-6
économie *f.* economics I-2
écotourisme *m.* ecotourism II-6
écouter *v.* to listen (to) I-2
écouteurs *m.* headphones II-3
écran *m.* screen 11
écrire *v.* to write I-7
écrivain/femme écrivain *m., f.* writer II-7
écrit (écrire) *p.p., adj.* written I-7
écureuil *m.* squirrel II-6
éducation physique *f.* physical education I-2

effacer *v.* to erase II-3
effet de serre *m.* greenhouse effect II-6
égaler *v.* to equal I-3
église *f.* church I-4
égoïste *adj.* selfish I-1
Eh! *interj.* Hey! I-2
électrique *adj.* electric I-8, II-P
  appareil électrique/ménager *m.* electrical/household appliance I-8, II-P
électricien/électricienne *m., f.* electrician II-5
élégant(e) *adj.* elegant 1
élevé *adj.* high II-5
élève *m., f.* pupil, student I-1
elle *pron., f.* she; it I-1; her I-3
  elle est… she/it is… I-1
elles *pron., f.* they I-1; them I-3
  elles sont… they are… I-1
e-mail *m.* e-mail II-3
emballage (en plastique) *m.* (plastic) wrapping/packaging II-6
embaucher *v.* to hire II-5
embrayage *m.* (*automobile*) clutch II-3
émission (de télévision) *f.* (television) program II-7
emménager *v.* to move in I-8, II-P
emmener *v.* to take (*someone*) I-5
emploi *m.* job II-5
  emploi à mi-temps/à temps partiel *m.* part-time job II-5
  emploi à plein temps *m.* full-time job II-5
employé(e) *m., f.* employee II-5
employer *v.* to use, to employ I-5
emprunter *v.* to borrow II-4
en *prep.* in I-3
  en automne in the fall I-5
  en avance early I-2
  en avoir marre to be fed up I-6
  en effet indeed; in fact I-6
  en été in the summer I-5
  en face (de) *prep.* facing, across (from) I-3
  en fait in fact I-7
  en général *adv.* in general I-8, II-P
  en hiver in the winter I-5
  en plein air in fresh air II-6
  en retard late I-2
  en tout cas in any case 6
  en vacances on vacation 7
  être en ligne to be online II-3
en *pron.* some of it/them; about it/them; of it/them; from it/them II-2
  Je vous en prie. *form.* Please.; You're welcome. I-1

Vocabulaire — French-English

Qu'en penses-tu? What do you think about that? II-6
enceinte *adj.* pregnant II-2
Enchanté(e). Delighted. I-1
encore *adv.* again; still I-3
endroit *m.* place I-4
énergie (nucléaire/solaire) *f.* (nuclear/solar) energy II-6
enfance *f.* childhood I-6
enfant *m., f.* child I-3
enfin *adv.* finally, at last I-7
enlever la poussière *v.* to dust I-8, II-P
ennuyeux/ennuyeuse *adj.* boring I-3
énorme *adj.* enormous, huge I-2
enregistrer *v.* to record II-3
enregistreur DVR *m.* DVR II-3
enseigner *v.* to teach I-2
ensemble *adv.* together I-6
ensuite *adv.* then, next I-7
entendre *v.* to hear I-6
entracte *m.* intermission II-7
entre *prep.* between I-3
entrée *f.* appetizer, starter II-1
entreprise *f.* firm, business II-5
entrer *v.* to enter I-7
entretien: passer un entretien to have an interview II-5
enveloppe *f.* envelope II-4
envie *f.* desire, envy I-2
   avoir envie (de) to feel like (*doing something*) I-2
environnement *m.* environment II-6
envoyer (à) *v.* to send (*to someone*) I-5
épargne *f.* savings II-4
   compte d'épargne *m.* savings account II-4
épicerie *f.* grocery store I-4
épouser *v.* to marry I-3
épouvantable *adj.* dreadful 5
   Il fait un temps épouvantable. The weather is dreadful. I-5
époux/épouse *m., f.* husband/wife I-3
équipe *f.* team I-5
escalier *m.* staircase I-8, II-P
escargot *m.* escargot, snail II-1
espace *m.* space II-6
Espagne *f.* Spain 7
espagnol(e) *adj.* Spanish I-1
espèce (menacée) *f.* (endangered) species II-6
espérer *v.* to hope I-5
essayer *v.* to try I-5
essence *f.* gas II-3
   réservoir d'essence *m.* gas tank II-3

voyant d'essence *m.* gas warning light II-3
essentiel(le) *adj.* essential II-6
   Il est essentiel que… It is essential that… II-6
essuie-glace *m.* (**essuie-glaces** *pl.*) windshield wiper(s) II-3
essuyer (la vaisselle/la table) *v.* to wipe (the dishes/the table) I-8, II-P
est *m.* east II-4
Est-ce que… ? (*used in forming questions*) I-2
et *conj.* and I-1
   Et toi? *fam.* And you? I-1
   Et vous? *form.* And you? I-1
étage *m.* floor I-7
étagère *f.* shelf I-8, II-P
étape *f.* stage I-6
état civil *m.* marital status I-6
États-Unis *m., pl.* United States I-7
été *m.* summer I-5
   en été in the summer I-5
été (être) *p.p.* been I-6
éteindre *v.* to turn off II-3
éternuer *v.* to sneeze II-2
étoile *f.* star II-6
étranger/étrangère *adj.* foreign I-2
   langues étrangères *f., pl.* foreign languages I-2
étranger *m.* (*places that are*) abroad, overseas I-7
   à l'étranger abroad, overseas I-7
étrangler *v.* to strangle II-5
être *v.* to be I-1
   être bien/mal payé(e) to be well/badly paid II-5
   être connecté(e) avec quelqu'un to be online with someone I-7, II-3
   être en ligne avec to be online with II-3
   être en pleine forme to be in good shape II-2
études (supérieures) *f., pl.* studies; (higher) education I-2
étudiant(e) *m., f.* student I-1
étudier *v.* to study I-2
eu (avoir) *p.p.* had I-6
eux *disj. pron., m., pl.* they, them I-3
évidemment *adv.* obviously, evidently; of course I-8, II-P
évident(e) *adj.* evident, obvious II-7
   Il est évident que… It is evident that… II-7
évier *m.* sink I-8, II-P

éviter (de) *v.* to avoid (*doing something*) II-2
exactement *adv.* exactly II-1
examen *m.* exam; test I-1
   être reçu(e) à un examen *v.* to pass an exam I-2
   passer un examen *v.* to take an exam I-2
Excuse-moi. *fam.* Excuse me. I-1
Excusez-moi. *form.* Excuse me. I-1
exercice *m.* exercise II-2
   faire de l'exercice *v.* to exercise II-2
exigeant(e) *adj.* demanding II-5
   profession (exigeante) *f.* a (demanding) profession II-5
exiger (que) *v.* to demand (that) II-6
expérience (professionnelle) *f.* (professional) experience II-5
expliquer *v.* to explain I-2
explorer *v.* to explore I-4
exposition *f.* exhibit II-7
extinction *f.* extinction II-6

F

facile *adj.* easy I-2
facilement *adv.* easily I-8, II-P
facteur *m.* mailman II-4
faculté *f.* university; faculty I-1
faible *adj.* weak I-3
faim *f.* hunger I-4
   avoir faim *v.* to be hungry I-4
faire *v.* to do; to make I-5
   faire attention (à) *v.* to pay attention (to) I-5
   faire quelque chose de beau *v.* to be up to something interesting II-4
   faire de l'aérobic *v.* to do aerobics I-5
   faire de la gym *v.* to work out I-5
   faire de la musique *v.* to play music II-5
   faire de la peinture *v.* to paint II-7
   faire de la planche à voile *v.* to go windsurfing I-5
   faire de l'exercice *v.* to exercise II-2
   faire des projets *v.* to make plans II-5
   faire du camping *v.* to go camping I-5
   faire du cheval *v.* to go horseback riding I-5
   faire du jogging *v.* to go jogging I-5

Vocabulaire — French-English

faire du shopping *v.* to go shopping I-7
faire du ski *v.* to go skiing I-5
faire du sport *v.* to do sports I-5
faire du vélo *v.* to go bike riding I-5
faire la connaissance de *v.* to meet (*someone*) I-5
faire la cuisine *v.* to cook I-5
faire la fête *v.* to party I-6
faire la lessive *v.* to do the laundry I-8, II-P
faire la poussière *v.* to dust I-8, II-P
faire la queue *v.* to wait in line II-4
faire la vaisselle *v.* to do the dishes I-8, II-P
faire le lit *v.* to make the bed I-8, II-P
faire le ménage *v.* to do the housework I-8, II-P
faire le plein *v.* to fill the tank II-3
faire les courses *v.* to run errands II-1
faire les musées *v.* to go to museums II-7
faire les valises *v.* to pack one's bags I-7
faire mal *v.* to hurt II-2
faire plaisir à quelqu'un *v.* to please someone II-5
faire sa toilette *v.* to wash up II-2
faire une piqûre *v.* to give a shot 10
faire une promenade *v.* to go for a walk I-5
faire une randonnée *v.* to go for a hike I-5
faire un séjour *v.* to spend time (*somewhere*) I-7
faire un tour (en voiture) *v.* to go for a walk (drive) I-5
faire visiter *v.* to give a tour I-8, II-P
fait (faire) *p.p., adj.* done; made I-6
falaise *f.* cliff II-6
faut (falloir) *v.* (*used with infinitive*) is necessary to… I-5
  Il a fallu… It was necessary to… I-6
  Il fallait… One had to… I-8, II-P
  Il faut que… One must…/It is necessary that… II-6
fallu (falloir) *p.p.* (*used with infinitive*) had to… I-6
  Il a fallu… It was necessary to… I-6

famille *f.* family I-3
fatigué(e) *adj.* tired I-3
fauteuil *m.* armchair I-8, II-P
favori/favorite *adj.* favorite I-3
fax *m.* fax (machine) II-3
félicitations congratulations II-7
femme *f.* woman; wife I-1
  femme d'affaires businesswoman I-3
  femme au foyer housewife II-5
  femme auteur author II-7
  femme cadre executive II-5
  femme écrivain writer II-7
  femme peintre painter II-7
  femme politique politician II-5
  femme pompier firefighter II-5
  femme sculpteur sculptor II-7
fenêtre *f.* window I-1
fer à repasser *m.* iron I-8, II-P
férié(e) *adj.* holiday I-6
  jour férié *m.* holiday I-6
fermé(e) *adj.* closed II-4
fermer *v.* to close; to shut off II-3
festival (festivals *pl.***)** *m.* festival II-7
fête *f.* party; celebration I-6
  faire la fête *v.* to party I-6
fêter *v.* to celebrate I-6
feu de signalisation *m.* traffic light II-4
feuille de papier *f.* sheet of paper I-1
feuilleton *m.* soap opera II-7
février *m.* February I-5
fiancé(e) *adj.* engaged I-3
fiancé(e) *m., f.* fiancé I-6
fichier *m.* file II-3
fier/fière *adj.* proud I-3
fièvre *f.* fever II-2
  avoir de la fièvre *v.* to have a fever II-2
fille *f.* girl; daughter I-1
film (d'aventures, d'horreur, de science-fiction, policier) *m.* (adventure, horror, science-fiction, crime) film II-7
fils *m.* son I-3
fin *f.* end II-7
finalement *adv.* finally I-7
fini (finir) *p.p., adj.* finished, done, over I-4
finir (de) *v.* to finish (*doing something*) I-4
fleur *f.* flower I-8, II-P
fleuve *m.* river II-6
fois *f.* time I-8, II-P
  une fois *adv.* once I-8, II-P
  deux fois *adv.* twice I-8, II-P
fonctionner *v.* to work, to function II-3
fontaine *f.* fountain II-4

foot(ball) *m.* soccer I-5
  football américain *m.* football I-5
forêt (tropicale) *f.* (tropical) forest II-6
formation *f.* education; training II-5
forme *f.* shape; form II-2
  être en pleine forme *v.* to be in good shape II-2
formidable *adj.* great I-7
formulaire *m.* form II-4
  remplir un formulaire to fill out a form II-4
fort(e) *adj.* strong I-3
fou/folle *adj.* crazy I-3
four (à micro-ondes) *m.* (microwave) oven I-8, II-P
fourchette *f.* fork II-1
frais/fraîche *adj.* fresh; cool I-5
  Il fait frais. (*weather*) It is cool. I-5
fraise *f.* strawberry II-1
français(e) *adj.* French I-1
France *f.* France I-7
franchement *adv.* frankly, honestly I-8, II-P
freiner *v.* to brake II-3
freins *m., pl.* brakes II-3
fréquenter *v.* to frequent; to visit I-4
frère *m.* brother I-3
  beau-frère *m.* brother-in-law I-3
  demi-frère *m.* half-brother, stepbrother I-3
frigo *m.* refrigerator I-8, II-P
frisé(e) *adj.* curly I-3
frites *f., pl.* French fries I-4
froid *m.* cold I-2
  avoir froid to be cold I-2
  Il fait froid. (*weather*) It is cold. I-5
fromage *m.* cheese I-4
fruit *m.* fruit II-1
fruits de mer *m., pl.* seafood II-1
fumer *v.* to smoke II-2
funérailles *f., pl.* funeral II-1
furieux/furieuse *adj.* furious II-6
  être furieux/furieuse que… *v.* to be furious that… II-6

G

gagner *v.* to win I-5; to earn II-5
gant *m.* glove I-6
garage *m.* garage I-8, II-P
garanti(e) *adj.* guaranteed 5
garçon *m.* boy I-1
garder la ligne *v.* to stay slim II-2
gare (routière) *f.* train station (bus station) I-7
gaspillage *m.* waste II-6

Vocabulaire

French-English

gaspiller *v.* to waste II-6
gâteau *m.* cake I-6
gauche *f.* the left (side) I-3
  à gauche (de) *prep.* to the left (of) I-3
gazeux/gazeuse *adj.* carbonated, fizzy 4
  boisson gazeuse *f.* carbonated drink/beverage I-4
généreux/généreuse *adj.* generous I-3
génial(e) *adj.* great I-3
genou *m.* knee II-2
genre *m.* genre II-7
gens *m., pl.* people I-7
gentil/gentille *adj.* nice I-3
gentiment *adv.* nicely I-8, II-P
géographie *f.* geography I-2
gérant(e) *m., f.* manager II-5
gestion *f.* business administration I-2
glace *f.* ice cream I-6
glaçon *m.* ice cube I-6
glissement de terrain *m.* landslide II-6
golf *m.* golf I-5
enfler *v.* to swell II-2
gorge *f.* throat II-2
goûter *m.* afternoon snack II-1; *v.* to taste II-1
gouvernement *m.* government II-6
grand(e) *adj.* big I-3
  grand magasin *m.* department store I-4
grand-mère *f.* grandmother I-3
grand-père *m.* grandfather I-3
grands-parents *m., pl.* grandparents I-3
gratin *m.* gratin II-1
gratuit(e) *adj.* free II-7
grave *adj.* serious II-2
  Ce n'est pas grave. It's okay.; No problem. I-6
graver *v.* to record, to burn (CD, DVD) II-3
grille-pain *m.* toaster I-8, II-P
grippe *f.* flu II-2
gris(e) *adj.* gray I-6
gros(se) *adj.* fat I-3
grossir *v.* to gain weight I-4
guérir *v.* to get better II-2
guitare *f.* guitar II-7
gym *f.* exercise I-5
  faire de la gym *v.* to work out I-5
gymnase *m.* gym I-4

H

habitat *m.* habitat II-6
  sauvetage des habitats *m.* habitat preservation II-6
habiter (à) *v.* to live (in/at) I-2
haricots verts *m., pl.* green beans II-1
Hein? *interj.* Huh?; Right? I-3
herbe *f.* grass II-6
hésiter (à) *v.* to hesitate (to do something) II-3
heure(s) *f.* hour, o'clock; time I-2
  à … heure(s) at … (o'clock) I-4
  À quelle heure? What time?; When? I-2
  À tout à l'heure. See you later. I-1
  Quelle heure avez-vous? *form.* What time do you have? I-2
  Quelle heure est-il? What time is it? I-2
heureusement *adv.* fortunately I-8, II-P
heureux/heureuse *adj.* happy I-3
  être heureux/heureuse que… to be happy that… II-6
hier (matin/après-midi/soir) *adv.* yesterday (morning/afternoon/evening) I-7
  avant-hier *adv.* day before yesterday I-7
histoire *f.* history; story I-2
hiver *m.* winter I-5
  en hiver in the winter I-5
homme *m.* man I-1
  homme d'affaires *m.* businessman I-3
  homme politique *m.* politician II-5
honnête *adj.* honest II-7
honte *f.* shame I-2
  avoir honte (de) *v.* to be ashamed (of) I-2
hôpital *m.* hospital I-4
horloge *f.* clock I-1
hors-d'œuvre *m.* hors d'œuvre, appetizer II-1
hôte/hôtesse *m., f.* host I-6
hôtel *m.* hotel I-7
hôtelier/hôtelière *m., f.* hotel keeper I-7
huile *f.* oil II-1
  huile *f.* (automobile) oil II-3
  huile d'olive *f.* olive oil II-1
  vérifier l'huile to check the oil II-3
  voyant d'huile *m.* oil warning light II-3
huit *m.* eight I-1
huitième *adj.* eighth I-7
humeur *f.* mood I-8, II-P
  être de bonne/mauvaise humeur *v.* to be in a good/bad mood I-8, II-P

I

ici *adv.* here I-1
idée *f.* idea I-3
il *sub. pron.* he; it I-1
  il est… he/it is… I-1
  Il n'y a pas de quoi. It's nothing.; You're welcome. I-1
  Il vaut mieux que… It is better that… II-6
Il faut (falloir) *v. (used with infinitive)* It is necessary to… I-6
  Il a fallu… It was necessary to… I-6
  Il fallait… One had to… I-8, II-P
  Il faut (que)… One must…/ It is necessary that… II-6
il y a there is/are I-1
  il y a eu there was/were 6
  il y avait there was/were I-8, II-P
  Qu'est-ce qu'il y a? What is it?; What's wrong? I-1
  Y a-t-il… ? Is/Are there… ? I-2
  il y a… *(used with an expression of time)* … ago II-1
île *f.* island II-6
ils *sub. pron., m., pl.* they I-1
  ils sont… they are… I-1
immeuble *m.* building I-8, II-P
impatient(e) *adj.* impatient I-1
imperméable *m.* rain jacket I-5
important(e) *adj.* important I-1
  Il est important que… It is important that… II-6
impossible *adj.* impossible II-7
  Il est impossible que… It is impossible that… II-7
imprimante *f.* printer II-3
imprimer *v.* to print II-3
incendie *m.* fire II-6
  prévenir l'incendie to prevent a fire II-6
incroyable *adj.* incredible II-3
indépendamment *adv.* independently I-8, II-P
indépendant(e) *adj.* independent I-1
indications *f.* directions II-4
indiquer *v.* to indicate I-5
indispensable *adj.* essential, indispensable II-6
  Il est indispensable que… It is essential that… II-6
individuel(le) *adj.* single, individual I-7
  chambre individuelle *f.* single (hotel) room I-7
infirmier/infirmière *m., f.* nurse II-2

Vocabulaire

French-English

informations (infos) *f., pl.* news II-7
informatique *f.* computer science I-2
ingénieur *m.* engineer I-3
inquiet/inquiète *adj.* worried I-3
instrument *m.* instrument I-1
intellectuel(le) *adj.* intellectual I-3
intelligent(e) *adj.* intelligent I-1
interdire *v.* to forbid, to prohibit II-6
intéressant(e) *adj.* interesting I-1
inutile *adj.* useless I-2
invité(e) *m., f.* guest I-6
inviter *v.* to invite I-4
irlandais(e) *adj.* Irish I-7
Irlande *f.* Ireland I-7
Italie *f.* Italy I-7
italien(ne) *adj.* Italian I-1

J

jaloux/jalouse *adj.* jealous I-3
jamais *adv.* never I-5
  ne… jamais never, not ever II-4
jambe *f.* leg II-2
jambon *m.* ham I-4
janvier *m.* January I-5
Japon *m.* Japan I-7
japonais(e) *adj.* Japanese I-1
jardin *m.* garden; yard I-8, II-P
jaune *adj.* yellow I-6
je/j' *sub. pron.* I I-1
  Je vous en prie. *form.* Please.; You're welcome. I-1
jean *m., sing.* jeans I-6
jeter *v.* to throw away II-6
jeu *m.* game I-5
  jeu télévisé *m.* game show II-7
  jeu vidéo (des jeux vidéo) *m.* video game(s) II-3
jeudi *m.* Thursday I-2
jeune *adj.* young I-3
  jeunes mariés *m., pl.* newlyweds I-6
jeunesse *f.* youth I-6
  auberge de jeunesse *f.* youth hostel I-7
jogging *m.* jogging I-5
  faire du jogging *v.* to go jogging I-5
joli(e) *adj.* handsome; beautiful I-3
joue *f.* cheek II-2
jouer (à/de) *v.* to play (a sport/a musical instrument) I-5
  jouer un rôle *v.* to play a role II-7
joueur/joueuse *m., f.* player I-5
jour *m.* day I-2

jour de congé *m.* day off I-7
jour férié *m.* holiday I-6
  Quel jour sommes-nous? What day is it? I-2
journal *m.* newspaper; journal I-7
journaliste *m., f.* journalist I-3
journée *f.* day I-2
juillet *m.* July I-5
juin *m.* June I-5
jungle *f.* jungle II-6
jupe *f.* skirt I-6
jus (d'orange/de pomme) *m.* (orange/apple) juice I-4
jusqu'à (ce que) *prep.* until II-4
juste *adv.* just; right I-3
  juste à côté right next door I-3

K

kilo(gramme) *m.* kilo(gram) II-1
kiosque *m.* kiosk I-4

L

l' *def. art., m., f. sing.* the I-1; *d.o. pron., m., f.* him; her; it I-7
la *def. art., f. sing.* the I-1; *d.o. pron., f.* her; it I-7
là(-bas) (over) there I-1
-là *(used with demonstrative adjective* **ce** *and noun or with demonstrative pronoun* **celui***)* there I-6
lac *m.* lake II-6
laid(e) *adj.* ugly I-3
laine *f.* wool II-4
laisser *v.* to let, to allow II-3
  laisser tranquille *v.* to leave alone II-2
  laisser un message *v.* to leave a message II-5
  laisser un pourboire *v.* to leave a tip I-4
lait *m.* milk I-4
laitue *f.* lettuce II-1
lampe *f.* lamp I-8, II-P
langues (étrangères) *f., pl.* (foreign) languages I-2
lapin *m.* rabbit II-6
laquelle *pron., f., sing.* which one II-5
  à laquelle *pron., f., sing.* which one II-5
  de laquelle *pron., f., sing.* which one II-5
large *adj.* loose; big I-6
lavabo *m.* bathroom sink I-8, II-P
lave-linge *m.* washing machine I-8, II-P
laver *v.* to wash I-8, II-P
laverie *f.* laundromat II-4

lave-vaisselle *m.* dishwasher I-8, II-P
le *def. art., m. sing.* the I-1; *d.o. pron.* him; it I-7
lecteur MP3 / (de) CD/ DVD *m.* MP3/CD/DVD player II-3
légume *m.* vegetable II-1
lent(e) *adj.* slow I-3
lequel *pron., m., sing.* which one II-5
  auquel (à + lequel) *pron., m., sing.* which one II-5
  duquel (de + lequel) *pron., m., sing.* which one II-5
les *def. art., m., f., pl.* the I-1; *d.o. pron., m., f., pl.* them I-7
lesquelles *pron., f., pl.* which ones II-5
  auxquelles (à + lesquelles) *pron., f., pl.* which ones II-5
  desquelles (de + lesquelles) *pron., f., pl.* which ones II-5
lesquels *pron., m., pl.* which ones II-5
  auxquels (à + lesquels) *pron., m., pl.* which ones II-5
  desquels (de + lesquels) *pron., m., pl.* which ones II-5
lessive *f.* laundry I-8, II-P
  faire la lessive *v.* to do the laundry I-8, II-P
lettre *f.* letter II-4
  boîte aux lettres *f.* mailbox II-4
  lettre de motivation *f.* letter of application II-5
  lettre de recommandation *f.* letter of recommendation, reference letter II-5
lettres *f., pl.* humanities I-2
leur *i.o. pron., m., f., pl.* them I-6
leur(s) *poss. adj., m., f.* their I-3
librairie *f.* bookstore I-1
libre *adj.* available I-7
lien *m.* link II-3
lieu *m.* place I-4
ligne *f.* figure, shape II-2
  garder la ligne *v.* to stay slim II-2
limitation de vitesse *f.* speed limit II-3
limonade *f.* lemon soda I-4
linge *m.* laundry I-8, II-P
  lave-linge *m.* washing machine I-8, II-P
  sèche-linge *m.* clothes dryer I-8, II-P
liquide *m.* cash *(money)* II-4
  payer en liquide *v.* to pay in cash II-4
lire *v.* to read I-7
lit *m.* bed I-7

Vocabulaire — French-English

faire le lit *v.* to make the bed I-8, II-P
littéraire *adj.* literary II-7
littérature *f.* literature I-1
livre *m.* book I-1
logement *m.* housing I-8, II-P
logiciel *m.* software, program II-3
loi *f.* law II-6
loin de *prep.* far from I-3
loisir *m.* leisure activity I-5
long(ue) *adj.* long I-3
   chemise à manches longues *f.* long-sleeved shirt I-6
longtemps *adv.* a long time I-5
louer *v.* to rent I-8, II-P
loyer *m.* rent I-8, II-P
lu (lire) *p.p.* read I-7
lui *pron., sing.* he I-1; him I-3; *i.o. pron. (attached to imperative)* to him/her II-1
l'un(e) à l'autre to one another II-3
l'un(e) l'autre one another II-3
lundi *m.* Monday I-2
Lune *f.* moon II-6
lunettes (de soleil) *f., pl.* (sun)glasses I-6
lycée *m.* high school I-1
lycéen(ne) *m., f.* high school student I-2

M

ma *poss. adj., f., sing.* my I-3
Madame *f.* Ma'am; Mrs. I-1
Mademoiselle *f.* Miss I-1
magasin *m.* store I-4
   grand magasin *m.* department store I-4
magazine *m.* magazine II-7
magnétophone *m.* tape recorder II-3
magnétoscope *m.* videocassette recorder (VCR) II-3
mai *m.* May I-5
maigrir *v.* to lose weight I-4
maillot de bain *m.* swimsuit, bathing suit I-6
main *f.* hand I-5
   sac à main *m.* purse, handbag I-6
maintenant *adv.* now I-5
maintenir *v.* to maintain II-1
mairie *f.* town/city hall; mayor's office II-4
mais *conj.* but I-1
   mais non (but) of course not; no I-2
maison *f.* house I-4
   rentrer à la maison *v.* to return home I-2
mal *adv.* badly I-7

Je vais mal. I am doing badly. I-1
le plus mal *super. adv.* the worst II-1
se porter mal *v.* to be doing badly II-2
mal *m.* illness; ache, pain II-2
   avoir mal *v.* to have an ache II-2
   avoir mal au cœur *v.* to feel nauseated II-2
   faire mal *v.* to hurt II-2
malade *adj.* sick, ill II-2
   tomber malade *v.* to get sick II-2
maladie *f.* illness II-5
   assurance maladie *f.* health insurance II-5
malheureusement *adv.* unfortunately I-2
malheureux/malheureuse *adj.* unhappy I-3
manche *f.* sleeve I-6
   chemise à manches courtes/longues *f.* short-/long-sleeved shirt I-6
manger *v.* to eat I-2
   salle à manger *f.* dining room I-8, II-P
manteau *m.* coat I-6
maquillage *m.* makeup II-2
marchand de journaux *m.* newsstand II-4
marché *m.* market I-4
   bon marché *adj.* inexpensive I-6
marcher *v.* to walk *(person)* I-5; to work *(thing)* II-3
mardi *m.* Tuesday I-2
mari *m.* husband I-3
mariage *m.* marriage; wedding *(ceremony)* I-6
marié(e) *adj.* married I-3
mariés *m., pl.* married couple I-6
   jeunes mariés *m., pl.* newlyweds I-6
marocain(e) *adj.* Moroccan I-1
marron *adj., inv.* (not for hair) brown I-3
mars *m.* March I-5
martiniquais(e) *adj.* from Martinique I-1
match *m.* game I-5
mathématiques (maths) *f., pl.* mathematics I-2
matin *m.* morning I-2
   ce matin *adv.* this morning I-2
   demain matin *adv.* tomorrow morning I-2
   hier matin *adv.* yesterday morning I-7
matinée *f.* morning I-2
mauvais(e) *adj.* bad I-3
   Il fait mauvais. The weather is bad. I-5

le/la plus mauvais(e) *super. adj.* the worst II-1
mayonnaise *f.* mayonnaise II-1
me/m' *pron., sing.* me; myself I-6
mec *m.* guy II-2
mécanicien *m.* mechanic II-3
mécanicienne *f.* mechanic II-3
méchant(e) *adj.* mean I-3
médecin *m.* doctor I-3
médicament (contre/pour) *m.* medication (against/for) II-2
meilleur(e) *comp. adj.* better II-1
   le/la meilleur(e) *super. adj.* the best II-1
membre *m.* member II-7
même *adj.* even I-5; same
-même(s) *pron.* -self/-selves I-6
menacé(e) *adj.* endangered II-6
   espèce menacée *f.* endangered species II-6
ménage *m.* housework I-8, II-P
   faire le ménage *v.* to do housework I-8, II-P
ménager/ménagère *adj.* household I-8, II-P
   appareil ménager *m.* household appliance I-8, II-P
   tâche ménagère *f.* household chore I-8, II-P
mention *f.* distinction II-5
menu *m.* menu II-1
mer *f.* sea I-7
Merci (beaucoup). Thank you (very much). I-1
mercredi *m.* Wednesday I-2
mère *f.* mother I-3
   belle-mère *f.* mother-in-law; stepmother I-3
mes *poss. adj., m., f., pl.* my I-3
message *m.* message II-5
   laisser un message *v.* to leave a message II-5
messagerie *f.* voicemail II-5
météo *f.* weather II-7
métier *m.* profession II-5
métro *m.* subway I-7
   station de métro *f.* subway station I-7
metteur en scène *m.* director *(of a play)* II-7
mettre *v.* to put, to place 6
   mettre la table to set the table I-8, II-P
meuble *m.* piece of furniture I-8, II-P
mexicain(e) *adj.* Mexican I-1
Mexique *m.* Mexico I-7
Miam! *interj.* Yum! I-5
micro-onde *m.* microwave oven I-8, II-P
   four à micro-ondes *m.* microwave oven I-8, II-P
midi *m.* noon I-2

Vocabulaire — French-English

après-midi *m.* afternoon I-2
mieux *comp. adv.* better II-1
   aimer mieux *v.* to prefer I-2
   le mieux *super. adv.* the best II-1
   se porter mieux *v.* to be doing better II-2
mille *m.* one thousand I-5
   cent mille *m.* one hundred thousand I-5
million, un *m.* one million I-5
   deux millions *m.* two million I-5
minuit *m.* midnight I-2
miroir *m.* mirror I-8, II-P
mis (mettre) *p.p.* put, placed I-6
mode *f.* fashion I-2
modeste *adj.* modest II-5
moi *disj. pron., sing.* I, me I-3; *pron. (attached to an imperative)* to me, to myself II-1
   Moi aussi. Me too. I-1
   Moi non plus. Me neither. I-2
moins *adv.* before ... (o'clock) I-2
moins (de) *adv.* less (of); fewer I-4
   le/la moins *super. adv. (used with verb or adverb)* the least II-1
   le moins de... *(used with noun to express quantity)* the least... II-6
   moins de... que... *(used with noun to express quantity)* less... than... II-6
mois *m.* month I-2
   ce mois-ci this month I-2
moment *m.* moment I-1
mon *poss. adj., m., sing.* my I-3
monde *m.* world I-7
moniteur *m.* monitor II-3
monnaie *f.* change, coins; money II-4
Monsieur *m.* Sir; Mr. I-1
montagne *f.* mountain I-4
monter *v.* to go up, to come up; to get in/on I-7
montre *f.* watch I-1
montrer (à) *v.* to show *(to someone)* I-6
morceau (de) *m.* piece, bit (of) I-4
mort *f.* death I-6
mort (mourir) *p.p., adj. (as past participle)* died; *(as adjective)* dead I-7
mot de passe *m.* password II-3
moteur *m.* engine II-3
mourir *v.* to die I-7
moutarde *f.* mustard II-1
moyen(ne) *adj.* medium I-3
   de taille moyenne of medium height I-3
MP3 *m.* MP3 II-3
mur *m.* wall I-8, II-P
musée *m.* museum I-4
faire les musées *v.* to go to museums II-7
musical(e) *adj.* musical II-7
   comédie musicale *f.* musical II-7
musicien(ne) *m., f.* musician I-3
musique: faire de la musique *v.* to play music II-7

N

nager *v.* to swim I-4
naïf/naïve *adj.* naïve I-3
naissance *f.* birth I-6
naître *v.* to be born I-7
nappe *f.* tablecloth II-1
nationalité *f.* nationality I-1
   Je suis de nationalité... I am of ... nationality. I-1
   Quelle est ta nationalité? *fam.* What is your nationality? I-1
   Quelle est votre nationalité? *fam., pl., form.* What is your nationality? I-1
nature *f.* nature II-6
naturel(le) *adj.* natural II-6
   ressource naturelle *f.* natural resource II-6
né (naître) *p.p., adj.* born I-7
ne/n' no, not I-1
   ne... aucun(e) none, not any II-4
   ne... jamais never, not ever II-4
   ne... ni... ni... neither... nor... II-4
   ne... pas no, not I-2
   ne... personne nobody, no one II-4
   ne... plus no more, not anymore II-4
   ne... que only II-4
   ne... rien nothing, not anything II-4
   N'est-ce pas? *(tag question)* Isn't it? I-2
nécessaire *adj.* necessary II-6
   Il est nécessaire que... It is necessary that... II-6
neiger *v.* to snow I-5
   Il neige. It is snowing. I-5
nerveusement *adv.* nervously I-8, II-P
nerveux/nerveuse *adj.* nervous I-3
nettoyer *v.* to clean I-5
neuf *m.* nine I-1
neuvième *adj.* ninth I-7
neveu *m.* nephew I-3
nez *m.* nose II-2
ni nor II-4
   ne... ni... ni... neither... nor II-4
nièce *f.* niece I-3
niveau *m.* level II-5
noir(e) *adj.* black I-3
non no I-2
   mais non (but) of course not; no I-2
nord *m.* north II-4
nos *poss. adj., m., f., pl.* our I-3
note *f. (academics)* grade I-2
notre *poss. adj., m., f., sing.* our I-3
nourriture *f.* food, sustenance II-1
nous *pron.* we I-1; us I-3; ourselves II-2
nouveau/nouvelle *adj.* new I-3
nouvelles *f., pl.* news II-7
novembre *m.* November I-5
nuage de pollution *m.* pollution cloud II-6
nuageux/nuageuse *adj.* cloudy I-5
   Le temps est nuageux. It is cloudy. I-5
nucléaire *adj.* nuclear II-6
   centrale nucléaire *f.* nuclear plant II-6
   énergie nucléaire *f.* nuclear energy II-6
nuit *f.* night I-2
   boîte de nuit *f.* nightclub I-4
nul(le) *adj.* useless I-2
numéro *m.* (telephone) number II-3
   composer un numéro *v.* to dial a number II-3
   recomposer un numéro *v.* to redial a number II-3

O

objet *m.* object I-1
obtenir *v.* to get, to obtain II-5
occupé(e) *adj.* busy I-1
octobre *m.* October I-5
œil (les yeux) *m.* eye (eyes) II-2
œuf *m.* egg II-1
œuvre *f.* artwork, piece of art II-7
   chef-d'œuvre *m.* masterpiece II-7
   hors-d'œuvre *m.* hors d'œuvre, starter II-1
offert (offrir) *p.p.* offered II-3
office du tourisme *m.* tourist office II-4
offrir *v.* to offer II-3
oignon *m.* onion II-1
oiseau *m.* bird I-3
olive *f.* olive II-1
   huile d'olive *f.* olive oil II-1
omelette *f.* omelette I-5
on *sub. pron., sing.* one (we) I-1
   on y va let's go II-2

Vocabulaire — French-English

oncle *m.* uncle I-3
onze *m.* eleven I-1
onzième *adj.* eleventh I-7
opéra *m.* opera II-7
optimiste *adj.* optimistic I-1
orageux/orageuse *adj.* stormy I-5
   Le temps est orageux. It is stormy. I-5
orange *adj. inv.* orange I-6; *f.* orange II-1
orchestre *m.* orchestra II-7
ordinateur *m.* computer I-1
ordonnance *f.* prescription II-2
ordures *f., pl.* trash II-6
   ramassage des ordures *m.* garbage collection II-6
oreille *f.* ear II-2
oreiller *m.* pillow I-8, II-P
organiser (une fête) *v.* to organize/to plan (a party) I-6
origine *f.* heritage I-1
   Je suis d'origine… I am of… heritage. I-1
orteil *m.* toe II-2
ou *or* I-3
où *adv., rel. pron.* where 4
ouais *adv.* yeah I-2
oublier (de) *v.* to forget (to do something) I-2
ouest *m.* west II-4
oui *adv.* yes I-2
ouvert (ouvrir) *p.p., adj. (as past participle)* opened; *(as adjective)* open II-3
ouvrier/ouvrière *m., f.* worker, laborer II-5
ouvrir *v.* to open II-3
ozone *m.* ozone II-6
   trou dans la couche d'ozone *m.* hole in the ozone layer II-6

P

page d'accueil *f.* home page II-3
pain (de campagne) *m.* (country-style) bread I-4
panne *f.* breakdown, malfunction II-3
   tomber en panne *v.* to break down II-3
pantalon *m., sing.* pants I-6
pantoufle *f.* slipper II-2
papeterie *f.* stationery store II-4
papier *m.* paper I-1
   corbeille à papier *f.* wastebasket I-1
   feuille de papier *f.* sheet of paper I-1
paquet cadeau *m.* wrapped gift I-6
par *prep.* by I-3
par jour/semaine/mois/an per day/week/month/year I-5
parapluie *m.* umbrella I-5
parc *m.* park I-4
parce que *conj.* because I-2
Pardon. Pardon (me). I-1
Pardon? What? I-4
pare-brise *m.* windshield II-3
pare-chocs *m.* bumper II-3
parents *m., pl.* parents I-3
paresseux/paresseuse *adj.* lazy I-3
parfait(e) *adj.* perfect I-4
parfois *adv.* sometimes I-5
parking *m.* parking lot II-3
parler (à) *v.* to speak (to) I-6
   parler (au téléphone) *v.* to speak (on the phone) I-2
partager *v.* to share I-2
partir *v.* to leave I-5
   partir en vacances *v.* to go on vacation I-7
pas (de) *adv.* no, none II-4
   ne… pas no, not I-2
   pas de problème no problem II-4
   pas du tout not at all I-2
   pas encore not yet I-8, II-P
   Pas mal. Not badly. I-1
passager/passagère *m., f.* passenger I-7
passeport *m.* passport I-7
passer *v.* to pass by; to spend time I-7
   passer chez quelqu'un *v.* to stop by someone's house I-4
   passer l'aspirateur *v.* to vacuum I-8, II-P
   passer un examen *v.* to take an exam I-2
passe-temps *m.* pastime, hobby I-5
pâté (de campagne) *m.* pâté, meat spread II-1
pâtes *f., pl.* pasta II-1
patiemment *adv.* patiently I-8, II-P
patient(e) *m., f.* patient II-2; *adj.* patient I-1
patienter *v.* to wait (on the phone), to be on hold II-5
patiner *v.* to skate I-4
pâtisserie *f.* pastry shop, bakery, pastry II-1
patron(ne) *m., f.* boss II-5
pauvre *adj.* poor I-3
payé (payer) *p.p., adj.* paid II-5
   être bien/mal payé(e) *v.* to be well/badly paid II-5
payer *v.* to pay I-5
   payer avec une carte de crédit *v.* to pay with a credit card II-4
payer en liquide *v.* to pay in cash II-4
payer par chèque *v.* to pay by check II-4
pays *m.* country I-7
peau *f.* skin II-2
pêche *f.* fishing I-5; peach II-1
   aller à la pêche *v.* to go fishing I-5
peigne *m.* comb II-2
peintre/femme peintre *m., f.* painter II-7
peinture *f.* painting II-7
pendant (que) *prep.* during, while I-7
pendant *(with time expression) prep.* for II-1
pénible *adj.* tiresome I-3
penser (que) *v.* to think (that) I-2
   ne pas penser que… to not think that… II-7
   Qu'en penses-tu? What do you think about that? II-6
perdre *v.* to lose I-6
   perdre son temps *v.* to lose/to waste time I-6
perdu *p.p., adj.* lost II-4
   être perdu(e) to be lost II-4
père *m.* father I-3
   beau-père *m.* father-in-law; stepfather I-3
permettre (de) *v.* to allow (to do something) I-6
permis *m.* permit; license II-3
   permis de conduire *m.* driver's license II-3
permis (permettre) *p.p., adj.* permitted, allowed I-6
personnage (principal) *m.* (main) character II-7
personne *f.* person I-1; *pron.* no one II-4
   ne… personne nobody, no one II-4
pessimiste *adj.* pessimistic I-1
petit(e) *adj.* small I-3; short (stature) I-3
   petit(e) ami(e) *m., f.* boyfriend/girlfriend I-1
petit-déjeuner *m.* breakfast II-1
petite-fille *f.* granddaughter I-3
petit-fils *m.* grandson I-3
petits-enfants *m., pl.* grandchildren I-3
petits pois *m., pl.* peas II-1
peu (de) *adv.* little; not much (of) I-2
peur *f.* fear I-2
   avoir peur (de/que) *v.* to be afraid (of/that) I-2
peut-être *adv.* maybe, perhaps I-2
phares *m., pl.* headlights II-3
pharmacie *f.* pharmacy II-2

Vocabulaire — French-English

pharmacien(ne) *m., f.* pharmacist II-2
philosophie *f.* philosophy I-2
photo(graphie) *f.* photo (graph) I-3
physique *f.* physics I-2
piano *m.* piano II-7
pièce *f.* room I-8, II-P
pièce de théâtre *f.* play II-7
pièces de monnaie *f., pl.* change II-4
pied *m.* foot II-2
pierre *f.* stone II-6
pilule *f.* pill II-2
pique-nique *m.* picnic II-6
piqûre *f.* shot, injection II-2
  faire une piqûre *v.* to give a shot II-2
pire *comp. adj.* worse II-1
  le/la pire *super. adj.* the worst II-1
piscine *f.* pool I-4
placard *m.* closet; cupboard I-8, II-P
place *f.* square; place I-4; *f.* seat II-7
plage *f.* beach I-7
plaisir *m.* pleasure, enjoyment II-5
  faire plaisir à quelqu'un *v.* to please someone II-5
plan *m.* map I-7
  utiliser un plan *v.* to use a map I-7
planche à voile *f.* windsurfing I-5
  faire de la planche à voile *v.* to go windsurfing I-5
planète *f.* planet II-6
  sauver la planète *v.* to save the planet II-6
plante *f.* plant II-6
plastique *m.* plastic II-6
  emballage en plastique *m.* plastic wrapping/packaging II-6
plat (principal) *m.* (main) dish II-1
plein air *m.* outdoor, open-air II-6
pleine forme *f.* good shape, good state of health II-2
  être en pleine forme *v.* to be in good shape II-2
pleurer *v.* to cry
pleuvoir *v.* to rain I-5
  Il pleut. It is raining. I-5
plombier *m.* plumber II-5
plu (pleuvoir) *p.p.* rained I-6
pluie acide *f.* acid rain II-6
plus *adv.* (used in comparatives, superlatives, and expressions of quantity) more I-4
  le/la plus ... *super. adv.* (used with adjective) the most II-1
  le/la plus mauvais(e) *super. adj.* the worst II-1

le plus *super. adv.* (used with verb or adverb) the most II-1
le plus de... (used with noun to express quantity) the most... II-6
le plus mal *super. adv.* the worst II-1
plus... que (used with adjective) more... than II-1
plus de more of I-4
plus de... que (used with noun to express quantity) more... than II-6
plus mal *comp. adv.* worse II-1
plus mauvais(e) *comp. adj.* worse II-1
plus *adv.* no more, not anymore II-4
  ne... plus no more, not anymore II-4
plusieurs *adj.* several I-4
plutôt *adv.* rather I-2
pneu (crevé) *m.* (flat) tire II-3
  vérifier la pression des pneus *v.* to check the tire pressure II-3
poème *m.* poem II-7
poète/poétesse *m., f.* poet II-7
point *m.* (punctuation mark) period II-3
poire *f.* pear II-1
poisson *m.* fish I-3
poissonnerie *f.* fish shop II-1
poitrine *f.* chest II-2
poivre *m.* (spice) pepper II-1
poivron *m.* (vegetable) pepper II-1
poli(e) *adj.* polite I-1
police *f.* police II-3
  agent de police *m.* police officer II-3
  commissariat de police *m.* police station II-4
policier *m.* police officer II-3
  film policier *m.* detective film II-7
policière *f.* police officer II-3
poliment *adv.* politely I-8, II-P
politique *adj.* political I-2
  femme politique *f.* politician II-5
  homme politique *m.* politician II-5
  sciences politiques (sciences po) *f., pl.* political science I-2
polluer *v.* to pollute II-6
pollution *f.* pollution II-6
  nuage de pollution *m.* pollution cloud II-6
pomme *f.* apple II-1
pomme de terre *f.* potato II-1
pompier/femme pompier *m., f.* firefighter II-5
pont *m.* bridge II-4

population croissante *f.* growing population II-6
porc *m.* pork II-1
portable *m.* cell phone II-3
porte *f.* door I-1
porter *v.* to wear I-6
portière *f.* car door II-3
portrait *m.* portrait I-5
poser une question (à) *v.* to ask (someone) a question I-6
posséder *v.* to possess, to own I-5
possible *adj.* possible II-7
  Il est possible que... It is possible that... II-6
poste *f.* postal service; post office II-4
  bureau de poste *m.* post office II-4
poste *m.* position II-5
poste de télévision *m.* television set II-3
poster une lettre *v.* to mail a letter II-4
postuler *v.* to apply II-5
poulet *m.* chicken II-1
pour *prep.* for I-5
  pour qui? for whom? I-4
  pour rien for no reason I-4
  pour que so that II-7
pourboire *m.* tip I-4
  laisser un pourboire *v.* to leave a tip I-4
pourquoi? *adv.* why? I-2
poussière *f.* dust I-8, II-P
  enlever/faire la poussière *v.* to dust I-8, II-P
pouvoir *v.* to be able to; can II-1
pratiquer *v.* to play regularly, to practice I-5
préféré(e) *adj.* favorite, preferred I-2
préférer (que) *v.* to prefer (that) I-5
premier *m.* the first (day of the month) I-5
  C'est le 1er (premier) octobre. It is October first. I-5
premier/première *adj.* first I-2
prendre *v.* to take I-4; to have I-4
  prendre sa retraite *v.* to retire I-6
  prendre un train/avion/ taxi/autobus/bateau *v.* to take a train/plane/taxi/bus/boat I-7
  prendre un congé *v.* to take time off II-5
  prendre une douche *v.* to take a shower II-2
  prendre (un) rendez-vous *v.* to make an appointment II-5
préparer *v.* to prepare (for) I-2

Vocabulaire

French-English

près (de) *prep.* close (to), near I-3
  tout près (de) very close (to) II-4
présenter *v.* to present, to introduce II-7
  Je te présente… *fam.* I would like to introduce… to you. I-1
  Je vous présente… *fam., form.* I would like to introduce… to you. I-1
préservation *f.* protection II-6
préserver *v.* to preserve II-6
presque *adv.* almost I-2
pressé(e) *adj.* hurried II-1
pression *f.* pressure II-3
  vérifier la pression des pneus to check the tire pressure II-3
prêt(e) *adj.* ready I-3
prêter (à) *v.* to lend (*to someone*) I-6
prévenir l'incendie *v.* to prevent a fire II-6
principal(e) *adj.* main, principal II-1
  personnage principal *m.* main character II-7
  plat principal *m.* main dish II-1
printemps *m.* spring I-5
  au printemps in the spring I-5
pris (prendre) *p.p., adj.* taken I-6
prix *m.* price I-4
problème *m.* problem I-1
prochain(e) *adj.* next I-2
produire *v.* to produce I-6
produit *m.* product II-6
produit (produire) *p.p., adj.* produced I-6
professeur *m.* teacher, professor I-1
profession (exigeante) *f.* (demanding) profession II-5
professionnel(le) *adj.* professional II-5
  expérience professionnelle *f.* professional experience II-5
profiter (de) *v.* to take advantage (of); to enjoy II-7
programme *m.* program II-7
projet *m.* project II-5
  faire des projets *v.* to make plans I-5
promenade *f.* walk, stroll I-5
  faire une promenade *v.* to go for a walk I-5
promettre *v.* to promise I-6
promis (promettre) *p.p., adj.* promised I-6
promotion *f.* promotion II-5
proposer (que) *v.* to propose (that) II-6
  proposer une solution *v.* to propose a solution II-6
propre *adj.* clean I-8, II-P

propriétaire *m., f.* owner I-8, II-P; landlord/landlady I-8, II-P
protection *f.* protection II-6
protéger *v.* to protect 5
psychologie *f.* psychology I-2
psychologique *adj.* psychological II-7
psychologue *m., f.* psychologist II-5
pu (pouvoir) *p.p.* (*used with infinitive*) was able to 9
publicité (pub) *f.* advertisement II-7
publier *v.* to publish II-7
puis *adv.* then I-7
pull *m.* sweater I-6
pur(e) *adj.* pure II-6

Q

quand *adv.* when I-4
  C'est quand l'anniversaire de … ? When is …'s birthday? I-5
  C'est quand ton/votre anniversaire? When is your birthday? I-5
quarante *m.* forty I-1
quart *m.* quarter I-2
  et quart a quarter after… (o'clock) I-2
quartier *m.* area, neighborhood I-8, II-P
quatorze *m.* fourteen I-1
quatre *m.* four I-1
quatre-vingts *m.* eighty I-3
quatre-vingt-dix *m.* ninety I-3
quatrième *adj.* fourth I-7
que/qu' *rel. pron.* that; which II-3; *conj.* than II-1, II-6
  plus/moins … que (*used with adjective*) more/less … than II-1
  plus/moins de … que (*used with noun to express quantity*) more/less … than II-6
que/qu'…? *interr. pron.* what? I-4
  Qu'en penses-tu? What do you think about that? II-6
  Qu'est-ce que c'est? What is it? I-1
  Qu'est-ce qu'il y a? What is it?; What's wrong? I-1
que *adv.* only II-4
  ne… que only II-4
québécois(e) *adj.* from Quebec I-1
quel(le)(s)? *interr. adj.* which? I-4; what? I-4
  À quelle heure? What time?; When? I-2
  Quel jour sommes-nous? What day is it? I-2
  Quelle est la date? What is the date? I-5

Quelle est ta nationalité? *fam.* What is your nationality? I-1
Quelle est votre nationalité? *form.* What is your nationality? I-1
Quelle heure avez-vous? *form.* What time do you have? I-2
Quelle heure est-il? What time is it? I-2
Quelle température fait-il? (*weather*) What is the temperature? I-5
Quel temps fait-il? What is the weather like? I-5
quelqu'un *pron.* someone II-4
quelque chose *m.* something; anything I-4
  Quelque chose ne va pas. Something's not right. I-5
quelquefois *adv.* sometimes I-8, II-P
quelques *adj.* some I-4
question *f.* question I-6
  poser une question (à) to ask (*someone*) a question I-6
queue *f.* line II-4
  faire la queue *v.* to wait in line II-4
qui? *interr. pron.* who? I-4; whom? I-4; *rel. pron.* who, that II-3
  à qui? to whom? I-4
  avec qui? with whom? I-4
  C'est de la part de qui? On behalf of whom? II-5
  Qui est à l'appareil? Who's calling, please? II-5
  Qui est-ce? Who is it? I-1
quinze *m.* fifteen I-1
quitter (la maison) *v.* to leave (the house) I-4
  Ne quittez pas. Please hold. II-5
quoi? *interr. pron.* what? I-1
  Il n'y a pas de quoi. It's nothing.; You're welcome. I-1
  quoi que ce soit whatever it may be II-5

R

raccrocher *v.* to hang up II-5
radio *f.* radio II-7
  à la radio on the radio II-7
raide *adj.* straight I-3
raison *f.* reason; right I-2
  avoir raison *v.* to be right I-2
ramassage des ordures *m.* garbage collection II-6
randonnée *f.* hike I-5
  faire une randonnée *v.* to go for a hike I-5
ranger *v.* to tidy up, to put away I-8, II-P

Vocabulaire — French-English

rapide *adj.* fast I-3
rapidement *adv.* rapidly I-8, II-P
rarement *adv.* rarely I-5
rasoir *m.* razor II-2
ravissant(e) *adj.* beautiful; delightful II-5
réalisateur/réalisatrice *m., f.* director (*of a movie*) II-7
récent(e) *adj.* recent II-7
réception *f.* reception desk I-7
recevoir *v.* to receive II-4
réchauffement de la Terre *m.* global warming II-6
rechercher *v.* to search for, to look for II-5
recommandation *f.* recommendation II-5
recommander (que) *v.* to recommend (that) II-6
recomposer (un numéro) *v.* to redial (a number) II-3
reconnaître *v.* to recognize I-8, II-P
reconnu (reconnaître) *p.p., adj.* recognized I-8, II-P
reçu *m.* receipt II-4
reçu (recevoir) *p.p., adj.* received I-7
   être reçu(e) à un examen to pass an exam I-2
recyclage *m.* recycling II-6
recycler *v.* to recycle II-6
redémarrer *v.* to restart, to start again II-3
réduire *v.* to reduce I-6
réduit (réduire) *p.p., adj.* reduced I-6
référence *f.* reference II-5
réfléchir (à) *v.* to think (about), to reflect (on) I-4
refuser (de) *v.* to refuse (*to do something*) II-3
regarder *v.* to watch I-2
   Ça ne nous regarde pas. That has nothing to do with us.; That is none of our business. II-6
régime *m.* diet II-2
   être au régime *v.* to be on a diet II-1
région *f.* region II-6
regretter (que) *v.* to regret (that) II-6
remplir (un formulaire) *v.* to fill out (a form) II-4
rencontrer *v.* to meet I-2
rendez-vous *m.* date; appointment I-6
   prendre (un) rendez-vous *v.* to make an appointment II-5
rendre (à) *v.* to give back, to return (to) I-6
   rendre visite (à) *v.* to visit I-6

rentrer (à la maison) *v.* to return (home) I-2
   rentrer (dans) *v.* to hit II-3
renvoyer *v.* to dismiss, to let go II-5
réparer *v.* to repair II-3
repartir *v.* to go back II-7
repas *m.* meal II-1
repasser *v.* to take again II-7
   repasser (le linge) *v.* to iron (the laundry) I-8, II-P
   fer à repasser *m.* iron I-8, II-P
répéter *v.* to repeat; to rehearse I-5
répondeur (téléphonique) *m.* answering machine II-3
répondre (à) *v.* to respond, to answer (to) I-6
réseau (social) *m.* (social) network II-3
réservation *f.* reservation I-7
   annuler une réservation *v.* to cancel a reservation I-7
réservé(e) *adj.* reserved I-1
réserver *v.* to reserve I-7
réservoir d'essence *m.* gas tank II-3
résidence universitaire *f.* dorm I-8, II-P
ressource naturelle *f.* natural resource II-6
restaurant *m.* restaurant I-4
   restaurant universitaire (resto U) *m.* university cafeteria I-2
rester *v.* to stay I-7
résultat *m.* result I-2
retenir *v.* to keep, to retain II-1
retirer (de l'argent) *v.* to withdraw (money) II-4
retourner *v.* to return I-7
retraite *f.* retirement I-6
   prendre sa retraite *v.* to retire I-6
retraité(e) *m., f.* retired person II-5
retrouver *v.* to find (again); to meet up with I-2
rétroviseur *m.* rear-view mirror II-3
réunion *f.* meeting II-5
réussir (à) *v.* to succeed (*in doing something*) I-4
réussite *f.* success II-5
réveil *m.* alarm clock II-2
revenir *v.* to come back II-1
rêver (de) *v.* to dream about II-3
revoir *v.* to see again II-7
   Au revoir. Good-bye. I-1
revu (revoir) *p.p.* seen again II-7
rez-de-chaussée *m.* ground floor I-7

rhume *m.* cold II-2
ri (rire) *p.p.* laughed I-6
rideau *m.* curtain I-8, II-P
rien *m.* nothing II-4
   De rien. You're welcome. I-1
   ne… rien nothing, not anything II-4
   ne servir à rien *v.* to be good for nothing II-1
rire *v.* to laugh I-6
rivière *f.* river II-6
riz *m.* rice II-1
robe *f.* dress I-6
rôle *m.* role II-6
   jouer un rôle *v.* to play a role II-7
roman *m.* novel II-7
rose *adj.* pink I-6
roue (de secours) *f.* (emergency) tire II-3
rouge *adj.* red I-6
rouler en voiture *v.* to ride in a car I-7
rue *f.* street II-3
   suivre une rue *v.* to follow a street II-4

S

s'adorer *v.* to adore one another II-3
s'aider *v.* to help one another II-3
s'aimer (bien) *v.* to love (like) one another II-3
s'allumer *v.* to light up II-3
s'amuser *v.* to play; to have fun II-2
   s'amuser à *v.* to pass time by II-3
s'apercevoir *v.* to notice; to realize II-4
s'appeler *v.* to be named, to be called II-2
   Comment t'appelles-tu? *fam.* What is your name? I-1
   Comment vous appelez-vous? *form.* What is your name? I-1
   Je m'appelle… My name is… I-1
s'arrêter *v.* to stop II-2
s'asseoir *v.* to sit down II-2
sa *poss. adj., f., sing.* his; her; its I-3
sac *m.* bag I-1
   sac à dos *m.* backpack I-1
   sac à main *m.* purse, handbag I-6
sain(e) *adj.* healthy II-2
saison *f.* season I-5
salade *f.* salad II-1
salaire (élevé/modeste) *m.* (high/low) salary II-5
   augmentation de salaire *f.* raise in salary II-5

Vocabulaire — French-English

sale *adj.* dirty I-8, II-P
salir *v.* to soil, to make dirty I-8, II-P
salle *f.* room I-8, II-P
  salle à manger *f.* dining room I-8, II-P
  salle de bains *f.* bathroom I-8, II-P
  salle de classe *f.* classroom I-1
  salle de séjour *f.* living/family room I-8, II-P
salon *m.* formal living room, sitting room I-8, II-P
  salon de beauté *m.* beauty salon II-4
Salut! Hi!; Bye! I-1
samedi *m.* Saturday I-2
sandwich *m.* sandwich I-4
sans *prep.* without I-8, II-P
  sans que *conj.* without II-7
santé *f.* health II-2
  être en bonne/mauvaise santé *v.* to be in good/bad health II-2
saucisse *f.* sausage II-1
sauvegarder *v.* to save II-3
sauver (la planète) *v.* to save (the planet) II-6
sauvetage des habitats *m.* habitat preservation II-6
savoir *v.* to know (*facts*), to know how to do something I-8, II-P
  savoir (que) *v.* to know (that) II-7
  Je n'en sais rien. I don't know anything about it. II-6
savon *m.* soap II-2
sciences *f., pl.* science I-2
  sciences politiques (sciences po) *f., pl.* political science I-2
sculpture *f.* sculpture II-7
sculpteur/femme sculpteur *m., f.* sculptor II-7
se/s' *pron., sing., pl.* (*used with reflexive verb*) himself; herself; itself; 10 (*used with reciprocal verb*) each other II-3
séance *f.* show; screening II-7
se blesser *v.* to hurt oneself II-2
se brosser (les cheveux/les dents) *v.* to brush one's (hair/teeth) II-1
se casser *v.* to break II-2
sèche-linge *m.* clothes dryer I-8, II-P
se coiffer *v.* to do one's hair II-2
se connaître *v.* to know one another II-3
se coucher *v.* to go to bed II-2
secours *m.* help II-3
  Au secours! Help! II-3
s'écrire *v.* to write one another II-3

sécurité *f.* security; safety
  attacher sa ceinture de sécurité *v.* to buckle one's seatbelt II-3
se dépêcher *v.* to hurry II-2
se déplacer *v.* to move, to change location II-4
se déshabiller *v.* to undress II-2
se détendre *v.* to relax II-2
se dire *v.* to tell one another II-3
se disputer (avec) *v.* to argue (with) II-2
se donner *v.* to give one another II-3
se fouler (la cheville) *v.* to twist/to sprain one's (ankle) II-2
se garer *v.* to park II-3
seize *m.* sixteen I-1
séjour *m.* stay I-7
  faire un séjour *v.* to spend time (*somewhere*) I-7
  salle de séjour *f.* living room I-8, II-P
sel *m.* salt II-1
se laver (les mains) *v.* to wash oneself (one's hands) II-2
se lever *v.* to get up, to get out of bed II-2
semaine *f.* week I-2
  cette semaine this week I-2
s'embrasser *v.* to kiss one another II-3
se maquiller *v.* to put on makeup II-2
se mettre *v.* to put (*something*) on (*yourself*) II-2
  se mettre à *v.* to begin to II-2
  se mettre en colère *v.* to become angry II-2
s'endormir *v.* to fall asleep, to go to sleep II-2
s'énerver *v.* to get worked up, to become upset II-2
sénégalais(e) *adj.* Senegalese I-1
s'ennuyer *v.* to get bored II-2
s'entendre bien (avec) *v.* to get along well (with one another) II-2
sentier *m.* path II-6
sentir *v.* to feel; to smell; to sense I-5
séparé(e) *adj.* separated I-3
se parler *v.* to speak to one another II-3
se porter mal/mieux *v.* to be ill/better II-2
se préparer (à) *v.* to get ready; to prepare (*to do something*) II-2
se promener *v.* to take a walk II-2
sept *m.* seven I-1
septembre *m.* September I-5
septième *adj.* seventh I-7
se quitter *v.* to leave one another II-3

se raser *v.* to shave oneself II-2
se réconcilier *v.* to make up II-7
se regarder *v.* to look at oneself; to look at each other II-2
se relever *v.* to get up again II-2
se rencontrer *v.* to meet one another, to make each other's acquaintance II-3
se rendre compte *v.* to realize II-2
se reposer *v.* to rest II-2
se retrouver *v.* to meet one another (*as planned*) II-3
se réveiller *v.* to wake up II-2
se sécher *v.* to dry oneself II-2
se sentir *v.* to feel II-2
sérieux/sérieuse *adj.* serious I-3
serpent *m.* snake II-6
serre *f.* greenhouse II-6
  effet de serre *m.* greenhouse effect II-6
serré(e) *adj.* tight I-6
serveur/serveuse *m., f.* server I-4
serviette *f.* napkin II-1
  serviette (de bain) *f.* (bath) towel II-2
servir *v.* to serve I-5
ses *poss. adj., m., f., pl.* his; her; its I-3
se souvenir (de) *v.* to remember II-2
se téléphoner *v.* to phone one another II-3
se tourner *v.* to turn (oneself) around II-2
se tromper (de) *v.* to be mistaken (about) II-2
se trouver *v.* to be located II-2
seulement *adv.* only I-8, II-P
s'habiller *v.* to dress II-2
shampooing *m.* shampoo II-2
shopping *m.* shopping I-7
  faire du shopping *v.* to go shopping I-7
short *m., sing.* shorts I-6
si *conj.* if II-5
si *adv.* (*when contradicting a negative statement or question*) yes I-2
signer *v.* to sign II-4
S'il te plaît. *fam.* Please. I-1
S'il vous plaît. *form.* Please. I-1
sincère *adj.* sincere I-1
s'inquiéter *v.* to worry II-2
s'intéresser (à) *v.* to be interested (in) II-2
site Internet/web *m.* web site II-3
six *m.* six I-1
sixième *adj.* sixth I-7
ski *m.* skiing I-5
  faire du ski *v.* to go skiing I-5
  station de ski *f.* ski resort I-7
skier *v.* to ski I-5

Vocabulaire — French-English

smartphone *m.* smartphone II-3
SMS *m.* text message II-3
s'occuper (de) *v.* to take care (*of something*), to see to II-2
sociable *adj.* sociable I-1
sociologie *f.* sociology I-1
sœur *f.* sister I-3
  belle-sœur *f.* sister-in-law I-3
  demi-sœur *f.* half-sister, stepsister I-3
soie *f.* silk II-4
soif *f.* thirst I-4
  avoir soif *v.* to be thirsty I-4
soir *m.* evening I-2
  ce soir *adv.* this evening I-2
  demain soir *adv.* tomorrow evening I-2
  du soir *adv.* in the evening I-2
  hier soir *adv.* yesterday evening I-7
soirée *f.* evening I-2
sois (être) *imp. v.* be I-2
soixante *m.* sixty I-1
soixante-dix *m.* seventy I-3
solaire *adj.* solar II-6
  énergie solaire *f.* solar energy II-6
soldes *f., pl.* sales I-6
soleil *m.* sun I-5
  Il fait (du) soleil. It is sunny. I-5
solution *f.* solution II-6
  proposer une solution *v.* to propose a solution II-6
sommeil *m.* sleep I-2
  avoir sommeil *v.* to be sleepy I-2
son *poss. adj., m., sing.* his; her; its I-3
sonner *v.* to ring II-3
s'orienter *v.* to get one's bearings II-4
sorte *f.* sort, kind II-7
sortie *f.* exit I-7
sortir *v.* to go out, to leave I-5; to take out I-8, II-P
  sortir la/les poubelle(s) *v.* to take out the trash I-8, II-P
soudain *adv.* suddenly I-8, II-P
souffrir *v.* to suffer II-3
souffert (souffrir) *p.p.* suffered II-3
souhaiter (que) *v.* to wish (that) II-6
soupe *f.* soup I-4
  cuillère à soupe *f.* soupspoon II-1
sourire *v.* to smile I-6; *m.* smile II-4
souris *f.* mouse II-3
sous *prep.* under I-3
sous-sol *m.* basement I-8, II-P
sous-vêtement *m.* underwear I-6
souvent *adv.* often I-5
soyez (être) *imp. v.* be I-7
soyons (être) *imp. v.* let's be I-7
spécialiste *m., f.* specialist II-5
spectacle *m.* show I-5
spectateur/spectatrice *m., f.* spectator II-7
sport *m.* sport(s) I-5
  faire du sport *v.* to do sports I-5
sportif/sportive *adj.* athletic I-3
stade *m.* stadium I-5
stage *m.* internship; professional training II-5
station (de métro) *f.* (subway) station I-7
station de ski *f.* ski resort I-7
station-service *f.* service station II-3
statue *f.* statue II-4
steak *m.* steak II-1
studio *m.* studio (*apartment*) I-8, II-P
stylisme *m.* **de mode** *f.* fashion design I-2
stylo *m.* pen I-1
su (savoir) *p.p.* known I-8, II-P
sucre *m.* sugar I-4
sud *m.* south II-4
suggérer (que) *v.* to suggest (that) II-6
sujet *m.* subject II-6
  au sujet de on the subject of; about II-6
suisse *adj.* Swiss I-1
Suisse *f.* Switzerland I-7
suivre (un chemin/une rue/ un boulevard) *v.* to follow (a path/a street/a boulevard) II-4
supermarché *m.* supermarket II-1
sur *prep.* on I-3
sûr(e) *adj.* sure, certain II-1
  bien sûr of course I-2
  Il est sûr que… It is sure that… II-7
  Il n'est pas sûr que… It is not sure that… II-7
surfer sur Internet *v.* to surf the Internet II-1
surpopulation *f.* overpopulation II-6
surpris (surprendre) *p.p., adj.* surprised I-6
  être surpris(e) que… *v.* to be surprised that… II-6
  faire une surprise à quelqu'un *v.* to surprise someone I-6
surtout *adv.* especially; above all I-2
sympa(thique) *adj.* nice I-1
symptôme *m.* symptom II-2
syndicat *m.* (*trade*) union II-5

T

ta *poss. adj., f., sing.* your I-3
table *f.* table I-1
  À table! Let's eat! Food is ready! II-1
  débarrasser la table *v.* to clear the table I-8, II-P
  mettre la table *v.* to set the table I-8, II-P
tableau *m.* blackboard; picture I-1; *m.* painting II-7
tablette (tactile) *f.* tablet computer II-3
tâche ménagère *f.* household chore I-8, II-P
taille *f.* size; waist I-6
  de taille moyenne of medium height I-3
tailleur *m.* (*woman's*) suit; tailor I-6
tante *f.* aunt I-3
tapis *m.* rug I-8, II-P
tard *adv.* late I-2
  À plus tard. See you later. I-1
tarte *f.* pie; tart I-8, II-P
tasse (de) *f.* cup (of) I-4
taxi *m.* taxi I-7
  prendre un taxi *v.* to take a taxi I-7
te/t' *pron., sing., fam.* you I-7; yourself II-2
tee-shirt *m.* tee shirt I-6
télécarte *f.* phone card II-5
télécharger *v.* to download II-3
télécommande *f.* remote control II-3
téléphone *m.* telephone I-2
  parler au téléphone *v.* to speak on the phone I-2
téléphoner (à) *v.* to telephone (*someone*) I-2
téléphonique *adj.* (*related to the*) telephone II-4
  cabine téléphonique *f.* phone booth II-4
télévision *f.* television I-1
  à la télé(vision) on television II-7
  chaîne (de télévision) *f.* television channel II-3
tellement *adv.* so much I-2
  Je n'aime pas tellement… I don't like… very much. I-2
température *f.* temperature I-5
  Quelle température fait-il? What is the temperature? I-5
temps *m., sing.* weather I-5
  Il fait un temps épouvantable. The weather is dreadful. I-5
  Le temps est nuageux. It is cloudy. I-5
  Le temps est orageux. It is stormy. I-5

deux cent onze **211**

Vocabulaire — French-English

Quel temps fait-il? What is the weather like? I-5
temps *m., sing.* time I-5
  de temps en temps *adv.* from time to time I-8, II-P
  emploi à mi-temps/à temps partiel *m.* part-time job II-5
  emploi à plein temps *m.* full-time job II-5
  temps libre *m.* free time I-5
Tenez! (tenir) *imp. v.* Here! II-1
tenir *v.* to hold II-1
tennis *m.* tennis I-5
terrasse (de café) *f.* (café) terrace I-4
Terre *f.* Earth II-6
  réchauffement de la Terre *m.* global warming II-6
tes *poss. adj., m., f., pl.* your I-3
tête *f.* head II-2
texto *m.* text message II-3
thé *m.* tea I-4
théâtre *m.* theater II-7
thon *m.* tuna II-1
ticket de bus/métro *m.* bus/subway ticket I-7
Tiens! (tenir) *imp. v.* Here! II-1
timbre *m.* stamp II-4
timide *adj.* shy I-1
tiret *m. (punctuation mark)* dash; hyphen II-3
tiroir *m.* drawer I-8, II-P
toi *disj. pron., sing., fam.* you I-3; *refl. pron., sing., fam. (attached to imperative)* yourself II-2
  toi non plus you neither I-2
toilette *f.* washing up, grooming II-2
  faire sa toilette to wash up II-2
toilettes *f., pl.* restroom(s) I-8, II-P
tomate *f.* tomato II-1
tomber *v.* to fall I-7
  tomber amoureux/amoureuse *v.* to fall in love I-6
  tomber en panne *v.* to break down II-3
  tomber/être malade *v.* to get/be sick II-2
  tomber sur quelqu'un *v.* to run into someone I-7
ton *poss. adj., m., sing.* your I-3
tort *m.* wrong; harm I-2
  avoir tort *v.* to be wrong I-2
tôt *adv.* early I-2
toujours *adv.* always I-8, II-P
tour *m.* tour I-5
  faire un tour (en voiture) *v.* to go for a walk (drive) I-5
tourisme *m.* tourism II-4
  office du tourisme *m.* tourist office II-4
tourner *v.* to turn II-4

tousser *v.* to cough II-2
tout *m., sing.* all I-4
  tous les *(used before noun)* all the... I-4
  tous les jours *adv.* every day I-8, II-P
  toute la *f., sing. (used before noun)* all the... I-4
  toutes les *f., pl. (used before noun)* all the... I-4
  tout le *m., sing. (used before noun)* all the... I-4
  tout le monde everyone II-1
tout(e) *adv. (before adjective or adverb)* very, really I-3
  À tout à l'heure. See you later. I-1
  tout à coup suddenly I-7
  tout à fait absolutely; completely II-4
  tout de suite right away I-7
  tout droit straight ahead II-4
  tout d'un coup *adv.* all of a sudden I-8, II-P
  tout près (de) really close by, really close (to) I-3
toxique *adj.* toxic II-6
  déchets toxiques *m., pl.* toxic waste II-6
trac *m.* stage fright II-5
traduire *v.* to translate I-6
traduit (traduire) *p.p., adj.* translated I-6
tragédie *f.* tragedy II-7
train *m.* train I-7
tranche *f.* slice II-1
tranquille *adj.* calm, serene II-2
  laisser tranquille *v.* to leave alone II-2
travail *m.* work II-4
  chercher un/du travail *v.* to look for work II-4
  trouver un/du travail *v.* to find a job II-5
travailler *v.* to work I-2
travailleur/travailleuse *adj.* hard-working I-3
traverser *v.* to cross II-4
treize *m.* thirteen I-1
trente *m.* thirty I-1
très *adv. (before adjective or adverb)* very, really I-8, II-P
  Très bien. Very well. I-1
triste *adj.* sad I-3
  être triste que... *v.* to be sad that... II-6
trois *m.* three I-1
troisième *adj.* third 7
trop (de) *adv.* too many/much (of) I-4
tropical(e) *adj.* tropical II-6
  forêt tropicale *f.* tropical forest II-6

trou (dans la couche d'ozone) *m.* hole (in the ozone layer) II-6
troupe *f.* company, troupe II-7
trouver *v.* to find; to think I-2
  trouver un/du travail *v.* to find a job II-5
truc *m.* thing I-7
tu *sub. pron., sing., fam.* you I-1

U

un *m. (number)* one I-1
un(e) *indef. art.* a; an I-1
universitaire *adj. (related to the)* university I-1
  restaurant universitaire (resto U) *m.* university cafeteria I-2
université *f.* university I-1
urgences *f., pl.* emergency room II-2
  aller aux urgences *v.* to go to the emergency room II-2
usine *f.* factory II-6
utile *adj.* useful I-2
utiliser (un plan) *v.* use (a map) I-7

V

vacances *f., pl.* vacation I-7
  partir en vacances *v.* to go on vacation I-7
vache *f.* cow II-6
vaisselle *f.* dishes I-8, II-P
  faire la vaisselle *v.* to do the dishes I-8, II-P
  lave-vaisselle *m.* dishwasher I-8, II-P
valise *f.* suitcase I-7
  faire les valises *v.* to pack one's bags I-7
vallée *f.* valley II-6
variétés *f., pl.* popular music II-7
vaut (valoir) *v.*
  Il vaut mieux que It is better that II-6
vélo *m.* bicycle I-5
  faire du vélo *v.* to go bike riding I-5
velours *m.* velvet II-4
vendeur/vendeuse *m., f.* seller I-6
vendre *v.* to sell I-6
vendredi *m.* Friday I-2
venir *v.* to come II-1
  venir de *v. (used with an infinitive)* to have just II-1
vent *m.* wind I-5
  Il fait du vent. It is windy. I-5
ventre *m.* stomach II-2

Vocabulaire

French-English

vérifier (l'huile/la pression des pneus) *v.* to check (the oil/the tire pressure) II-3
véritable *adj.* true, real II-4
verre (de) *m.* glass (of) I-4
vers *adv.* about I-2
vert(e) *adj.* green I-3
   haricots verts *m., pl.* green beans II-1
vêtements *m., pl.* clothing I-6
   sous-vêtement *m.* underwear I-6
vétérinaire *m., f.* veterinarian II-5
veuf/veuve *adj.* widowed I-3
veut dire (vouloir dire) *v.* means, signifies II-1
viande *f.* meat II-1
vie *f.* life I-6
   assurance vie *f.* life insurance II-5
vieille *adj., f. (feminine form of* **vieux)** old I-3
vieillesse *f.* old age I-6
vietnamien(ne) *adj.* Vietnamese I-1
vieux/vieille *adj.* old I-3
ville *f.* city; town I-4
vin *m.* wine I-6
vingt *m.* twenty I-1
vingtième *adj.* twentieth I-7
violet(te) *adj.* purple; violet I-6
violon *m.* violin II-7
visage *m.* face II-2
visite *f.* visit I-6
   rendre visite (à) *v.* to visit (*a person or people*) I-6
visiter *v.* to visit (*a place*) I-2
   faire visiter *v.* to give a tour I-8, II-P
vite *adv.* quickly I-1; quick, hurry I-4
vitesse *f.* speed II-3
voici here is/are I-1
voilà there is/are I-1
voir *v.* to see II-7
voisin(e) *m., f.* neighbor I-3
voiture *f.* car II-3
   faire un tour en voiture *v.* to go for a drive I-5
   rouler en voiture *v.* to ride in a car I-7
vol *m.* flight I-7
volant *m.* steering wheel II-3
volcan *m.* volcano II-6
volley(-ball) *m.* volleyball I-5
volontiers *adv.* willingly II-2
vos *poss. adj., m., f., pl.* your I-3
votre *poss. adj., m., f., sing.* your I-3
vouloir *v.* to want; to mean (*with* **dire**) II-1
   ça veut dire that is to say II-2
   veut dire *v.* means, signifies II-1

vouloir (que) *v.* to want (that) II-6
voulu (vouloir) *p.p., adj. (used with infinitive)* wanted to... ; *(used with noun)* planned to/for II-1
vous *pron., sing., pl., fam., form.* you I-1; *d.o. pron.* you I-7; yourself, yourselves II-2
voyage *m.* trip I-7
   agence de voyages *f.* travel agency I-7
   agent de voyages *m.* travel agent I-7
voyager *v.* to travel I-2
voyant (d'essence/d'huile) *m.* (gas/oil) warning light 11
vrai(e) *adj.* true; real I-3
   Il est vrai que... It is true that... II-7
   Il n'est pas vrai que... It is untrue that... II-7
vraiment *adv.* really, truly I-5
vu (voir) *p.p.* seen II-7

W

W.-C. *m., pl.* restroom(s) I-8, II-P
week-end *m.* weekend I-2
   ce week-end this weekend I-2

Y

y *pron.* there; at (*a place*) II-2
   j'y vais I'm going/coming I-8, II-P
   nous y allons we're going/coming II-1
   on y va let's go II-2
   Y a-t-il... ? Is/Are there... ? I-2
yaourt *m.* yogurt II-1
yeux (œil) *m., pl.* eyes I-3

Z

zéro *m.* zero I-1
zut *interj.* darn I-6

Vocabulaire

English-French

A

a **un(e)** *indef. art.* I-1
able: to be able to **pouvoir** *v.* II-1
abolish **abolir** *v.* II-6
about **vers** *adv.* I-2
abroad **à l'étranger** I-7
absolutely **absolument** *adv.* I-8, II-P; **tout à fait** *adv.* I-6
accident **accident** *m.* II-2
 to have/to be in an accident **avoir un accident** *v.* II-3
accompany **accompagner** *v.* II-4
account (at a bank) **compte** *m.* II-4
 checking account **compte** *m.* **de chèques** II-4
 to have a bank account **avoir un compte bancaire** *v.* II-4
accountant **comptable** *m., f.* II-5
acid rain **pluie acide** *f.* II-6
across from **en face de** *prep.* I-3
acquaintance **connaissance** *f.* I-5
active **actif/active** *adj.* I-3
actively **activement** *adv.* I-8, II-P
actor **acteur/actrice** *m., f.* I-1
address **adresse** *f.* II-4
administration: business administration **gestion** *f.* I-2
adolescence **adolescence** *f.* I-6
adore **adorer** I-2
 I love… **J'adore…** I-2
 to adore one another **s'adorer** *v.* II-3
adulthood **âge adulte** *m.* I-6
adventure **aventure** *f.* II-7
 adventure film **film** *m.* **d'aventures** II-7
advertisement **publicité (pub)** *f.* II-7
advice **conseil** *m.* II-5
advisor **conseiller/conseillère** *m., f.* II-5
aerobics **aérobic** *m.* I-5
 to do aerobics **faire de l'aérobic** *v.* I-5
afraid: to be afraid of/that **avoir peur de/que** *v.* II-6
after **après (que)** *adv.* I-7
afternoon **après-midi** *m.* I-2
 … (o'clock) in the afternoon … **heure(s) de l'après-midi** I-2
afternoon snack **goûter** *m.* II-1
again **encore** *adv.* I-3
age **âge** *m.* I-6

agent: travel agent **agent de voyages** *m.* I-7
 real estate agent **agent immobilier** *m.* II-5
ago (with an expression of time) **il y a…** II-1
agree: to agree (with) **être d'accord (avec)** *v.* I-2
airport **aéroport** *m.* I-7
alarm clock **réveil** *m.* II-2
Algerian **algérien(ne)** *adj.* I-1
all **tout** *m., sing.* I-4
 all of a sudden **soudain** *adv.* I-8, II-P; **tout à coup** *adv.*; **tout d'un coup** *adv.* I-7
all right? (tag question) **d'accord?** I-2
allergy **allergie** *f.* II-2
allow (to do something) **laisser** *v.* II-3; **permettre (de)** *v.* I-6
allowed **permis (permettre)** *p.p., adj.* I-6
all the… (agrees with noun that follows) **tout le…** *m., sing;* **toute la…** *f., sing;* **tous les…** *m., pl.;* **toutes les…** *f., pl.* I-4
almost **presque** *adv.* I-5
a lot (of) **beaucoup (de)** *adv.* I-4
alone: to leave alone **laisser tranquille** *v.* II-2
already **déjà** *adv.* I-3
always **toujours** *adv.* I-8, II-P
American **américain(e)** *adj.* I-1
an **un(e)** *indef. art.* I-1
ancient (placed after noun) **ancien(ne)** *adj.* II-7
and **et** *conj.* I-1
 And you? **Et toi?**, *fam.;* **Et vous?** *form.* I-1
angel **ange** *m.* I-1
angry: to become angry **s'énerver** *v.* II-2; **se mettre en colère** *v.* II-2
animal **animal** *m.* II-6
ankle **cheville** *f.* II-2
answering machine **répondeur téléphonique** *m.* II-3
apartment **appartement** *m.* I-7
appetizer **entrée** *f.* II-1; **hors-d'œuvre** *m.* II-1
applaud **applaudir** *v.* II-7
applause **applaudissement** *m.* II-7
apple **pomme** *f.* II-1
appliance **appareil** *m.* I-8, II-P
 electrical/household appliance **appareil** *m.* **électrique/ménager** I-8, II-P
applicant **candidat(e)** *m., f.* II-5
apply **postuler** *v.* II-5

appointment **rendez-vous** *m.* II-5
 to make an appointment **prendre (un) rendez-vous** *v.* II-5
April **avril** *m.* I-5
architect **architecte** *m., f.* I-3
architecture **architecture** *f.* I-2
Are there…? **Y a-t-il…?** I-2
area **quartier** *m.* I-8, II-P
argue (with) **se disputer (avec)** *v.* II-2
arm **bras** *m.* II-2
armchair **fauteuil** *m.* I-8, II-P
armoire **armoire** *f.* I-8, II-P
around **autour (de)** *prep.* II-4
arrival **arrivée** *f.* I-7
arrive **arriver (à)** *v.* I-2
art **art** *m.* I-2
 artwork, piece of art **œuvre** *f.* II-7
 fine arts **beaux-arts** *m., pl.* II-7
artist **artiste** *m., f.* I-3
as (like) **comme** *adv.* I-6
 as … as (used with adjective to compare) **aussi … que** II-1
 as much … as (used with noun to express comparative quantity) **autant de … que** II-6
as soon as **dès que** *adv.* II-5
ashamed: to be ashamed of **avoir honte de** *v.* I-2
ask **demander** *v.* I-2
 to ask (someone) **demander (à)** *v.* I-6
 to ask (someone) a question **poser une question (à)** *v.* I-6
 to ask that… **demander que…** II-6
aspirin **aspirine** *f.* II-2
at **à** *prep.* I-4
 at … (o'clock) **à … heure(s)** I-4
 at the doctor's office **chez le médecin** *prep.* I-2
 at (someone's) house **chez…** *prep.* I-2
 at the end (of) **au bout (de)** *prep.* II-4
 at last **enfin** *adv.* II-3
athlete **athlète** *m., f.* I-3
ATM **distributeur** *m.* **automatique/de billets** *m.* II-4
attend **assister** *v.* I-2
August **août** *m.* I-5
aunt **tante** *f.* I-3
author **auteur/femme auteur** *m., f.* II-7
autumn **automne** *m.* I-5
 in autumn **en automne** I-5
available (free) **libre** *adj.* I-7
avenue **avenue** *f.* II-4
avoid **éviter de** *v.* II-2

Vocabulaire

English-French

B

back **dos** *m.* II-2
backpack **sac à dos** *m.* I-1
bad **mauvais(e)** *adj.* I-3
  to be in a bad mood **être de mauvaise humeur** I-8, II-P
  to be in bad health **être en mauvaise santé** II-2
badly **mal** *adv.* I-7
  I am doing badly. **Je vais mal.** I-1
  to be doing badly **se porter mal** *v.* II-2
baguette **baguette** *f.* I-4
bakery **boulangerie** *f.* II-1
balcony **balcon** *m.* I-8, II-P
banana **banane** *f.* II-1
bank **banque** *f.* II-4
  to have a bank account **avoir un compte bancaire** *v.* II-4
banker **banquier/banquière** *m., f.* II-5
banking **bancaire** *adj.* II-4
baseball **baseball** *m.* I-5
baseball cap **casquette** *f.* I-6
basement **sous-sol** *m.*; **cave** *f.* I-8, II-P
basketball **basket(-ball)** *m.* I-5
bath **bain** *m.* I-6
bathing suit **maillot de bain** *m.* I-6
bathroom **salle de bains** *f.* I-8, II-P
bathtub **baignoire** *f.* I-8, II-P
be **être** *v.* I-1
  sois (être) *imp. v.* I-7;
  soyez (être) *imp. v.* I-7
beach **plage** *f.* I-7
beans **haricots** *m., pl.* II-1
  green beans **haricots verts** *m., pl.* II-1
bearings: to get one's bearings **s'orienter** *v.* II-4
beautiful **beau (belle)** *adj.* I-3
beauty salon **salon** *m.* **de beauté** II-4
because **parce que** *conj.* I-2
become **devenir** *v.* II-1
bed **lit** *m.* I-7
  to go to bed **se coucher** *v.* II-2
bedroom **chambre** *f.* I-8, II-P
beef **bœuf** *m.* II-1
been **été (être)** *p.p.* I-6
beer **bière** *f.* I-6
before **avant (de/que)** *adv.* I-7
  before (o'clock) **moins** *adv.* I-2
begin (to do something) **commencer (à)** *v.* I-2; **se mettre à** *v.* II-2
beginning **début** *m.* II-7
behind **derrière** *prep.* I-3

Belgian **belge** *adj.* I-7
Belgium **Belgique** *f.* I-7
believe (that) **croire (que)** *v.* II-7
believed **cru (croire)** *p.p.* II-7
belt **ceinture** *f.* I-6
  to buckle one's seatbelt **attacher sa ceinture de sécurité** *v.* II-3
bench **banc** *m.* II-4
best: the best **le mieux** *super. adv.* II-1; **le/la meilleur(e)** *super. adj.* II-1
better **meilleur(e)** *comp. adj.*; **mieux** *comp. adv.* II-1
  It is better that… **Il vaut mieux que/qu'…** II-6
  to be doing better **se porter mieux** *v.* II-2
  to get better (from illness) **guérir** *v.* II-2
between **entre** *prep.* I-3
beverage (carbonated) **boisson** *f.* **(gazeuse)** I-4
bicycle **vélo** *m.* I-5
  to go bike riding **faire du vélo** *v.* I-5
big **grand(e)** *adj.* I-3; (clothing) **large** *adj.* I-6
bill (in a restaurant) **addition** *f.* I-4
bills (money) **billets** *m., pl.* II-4
biology **biologie** *f.* I-2
bird **oiseau** *m.* I-3
birth **naissance** *f.* I-6
birthday **anniversaire** *m.* I-5
bit (of) **morceau (de)** *m.* I-4
black **noir(e)** *adj.* I-3
blackboard **tableau** *m.* I-1
blanket **couverture** *f.* I-8, II-P
blonde **blond(e)** *adj.* I-3
blouse **chemisier** *m.* I-6
blue **bleu(e)** *adj.* I-3
boat **bateau** *m.* I-7
body **corps** *m.* II-2
book **livre** *m.* I-1
bookstore **librairie** *f.* I-1
bored: to get bored **s'ennuyer** *v.* II-2
boring **ennuyeux/ennuyeuse** *adj.* I-3
born: to be born **naître** *v.* I-7; **né (naître)** *p.p., adj.* I-7
borrow **emprunter** *v.* II-4
bottle (of) **bouteille (de)** *f.* I-4
boulevard **boulevard** *m.* II-4
boutique **boutique** *f.* II-4
bowl **bol** *m.* II-1
box **boîte** *f.* II-1
boy **garçon** *m.* I-1
boyfriend **petit ami** *m.* I-1
brake **freiner** *v.* II-3
brakes **freins** *m., pl.* II-3
brave **courageux/courageuse** *adj.* I-3

Brazil **Brésil** *m.* I-7
Brazilian **brésilien(ne)** *adj.* I-7
bread **pain** *m.* I-4
  country-style bread **pain** *m.* **de campagne** I-4
bread shop **boulangerie** *f.* II-1
break **se casser** *v.* II-2
breakdown **panne** *f.* II-3
break down **tomber en panne** *v.* II-3
break up (to leave one another) **se quitter** *v.* II-3
breakfast **petit-déjeuner** *m.* II-1
bridge **pont** *m.* II-4
bright **brillant(e)** *adj.* I-1
bring (a person) **amener** *v.* I-5; (a thing) **apporter** *v.* I-4
broom **balai** *m.* I-8, II-P
brother **frère** *m.* I-3
brother-in-law **beau-frère** *m.* I-3
brown **marron** *adj., inv.* I-3
  brown (hair) **châtain** *adj.* I-3
brush (hair/tooth) **brosse** *f.* **(à cheveux/à dents)** II-2
  to brush one's hair/teeth **se brosser les cheveux/les dents** *v.* II-1
buckle: to buckle one's seatbelt **attacher sa ceinture de sécurité** *v.* II-3
build **construire** *v.* I-6
building **bâtiment** *m.* II-4; **immeuble** *m.* I-8, II-P
bumper **pare-chocs** *m.* II-3
burn (CD/DVD) **graver** *v.* II-3
bus **autobus** *m.* I-7
bus stop **arrêt d'autobus (de bus)** *m.* I-7
bus terminal **gare** *f.* **routière** I-7
business (profession) **affaires** *f., pl.* I-3; (company) **entreprise** *f.* II-5
business administration **gestion** *f.* I-2
businessman **homme d'affaires** *m.* I-3
businesswoman **femme d'affaires** *f.* I-3
busy **occupé(e)** *adj.* I-1
but **mais** *conj.* I-1
butcher's shop **boucherie** *f.* II-1
butter **beurre** *m.* I-4
buy **acheter** *v.* I-5
by **par** *prep.* I-3
Bye! **Salut!** *fam.* I-1

C

cabinet **placard** *m.* I-8, II-P
café **café** *m.* I-1; **brasserie** *f.* II-4
  café terrace **terrasse** *f.* **de café** I-4

Vocabulaire

English-French

cybercafé **cybercafé** *m.* II-4
cafeteria (school) **cantine** *f.* II-1
cake **gâteau** *m.* I-6
calculator **calculatrice** *f.* I-1
call **appeler** *v.* II-5
calm **calme** *adj.* I-1; **calme** *m.* I-1
camcorder **caméra vidéo** *f.* II-3; **caméscope** *m.* II-3
camera **appareil photo** *m.* II-3
   digital camera **appareil photo** *m.* **numérique** II-3
camping **camping** *m.* I-5
   to go camping **faire du camping** *v.* I-5
can (of food) **boîte (de conserve)** *f.* II-1
Canada **Canada** *m.* I-7
Canadian **canadien(ne)** *adj.* I-1
cancel (a reservation) **annuler (une réservation)** *v.* I-7
candidate **candidat(e)** *m., f.* II-5
candy **bonbon** *m.* I-6
cap: baseball cap **casquette** *f.* I-6
capital **capitale** *f.* I-7
car **voiture** *f.* II-3
   to ride in a car **rouler en voiture** *v.* I-7
card *(letter)* **carte postale** *f.* II-4; credit card **carte** *f.* **de crédit** II-4
   to pay with a credit card **payer avec une carte de crédit** *v.* II-4
   cards *(playing)* **cartes** *f.* I-5
carbonated drink/beverage **boisson** *f.* **gazeuse** I-4
career **carrière** *f.* II-5
carpooling **covoiturage** *m.* II-6
carrot **carotte** *f.* II-1
carry **apporter** *v.* I-4
cartoon **dessin animé** *m.* II-7
case: in any case **en tout cas** I-6
cash **liquide** *m.* II-4
   to pay in cash **payer en liquide** *v.* II-4
cat **chat** *m.* I-3
catastrophe **catastrophe** *f.* II-6
catch sight of **apercevoir** *v.* II-4
CD(s) **CD** *m.* II-3
CD/DVD /MP3 player **lecteur (de) CD/DVD / lecteur MP3** *m.* II-3
celebrate **célébrer** *v.* I-5; **fêter** *v.* I-6
celebration **fête** *f.* I-6
cellar **cave** *f.* I-8, II-P
cell(ular) phone **portable** *m.* II-3
center: city/town center **centre-ville** *m.* II-4
certain **certain(e)** *adj.* II-1; **sûr(e)** *adj.* II-7

It is certain that… **Il est certain que…** II-7
It is uncertain that… **Il n'est pas certain que…** II-7
chair **chaise** *f.* I-1
champagne **champagne** *m.* I-6
change *(coins)* **(pièces** *f. pl.* **de) monnaie** II-4
channel (television) **chaîne** *f.* **(de télévision)** II-3
character **personnage** *m.* II-7
   main character **personnage principal** *m.* II-7
charming **charmant(e)** *adj.* I-1
chat **bavarder** *v.* I-4
check **chèque** *m.* II-4; *(bill)* **addition** *f.* I-4
   to pay by check **payer par chèque** *v.* II-4;
   to check (the oil/the air pressure) **vérifier (l'huile/la pression des pneus)** *v.* II-3
checking account **compte** *m.* **de chèques** II-4
cheek **joue** *f.* II-2
cheese **fromage** *m.* I-4
chemistry **chimie** *f.* I-2
chess **échecs** *m., pl.* I-5
chest **poitrine** *f.* II-2
   chest of drawers **commode** *f.* I-8, II-P
chic **chic** *adj.* I-4
chicken **poulet** *m.* II-1
child **enfant** *m., f.* I-3
childhood **enfance** *f.* I-6
China **Chine** *f.* I-7
Chinese **chinois(e)** *adj.* I-7
choir **chœur** *m.* II-7
choose **choisir** *v.* I-4
chorus **chœur** *m.* II-7
chrysanthemums **chrysanthèmes** *m., pl.* II-1
church **église** *f.* I-4
city **ville** *f.* I-4
city hall **mairie** *f.* II-4
city/town center **centre-ville** *m.* II-4
class *(group of students)* **classe** *f.* I-1; *(course)* **cours** *m.* I-2
classmate **camarade de classe** *m., f.* I-1
classroom **salle** *f.* **de classe** I-1
clean **nettoyer** *v.* I-5; **propre** *adj.* I-8, II-P
clear **clair(e)** *adj.* II-7
   It is clear that… **Il est clair que…** II-7
   to clear the table **débarrasser la table** I-8, II-P
client **client(e)** *m., f.* I-7
cliff **falaise** *f.* II-6
clock **horloge** *f.* I-1
   alarm clock **réveil** *m.* II-2

close (to) **près (de)** *prep.* I-3
   very close (to) **tout près (de)** II-4
close **fermer** *v.* II-3
closed **fermé(e)** *adj.* II-4
closet **placard** *m.* I-8, II-P
clothes dryer **sèche-linge** *m.* I-8, II-P
clothing **vêtements** *m., pl.* I-6
cloudy **nuageux/nuageuse** *adj.* I-5
   It is cloudy. **Le temps est nuageux.** I-5
clutch **embrayage** *m.* II-3
coast **côte** *f.* II-6
coat **manteau** *m.* I-6
coffee **café** *m.* I-1
coffeemaker **cafetière** *f.* I-8, II-P
coins **pièces** *f. pl.* **de monnaie** II-4
cold **froid** *m.* I-2
   to be cold **avoir froid** *v.* I-2
   (weather) It is cold. **Il fait froid.** I-5
cold **rhume** *m.* II-2
color **couleur** *f.* I-6
   What color is…? **De quelle couleur est…?** I-6
comb **peigne** *m.* II-2
come **venir** *v.* I-7
come back **revenir** *v.* II-1
Come on. **Allez.** I-2
comedy **comédie** *f.* II-7
comic strip **bande dessinée (B.D.)** *f.* I-5
compact disc **compact disque** *m.* II-3
company *(troop)* **troupe** *f.* II-7
completely **tout à fait** *adv.* I-6
composer **compositeur** *m.* II-7
computer **ordinateur** *m.* I-1
computer science **informatique** *f.* I-2
concert **concert** *m.* II-7
congratulations **félicitations** II-7
consider **considérer** *v.* I-5
constantly **constamment** *adv.* I-8, II-P
construct **construire** *v.* I-6
consultant **conseiller/conseillère** *m., f.* II-5
continue *(doing something)* **continuer (à)** *v.* II-4
cook **cuisiner** *v.* II-1; **faire la cuisine** *v.* I-5; **cuisinier/cuisinière** *m., f.* II-5
cookie **biscuit** *m.* I-6
cooking **cuisine** *f.* I-5
cool: *(weather)* It is cool. **Il fait frais.** I-5
corner **angle** *m.* II-4; **coin** *m.* II-4
cost **coûter** *v.* I-4

Vocabulaire — English-French

cotton **coton** *m.* I-6
couch **canapé** *m.* I-8, II-P
cough **tousser** *v.* II-2
count (on someone) **compter (sur quelqu'un)** *v.* I-8, II-P
country **pays** *m.* I-7
   country(side) **campagne** *f.* I-7
country-style **de campagne** *adj.* I-4
couple **couple** *m.* I-6
courage **courage** *m.* II-5
courageous **courageux/ courageuse** *adj.* I-3
course **cours** *m.* I-2
cousin **cousin(e)** *m., f.* I-3
cover **couvrir** *v.* II-3
covered **couvert (couvrir)** *p.p.* II-3
cow **vache** *f.* II-6
crazy **fou/folle** *adj.* I-3
cream **crème** *f.* II-1
credit card **carte** *f.* **de crédit** II-4
   to pay with a credit card **payer avec une carte de crédit** *v.* II-4
crêpe **crêpe** *f.* I-5
crime film **film policier** *m.* II-7
croissant **croissant** *m.* I-4
cross **traverser** *v.* II-4
cruel **cruel/cruelle** *adj.* I-3
cry **pleurer** *v.*
cup (of) **tasse (de)** *f.* I-4
cupboard **placard** *m.* I-8, II-P
curious **curieux/ curieuse** *adj.* I-3
curly **frisé(e)** *adj.* I-3
currency **monnaie** *f.* II-4
curtain **rideau** *m.* I-8, II-P
customs **douane** *f.* I-7
cybercafé **cybercafé** *m.* II-4

D

dance **danse** *f.* II-7
   to dance **danser** *v.* I-4
danger **danger** *m.* II-6
dangerous **dangereux/ dangereuse** *adj.* II-3
dark (*hair*) **brun(e)** *adj.* I-3
darling **chéri(e)** *adj.* I-2
darn **zut** II-3
dash (*punctuation mark*) **tiret** *m.* II-3
date (*day, month, year*) **date** *f.* I-5; (*meeting*) **rendez-vous** *m.* I-6
   to make a date **prendre (un) rendez-vous** *v.* II-5
daughter **fille** *f.* I-1
day **jour** *m.* I-2; **journée** *f.* I-2
   day after tomorrow **après-demain** *adv.* I-2
   day before yesterday **avant-hier** *adv.* I-7
   day off **congé** *m.*, **jour de congé** I-7
dear **cher/chère** *adj.* I-2
death **mort** *f.* I-6
December **décembre** *m.* I-5
decide (*to do something*) **décider (de)** *v.* II-3
deforestation **déboisement** *m.* II-6
degree **diplôme** *m.* I-2
degrees (*temperature*) **degrés** *m., pl.* I-5
   It is… degrees. **Il fait… degrés.** I-5
delicatessen **charcuterie** *f.* II-1
delicious **délicieux/délicieuse** *adj.* I-4
Delighted. **Enchanté(e).** *p.p., adj.* I-1
demand (that) **exiger (que)** *v.* II-6
demanding **exigeant(e)** *adj.*
   demanding profession **profession** *f.* **exigeante** II-5
dentist **dentiste** *m., f.* I-3
department store **grand magasin** *m.* I-4
departure **départ** *m.* I-7
deposit: to deposit money **déposer de l'argent** *v.* II-4
depressed **déprimé(e)** *adj.* II-2
describe **décrire** *v.* I-7
described **décrit (décrire)** *p.p., adj.* I-7
desert **désert** *m.* II-6
design (*fashion*) **stylisme (de mode)** *m.* I-2
desire **envie** *f.* I-2
desk **bureau** *m.* I-1
dessert **dessert** *m.* I-6
destroy **détruire** *v.* I-6
destroyed **détruit (détruire)** *p.p., adj.* I-6
detective film **film policier** *m.* II-7
detest **détester** *v.* I-2
   I hate… **Je déteste…** I-2
develop **développer** *v.* II-6
dial (*a number*) **composer (un numéro)** *v.* II-3
dictionary **dictionnaire** *m.* I-1
die **mourir** *v.* I-7
died **mort (mourir)** *p.p., adj.* I-7
diet **régime** *m.* II-2
   to be on a diet **être au régime** II-1
difference **différence** *f.* I-1
different **différent(e)** *adj.* I-1
differently **différemment** *adv.* I-8, II-P
difficult **difficile** *adj.* I-1

digital camera **appareil photo** *m.* **numérique** II-3
dining room **salle à manger** *f.* I-8, II-P
dinner **dîner** *m.* II-1
   to have dinner **dîner** *v.* I-2
diploma **diplôme** *m.* I-2
directions **indications** *f.* II-4
director (*movie*) **réalisateur/ réalisatrice** *m., f.*; (*play/show*) **metteur en scène** *m.* II-7
dirty **sale** *adj.* I-8, II-P
discover **découvrir** *v.* II-3
discovered **découvert (découvrir)** *p.p.* II-3
discreet **discret/discrète** *adj.* I-3
discuss **discuter** *v.* II-3
dish (*food*) **plat** *m.* II-1
   to do the dishes **faire la vaisselle** *v.* I-8, II-P
dishwasher **lave-vaisselle** *m.* I-8, II-P
dismiss **renvoyer** *v.* II-5
distinction **mention** *f.* II-5
divorce **divorce** *m.* I-6
   to divorce **divorcer** *v.* I-3
divorced **divorcé(e)** *p.p., adj.* I-3
do (*make*) **faire** *v.* I-5
   to do odd jobs **bricoler** *v.* I-5
doctor **médecin** *m.* I-3
documentary **documentaire** *m.* II-7
dog **chien** *m.* I-3
done **fait (faire)** *p.p., adj.* I-6
door (*building*) **porte** *f.* I-1; (*automobile*) **portière** *f.* II-3
dorm **résidence** *f.* **universitaire** I-8, II-P
doubt (that)… **douter (que)…** *v.* II-7
doubtful **douteux/douteuse** *adj.* II-7
   It is doubtful that… **Il est douteux que…** II-7
download **télécharger** *v.* II-3
downtown **centre-ville** *m.* I-4
drag **barbant** *adj.* I-3; **barbe** *f.* I-3
drape **rideau** *m.* I-8, II-P
draw **dessiner** *v.* I-2
drawer **tiroir** *m.* I-8, II-P
dreadful **épouvantable** *adj.* I-5
dream (about) **rêver (de)** *v.* II-3
dress **robe** *f.* I-6
   to dress **s'habiller** *v.* II-2
dresser **commode** *f.* I-8, II-P
drink (carbonated) **boisson** *f.* **(gazeuse)** I-4
   to drink **boire** *v.* I-4
drive **conduire** *v.* I-6
   to go for a drive **faire un tour en voiture** I-5
driven **conduit (conduire)** *p.p.* I-6

Vocabulaire — English-French

driver (taxi/truck) **chauffeur (de taxi/de camion)** *m.* II-5
driver's license **permis** *m.* **de conduire** II-3
drums **batterie** *f.* II-7
drunk **bu (boire)** *p.p.* I-6
dryer (clothes) **sèche-linge** *m.* I-8, II-P
dry oneself **se sécher** *v.* II-2
due **dû(e) (devoir)** *adj.* II-1
during **pendant** *prep.* I-7
dust **enlever/faire la poussière** *v.* I-8, II-P
DVR **enregistreur DVR** *m.* II-3

E

each **chaque** *adj.* I-6
ear **oreille** *f.* II-2
early **en avance** *adv.* I-2; **tôt** *adv.* I-2
earn **gagner** *v.* II-5
Earth **Terre** *f.* II-6
easily **facilement** *adv.* I-8, II-P
east **est** *m.* II-4
easy **facile** *adj.* I-2
eat **manger** *v.* I-2
   to eat lunch **déjeuner** *v.* I-4
éclair **éclair** *m.* I-4
ecological **écologique** *adj.* II-6
ecology **écologie** *f.* II-6
economics **économie** *f.* I-2
ecotourism **écotourisme** *m.* II-6
education **formation** *f.* II-5
effect: in effect **en effet** II-6
egg **œuf** *m.* II-1
eight **huit** *m.* I-1
eighteen **dix-huit** *m.* I-1
eighth **huitième** *adj.* I-7
eighty **quatre-vingts** *m.* I-3
eighty-one **quatre-vingt-un** *m.* I-3
elder **aîné(e)** *adj.* I-3
electric **électrique** *adj.* I-8, II-P
   electrical appliance **appareil** *m.* **électrique** I-8, II-P
electrician **électricien/électricienne** *m., f.* II-5
elegant **élégant(e)** *adj.* I-1
elevator **ascenseur** *m.* I-7
eleven **onze** *m.* I-1
eleventh **onzième** *adj.* I-7
e-mail **e-mail** *m.* II-3
emergency room **urgences** *f., pl.* II-2
   to go to the emergency room **aller aux urgences** *v.* II-2
employ **employer** *v.* I-5
end **fin** *f.* II-7
endangered **menacé(e)** *adj.* II-6
   endangered species **espèce** *f.* **menacée** II-6
engaged **fiancé(e)** *adj.* I-3

engine **moteur** *m.* II-3
engineer **ingénieur** *m.* I-3
England **Angleterre** *f.* I-7
English **anglais(e)** *adj.* I-1
enormous **énorme** *adj.* I-2
enough (of) **assez (de)** *adv.* I-4
   not enough (of) **pas assez (de)** I-4
enter **entrer** *v.* I-7
envelope **enveloppe** *f.* II-4
environment **environnement** *m.* II-6
equal **égaler** *v.* I-3
erase **effacer** *v.* II-3
errand **course** *f.* II-1
escargot **escargot** *m.* II-1
especially **surtout** *adv.* I-2
essay **dissertation** *f.* II-3
essential **essentiel(le)** *adj.* II-6
   It is essential that… **Il est essentiel/indispensable que…** II-6
even **même** *adv.* I-5
evening **soir** *m.*; **soirée** *f.* I-2
   … (o'clock) in the evening … **heures du soir** I-2
every day **tous les jours** *adv.* I-8, II-P
everyone **tout le monde** *m.* II-1
evident **évident(e)** *adj.* II-7
   It is evident that… **Il est évident que…** II-7
evidently **évidemment** *adv.* I-8, II-P
exactly **exactement** *adv.* II-1
exam **examen** *m.* I-1
Excuse me. **Excuse-moi.** *fam.* I-1; **Excusez-moi.** *form.* I-1
executive **cadre/femme cadre** *m., f.* II-5
exercise **exercice** *m.* II-2
   to exercise **faire de l'exercice** *v.* II-2
exhibit **exposition** *f.* II-7
exit **sortie** *f.* I-7
expenditure **dépense** *f.* II-4
expensive **cher/chère** *adj.* I-6
explain **expliquer** *v.* I-2
explore **explorer** *v.* I-4
extinction **extinction** *f.* II-6
eye (eyes) **œil (yeux)** *m.* II-2

F

face **visage** *m.* II-2
facing **en face (de)** *prep.* I-3
fact: in fact **en fait** I-7
factory **usine** *f.* II-6
fail **échouer** *v.* I-2
fall **automne** *m.* I-5
   in the fall **en automne** I-5
   to fall **tomber** *v.* I-7

to fall in love **tomber amoureux/amoureuse** *v.* I-6
to fall asleep **s'endormir** *v.* II-2
family **famille** *f.* I-3
famous **célèbre** *adj.* II-7; **connu (connaître)** *p.p., adj.* I-8, II-P
far (from) **loin (de)** *prep.* I-3
farewell **adieu** *m.* II-6
farmer **agriculteur/agricultrice** *m., f.* II-5
fashion **mode** *f.* I-2
   fashion design **stylisme de mode** *m.* I-2
fast **rapide** *adj.* I-3; **vite** *adv.* I-8, II-P
fat **gros(se)** *adj.* I-3
father **père** *m.* I-3
father-in-law **beau-père** *m.* I-3
favorite **favori/favorite** *adj.* I-3; **préféré(e)** *adj.* I-2
fax machine **fax** *m.* II-3
fear **peur** *f.* I-2
   to fear that **avoir peur que** *v.* II-6
February **février** *m.* I-5
fed up: to be fed up **en avoir marre** *v.* I-3
feel (to sense) **sentir** *v.* I-5; (state of being) **se sentir** *v.* II-2
   to feel like (doing something) **avoir envie (de)** I-2
   to feel nauseated **avoir mal au cœur** II-2
festival (festivals) **festival (festivals)** *m.* II-7
fever **fièvre** *f.* II-2
   to have fever **avoir de la fièvre** *v.* II-2
fiancé **fiancé(e)** *m., f.* I-6
field (terrain) **champ** *m.* II-6; (of study) **domaine** *m.* II-5
fifteen **quinze** *m.* I-1
fifth **cinquième** *adj.* I-7
fifty **cinquante** *m.* I-1
figure (physique) **ligne** *f.* II-2
file **fichier** *m.* II-3
fill: to fill out a form **remplir un formulaire** *v.* II-4
   to fill the tank **faire le plein** *v.* II-3
film **film** *m.* II-7
   adventure/crime film **film** *m.* **d'aventures/policier** II-7
finally **enfin** *adv.* I-7; **finalement** *adv.* I-7; **dernièrement** *adv.* I-8, II-P
find (a job) **trouver (un/du travail)** *v.* II-5
   to find again **retrouver** *v.* I-2
fine **amende** *f.* II-3
fine arts **beaux-arts** *m., pl.* II-7
finger **doigt** *m.* II-2

Vocabulaire — English-French

finish (*doing something*) **finir (de)** *v.* I-4, II-3
fire **incendie** *m.* II-6
firefighter **pompier/femme pompier** *m., f.* II-5
firm (*business*) **entreprise** *f.* II-5;
first **d'abord** *adv.* I-7; **premier/première** *adj.* I-2; **premier** *m.* I-5
   It is October first. **C'est le 1ᵉʳ (premier) octobre.** I-5
fish **poisson** *m.* I-3
fishing **pêche** *f.* I-5
   to go fishing **aller à la pêche** *v.* I-5
fish shop **poissonnerie** *f.* II-1
five **cinq** *m.* I-1
flat tire **pneu** *m.* **crevé** II-3
flight (*air travel*) **vol** *m.* I-7
floor **étage** *m.* I-7
flower **fleur** *f.* I-8, II-P
flu **grippe** *f.* II-2
fluently **couramment** *adv.* I-8, II-P
follow (*a path/a street/a boulevard*) **suivre (un chemin/une rue/un boulevard)** *v.* II-4
food item **aliment** *m.* II-1; **nourriture** *f.* II-1
foot **pied** *m.* II-2
football **football américain** *m.* I-5
for **pour** *prep.* I-5; **pendant** *prep.* II-1
   For whom? **Pour qui?** I-4
forbid **interdire** *v.* II-6
foreign **étranger/étrangère** *adj.* I-2
   foreign languages **langues** *f., pl.* **étrangères** I-2
forest **forêt** *f.* II-6
   tropical forest **forêt tropicale** *f.* II-6
forget (*to do something*) **oublier (de)** *v.* I-2
fork **fourchette** *f.* II-1
form **formulaire** *m.* II-4
former (*placed before noun*) **ancien(ne)** *adj.* II-7
fortunately **heureusement** *adv.* I-8, II-P
forty **quarante** *m.* I-1
fountain **fontaine** *f.* II-4
four **quatre** *m.* I-1
fourteen **quatorze** *m.* I-1
fourth **quatrième** *adj.* I-7
France **France** *f.* I-7
frankly **franchement** *adv.* I-8, II-P
free (*at no cost*) **gratuit(e)** *adj.* II-7
   free time **temps libre** *m.* I-5
freezer **congélateur** *m.* I-8, II-P
French **français(e)** *adj.* I-1
French fries **frites** *f., pl.* I-4
frequent (*to visit regularly*) **fréquenter** *v.* I-4
fresh **frais/fraîche** *adj.* I-5
Friday **vendredi** *m.* I-2
friend **ami(e)** *m., f.* I-1; **copain/copine** *m., f.* I-1
friendship **amitié** *f.* I-6
from **de/d'** *prep.* I-1
   from time to time **de temps en temps** *adv.* I-8, II-P
front: in front of **devant** *prep.* I-3
fruit **fruit** *m.* II-1
full (*no vacancies*) **complet (complète)** *adj.* I-7
full-time job **emploi** *m.* **à plein temps** II-5
fun **amusant(e)** *adj.* I-1
   to have fun (*doing something*) **s'amuser (à)** *v.* II-3
funeral **funérailles** *f., pl.* II-1
funny **drôle** *adj.* I-3
furious **furieux/furieuse** *adj.* II-6
   to be furious that… **être furieux/furieuse que…** *v.* II-6

G

gain: gain weight **grossir** *v.* I-4
game (*amusement*) **jeu** *m.* I-5; (*sports*) **match** *m.* I-5
game show **jeu télévisé** *m.* II-7
garage **garage** *m.* I-8, II-P
garbage **ordures** *f., pl.* II-6
garbage collection **ramassage** *m.* **des ordures** II-6
garden **jardin** *m.* I-8, II-P
garlic **ail** *m.* II-1
gas **essence** *f.* II-3
gas tank **réservoir d'essence** *m.* II-3
gas warning light **voyant** *m.* **d'essence** II-3
generally **en général** *adv.* I-8, II-P
generous **généreux/généreuse** *adj.* I-3
genre **genre** *m.* II-7
gentle **doux/douce** *adj.* I-3
geography **géographie** *f.* I-2
German **allemand(e)** *adj.* I-1
Germany **Allemagne** *f.* I-7
get (*to obtain*) **obtenir** *v.* II-5
get along well (with) **s'entendre bien (avec)** *v.* II-2
get off **descendre (de)** *v.* I-6
get up **se lever** *v.* II-2
   get up again **se relever** *v.* II-2
gift **cadeau** *m.* I-6
   wrapped gift **paquet cadeau** *m.* I-6
gifted **doué(e)** *adj.* II-7
girl **fille** *f.* I-1
girlfriend **petite amie** *f.* I-1
give (*to someone*) **donner (à)** *v.* I-2
   to give a shot **faire une piqûre** *v.* II-2
   to give a tour **faire visiter** *v.* I-8, II-P
   to give back **rendre (à)** *v.* I-6
   to give one another **se donner** *v.* II-3
glass (of) **verre (de)** *m.* I-4
glasses **lunettes** *f., pl.* I-6
   sunglasses **lunettes de soleil** *f., pl.* I-6
global warming **réchauffement** *m.* **de la Terre** II-6
glove **gant** *m.* I-6
go **aller** *v.* I-4
   Let's go! **Allons-y!** I-4; **On y va!** II-2
   I'm going. **J'y vais.** I-8, II-P
   to go back **repartir** *v.* II-7
   to go downstairs **descendre (de)** *v.* I-6
   to go out **sortir** *v.* I-7
   to go over **dépasser** *v.* II-3
   to go up **monter** *v.* I-7
   to go with **aller avec** *v.* I-6
golf **golf** *m.* I-5
good **bon(ne)** *adj.* I-3
   Good evening. **Bonsoir.** I-1
   Good morning. **Bonjour.** I-1
   to be good for nothing **ne servir à rien** *v.* II-1
   to be in a good mood **être de bonne humeur** *v.* I-8, II-P
   to be in good health **être en bonne santé** *v.* II-2
   to be in good shape **être en pleine forme** *v.* II-2
   to be up to something interesting **faire quelque chose de beau** *v.* II-4
Good-bye. **Au revoir.** I-1
government **gouvernement** *m.* II-6
grade (*academics*) **note** *f.* I-2
grandchildren **petits-enfants** *m., pl.* I-3
granddaughter **petite-fille** *f.* I-3
grandfather **grand-père** *m.* I-3
grandmother **grand-mère** *f.* I-3
grandparents **grands-parents** *m., pl.* I-3
grandson **petit-fils** *m.* I-3
grant **bourse** *f.* I-2
grass **herbe** *f.* II-6
gratin **gratin** *m.* II-1
gray **gris(e)** *adj.* I-6
great **formidable** *adj.* I-7; **génial(e)** *adj.* I-3
green **vert(e)** *adj.* I-3
green beans **haricots verts** *m., pl.* II-1
greenhouse **serre** *f.* II-6
   greenhouse effect **effet de serre** *m.* II-6
grocery store **épicerie** *f.* I-4

Vocabulaire — English-French

groom: to groom oneself *(in the morning)* **faire sa toilette** *v.* II-2
ground floor **rez-de-chaussée** *m.* I-7
growing population **population** *f.* **croissante** II-6
guaranteed **garanti(e)** *p.p., adj.* I-5
guest **invité(e)** *m., f.* I-6; **client(e)** *m., f.* I-7
guitar **guitare** *f.* II-7
guy **mec** *m.* II-2
gym **gymnase** *m.* I-4

H

habitat **habitat** *m.* II-6
   habitat preservation **sauvetage des habitats** *m.* II-6
had **eu (avoir)** *p.p.* I-6
had to **dû (devoir)** *p.p.* II-1
hair **cheveux** *m., pl.* II-1
   to brush one's hair **se brosser les cheveux** *v.* II-1
   to do one's hair **se coiffer** *v.* II-2
hairbrush **brosse** *f.* **à cheveux** II-2
hairdresser **coiffeur/coiffeuse** *m., f.* I-3
half **demie** *f.* I-2
   half past ... *(o'clock)* **... et demie** I-2
half-brother **demi-frère** *m.* I-3
half-sister **demi-sœur** *f.* I-3
half-time job **emploi** *m.* **à mi-temps** II-5
hallway **couloir** *m.* I-8, II-P
ham **jambon** *m.* I-4
hand **main** *f.* I-5
handbag **sac à main** *m.* I-6
handsome **beau** *adj.* I-3
hang up **raccrocher** *v.* II-5
happiness **bonheur** *m.* I-6
happy **heureux/heureuse** *adj.;* **content(e)** II-5
   to be happy that... **être content(e) que...** *v.* II-6; **être heureux/heureuse que...** *v.* II-6
hard drive **disque (dur)** *m.* II-3
hard-working **travailleur/travailleuse** *adj.* I-3
hat **chapeau** *m.* I-6
hate **détester** *v.* I-2
   I hate... **Je déteste...** I-2
have **avoir** *v.* I-2; **aie (avoir)** *imp. v.* I-7; **ayez (avoir)** *imp. v.* I-7; **prendre** *v.* I-4
   to have an ache **avoir mal** *v.* II-2

to have to *(must)* **devoir** *v.* II-1
he **il** *sub. pron.* I-1
head *(body part)* **tête** *f.* II-2; *(of a company)* **chef** *m.* **d'entreprise** II-5
headache: to have a headache **avoir mal à la tête** *v.* II-2
headlights **phares** *m., pl.* II-3
headphones **écouteurs** *m.* II-3
health **santé** *f.* II-2
   to be in good health **être en bonne santé** *v.* II-2
health insurance **assurance** *f.* **maladie** II-5
healthy **sain(e)** *adj.* II-2
hear **entendre** *v.* I-6
heart **cœur** *m.* II-2
heat **chaud** *m.* 2
hello *(on the phone)* **allô** I-1; *(in the evening)* **Bonsoir.** I-1; *(in the morning or afternoon)* **Bonjour.** I-1
help **au secours** II-3
   to help *(to do something)* **aider (à)** *v.* I-5
   to help one another **s'aider** *v.* II-3
her **la/l'** *d.o. pron.* I-7; **lui** *i.o. pron.* I-6; *(attached to an imperative)* **-lui** *i.o. pron.* II-1
her **sa** *poss. adj., f., sing.* I-3; **ses** *poss. adj., m., f., pl.* I-3; **son** *poss. adj., m., sing.* I-3
Here! **Tenez!** *form., imp. v.* II-1; **Tiens!** *fam., imp. v.* II-1
here **ici** *adv.* I-1; *(used with demonstrative adjective* **ce** *and noun or with demonstrative pronoun* **celui***);* **-ci** I-6; Here is.... **Voici...** I-1
heritage: I am of... heritage. **Je suis d'origine...** I-1
herself *(used with reflexive verb)* **se/s'** *pron.* II-2
hesitate *(to do something)* **hésiter (à)** *v.* II-3
Hey! **Eh!** *interj.* 2
Hi! **Salut!** *fam.* I-1
high **élevé(e)** *adj.* II-5
high school **lycée** *m.* I-1
   high school student **lycéen(ne)** *m., f.* 2
higher education **études supérieures** *f., pl.* 2
highway **autoroute** *f.* II-3
hike **randonnée** *f.* I-5
   to go for a hike **faire une randonnée** *v.* I-5
him **lui** *i.o. pron.* I-6; **le/l'** *d.o. pron.* I-7; *(attached to imperative)* **-lui** *i.o. pron.* II-1
himself *(used with reflexive verb)* **se/s'** *pron.* II-2
hire **embaucher** *v.* II-5

his **sa** *poss. adj., f., sing.* I-3; **ses** *poss. adj., m., f., pl.* I-3; **son** *poss. adj., m., sing.* I-3
history **histoire** *f.* I-2
hit **rentrer (dans)** *v.* II-3
hold **tenir** *v.* II-1
   to be on hold **patienter** *v.* II-5
hole in the ozone layer **trou dans la couche d'ozone** *m.* II-6
holiday **jour férié** *m.* I-6; **férié(e)** *adj.* I-6
home *(house)* **maison** *f.* I-4
   at (someone's) home **chez...** *prep.* 4
home page **page d'accueil** *f.* II-3
homework **devoir** *m.* I-2
honest **honnête** *adj.* II-7
honestly **franchement** *adv.* I-8, II-P
hood **capot** *m.* II-3
hope **espérer** *v.* I-5
hors d'œuvre **hors-d'œuvre** *m.* II-1
horse **cheval** *m.* I-5
   to go horseback riding **faire du cheval** *v.* I-5
hospital **hôpital** *m.* I-4
host **hôte/hôtesse** *m., f.* I-6
hot **chaud** *m.* I-2
   It is hot *(weather)*. **Il fait chaud.** I-5
   to be hot **avoir chaud** *v.* I-2
hot chocolate **chocolat chaud** *m.* I-4
hotel **hôtel** *m.* I-7
   (single) hotel room **chambre** *f.* **(individuelle)** I-7
hotel keeper **hôtelier/hôtelière** *m., f.* I-7
hour **heure** *f.* I-2
house **maison** *f.* I-4
   at (someone's) house **chez...** *prep.* I-2
   to leave the house **quitter la maison** *v.* I-4
   to stop by someone's house **passer chez quelqu'un** *v.* I-4
household **ménager/ménagère** *adj.* I-8, II-P
household appliance **appareil** *m.* **ménager** I-8, II-P
household chore **tâche ménagère** *f.* I-8, II-P
housewife **femme au foyer** *f.* II-5
housework: to do the housework **faire le ménage** *v.* I-8, II-P
housing **logement** *m.* I-8, II-P
how **comme** *adv.* I-2; **comment?** *interr. adv.* I-4
   How are you? **Comment allez-vous?** *form.* I-1; **Comment vas-tu?** *fam.* I-1
   How many/How much (of)? **Combien (de)?** I-1

Vocabulaire — English-French

How much is…? **Combien coûte…?** I-4
huge **énorme** adj. I-2
Huh? **Hein?** interj. I-3
humanities **lettres** f., pl. I-2
hundred: one hundred **cent** m. I-5
　five hundred **cinq cents** m. I-5
　one hundred one **cent un** m. I-5
　one hundred thousand **cent mille** m. I-5
hundredth **centième** adj. I-7
hunger **faim** f. I-4
hungry: to be hungry **avoir faim** v. I-4
hunt **chasse** f. II-6
　to hunt **chasser** v. II-6
hurried **pressé(e)** adj. II-1
hurry **se dépêcher** v. II-2
hurt **faire mal** v. II-2
　to hurt oneself **se blesser** v. II-2
husband **mari** m.; **époux** m. I-3
hyphen (punctuation mark) **tiret** m. II-3

I

I **je** sub. pron. I-1; **moi** disj. pron., sing. I-3
ice cream **glace** f. I-6
ice cube **glaçon** m. I-6
idea **idée** f. I-3
if **si** conj. II-5
ill: to become ill **tomber malade** v. II-2
illness **maladie** f. II-5
immediately **tout de suite** adv. I-4
impatient **impatient(e)** adj. I-1
important **important(e)** adj. I-1
　It is important that… **Il est important que…** II-6
impossible **impossible** adj. II-7
　It is impossible that… **Il est impossible que…** II-7
improve **améliorer** v. II-5
in **dans** prep. I-3; **en** prep. I-3; **à** prep. I-4
included **compris (comprendre)** p.p., adj. I-6
incredible **incroyable** adj. II-3
independent **indépendant(e)** adj. I-1
independently **indépendamment** adv. I-8, II-P
indicate **indiquer** v. 5
indispensable **indispensable** adj. II-6
inexpensive **bon marché** adj. I-6
injection **piqûre** f. II-2

to give an injection **faire une piqûre** v. II-2
injury **blessure** f. II-2
instrument **instrument** m. I-1
insurance (health/life) **assurance** f. **(maladie/vie)** II-5
intellectual **intellectuel(le)** adj. I-3
intelligent **intelligent(e)** adj. I-1
interested: to be interested (in) **s'intéresser (à)** v. II-2
interesting **intéressant(e)** adj. I-1
intermission **entracte** m. II-7
internship **stage** m. II-5
intersection **carrefour** m. II-4
interview: to have an interview **passer un entretien** II-5
introduce **présenter** v. I-1
　I would like to introduce (name) to you. **Je te présente…** , fam. I-1
　I would like to introduce (name) to you. **Je vous présente…** , form. I-1
invite **inviter** v. I-4
Ireland **Irlande** f. I-7
Irish **irlandais(e)** adj. I-7
iron **fer à repasser** m. I-8, II-P
　to iron (the laundry) **repasser (le linge)** v. I-8, II-P
isn't it? (tag question) **n'est-ce pas?** I-2
island **île** f. II-6
Italian **italien(ne)** adj. I-1
Italy **Italie** f. I-7
it: It depends. **Ça dépend.** I-4
　It is… **C'est…** I-1
itself (used with reflexive verb) **se/s'** pron. II-2

J

jacket **blouson** m. I-6
jam **confiture** f. II-1
January **janvier** m. I-5
Japan **Japon** m. I-7
Japanese **japonais(e)** adj. I-1
jealous **jaloux/jalouse** adj. I-3
jeans **jean** m. sing. I-6
jewelry store **bijouterie** f. II-4
jogging **jogging** m. I-5
　to go jogging **faire du jogging** v. I-5
joke **blague** f. I-2
journalist **journaliste** m., f. I-3
juice (orange/apple) **jus** m. **(d'orange/de pomme)** I-4
July **juillet** m. I-5
June **juin** m. I-5
jungle **jungle** f. II-6
just (barely) **juste** adv. I-3

K

keep **retenir** v. II-1
key **clé** f. I-7
keyboard **clavier** m. II-3
kilo(gram) **kilo(gramme)** m. II-1
kind **bon(ne)** adj. I-3
kiosk **kiosque** m. I-4
kiss one another **s'embrasser** v. II-3
kitchen **cuisine** f. I-8, II-P
knee **genou** m. II-2
knife **couteau** m. II-1
know (as a fact) **savoir** v. I-8, II-P; (to be familiar with) **connaître** v. I-8, II-P
　to know one another **se connaître** v. II-3
　I don't know anything about it. **Je n'en sais rien.** II-6
　to know that… **savoir que…** II-7
known (as a fact) **su (savoir)** p.p. I-8, II-P; (famous) **connu (connaître)** p.p., adj. I-8, II-P

L

laborer **ouvrier/ouvrière** m., f. II-5
lake **lac** m. II-6
lamp **lampe** f. I-8, II-P
landlord **propriétaire** m., f. I-3
landslide **glissement de terrain** m. II-6
language **langue** f. I-2
　foreign languages **langues** f., pl. **étrangères** I-2
last **dernier/dernière** adj. I-2
lastly **dernièrement** adv. I-8, II-P
late (when something happens late) **en retard** adv. I-2; (in the evening, etc.) **tard** adv. I-2
laugh **rire** v. I-6
laughed **ri (rire)** p.p. I-6
laundromat **laverie** f. II-4
laundry: to do the laundry **faire la lessive** v. I-8, II-P
law (academic discipline) **droit** m. I-2; (ordinance or rule) **loi** f. II-6
lawyer **avocat(e)** m., f. I-3
lay off (let go) **renvoyer** v. II-5
lazy **paresseux/paresseuse** adj. I-3
learned **appris (apprendre)** p.p. I-6
least **moins** II-1
　the least… (used with adjective) **le/la moins…** super. adv. II-1
　the least… , (used with noun to express quantity) **le moins de…** II-6

Vocabulaire — English-French

the least... *(used with verb or adverb)* **le moins...** *super. adv.* II-1
leather **cuir** *m.* I-6
leave **partir** *v.* I-5; **quitter** *v.* I-4
   to leave alone **laisser tranquille** *v.* II-2
   to leave one another **se quitter** *v.* II-3
   I'm leaving. **Je m'en vais.** I-8, II-P
left: to the left (of) **à gauche (de)** *prep.* I-3
leg **jambe** *f.* II-2
leisure activity **loisir** *m.* I-5
lemon soda **limonade** *f.* I-4
lend (to someone) **prêter (à)** *v.* I-6
less **moins** *adv.* I-4
   less of... *(used with noun to express quantity)* **moins de...** I-4
   less ... than *(used with noun to compare quantities)* **moins de... que** II-6
   less... than *(used with adjective to compare qualities)* **moins... que** II-1
let **laisser** *v.* II-3
   to let go *(to fire or lay off)* **renvoyer** *v.* II-5
   Let's go! **Allons-y!** I-4; **On y va!** II-2
letter **lettre** *f.* II-4
   letter of application **lettre** *f.* **de motivation** II-5
   letter of recommendation/reference **lettre** *f.* **de recommandation** II-5
lettuce **laitue** *f.* II-1
level **niveau** *m.* II-5
library **bibliothèque** *f.* I-1
license: driver's license **permis** *m.* **de conduire** II-3
life **vie** *f.* I-6
life insurance **assurance** *f.* **vie** II-5
light: warning light *(automobile)* **voyant** *m.* II-3
   oil/gas warning light **voyant** *m.* **d'huile/d'essence** II-3
   to light up **s'allumer** *v.* II-3
like *(as)* **comme** *adv.* I-6; to like **aimer** *v.* I-2
   I don't like ... very much. **Je n'aime pas tellement...** I-2
   I really like... **J'aime bien...** I-2
   to like one another **s'aimer bien** *v.* II-3
   to like that... **aimer que...** *v.* II-6
line **queue** *f.* II-4
   to wait in line **faire la queue** *v.* II-4
link **lien** *m.* II-3

listen (to) **écouter** *v.* I-2
literary **littéraire** *adj.* II-7
literature **littérature** *f.* I-1
little *(not much)* (of) **peu (de)** *adv.* I-4
live (in) **habiter (à)** *v.* I-2
living room *(informal room)* **salle de séjour** *f.* I-8, II-P; *(formal room)* **salon** *m.* I-8, II-P
located: to be located **se trouver** *v.* II-2
long **long(ue)** *adj.* I-3
   a long time **longtemps** *adv.* I-5
look *(at one another)* **se regarder** *v.* II-3; *(at oneself)* **se regarder** *v.* II-2
look for **chercher** *v.* I-2
   to look for work **chercher du/un travail** II-4
loose *(clothing)* **large** *adj.* I-6
lose: to lose (time) **perdre (son temps)** *v.* I-6
   to lose weight **maigrir** *v.* I-4
lost: to be lost **être perdu(e)** *v.* II-4
lot: a lot of **beaucoup de** *adv.* I-4
love **amour** *m.* I-6
   to love **adorer** *v.* I-2
   I love... **J'adore...** I-2
   to love one another **s'aimer** *v.* II-3
   to be in love **être amoureux/amoureuse** *v.* I-6
luck **chance** *f.* I-2
   to be lucky **avoir de la chance** *v.* I-2
lunch **déjeuner** *m.* II-1
   to eat lunch **déjeuner** *v.* I-4

M

ma'am **Madame.** *f.* I-1
machine: answering machine **répondeur** *m.* II-3
mad: to get mad **s'énerver** *v.* II-2
made **fait (faire)** *p.p., adj.* I-6
magazine **magazine** *m.* II-7
mail **courrier** *m.* II-4
mailbox **boîte** *f.* **aux lettres** II-4
mailman **facteur** *m.* II-4
main character **personnage principal** *m.* II-7
main dish **plat (principal)** *m.* II-1
maintain **maintenir** *v.* II-1
make **faire** *v.* I-5
makeup **maquillage** *m.* II-2
   to put on makeup **se maquiller** *v.* II-2
make up **se réconcilier** *v.* II-7
malfunction **panne** *f.* II-3
man **homme** *m.* I-1
manage *(in business)* **diriger** *v.* II-5; *(to do something)* **arriver à** *v.* I-2

manager **gérant(e)** *m., f.* II-5
many (of) **beaucoup (de)** *adv.* I-4
   How many (of)? **Combien (de)?** I-1
map *(of a city)* **plan** *m.* I-7; *(of the world)* **carte** *f.* I-1
March **mars** *m.* I-5
marital status **état civil** *m.* I-6
market **marché** *m.* I-4
marriage **mariage** *m.* I-6
married **marié(e)** *adj.* I-3
   married couple **mariés** *m., pl.* I-6
marry **épouser** *v.* I-3
Martinique: from Martinique **martiniquais(e)** *adj.* I-1
masterpiece **chef-d'œuvre** *m.* II-7
mathematics **mathématiques (maths)** *f., pl.* I-2
May **mai** *m.* I-5
maybe **peut-être** *adv.* I-2
mayonnaise **mayonnaise** *f.* II-1
mayor's office **mairie** *f.* II-4
me **moi** *disj. pron., sing.* I-3; *(attached to imperative)* **-moi** *pron.* II-1; **me/m'** *i.o. pron.* I-6; **me/m'** *d.o. pron.* I-7
   Me too. **Moi aussi.** I-1
   Me neither. **Moi non plus.** I-2
meal **repas** *m.* II-1
mean **méchant(e)** *adj.* I-3
   to mean *(with* **dire***)* **vouloir** *v.* II-1
means: that means **ça veut dire** *v.* II-1
meat **viande** *f.* II-1
mechanic **mécanicien/mécanicienne** *m., f.* II-3
medication *(against/for)* **médicament (contre/pour)** *m., f.* II-2
meet *(to encounter, to run into)* **rencontrer** *v.* I-2; *(to make the acquaintance of)* **faire la connaissance de** *v.* I-5, **se rencontrer** *v.* II-3; *(planned encounter)* **se retrouver** *v.* II-3
meeting **réunion** *f.* II-5; **rendez-vous** *m.* I-6
member **membre** *m.* II-7
menu **menu** *m.* II-1; **carte** *f.* II-1
message **message** *m.* II-5
   to leave a message **laisser un message** *v.* II-5
Mexican **mexicain(e)** *adj.* I-1
Mexico **Mexique** *m.* I-7
microwave oven **four à micro-ondes** *m.* I-8, II-P
midnight **minuit** *m.* II-2
milk **lait** *m.* I-4
mineral water **eau** *f.* **minérale** I-4
mirror **miroir** *m.* I-8, II-P
Miss **Mademoiselle** *f.* I-1

Vocabulaire — English-French

mistaken: to be mistaken (*about something*) **se tromper (de)** *v.* II-2
modest **modeste** *adj.* II-5
moment **moment** *m.* I-1
Monday **lundi** *m.* I-2
money **argent** *m.* II-4; (*currency*) **monnaie** *f.* II-4
 to deposit money **déposer de l'argent** *v.* II-4
monitor **moniteur** *m.* II-3
month **mois** *m.* I-2
 this month **ce mois-ci** I-2
moon **Lune** *f.* II-6
more **plus** *adv.* I-4
 more of **plus de** I-4
 more … than (*used with noun to compare quantities*) **plus de… que** II-6
 more … than (*used with adjective to compare qualities*) **plus… que** II-1
morning **matin** *m.* I-2; **matinée** *f.* I-2
 this morning **ce matin** I-2
Moroccan **marocain(e)** *adj.* I-1
most **plus** II-1
 the most… (*used with adjective*) **le/la plus…** *super. adv.* II-1
 the most… (*used with noun to express quantity*) **le plus de…** II-6
 the most… (*used with verb or adverb*) **le plus…** *super. adv.* II-1
mother **mère** *f.* I-3
mother-in-law **belle-mère** *f.* I-3
mountain **montagne** *f.* I-4
mouse **souris** *f.* II-3
mouth **bouche** *f.* II-2
move (*to get around*) **se déplacer** *v.* II-4
 to move in **emménager** *v.* I-8, II-P
 to move out **déménager** *v.* I-8, II-P
movie **film** *m.* II-7
 adventure/horror/science-fiction/crime movie **film** *m.* **d'aventures/d'horreur/de science-fiction/policier** II-7
movie theater **cinéma (ciné)** *m.* I-4
MP3 **MP3** *m.* II-3
much (as much … as) (*used with noun to express quantity*) **autant de … que** *adv.* II-6
 How much (*of something*)? **Combien (de)?** I-1
 How much is… ? **Combien coûte… ?** I-4
museum **musée** *m.* I-4
 to go to museums **faire les musées** *v.* II-7
mushroom **champignon** *m.* II-1
music: to play music **faire de la musique** II-7
musical **comédie** *f.* **musicale** II-7; **musical(e)** *adj.* II-7
musician **musicien(ne)** *m., f.* I-3
must (*to have to*) **devoir** *v.* II-1
 One must **Il faut…** I-5
mustard **moutarde** *f.* II-1
my **ma** *poss. adj., f., sing.* I-3; **mes** *poss. adj., m., f., pl.* I-3; **mon** *poss. adj., m., sing.* I-3
myself **me/m'** *pron., sing.* II-2; (*attached to an imperative*) **-moi** *pron.* II-1

N

naïve **naïf (naïve)** *adj.* I-3
name: My name is… **Je m'appelle…** I-1
named: to be named **s'appeler** *v.* II-2
napkin **serviette** *f.* II-1
nationality **nationalité** *f.*
 I am of … nationality. **Je suis de nationalité…** I-1
natural **naturel(le)** *adj.* II-6
natural resource **ressource naturelle** *f.* II-6
nature **nature** *f.* II-6
nauseated: to feel nauseated **avoir mal au cœur** *v.* II-2
near (to) **près (de)** *prep.* I-3
 very near (to) **tout près (de)** II-4
necessary **nécessaire** *adj.* II-6
 It was necessary… (*followed by infinitive or subjunctive*) **Il a fallu…** I-6
 It is necessary…. (*followed by infinitive or subjunctive*) **Il faut que…** I-5
 It is necessary that… (*followed by subjunctive*) **Il est nécessaire que/qu'…** II-6
neck **cou** *m.* II-2
need **besoin** *m.* I-2
 to need **avoir besoin (de)** *v.* I-2
neighbor **voisin(e)** *m., f.* I-3
neighborhood **quartier** *m.* I-8, II-P
neither… nor **ne… ni… ni…** *conj.* II-4
nephew **neveu** *m.* I-3
nervous **nerveux/nerveuse** *adj.* I-3
nervously **nerveusement** *adv.* I-8, II-P
network (social) **réseau (social)** *m.* II-3
never **jamais** *adv.* I-5; **ne… jamais** *adv.* II-4

new **nouveau/nouvelle** *adj.* I-3
newlyweds **jeunes mariés** *m., pl.* I-6
news **informations (infos)** *f., pl.* II-7; **nouvelles** *f., pl.* II-7
newspaper **journal** *m.* I-7
newsstand **marchand de journaux** *m.* II-4
next **ensuite** *adv.* I-7; **prochain(e)** *adj.* I-2
 next to **à côté de** *prep.* I-3
nice **gentil/gentille** *adj.* I-3; **sympa(thique)** *adj.* I-1
nicely **gentiment** *adv.* I-8, II-P
niece **nièce** *f.* I-3
night **nuit** *f.* I-2
nightclub **boîte (de nuit)** *f.* I-4
nine **neuf** *m.* I-1
nine hundred **neuf cents** *m.* I-5
nineteen **dix-neuf** *m.* I-1
ninety **quatre-vingt-dix** *m.* I-3
ninth **neuvième** *adj.* I-7
no (*at beginning of statement to indicate disagreement*) **(mais) non** I-2; **aucun(e)** *adj.* II-2
 no more **ne… plus** II-4
 no problem **pas de problème** II-4
 no reason **pour rien** I-4
 no, none **pas (de)** II-4
nobody **ne… personne** II-4
none (not any) **ne… aucun(e)** II-4
noon **midi** *m.* I-2
no one **personne** *pron.* II-4
north **nord** *m.* II-4
nose **nez** *m.* II-2
not **ne… pas** I-2
 not at all **pas du tout** *adv.* I-2
 Not badly. **Pas mal.** I-1
 to not believe that **ne pas croire que** *v.* II-7
 to not think that **ne pas penser que** *v.* II-7
 not yet **pas encore** *adv.* I-8, II-P
notebook **cahier** *m.* I-1
notes **billets** *m., pl.* II-3
nothing **rien** *indef. pron.* II-4
 It's nothing. **Il n'y a pas de quoi.** I-1
notice **s'apercevoir** *v.* II-4
novel **roman** *m.* II-7
November **novembre** *m.* I-5
now **maintenant** *adv.* I-5
nuclear **nucléaire** *adj.* II-6
nuclear energy **énergie nucléaire** *f.* II-6
nuclear plant **centrale nucléaire** *f.* II-6
nurse **infirmier/infirmière** *m., f.* II-2

Vocabulaire

English-French

O

object **objet** *m.* I-1
obtain **obtenir** *v.* II-5
obvious **évident(e)** *adj.* II-7
    It is obvious that… **Il est évident que…** II-7
obviously **évidemment** *adv.* I-8, II-P
o'clock: It's… (o'clock). **Il est… heure(s).** I-2
    at … (o'clock) **à … heure(s)** I-4
October **octobre** *m.* I-5
of **de/d'** *prep.* I-3
    of medium height **de taille moyenne** *adj.* I-3
    of the **des (de + les)** I-3
    of the **du (de + le)** I-3
    of which, of whom **dont** *rel. pron.* II-3
of course **bien sûr** *adv.*; **évidemment** *adv.* I-2
    of course not *(at beginning of statement to indicate disagreement)* **(mais) non** I-2
offer **offrir** *v.* II-3
offered **offert (offrir)** *p.p.* II-3
office **bureau** *m.* I-4
    at the doctor's office **chez le médecin** *prep.* I-2
often **souvent** *adv.* I-5
oil **huile** *f.* II-1
    automobile oil **huile** *f.* II-3
    oil warning light **voyant** *m.* **d'huile** II-3
    olive oil **huile** *f.* **d'olive** II-1
    to check the oil **vérifier l'huile** *v.* II-3
okay **d'accord** I-2
old **vieux/vieille** *adj.*; *(placed after noun)* **ancien(ne)** *adj.* I-3
old age **vieillesse** *f.* I-6
olive **olive** *f.* II-1
olive oil **huile** *f.* **d'olive** II-1
omelette **omelette** *f.* I-5
on **sur** *prep.* I-3
    On behalf of whom? **C'est de la part de qui?** II-5
    on the condition that… **à condition que** II-7
    on television **à la télé(vision)** II-7
    on the contrary **au contraire** II-7
    on the radio **à la radio** II-7
    on the subject of **au sujet de** II-6
    on vacation **en vacances** I-7
once **une fois** *adv.* I-8, II-P
one **un** *m.* I-1
    one **on** *sub. pron., sing.* I-1
    one another **l'un(e) à l'autre** II-3
one another **l'un(e) l'autre** II-3
one had to… **il fallait…** I-8, II-P
One must… **Il faut que/qu'…** II-6
One must… **Il faut…** *(followed by infinitive or subjunctive)* I-5
one million **un million** *m.* I-5
    one million *(things)* **un million de…** I-5
onion **oignon** *m.* II-1
online **en ligne** II-3
    to be online **être en ligne** *v.* II-3
    to be online (with someone) **être connecté(e) (avec quelqu'un)** *v.* I-7, II-3
only **ne… que** II-4; **seulement** *adv.* I-8, II-P
open **ouvrir** *v.* II-3; **ouvert(e)** *adj.* II-3
opened **ouvert (ouvrir)** *p.p.* II-3
opera **opéra** *m.* II-7
optimistic **optimiste** *adj.* I-1
or **ou** I-3
orange **orange** *f.* II-1; **orange** *inv.adj.* I-6
orchestra **orchestre** *m.* II-7
order **commander** *v.* II-1
organize (a party) **organiser (une fête)** *v.* I-6
orient oneself **s'orienter** *v.* II-4
others **d'autres** I-4
our **nos** *poss. adj., m., f., pl.* I-3; **notre** *poss. adj., m., f., sing.* I-3
outdoor *(open-air)* **plein air** II-6
over **fini** *adj., p.p.* I-7
overpopulation **surpopulation** *f.* II-6
overseas **à l'étranger** *adv.* I-7
over there **là-bas** *adv.* I-1
owed **dû (devoir)** *p.p., adj.* II-1
own **posséder** *v.* I-5
owner **propriétaire** *m., f.* I-3
ozone **ozone** *m.* II-6
    hole in the ozone layer **trou dans la couche d'ozone** *m.* II-6

P

pack: to pack one's bags **faire les valises** I-7
package **colis** *m.* II-4
paid **payé (payer)** *p.p., adj.* II-5
    to be well/badly paid **être bien/mal payé(e)** II-5
pain **douleur** *f.* II-2
paint **faire de la peinture** *v.* II-7
painter **peintre/femme peintre** *m., f.* II-7
painting **peinture** *f.* II-7; **tableau** *m.* II-7
Palm Pilot **palm** *m.* I-1
pants **pantalon** *m., sing.* I-6
paper **papier** *m.* I-1
Pardon (me). **Pardon.** I-1
parents **parents** *m., pl.* I-3
park **parc** *m.* I-4
    to park **se garer** *v.* II-3
parka **anorak** *m.* I-6
parking lot **parking** *m.* II-3
part-time job **emploi** *m.* **à mi-temps/à temps partiel** *m.* II-5
party **fête** *f.* I-6
    to party **faire la fête** *v.* I-6
pass **dépasser** *v.* II-3; **passer** *v.* I-7
    to pass an exam **être reçu(e) à un examen** *v.* I-2
passenger **passager/passagère** *m., f.* I-7
passport **passeport** *m.* I-7
password **mot de passe** *m.* II-3
past: in the past **autrefois** *adv.* I-8, II-P
pasta **pâtes** *f., pl.* II-1
pastime **passe-temps** *m.* I-5
pastry **pâtisserie** *f.* II-1
pastry shop **pâtisserie** *f.* II-1
pâté **pâté (de campagne)** *m.* II-1
path **sentier** *m.* II-6; **chemin** *m.* II-4
patient **patient(e)** *adj.* I-1
patiently **patiemment** *adv.* I-8, II-P
pay **payer** *v.* I-5
    to pay by check **payer par chèque** *v.* II-4
    to pay in cash **payer en liquide** *v.* II-4
    to pay with a credit card **payer avec une carte de crédit** *v.* II-4
    to pay attention (to) **faire attention (à)** *v.* I-5
peach **pêche** *f.* II-1
pear **poire** *f.* II-1
peas **petits pois** *m., pl.* II-1
pen **stylo** *m.* I-1
pencil **crayon** *m.* I-1
people **gens** *m., pl.* I-7
pepper *(spice)* **poivre** *m.* II-1; *(vegetable)* **poivron** *m.* II-1
per day/week/month/year **par jour/semaine/mois/an** I-5
perfect **parfait(e)** *adj.* I-2
perhaps **peut-être** *adv.* I-2
period *(punctuation mark)* **point** *m.* II-3
permit **permis** *m.* II-3
permitted **permis (permettre)** *p.p., adj.* I-6
person **personne** *f.* I-1

Vocabulaire — English-French

pessimistic **pessimiste** *adj.* I-1
pharmacist **pharmacien(ne)** *m., f.* II-2
pharmacy **pharmacie** *f.* II-2
philosophy **philosophie** *f.* I-2
phone booth **cabine téléphonique** *f.* II-4
phone card **télécarte** *f.* II-5
phone one another **se téléphoner** *v.* II-3
photo(graph) **photo(graphie)** *f.* I-3
physical education **éducation physique** *f.* I-2
physics **physique** *f.* I-2
piano **piano** *m.* II-7
pick up **décrocher** *v.* II-5
picnic **pique-nique** *m.* II-6
picture **tableau** *m.* I-1
pie **tarte** *f.* II-1
piece (of) **morceau (de)** *m.* I-4
   piece of furniture **meuble** *m.* I-8, II-P
pill **pilule** *f.* II-2
pillow **oreiller** *m.* I-8, II-P
pink **rose** *adj.* I-6
pitcher (of water) **carafe (d'eau)** *f.* II-1
place **endroit** *m.* I-4; **lieu** *m.* I-4
planet **planète** *f.* II-6
plans: to make plans **faire des projets** *v.* II-5
plant **plante** *f.* II-6
plastic **plastique** *m.* II-6
plastic wrapping **emballage en plastique** *m.* II-6
plate **assiette** *f.* II-1
play **pièce de théâtre** *f.* II-7
play **s'amuser** *v.* II-2; (*a sport/a musical instrument*) **jouer (à/de)** *v.* I-5
   to play regularly **pratiquer** *v.* I-5
   to play sports **faire du sport** *v.* I-5
   to play a role **jouer un rôle** *v.* II-7
player **joueur/joueuse** *m., f.* I-5
playwright **dramaturge** *m.* II-7
pleasant **agréable** *adj.* I-1
please: to please someone **faire plaisir à quelqu'un** *v.* II-5
   Please. **S'il te plaît.** *fam.* I-1
   Please. **S'il vous plaît.** *form.* I-1
   Please. **Je vous en prie.** *form.* I-1
   Please hold. **Ne quittez pas.** II-5
plumber **plombier** *m.* II-5
poem **poème** *m.* II-7
poet **poète/poétesse** *m., f.* II-7
police **police** *f.* II-3; **policier** *adj.* II-7
police officer **agent de police** *m.* II-3; **policier** *m.* II-3; **policière** *f.* II-3
police station **commissariat de police** *m.* II-4
polite **poli(e)** *adj.* I-1
politely **poliment** *adv.* I-8, II-P
political science **sciences politiques (sciences po)** *f., pl.* I-2
politician **homme/femme politique** *m., f.* II-5
pollute **polluer** *v.* II-6
pollution **pollution** *f.* II-6
   pollution cloud **nuage de pollution** *m.* II-6
pool **piscine** *f.* I-4
poor **pauvre** *adj.* I-3
popular music **variétés** *f., pl.* II-7
population **population** *f.* II-6
   growing population **population croissante** *f.* II-6
pork **porc** *m.* II-1
portrait **portrait** *m.* I-5
position (*job*) **poste** *m.* II-5
possess (*to own*) **posséder** *v.* I-5
possible **possible** *adj.* II-7
   It is possible that… **Il est possible que…** II-6
post **afficher** *v.* II-5
post office **bureau de poste** *m.* II-4
postal service **poste** *f.* II-4
postcard **carte postale** *f.* II-4
poster **affiche** *f.* I-8, II-P
potato **pomme de terre** *f.* II-1
practice **pratiquer** *v.* I-5
prefer **aimer mieux** *v.* I-2; **préférer (que)** *v.* I-5
pregnant **enceinte** *adj.* II-2
prepare (for) **préparer** *v.* I-2
   to prepare (*to do something*) **se préparer (à)** *v.* II-2
prescription **ordonnance** *f.* II-2
present **présenter** *v.* II-7
preservation: habitat preservation **sauvetage des habitats** *m.* II-6
preserve **préserver** *v.* II-6
pressure **pression** *f.* II-3
   to check the tire pressure **vérifier la pression des pneus** *v.* II-3
pretty **joli(e)** *adj.* I-3; (*before an adjective or adverb*) **assez** *adv.* I-8, II-P
prevent: to prevent a fire **prévenir l'incendie** *v.* II-6
price **prix** *m.* I-4
principal **principal(e)** *adj.* II-4
print **imprimer** *v.* II-3
printer **imprimante** *f.* II-3
problem **problème** *m.* I-1
produce **produire** *v.* I-6
produced **produit (produire)** *p.p., adj.* I-6
product **produit** *m.* II-6
profession **métier** *m.* II-5; **profession** *f.* II-5
   demanding profession **profession** *f.* **exigeante** II-5
professional **professionnel(le)** *adj.* II-5
   professional experience **expérience professionnelle** *f.* II-5
program **programme** *m.* II-7; (*software*) **logiciel** *m.* II-3; (*television*) **émission** *f.* **de télévision** II-7
prohibit **interdire** *v.* II-6
project **projet** *m.* II-5
promise **promettre** *v.* I-6
promised **promis (promettre)** *p.p., adj.* I-6
promotion **promotion** *f.* II-5
propose that… **proposer que…** *v.* II-6
   to propose a solution **proposer une solution** *v.* II-6
protect **protéger** *v.* I-5
protection **préservation** *f.* II-6; **protection** *f.* II-6
proud **fier/fière** *adj.* I-3
psychological **psychologique** *adj.* II-7
psychological drama **drame psychologique** *m.* II-7
psychology **psychologie** *f.* I-2
psychologist **psychologue** *m., f.* II-5
publish **publier** *v.* II-7
pure **pur(e)** *adj.* II-6
purple **violet(te)** *adj.* I-6
purse **sac à main** *m.* I-6
put **mettre** *v.* I-6
   to put (on) (yourself) **se mettre** *v.* II-2
   to put away **ranger** *v.* I-8, II-P
   to put on makeup **se maquiller** *v.* II-2
   put **mis (mettre)** *p.p.* I-6

Q

quarter **quart** *m.* I-2
   a quarter after … (o'clock) **… et quart** I-2
Quebec: from Quebec **québécois(e)** *adj.* I-1
question **question** *f.* I-6
   to ask (*someone*) a question **poser une question (à)** *v.* I-6
quick **vite** *adv.* I-4
quickly **vite** *adv.* I-1
quite (*before an adjective or adverb*) **assez** *adv.* I-8, II-P

Vocabulaire — English-French

R

rabbit **lapin** *m.* II-6
rain **pleuvoir** *v.* I-5
   acid rain **pluie** *f.* **acide** II-6
   It is raining. **Il pleut.** I-5
   It was raining. **Il pleuvait.** I-8, II-P
rain forest **forêt tropicale** *f.* II-6
rain jacket **imperméable** *m.* I-5
rained **plu (pleuvoir)** *p.p.* I-6
raise (in salary) **augmentation (de salaire)** *f.* II-5
rapidly **rapidement** *adv.* I-8, II-P
rarely **rarement** *adv.* I-5
rather **plutôt** *adv.* I-1
ravishing **ravissant(e)** *adj.* II-5
razor **rasoir** *m.* II-2
read **lire** *v.* I-7
read **lu (lire)** *p.p., adj.* I-7
ready **prêt(e)** *adj.* I-3
real (*true*) **vrai(e)** *adj.*; **véritable** *adj.* I-3
real estate agent **agent immobilier** *m., f.* II-5
realize **se rendre compte** *v.* II-2
really **vraiment** *adv.* I-5; (*before adjective or adverb*) **tout(e)** *adv.* I-3; (*before adjective or adverb*) **très** *adv.* I-8, II-P
   really close by **tout près** I-3
rear-view mirror **rétroviseur** *m.* II-3
reason **raison** *f.* I-2
receive **recevoir** *v.* II-4
received **reçu (recevoir)** *p.p., adj.* II-4
receiver **combiné** *m.* II-5
recent **récent(e)** *adj.* II-7
reception desk **réception** *f.* I-7
recognize **reconnaître** *v.* I-8, II-P
recognized **reconnu (reconnaître)** *p.p., adj.* I-8, II-P
recommend that… **recommander que…** *v.* II-6
recommendation **recommandation** *f.* II-5
record **enregistrer** *v.* II-3
   (*CD, DVD*) **graver** *v.* II-3
recycle **recycler** *v.* II-6
recycling **recyclage** *m.* II-6
red **rouge** *adj.* I-6
redial **recomposer (un numéro)** *v.* II-3
reduce **réduire** *v.* I-6
reduced **réduit (réduire)** *p.p., adj.* I-6
reference **référence** *f.* II-5
reflect (on) **réfléchir (à)** *v.* II-4
refrigerator **frigo** *m.* I-8, II-P
refuse (*to do something*) **refuser (de)** *v.* II-3
region **région** *f.* II-6

regret that… **regretter que…** II-6
relax **se détendre** *v.* II-2
remember **se souvenir (de)** *v.* II-2
remote control **télécommande** *f.* II-3
rent **loyer** *m.* I-8, II-P
   to rent **louer** *v.* I-8, II-P
repair **réparer** *v.* II-3
repeat **répéter** *v.* I-5
research **rechercher** *v.* II-5
researcher **chercheur/chercheuse** *m., f.* II-5
reservation **réservation** *f.* I-7
   to cancel a reservation **annuler une réservation** I-7
reserve **réserver** *v.* I-7
reserved **réservé(e)** *adj.* I-1
resign **démissionner** *v.* II-5
resort (ski) **station** *f.* **(de ski)** I-7
respond **répondre (à)** *v.* I-6
rest **se reposer** *v.* II-2
restart **redémarrer** *v.* II-3
restaurant **restaurant** *m.* I-4
restroom(s) **toilettes** *f., pl.* I-8, II-P; **W.-C.** *m., pl.*
result **résultat** *m.* I-2
résumé **curriculum vitæ (C.V.)** *m.* II-5
retake **repasser** *v.* II-7
retire **prendre sa retraite** *v.* I-6
retired person **retraité(e)** *m., f.* II-5
retirement **retraite** *f.* I-6
return **retourner** *v.* I-7
   to return (home) **rentrer (à la maison)** *v.* I-2
review (*criticism*) **critique** *f.* II-7
rice **riz** *m.* II-1
ride: to go horseback riding **faire du cheval** *v.* I-5
   to ride in a car **rouler en voiture** *v.* I-7
right **juste** *adv.* I-3
   to the right (of) **à droite (de)** *prep.* I-3
   to be right **avoir raison** I-2
   right away **tout de suite** I-7
   right next door **juste à côté** I-3
ring **sonner** *v.* II-3
river **fleuve** *m.* II-6; **rivière** *f.* II-6
riverboat **bateau-mouche** *m.* I-7
role **rôle** *m.* II-6
room **pièce** *f.* I-8, II-P; **salle** *f.* I-8, II-P
   bedroom **chambre** *f.* I-7
   classroom **salle** *f.* **de classe** I-1
   dining room **salle** *f.* **à manger** I-8, II-P
   single hotel room **chambre** *f.* **individuelle** I-7

roommate **camarade de chambre** *m., f.* I-1
   (*in an apartment*) **colocataire** *m., f.* I-1
round-trip **aller-retour** *adj.* I-7
   round-trip ticket **billet** *m.* **aller-retour** I-7
rug **tapis** *m.* I-8, II-P
run **courir** *v.* I-5; **couru (courir)** *p.p., adj.* I-6
   to run into someone **tomber sur quelqu'un** *v.* I-7

S

sad **triste** *adj.* I-3
   to be sad that… **être triste que…** *v.* II-6
safety **sécurité** *f.* II-3
said **dit (dire)** *p.p., adj.* I-7
salad **salade** *f.* II-1
salary (a high, low) **salaire (élevé, modeste)** *m.* II-5
sales **soldes** *f., pl.* I-6
salon: beauty salon **salon** *m.* **de beauté** II-4
salt **sel** *m.* II-1
sandwich **sandwich** *m.* I-4
sat (down) **assis (s'asseoir)** *p.p.* II-2
Saturday **samedi** *m.* I-2
sausage **saucisse** *f.* II-1
save **sauvegarder** *v.* II-3
   save the planet **sauver la planète** *v.* II-6
savings **épargne** *f.* II-4
savings account **compte d'épargne** *m.* II-4
say **dire** *v.* I-7
scarf **écharpe** *f.* I-6
scholarship **bourse** *f.* I-2
school **école** *f.* I-2
science **sciences** *f., pl.* I-2
   political science **sciences politiques (sciences po)** *f., pl.* I-2
screen **écran** *m.* II-3
screening **séance** *f.* II-7
sculpture **sculpture** *f.* II-7
sculptor **sculpteur/femme sculpteur** *m., f.* II-7
sea **mer** *f.* I-7
seafood **fruits de mer** *m., pl.* II-1
search for **chercher** *v.* I-2
   to search for work **chercher du travail** *v.* II-4
season **saison** *f.* I-5
seat **place** *f.* II-7
seatbelt **ceinture de sécurité** *f.* II-3
   to buckle one's seatbelt **attacher sa ceinture de sécurité** *v.* II-3

Vocabulaire — English-French

seated **assis(e)** *p.p., adj.* II-2
second **deuxième** *adj.* I-7
security **sécurité** *f.* II-3
see **voir** *v.* II-7; (*catch sight of*) **apercevoir** *v.* II-4
  to see again **revoir** *v.* II-7
  See you later. **À plus tard.** I-1
  See you later. **À tout à l'heure.** I-1
  See you soon. **À bientôt.** I-1
  See you tomorrow. **À demain.** I-1
seen **aperçu (apercevoir)** *p.p.* II-4; **vu (voir)** *p.p.* II-7
  seen again **revu (revoir)** *p.p.* II-7
self/-selves **même(s)** *pron.* I-6
selfish **égoïste** *adj.* I-1
sell **vendre** *v.* I-6
seller **vendeur/vendeuse** *m., f.* I-6
send **envoyer** *v.* I-5
  to send (*to someone*) **envoyer (à)** *v.* I-6
  to send a letter **poster une lettre** II-4
Senegalese **sénégalais(e)** *adj.* I-1
sense **sentir** *v.* I-5
separated **séparé(e)** *adj.* I-3
September **septembre** *m.* I-5
serious **grave** *adj.* II-2; **sérieux/sérieuse** *adj.* I-3
serve **servir** *v.* I-5
server **serveur/serveuse** *m., f.* I-4
service station **station-service** *f.* II-3
set the table **mettre la table** *v.* I-8, II-P
seven **sept** *m.* I-1
seven hundred **sept cents** *m.* I-5
seventeen **dix-sept** *m.* I-1
seventh **septième** *adj.* I-7
seventy **soixante-dix** *m.* I-3
several **plusieurs** *adj.* I-4
shame **honte** *f.* I-2
  It's a shame that… **Il est dommage que…** II-6
shampoo **shampooing** *m.* II-2
shape (*state of health*) **forme** *f.* II-2
share **partager** *v.* I-2
shave (oneself) **se raser** *v.* II-2
shaving cream **crème à raser** *f.* II-2
she **elle** *pron.* I-1
sheet of paper **feuille de papier** *f.* I-1
sheets **draps** *m., pl.* I-8, II-P
shelf **étagère** *f.* I-8, II-P
shh **chut** II-7
shirt (short-/long-sleeved) **chemise (à manches courtes/longues)** *f.* I-6
shoe **chaussure** *f.* I-6

shopkeeper **commerçant(e)** *m., f.* II-1
shopping **shopping** *m.* I-7
  to go shopping **faire du shopping** *v.* I-7
  to go (grocery) shopping **faire les courses** *v.* I-1
shopping center **centre commercial** *m.* I-4
short **court(e)** *adj.* I-3; (*stature*) **petit(e)** I-3
shorts **short** *m.* I-6
shot (*injection*) **piqûre** *f.* II-2
  to give a shot **faire une piqûre** *v.* II-2
show **spectacle** *m.* I-5; (*movie or theater*) **séance** *f.* II-7
  to show (*to someone*) **montrer (à)** *v.* I-6
shower **douche** *f.* I-8, II-P
shut off **fermer** *v.* II-3
shy **timide** *adj.* I-1
sick: to get/be sick **tomber/être malade** *v.* II-2
sign **signer** *v.* II-4
silk **soie** *f.* I-6
since **depuis** *adv.* II-1
sincere **sincère** *adj.* I-1
sing **chanter** *v.* I-5
singer **chanteur/chanteuse** *m., f.* I-1
single (*marital status*) **célibataire** *adj.* I-3
  single hotel room **chambre** *f.* **individuelle** I-7
sink **évier** *m.* I-8, II-P; (*bathroom*) **lavabo** *m.* I-8, II-P
sir **Monsieur** *m.* I-1
sister **sœur** *f.* I-3
sister-in-law **belle-sœur** *f.* I-3
sit down **s'asseoir** *v.* II-2
sitting **assis(e)** *adj.* II-2
six **six** *m.* I-1
six hundred **six cents** *m.* I-5
sixteen **seize** *m.* I-1
sixth **sixième** *adj.* I-7
sixty **soixante** *m.* I-1
size **taille** *f.* I-6
skate **patiner** *v.* I-4
ski **skier** *v.* I-5; **faire du ski** I-5
skiing **ski** *m.* I-5
ski jacket **anorak** *m.* I-6
ski resort **station** *f.* **de ski** I-7
skin **peau** *f.* II-2
skirt **jupe** *f.* I-6
sky **ciel** *m.* II-6
sleep **sommeil** *m.* II-2
  to sleep **dormir** *v.* I-5
  to be sleepy **avoir sommeil** *v.* I-2
sleeve **manche** *f.* I-6
slice **tranche** *f.* II-1
slipper **pantoufle** *f.* II-2

slow **lent(e)** *adj.* I-3
small **petit(e)** *adj.* I-3
smartphone **smartphone** *m.* II-3
smell **sentir** *v.* I-5
smile **sourire** *m.* I-6
  to smile **sourire** *v.* I-6
smoke **fumer** *v.* II-2
snack (afternoon) **goûter** *m.* II-1
snake **serpent** *m.* II-6
sneeze **éternuer** *v.* II-2
snow **neiger** *v.* I-5
  It is snowing. **Il neige.** I-5
  It was snowing… **Il neigeait…** I-8, II-P
so **si** II-3; **alors** *adv.* I-1
  so that **pour que** II-7
soap **savon** *m.* II-2
soap opera **feuilleton** *m.* II-7
soccer **foot(ball)** *m.* I-5
sociable **sociable** *adj.* I-1
sociology **sociologie** *f.* I-1
sock **chaussette** *f.* I-6
software **logiciel** *m.* II-3
soil (*to make dirty*) **salir** *v.* I-8, II-P
solar **solaire** *adj.* II-6
solar energy **énergie solaire** *f.* II-6
solution **solution** *f.* II-6
some **de l'** *part. art., m., f., sing.* I-4
  some **de la** *part. art., f., sing.* I-4
  some **des** *part. art., m., f., pl.* I-4
  some **du** *part. art., m., sing.* I-4
  some **quelques** *adj.* I-4
  some (of it/them) **en** *pron.* II-2
someone **quelqu'un** *pron.* II-4
something **quelque chose** *m.* I-4
  Something's not right. **Quelque chose ne va pas.** I-5
sometimes **parfois** *adv.* I-5; **quelquefois** *adv.* I-8, II-P
son **fils** *m.* I-3
song **chanson** *f.* II-7
sorry **désolé(e)** II-3
  to be sorry that… **être désolé(e) que…** *v.* II-6
sort **sorte** *f.* II-7
So-so. **Comme ci, comme ça.** I-1
soup **soupe** *f.* I-4
soupspoon **cuillère à soupe** *f.* II-1
south **sud** *m.* II-4
space **espace** *m.* II-6
Spain **Espagne** *f.* I-7
Spanish **espagnol(e)** *adj.* I-1
speak (on the phone) **parler (au téléphone)** *v.* I-2
  to speak (to) **parler (à)** *v.* I-6
  to speak to one another **se parler** *v.* II-3
specialist **spécialiste** *m., f.* II-5
species **espèce** *f.* II-6

Vocabulaire — English-French

endangered species **espèce** f. **menacée** II-6
spectator **spectateur/spectatrice** m., f. II-7
speed **vitesse** f. I-3
speed limit **limitation de vitesse** f. II-3
spend **dépenser** v. I-4
  to spend money **dépenser de l'argent** I-4
  to spend time **passer** v. I-7
  to spend time (*somewhere*) **faire un séjour** I-7
spoon **cuillère** f. II-1
sport(s) **sport** m. I-5
  to play sports **faire du sport** v. I-5
sporty **sportif/sportive** adj. I-3
sprain one's ankle **se fouler la cheville** II-2
spring **printemps** m. I-5
  in the spring **au printemps** I-5
square (*place*) **place** f. I-4
squirrel **écureuil** m. II-6
stadium **stade** m. I-5
stage (*phase*) **étape** f. I-6
stage fright **trac** II-5
staircase **escalier** m. I-8, II-P
stamp **timbre** m. II-4
star **étoile** f. II-6
starter **entrée** f. II-1
start up **démarrer** v. II-3
station **station** f. I-7
  subway station **station** f. **de métro** I-7
  train station **gare** f. I-7
stationery store **papeterie** f. II-4
statue **statue** f. II-4
stay **séjour** m. I-7; **rester** v. I-7
  to stay slim **garder la ligne** v. II-2
steak **steak** m. II-1
steering wheel **volant** m. II-3
stepbrother **demi-frère** m. I-3
stepfather **beau-père** m. I-3
stepmother **belle-mère** f. I-3
stepsister **demi-sœur** f. I-3
stereo system **chaîne stéréo** f. II-3
still **encore** adv. I-3
stomach **ventre** m. II-2
  to have a stomach ache **avoir mal au ventre** v. II-2
stone **pierre** f. II-6
stop (*doing something*) **arrêter (de faire quelque chose)** v.; (*to stop oneself*) **s'arrêter** v. II-2
  to stop by someone's house **passer chez quelqu'un** v. I-4
  bus stop **arrêt d'autobus (de bus)** m. I-7
store **magasin** m.; **boutique** f. II-4
  grocery store **épicerie** f. I-4

stormy **orageux/orageuse** adj. I-5
  It is stormy. **Le temps est orageux.** I-5
story **histoire** f. I-2
stove **cuisinière** f. I-8, II-P
straight **raide** adj. I-3
  straight ahead **tout droit** adv. II-4
strangle **étrangler** v. II-5
strawberry **fraise** f. II-1
street **rue** f. II-3
  to follow a street **suivre une rue** v. II-4
strong **fort(e)** adj. I-3
student **étudiant(e)** m., f. I; **élève** m., f. I-1
  high school student **lycéen(ne)** m., f. I-2
studies **études** f. I-2
studio (*apartment*) **studio** m. I-8, II-P
study **étudier** v. I-2
suburbs **banlieue** f. I-4
subway **métro** m. I-7
subway station **station** f. **de métro** I-7
succeed (*in doing something*) **réussir (à)** v. I-4
success **réussite** f. II-5
suddenly **soudain** adv. I-8, II-P; **tout à coup** adv. I-7.; **tout d'un coup** adv. I-8, II-P
suffer **souffrir** v. II-3
suffered **souffert (souffrir)** p.p. II-3
sugar **sucre** m. I-4
suggest (that) **suggérer (que)** v. II-6
suit (*man's*) **costume** m. I-6; (*woman's*) **tailleur** m. I-6
suitcase **valise** f. I-7
summer **été** m. I-5
  in the summer **en été** I-5
sun **soleil** m. I-5
  It is sunny. **Il fait (du) soleil.** I-5
Sunday **dimanche** m. I-2
sunglasses **lunettes de soleil** f., pl. I-6
supermarket **supermarché** m. II-1
sure **sûr(e)** II-1
  It is sure that… **Il est sûr que…** II-7
  It is unsure that… **Il n'est pas sûr que…** II-7
surf on the Internet **surfer sur Internet** II-3
surprise (someone) **faire une surprise (à quelqu'un)** v. I-6
surprised **surpris (surprendre)** p.p., adj. I-6
  to be surprised that… **être surpris(e) que…** v. II-6

sweater **pull** m. I-6
sweep **balayer** v. I-8, II-P
swell **enfler** v. II-2
swim **nager** v. I-4
swimsuit **maillot de bain** m. I-6
Swiss **suisse** adj. I-1
Switzerland **Suisse** f. I-7
symptom **symptôme** m. II-2

T

table **table** f. I-1
  to clear the table **débarrasser la table** v. I-8, II-P
tablecloth **nappe** f. II-1
tablet computer **tablette (tactile)** f. II-3
take **prendre** v. I-4
  to take a shower **prendre une douche** II-2
  to take a train (plane, taxi, bus, boat) **prendre un train (un avion, un taxi, un autobus, un bateau)** v. I-7
  to take a walk **se promener** v. II-2
  to take advantage of **profiter de** v. II-7
  to take an exam **passer un examen** v. I-2
  to take care (of something) **s'occuper (de)** v. II-2
  to take out the trash **sortir la/les poubelle(s)** v. I-8, II-P
  to take time off **prendre un congé** v. II-5
  to take (someone) **emmener** v. I-5
taken **pris (prendre)** p.p., adj. I-6
tale **conte** m. II-7
talented (*gifted*) **doué(e)** adj. II-7
tan **bronzer** v. I-6
tape recorder **magnétophone** m. II-3
tart **tarte** f. II-1
taste **goûter** v. II-1
taxi **taxi** m. I-7
tea **thé** m. I-4
teach **enseigner** v. I-2
  to teach (*to do something*) **apprendre (à)** v. I-4
teacher **professeur** m. I-1
team **équipe** f. I-5
teaspoon **cuillère à café** f. II-1
tee shirt **tee-shirt** m. I-6
teeth **dents** f., pl. II-1
  to brush one's teeth **se brosser les dents** v. II-1
telephone (*receiver*) **appareil** m. II-5
  to telephone (*someone*) **téléphoner (à)** v. I-2

Vocabulaire

English-French

It's Mr./Mrs./Miss … (on the phone.) **C'est M./Mme/ Mlle … (à l'appareil.)** II-5
television **télévision** *f.* I-1
   television channel **chaîne** *f.* **(de télévision)** II-3
   television program **émission** *f.* **de télévision** II-7
   television set **poste de télévision** *m.* II-3
tell one another **se dire** *v.* II-3
temperature **température** *f.* I-5
ten **dix** *m.* I-1
tennis **tennis** *m.* I-5
tennis shoes **baskets** *f., pl.* I-6
tenth **dixième** *adj.* I-7
terminal (bus) **gare** *f.* **routière** I-7
terrace (café) **terrasse** *f.* **de café** I-4
test **examen** *m.* I-1
text message **texto, SMS** *m.* II-3
than **que/qu'** *conj.* II-1, II-6
thank: Thank you (very much). **Merci (beaucoup).** I-1
that **ce/c', ça** I-1; **que** *rel. pron.* II-3
   Is that… ? **Est-ce… ?** I-2
   That's enough. **Ça suffit.** I-5
   That has nothing to do with us. That is none of our business. **Ça ne nous regarde pas.** II-6
   that is… **c'est…** I-1
   that is to say **ça veut dire** II-2
theater **théâtre** *m.* II-7
their **leur(s)** *poss. adj., m., f.* I-3
them **les** *d.o. pron.* I-7, **leur** *i.o. pron., m., f., pl.* I-6
then **ensuite** *adv.* I-7, **puis** *adv.* I-7, **puis** I-4; **alors** *adv.* I-7
there **là** I-1; **y** *pron.* II-2
   Is there… ? **Y a-t-il… ?** I-2
   over there **là-bas** *adv.* I-1
   (over) there (*used with demonstrative adjective* **ce** *and noun or with demonstrative pronoun* **celui**) **-là** I-6
   There is/There are… **Il y a…** I-1
   There is/There are…. **Voilà…** I-1
   There was… **Il y a eu…** I-6; **Il y avait…** I-8, II-P
therefore **donc** *conj.* I-7
these/those **ces** *dem. adj., m., f., pl.* I-6
   these/those **celles** *pron., f., pl.* II-6
   these/those **ceux** *pron., m., pl.* II-6
they **ils** *sub. pron., m.* I-1; **elles** *sub. and disj. pron., f.* I-1; **eux** *disj. pron., pl.* I-3
thing **chose** *f.* I-1, **truc** *m.* I-7
think (about) **réfléchir (à)** *v.* I-4
   to think (that) **penser (que)** *v.* I-2

third **troisième** *adj.* I-7
thirst **soif** *f.* I-4
   to be thirsty **avoir soif** *v.* I-4
thirteen **treize** *m.* I-1
thirty **trente** *m.* I-1
thirty-first **trente et unième** *adj.* I-7
this/that **ce** *dem. adj., m., sing.* I-6; **cet** *dem. adj., m., sing.* I-6; **cette** *dem. adj., f., sing.* I-6
   this afternoon **cet après-midi** I-2
   this evening **ce soir** I-2
   this one/that one **celle** *pron., f., sing.* II-6; **celui** *pron., m., sing.* II-6
   this week **cette semaine** I-2
   this weekend **ce week-end** I-2
   this year **cette année** I-2
those are… **ce sont…** I-1
thousand: one thousand **mille** *m.* I-5
   one hundred thousand **cent mille** *m.* I-5
threat **danger** *m.* II-6
three **trois** *m.* I-1
three hundred **trois cents** *m.* I-5
throat **gorge** *f.* II-2
throw away **jeter** *v.* II-6
Thursday **jeudi** *m.* I-2
ticket **billet** *m.* I-7
   round-trip ticket **billet** *m.* **aller-retour** I-7 bus/subway ticket **ticket de bus/de métro** *m.* I-7
tie **cravate** *f.* I-6
tight **serré(e)** *adj.* I-6
time (occurence) **fois** *f.*; (general sense) **temps** *m., sing.* I-5
   a long time **longtemps** *adv.* I-5
   free time **temps libre** *m.* I-5
   from time to time **de temps en temps** *adv.* I-8, II-P
   to lose time **perdre son temps** *v.* I-6
tinker **bricoler** *v.* I-5
tip **pourboire** *m.* I-4
   to leave a tip **laisser un pourboire** *v.* I-4
tire **pneu** *m.* II-3
   flat tire **pneu** *m.* **crevé** II-3
   (emergency) tire **roue (de secours)** *f.* II-3
   to check the tire pressure **vérifier la pression des pneus** *v.* II-3
tired **fatigué(e)** *adj.* I-3
tiresome **pénible** *adj.* I-3
to **à** *prep.* I-4; **au (à + le)** I-4; **aux (à + les)** I-4
toaster **grille-pain** *m.* I-8, II-P
today **aujourd'hui** *adv.* I-2

toe **orteil** *m.* II-2; **doigt de pied** *m.* II-2
together **ensemble** *adv.* I-6
tomato **tomate** *f.* II-1
tomorrow (morning, afternoon, evening) **demain (matin, après-midi, soir)** *adv.* I-2
   day after tomorrow **après-demain** *adv.* I-2
too **aussi** *adv.* I-1
   too many/much (of) **trop (de)** I-4
tooth **dent** *f.* II-1
   to brush one's teeth **se brosser les dents** *v.* II-1
toothbrush **brosse** *f.* **à dents** II-2
toothpaste **dentifrice** *m.* II-2
tour **tour** *m.* I-5
tourism **tourisme** *m.* II-4
tourist office **office du tourisme** *m.* II-4
towel (bath) **serviette (de bain)** *f.* II-2
town **ville** *f.* I-4
town hall **mairie** *f.* II-4
toxic **toxique** *adj.* II-6
toxic waste **déchets toxiques** *m., pl.* II-6
traffic **circulation** *f.* II-3
traffic light **feu de signalisation** *m.* II-4
tragedy **tragédie** *f.* II-7
train **train** *m.* I-7
train station **gare** *f.* I-7; **station** *f.* **de train** I-7
training **formation** *f.* II-5
translate **traduire** *v.* I-6
translated **traduit (traduire)** *p.p., adj.* I-6
trash **ordures** *f., pl.* II-6
travel **voyager** *v.* I-2
travel agency **agence de voyages** *f.* I-7
travel agent **agent de voyages** *m.* I-7
tree **arbre** *m.* II-6
trip **voyage** *m.* I-7
troop (company) **troupe** *f.* II-7
tropical **tropical(e)** *adj.* II-6
   tropical forest **forêt tropicale** *f.* II-6
true **vrai(e)** *adj.* I-3; **véritable** *adj.* I-6
   It is true that… **Il est vrai que…** II-7
   It is untrue that… **Il n'est pas vrai que…** II-7
trunk **coffre** *m.* II-3
try **essayer** *v.* I-5
Tuesday **mardi** *m.* I-2
tuna **thon** *m.* II-1
turn **tourner** *v.* II-4
   to turn off **éteindre** *v.* II-3

Vocabulaire — English-French

to turn on **allumer** *v.* II-3
to turn (oneself) around **se tourner** *v.* II-2
twelve **douze** *m.* I-1
twentieth **vingtième** *adj.* I-7
twenty **vingt** *m.* I-1
twenty-first **vingt et unième** *adj.* I-7
twenty-second **vingt-deuxième** *adj.* I-7
twice **deux fois** *adv.* I-8, II-P
twist one's ankle **se fouler la cheville** *v.* II-2
two **deux** *m.* I-1
two hundred **deux cents** *m.* I-5
two million **deux millions** *m.* I-5
type **genre** *m.* II-7

U

ugly **laid(e)** *adj.* I-3
umbrella **parapluie** *m.* I-5
uncle **oncle** *m.* I-3
under **sous** *prep.* I-3
understand **comprendre** *v.* I-4
understood **compris (comprendre)** *p.p., adj.* I-6
underwear **sous-vêtement** *m.* I-6
undress **se déshabiller** *v.* II-2
unemployed person **chômeur/chômeuse** *m., f.* II-5
  to be unemployed **être au chômage** *v.* II-5
unemployment **chômage** *m.* II-5
unfortunately **malheureusement** *adv.* I-2
unhappy **malheureux/malheureuse** *adj.* I-3
union **syndicat** *m.* II-5
United States **États-Unis** *m., pl.* I-7
university **faculté** *f.* I-1; **université** *f.* I-1
university cafeteria **restaurant universitaire (resto U)** *m.* I-2
unless **à moins que** *conj.* II-7
unpleasant **antipathique** *adj.* I-3; **désagréable** *adj.* I-1
until **jusqu'à** *prep.* II-4; **jusqu'à ce que** *conj.* II-7
upset: to become upset **s'énerver** *v.* II-2
us **nous** *i.o. pron.* I-6; **nous** *d.o. pron.* I-7
use **employer** *v.* I-5
  to use a map **utiliser un plan** *v.* I-7
useful **utile** *adj.* I-2
useless **inutile** *adj.* I-2; **nul(le)** *adj.* I-2
usually **d'habitude** *adv.* I-8, II-P

V

vacation **vacances** *f., pl.* I-7
  vacation day **jour de congé** *m.* I-7
vacuum **aspirateur** *m.* I-8, II-P
  to vacuum **passer l'aspirateur** *v.* I-8, II-P
valley **vallée** *f.* II-6
vegetable **légume** *m.* II-1
velvet **velours** *m.* I-6
very (before adjective) **tout(e)** *adv.* I-3; (before adverb) **très** *adv.* I-8, II-P
  Very well. **Très bien.** I-1
veterinarian **vétérinaire** *m., f.* II-5
videocassette recorder (VCR) **magnétoscope** *m.* II-3
video game(s) **jeu vidéo (des jeux vidéo)** *m.* II-3
videotape **cassette vidéo** *f.* II-3
Vietnamese **vietnamien(ne)** *adj.* I-1
violet **violet(te)** *adj.* I-6
violin **violon** *m.* II-7
visit **visite** *f.* I-6
  to visit (a place) **visiter** *v.* I-2; (a person or people) **rendre visite (à)** *v.* I-6; (to visit regularly) **fréquenter** *v.* I-4
voicemail **messagerie** *f.* II-5
volcano **volcan** *m.* II-6
volleyball **volley(-ball)** *m.* I-5

W

waist **taille** *f.* I-6
wait **attendre** *v.* I-6
  to wait (on the phone) **patienter** *v.* II-5
  to wait in line **faire la queue** *v.* II-4
wake up **se réveiller** *v.* II-2
walk **promenade** *f.* I-5; **marcher** *v.* I-5
  to go for a walk **faire une promenade** I-5; **faire un tour** I-5
wall **mur** *m.* I-8, II-P
want **désirer** *v.* I-5; **vouloir** *v.* II-1
wardrobe **armoire** *f.* I-8, II-P
warming: global warming **réchauffement de la Terre** *m.* II-6
warning light (gas/oil) **voyant** *m.* **(d'essence/d'huile)** II-3
wash **laver** *v.* I-8, II-P
  to wash oneself (one's hands) **se laver (les mains)** *v.* II-2
  to wash up (in the morning) **faire sa toilette** *v.* II-2
washing machine **lave-linge** *m.* I-8, II-P
waste **gaspillage** *m.* II-6; **gaspiller** *v.* II-6
wastebasket **corbeille (à papier)** *f.* I-1
waste time **perdre son temps** *v.* I-6
watch **montre** *f.* I-1; **regarder** *v.* I-2
water **eau** *f.* I-4
  mineral water **eau f. minérale** I-4
way (by the way) **au fait** I-3; (path) **chemin** *m.* II-4
we **nous** *pron.* I-1
weak **faible** *adj.* I-3
wear **porter** *v.* I-6
weather **temps** *m., sing.* I-5; **météo** *f.* II-7
  The weather is bad. **Il fait mauvais.** I-5
  The weather is dreadful. **Il fait un temps épouvantable.** I-5
  The weather is good/warm. **Il fait bon.** I-5
  The weather is nice. **Il fait beau.** I-5
web site **site Internet/web** *m.* II-3
wedding **mariage** *m.* I-6
Wednesday **mercredi** *m.* I-2
weekend **week-end** *m.* I-2
  this weekend **ce week-end** *m.* I-2
welcome **bienvenu(e)** *adj.* I-1
  You're welcome. **Il n'y a pas de quoi.** I-1
well **bien** *adv.* I-7
  I am doing well/badly. **Je vais bien/mal.** I-1
west **ouest** *m.* II-4
What? **Comment?** *adv.* I-4; **Pardon?** I-4; **Quoi?** I-1 *interr. pron.* I-4
  What day is it? **Quel jour sommes-nous?** I-2
  What is it? **Qu'est-ce que c'est?** *prep.* I-1
  What is the date? **Quelle est la date?** I-5
  What is the temperature? **Quelle température fait-il?** I-5
  What is the weather like? **Quel temps fait-il?** I-5
  What is your name? **Comment t'appelles-tu?** *fam.* I-1
  What is your name? **Comment vous appelez-vous?** *form.* I-1
  What is your nationality? **Quelle est ta nationalité?** *sing., fam.* I-1
  What is your nationality? **Quelle est votre nationalité?** *sing., pl., fam., form.* I-1

Vocabulaire

English-French

What time do you have?
Quelle heure avez-vous?
form. I-2
What time is it? **Quelle heure est-il?** I-2
What time? **À quelle heure?** I-2
What do you think about that?
Qu'en penses-tu? II-6
What's up? **Ça va?** I-1
whatever it may be **quoi que ce soit** II-5
What's wrong? **Qu'est-ce qu'il y a?** I-1
when **quand** *adv.* I-4
When is …'s birthday? **C'est quand l'anniversaire de …?** I-5
When is your birthday?
C'est quand ton/votre anniversaire? I-5
where **où** *adv., rel. pron.* I-4
which? **quel(le)(s)?** *adj.* I-4
which one **à laquelle** *pron., f., sing.* II-5
which one **auquel (à + lequel)** *pron., m., sing.* II-5
which one **de laquelle** *pron., f., sing.* II-5
which one **duquel (de + lequel)** *pron., m., sing.* II-5
which one **laquelle** *pron., f., sing.* II-5
which one **lequel** *pron., m., sing.* II-5
which ones **auxquelles (à + lesquelles)** *pron., f., pl.* II-5
which ones **auxquels (à + lesquels)** *pron., m., pl.* II-5
which ones **desquelles (de + lesquelles)** *pron., f., pl.* II-5
which ones **desquels (de + lesquels)** *pron., m., pl.* II-5
which ones **lesquelles** *pron., f., pl.* II-5
which ones **lesquels** *pron., m., pl.* II-5
while **pendant que** *prep.* I-7
white **blanc(he)** *adj.* I-6
who? **qui?** *interr. pron.* I-4; **qui** *rel. pron.* II-3
Who is it? **Qui est-ce?** I-1
Who's calling, please? **Qui est à l'appareil?** II-5
whom? **qui?** *interr.* I-4
For whom? **Pour qui?** I-4
To whom? **À qui?** I-4
why? **pourquoi?** *adv.* I-2, I-4
widowed **veuf/veuve** *adj.* I-3
wife **femme** *f.* I-1; **épouse** *f.* I-3
willingly **volontiers** *adv.* II-2
win **gagner** *v.* I-5

wind **vent** *m.* I-5
It is windy. **Il fait du vent.** I-5
window **fenêtre** *f.* I-1
windshield **pare-brise** *m.* II-3
windshield wiper(s) **essuie-glace (essuie-glaces** *pl.***)** *m.* II-3
windsurfing **planche à voile** *v.* I-5
to go windsurfing **faire de la planche à voile** *v.* I-5
wine **vin** *m.* I-6
winter **hiver** *m.* I-5
in the winter **en hiver** I-5
wipe (the dishes/the table)
essuyer (la vaisselle/la table) *v.* I-8, II-P
wish that… **souhaiter que…** *v.* II-6
with **avec** *prep.* I-1
with whom? **avec qui?** I-4
withdraw money **retirer de l'argent** *v.* II-4
without **sans** *prep.* I-8, II-P; **sans que** *conj.* I-5
woman **femme** *f.* I-1
wood **bois** *m.* II-6
wool **laine** *f.* I-6
work **travail** *m.* II-4
to work **travailler** *v.* I-2; **marcher** *v.* II-3; **fonctionner** *v.* II-3
work out **faire de la gym** *v.* I-5
worker **ouvrier/ouvrière** *m., f.* II-5
world **monde** *m.* I-7
worried **inquiet/inquiète** *adj.* I-3
worry **s'inquiéter** *v.* II-2
worse **pire** *comp. adj.* II-1; **plus mal** *comp. adv.* II-1; **plus mauvais(e)** *comp. adj.* II-1
worst: the worst **le plus mal** *super. adv.* II-1; **le/la pire** *super. adj.* II-1; **le/la plus mauvais(e)** *super. adj.* II-1
wound **blessure** *f.* II-2
wounded: to get wounded **se blesser** *v.* II-2
write **écrire** *v.* I-7
to write one another **s'écrire** *v.* II-3
writer **écrivain/femme écrivain** *m., f.* II-7
written **écrit (écrire)** *p.p., adj.* I-7
wrong **tort** *m.* I-2
to be wrong **avoir tort** *v.* I-2

Y

yeah **ouais** I-2
year **an** *m.* I-2; **année** *f.* I-2
yellow **jaune** *adj.* I-6

yes **oui** I-2; *(when making a contradiction)* **si** I-2
yesterday (morning/afternoon evening) **hier (matin/après-midi/soir)** *adv.* I-7
day before yesterday **avant-hier** *adv.* I-7
yogurt **yaourt** *m.* II-1
you **toi** *disj. pron., sing., fam.* I-3; **tu** *sub. pron., sing., fam.* I-1; **vous** *pron., sing., pl., fam., form.* I-1
you neither **toi non plus** I-2
You're welcome. **De rien.** I-1
young **jeune** *adj.* I-3
younger **cadet(te)** *adj.* I-3
your **ta** *poss. adj., f., sing.* I-3; **tes** *poss. adj., m., f., pl.* I-3; **ton** *poss. adj., m., sing.* I-3; **vos** *poss. adj., m., f., pl.* I-3; **votre** *poss. adj., m., f., sing.* I-3;
yourself **te/t'** *refl. pron., sing., fam.* II-2; **toi** *refl. pron., sing., fam.* II-2; **vous** *refl. pron., form.* II-2
youth **jeunesse** *f.* I-6
youth hostel **auberge de jeunesse** *f.* I-7
Yum! **Miam!** *interj.* I-5

Z

zero **zéro** *m.* I-1

Vocabulaire supplémentaire

Mots utiles

absent(e) *absent*
un département *department*
une dictée *dictation*
une phrase *sentence*
une feuille d'activités *activity sheet*
l'horaire des cours (*m.*) *class schedule*
un paragraphe *paragraph*
une épreuve *quiz*
un examen *exam; test*
suivant(e) *following*

Expressions utiles

Asseyez-vous, s'il vous plaît. *Sit down, please.*
Avez-vous des questions? *Do you have any questions?*
Comment dit-on _____ en français? *How do you say _____ in French?*
Comment écrit-on _____ en français? *How do you write _____ in French?*
Écrivez votre nom. *Write your name.*
Étudiez la leçon trois. *Study lesson 3.*
Fermez votre livre. *Close your book(s).*
Je ne comprends pas. *I don't understand.*
Je ne sais pas. *I don't know.*
Levez la main. *Raise your hand(s).*
Lisez la phrase à voix haute. *Read the sentence aloud.*
Ouvrez votre livre à la page deux. *Open your book to page two.*
Plus lentement, s'il vous plaît. *Slower, please.*
Que signifie _____? *What does _____ mean?*
Répétez, s'il vous plaît. *Repeat, please.*
Répondez à la/aux question(s). *Answer the question(s).*
Vous comprenez? *Do you understand?*

Titres des sections du livre

À l'écoute *Listening*
Après la lecture *After Reading*
Avant la lecture *Before Reading*
Coup de main *Helping Hand*
Culture à la loupe *Culture through a magnifying glass*
Écriture *Writing*
Essayez! *Try it!*
Incroyable mais vrai! *Incredible But True!*
Le français quotidien *Everyday French*
Le français vivant *French Live*
Lecture *Reading*
Les sons et les lettres *Sounds and Letters*
Mise en pratique *Putting it into Practice*
Le monde francophone *The Francophone World*
Pour commencer *To Begin*
Projet *Project*
Roman-photo *Story based on photographs*
Savoir-faire *Know-how*
Structures *Structures; Grammar*
Le zapping *Channel-surfing*

D'autres adjectifs de nationalité en Europe

autrichien(ne) *Austrian*
belge *Belgian*
bulgare *Bulgarian*
danois(e) *Danish*
écossais(e) *Scottish*
finlandais(e) *Finnish*
grec/grecque *Greek*
hongrois(e) *Hungarian*
norvégien(ne) *Norwegian*
polonais(e) *Polish*
portugais(e) *Portuguese*
roumain(e) *Romanian*
russe *Russian*
slovaque *Slovakian*
slovène *Slovene; Slovenian*
suédois(e) *Swedish*
tchèque *Czech*
tunisien(ne) *Tunisian*

D'autres adjectifs de nationalité en Afrique

africain(e) *African*
angolais(e) *Angolan*
béninois(e) *Beninese*
camerounais(e) *Cameroonian*
congolais(e) *Congolese*
égyptien(ne) *Egyptian*
éthiopien(ne) *Ethiopian*
kenyan(e) *Kenyan*
ivoirien(ne) *of the Ivory Coast*
nigérien(ne) *Nigerian*
somalien(ne) *Somali*
soudanais(e) *Sudanese*
sud-africain(e) *South African*
tchadien(ne) *Chadian*
togolais(e) *Togolese*
tunisien(ne) *Tunisian*

D'autres adjectifs de nationalité dans le monde

antillais(e) *Caribbean, West Indian*
argentin(e) *Argentinian*
asiatique *Asian*
australien(ne) *Australian*
bolivien(ne) *Bolivian*
chilien(ne) *Chilean*
chinois(e) *Chinese*
colombien(ne) *Colombian*
cubain(e) *Cuban*
haïtien(ne) *Haitian*
indien(ne) *Indian*
irakien(ne) *Iraqi*
iranien(ne) *Iranian*
israélien(ne) *Israeli*
libanais(e) *Lebanese*
néo-zélandais(e) *New Zealander*
pakistanais(e) *Pakistani*
péruvien(ne) *Peruvian*
portoricain(e) *Puerto Rican*
syrien(ne) *Syrian*
turc/turque *Turkish*
vénézuélien(ne) *Venezuelan*

Vocabulaire supplémentaire

D'autres cours

l'agronomie (f.) agriculture
l'algèbre (m.) algebra
l'anatomie (f.) anatomy
l'anthropologie (f.) anthropology
l'archéologie (f.) archaeology
l'architecture (f.) architecture
l'astronomie (f.) astronomy
la biochimie biochemistry
la botanique botany
le commerce business
l'éducation physique (f.) physical education
une filière course of study
le latin Latin
les langues romanes romance languages
la linguistique linguistics
le marketing marketing
les mathématiques supérieures, spéciales calculus
la médecine medicine
la musique music
la trigonométrie trigonometry
la zoologie zoology

D'autres mots utiles

une cantine cafeteria
un classeur binder
une gomme eraser
l'infirmerie (f.) infirmary
une règle ruler

D'autres animaux familiers

un cochon d'Inde guinea pig
un furet ferret
une gerbille gerbil
un hamster hamster
un rongeur rodent
une souris mouse
une tortue turtle

D'autres adjectifs pour décrire les gens

ambitieux/ambitieuse ambitious
arrogant(e) arrogant
calme calm
compétent(e) competent
excellent(e) excellent
franc/franche frank, honest
(mal)honnête (dis)honest
idéaliste idealistic
immature immature
mûr(e) mature
(ir)responsable (ir)responsible
romantique romantic
séduisant(e) attractive
sentimental(e) sentimental
sincère sincere
souple flexible
studieux/ieuse studious
tranquille quiet

D'autres professions

un boucher/une bouchère butcher
un boulanger/une boulangère baker
un caissier/une caissière cashier
un cordonnier cobbler
un dessinateur/une dessinatrice illustrator
un fermier/une fermière farmer
un(e) informaticien(ne) computer scientist
un instituteur/une institutrice nursery/elementary school teacher
un(e) photographe photographer
un(e) pilote pilot
un(e) styliste fashion designer
un tailleur (pour dames) (ladies') tailor
un teinturier dry cleaner

Au café

une brioche brioche, bun
un café crème espresso with milk
un croque-monsieur toasted ham and cheese sandwich
de l'eau gazeuse (f.) sparkling mineral water
de l'eau plate (f.) plain water
un garçon de café waiter
une omelette au jambon/au fromage omelet with ham/with cheese
des œufs au/sur le plat (m.) fried eggs
une part de tarte slice of a pie
une tartine de beurre slice of bread and butter

Quelques fromages

du bleu des Causses blue cheese made with cow's milk
du camembert soft cheese made with cow's milk
du fromage de chèvre goat cheese
du gruyère Swiss cheese
du munster semisoft cheese that can be sharp in flavor, made with cow's milk
du reblochon soft cheese made with cow's milk
du roquefort blue cheese made with sheep's milk
de la tomme de Savoie cheese from the Alps made of scalded curds

Vocabulaire supplémentaire

D'autres loisirs

une **bicyclette** *bicycle*
bricolage (faire du) *fixing things*
collectionner les timbres *to collect stamps*
faire des mots croisés *to do a crossword puzzle*
une **fête foraine/une foire** *fair*
jouer à la pétanque/aux boules (f.) *to play the game of petanque*
jouer aux dames (f.) *to play checkers*
louer une vidéo/un DVD *to rent a video/DVD*
la natation (faire de) *swimming*
un **parc d'attractions** *amusement park*
tapisserie (faire de la) *needlework*
tricoter *knitting*
un **vidéoclub** *video store*

Des mots liés à la météo

une **averse** *shower*
la **bise** *North wind*
la **brise** *breeze*
un **ciel couvert** *overcast sky*
un **ciel dégagé** *clear sky*
une **éclaircie** *break in the weather; sunny spell*
la **grêle** *hale*
la **grisaille** *grayness*
de la **neige fondue** *sleet*
un **nuage** *cloud*
un **orage** *thunder storm*
une **vague de chaleur** *heat wave*
le **verglas** *black ice*

Des fêtes de famille

une **bague de fiançailles** *engagement ring*
un **baptême** *christening*
les **fiançailles** *engagement*
les **noces d'argent** *silver wedding anniversary*
les **noces d'or** *golden wedding anniversary*
un **enterrement** *funeral*

Des jours fériés

l'**Action de grâce** *Thanksgiving*
la **fête de l'Indépendance** *Independence Day*
une **fête nationale** *National holiday*
le **Jour de l'an/la Saint-Sylvestre** *New Year's Day*
le **14 juillet** *Bastille Day*
la **Saint-Valentin** *Valentine's Day*

D'autres mots pour faire la fête

des **accessoires de cotillon (m.)** *party accessories*
des **amuse-gueule (m.)** *appetizers; nibbles*
un **bal** *ball*
des **confettis** *confetti*
une **coupe** *glass (champagne)*
des **feux d'artifice** *fireworks*
une **flûte** *flute (champagne)*
un **serpentin** *streamer*

Quelques vêtements

une **doudoune** *down coat*
un **foulard** *headscarf*
un **gilet** *cardigan; vest*
un **moufle** *mitten*
un **pantacourt** *capri pants*
un **pull à col roulé** *turtleneck*
un **sweat-shirt** *sweatshirt*
une **veste** *jacket*

Quelques pays d'Europe

l'/en **Autriche (f.)** *Austria*
la/en **Bulgarie** *Bulgaria*
le/au **Danemark** *Denmark*
l'/en **Écosse (f.)** *Scotland*
la/en **Finlande** *Finland*
la/en **Grèce** *Greece*
la/en **Hongrie** *Hungary*
la/en **Norvège** *Norway*
la/en **Pologne** *Poland*
le/au **Portugal** *Portugal*
la/en **République tchèque** *Czech Republic*
la/en **Roumanie** *Romania*
le/au **Royaume-Uni** *United Kingdom*
la/en **Russie** *Russia*
la/en **Slovaquie** *Slovakia*
la/en **Slovénie** *Slovenia*
la/en **Suède** *Sweden*

Quelques pays d'Afrique

l'/en **Afrique du Sud (f.)** *South Africa*
l'/en **Algérie (f.)** *Algeria*
l'/en **Angola (f.)** *Angola*
le/au **Bénin** *Benin*
le/au **Cameroun** *Cameroon*
le/au **Congo** *Congo*
la/en **Côte d'Ivoire** *Ivory Coast*
l'/en **Égypte (f.)** *Egypt*
l'/en **Éthiopie (f.)** *Ethiopia*
le/au **Kenya** *Kenya*
le/au **Maroc** *Morocco*
le/au **Niger** *Niger*
le/au **Sénégal** *Senegal*
la/en **Somalie** *Somalia*
le/au **Soudan** *Sudan*
le/au **Tchad** *Chad*
le/au **Togo** *Togo*
la/en **Tunisie** *Tunisia*

D'autres pays

l'/en **Argentine (f.)** *Argentina*
l'/en **Australie (f.)** *Australia*
la/en **Bolivie** *Bolivia*
le/au **Chili** *Chile*
la/en **Colombie** *Colombia*
(à) **Cuba (f.)** *Cuba*
(à) **Haïti** *Haiti*
l'/en **Inde (f.)** *India*
l'/en **Irak (m.)** *Iraq*
l'/en **Iran (m.)** *Iran*
(en) **Israël (m.)** *Israel*
le/au **Liban** *Lebanon*
la/en **Nouvelle-Zélande** *New Zealand*
le/au **Pakistan** *Pakistan*
le/au **Pérou** *Peru*
(à) **Porto Rico (f.)** *Puerto Rico*
la/en **Syrie** *Syria*
la/en **Turquie** *Turkey*
le/au **Venezuela** *Venezuela*

Vocabulaire supplémentaire

Partir en vacances

atterrir *to land*
l'atterrissage (m.) *landing*
une compagnie aérienne *airline*
une crème solaire *sunscreen*
une croisière *cruise*
le décollage *take-off*
décoller *to take off*
défaire ses valises *to unpack*
un douanier *customs officer*
une frontière *border*
un groom *bellhop*
un numéro de vol *flight number*
dormir à la belle étoile *to sleep out in the open*
une station balnéaire *seaside resort*

Dans la maison

allumer la lumière *to turn on the light*
du bois *wood*
le chauffage central *central heating*
la cheminé *chimney; fireplace*
la climatisation *air-conditioning*
la décoration intérieure *interior design*
en bas *downstairs*
en haut *upstairs*
éteindre la lumière *to turn off the light*
le fioul *heating oil*
le gaz *natural gas*
le grenier *attic*
la lumière *light*
une penderie *walk-in closet*
un plafond *ceiling*
le sol *floor*
le toit *roof*

Des tâches ménagères

aérer une pièce *to air a room*
arroser les plantes *to water the plants*
étendre le linge *to hang out/hang up washing*
laver les vitres *to clean the windows*
une vitre *windowpane*

Des meubles et des objets de la maison

une ampoule *light bulb*
une bougie *candle*
un buffet *sideboard*
une corde à linge *clothesline*
une couette *comforter*
le linge de maison *linen*
une persienne *shutter*
une pince à linge *clothes pin*
un portemanteau *coat rack*
un radiateur *radiator*
un robot ménager *food processor*
un store *blind*
un volet *shutter*

Index

A

à
  contractions with (4) 135, 143
accent marks (3), 93, 111
adjectives
  agreement (1) 32, 33
  descriptive (1), (3) 32, 33, 98, 99, 132
  position of (3) 99
  possessive (3) 102, 103
agreement
  adjectives (1) 32, 33
  possessive adjectives (3) 102, 103
aller
  imperative (2) 55
  present (4) 142
  with infinitive (near future) (4) 142
alphabet (1) 5
articles
  definite (1), (2) 10, 11, 65
  indefinite (1) 10
  partitive (4) 161, 162
au (contraction) (4) 143
avoir
  expressions with (2), (4) 73, 88, 152, 176
  present (2) 72

B

boire (4) 160, 161, 176

C

capitalization (1) 33
ce
  vs. il/elle (1) 29
c'est, ce sont (1) 29
  vs. il est, ils sont (1) 29
chez (3) 121
commencer, verbs like (2) 54, 88
contractions
  with à (4) 143
  with de (3) 103

D

de
  contractions with (3) 103
  with expressions of quantity (4) 164, 176
  for possession (3) 103
definite articles (1) 11
du (contraction) (3) 103

E

-er verbs
  present (2) 54, 55
  with spelling changes (2), 55
errands vocabulary (4), 134, 176
est-ce que (2) 58, 88
être
  present (1) 29

with adjectives (1), (3), 32, 33, 98
expressions
  of quantity (4) 152, 176
  with avoir (2), (4), 73, 88, 152, 176

F

family members and relatives (3) 90, 132
farewells (1) 2, 44
finir (4) 164, 176
forming questions (2) 58
future
  near (aller + infinitive) (4) 142

G

gender (1) 10
greetings (1) 2, 44

I

il y a (1) 11, 44
impératif (2) (4) 55, 73, 164
indefinite articles (1) 11
information questions (2) 58, 88
interrogative words (4), 146, 176
intonation, questions (2) 58
introductions (1) 2, 44
-ir verbs
  regular (4) 164, 176

L

le, la, l', les (1) 11

N

near future (4) 142
negation
  ne... pas (2) 59, 88
  negative words (2), 59, 88
n'est-ce pas (2) 58, 88
nouns (1) 10
nous commands (2) (4) 55, 73, 164
numbers
  0–60 (1) 14
  61–100 (3) 116

O

on (1) 28
où (4), 146, 176

P

partitives (4) 161
position of adjectives (1), (3) 33, 99
possessive adjectives (3) 102
prendre
  present (4) 160, 176
prepositions
  chez (3) 121
  of location (3) 120
pronouns
  disjunctive (3), 121

on (1) 28
  subject (1) 28
pronunciation
  l'accent aigu (3) 93
  l'accent circonflexe (3) 111
  l'accent grave (3) 93
  the alphabet (1) 5
  la cédille (3) 111
  the letter r (2) 67
  liaisons (2) 49
  nasal vowels (4) 155
  oral vowels (4) 137
  silent letters (1) 23
  le tréma (3) 111

Q

quantity, expressions of (4) 152, 164, 176
que (4), 146, 176
questions
  age (2) 73, 88
  est-ce que (2) 58, 88
  formation (2) 58
  inversion (2) 58
  n'est-ce pas (2) 58
  question words (4) 146, 176
  tag questions (2) 58, 88

S

subject pronouns (1) 28

T

tag questions (2) 58, 88
telling time (2) 76

U

un, une (1) 11

V

vous vs. tu (1) 3, 28

W

written accents (3), 93, 111

Z

Le Zapping sections (1), (2), (3), (4), 19, 63, 107, 151

Credits

Photography and Art Credits

All images ©Vista Higher Learning unless otherwise noted.

Cover: (tl) VHL; (tr) © Selitbul/iStockphoto; (bl) © Garry Black/Media Bakery; (br) © David Freund/Media Bakery.

Master Art: (banner background image) Jessica Beets.

Front Matter (SE): i: (tl) VHL; (tr) © Selitbul/iStockphoto; (bl) © Garry Black/Media Bakery; (br) © David Freund/Media Bakery; **xviii:** (l, r) © North Wind Picture Archives/Alamy; **xix:** (l) From Frank Bond, "Louisiana" and the Louisiana Purchase, Washington, Government Printing Office, 1912 Map No. 4. Courtesy of the Library of Congress; (r) © Design Pics Inc/Alamy; **xx:** Renoir, Pierre-Auguste *Dance in the Country* 1883. Oil on canvas 180cm x 90cm (71in x 35in). Location: Musée d'Orsay, Paris. Photo credit: © The Gallery Collection/Corbis; **xxi:** (tl) © Moodboard/Fotolia; (bl) © Moshimochi/Shutterstock; (br) © Wavebreakmedia Ltd/Shutterstock; **xxii:** © JTB Media Creation, Inc/Alamy; **xxiii:** (l) © Dave & Les Jacobs/Blend Images/Corbis; (r) © Yuri/iStockphoto; **xxiv:** © Pascal Fayolle/NRJ/SIPA/Newscom; **xxv:** (t) © Monkey Business Images/Fotolia; (b) © Yuri Arcurs/Fotolia; **xxvi:** (t) © Monkeybusinessimages/iStockphoto; (b) © Masterfile Royalty-Free; **xxvii:** © H. Schmid/Corbis.

Front Matter (TE): T1: (tl) VHL; (tr) © Selitbul/iStockphoto; (bl) © Garry Black/Media Bakery; (br) © David Freund/Media Bakery; **T10:** (l) © Mike Flippo/Shutterstock; (r) © Mr. Aesthetics/Shutterstock; **T11:** © Jordache/Dreamstime; **T12:** (l) © Mike Flippo/Shutterstock; **T29:** © SimmiSimons/iStockphoto; **T30:** © Monkeybusinessimages/Bigstock.

Unit 1: 1: Anne Loubet; **4:** (t) VHL; (b) Rossy Llano; **8:** (t, b) Anne Loubet; **9:** © Ian G. Dagnall/Alamy; **13:** (tl) © LdF/iStockphoto; (tm) Martín Bernetti; (tr, bmr) Rossy Llano; (bl) © 2009 Jupiterimages Corporation; (bml) © Auris/iStockphoto; (br) Anne Loubet; **15:** (bl, br) Anne Loubet; **17:** Pascal Pernix; **22:** Martín Bernetti; **26:** (r) Anne Loubet; (l) © Sam Edwards/Getty Images; **27:** Extrait de Superdupont – Tome 2 © Solé/Fluide Glacial; **28:** (l, r) Anne Loubet; **29:** (tl) Annie Pickert Fuller; (tr, bl) VHL; (br) © Masson/Shutterstock; **30:** (tl, tr) Martín Bernetti; (tm, br) VHL; (bl) © Niko Guido/iStockphoto; (bm) Anne Loubet; **31:** (tl) © Reuters/Corbis; (tm) © EdStock/iStockphoto; (tr) Darío Eusse Tobón; (bl) Anne Loubet; (bml, bmr) Martín Bernetti; (br) © Rasmus Rasmussen/iStockphoto; **33:** (l, r) VHL; **35:** © Masterfile Royalty-Free; **36:** (tl, tr, mtr, mbr, bl, br) Anne Loubet; (mtl) © Robert Lerich/Fotolia; (mbl) Rossy Llano; **37:** Pascal Pernix; **38:** (left col: t) © Hulton-Deutsch Collection/Corbis; (left col: mt) © Caroline Penn/Corbis; (left col: mb) © Allstar Picture Library/Alamy; (left col: b) © Eddy Lemaistre/For Picture/Corbis; (t) Photo courtesy of www.Tahiti-Tourisme.com; (m) © Lonely Planet Images/Ariadne Van Zandbergen/Getty Images; (b) © Eddy Lemaistre/For Picture/Corbis; **39:** (tl) Rossy Llano; (tr) © Antoine Gyori/Sygma/Corbis; (bl) © Owen Franken/Corbis; (br) Published with the kind authorization of the *Service de communication pour la Francophonie*; **42:** © Inspirestock Royalty-Free/Inmagine.

Unit 2: 45: © Auremar/Fotolia; **52:** Anne Loubet; **53:** © Jose Luis Pelaez, Inc/Blend Images/MaXx Images; **60:** Anne Loubet; **66:** (l) Martín Bernetti; (r) Pascal Pernix; **70:** Pascal Pernix; **71:** Pascal Pernix; **72:** (all) VHL; **73:** (all) Anne Loubet; **81:** Anne Loubet; **82:** (left col: t) Dante Gabriel Rossetti (1828–1882). *Joan of Arc Kissing the Sword of Deliverance*, 1863. Oil on canvas, 61 cm x 53 cm. Inv.55.996.8.1. Location: Musée d'Art Moderne et Contemporain, Strasbourg, France. Photo credit: © Christie's Images/Corbis; (left col: m) © Bettmann/Corbis; (left col: b) © Antoine Gyori/Sygma/Corbis; (t, b) Anne Loubet; (ml) © Claude Coquilleau/Fotolia; (mr) © Daniel Haller/iStockphoto; **83:** (tl) © David Gregs/Alamy; (tr, bl) Anne Loubet; (br) © Caroline Beecham/iStockphoto; **84:** (inset) Martín Bernetti; **84-85:** (background) © Art Kowalsky/Alamy; **85:** (inset) © Jon Feingersh/Blend Images/MaXx Images; **86:** Pascal Pernix; **87:** (l) Martín Bernetti; (r) Darío Eusse Tobón.

Unit 3: 89: Anne Loubet; **92:** Martín Bernetti; **96:** Anne Loubet; **97:** (l) © Elise Amendola/AP Images; (r) © Icon Sports Media/Corbis; **98:** (l) Martín Bernetti; (r) © FogStock LLC/Photolibrary; **100:** © Hemera Technologies/AbleStock.com/Jupiterimages; **101:** (t) © Tomasz Trojanowski/Shutterstock; (tl) © Brian McEntire/iStockphoto; (tm) © Anna Lurye/Shutterstock; (tr) © RJGrant/Bigstock; (bl) © Linda Kloosterhof/iStockphoto; (bm) © Dmitry Pistrov/Shutterstock; (br) © Oliveromg/Shutterstock; **104:** (tl, tr, bl, br) Martín Bernetti; (tm) © Dmitry Kutlayev/iStockphoto; (bml) VHL; (bmr) Anne Loubet; **105:** (t) © Gladiolus/iStockphoto; (bl) © Dynamic Graphics/Jupiterimages; (br) Rossy Llano; **109:** (l) Martín Bernetti; (m, r) Anne Loubet; **110:** (t, mml, mmr, br) Anne Loubet; (ml) © Hemera Technologies/Photos.com; (mr) © Vstock, LLC/Photolibrary; (bl) Martín Bernetti; (bml) © Photolibrary; (bmr) © Keith Levit Photography/Photolibrary; **114:** Anne Loubet; **115:** (l) © Anita Bugge/Getty Images; (tr) © Patrick Roncen/Kipa/Corbis; (br) © Pascalito/Sygma/Corbis; **117:** (inset: t) Ray Levesque; (inset: background) © Nigel Riches/Media Bakery; (inset: b) Anne Loubet; **119:** (t, br) Martín Bernetti; (tl) © David Lee/Alamy; (tml) © Nike Sh/Dreamstime; (tmr) © TpaBMa/Age Fotostock; (tr) © Igor Tarasov/Fotolia; (bl) © Creative Jen Designs/Shutterstock; (bmm) © Photofriday/Shutterstock; (bmr) © F9photos/Shutterstock; **122:** (tl) © Valua Vitaly/Shutterstock; (tm) © Roy Hsu/Media Bakery; (tr) © Don Mason/Getty Images; (bl) © Simon Kolton/Alamy; (bml) © Blend Images/Ariel Skelley/Getty Images; (bmr) © Jacek Chabraszewski/iStockphoto; (br) © Sergei Telegin/Shutterstock; **124:** Anne Loubet; **125:** Anne Loubet; **126:** (left col: t) © Stapleton Collection/Corbis; (left col: bl) © Kurt Krieger/Corbis; (left col: br) © Keystone Pictures USA/Alamy; (t) © Jeremy Reddington/Shutterstock; (ml) © Abadesign/Shutterstock; (mr) Anne Loubet; (b) © Benjamin Herzog/Fotolia; **127:** (tl) Tom Delano; (tr, br) Anne Loubet; (bl) Janet Dracksdorf; **128:** (t) © Juniors Bildarchiv/Alamy; (b) Martín Bernetti; **129:** Anne Loubet; **130:** Anne Loubet; **131:** Anne Loubet.

Credits

Unit 4: 133: Pascal Pernix; **136:** (t) © Buzzshotz/Alamy; (b) Martín Bernetti; **140:** Anne Loubet; **141:** (t) © Inge Yspeert/Corbis; (b) © Philippe Cabaret/Sygma/Corbis; **145:** © David Hughes/Photolibrary; **153:** © Tetra Images/SuperStock; **154:** Anne Loubet; **158:** Pascal Pernix; **159:** (t) © Kevin Foy/Alamy; (b) © Yadid Levy/Alamy; **161:** VHL; **165:** (inset) Ana Cabezas Martín; **169:** Anne Loubet; **170:** (left col: t) © Chris Hellier/Corbis; (left col: b) © Hulton-Deutsch Collection/Corbis; (t) © Christophe Boisvieux/Corbis; (ml) © David Osborne/Alamy; (mr) © Dan Moore/iStockphoto; (b) © Daniel Brechwoldt/iStockphoto; **171:** (tl) Janet Dracksdorf; (tr) © Leslie Garland Picture Library/Alamy; (bl) © Brian Harris/Alamy; (br) © Walid Nohra/Shutterstock; **172-173:** (background) Anne Loubet; **173:** (t, b) Anne Loubet; **174:** Martín Bernetti; **175:** © Patrick Sheandell O'Carroll/Getty Images.

Video Credits

Production Company: Klic Video Productions, Inc.

Lead Photographer: Pascal Pernix

Photographer, Assistant Director: Barbara Ryan Malcolm

Photography Assistant: Pierre Halart

Television Credits

19 By permission of INPES.

63 By permission of Université de Moncton.

107 By permission of Pages d'Or.

151 By permission of Swiss International Airlines.